Sydney Lynch

W9-CZL-782

ACT Guide, Edition 1.1

Introduction   1

English   37

Math   155

Reading   335

Science   451

Writing   533

Practice Tests   609

Answers   785

 +

Resources & Downloads:

IVYGLOBAL.COM/STUDY

ACT Guide, Edition 1.1

This publication was written and edited by the team at Ivy Global.

Editor-in-Chief: Nathan Létourneau
Producers: Lloyd Min and Junho Suh

Editors: Sacha Azor, Corwin Henville, Sarah Pike, Kristin Rose, and Nathan TeBokkel

Contributors: Thea Bélanger-Polak, Stephanie Bucklin, Alexandra Candib, Isabel Carlin, Aleah Gornbein, Ali Haydaroglu, Elizabeth Hilts, Lei Huang, Heeju Kim, Zoë Martin, Amelia McLeod, Mark Mendola, Geoffrey Morrison, Rachel Schloss, Yolanda Song, Meena Sundararaj, Isabel Villeneuve, and Charlie Wolock

Interns: Matthew Chung, Ian Hu, Philip Tsang, and Lily Wang

About the Publisher

Ivy Global is a pioneering education company that delivers a wide range of educational services.

Email: publishing@ivyglobal.com
Website: www.ivyglobal.com

Contents

Introduction

Preface 3

Test-Taking Basics 11

Key Strategies 17

English

Approaching the English Test 39

Grammar 51

Sentence Structure 75

Punctuation 95

Writing Strategy 109

Organization 127

Style 143

Math

Approaching the Math Test 157

Pre-Algebra 169

Elementary Algebra 201

Intermediate Algebra 219

Coordinate Geometry 247

Plane Geometry 287

Trigonometry 317

Reading

Approaching the Reading Test 337

Passage Types 367

Details and Implicit Meaning 389

Generalizations and Main Ideas 401

Author's Voice and Method 411

Meaning of Words and Phrases 425

Relationships 439

Science

Approaching the Science Test 453

Passage Types 463

Question Types 505

Writing

Approaching the Writing Test 535

Writing the Essay 547

Scoring Rubric and Sample Essays 565

Practice Essay Prompts 585

Practice Tests

Practice Test 1 611

Practice Test 2 669

Practice Test 3 727

Answers

English 787

Math 789

Reading 791

Science 795

Practice Tests 797

Scoring Your Practice Tests 801

Introduction
Chapter 1

Section 1
Preface

Welcome, students, parents, and teachers! This book is intended to help students prepare for the ACT, a test created and administered by ACT, Inc.

Many colleges and universities in the United States require the ACT as part of the application process. It's our goal to help you do your best on the ACT by offering you tips, tricks, and plenty of practice. This book will help you turn this challenging admissions requirement into an opportunity to demonstrate your skills and preparation to colleges.

We'll provide you with a comprehensive breakdown of the ACT and proven test-taking strategies for the different sections and question types. There are chapters about each of the ACT's test sections, as well as multiple practice exams. You'll find:

- Key test-taking strategies
- A breakdown and detailed review of the content of each section
- 3 full-length practice tests and more than 500 practice problems and drills
- Answer keys at the back of this book
- Full answer explanations and scoring online

The first key to succeeding on the ACT is knowing the exam, so the rest of this chapter provides details about its structure, format, and timing along with key strategies to use in all sections. Chapters 2–6 delve into the question types and content you will encounter in each section. We recommend working through these chapters, taking the practice exams in Chapter 7, and then reviewing any challenging material.

Visit our website for additional resources, including review of foundational concepts, extra practice, answer explanations, and interactive scoring and personal reports. You'll also find information about upcoming tests, tutoring services, prep classes, and other tips to help you succeed. Happy studying!

 For additional resources, please visit **ivyglobal.com/study**.

What is the ACT?
Part 1

Introduction

The ACT is a standardized examination designed to measure students' abilities in four areas: English, Math, Reading, and Science. There is also an optional Writing component. Many American colleges and universities require ACT scores for admission and consider these scores an important factor in assessing applications.

Why do colleges care about the ACT? Since grading standards vary from one high school to another, it can be hard for colleges to know whether two applicants with the same grades are performing at the same level. Therefore, having everyone take the same standardized test gives colleges another metric for comparing students' abilities.

Of course, ACT scores aren't the only things that colleges consider when assessing applicants. Your high school grades, course selection, extracurricular activities, recommendation letters, and application essays are all factors that colleges will use to decide whether you are a good fit for their school. However, in today's highly competitive admissions process, a solid ACT score may provide you with the extra edge needed to be successful.

What's New?

ACT, Inc. continues to implement changes to the ACT content. Changes for 2015 included the addition of paired passages to the Reading Test, the consolidation of the Science Test to 6 passages from 7 passages (with the same number of questions), and a large-scale redesign of the Writing Test. This book reflects all of these changes.

Changes for fall of 2016 include expanding and redesigning ACT, Inc.'s reporting tools, and replacing test subscores with reporting categories. We will discuss these changes in detail in the following section.

The ACT in Detail
Part 2

Understanding the format and scoring of the new ACT will help you pick appropriate strategies and know what to expect on test day.

The Format

The ACT is 2 hours and 55 minutes long (plus 40 minutes for the optional essay). It is composed of the following sections:

- English Test (45 minutes, 75 questions)
- Math Test (60 minutes, 60 questions)
- Reading Test (35 minutes, 40 questions)
- Science Test (35 minutes, 40 questions)
- Optional Writing Test/Essay section (40 minutes)

The ACT also includes two breaks, one approximately 10 minutes long between the Math and Reading Tests, and one approximately 5 minutes long between the Science Test and the optional Writing Test.

The Scoring System

The ACT uses scaled test scores. First, the ACT calculates how many questions you correctly answered in each section; this is your **raw score**. **Scaled scores** are calculated by taking your raw test scores and adjusting them to a score from 1 to 36 according to a chart that the ACT develops. These charts are exam-specific, and so may vary slightly from one exam to the next. There are four scaled scores, one for each test: the English Test, the Math Test, the Reading Test, and the Science Test. Together, the average of these four scaled scores generates the ACT **composite score**, which is also scored from 1 to 36.

If you take the Writing Test, you will receive an additional scored average, from 2 to 12. This optional component is scored separately and does not affect your scores in other areas, or your overall ACT composite score.

The ACT also provides you with **subscores**, which are subject- or area-specific results. These do not affect your scaled test scores, but rather provide institutions with more detailed information about your exam results. Subscores for three of the four main tests (the Science Test does not have subscores) are each calculated from 1 to 18. The English test is subdivided into Usage/Mechanics and Rhetorical Skills. The Math Test is subdivided into Pre-Algebra/Elementary Algebra, Algebra/Coordinate Geometry, and

Plane Geometry/Trigonometry. The Reading Test is subdivided into Social Studies/Sciences and Arts/Literature.

The optional Writing Test is scored on a scale from 1 to 36. The Writing Test also reports four subscores: Ideas and Analysis, Development and Support, Organization, and Language Use and Conventions. Each area score is reported on a scale from 2 to 12. The average of these four scores, from 2 to 12, is reported to you when you get your results.

The ACT includes two additional scores. The first is the Science, Technology, Engineering, and Mathematics or STEM score. The second is for English Language Arts or ELA, and is only included if the optional Writing Test is taken. These scores are each calculated from 1 to 36. The following table summarizes the scoring for the ACT:

ACT Scoring	
Raw Test Scores	<ul><li>English Test (75)</li><li>Math Test (60)</li><li>Reading Test (40)</li><li>Science Test (40)</li><li>Optional Writing Test (36), changing to (48) after September 2016</li></ul>
Scaled Scores (1 to 36)	<ul><li>English Test</li><li>Math Test</li><li>Reading Test</li><li>Science Test</li><li>Optional Writing Test (not included in the ACT exam final subscore)</li></ul>
Optional Writing Test (2 to 12)	• The rounded average of the four Writing Test subscores
Composite ACT Score (1 to 36)	• The average of the English, Math, Reading, and Science scaled scores
Subscores (1 to 18—before September 2016)	<ul><li>English: Usage/Mechanics and Rhetorical Skills</li><li>Math: Pre-Algebra/Elementary Algebra, Algebra/Coordinate Geometry, and Plane Geometry/Trigonometry</li><li>Reading: Social Studies/Sciences and Arts/Literature</li><li>Writing: Ideas and Analysis, Development and Support, Organization, and Language Use and Conventions (2 to 12)</li></ul>

Check if needed →

The Scoring System After September 2016

ACT, Inc. has announced that it will be altering scoring of the ACT exam after September of 2016. The scaled scores of the test will not change, but the current subscore system will be replaced by reporting categories. The reporting categories will be defined as shown in the table below:

ACT Reporting Categories	
English	<ul><li>Production of Writing</li><li>Knowledge of Language</li><li>Conventions of Standard English</li></ul>
Mathematics	<ul><li>Preparing for Higher Math</li><li>Number and Quantity</li><li>Algebra</li><li>Functions</li><li>Geometry</li><li>Statistics and Probability</li><li>Integrating Essential Skills</li><li>Modeling</li></ul>
Reading	<ul><li>Key Ideas and Details</li><li>Craft and Structure</li><li>Integration of Knowledge and Ideas</li></ul>
Science	<ul><li>Interpretation of Data</li><li>Scientific Investigation</li><li>Evaluation of Models, Inferences, and Experimental Results</li></ul>

Taking the ACT
Part 3

The ACT is administered only on specific dates at designated testing locations worldwide throughout the academic year. These standard dates fall in February, April, May, June, September, October, and December, with some exceptions. You can see the upcoming dates in your location on the ACT, Inc. website: www.act.org.

How Do I Register?

The easiest way to sign up for the exam is on the ACT website. You'll need to fill out a personal profile form, including your high school course information, and upload a recognizable photo, which will be included on your admission ticket.

You can also register by mail. To do this, ask your school counselor for the ACT Register-by-Mail packet or request this packet online at www.act.org.

When you register, you can sign up for your preferred date and location. However, testing centers often run out of room, so make sure you sign up early in order to reserve your place! There is also a cut-off for registrations approximately one month before the test date; after this point you'll need to contact the ACT to see if late registration or standby testing is an option.

When Should I Take the ACT?

Typically, students take the ACT during 11th grade or the beginning of 12th grade. You should plan to take the exam when you feel prepared, keeping in mind that you may wish to take the exam more than once and that you must take the exam in time to provide colleges with your scores.

Almost all schools will accept scores through December of your 12th grade year. After December, it really depends on the school to which you are applying. If you are planning to apply for Early Admission to any school, you'll need to take the test by November of 12th grade at the very latest.

Choosing an initial exam date several months ahead of the last available date that works for your application schedule will give you the opportunity to take the exam again if you need to. If you take the ACT in December, April, or June, certain centers may allow you to order a Test Information Release (TIR). If you order a TIR, you will receive a copy of the multiple choice test questions used to determine your score, a list of your answers, and the answer key. This may be very helpful in guiding your studies if you decide to take the exam more than once.

How Many Times Can I Take the ACT?

ACT, Inc. has no limits on how many times you can take the ACT. Many students take the exam two or three times to ensure their scores represent the best they can do. However, we don't recommend taking the exam more than two or three times, because you'll get fatigued and your score will start to plateau. Prepare to do your best each time you take the test, and you shouldn't have to re-take it too many times.

How Do I Send My Score to Colleges?

When you sign up for the ACT, you can select which schools you'd like to receive your scores. You can also do this after taking the ACT by logging onto your account on the ACT website. If you have taken the ACT more than once, the ACT "Score Choice" program allows you to choose which test results you would like to report to schools. You can't "divide up" the scores of different tests—all sections of the ACT from a single test date must be sent together.

However, certain schools don't participate in the "Score Choice" program. These schools request that applicants send the results of every ACT test they have taken. Even so, most schools have a policy of only considering your highest scores. Some schools will take your best overall score from a single administration while others will mix and match your best section scores from your entire test history, creating a new composite "Superscore." You can see how your prospective schools consider your scores by visiting their admissions websites.

How Do I Improve My Score?

The key to raising your ACT score is to adopt a long-term strategy. Score improvement on the ACT occurs only after consistently practicing and learning concepts over a long period of time. Early on in your high school career, focus on building vocabulary and improving essay-writing skills. Read as much as you can beyond your school curriculum—materials like novels, biographies, and current-event magazines. Keep up with the math taught in your classes and ask questions if you need help.

In addition to keeping up with the fundamental concepts and skills tested on the ACT, you'll need to learn how to approach the specific types of questions included on the exam. In the next section, we'll talk about some general test-taking strategies that will help you tackle the format of the ACT as a whole. Then, you can work through Chapters 2–6 to learn specific strategies for each part of the test. In Chapter 7, you'll be able to apply these strategies to three full-length practice tests. If you only have a short time to prepare, you can start with the practice tests to identify the areas you most need to focus on.

With enough practice, you'll be prepared to score your personal best on test day! Let's get started.

Section 2
Test-Taking Basics

In this section, we will help you prepare for the ACT with effective ways to approach studying and test taking. We will cover:

- Tips to keep in mind to help you as you approach the ACT exam
- How to create a study schedule, with a sample template to help you get started
- Important things to remember on the day of the exam

These essential strategies will help you before, during, and after the exam, providing you with key information so that you are prepared on the test day for what it is like to take the ACT.

How to Approach the ACT Exam
Part 1

Now that you're familiar with the ACT, here are a few key tips for taking the test:

- **Know the Test**: Because it is a standardized exam, the format of the ACT is the same every time it's administered. By knowing the time limit, number of questions, and directions for each section, you'll save time by skipping over the directions, and can relax knowing there won't be any surprises!

- **Manage Your Time**: Unlike a normal hour-long high school test, the ACT runs between three and four hours long—so you'll want to practice building your stamina! Doing timed practice tests or timed sections will help you learn to stay focused for the duration of the test. The Key Strategies section of this chapter discusses pacing for the ACT and how you can make the most of the time given to you.

- **Guess Effectively**: There is no downside to guessing! You should always guess on any questions you cannot answer with certainty. The Predicting and Process of Elimination strategies, found in the Key Strategies section of this chapter, will help you to make informed guesses. You may, however, not have time to attempt every question in a section. Because of this, it is a good idea to choose a letter beforehand that you will always use when guessing. This will save you from spending time deciding what answer choice to pick, and makes it easier to bubble in guesses.

- **Write and Bubble Clearly**: All of your work on the ACT, with the exception of the Writing Test, will be graded entirely by a machine. Make sure to fill in each bubble on your answer sheet completely using only a No. 2 pencil. Before beginning each section, double check that you are working on the corresponding section of the answer sheet.

For the Writing Test, remember to write your essay only in the lines of the lined pages provided in your answer sheet—your readers won't be able to see anything you write outside of these margins! Even though you are writing quickly, write as legibly as you can. Your readers need to be able to read your handwriting in order to give you points. Don't write any part of your essay in your test booklet, though you can use this space for jotting down notes or an outline for your essay.

Create a Study Schedule
Part 2

To prepare to do your best on test day, you'll need to organize your time leading up to the exam. First, you'll need to assess your strengths and weaknesses in order to figure out *what* to study. Then, you'll need to organize *how* you will study in order to make the best use of your time before your test date.

Identify Your Strengths and Weaknesses

To determine your areas of strength and weakness and to get an idea of which concepts you need to review, work through some practice questions. You can try out the questions for the English, Math, Reading, Science, and Writing tests in Chapters 2–6 of this book, or you can take one of the full-length practice tests in Chapter 7. Circle questions that you find more challenging.

After completing a section or a test, check your answers against the correct answers. Write down how many questions you missed, and review these questions. Also take a look at the topics or types of questions you found most difficult. What was challenging for you? What did you feel good about? Did you get questions wrong because you made an avoidable error, or did you get questions wrong because you did not know how to solve them? Reflecting on these questions will help you determine your individual strengths and weaknesses, and will help you decide what to focus on before your test date.

Plan Your Study Time

After determining your areas of strength and weakness, create a study plan and schedule for your ACT preparation. Work backward from your test date until you arrive at your starting point for studying. The number of weeks you have until your exam will determine how much time you can (and should) devote to your preparation. Make sure you leave enough time to review and practice each concept you'd like to improve—remember, practice is essential!

To begin, try using this sample study plan as a model for your own personalized study schedule.

My test date is: _____.

I have _____ weeks to study. I will make an effort to study _____ minutes/hours every day/week, and I will set aside extra time on _____ to take timed sections.

I plan to take _____ full-length tests between now and my test date. I will study for _____ weeks and then take a practice test. My goal for this test is to improve my score in the following specific areas:

_____

_____

_____

_____

_____

If I do not make this goal, then I will spend more time studying.

Study Schedule				
Date	Plan of Study	Time Allotted	Goal Reached?	Further Action
Jan 1	Review 10 vocabulary words and quadratic equations	1 hr	Yes, I know these 10 words and feel comfortable with quadratic equations.	
Jan 3	Review the next 10 vocabulary words and parts of speech	1 hr	I know these 10 words, but I'm still a bit shaky on parts of speech.	I'll review this again tomorrow and ask my English teacher for advice.

Be Prepared on Test Day
Part 3

After you've prepared by reviewing and practicing each area you need to improve, you'll be ready for test day! Here are some tips to make sure you can do your best.

Before the Test

On the night before the test, review only lightly, if at all. You can review a few concepts you find challenging, but don't try to learn anything new. Pick out what you are going to wear to the test—try wearing layers in case the exam room is hotter or colder than you expect. Organize everything you need to bring. Know where the test center is located and how long it will take to get there. Have a nutritious meal and get plenty of rest!

On the morning of the exam, let your adrenaline kick in naturally. Eat a good breakfast and stay hydrated; your body needs fuel to help you perform. Allow enough time for traveling to the test center, and be sure to follow your admissions ticket for directions on how early you should arrive.

Remember to bring the following items with you:

Test Day Checklist

- [ ] Admission ticket
- [ ] Approved photo ID
- [ ] No. 2 pencils and erasers
- [ ] Calculator with new batteries and back-up batteries
- [ ] Non-beeping watch
- [ ] Healthy snacks and a water bottle
- [ ] Directions to the test center and instructions for finding the entrance

Make sure you set your alarm and plan a time to leave that allows for delays. You need to be on time, or you can't take the test!

During the Test

Stay focused. Keep your mind on the task at hand, which should be nothing but the question in front of you. If you find your mind wandering, pull your focus back to the test. Don't look around the room to compare your progress to that of your neighbors. Everyone works at their own pace, and you have no idea which particular part of the section your neighbors are working on.

Remember the test-taking strategies that you've practiced. Read and think carefully. Be sure to read each question in its entirety, and consider each answer choice. Work at a good, even pace, and keep moving. Keep an eye on your time throughout each section (and make sure your watch's time matches the proctor's clock). Frequently double check that you are bubbling answers in the correct section of your answer sheet.

Remember to utilize the 5 Ps and other relevant strategies that you'll learn in the following sections. Use your test booklet to cross out answers that you know are wrong, work out math problems, and annotate reading passages. Answer the easy questions first, and make a guess for those you're not sure of. Be sure to mark questions where you guessed so that you can quickly turn back to them after you finish all the other questions in the section.

You cannot overestimate the importance of a positive outlook during the test. You have spent months preparing for the ACT—now it is time to be confident in the work you have done and in the knowledge you have acquired. Stay confident. Trust yourself, your abilities, and all of your preparation. Walk into the test room with every expectation that you will do well and remember: you are smart and accomplished!

After the Test

First things first: give yourself a pat on the back! You have just completed a huge step in your educational career. Take some time to relax and unwind with friends or family.

Your score report should become available to you about two weeks after you take the test. This score report will contain your composite score, test scores, and subscores. While these scores are important, remember to keep things in perspective. College applications will also entail submitting essays, letters of recommendation, high school grades, an activities list, and more. Even if you feel that your ACT scores are not an accurate reflection of your capabilities, you have many opportunities to shine in the other areas of your applications.

Remember that you can also retake the ACT. After you take the ACT the first time, you can pinpoint which areas you need to practice more. Students often improve their scores after taking the test a second time.

Either way, congratulate yourself on completing this challenge!

Section 3
Key Strategies

In addition to learning the material tested on the ACT, to perform your best you must also use the best strategies for tackling the questions. Below are five key techniques that will help you greatly on the test: the **5 Ps**. They can be used across the test to help you choose answers confidently and improve your score. The strategies are:

- Pencil on Paper   ← #2 pencil, writing on booklet doesn't matter
- Prediction
- Process of Elimination ← Only if you don't know
- Plugging in Options
- Pacing   ← Watches are OK to pace yourself

Too much time = OK
Too little time = NO

The problem
X X X
↑ ↑ ↑
Wrong
Answers
The correct ←
answer ✓

Pencil on Paper
Part 1

As you take the ACT, you don't want to passively read the information presented to you, but rather engage with and understand it. We call this the **Pencil on Paper** strategy. The best way to do this is to be an **active reader**, meaning to pay attention and engage while you are reading a passage, question, or answer option. Doing this will not only allow you to understand the information you will be tested on, but will also save you from reviewing the same information multiple times. One way of doing this is to use your pencil to **mark up** or add information in your test booklet.

You can use active reading in the English Test to mark up or underline elements of a passage that you believe will be important, or to identify and underline key parts of a sentence in questions about grammar or sentence structure. Consider the following example:

Example
<u>Standard safety features</u>, like the seatbelt in your car, is a good example of how consumer protection has advanced over time. These required safety features once cost extra—when they were available at all.	**A.** NO CHANGE **B.** are **C.** am **D.** was

This question focuses on subject-verb agreement, a concept we'll discuss further in Chapter 3, Section 2. To correctly answer this type of question, you need to identify the subject of a verb. The ACT will often try to trick you by placing other phrases between the subject and the verb, but by consciously hunting for the subject and underlining it in the sentence you can avoid being tricked by other phrases. In this example, the correct answer is (B), "are," because that is the only verb that agrees with the plural subject "standard safety features," which has been marked up using a wavy line.

Some English passages will also seem to be missing information or have sentences that are in the wrong place in the paragraph. If you can identify and mark these types of errors while you're reading, selecting the correct answer choice will be much easier!

In the Math Test, you can use active reading techniques by underlining what the question is asking you to find. This will help you determine what is important to solve each problem, so that you can focus on key information rather than being distracted by details.

You can also actively use your pencil by drawing a diagram for questions where no diagram is provided. ACT Math Test diagrams are not necessarily drawn to scale, so redrawing them may help you visualize a challenging problem, even if a diagram is provided.

Example

A square and a rectangle have the same perimeter. The area of the square is 16 and the rectangle has a length of 5. What is the area of the rectangle?

F. 3

G. 6

H. 15

J. 30

K. 60

To begin this problem, you will first want to draw a diagram of the square and rectangle with the given information and with the question's unknowns:

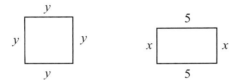

Next, you want to make sure that you have all of the question's information on your diagram. The question says that the area of the square is 16. You know that y^2 = the square's area; thus y, one side of the square, is equal to 4. $4y$, the perimeter of the square, is 16, and you know that the perimeter of the rectangle is also 16. Add the units for the square to your drawing:

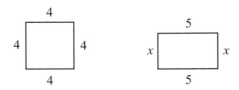

Drawing a diagram like this can help you more easily find the correct answer. We'll finish solving this problem when we talk about the Process of Elimination strategy later in this section.

In the Reading Test, like the English Test, you can be an active reader by using your pencil to mark up passages as you read. This will help you stay focused, understand what you read, and make it easy to find ideas in the passage when you refer back to the text. We will discuss active reading further in Chapter 4, Section 1.

Here's how a reading passage might look once it has been marked up. Aim to circle or underline two to three **main ideas** per paragraph that relate to the **5 Ws**: "who," "what," "where," "when," and "why."

Social Science: This passage is adapted from the article "Paid Sick Days and Physicians at Work: Ancient Egyptians Had State-Supported Health Care" by Anne Austin (©2015 by Anne Austin).

We might think of state-supported health care as an innovation of the 20th century, but it's a much older tradition than that. In fact, texts from a village dating back
5 to Egypt's New Kingdom period, about 3,100–3,600 years ago, suggest that in ancient Egypt there was a state-supported health care network designed to ensure that workers making the king's tomb were
10 productive.

The village of Deir el-Medina was built for the workmen who made the royal tombs during the New Kingdom (1550–1070 BCE). During this period, kings were buried in the
15 Valley of the Kings in a series of rock-cut tombs, not the enormous pyramids of the past.

The village was purposely built close enough to the royal tomb to ensure that workers could hike there on a weekly basis. These
20 workmen were not what we normally picture when we think about the men who built and decorated ancient Egyptian royal tombs— they were highly skilled craftsmen. The workmen at Deir el-Medina were given a
25 variety of amenities afforded only to those with the craftsmanship and knowledge necessary to work on something as important as the royal tomb. The village was allotted extra support: the Egyptian state
30 paid them monthly wages in the form of grain and provided them with housing and servants to assist with tasks like washing laundry, grinding grain, and porting water. Their families lived with them in the village,
35 and their wives and children could also benefit from these provisions from the state.

You can use the same approach for the Science Test. On the Science Test, you aren't looking for repeated words or for the 5 Ws, but instead for the **3 Ds**: details, differences, and definitions. Normally, you only need to look at the figures and their labels, axes, keys, and notes, in order to find and circle these things. However, in the Conflicting Viewpoints passage, you'll need to put your pencil on the paper for longer and do some actual reading.

As you read each viewpoint, circle its main idea. Then, note key differences between the viewpoints. Finally, write down the relationships that the viewpoint explains. In the example below, both viewpoints are marked up with circles and relationships—more on this in Chapter 5.

Over the past 200 years, the temperature of the Earth has exponentially increased in a process many scientists call global warming. Global warming has an effect on all ecosystems through the destruction and creation of habitats and through exceeding the heat tolerance of different organisms.

One organism influenced by global warming is the polar bear (Ursus maritimus). Polar bears typically reside in or near the Arctic Circle, but have recently been spotted far south of their natural habitat. Two scientists discuss the appearance of polar bears in southern regions and its relation to global warming.

Scientist 1

Polar bears primarily prey on seals that live in the Arctic Ocean. Polar bears can swim for extended periods of time, but they need dry ground where they can rest and breathe. Typically, polar bears have used sea ice to rest and breathe while they hunt seals, but global warming has caused sea ice in the Arctic Ocean to melt. Without (sea ice) polar bears cannot hunt seals, and lose their primary food source. They migrate southward, away from the Ocean and melting ice, in search of more food.

Scientist 2

Over thousands of years, polar bears have evolved translucent fur, which scatters and reflects visible light. This gives their fur the appearance of being white, which helps to camouflage them when they hunt for their prey in snow and ice. However, global warming has melted the snow and ice in much of the bears' habitats. Against the new habitat of grass and brush, the polar bears' (white-looking fur) is bright and obvious. No longer camouflaged, the bears are unable to successfully hunt for prey. They migrate northward in search of whiter habitats in which to hunt while camouflaged.

↑T = ↓S&I = ↑C =
North (This is the
relationship, which
explains the
viewpoint: as
temperature
increases, snow and
ice decrease,
camouflage
decreases, and
polar bears move
north.)

If you're taking the Writing Test, you can use the Pencil on Paper strategy to organize your thoughts and plan your essay. You should take some time before actually writing your essay to identify the key facts in the prompt that you will focus on when building your argument, make brief notes about your preliminary thoughts on the perspectives presented, and sketch an outline.

Consider the following example of how you might mark up an essay prompt:

Commercials in School

Schools distribute various type of media: textbooks, yearbooks, school newspapers, and TV and radio content. Many of these types of content include advertisements and commercially sponsored content, and some are compulsory. For example, students may be required to watch a school news program at the beginning of each school day, and some of those programs may include commercial content. Including advertisements in school media provides a source of revenue for schools or providers of free content to schools, and is a standard practice in many other forms of media. However, critics argue that it is exploitative to require students to view advertisements, or that promoting commercial content in school media is contrary to the values of education. Is it appropriate for schools to raise revenue by selling advertisements in school media, or to promote free media that includes commercial content—or should schools be ad-free zones?

Our paper
sells ads—
use example?

> Yes!

Read and carefully consider these perspectives. Each suggests a particular way of thinking about commercials in school.

Perspective 1	Perspective 2	Perspective 3
By providing advertisers with the opportunity to share relevant content with students, schools can raise revenues, allowing them to provide better services to students. It's a win-win situation.	Schools exist to provide students with an education, not to sell captive audiences to advertisers. School media has an ethical obligation to be educational—not commercial.	Students have to view ads all the time, so learning how to evaluate them is important. School media should both include ads and encourage students to evaluate them critically.

Seriously? (next to Perspective 2)

True! (next to Perspective 3)

Misses point:
COMPULSORY is not a "win"

Not realistic!

Closest to my view,
but no compulsory ads

By underlining items that are important to your own analysis and sketching out some of your thoughts as you read, you can begin to develop your thesis and select some areas for discussion. We'll talk about outlining your essay in Chapter 6.

Prediction
Part 2

When you are selecting your answer choices, one of the best ways to increase your accuracy is by using **Prediction**: coming up with an expected answer on your own rather than relying on the given choices. Imagine you are answering an open-ended question, rather than a multiple choice question. How would you rewrite an English sentence? What number would you arrive at for a Math calculation? How would you put a Reading or Science answer in your own words? While this technique seems simple, it has huge benefits when used consistently, as it helps you think critically and avoid common wrong answers, which you will learn about in the Process of Elimination strategy that follows.

In the English Test, there are some questions for which you may be able to easily anticipate the correct answer, and looking for the answer that you already know is correct can be the quickest option. Consider the following example:

Example	
Some fads have <u>went</u> in and out of style in generational cycles.	**A.** NO CHANGE **B.** go **C.** going **D.** gone

In English, we use helping verbs with main verbs to express tense, and there are only so many combinations that are allowed. The rule is pretty strict, and it's one of the rules that applies not only in formal writing, but also in our casual, everyday speech. So, even if you don't necessarily know all of the words to explain the rule, if you speak English regularly then there's a good chance that you just plain know—for a fact—that you don't say "have went."

You may also know, even before you look at the options, that what you *should* say is "have gone." In that case, you don't need to figure out exactly why the other choices are wrong and eliminate them— just look for the answer that you know must be there, because you already know that it's correct, and pick it.

Prediction can also be used on the Math Test by determining what must be true, given the information in a question.

If $y = x^2$ and $-1 < x < 1$, which of the following could be a possible value for y?

F. $-\dfrac{5}{4}$

G. $-\dfrac{1}{4}$

H. $\dfrac{1}{4}$

J. $\dfrac{5}{4}$

K. $\dfrac{3}{2}$

You know that any number squared *must* be positive, so you can predict that your answer will be positive. Because of this, you can think of the values for x as anything from zero to slightly smaller than 1, so either a positive fraction, decimal, or 0. You know that the square of any number smaller than 1 but not equal to zero is going to be smaller the number itself, so $x > x^2$, when $0 < x < 1$. This means that y also cannot be greater than 1.

You can predict, therefore, even before you look at the answer choices, that your answer will be either 0 or a number between 0 and 1, but not greater than 1. Now you are ready to look at the answer choices. The only answer choice that works with this prediction is (H). (F) and (G) are negative numbers, and (J) and (K) are both fractions with values greater than 1. If you plug this answer back into your question to double check, you can confirm that it works as a possible value for y.

In the Reading Test, you can use the information you gained from marking up passages with the Pencil on Paper strategy to predict what the correct answer will be for a question, before even reading the given options. Let's look at a question about the Egyptian health care passage. Here's the passage again, with key ideas underlined.

Example

Social Science: This passage is adapted from the article "Paid Sick Days and Physicians at Work: Ancient Egyptians Had State-Supported Health Care" by Anne Austin (©2015 by Anne Austin).

We might think of <u>state-supported health care</u> as an innovation of the 20th century, but it's a <u>much older tradition</u> than that. In fact, <u>texts from a village</u> dating back
5 to Egypt's New Kingdom period, about 3,100–3,600 years ago, suggest that in <u>ancient Egypt</u> there was a <u>state-supported health care network</u> designed to ensure that

<u>workers making the king's tomb were</u>
10 <u>productive.</u>

The <u>village of Deir el-Medina</u> was built for the workmen who made the royal tombs during the <u>New Kingdom (1550–1070 BCE)</u>. During this period, kings were buried in the
15 Valley of the Kings in a series of rock-cut tombs, not the enormous pyramids of the past. The village was <u>purposely built close enough</u> to the royal tomb to ensure that <u>workers</u> <u>could hike there</u> on a weekly basis. These

workmen were not what we normally picture when we think about the men who built and decorated ancient Egyptian royal tombs—they were <u>highly skilled craftsmen</u>. The workmen at Deir el-Medina were given a variety of amenities afforded only to those with the craftsmanship and knowledge necessary to work on something as important as the royal tomb. The village was allotted <u>extra support</u>: the Egyptian state paid them <u>monthly wages</u> in the form of grain and provided them with <u>housing and servants</u> to assist with tasks like washing laundry, grinding grain, and porting water. <u>Their families lived with them in the village</u>, and their wives and children could also benefit from these provisions from the state.

Which of the following statements would the author most likely make with regard to state-supported health care?

Even though this question is quite open-ended, by referring back to the passage, you should already be able to predict a general answer. From the underlined portions above, the author asserts that state-supported heath care is an old tradition, that documents show it occurred in a village in ancient Egypt (and included support for families), and that it was designed on purpose to keep workers productive. A correct answer choice could refer to any of these claims made by the author. Here are the answer options:

A. It is an effective policy for states hoping to boost productivity.
B. Historical evidence shows that such practices existed three millennia ago.
C. It is an ineffective policy because it must be supplemented by family help.
D. Written evidence for its existence in Deir el-Medina is not very detailed.

Here, (B) directly matches the second assertion listed above, making it easy to locate the correct response. (A) and (C) are both incorrect as they have no support in the passage; there are no arguments made about whether or not state-supported health care is an effective policy. (D) is incorrect as it contradicts information from the passage; the written evidence from Deir el-Medina in fact appears to be quite detailed, as it covers what provisions workers and their families were given.

Process of Elimination
Part 3

Sometimes the easiest way to answer a question is by finding the wrong answers. You may have used the **Process of Elimination** before; it's a great technique to narrow down your possible answer choices. This technique is especially useful if you are having a hard time predicting answer choices. Using Process of Elimination in combination with Prediction will increase your speed and accuracy on the exam.

Don't select an answer on your first read-through. Assess each answer choice one by one. If you know an option is incorrect, cross it out with a line or X in your test booklet. If an answer choice seems possible, leave it open to reconsider. Once you have assessed all of the answer choices, compare any that you left open and select the best one. In some cases you may even be able to knock out every answer except for one. In this case, you will have found the correct answer!

In the English Test, you can use the Process of Elimination to help you work through questions about grammar errors in a couple of ways. First, you should eliminate answer choices that don't correct an error in the underlined section. Then, you should eliminate answer choices that correct the error but introduce new errors. Any answers that have grammatical or stylistic errors cannot be the correct choice and should be eliminated.

You can also use the Process of Elimination to narrow down your choices in questions that don't involve grammar errors. Consider the following example:

Example	
Age-related hearing loss is a familiar condition in modern society. About one in three Americans experience hearing loss as they age. <u>In contrast,</u> hearing loss doesn't necessarily have to be a part of normal aging. Chronic exposure to loud noise is a risk factor for hearing loss, and minimizing your exposure can help to preserve your hearing as you age.	**F.** NO CHANGE **G.** Furthermore **H.** However **J.** Therefore

This example focuses on a transitional phrase in a paragraph, and your task is to select the phrase that best illustrates the relationship between the text before the transitional phrase and the text after it. At first glance, it may not be obvious which choice is correct.

First of all, you should consider the whole context: the portion of the paragraph before the underlined phrase discusses how common hearing loss is, while the second part discusses how you can minimize your risk of hearing loss. These two ideas aren't exactly opposite, but there is a contrast—so you might not want to eliminate (F) immediately.

(G) and (J) signal different types of relationships altogether. (G) signals a simple addition or continuation, and (J) signals the conclusion of an argument. Neither of these is the correct relationship, so you can eliminate both of these choices.

Next, compare (F) and (H). Both signal a contrast, but (F) signals a strong, direct contrast. (H) signals a more subtle, nuanced contrast. In this case, the contrast isn't between direct opposites, so you should eliminate (F) and select (H) as your answer.

Let's look at how Process of Elimination works for the previous math problem and the drawing that you created:

A square and a rectangle have the same perimeter. The area of the square is 16 and the rectangle has a length of 5. What is the area of the rectangle?

F. 3
G. 6
H. 15
J. 30
K. 60

Using the drawing, you can predict that it would be impossible for the rectangle's area to be 3 or (F). You can also determine that it is highly unlikely for the answer to be (G) or (K), so you can expect your answer to be either (H) or (J).

The perimeter is $2 \times 5 + 2x$, so you set this expression equal to 16 and solve for x:

$$2 \times 5 + 2x = 16$$
$$10 + 2x = 16$$
$$2x = 6$$
$$x = 3$$

Remember that you are solving for the area, not x!

From your diagram, you can calculate the area as $3 \times 5 = 15$, so (H) is the correct answer. You can also check this answer using the figures you drew. The area of the rectangle is close to the area of the square. None of the other answer choices are close to 15. Notice that if you didn't have the time to solve this questions, Process of Elimination gave you a 50% chance of guessing the correct answer.

A big part of eliminating answers is recognizing which answers are wrong and *why* they're wrong. Fortunately, the ACT's wrong answers, especially in the Reading and Science Tests, tend to fall into three general categories: irrelevant, confused content, and out-of-scope. **Irrelevant** answers use a word or phrase that does not come from the passage. **Confused content** answers use words or phrases from the passage but in the wrong order or with faulty causality, often stating exactly the opposite of what the passage states. **Out-of-focus** answers miss the scope of the question.

Irrelevant answers are tricky because they appeal to your reason rather than to the passage. Confused content and out-of-focus answers are even more challenging because they use stuff right from the passage, which you may recognize. However, understanding the wrong answer types you'll see on the ACT means you can avoid these common traps. It also helps you avoid the kind of thinking that leads to choosing these wrong answers.

English grammar and Math Test questions involve the application of specific rules and formulas. Rather than these Wrong Answer Types, their wrong answers most often consist of misusing or not applying the correct rule or formula. However, you can still use the Process of Elimination on these sections, as you've just seen. The Wrong Answer Types are particularly useful for questions on the Reading and Science Tests, and the English Test's Rhetorical Skills questions. We'll review Reading and Science examples next.

Take a look at how the Process of Elimination can be used in the following Reading example:

Example

Despite paid sick leave, medical rations, and a state-supported physician, it is clear that in some cases the workmen were actually working through their illnesses. For
80 example, in one text, the workman Merysekhmet attempted to go to work after being sick. The text tells us that he descended to the King's Tomb on two consecutive days, but was unable to work. He then hiked back
85 to the village of Deir el-Medina where he stayed for the next ten days until he was able to work again. Though short, these hikes were steep: the trip from Deir el-Medina to the royal tomb involved an ascent greater
90 than climbing to the top of the Great Pyramid. Merysekhmet's movements across the Theban valleys were likely at the expense of his own health. This suggests that sick days and medical care were not
95 magnanimous gestures of the Egyptian state, but were rather calculated health care provisions designed to ensure that men like Merysekhmet were healthy enough to work.

One of the main points of the fifth paragraph (lines 76–98) is that:

A. the King's Tomb was a greater feat of engineering than the Great Pyramid.

B. the Egyptian state failed to provide time off for its sick workers.

C. worker illness was likely worsened by the journey to the King's Tomb.

D. ancient Egyptians typically took about ten days to recover when sick.

Here, read the full paragraph in order to understand the point it is trying to make. The first sentence sets up the issue of workers working even when they are sick. However, even if that is not clear to you, you can immediately eliminate (B), as it is a confused content choice that contradicts the first line of the passage. Since the paragraph does not compare the impressiveness of the King's Tomb to the Great Pyramid, (A) can also be eliminated. The passage doesn't indicate the typical sick leave; it just discusses a single worker's time off, so (D) is not the correct choice.

You are then left with choice (C), which accurately captures a key idea in the paragraph. You can learn more about using the Process of Elimination in Reading in Chapter 4, Section 1.

Finally, you can use the Process of Elimination in the Science Test. Consider the following example:

Example

Scientists studied how plant growth is affected by different levels of *irradiance*, which is a measure of light intensity (watts, W) per unit area (meters squared, m^2). They examined three species of plants: *Arabidopsis thaliana*, *Phaseolus vulgaris*, and *Nicotiana tabacum*.

Study 1

Five trays of *A. thaliana*, each with ten 4-day-old plants per tray, were placed under 5 different lights. One tray was placed under each light at a distance of 25 cm from the light. Table 1 shows the different irradiance provided by the 5 lights. The growth of the *A. thaliana* plants in each tray was measured, averaged, and recorded over a period of 30 days, as shown in Figure 1. Every day, each tray received 20 mL of water and 10 mg of fertilizer, and temperatures were kept constant at 25°C.

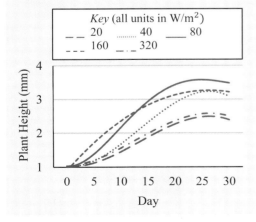

According to Study 1, which of the following statements best explains why the scientists controlled the temperature of each light and tray at 25°C?

F. Maintaining a constant temperature of 25°C is optimal for the growth of *A. thaliana* plants at a given irradiance.

G. Maintaining a constant temperature of 25°C ensures the distance from the plant trays to the light is the same for all 5 trays.

H. Maintaining a constant temperature of 25°C ensures the temperature does not have an effect on plant growth.

J. Maintaining a constant temperature of 25°C is important for the growth of *A. thaliana, P. vulgaris,* and *N. tabacum.*

This is an Experimental Design question, which doesn't require you to read the figures, but instead to read the experimental method explained in the paragraph before the figures. Since the question and its answer choices are long-winded, using process of elimination with special attention to Wrong Answer Types should help you get to the right answer in as little time as possible.

(F) is wrong because it's irrelevant; it doesn't relate to the information given in the passage. While it's a reasonable guess, the passage never mentions optimal growth. Science questions will sometimes expect you to use your outside knowledge, but only for basic concepts, not the specific optimal growth conditions for a particular plant. (G) is a confused concept, a misinterpretation of the information given. The distance and the temperature were both kept constant, but they have no effect on each other according to the passage.

(J) is out-of-scope; it relates to, but does not match the scope of the question. In this case, the choice talks about all plants, whereas the question asks about Study 1, which only talks about *A. thaliana*. (J) is too big-picture to adequately address the scope of the question. This leaves answer choice (H) as correct. The passage specifically states that the scientists were investigating the effect of irradiance on plant growth.

Plugging in Options
Part 4

Even if you're not sure how to approach a multiple choice question, because you are given 4 answer options you will always have somewhere to start—you can plug in the answer choices to see which might work. We call this **Plugging in Options**.

In the English Test, you can apply this strategy by plugging each answer choice in to the original passage, and reading the resulting sentence in your head. Even if you can't say exactly what the error is, your everyday English skills can help you to eliminate choices that clearly sound wrong. Consider the following example:

Example	
Yesterday, John ran the store until 5:00, then Lisa will take over. _____	**A.** NO CHANGE **B.** took **C.** is taking **D.** DELETE the underlined portion

This type of error is called an "inappropriate shift in verb tense," and it's discussed in Chapter 2, Section 3. "John ran the store" is in the past tense, and since Lisa took over at 5:00 yesterday, that should also be in the past tense. But even if you can't name and explain the error, you can probably guess that (D) is wrong by imagining the sentence with that option plugged in: "John ran the store until 5:00, then Lisa over." The phrase "then Lisa over" doesn't really make any sense, because there's no verb.

You might also be able to eliminate (A) and (C) by plugging them into the sentence and noticing that they just don't sound right. (B) solves the error, sounds right, and is the correct answer. This is a fast and easy way of handling many English Test problems, but be careful: if you only go by what sounds right, and you're never sure exactly what sort of errors you're looking at, then it's possible that you'll make a careless mistake by picking something that sounds okay but is technically wrong. You'll have a chance to learn about specific grammar errors in Chapter 2.

Plugging in answer choices can be especially helpful on the Math Test, as it can often help you avoid completing long calculations. When you use this strategy, it is best to start with the third answer choice, as most answer choices are listed in increasing or decreasing numerical order. If you start with the middle, you may be able to eliminate multiple answers based on the result. For example, if the answers increase in value from (F) to (J) and you determine that (H) is too small, you can eliminate (F), (G), and (H).

Here's a simple math problem that shows this approach:

Example

If $\dfrac{9}{4x} = \dfrac{3}{8}$, what is the value of x?

F. 4

G. 6

H. 8

J. 10

K. 12

To solve by testing answer choices, start with (G) or (H). If you start with (H), then substitute 8 for x:

$$\frac{9}{4 \times 8} = \frac{9}{32}$$

Next, check your answer with the question:

$$\frac{9}{32} \neq \frac{3}{8}$$

Your answer $\dfrac{9}{32}$ does not reduce to $\dfrac{3}{8}$, so (H) is not the right answer. However, you can use this to eliminate more than one answer choice. $\dfrac{9}{32}$ is smaller than $\dfrac{3}{8}$, so you know that 8 is too great a value of x. Therefore, you can also eliminate any other values greater than 8, such as (J) and (K).

Next, try (G), substituting 6 for x:

$$\frac{9}{4 \times 6} = \frac{9}{24}$$

This fraction can be simplified by dividing both the numerator and denominator by three. Check this with the original answer:

$$\frac{9}{24} = \frac{3}{8}$$

Since $\dfrac{9}{24}$ can be reduced to $\dfrac{3}{8}$, (G) is the correct answer.

Plugging in Options can also be used on the Reading Test for Meanings of Words in Context questions, which ask about specific vocabulary in a passage. To answer these questions, you can sub the answer choices back into the original sentence to see which choice works best in context.

Example

65 Just like today, some of these ancient Egyptian medical treatments required expensive and rare ingredients that limited who could actually afford to be treated, but the most frequent ingredients 70 found in these texts tended to be common household items like honey and grease.	As used in line 70, "common" most nearly means: **A.** accepted. **B.** ordinary. **C.** vulgar. **D.** recurrent.

Here, only answer choice (B) makes sense when you plug it into the original sentence. While all the other answer choices are valid synonyms of "common," they do not provide the same contrast with the rest of the sentence, which suggests that rather than being "expensive and rare" most ingredients were regular, everyday items. You can learn more about this strategy and question type in Chapter 4, Section 6.

Pacing
Part 5

There are a lot of questions on the ACT, and you need to answer them under timed conditions, so it's important to consider your **Pacing**. The following table shows the time allowed (in minutes) for each of the ACT tests, and the number of questions on each test.

English	Math	Reading	Science	Total
45 minutes	60 minutes	35 minutes	35 minutes	175 minutes
75 questions	60 questions	40 questions	40 questions	215 questions

As you can see, there are more questions on the ACT than there are minutes to answer them. That means that you have to move pretty quickly. You can divide the time allowed for each test by the number of questions to figure out how much time, on average, you can spend on each question. Pacing *isn't* about spending exactly the right amount of time on each question. The more you check your watch, the less time you have to answer questions.

The challenge of effective pacing is to find the combination of strategies that best allows you to complete the exam with confidence and accuracy, and to practice your pacing so that you have a feel for it on test day—without needing to watch the clock. The best way to get a feel for the pace of the exam is to develop a conscious pacing strategy, then do timed practice until you begin to get a sense of how it feels to move at the right pace.

To begin developing your pace, you should set a target pace for a section of the exam. Then, pick a few **checkpoints**: predetermined points where you will check how much time has elapsed so far and quickly compare it to your plan. To determine your checkpoints, pick a few fairly evenly spaced points on the exam, and determine how much time you should have used up when you have reached each checkpoint, and therefore how much you should have remaining.

It's a good idea to remember no more than you have to. Remember the checkpoint location and the time that should've elapsed by that point. Don't worry about the time remaining. As long as you're on track (or close to it), you'll be in good shape.

Here are some examples of what checkpoints might look like on each section of the ACT:

English (Average time: 9 minutes per passage)	
Checkpoint	Time Elapsed
Question 30 (end of Passage II)	18 minutes
Question 45 (end of Passage III)	27 minutes
Question 60 (end of Passage IV)	36 minutes

Math (Average time: 1 minute per question)	
Checkpoint	Time Elapsed
Question 30 (halfway)	20 minutes
Question 45 (three-quarters)	40 minutes

Reading (Average time: 8 minutes and 30 seconds per passage)	
Checkpoint	Time Elapsed
Question 20 (end of Passage II, halfway)	17 minutes
Question 30 (end of Passage III)	25 minutes

Science (Average time: 5 minutes and 50 seconds per passage)	
Checkpoint	Time Elapsed
End of Passage II	11 minutes
End of Passage III (halfway)	17 minutes
End of Passage IV	23 minutes

If you're behind your checkpoints, you can consider using a time-saving pacing strategy we call **Pick and Skip**. This refers to working on questions that are easier for you first, and leaving more challenging or time-consuming questions for later, or simply making your best guess.

Remember that every question on the ACT is worth one point, no matter how easy or difficult it is. That means it is to your advantage to earn points by first answering questions you find easy. Noting which kinds of questions you can answer quickly versus those that take more time, and which questions you answer accurately versus incorrectly, is crucial if you wish to apply the Pick and Skip strategy

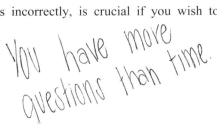

You have more questions than time.

effectively. However, be sure to use it with caution, as it can increase your chances of making errors when bubbling in your answers.

In the end, make sure to pay attention to how different strategies affect your pacing and accuracy. Some of the strategies described in this section, like Pick and Skip, increase your speed at the expense of your accuracy. Others, like Pencil on Paper, increase your accuracy at the expense of your speed. Ultimately, you should use the combination of strategies that allows you to answer each question as accurately as you can without running out of time.

English
Chapter 2

Section 1
Approaching the English Test

The ACT English Test is a test of writing and editing skills. You will be presented with a series of passages written in a few different styles and about various subjects. Questions in this section will test your knowledge of grammar rules and the elements of effective writing. Some questions will prompt you to correct errors of Usage and Mechanics in the areas of Punctuation, Grammar, and Sentence Structure, which we'll discuss in Sections 2–4. You'll also be prompted to improve or answer questions about the passages to demonstrate Rhetorical Skills in the areas of Writing Strategy, Organization, and Style, which we'll discuss in Sections 5–7.

In this section, we're going to explain the basic format of the English Test and how it is scored, explain how to interpret the questions and provide some examples, and tell you how you can best plan your overall approach to the English Test.

- The Basics
- Reading the English Test
- Planning your Approach

While the passages and questions will be new every time, the overall structure of the ACT English Test will always be the same. By becoming familiar with the ACT English Test now, you'll be well-prepared on test day!

The Basics
Part 1

Before we discuss strategies for tackling the test, we want to tell you about the format of the exam and how it is scored. Learning these basic facts will help you to understand the strategies that we recommend, and avoid surprises on test day.

ACT English Test by the Numbers

You will have 45 minutes to complete the ACT English Test, which is made up of five passages. Each passage will also be accompanied by 15 questions, for a total of 75 multiple choice questions.

The English Test		
Time	45 minutes	~9 minutes per passage
Text	5 passages	300–350 words per passage
Questions	75 questions	15 questions per passage

45 minutes to work through five passages averages out to nine minutes per passage. It also works out to about 36 seconds per question.

That may seem daunting, but the reality is that you'll probably answer a lot of the questions in just a few seconds and spend most of your time on a handful of the more challenging questions. Later in this section, we will discuss some strategies for reading the passages effectively and approaching the questions within the time limit.

There are two basic question types on the ACT English Test. The ACT is renaming the categories on score reports for September 2016 and later, but they still contain the same types of questions. We'll talk more about these question types later in this section.

Usage and Mechanics (40 Questions)		
Punctuation	10	~13% of test
Grammar	12	~16% of test
Sentence Structure	18	~24% of test

Rhetorical Skills (35 Questions)		
Writing Strategy	12	~16% of test
Organization	11	~15% of test
Style	12	~16% of test

Each of the Rhetorical Skills question types appears about as frequently as any other, but Sentence Structure is the most common question type in Usage and Mechanics and on the exam overall. That means that understanding Sentence Structure questions is key to doing well on the ACT.

Scoring

You will receive a couple of different scores based on your answers on the English Test. You will receive an English Test score on a scale of 1–36. You'll also receive a percentile score, which shows what percentage of students received a lower score than you. For example: if you scored in the 55th percentile, you did better than 55% of students.

The English portion of your score report will look a bit like this:

	Score	U.S. Rank
English	20	51%

The English score is based on your answers to all of the questions on the English Test. You have a raw score that isn't reported, which is equal to the number of questions you answer correctly. This is converted to a scaled score on a scale of 1–36. The scaled score is the score that is reported on your score report. The scale for the exam is set by the performance of all of the students taking the exam, so the conversion of a specific raw score to a specific scaled score varies from one exam to another—but usually not by very much.

The Passages

The passages on the English Test will be similar to passages you have read in the classroom. They will be 300–350 words in length, broken up into paragraphs. That's a relatively short length for a passage: there are 333 words just on this page. However, because of the way that the ACT is formatted, each passage will be spread out across two or three pages. The passages will not be ordered by subject or difficulty.

The ACT English Test also asks you to demonstrate skills that you might not have been tested on in English class. Rather than just composing sentences without errors, you'll need to actually correct errors in a longer passage.

The English Test also focuses on very different skills than the Reading Test does. It will still pay to read passages carefully on the English Test, but you won't be asked detailed questions about their implicit or stated meanings as you would in a reading comprehension quiz or the ACT Reading Test. ACT English passages are also shorter than those on the Reading Test, and generally easier to read and understand.

ACT passages will cover a variety of subject areas and a variety of topics, and can be written in a variety of styles:

Subject Area	Example Topics
Science	Topics can include anatomy, astronomy, biology, botany, chemistry, ecology, geology, medicine, meteorology, microbiology, natural history, physiology, physics, technology, and zoology.
History	Topics can range from ancient history to global contemporary history.
Humanities	Topics can include architecture, art, dance, ethics, film, language, literary criticism, music, philosophy, radio, television, and theater.
Narrative	Topics can include a wide range of personal narratives including memoirs, biographies, profiles, and anecdotes.

Style	Description
Anecdote	Anecdotes are personal stories. These will generally be written in the first-person ("I," "me," etc.), and can be fairly informal.
Nonfiction Narrative	Some of the stories on the ACT will be a little more formal in tone, and might be written in the third-person ("he," "she," etc.), while still describing a series of events.
Informative	Most of the ACT passages will fall into this fairly broad category. These will usually be written in the third-person, but less formal ones may include second-person ("you") components. The most formal passages on the ACT will fall into this category, but the category can also include some less formal writing.

In general, your approach to passages on different subjects should be similar. However, you'll need to pay attention to the style and tone of each passage in order to correctly answer certain question types. We'll discuss those question types further in the Style section of this chapter.

The Questions

The English Test is not like most classroom grammar or vocabulary tests. You won't be asked direct questions about grammatical rules, such as "What tense do you use for completed actions?" You also won't be quizzed on the meanings of obscure words.

Passages in the English Test will contain errors. The questions in this section mainly ask you to select revisions for selected portions of each passage to correct errors, or improve the writing of the passage. A few questions will ask about the likely effects of certain changes, or about the writing of the passage as a whole. Some of the questions will also ask you to add or remove information on the basis of its relevance or appropriateness, but you won't have to fact-check the information. The mistakes in the passages are grammatical, stylistic, and logical—not factual.

Some types of questions will appear only at the end of a passage. These questions ask you to think about the entire passage, so they can be more challenging than some other question types. Other than these, questions are not ordered by difficulty.

You will be asked questions about Punctuation, Grammar, Sentence Structure, Writing Strategy, Organization, and Style. The rest of this chapter will introduce you to all of these concepts in more detail, and will teach you strategies for approaching each question type.

You can work through the practice questions and exams in this book to figure out which question types are the most challenging for you, and focus on studying those question types. If you have room for improvement in more than one subject area, you can focus first on improving in the areas that make up more of the test.

Reading the English Test
Part 2

The English Test has a complicated format. You don't want to be confused on test day, so it's a good idea to familiarize yourself with this format now.

First of all, there are two basic formats for questions on the English Test: the **unstated question** format, which provides answer choices but no specific question, and the **stated question** format, which poses a specific question before the answer choices.

Unstated questions are the most common format, and simply provide answer options. There is always a portion of the passage underlined next to them, and the implied question is "Which choice best replaces the underlined portion of the passage?" "NO CHANGE" is provided as an option for those cases in which the underlined portion of the passage is best as it is currently written.

Example	
The Supremes hold the record for the most number-one hit's by an American vocal group.	**A.** NO CHANGE **B.** hits' **C.** hit **D.** hits

Stated questions can appear with or without an underlined portion of the passage next to them. When there is no underlined portion, the question will state which part of the passage, if any, the writer is considering changing.

Example	
For good oral hygiene, we should limit our intake of certain foods and beverages. Soft drinks, for instance, are bad for teeth on account of their high acid levels. Sugary sweets also promote tooth decay, by fostering harmful bacteria; these bacteria then produce acids that erode teeth. [1]	The writer is considering deleting the phrase "by fostering harmful bacteria" from the preceding sentence. Should the writer make this change? **F.** Yes, because the specific details about how sugar promotes tooth decay are distracting. **G.** Yes, because additional details about bacteria are redundant. **H.** No, because deleting this phrase would make the later reference to the bacteria confusing. **J.** No, because these details are necessary to support the main idea of the paragraph.

You may have heard the saying, "An apple a day keeps the doctor away." Apples, for example, have a rough texture that cleans teeth and gums.

Which choice most effectively guides the reader from the preceding paragraph into this new paragraph?

A. NO CHANGE

B. Yet some foods have the opposite effect, and help to keep teeth healthy.

C. It is therefore very important to avoid consuming acids.

D. Apples are very crunchy.

Two-part questions will ask you to choose both the best answer and the best supporting reason for that answer. These questions always provide two "yes, because" and two "no, because" options.

Example

Georgia O'Keeffe moved to New Mexico in 1929. She loved the desert landscapes of the northern part of the state, and they greatly influenced her art. [1]

At this point, the writer is considering adding the following true statement:

> The second largest city in New Mexico is Las Cruces.

Should the writer add this sentence here?

F. Yes, because it provides interesting background information about the state of New Mexico.

G. Yes, because it reminds readers that the second largest city in New Mexico is not Santa Fe.

H. No, because it distracts the reader from the main point of this paragraph.

J. No, because it does not provide specific enough information about Las Cruces.

Interrelated questions may ask about different elements of the same sentence or nearby parts of the passage. While you can always find the answers independently, sometimes it's easier to answer one question after answering the other.

Example

When she first started teaching, the teacher worried that her students would see group work as a chance to cheat on assignments. The teacher realized, regardless, that working together

A. NO CHANGE

B. thus,

C. however,

D. specifically,

gave the students a chance to <u>practice</u> and it wasn't

cheating at all.

F. NO CHANGE
G. practicing
H. practiced
J. practices

When you answer interrelated questions, don't feel obligated to answer them in order. You might want to clear up the Sentence Structure error in Question 2 first, and then turn to the Organization error in Question 1. The answer that you choose for the second question doesn't directly affect the answer to the first question, but the sentence is easier to understand as a whole when you correct the smaller errors first. This can make it easier to think about broader questions.

Whole-paragraph questions will usually focus on the placement of a sentence within a paragraph.

Example

I was shy of speaking as a child, and yet remarkably unembarrassed by public silliness. When I was called upon to speak up in class, I could only just squeak out the minimum required to satisfy the teacher. [A] However, I was happy to boldly stroll down the street caked in mud after a rainy afternoon spent sliding down a muddy hill with friends. [B] I was perfectly happy to join the other children at play as a dog, going down on all fours in the dirt and barking—but I struggled to invite them to my birthday party. [C] Now that I've entered the adult world, my behavior is almost entirely reversed. [D] I'm perfectly happy to speak before a room of colleagues on the details of a project, but I would be incredibly embarrassed to even stand quietly in the room with muddy clothes. I'd be absolutely mortified to be tickled in public, but I can unabashedly express the very strongest opinions about the weather to just about anyone.

The writer wants to divide this paragraph in order to separate details about the narrator's childhood and adulthood. The best place to begin a new paragraph would be:

A. at Point A.
B. at Point B.
C. at Point C.
D. at Point D.

The example above uses alphabetical "points" to indicate the places where you might begin a new paragraph. Some questions will employ numbered sentences instead, as below:

Questions about the passage as a whole occur at the very end of a set of questions. They may focus on the order of paragraphs within the passage, the introduction of new material, or the writer's purpose in writing the passage. Questions of this type are easily identified by a box indicating that they are about the whole passage.

Planning Your Approach
Part 3

Now that you know the general structure of the English Test, you can begin to plan your approach. You should have a plan for tackling the test as a whole, strategies for answering questions, and a study schedule that you can stick to.

First, consider these general strategies for planning how to approach the section:

- **Read passages in order.** You may have been advised at some point that you can do better if you skim each passage before starting and then start with the easiest one. That can make sense on some other exams, but not the ACT. All of the passages on the ACT are pretty similar in difficulty, so it's not really worth the extra time and effort to take them out of order.
- **Read every part of the passage.** You should not "skim" the passages, trying to read only the important parts. Assume that every sentence is important! Even if sentences don't have underlined portions, they may give you valuable information that you will use to answer the questions.
- **Attempt the questions in order.** When you come to the point of a question in the passage, try it. The questions are placed so that you should have enough context to answer them by the time you reach their number in the passage; if you can't answer a question when you first encounter it, circle it in your test booklet and come back to it before you move on to the next passage.
- **Complete each passage before you move on**. Make sure you attempt all questions for a passage before moving on. It is easiest to answer the questions while the passage is fresh in your mind. If you're not sure about a question, circle it in your test booklet and enter a guess on your answer sheet. That way, you can easily go back to the question if you have extra time to check your answers after finishing the last passage.

Using this overall approach will help you to keep a steady pace as you proceed through the exam and maximize your chances of answering every question.

Strategies for Answering Questions

Once you have an overall strategy, you can start thinking about how you're going to handle individual questions. You should review the 5 Ps in the first chapter of this book to see how you can apply some of those essential test-taking strategies in the English section.

Pay special attention to Process of Elimination, which is one of the most important test-taking strategies that you can use on the English section. Also pay attention to Predicting, which can help you quickly answer Rhetorical Skills questions that could otherwise eat into your time.

There are also a couple of tips that apply only in this section. You should learn when to pick "NO CHANGE," and you should practice building your English skills every day, using the content in this book and from other sources.

Choosing "NO CHANGE"

Much of this chapter will be focused on how to spot and correct errors in the passages on the English Test. However, some portions of the passages will need no correction. In these cases, you should choose (A) or (F), for "NO CHANGE."

When questions have "NO CHANGE" as a possible answer, you should not be afraid to pick it! Many students are hesitant to pick "NO CHANGE" because it seems "too easy." However, there *are* portions of the passage that are already in their best form. Remember to read the underlined portion and predict what the answer should be based on context, then go through the answers and eliminate bad choices. If you do this and still think that the portion is best unchanged, then it probably is! Go ahead and bubble in (A) or (F) as your answer.

Example	
He was nearly forty years younger, yet his writing was <u>stronger and more popular</u> than his mentor's writing.	**F.** NO CHANGE **G.** was stronger and most popular **H.** was more stronger and more popular **J.** was strongest and most popular

This sentence doesn't have any grammatical or stylistic errors, so the original version is correct. However, you also want to check the other answer choices to make sure that (F) is the best answer before you select it. Answer choices (G), (H), and (J) all contain grammatical errors, so they cannot be the correct answer. Therefore, you would choose (F), "NO CHANGE."

You may find that (A) or (F), "NO CHANGE," is the answer for more than one question in a single passage. Again, don't second guess your answer just because you think there isn't an error. Follow the strategies above and feel confident in your choice!

Practicing Your English Skills Daily

A little bit of studying every day for a long time is better than a lot of studying just before the exam. Plan to practice daily, and mix your practice on the English Test with other sections. By studying consistently, you'll learn the material more deeply and have an easier time applying your English skills on test day.

One final, important way to improve the skills tested on the English Test is to practice standard English even when you're not being graded for it. When writing emails, sending texts, or writing for fun, get in the habit of using punctuation, capitalization, complete sentences, and proper grammar, and read what you write, making any necessary corrections. Finally, read material that challenges you every day. You can find a reading list organized by grade and subject matter in our supplementary materials online.

 For additional resources, please visit **ivyglobal.com/study**.

Section 2
Grammar

Grammar is a very broad term. The grammar of a language is the set of rules that governs how words and phrases are formed, what order they should go in, and even which words and phrases should be used to express certain ideas.

On the ACT English Test, Grammar questions test your ability to apply the rules of English grammar to correct the formation of certain words and phrases, the agreement of words and phrases within a sentence, and the uses of words and phrases in order to express certain ideas. In order to master the grammatical rules tested in this section, you need to have a good understanding of a few more basic concepts that we'll review before discussing the kinds of questions that you'll see on the ACT. In this section, we will cover:

- Parts of Speech
- Grammatical Agreement
- Verb Forms
- Pronoun Forms
- Comparatives and Superlatives
- Idioms

Grammar questions on the ACT are usually not designed to trick you. There are a few tricks and traps that we will discuss, but if you are able to memorize and apply the rules that we discuss in this section, then correctly answering most Grammar questions should be a straightforward task.

There are 12 Grammar questions on the ACT English Test, which is 16% of the test.

Parts of Speech
Part 1

Parts of speech are the types of words used in sentences. Knowing what part of speech a word is tells you what it does in a sentence. In order to learn rules for words and sentences, you need to know how to identify what part of speech you're working with.

Nouns are words that refer to people, places, things, or ideas. In the following sentences, nouns are underlined.

> Friday is usually my favorite day of the week.
> My dog ate my shoes this morning.
> I put on my furry slippers.
> The whole class laughed.
> Ms. Samuels liked my humor!

Nouns can be in a **singular** form, meaning that they refer to one of the type of thing that they represent. "Dog" is singular: that form of the word refers to only one dog.

Nouns can also take a **plural** form, meaning that they refer to more than one of the thing that they represent. "Dogs" is plural: that form of the word refers to two or more dogs. The plural form of a noun is most often formed by adding an "s" to the end of the singular form, though some plural nouns have different spellings.

Possessive nouns show ownership. Instead of saying, "the sweater that Cindy owns," we say, "Cindy's sweater." In a sentence, the possessive noun is the noun that is "doing" the owning: possessive nouns modify other nouns, and the nouns they modify describe what is owned.

Most possessive nouns have an apostrophe and an extra "s" added to the end, though some don't need an "s." We'll talk more about making possessive nouns in the Punctuation part of this book.

Sometimes nouns will be replaced by **pronouns**. In the following sentences, pronouns are underlined.

> My sisters don't like to watch TV, but they love when my parents take them to the movies.
> Maybe my parents will take me too!
> We should see the scary movie.

The noun that a pronoun replaces is called its **antecedent**. The antecedent has to be somewhere close to the pronoun so it can give us the context we need to understand who or what a pronoun is talking about. In the first example on the previous page, "sisters" is the antecedent of "they."

In the following sentences, pronoun/antecedent pairs are underlined.

Marcus never tries any food that he thinks he won't like.
Claire and Jordan are very adventurous, so they try new food often.

Pronouns also express **grammatical person**. The three grammatical persons are the **first person**, indicated by "I" and "me," the **second person**, indicated by "you," and the **third person**, indicated by "he," "she," "it," "they," or any noun that could be replaced by one of those pronouns.

Verbs are words that refer to actions or states of being. In the following sentences, verbs are underlined.

I learned new Spanish words in class, but I forgot them all by the next day.
I became embarrassed when I couldn't even remember how to say my name!
Kat always laughs way too hard at her own jokes.
Brianna, on the other hand, is actually funny.

The two main types of verbs are **action verbs** (words for actions, like "learned," "laughs," or "say") and **linking verbs** (words for states of being, like "is," "became," or "could").

All verbs have **subjects**: the subject of a verb is the noun that's performing an action, or that is in the state of being.

Some verbs also have **objects**, which are the nouns that are receiving an action. **Transitive verbs** are verbs that have an object. We've underlined the verb, its subject, and its object in the following sentence:

Luisa carries the box.

"Carries" is the verb. Luisa is the one doing the carrying, so she's the subject. The box is being carried, so it's the object. Because "carries" has an object, it's a transitive verb.

Intransitive verbs are verbs that have no object. Consider the following example:

Helen runs.

"Helen" is the one doing the running, so she is the subject. "Runs" is the action, so it's the verb. There is no object, because Helen isn't running something: she's just running.

Many verbs can be either transitive or intransitive, depending on the context of the sentence.

Verbs also change to show their **tense**. This feature of a verb tells us when an action takes place. You must be careful to make sure that verbs in ACT questions are in the right tense. Let's review the most commonly tested tenses on the ACT.

The **present tense** is used to talk about actions that are currently happening, that happen generally or regularly, or that happen in literature.

> You <u>are</u> reading. (currently happening)
> He <u>cries</u> every time he <u>goes</u> to a sad movie. (regularly)
> In Oscar Wilde's novel, Dorian Gray <u>descends</u> into a life of sin. (literature)

The **past tense** is used to talk about events that occurred and were completed in the past. It is often formed by adding "-d" or "-ed" to the end of a verb, but some English verbs form their past tense in different ways. These are called **irregular verbs**, and you can find a list of irregular verbs with our other online resources.

 For additional resources, please visit **ivyglobal.com/study**.

> I <u>unzipped</u> my backpack to find it full of eggs.
> She <u>ran</u> as fast as she could.

The **imperfect past tense** is used to talk about continuous or ongoing actions in the past. It is formed by adding "was" or "were" before the –ing form of a verb.

> To be fair, you <u>were trying</u> to steal my sandals.
> She <u>was looking</u> intently at the paintings.

You can use the imperfect and regular past tenses together to talk about events in the past. This means that both events happened at the same time, or one event interrupted the other.

> We <u>were going</u> to the bookstore when the bicycle <u>hit</u> us.
> My leg <u>cramped</u> while I <u>was swimming</u>.

The **present perfect tense** is used to talk about actions that occurred in the past, but are continuing in the present. It is formed by adding "has" or "have" before a special form of the verb called the **past participle**.

Lucy <u>has played</u> the cello for years.

Tomás and David <u>have eaten</u> way too many chicken nuggets.

The past participle of irregular verbs is often different from the regular past tense form of the verb. For example, the perfect past tense of "go" is "have gone," not "have went." Refer to the list of irregular verbs included in our online resources to learn the past tense and past participle of some common irregular verbs.

 For additional resources, please visit **ivyglobal.com/study**.

The **remote past** or **perfect past tense** is used to talk about past events that took place before some other event or point in time that is already in the past. It is formed by adding "had" to the past participle.

The movie bored me because I <u>had seen</u> it twice already.

You weren't interested in the gossip because you <u>had</u> already <u>heard</u> the truth.

The **future tense** is used to talk about events that will happen in the future. It is formed by adding "will" or "shall" to the verb.

We <u>will talk</u> about this later.

Tomorrow I <u>shall be</u> in Aruba.

You may also want to talk about the future but from a time in the past. For example, you can discuss beliefs or thoughts about the future that you had at a previous time. When talking about hypothetical events or future events from a past perspective, use "would" rather than "will."

Medieval warriors believed they <u>would</u> win if they were strong in their faith.

I thought that she <u>would</u> get the best score in the class.

Take a look at the timeline below if you get confused about what verb tense to use:

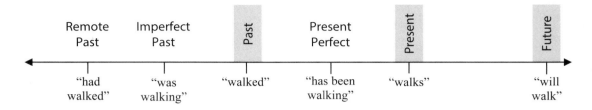

Finally, verbs also vary in **voice**. When a verb's voice changes, the entire sentence gets rearranged. When a sentence is in the **active voice**, the subject is the "doer" of the sentence's action:

My brother ate the cookies.

In this sentence, the subject (my brother) performs the action (eating), and the object (the cookies) receives that action. You can flip the order of the subject and object by making some changes to the sentence. In the **passive voice**, the subject doesn't actually perform the action:

The cookies were eaten by my brother.

Now the cookies are the subject of the sentence, even though they aren't performing the "eating"—my brother is the one who is eating. This rearrangement is written in the passive voice. The passive voice may sound more awkward to your ear than the active voice. In general, the ACT will want you to change sentences from the passive voice to the active voice.

Adjectives are words that describe or give more information about nouns—in technical terms, they "modify" nouns. In the following sentences, adjectives are underlined.

The food in the <u>new</u> cafeteria is very <u>flavorful</u>.
They only serve <u>raw</u>, <u>organic</u>, and <u>vegan</u> foods.

Adjectives usually come before the nouns they modify or are connected to them by linking verbs.

Possessive nouns and pronouns often behave the same way as adjectives: instead of standing on their own, they modify another noun. When you see a possessive noun or pronoun, it will usually be next to the noun that it modifies. When it's not, it modifies a noun that appears somewhere else in the passage. Possessive nouns and pronouns are punctuated in different ways: we'll discuss them further in the Punctuation section.

Adjectives should not be confused with **adverbs**, which describe or give more information about adjectives, verbs, or other adverbs. In the following sentences, adverbs are underlined.

I can run pretty quickly when I put my mind to it.
My first race went well, but I could have done better.
Sophia and I went to the play, but it clearly wasn't a date.
I'm a very good cook, but I really hate doing the dishes.

As you can see, some adverbs end in the suffix "-ly," although many do not. Adverbs usually answer questions about the adjective or verb, like "where?", "why?", "when?", "to what extent?", or "how?".

There is also a special kind of adjective called an **article**. There are two articles, and they are some of the most common words in English: "a" and "the" ("an" is a form of "a"). You won't be tested directly on articles by the ACT, but you should know two things about them:

- They're *not* nouns or pronouns, so they won't be an antecedent, subject, or object.
- "A" always describes a singular noun, but "the" can describe singular or plural nouns.

Prepositions describe the relationships between other words in a sentence. In the following sentences, prepositions are underlined.

I'm thinking about walking to school today.
Marwan handed his phone to Sofia, who plugged it into the charger.

Prepositional phrases are phrases that begin with prepositions and add descriptive information to a sentence. We'll talk more about them in Section 3, Sentence Structure.

Keep in mind that many prepositions can also be other parts of speech. This can be especially tricky with the word "to," because it has two very common roles: as a preposition, and as part of a verb. We've underlined the preposition in the following sentence:

I like to ride my bike to the coffee shop.

You should notice that "to" is not underlined the first time it pops up, but is underlined the second time. That's because the first instance is part of the verb "to ride." When "to" comes right before a verb, it's not a preposition: it's part of the verb. The second instance, "to the coffee shop," is a prepositional phrase describing the place I'd like to go on my bike.

You should become comfortable naming and identifying all of these parts of speech, because you're going to see them in a lot of explanations!

Agreement
Part 2

Some words in English change their form depending on certain factors. Words may have to take similar forms across a sentence, and this is called **agreement**. Some questions on the English Test will test your ability to tell if different types of words correctly agree with other words in the sentence. Here's an example of the sort of Agreement questions you might see on the ACT:

Example
A Japanese *bunraku* puppet is operated by three puppeteers—one for the legs, one for the left arm, and one for the right arm and head—who <u>controls</u> the puppet using long, thin rods.   **A.** NO CHANGE **B.** has been controlling **C.** control **D.** is controlling

This question focuses on **subject-verb agreement**, which is one form of agreement the ACT will test. Verbs must always agree with their subjects, and these questions require you to identify and correct the verbs that don't agree.

In this question, the phrase between em-dashes ("—") separates the subject from the verb. When you ask yourself "who's doing the controlling?" the answer should be "the puppeteers," which is a plural subject. (A), (B), and (D) each take singular subjects. (C) is the only form of the verb that agrees with a plural subject, so it's the correct answer.

Most verbs use the same form in the present tense for every combination of person and number except the third-person singular ("he," "she," or "it"). Verbs in the simple future and simple past tenses almost always use the same form, regardless of the number and person. Here are some forms of "control":

To Control			
Present Tense			
Singular	I control	You control	He/she/it controls
Plural	We control	You control	They control

Past Tense	
I/We/You/He/She/It/They	controlled

Future Tense	
I/We/You/He/She/It/They	will control

Many verbs are like "control": you can tell what form they should take even if you've never seen the verb before. Add an "s" for he/she/it subjects, an "ed" for past tense, or "will" for the future.

Verbs that have different forms than these are called **irregular verbs**. One very common exception is the verb "to be." This verb has different forms for the singular and plural first person in the present and past tenses:

To Be			
Present Tense			
Singular	I am	You are	He/she/it is
Plural	We are	You are	They are
Past Tense			
Singular	I was	You were	He/she/it was
Plural	We were	You were	They were
Future Tense			
I/We/You/He/She/It/They		will be	

It's important to learn the forms of the verb "to be," because it is commonly used as a helping verb to express the tense, number, and person of another verb.

The ACT may also try to trick you with subjects that are ambiguously singular or plural. This can happen when parts of the subject are connected by "and" or "or."

Subjects with "and" are always plural.

The bowl and the spoon are in the cabinet.	**F.**	NO CHANGE
	G.	is
	H.	am
	J.	was

Because the subject "the bowl and the spoon" is plural, the correct answer is (F), "are."

When the subject uses "or," the verb agrees with the *closer* word.

| Example |

Either Brian or his colleagues is bringing donuts.	**A.**	NO CHANGE
	B.	has been
	C.	was
	D.	are

Since the subject is "Brian or his colleagues," the verb has to agree with the closer part of the subject. In this case, that's the plural noun "colleagues." (D), "are," is the only verb that agrees with a plural subject, so it's the correct choice.

Certain pronouns can also make it difficult to figure out whether the subject is singular or plural.

Neither of my sisters is/are good at sports.
Each of the princes has/have a chance to take the throne.

In these cases, it may be tempting to use the plural verb form, especially if you think that the plural nouns ("sisters" or "princes") are the subjects. However, those plural nouns are both objects of the preposition "of," which means that they can't be the subjects. The true subjects here are the pronouns "neither" and "each," which are both singular.

Neither of my sisters is good at sports.
Each of the princes has a chance to take the throne.

Here are some other pronouns that are always singular:

Singular Pronouns	
Either	Either of those gifts is a good choice.
Someone	I hope someone brings the cake!
Anyone	If anyone speaks, we will lose the game.
Somebody	Somebody always forgets to close the garage.
Nobody	By the time I got there, nobody was awake.
Everything	Everything in the kitchen seems clean.
Anybody	Let me know if anybody finds my keys.
Everyone	Everyone in my town loves football.

The ACT might also try to make agreement questions trickier by separating verbs from their subjects and pronouns from their antecedents. Consider the following example:

Example	
The best part about living in big cities, like New York City, is that they has a lot of concerts, art exhibitions, and other cultural events to enjoy.	F. NO CHANGE G. it has H. they have J. it have

Reading this sentence quickly, you might see the singular New York City mentioned and think the pronoun and verb should be singular ("it has"). However, try removing the part of the sentence that is set off between two commas. Material set off by commas in this way is often additional information that can be removed. Take out this phrase, and you are left with:

The best part about living in big cities is that ~~they has~~ a lot of concerts, art exhibitions, and other cultural events to enjoy.	F. NO CHANGE G. it has H. they have J. it have

The pronoun refers to "big cities," which is plural. This means the pronoun and its verb should also be plural, so (H) is correct.

The ACT will also occasionally leave a word out, allowing it to be implied in a particular sentence because it appears elsewhere in a passage. Keep an eye out for cases that call for an implied word:

> Julie and Bob both collect rocks. Julie's <u>are</u> mostly rare and valuable minerals, while Bob's <u>are</u> mostly common minerals with interesting shapes.

In this example, the verb "are" is taking the subject "rocks." That word doesn't actually even appear in the sentence with the underlined verb: only the possessive nouns "Julie's" and "Bob's" are used. However, those are acting as modifiers—and they *imply* the noun that they modify. Here's how the sentence reads with the implied words inserted:

> Julie and Bob both collect rocks. Julie's [rocks] <u>are</u> mostly rare and valuable minerals, while Bob's [rocks] <u>are</u> mostly common minerals with interesting shapes.

In this version, it's clear that the verb "are" takes the plural subject "rocks."

Finally, the ACT will sometimes test **adjective-noun agreement** and **adverb-verb** agreement. Many descriptive words have both adjective and adverb forms. The ACT will test your ability to choose between the adverb and adjective forms of a modifier depending on whether it modifies a noun or a verb. Here's an example of this type of agreement question:

Example	
Researchers <u>diligently record even</u> <u>uninterestingly</u> findings, because they know that all of the data matter.	**A.** NO CHANGE **B.** diligent record even uninteresting **C.** diligent record even uninterestingly **D.** diligently record even uninteresting

To answer these questions, you just need to remember that:

1. Adjectives modify nouns, and adverbs modify verbs, adjectives, or other adverbs.
2. Adjectives and adverbs are typically placed right next to the words that they modify.

In this question, "record" is acting as a verb and "findings" is a noun, so we should select the answer choice that modifies "record" with an adverb and "findings" with an adjective. In this case, that's (D), "diligently record even uninteresting findings."

If you're unsure whether a word is an adjective or an adverb, remember that descriptive words ending in "-ly" are usually adverbs.

Verb Forms
Part 3

The ACT won't just test your ability to recognize the form that's correct in a particular context. Sometimes, the ACT will also test your ability to recognize verb forms that would not be correct in *any* context and replace them with correct verb forms. Consider the following example:

Example	
I would have <u>drove</u> you home, but I was out of gas.	**F.** NO CHANGE **G.** drive **H.** driven **J.** driving

"Drove" is a past tense form of "drive," and we're talking about events that occurred in the past. However, that's not the correct answer. The helping verb "have" is *part of this verb*, and that gives it its tense. (F), (G), and (J) each fail to complete a correct verb form. Only (H), "have driven," is a correct verb form. This isn't a matter of agreement: "have drive," "have drove," and "have driving" are never correct verb forms.

Verb forms can change depending on tense and voice. You need to know the simple present and simple past tenses of a verb, which we've already discussed. On top of that, you need at least two more forms.

You need to be able to identify the **past participle**. The past participle is usually the same as the simple past tense, but there are enough exceptions that you should keep a second rule in mind: to figure out the past participle, think of how you would describe an object of the verb. If I "drive" you home, you are being "driven" home. If I "fly" you home, you are being "flown" home. If I "help" you home, you are being "helped" home. "Driven," "flown," and "helped" are the past participles of "drive," "fly," and "help."

You also need to be able to identify the **present participle**: this is sometimes also called the "-ing" form because it is usually the base form of the verb with "-ing" added to the end. "Driving," "flying," and "throwing" are the present participles or "-ing" forms of "drive," "fly," and "throw."

Once you know these two forms of a verb, you can complete the other tenses correctly by paying attention to **helping verbs** (also called **auxiliary verbs**) in the sentence. Helping verbs are verbs that add on to the main verb in the sentence and change its tense. They also determine which form of the verb you should use. Sometimes, there are two or more helping verbs before a main verb. In that case, the helping verb closest to the main verb determines the form that you should use.

Note that the forms of the verb "to be" behave differently depending on whether a sentence is in the active or passive voice. You can check the following table to see how helping verbs and voice determine the form of the main verb.

Active Voice be / been / is / are / was / were	Present Participle	Lisa is driving Peter to the store.
Passive Voice be / been / is / are / was / were	Past Participle	Peter was driven to the store by Lisa.
being / have / has / had / having	Past Participle	Peter is being driven to the store by Lisa.
can / could / do / does / did / may / might / must / should / will / would	Base Form	Lisa can drive Peter to the store.

Let's look again at our example:

I would have drove you home, but I was out of gas.

F. NO CHANGE
G. drive
H. driven
J. driving

The past tense of "drive" is "drove," but the helping verb "have" lets us know that we need to use the past participle "driven" to complete the verb tense that "have" is making us use. "Drove" isn't wrong because the tense isn't logical, or it doesn't agree with the subject; it just doesn't correctly complete the verb. It's never correct to write "would have drove" in any context.

When you look for helping verbs, keep in mind that they aren't always right next to the verb that they modify. Consider the following example:

Example

He would gladly drives you home, but he is out of gas.

A. NO CHANGE
B. driving
C. driven
D. drive

Although the adverb "gladly" falls between "would" and "drive," the helping verb "would" still determines the tense of "drive," and we have to use the base form of the verb—(D), "drive."

Every action verb also has an **infinitive** form, which might also be incorrectly formed in a Verb Forms question. The infinitive form of a verb is just the word "to" and the base form of the verb. Any other tense or form of the verb after "to" will not form a correct infinitive. Here's an example:

Example	
I wanted to <u>driven</u> you home, but I was out of gas.	**F.** NO CHANGE **G.** drove **H.** drive **J.** had driven

You always combine the base form of the verb with "to" to make the infinitive: it doesn't matter what tense the rest of the sentence is in. The example sentence above discusses events that occurred in the past, but it's still not correct to write "wanted to drove." (H) correctly uses the base form of the verb.

Note that you can still combine other helping verbs with "to," but they have to use their base form. (J), "had driven," isn't incorrect because it uses another helping verb, but only because it uses the past-tense "had" instead of the base form of the verb "have," which would correctly complete the infinitive "to have driven."

Finally, the ACT may also test your knowledge of the forms of irregular verbs. Since these verbs don't follow the regular rules for forming the simple past tense and past participle, you just need to learn and memorize their various forms. You can find a list of common irregular verbs on our website.

For additional resources, please visit **ivyglobal.com/study**.

Pronoun Forms
Part 4

Pronouns can take different forms in a sentence depending on their role, and the ACT will test your ability to identify the correct form of pronoun to use, and to distinguish between commonly confused forms.

Here's an example of a Pronoun Forms and Cases question like those you will see on the ACT:

Example	
<u>Them</u> have reported that landfills were a significant source of methane, accounting for nearly a fifth of U.S. methane emissions.	**A.** NO CHANGE **B.** Their **C.** They're **D.** They

(A), "them," is incorrect because it should be used only when it's the object of a verb, but in this sentence it's the subject. (B), "their," is incorrect because it's possessive—and that's not necessary in this sentence. (C), "they're," is incorrect because it's a contraction of "they" and "are." If you unpacked the contraction, the sentence would read "They are have reported," which has one too many verbs. Only (D), "they," uses the correct form of a pronoun for this sentence.

Pronouns have a variety of forms for different situations. Pronouns change forms when they're possessive. However, unlike nouns, most possessive pronouns aren't formed by just adding an apostrophe and an "s" to a pronoun. Instead, pronouns have possessive forms. Some possessive pronouns, like "their," are commonly confused with contractions that look or sound similar, like "they're." Although the ACT doesn't usually test you on the spelling of similar-sounding words, they do make an exception for these commonly confused words.

Pronouns also change forms depending on whether they are the subject or object of a verb. **Subjective pronouns** are used when they are the subject of a verb—in other words, when they are doing the action. **Objective pronouns** are used when they are the object of a verb—in other words, when the action is being done to them.

There is also a kind of modifier called a **possessive determiner** that modifies a noun to show possession. You use the determiner instead of the possessive pronoun when it comes before a noun to show possession of that noun by the antecedent of the pronoun. In the following examples, possessive determiners are underlined.

<u>My</u> sister lost <u>her</u> credit card, and we had to spend the rest of <u>our</u> day looking for it.

There's a Procrastinator Club at <u>my</u> high school, but <u>its</u> members haven't organized <u>their</u> first meeting yet.

Here's a list of common pronouns in their subjective, objective, and possessive forms, and the determiners based on those pronouns:

Subjective	Objective	Possessive	Determiner
I	me	mine	my
you	you	yours	your
we	us	ours	our
he	him	his	his
she	her	hers	her
they	them	theirs	their
it	it	its	its
who	whom	whose	whose

Finally, some pronoun forms are commonly confused with other words that look or sound similar. The ACT might try to trip you up with these, so look out for them:

	Rule	Correct Usage
Its vs. It's	**Its** is the possessive form of "it." **It's** means "it is."	**It's** hard to tell when the baby will start crying. **Its** arched brows make it look upset all the time!
Their vs. They're vs. There	**Their** is the possessive form of "they." **They're** means "they are." **There** indicates a location.	The team practiced all year, and **their** hard work paid off. **They're** going to the championship. I'll just walk **there**.
Whose vs. Who's	**Whose** is the possessive form of "who." **Who's** means "who is."	**Who's** going to the store with me? Judy is. Now **whose** car should we take?
Your vs. You're	**Your** is the possessive form of "you." **You're** means "you are."	**You're** too talented to give up acting. Plus, **your** voice is incredible!

Comparatives and Superlatives
Part 5

As we discussed earlier, adjectives and adverbs can be used to describe the properties of nouns and verbs. They can also be used to compare the properties of nouns and adverbs. Consider the following examples:

> The grass is always <u>greener</u> on the other side.
> The peanut butter cookies are <u>tastier</u> than the sugar cookies.
> Charlie plays chess <u>more often</u> than Jane does, but Jane still plays <u>better</u> than Charlie does.

These are **comparative modifiers**, sometimes called **comparatives**. They are adjectives and adverbs that not only describe the properties of objects, but express that one has more or less of a property than the other.

Comparative modifiers are sometimes formed by adding "-er" to the end of an adjective or adverb. Not all words can be turned into comparatives by adding "-er" to the end, and sometimes the spelling of a comparative form of a word has to be changed more than that.

Comparatives can also be formed by adding either of the adverbs "more" or "less" in front of an adjective or adverb. When two objects are being directly compared, the word "than" is often used to connect them. When "than" appears between two nouns in a sentence, it almost always indicates a comparison.

Superlative modifiers, sometimes called **superlatives**, also express a kind of comparison, but they indicate that the object they're describing has the *most* or *least* of a certain property—not just more or less of it. Consider the following examples of superlatives:

> Mr. Jones has the <u>greenest</u> grass in the neighborhood.
> Peanut butter cookies are the <u>tastiest</u> kind of cookie.
> Of all the players in the chess club, Charlie plays <u>most</u> often, but Jane still plays <u>best</u>.

Superlative modifiers are sometimes formed by adding "-est" to the end of an adjective or adverb. Again, there are some exceptions and not all superlatives are spelled this way, but the ACT won't test you simply on the spelling of superlatives.

Superlatives can also be formed by adding the adverbs "most" or "least" in front of an adjective or adverb. However, "than" is not used with superlatives. "Than" indicates a comparison between two things, while superlatives compare one thing to every other thing in a category.

Here's a typical Comparative and Superlative Modifiers question:

Example	
Nobody was more <u>angriest</u> about the rule change than Pete, but he kept his cool and enforced the new rules.	**F.** NO CHANGE **G.** angrier **H.** angry **J.** most angry

A modifier can be either comparative or superlative, but not both. That means that you can eliminate any option that combines superlatives and comparatives. Since the word "more" isn't underlined, it will apply to any choice you make, and you can eliminate (F) and (J) because they would combine the superlative forms with the comparative form.

Some modifiers can be formed correctly in more than one way, but only in one way at a time. "More angry" and "angrier" are both correct comparative forms of "angry," but "more angrier" uses both methods of forming a comparative—so you can also eliminate that choice. Only (H), which makes "more angry," correctly forms a comparative in this sentence.

Let's look at one more example:

Example	
I thought that I was <u>smart</u> than my parents, but they still caught me when I tried to sneak out.	**A.** NO CHANGE **B.** smarter **C.** smartest **D.** most smart

There's nothing preceding "smart" in this sentence, so every choice besides (A) correctly forms a superlative or comparative of "smart." However, the word "than" shows you that you need to select the comparative form—not the base adjective "smart" or the superlatives "most smart" or "smartest." Therefore, (B), "smarter," is the correct choice.

Idioms
Part 6

Sometimes, a phrase doesn't make sense unless you already know what it means—like an inside joke. **Idioms** are phrases that have specific meanings that can't necessarily be figured out just by understanding the individual words. Idioms fall into two general categories: informal expressions, like "it's raining cats and dogs," won't really be tested on the ACT. On the other hand, **prepositional idioms**, phrases that use specific prepositions for reasons that might be more historical than grammatical, will be tested on the ACT.

You already know a lot of idioms, because they're a part of how we talk in everyday life. However, there's no specific rule for how idioms are constructed—so if you don't know an idiom, there's no reliable way to figure it out. Also, because there is no "idiom rule," you can't always easily say *why* the answer to an Idioms question is correct. Sometimes, it "just is." For these questions, the best approach is usually to pick the option that *sounds right in context*. Just plug your choices in, and see which one makes sense!

If you're having trouble with Idioms questions, review and memorize this list of idioms that usually use the same preposition, and try to spend a lot of your free time doing recreational reading so that you become more familiar with common idioms.

Some Common Prepositional Idioms			
Able to	Conscious of	Escape from	Opposed to
Believe in	Consists of	Excuse for	Preoccupied with
Blamed for	Depends on	Hope for	Protect from
Capable of	Differ from	Identical to	Recover from
Compared to	Discriminate against	Method of	Relevant to
Comply with	Equivalent to	Object to	Succeed in

Grammar Practice Questions
Part 7

Polynesian sailors left modern-day Samoa and Tonga about two thousand years ago for Pacific island chains to the east. As they journeyed up the open ocean, they developed a body of orally-preserved seafaring knowledge

1. A. NO CHANGE
    B. journeyed aboard
    C. journeyed within
    (D) journeyed across

that enabled them to safe travel extraordinary distances. From the subantarctic Enderby Island (290 miles south of New Zealand's South Island), to as far east as Rapa Nui (which is now a Chilean territory), to as far north as Hawaii, Polynesian navigators reached land without the aid of maps or compasses. What navigational methods did they use instead, and how do we know about they?

2. F. NO CHANGE
    G. safe travel extraordinarily
    (H) safely travel extraordinary
    J. safely travel extraordinarily

3. A. NO CHANGE
    (B) them?
    C. their?
    D. they're?

The idea of being many hundreds of miles from land without a compass might seems frightening, but the Pacific voyagers were surrounded by signs. Non-instrumental navigation

4. F. NO CHANGE
    (G) seem
    H. seeming
    J. seemed

was a high sophisticated system of stellar and sea-current observation. The sailors oriented themselves by memorizing the location of up to two hundred stars in the night sky, so that if clouds covered one important star their could still navigate by the other ones. During the day,

and on cloudy nights that were more cloudier than usual, the patterns of oceanic swells would have also aided navigation. Other useful signs

would have include seabirds, fish shoals, and floating debris.

The reason we in the modern world still have such an excellent sense of what these practices involved is because they were preserved in neighboring Micronesia up to modern times. The master-sailor Mau Piailug of Satawal was instructed with the art by his grandfather, and in

the 1970s he begin to teach young Hawaiians in order to prevent the traditional techniques from dying out. In 1980, Piailug's student Nainoa Thompson made the journey from Hawaii to Tahiti without navigational instruments, and in 1985 the two also sailed to New Zealand in a journey that lasted two years. This effort

5. **A.** NO CHANGE
   B. high sophisticatedly
   C. highly sophisticatedly
   D. highly sophisticated

6. **F.** NO CHANGE
   G. them
   H. he
   J. they

7. **A.** NO CHANGE
   B. most cloudy
   C. cloudiest
   D. cloudier

8. **F.** NO CHANGE
   G. including
   H. included
   J. includes

9. **A.** NO CHANGE
   B. has
   C. having
   D. has had

10. **F.** NO CHANGE
    G. of the art with
    H. by the art by
    J. in the art by

11. **A.** NO CHANGE
    B. began
    C. beginned
    D. begun

showed how the Polynesian sailors whom first
peopled the islands could have made long,
intentional voyages centuries ago, overturning
earlier theories that they drifted to their
destinations with accident.

      Thanks to Piailug, Thompson, and
others, a time-honored art has been preserved and
shared throughout the Pacific islands where
they first flourished, thousands of years ago, and

instructors in modern Polynesia still teach the
ancient art of navigation to students today.

12.
- F. NO CHANGE
- G. who've
- H. whose
- (J) who

13.
- A. NO CHANGE
- (B) by accident
- C. to accident
- D. in accident

14.
- F. NO CHANGE
- G. he
- (H) it
- J. these

15.
- (A) NO CHANGE
- B. teaches
- C. teaching
- D. is teaching

Section 3
Sentence Structure

On the ACT English Test, **Sentence Structure** questions test your ability to identify and correct sentences that try to put too much in one sentence, don't have all the required parts of a complete sentence, misplace certain elements, or use an inconsistent structure or style.

In order to master the rules discussed in this section, you will need to have a good understanding of a few more basic concepts before tackling the kinds of questions that you'll see on the ACT. In this section, we will cover:

- Clauses and Phrases
- Subordinate and Dependent Clauses
- Run-on Sentences
- Sentence Fragments
- Misplaced Modifiers
- Sentence Shifts

Often, the best way to solve Sentence Structure questions is to mentally plug in your options and think about which ones sound best; if a sentence feels incomplete, or suggests something that sounds silly, then it's probably wrong. You can get better at spotting these errors before test day by reviewing this section alongside the "Clauses and Phrases" refresher earlier in this chapter.

There are 18 Sentence Structure questions on the English Test, so they make up about 24% of all English questions. In fact, Sentence Structure questions are the single most common English question type!

Clauses and Phrases
Part 1

Some ACT English questions will ask you to rearrange or combine different parts of a sentence in order to fix a sentence that is structured incorrectly.

A **clause** consists of a subject and a verb. Think of a clause as the basic building block of a sentence: every grammatically correct sentence contains one or more clauses.

Some clauses can be complete sentences all on their own. These are called **independent clauses**. Sentences with just one clause are called **simple sentences**. In the following simple sentences, the subject is in bold and the verb is underlined:

> The **bird** <u>flew</u> away.
> My **mother** <u>sings</u> often.
> **Professor Ahmed** <u>taught</u> us history.
> **We** <u>wrote</u> her a thank you card.

Some clauses, called **dependent clauses**, cannot stand alone as grammatically complete sentences. The idea they express is incomplete. They begin with a **dependent marker word**, a pronoun or subordinate conjunction that makes the clause refer to other information, and must be joined up with an independent clause to make a whole sentence. A clause that would otherwise be independent becomes dependent when you add a dependent marker word. In the following dependent clauses, the subject is in bold, the verb is underlined, and the dependent marker word is in italics:

> *as* **we** <u>watched</u> from the window
> *because* **she** <u>loves</u> music
> *since* **we** <u>enjoyed</u> the class so much
> *when* **the semester** <u>ended</u>

A sentence with two or more clauses is a **complex sentence**. One of these clauses must be an independent clause. Here are some examples of complex sentences formed from the independent and dependent clauses above:

> The **bird** <u>flew</u> away *as* **we** <u>watched</u> from the window. (two clauses)
> My **mother** <u>sings</u> often *because* **she** <u>loves</u> music. (two clauses)

Professor Ahmed <u>taught</u> us history, and, *since* **we** <u>enjoyed</u> the class so much, **we** <u>wrote</u> her a thank you card *when* **the semester** <u>ended</u>. (four clauses)

It is also possible to join two or more independent clauses together. There are two basic ways of doing so.

First, you can use a comma followed by a coordinating conjunction (you can remember these conjunctions by using the acronym FANBOYS: for, and, nor, but, or, yet, so). Here are some independent clauses written as their own sentences:

It's raining a little bit.
I should take my umbrella.
I learned an important lesson about snow.
It's cold.

Now, here are a couple of those clauses joined with a conjunction and a comma:

It's raining a little bit, so I should take my umbrella.

You can also join independent clauses using a semicolon or a colon. Consider the following examples:

It's raining a little bit; I should take my umbrella.
I learned an important lesson about snow: it's cold.

You can always use a semicolon to join two independent clauses, but the clauses should be related. It's bad form to connect unrelated clauses with a semicolon, especially when it would make a very long sentence. The rules for colons are a little bit more complicated. We'll talk more about using punctuation to connect the parts of a sentence in the Punctuation section.

In addition to clauses, **phrases** are another important component of many sentences: phrases must be at least two words long, but unlike clauses, phrases do not combine a subject and a verb to express a complete idea. This section will look more closely at the kinds of phrases you should know about as you prepare for the ACT.

Noun Phrases

Noun phrases contain a noun and one or more modifiers. In the following examples, the noun is in bold and the modifiers are underlined:

thank-you **card**

the huge **cheese**

several extremely exciting **dunks**

Verb Phrases

A verb phrase employs a **main verb** and one or more **helping verbs** (also called auxiliary verbs). While there are an enormous number of main verbs, only a few words function as helping verbs:

Helping Verbs
can, could, shall, should, will, would, may, might, must, ought, be, am, is, are, was, were, been, being, have, has, had, do, does, did

When you combine these helping verbs with main verbs, you create phrases. In these examples, the main verb is in bold and the helping verbs are underlined:

has been **whistling**

will be **attending**

does not **want** (in this case, "not," an adverb, isn't considered a part of the verb phrase)

Prepositional Phrases

These phrases, as you might expect, open with a preposition (we discussed prepositions earlier, in the Grammar section). In a sentence, prepositional phrases play the part of either an adjective or an adverb. Here are some examples in which prepositional phrases modify nouns and verbs. The prepositional phrases are underlined.

I dropped it from the window.

He put it in the bucket near the crowd of jugglers.

After Alma's story, I left.

Pay close attention to prepositional phrases in sentences on the ACT, because sometimes they're slipped in between a verb and its subject or object. Since prepositional phrases contain nouns, they can look like they should be the subject or object of a verb—even though they actually act like adjectives or adverbs.

Run-on Sentences
Part 2

As you might expect from the name, a **run-on** or **fused sentence** is actually two potential sentences crammed together without punctuation. The ACT will sometimes prompt you to correct errors of this kind. Consider the following example:

<table>
<tr><td colspan="2">Example</td></tr>
<tr>
<td>

<u>Luisa is learning how to DJ she borrowed her</u>

<u>dad's records.</u>
</td>
<td>

Which of the following suggested alternatives to the underlined portion would be LEAST acceptable?

  A. Luisa is learning how to DJ. She borrowed her dad's records.

  B. Luisa is learning how to DJ, so she borrowed her dad's records.

  C. Luisa is learning how to DJ; she borrowed her dad's records.

  D. Luisa, learning how to DJ borrowed her dad's records.
</td>
</tr>
</table>

This sentence is made of two independent clauses, each of which would be acceptable as a stand-alone sentence. The simplest way to fix a run-on is to separate the clauses with a period, as (A) does. However, they can also be joined into one sentence if you use the appropriate conjunctions and/or punctuation. (B) links the two clauses with a comma and a conjunction, and (C) joins them with a semicolon. (D) attempts to rearrange the sentence so that "learning how to DJ" becomes a parenthetical phrase, but does not punctuate it appropriately. It is missing a comma after "DJ." Thus, (D) is the least acceptable.

The next question further emphasizes the many ways you can avoid a run-on sentence:

<table>
<tr><td colspan="2">Example</td></tr>
<tr>
<td>

Nadiya won a gold ribbon at the district

science <u>fair, and she</u> will compete in the regional

fair next week.
</td>
<td>

Which of the following alternatives to the underlined portion would be LEAST acceptable?

  F. fair. She

  G. fair she

  H. fair; she

  J. fair; therefore, she
</td>
</tr>
</table>

The sentence as it stands is grammatically correct. It joins two independent clauses with a comma and a conjunction ("and"). Your task, in this case, is to identify the grammatically incorrect option. It can't be (F) because this answer aptly separates the clauses with a period, making two complete sentences. It can't be (H), because it's also possible to link two independent clauses with a semicolon alone. (J) represents a final acceptable alternative, joining the clauses with a semicolon, a conjunctive adverb ("therefore"), and a comma. The least acceptable alternative, and correct answer to the question, must be (G), which creates a run-on sentence.

A **comma splice** is similar to a fused sentence. While a fused sentence fails to punctuate two linked independent clauses, a comma splice punctuates them inadequately using only a comma. Look at the following example:

Example

<table>
<tr>
<td>

Those superheroes are always flexing their muscles, I wonder if they ever get tired.

</td>
<td>

Which of the following alternatives to the underlined portion would be LEAST acceptable?

A. Those superheroes are always flexing their muscles. I wonder if they ever get tired.

B. Those superheroes are always flexing their muscles; I wonder if they ever get tired.

C. Those superheroes are always flexing their muscles, and it makes me wonder if they ever get tired.

D. Those superheroes are always flexing their muscles I wonder if they ever get tired.

</td>
</tr>
</table>

The underlined sentence contains an error because a comma on its own isn't sufficient to join two independent clauses. As with fused sentences, there are several ways to fix comma splices. (A), the first acceptable choice, splits the clauses into two sentences. (B) uses a semicolon and is likewise correct. In (C), you'll notice a slightly different tactic: this edit adds a conjunction and a comma. That's a perfectly acceptable solution! Only (D) is an unacceptable revision. It removes the comma, so the sentence is no longer a comma splice. However, it doesn't insert any other punctuation—creating a fused sentence.

Be especially careful with sentences that include **introductory** or **transitional** words. You can find a list of transitional words in the Organization section of this chapter. Most transitional words, like "however," "consequently," and "nevertheless," are adverbs. Sometimes, in informal conversation, they can sound like conjunctions—but they don't do the job of a conjunction in a formal English sentence.

Consider the following example:

X   I needed to get a 97 on the exam to <u>pass the course, consequently, I studied</u> for weeks.

This is a comma splice. The word "consequently" is an adverb, which modifies the verb "studied." A new independent clause begins between the words "course" and "consequently," so you must either split this sentence with a period or semicolon, or correctly join the clauses with a conjunction.

✓   I needed to get a 97 on the exam to <u>pass the course; consequently, I studied</u> for weeks.
✓   I needed to get a 97 on the exam to <u>pass the course, and, consequently, I studied</u> for weeks.

The next example shows what a comma splice question might look like on the ACT English Test:

Example	
Last night, I had a dream about a duck who became <u>President, his</u> name was Quackery Taylor.	**F.** NO CHANGE **G.** President his **H.** President. His **J.** President and his

The sentence, as it is, is a comma splice. If you select (F), then it remains in its incorrect state. (G) makes things even worse by removing the internal punctuation altogether; the comma splice has transformed into a fused sentence. (J), while introducing a conjunction ("and"), removes the comma. It, too, is a run-on sentence. The correct answer is (H), which solves the splice by making two sentences.

Subordinate and Dependent Clauses
Part 3

Earlier in this chapter, you read about the basic rules of English clauses. The ACT will ask you to correct sentences that, in one way or another, break those rules. One way that they can break the rules is by mixing up dependent and independent clauses, thereby creating fragments and run-ons. Here's an example of a Subordinate or Dependent Clauses question like those you will see on the ACT:

Example	
Tim doesn't know how to make cakes, <u>although bakes delicious pies.</u>	**A.** NO CHANGE **B.** although baking delicious pies. **C.** he bakes delicious pies. **D.** although he bakes delicious pies.

In this example, you can see an incomplete dependent clause. While the clause has a verb, "bakes," it's missing a subject. Clearly, then, (A) is not the right answer. Answer (B) doesn't help things either, as it still fails to introduce a subject. (C) is also no good. While the clause now has both a subject ("he") and a verb ("bakes"), it has removed the conjunction that makes it a dependent clause, creating a comma splice. (D) is correct, because it has a subject, a verb, and a subordinate conjunction.

Because this concept can be a bit confusing, consider an additional, perhaps trickier, example:

Example	
Mr. Mercer told us that, while <u>his popular first album</u> and inspired comparisons with the greats, he was more proud of his third one.	**F.** NO CHANGE **G.** his first popular album **H.** his first album **J.** his first album was popular

The last example showed you an incomplete dependent clause without a subject; this time, a verb is missing. If you stick with (F), you will have a marker word ("while") linked with a noun phrase ("his popular first album"), but no verb—you will not, in other words, explain what the first album *does*. (G) merely shuffles the word order, and (H) just removes the adjective. Only (J) introduces a verb ("was"), making "his first album" the subject.

Sentence Fragments
Part 4

You may encounter sentence fragments on the ACT. A **fragment** is a set of words or a clause that cannot stand on its own, but that a writer has tried to use as a complete sentence. Fragments consist entirely of dependent clauses or phrases.

> X   Emma didn't show up <u>until 9 PM. Even though</u> she said she'd arrive at 7.

Although the second "sentence" has a subject and a verb, it is not complete. You can see that it is a dependent clause because the phrase "even though" is a dependent marker. To fix this problem, you can attach it to the first sentence with a comma.

> ✓   Emma didn't show up <u>until 9 PM, even though</u> she said she'd arrive at 7.

Sometimes phrases will occur as fragments as well. A **phrase** isn't even a clause—it doesn't have both a subject and a verb.

> X   She got stuck in traffic, but tried her <u>hardest to get there. Driving like a maniac and weaving</u> in and out of traffic.

You'll notice that the second "sentence" here doesn't have a subject. In general, if you see a "sentence" with verbs all ending in "-ing" form, chances are there is a problem with it. To fix the sentence in this example, you have a couple of options. Attaching it to the main sentence with a comma makes it clear that "she" was the one driving like a maniac and weaving in and out of traffic:

> ✓   She got stuck in traffic, but tried her <u>hardest to get there, driving like a maniac and weaving</u> in and out of traffic.

You can also fix the problem by making the fragment into a stand-alone sentence:

> ✓   She got stuck in traffic, but tried her <u>hardest to get there. She drove like a maniac, weaving</u> in and out of traffic.

The second sentence now has a subject ("she") and two verbs that agree with it ("drove" and "weaved"). Both are appropriately in the past tense, since the narrator is describing a completed past event.

Some other fragments might be a little harder to spot:

> Music rising to a thundering crescendo as the percussionists frantically bang their drums.

What's wrong here? The dependent clause beginning with "as the percussionists" is well-formed, but recall that dependent clauses can never make up a complete sentence without an independent clause too. The rest of the sentence does not even constitute a clause. It might seem like "Music rising" provides a subject and verb pair, but "rising" actually doesn't behave as a verb; here, it makes up what is called a **gerund phrase**, and behaves as a noun. As a result, this sentence has no independent clause and is a fragment.

The final example shows what an ACT sentence fragment question might look like on the test:

Example

Found in Central and South America, <u>where</u> the two-toed sloth lives on a diet of leaves.

A. NO CHANGE
B. wherever
C. because
D. OMIT the underlined portion

The original sentence is a fragment, so you can eliminate (A). Both (B) and (C) fail to introduce a much-need independent clause into the sentence; each simply repeats the mistake of (A) by keeping a subordinate conjunction at the front of the clause. If we remove the subordinate conjunction, however, we come away with a proper independent clause: "the two-toed sloth lives on a diet of leaves." This means that (D) is the correct answer, as it is the only choice that fixes the fragment.

Misplaced Modifiers
Part 5

The ACT will also ask you to move or revise misplaced modifiers. **Misplaced modifiers** are phrases or clauses that are separated from the words they are meant to describe, and thus create ambiguities or mistaken meanings. Let's take a look at an example:

X   While biking to work this morning, <u>an odd thought struck Alanna</u>.

What this sentence *means* to suggest is that Alanna was the one biking to work, but the misplaced modifier "While biking to work this morning" creates the impression that the "odd thought" was actually doing the biking. We know this can't be true, so the modifier must be misplaced.

We have a couple of options for how to fix misplaced modifiers. The general rule is that we need to reorder the sentence so that the modifier is as close as possible to the object it's meant to modify.

✓   While biking to work this morning, <u>Alanna was struck by an odd thought</u>.
✓   <u>An odd thought struck Alanna</u> while <u>she was</u> biking to work this morning.

You'll notice that for these types of questions, you'll often need to change more than just a word or two. Often, entire clauses or the sentence as a whole will need to be reorganized or rewritten.

Usually, these modifying phrases will contain verbs in their "-ing" or "-ed" forms. Here's an example of a misplaced modifier sentence with an "-ed" form verb:

X   <u>Seasoned with many spices</u>, <u>Sam's mouth</u> burned when he ate a bite of <u>the curry</u>.

This sentence makes it sound like Sam's mouth was seasoned with many spices, which is not very likely. The modifier is meant to refer to the hot curry, so we'll need to rearrange the sentence to reflect that.

✓   <u>Sam's mouth</u> burned when he ate a bite of <u>the curry</u>, which was <u>seasoned with many spices</u>.
✓   <u>Seasoned with many spices</u>, <u>the curry</u> burned <u>Sam's mouth</u> when he ate a bite of it.

You have multiple options when fixing a misplaced modifier, depending on how much you want to change the sentence. Some multiple choice options on the ACT will make relatively minor changes, whereas others will overhaul the sentence. Make sure that the answer you choose doesn't introduce any new mistakes.

Here's an example of a Misplaced Modifier question like those on the ACT:

<table>
<tr><td colspan="2">Example</td></tr>
<tr>
<td>The annual dinner was supplied by a local man with chicken fingers.</td>
<td>
F. NO CHANGE
G. A local man with chicken fingers supplied the annual dinner.
H. The supplier, a local man with chicken fingers, supplied the annual dinner.
J. A local man supplied the annual dinner with chicken fingers.
</td>
</tr>
</table>

The sentence, while grammatically correct, paints an evocative picture of a caterer whose fingers are made out of chicken. This means that we should not choose (F). (G) rearranges the order of the subject and object, but otherwise conveys the same misleading information. (H) introduces a new phrase and a different clause structure. However, it, too, maintains the misleading pairing of "local man" and "chicken fingers." Only in (J) is it clear that the local man merely brought chicken fingers to the dinner.

Consider this example, a variation on a famous Groucho Marx joke:

<table>
<tr><td colspan="2">Example</td></tr>
<tr>
<td>This morning I saw an elephant in my pajamas.</td>
<td>
A. NO CHANGE
B. I saw an elephant in my pajamas this morning.
C. I saw, this morning, in my pajamas, an elephant.
D. This morning, while I was still in my pajamas, I saw an elephant.
</td>
</tr>
</table>

The sentence in its original form is comically unclear. You can't tell whether it was the speaker, or the elephant, who was wearing pajamas. (A), then, is not the correct choice. (B) merely switches the noun phrase "this morning" from one end of the sentence to the other; the result is just as confusing. (C) adds commas and rearranges the order of the clause and phrases, but it doesn't improve the clarity of the sentence. Only (D) introduces new words, "while I was still," to clarify who was wearing the pajamas.

Sentence Shifts
Part 6

In addition to being grammatically complete, sentences need to be grammatically consistent. Sentences that have abrupt, illogical changes in their style or structure partway through won't make much sense to readers. **Sentence Shift** questions on the ACT test your ability to recognize and correct these inconsistencies.

Tense, Voice, and Mood Shifts

In Section 2, we talked about verb tense and voice. Some of the questions on the ACT will ask you to find the correct version of a verb based on its place in the sentence. As you've seen, many sentences involve more than one clause. Clauses presented one after another form a **sequence**, and the verbs in these sequences have to be in the correct tense and voice.

Verb tenses reflect changes in time. Many tense mistakes involve the past tense:

> X   Patty <u>began</u> high school thirty years after her mother <u>graduates</u> from college.

If one of the events happened before the other one—in other words, if one event is further in the past than the other—then you can use the remote past tense to help make the order of events more clear. In this sentence, Patty's mother graduated college before Patty began high school, so you should use the remote past tense of "graduate:"

> ✓   Patty <u>began</u> high school thirty years after her mother <u>had graduated</u> from college.

You should also watch out for verb tenses in conditional sentences. **Conditional sentences** have a "conditional" clause that starts with "if" or "when," connected to a "result" clause that explains what happens if or when the condition is satisfied. You use conditional sentences to talk about hypothetical or possible situations.

If the result clause contains the word "will," the conditional clause should use the present tense of the verb.

> ✓   If she <u>trains</u> rigorously, she <u>will be</u> able to run the marathon.

If the result clause contains the word "would," the condition clause should use the past tense of the verb.

    ✓ If she <u>trained</u> rigorously, she <u>would be</u> able to run the marathon.

What if the condition in the sentence has already failed to happen? If the result clause has "would have," use the remote past tense of the verb:

    ✓ If she <u>had trained</u> rigorously, she <u>would have been</u> able to run the marathon.

Let's take a look at another example:

    X   If you <u>study</u> more, you <u>would get</u> better grades.
    ✓   If you <u>studied</u> more, you <u>would get</u> better grades.
    ✓   If you <u>had studied</u> more, you <u>would have gotten</u> better grades.
    ✓   If you <u>study</u> more, you <u>will get</u> better grades.

In Section 2, you also learned about the voice of a verb. You may remember that the active voice is usually preferable to the passive voice. However, the most important thing is to keep the voice of your verbs the same within a sentence—that is, use a **consistent voice**:

    X   The clown <u>makes balloon animals</u> for adults, and <u>children are entertained by him</u>.

This sentence uses both the active voice ("makes") and the passive voice ("are entertained by"). Shifting voice in a sentence can be confusing. Be sure to keep the voice of verbs the same.

    ✓ The clown <u>makes balloon animals</u> for adults, and <u>he entertains the children</u>.

Another feature of verbs that can shift is the mood. The **mood** tells you if a sentence is a statement, question, command, suggestion, or desire. Just like voice, mood needs to be consistent within a sentence or group of sentences:

    X   Bring in the groceries. After that, <u>you should walk</u> the dog.

If the first sentence is a command, the second sentence should also be a command.

    ✓ Bring in the groceries. After that, <u>walk</u> the dog.

Consider the following example of a Sentence Shifts question like those that you'll see on the ACT:

<table>
<tr><td colspan="2">Example</td></tr>
<tr>
<td>Stephanie took the same train for three years, and she <u>was enjoying</u> looking out the window at the scenery. When she moved downtown, she stopped taking that train.</td>
<td>

F. NO CHANGE
G. enjoys
H. had been enjoying
J. had enjoyed

</td>
</tr>
</table>

The sentence shifts from simple past tense ("took") to past continuous ("was enjoying"). This creates a confusing inconsistency. The past continuous indicates more short-term actions than the content of the sentence suggests—remember that she took the train for three years. (F) is the wrong answer. (G) is also incorrect: it shifts to the present tense. In (H), the switch to the past perfect progressive ("had been enjoying") introduces a new error. The correct choice, (J), keeps the sentence in a consistent past tense with the remote past.

Shifts in Pronoun Person or Number

You will also need to watch out for inconsistencies in the use of pronouns. Pronouns need to use the same number and gender as the nouns they are referring to (their antecedents), and the same pronoun should be used to refer to the same antecedent throughout a sentence—even when a different pronoun could be correct if it were used consistently. The ACT may try to trick you by changing a pronoun inappropriately or by making it unclear which noun it refers to.

Avoid changing the pronoun you are using partway through the sentence:

X   If <u>one</u> changes pronouns midsentence, <u>you</u> are doing it wrong.

If you start a sentence with one pronoun, stick with it all the way through:

✓   If <u>you</u> change pronouns midsentence, <u>you</u> are doing it wrong.

Similarly, if you are using one pronoun to refer to something in one sentence, do not change to a different pronoun in the next sentence.

X   If <u>a doctor</u> prescribes too many antibiotics, <u>he or she</u> risks creating antibiotic-resistant strains of bacteria. However, <u>they</u> must also consider the welfare of patients in the here and now.

Instead, use the same pronoun in both sentences:

> ✓ If a doctor prescribes too many antibiotics, <u>he or she</u> risks creating antibiotic-resistant strains of bacteria. However, <u>he or she</u> must also consider the welfare of patients in the here and now.

Note that the correct sentence uses "he or she" as the pronoun. This is because the pronoun is replacing "a doctor," which is a singular noun. You may be accustomed to using "they" as a singular pronoun in your own everyday speech and writing, but on the ACT "they" should be used only to replace plural nouns.

Here is a sample pronoun question like those you'll see on the ACT:

Example	
The three friends, Daisy, John, and Oscar, have formed a group, and it looks very interesting. It is called the Stargazers Club, and <u>they meet</u> every Thursday.	**A.** NO CHANGE **B.** we meet **C.** one meets **D.** it meets

This sentence wants to trick you into selecting (A), "NO CHANGE." As a single entity, the club must be referred to with a singular pronoun in American English. However, the presence of "Daisy, John, and Oscar" in the previous sentence might lead you to believe that a plural pronoun is needed here. You might also be tricked by the club's plural name, the "Stargazers." Remember to be consistent in your pronoun use, within and among sentences. The club is referred to as "it" in the first sentence and in the first clause of the second one, so you must keep using "it."

(B) introduces the first-person plural "we," and so is also incorrect. (C) similarly shifts pronouns. Only (D) maintains the necessary consistency by referring to the club as "it."

You might see this done a little differently in some of the books that you read: in British English, plural verbs are sometimes used after collective nouns, as in, "the Scottish team are practicing." Don't worry about the difference—just remember that the ACT follows the American convention.

Sentence Structure Practice Questions
Part 7

The artist Lygia Clark was born in Brazil in 1920. Early in her career, Clark focused first on creating small-scale monochromatic paintings; when she was using mostly grays, [1] blacks, and whites in geometric shapes. In the late 1950s, she cofounds the Neo-Concrete [2] movement with fellow artist Helio Oiticica. Her work became even more conceptual by the 1960s, when she shifted her attention to making [3] sculptures.

The Neo-Concretists believed that an artwork should make the spectator more aware of her physical body and metaphysical existence, to [4] accomplish this goal, Clark began to make [4] sculptures that could be manipulated by the spectator. Prominently featured, these sculptures [5] are her best-known works, and were in a 2014 retrospective of her work at New York City's Museum of Modern Art.

1. **A.** NO CHANGE
   B. paintings when was using
   C. paintings; when she used
   (D.) paintings, using

2. **F.** NO CHANGE
   (G.) cofounded
   H. was cofounding
   J. will cofound

3. Which of the following alternatives to the underlined portion would NOT be acceptable?
   A. when she shifted her attention and started making
   (B.) when she shifts her attention and makes
   C. when she shifted to making
   D. when she started making

4. **F.** NO CHANGE
   (G.) existence. To accomplish
   H. existence; and to accomplish
   J. existence and to accomplish

5. The best placement for the underlined phrase, revising capitalization as needed, would be:
   A. where it is now.
   B. after the word *these*
   (C.) after the word *were*
   D. before the word *work*

Made of aluminum plates with hinges
embedded in the surfaces, Clark created a small,
foldable sculpture entitled *Bicho invertabrato* in
1960. The sculpture has no principle

shape, instead, it is designed to be played with;
the hinges allow the spectator to open up the
plates, to fold them and reconfigure the whole
thing into different shapes. These unique pieces
had no front, no back, no inside, and no outside.
The endless possibilities express Clark's idea that
a work has no representative meaning outside
of its manipulation by spectators, it might be
more accurate to call those who viewed her work
"participants." Many artists would forbid
spectators from touching a sculpture, Clark
invited her audience to do so. She believed art

should not be enjoyed only through the eyes.
Through many senses. By interacting with the
piece, the participants entered what Clark called
a "dialogue" or a discussion or what one might
call a conversation between two living
organisms, during which the participant and the
art could become one entity.

6. F. NO CHANGE
   G. Small and foldable, Clark created a sculpture entitled *Bicho invertabrato* in 1960, made of aluminum plates with hinges embedded in the surfaces.
   H. Clark's 1960 piece, *Bicho invertabrato*, is a small, foldable sculpture made of aluminum plates with hinges embedded in the surfaces.
   J. Created in 1960, Clark made the small, foldable *Bicho invertabrato* out of aluminum plates with hinges embedded in the surfaces.

7. A. NO CHANGE
   B. shape; instead it is
   C. shape. Instead it is
   D. shape. Instead, it is

8. F. NO CHANGE
   G. have
   H. would have had
   J. had had

9. A. NO CHANGE
   B. spectators though it
   C. spectators, though it
   D. spectators. Though it

10. F. NO CHANGE
    G. a sculpture Clark
    H. a sculpture so Clark
    J. a sculpture, but Clark

11. A. NO CHANGE
    B. eyes, but through
    C. eyes; through
    D. eyes through

12. F. NO CHANGE
    G. or a discussion, or a conversation
    H. or a discussion, or what one might call, a conversation
    J. OMIT the underlined portion

In the latter part of her career, Clark turned away from creating art, she decided to focus on art therapy. She was interested in ____13

memories of trauma and wanted to uncover ____14 why certain objects brought about vivid memories for her patients. Her interest may have been inspired by her own experience, which made creating sculptures a daunting prospect, of breaking her wrist. ____15

13. **A.** NO CHANGE
    B. creating art she decided to focus
    C. creating art, to focus,
    D. creating art to focus

14. Which of the following alternatives to the underlined portion would NOT be acceptable?
    F. trauma; she wanted
    G. trauma. She wanted
    H. trauma. Wanted
    J. trauma, and she wanted

15. The best placement for the underlined phrase (adjusting the punctuation accordingly) would be:
    A. where it is now.
    B. after the word *by*.
    C. after the word *experience*.
    D. after the word *which*.

Section 4
Punctuation

ACT **Punctuation** questions test your ability to recognize and correct incorrect punctuation. Punctuation is an essential element of writing, primarily because it shows the reader how sentences are constructed and how they should be read. The proper use of punctuation makes the meaning of a sentence clear. Improper punctuation can make it difficult or impossible to understand what a sentence is supposed to mean.

You've already read about some of the rules for punctuation in Sections 2 and 3. This section serves as a review of those rules, provides additional information about punctuation, and shows some examples of the Punctuation questions you're likely to see on the ACT. In this section, we'll cover:

- Commas
- Colons, Semicolons, and Dashes
- Apostrophes
- Periods, Question Marks, and Exclamation Points

There are 10 Punctuation questions on the ACT English Test, which is about 13% of the English Test.

Commas
Part 1

Commas (,) are used to separate sentence parts in order to avoid confusion. Consider the following example:

> X Let's eat Grandma.
> ✓ Let's eat, Grandma.

The first sentence implies that a group of people are planning on making a cannibalistic snack of their grandmother; the second is an invitation to Grandma to join the family for a meal. As you can see, proper punctuation can be a life saver.

There are more complex rules about using commas. The chart below explains when to use commas and provides examples of how they should be used:

When to Use a Comma	Examples
Before a coordinating conjunction joining independent clauses	"There are almost infinitely many chocolate cake recipes, but the best one is my grandmother's." The seven coordinating conjunctions for English are: *For, and, nor, but, or, yet, so.* You can remember them with the acronym "FANBOYS."
After an introductory clause or phrase	"When one pays attention, one can spot moments of great beauty in daily life."
Between items in a series	"Among the items that were available at the auction were dressers, beds, couches, sets of dining tables and chairs, and nightstands." Commas are not needed between two words if they go together as one item in the list. Because the dining tables and chairs were sold as sets, no comma is needed between "tables" and "and chairs." The comma before the "and" preceding the last item in a list is called a "serial comma" or "Oxford comma." Not everyone uses it, but the ACT does!

	"The storm caused severe, irreversible damage to the dune system that protected the beautiful barrier islands."
Between coordinate adjectives, but not cumulative adjectives	Adjectives are coordinate if they are equally important and can be connected with the word "and," as in "severe and irreversible."
	When one is more important and connecting the adjectives with "and" would sound wrong, as in "the beautiful and barrier islands," they are cumulative, and no comma is necessary.
To set off a nonrestrictive element, but not a restrictive element	NONRESTRICTIVE "The hikers needed sturdy boots, which are expensive." If you remove "which are expensive," there's no significant change to the meaning of this sentence. RESTRICTIVE "The hikers needed boots that were sturdy." If you remove "that were sturdy" from this sentence, the meaning changes significantly.
To set off parenthetical phrases	"Space travel, as we know, is not yet available to the average person." You need to put commas on both sides of the parenthetical phrase. You can also use dashes, but the punctuation at the beginning of the phrase has to match the punctuation at the end.
To set off direct quotations	Pablo Picasso once said, "Give me a museum and I will fill it."

Here's an example of a Commas question like those you'll see on the ACT:

Example	
This style known as flamenco originated in Spain.	**A.** NO CHANGE **B.** style known as flamenco, originated **C.** style, known as flamenco, originated **D.** style, known as flamenco originated

(C) is correct because the comma sets off the parenthetical phrase "known as flamenco." (A) is not the best answer because it fails to insert the commas required to set off the nonrestrictive element. (B) and (D) are both incorrect because they use only one of the two necessary commas around the phrase "known as flamenco."

Colons, Semicolons, and Dashes
Part 2

Colons (:) are used after an independent clause to signify that what follows is either a list, an appositive, or a quotation. Colons are used after independent clauses, but colons don't need to be followed by independent clauses.

The following table summarizes the rules for colon use:

Colons	
When to Use a Colon	**Example**
In front of a list	As the invitation suggested, I brought three small items to the potluck: my sense of humor, my charming smile, and a bag of chips.
In front of a noun or pronoun that renames or specifies something from the preceding clause	I have only one character flaw: an excess of humility.
Colons that alert readers to a quote	Let us remember what the dormouse said: "Feed your head; feed your head."

Here's an example of a Colon question you might encounter on the ACT:

Example	
Heirloom apples not only taste unique, they also have: unique names, Ashmead's Kernel, Hidden Rose, American Mother, and Sheepnose, to name a few.	**F.** NO CHANGE **G.** also: have unique names, **H.** also have unique names, **J.** also have unique names:

(J) is correct because the colon sets off a list of some of the names for heirloom apples. (F) misplaces the colon and inserts an unnecessary comma. (G) is incorrect because it misplaces the colon. Remember that a colon has to follow an independent clause: placing a colon after an adverb like this is a common error that messes up the clause before the colon. (H) is incorrect because the comma after *names* isn't enough to separate this list from the rest of the sentence.

A **semicolon** (;) looks like a cross between a comma and a period, but has a unique role. When a comma is used in a place that calls for a semicolon, it often creates a comma splice. Avoid that mistake on the

English Test! Semicolons can replace a period to merge two sentences into one, but there should be a good reason for doing so. If you're taking the Writing Test, you should only use semicolons in your essay if you have a clear reason! Semicolons have two main uses:

Semicolons	
When to Use a Semicolon	Examples
To separate independent clauses that are NOT joined by coordinating conjunctions	"There are a million reasons to go to college; preparing for the job market is the reason most students cite."
In lists of items that contain internal punctuation	"Classic slapstick comedies often feature trios of characters: the Marx Brothers, with Groucho, Chico, and Harpo; the Three Stooges, with Moe, Larry, Curly or, in the later years, Shep; and the Three Amigos, with Steve Martin, Chevy Chase, and Martin Short."

Here's an example of a Semicolons question like those that you'll see on the ACT:

Example	
No one needs to be reminded that astronauts are very brave they know that.	**A.** NO CHANGE **B.** are very brave, they know that. **Ⓒ** are very brave; they know that. **D.** are: very brave; they know that.

(C) is correct because the semicolon separates independent clauses that are not joined by a coordinating conjunction. (A) is not the best answer because the resulting sentence is a run-on. (B) incorrectly inserts a comma and creates a comma splice. (D) places the semicolon correctly, but it also incorrectly inserts a colon before "very brave."

Dashes (—) are used in a few different ways. There are some common misconceptions about dashes: that they are the same as commas, that they can always be replaced by a different punctuation mark, or that they are always incorrect on the ACT. A dash is a unique punctuation mark, and while it shares some uses with other punctuation marks it's not always interchangeable with them. Further, while it's true that dashes are often avoided in formal writing, not all English passages on the ACT have a formal style.

The following table describes the correct uses of dashes:

Dashes	
When to Use a Dash	**Examples**
To set off parenthetical elements	"Oatmeal cookies—with or without raisins—are almost as popular as chocolate chip cookies." Commas can also be used for this purpose, but—whether commas or dashes are used—the same punctuation mark should be used on both sides of the parenthetical element.
To introduce lists or explanations	"The last tsar of Russia, Nicholas II, had four daughters—Grand Duchess Olga, Grand Duchess Tatiana, Grand Duchess Maria, and Grand Duchess Anastasia." "Heating a home with only a woodstove is not for everyone—it's messy, time-consuming, and requires a lot of wood." Colons can also be used for this purpose.
To signal an abrupt change in thought or speech	"And this," said the tour guide, "is a priceless Ming Dynasty—No! Don't touch that!" But alas, it was too late.

Here's an example of a Dashes question like those you might see on the ACT:

Example	
Julia saw Bob take several bagels from the snack table without making the recommended donation, but Julia was new in the office—<u>in fact, it was her first day</u>—so she wasn't totally comfortable confronting him about it.	**F.** NO CHANGE **G.** in fact it was her first day **H.** in fact—it was her first day **J.** in fact, it was: her first day

As you can see, this question doesn't exclusively focus on dashes. However, you should notice that the underlined portion is a parenthetical element set off with dashes. As such, using another dash inside of it, as in (H), would be confusing and incorrect. (J) is incorrect because it incorrectly inserts a colon, and (G) is incorrect because it omits a necessary comma. In this case, (F) is correct, because the parenthetical element only needs a comma between "in fact" and "it was," to set off the introductory clause in that part of the sentence.

Apostrophes
Part 3

Apostrophes have two main uses that will be tested on the ACT: forming possessive nouns (and, rarely, pronouns) and punctuating contractions.

Here are some rules to remember about using apostrophes to form **possessive nouns**:

Possessive Nouns	
To make most singular nouns possessive, simply add an apostrophe and an "s" to the end of the word (even when the word ends in "s").	coach + apostrophe + "s" becomes coach's child + apostrophe + "s" becomes child's boss + apostrophe + "s" becomes boss's Cindy + apostrophe + "s" becomes Cindy's dog + apostrophe + "s" becomes dog's
To make most plural nouns (which often end in "s") possessive, add an apostrophe to the end of the word.	coaches + apostrophe becomes coaches' bosses + apostrophe becomes bosses' dogs + apostrophe becomes dogs'

There are exceptions to these rules, of course. Not all plural nouns end in "s," so in order to make the plural possessive, you would add both an "s" followed by an apostrophe—just as you do with singular nouns. For example, to form the possessive of "children," add an apostrophe and an "s" to form the plural possessive "children's."

This applies only to nouns. **Possessive pronouns** *almost never* need apostrophes. Here are the most common pronouns and their possessive forms:

Common Pronouns	Singular Possessive	Plural Possessive
I/me or we/us	my/mine	our/ours
you	your/yours	you/yours
he/him she/her or they/them	his/hers	their/theirs
it	its	their/theirs
one	one's	their/theirs
who/whom	whose	whose

You can find a list of pronouns in various forms in Section 2.

Note that "one" is the only common pronoun that needs an apostrophe to form its possessive. Other pronouns that are formed from "one," like "anyone," also need apostrophes.

ACT questions about using apostrophes to form possessives look like this:

Example	
One of the most beautiful times to visit Paris is during Christmas, when the cities streets' are festooned with lights.	**A.** NO CHANGE **B.** cities streets **C.** city's streets' **D.** city's streets

(D) is correct because "city" should be singular and possessive, showing that the streets belong to the single city of Paris. (A) is incorrect because "streets," not "cities," is punctuated as a possessive—and the streets are not possessive in this sentence. "Cities" is also plural, which doesn't make sense if we are only talking about the city of Paris. (B) repeats the error of using the plural "cities." (C) correctly punctuates the possessive "city's," but is not the correct answer because it also adds an apostrophe to "streets," which should not be possessive in the context of this sentence.

Example	
The coaches stopwatches always seemed to run slower when they were timing Casey.	**F.** NO CHANGE **G.** coach's **H.** coaches' **J.** coachs'

(H) is correct because the stopwatches belong to plural coaches. (F) is incorrect because it fails to make the plural noun possessive. (G) is not the best answer because, although a single coach may have multiple stopwatches, the use of "they" makes it clear that there are at least two coaches timing Casey. (J) is incorrect because "coachs" isn't punctuated like a possessive noun or spelled like a plural noun—it's incorrect no matter how you look at it.

The second use of apostrophes on the ACT is to punctuate **contractions**, which are words made by combining two or more other words to create a new, often shorter word. An apostrophe, in this case, replaces one or more of the letters that a contraction omits. Here are some examples:

It + is = it's	I + will = I'll	We + will = we'll
Is + not = isn't	Can + not = can't	Would + not = wouldn't

Not all contractions are easy to break down like this; some contractions are idioms. For example, "won't" is a contraction of "will" and "not."

The ACT will test you on the use of apostrophes in contractions. The questions will look something this this:

<table>
<tr><td colspan="2">Example</td></tr>
<tr><td>Michael Crichton, <u>whose best known for his'</u> suspense-filled novels, is also a physician.</td><td>**A.** NO CHANGE
B. who's best known for his
C. who'se best known for his'
D. who's best known for his'</td></tr>
</table>

(B) is correct because "who's" is the correct contraction of "who is." (A) is incorrect because "whose" indicates possession and "his'" is not a correct possessive form. (C) incorrectly inserts an apostrophe in "who'se" and repeats the error of the incorrect possessive form of "his'." (D) also repeats the error of the incorrect possessive form of "his'."

<table>
<tr><td colspan="2">Example</td></tr>
<tr><td>Karen reminds <u>her sisters' that they cant let</u> their mother know about the surprise party.</td><td>**F.** NO CHANGE
G. her's sisters that they cant'
H. her sister's that they can't
J. her sisters that they can't</td></tr>
</table>

(J) is correct because Karen has multiple sisters, and "can't" is the correct contraction of "cannot" in this context. (F) is not the best answer because in the context of this sentence, "sisters" is not a possessive noun and "cant" is not a contraction of "cannot" (the word "cant" means "hypocritical and sanctimonious talk"). (G) is not the best answer because neither "her's" nor "cant'" are correctly punctuated: "her's" is not the correct possessive of "her," and "cant" is supposed to be the contraction "can't." (H) is incorrect because the use of the singular "sister's" and "they" creates a disagreement between noun and pronoun.

Periods, Question Marks, and Exclamation Points
Part 4

Periods, question marks, and exclamation points usually end sentences, so they are often referred to as **end-of-sentence punctuation**. Each of these punctuation marks plays a specific role in the sentence, showing the reader how to determine what kind of sentence it is.

Periods end all sentences except direct questions or exclamations. Question marks signify that a direct question is being asked. Indirect questions, however, do not require a question mark:

> Direct question: Did you eat dinner?
> Indirect question: She asked if he had eaten dinner.

Exclamation points are used when a sentence expresses a strong feeling or requires special emphasis. The difference between when you should use an exclamation mark and a period can sometimes be subtle in everyday life, but the ACT won't be subtle about it. Look for strong signals, like the use of "shouted," "suddenly," or other very strong language.

ACT questions about end-of-sentence punctuation will usually use a combination of these three punctuation marks. Those questions will look like this:

Example	
When she won the award for outstanding employee, Clara realized that she really had made the right career choice? Before then, she'd had her doubts.	**A.** NO CHANGE **B.** choice! before then, **C.** choice before! Then, **D.** choice. Before then,

(A) is not the best answer because Clara is not questioning her career choice: receiving the award has made her realize it is correct. (B) is not the best option because the exclamation after "choice" should end the first sentence, in which case "before" should be capitalized. (C) inserts an exclamation point mid-sentence and creates a sentence fragment. (D) is the best option because the period properly ends the first sentence, while the comma after "then" properly sets off the transitional expression in the second sentence.

Punctuation Practice Questions
Part 5

How to Be a Coffee Connoisseur

In much of North America, for many decades, "coffee" meant one thing; ground beans brewed in a drip coffee maker or percolator. With the rise of blockbuster espresso-based café franchises in the 1990s, that all began to change, and terms like "latté," "americano," and "cappuccino" entered thousands of neighborhood conversations. Yet many people—sometimes even people who enjoy these drinks—do not know the finer points of distinction between espresso-based beverages. I must admit that for a long time I too was such a person. Today I'm going to explain some of these differences.

The basic building block of espresso-based drinks is the espresso shot! It is made by forcing extremely hot water through a compact "puck" of finely ground beans, yielding about 30 mL of thick liquid. I enjoy drinking espresso all on it's own, but others often find it quite bitter! An espresso combined with extra hot

1. A. NO CHANGE
   B. thing:
   C. thing,
   D. thing.

2. F. NO CHANGE
   G. drinks do
   H. drinks, do
   J. drinks; do

3. A. NO CHANGE
   B. for a long time I, too, was such a person.
   C. for a long time, I too was such a person!
   D. for a long time, I, too, was such a person.

4. F. NO CHANGE
   G. shot?
   H. shot
   J. shot.

5. A. NO CHANGE
   B. its'
   C. it is
   D. its

6. F. NO CHANGE
   G. bitter?
   H. bitter—
   J. bitter

water is called an americano because it resembles

an American-style drip coffee.

Adding steamed or foamed milk to the

mix creates many more varieties. The

cappuccinos characteristic froth comes from its

blend of more or less equal parts steamed milk

and milk foam: this is poured over a shot of

espresso. The latté is a close cousin to the

cappuccino, but calls for a much higher

proportion of steamed milk and only a little

foam. If you'd like a chocolatey drink, I'd

recommend, a mocha, which adds chocolate,

steamed milk, and—in some cases whipped

cream to espresso.

So far, so good, but the ingenuity of the

world's baristas doesnt stop here. How could I

forget delicious combinations like the cortado,

macchiato, and café cubano. Respectively, they

are: an espresso served with an equal amount of

warm milk, an espresso touched with a little

foam, and an espresso that's sweetened as it's

being pulled.

7. **A.** NO CHANGE
   B. americano,
   C. americano:
   D. americano;

8. **F.** NO CHANGE
   G. cappuccinos'
   H. cappuccino's
   J. cappuccinos's

9. **A.** NO CHANGE
   B. foam;
   C. foam,
   D. foam

10. **F.** NO CHANGE
    G. recommend:
    H. recommend
    J. recommend—

11. **A.** NO CHANGE
    B. milk, and—in some cases whipped cream—
    C. milk, and—in some cases—whipped cream
    D. milk and in some cases whipped cream

12. **F.** NO CHANGE
    G. world's baristas doesn't
    H. worlds baristas doesnt
    J. worlds' baristas doesn't

13. **A.** NO CHANGE
    B. cubano!
    C. cubano?
    D. cubano

14. **F.** NO CHANGE
    G. its
    H. its'
    J. is

When it comes to coffee varieties, we have barely scratched—or perhaps it should be "splashed"—the surface? At any rate, I hope my guide has helped to make your next visit to the café less mysterious!

15. **A.** NO CHANGE
    B. surface!?
    C. surface—
    D. surface.

Section 5
Writing Strategy

Writing Strategy questions will ask you to consider a variety of prompts. Some ask you to select a choice that correctly analyzes the effects of a proposed change. Others propose a specific change, and ask you to correctly indicate whether a change should be made and why. Some indicate a goal of the writer, and ask you which of several options for changing the passage would best accomplish the writer's stated goal.

Writing Strategy questions come in a variety of specific styles and subtypes, covering a range of topics. In this section, we'll review:

- Focus
- Unity
- Purpose
- Effects of Changes

Unlike many of the questions on the English Test, Writing Strategy questions will usually have a written prompt. They often also involve much broader changes to the passage than those in the Grammar, Sentence Structure, or Punctuation questions that we've discussed so far. Because they will sometimes require you to consider large portions of the passage, you won't always be able to mentally plug in options and select the one that sounds best.

Writing Strategy questions can also take a little bit longer to answer than the more straightforward question types. If you're short on time and you run into a broad Writing Strategy question, you might benefit from skipping it so that you can move on to easier questions. Just remember to come back to it if you have time, try to attempt the question before you move on to the next passage, and always bubble in a guess before your time is up!

There are 12 Writing Strategy questions on each English Test, so they make up about 16% of the English Test.

Focus

Part 1

Focus questions will ask you to consider specific information in the context of the passage or paragraph as a whole and determine whether it is relevant, or which piece of information from several options is most relevant. These questions may ask you to select the most relevant addition from several choices, to identify and delete irrelevant information, or to consider whether information is relevant enough to be added to a passage.

Here's an example of one kind of Focus question that you're likely to see on the ACT:

Example

While vitamins are essential to health, large doses of vitamins can actually be quite harmful. Vitamins A, C, and E can all cause headaches, nausea, and other unpleasant symptoms at excessive doses. [1] Because of the risks of excessive doses, many doctors recommend that healthy patients avoid most vitamin supplements.

Given that all of the following statements are true, which one provides the most relevant information at this point in the essay?

A. Some food products are fortified with extra vitamins and nutrients.

B. Other vitamins may also cause other harms.

C. There's even some evidence that long-term overuse of some vitamins could cause cancer.

D. Vitamin deficiencies also cause unpleasant symptoms: fatigue, muscle pain—even memory loss.

To tackle this kind of Focus question, you should consider the answer choices in the context of the other sentences in the paragraph. They should relate to some common idea, and there should be some kind of progression of ideas that can provide a clue about what specific additional idea would best fit at the point the question is asking about. In this case, all of the other sentences are related to the potential harms of vitamins. Furthermore, at this point, the paragraph is shifting from specific examples of those harms to a conclusion based on those risks.

That means that the best choice in this question should be about the potential harms of large doses of vitamins, and should make sense following specific examples of harms and preceding a conclusion based on those harms.

(A) is largely irrelevant. It's related to the broad theme of vitamins, but not to the specific ideas in this paragraph. (B) is certainly related, but it's very vague, and would serve mainly to repeat an idea rather than provide additional relevant information. (D) actually weakens the writer's argument by introducing information that seems to contradict it. (C), by providing additional examples of potential harms, provides the most relevant information.

Unity
Part 2

Each essay that you read in the English section is composed of related paragraphs that work together to accomplish the writer's goal. Each paragraph also has an internal structure, built around a connecting idea. **Unity** is the idea that all of the sentences in a paragraph should be built around a connecting idea, and Unity questions test your ability to recognize connecting ideas and appropriately sort information into paragraphs.

Unity questions might ask you where to divide an overly-long paragraph into two shorter paragraphs, or offer a new sentence and ask which paragraph in an essay it belongs with. In either case, you need to identify the unifying theme of a paragraph: consider what each sentence in a paragraph is about, and what the sentences have in common.

Here's an example of a Unity question like those that you might see on the ACT:

Example

I was shy of speaking as a child, and yet remarkably unembarrassed by public silliness. When I was called upon to speak up in class, I could only just squeak out the minimum required to satisfy the teacher. [F] However, I was happy to boldly stroll down the street caked in mud after a rainy afternoon spent sliding down a muddy hill with friends. [G] I was perfectly happy to join the other children at play as a dog, going down on all fours in the dirt and barking—but I struggled to invite them to my birthday party. [H] Now that I've entered the adult world, my behavior is almost entirely reversed. [J] I'm perfectly happy to speak before a room of colleagues on the details of a project, but I would be

The writer wants to divide this paragraph in order to separate details about the narrator's childhood and adulthood. The best place to begin a new paragraph would be at Point:

F. F
G. G
H. H
J. J

incredibly embarrassed to even stand quietly in the room with muddy clothes. I'd be absolutely mortified to be tickled in public, but I can unabashedly express the very strongest opinions about the weather to just about anyone.

This question requires you to divide a single rambling paragraph into two strongly unified paragraphs; furthermore, the question prompt actually tells you what the unifying theme of each paragraph should be. One should be about the narrator's childhood, and one should be about adulthood. Your task is just to identify which theme each sentence belongs to, and divide the paragraph at the point where its sentences stop focusing on the narrator's childhood and start discussing adulthood.

(F) isn't the best choice because the sentence before point (F) and the sentence after it both discuss the narrator's behavior as a child. The same is true for (G), which falls between two examples of the narrator's childhood behavior.

The sentence following (H) introduces the idea of adulthood, and the sentence following (J) provides an example of how the narrator behaves in adulthood. Because the sentence between (H) and (J) introduces adult behavior, it makes the most sense to group it with the paragraph that discusses this behavior—even though it doesn't provide a specific example. Therefore, the best place to start a new paragraph is point (H).

When you're trying to decide between two points like (H) and (J), keep in mind that Unity questions want you to group sentences by the theme of the information—not into groups of sentences that have exactly the same function. Just like paragraphs within an essay, sentences within a paragraph can have different functions.

Here's another example of a type of question you're likely to see on the ACT that will require you to consider the themes of paragraphs:

[1]

There are over 300 recognized breeds of dog in the world, yet all dogs are members of a single species, *Canis lupus*. This single species encompasses a huge variety of subspecies and domesticated breeds, with widely varying characteristics.

[2]

The differences between domesticated breeds can be really striking. For example, Chihuahuas weigh 1.5-3 kg, while English Mastiffs weigh 55-100 kg. That means that the heaviest breed is more than 30 times as massive as the lightest.

[3]

This wide variation between breeds is the result of selective breeding. Wild members of the species include wolves, dingoes, jackals, and wild dogs; while these subspecies differ from one another, the range of the differences between wild subgroups of the species is much smaller than the range of differences between domestic breeds.

After reviewing the essay and realizing that some information has been left out, the writer composes the following sentence, incorporating that information:

> Gray Wolves, the largest wild subspecies, weigh 79-99 kg, while the smallest wild species, the now-extinct Honshu Wolf, weighed around 20 kg—so the largest wild subspecies was only around 5 times as large as the smallest.

The most logical and effective place to add this sentence would be after the last sentence of Paragraph:

A. 1
B. 2
C. 3
D. 4

Given the fact that so much of the variation in the species is driven by selective breeding, it might sound odd to say that selective breeding works by reducing individual variation. However, because the species is divided into a large number of different breeding populations, and individual variation within those subgroups is minimized and pushed towards extreme forms, the differences between the groups become more and more extreme over time.

The proposed addition provides an example of the differences between wild subspecies of *Canis lupus*. It doesn't fit at the end of paragraph 1, because such a specific example of the sizes of wild subspecies doesn't fit the general, introductory theme of the paragraph—so (A) is incorrect. It doesn't fit at the end of paragraph 2 because, while it's very similar to the information provided in that paragraph, the proposed addition is about *wild subspecies* while paragraph 2 is about *domestic breeds*—so (B) is also incorrect. It doesn't fit at the end of paragraph 4, because that paragraph describes in general terms how the dynamics of selective breeding create such big differences between groups—and such a specific example doesn't fit with that theme. So, (D) is also incorrect.

Only paragraph 3 mainly provides information about differences between wild subspecies of *Canis lupus*, and so (C) is correct.

Purpose
Part 3

Writers have goals in mind when they write: **Purpose** questions ask you to consider a hypothetical goal, and determine whether a passage accomplishes that goal. Not only do you need to determine *whether* a passage accomplishes a stated goal, you also need to determine which answer option best explains *why* the passage does or does not accomplish the goal.

These questions always come at the end of an essay, and always require you to consider the *whole* essay. Consider this example of a Purpose question:

Example

Sugar is a prominent part of the American diet, largely because it plays an important role in many modern processes of food production.

Refined sugar is used not only in products typically considered sweets, like soda, candies, and sweet breakfast cereals, but also in processed meats, soups, and even canned vegetables. That's because sugar isn't just added to make products taste sweet: it is also used as a natural preservative, to change the texture of food, to help moist products like bread retain their moisture, and even as a browning agent to help obtain a certain color.

Concerns about the health impacts of the added sugar used in many food products have already spurred advances in the use of artificial sweeteners and preservatives, and will continue to change the way that we use

Suppose the writer had decided to write an essay explaining the health risks associated with consuming too much sugar. Would this essay successfully fulfill the writer's goal?

F.   Yes, because the essay explains that sugar can be very dangerous for certain people.

G.   Yes, because the essay reveals that sugar is hidden in more products than most people realize.

H.   No, because the essay limits itself to discussing only the uses of sugar.

J.   No, because the essay suggests that there are no health risks associated with sugar.

---

sugar and make food. However, no substitute has yet been found that can play all of sugar's many roles, and so—for now, at least—sugar remains an important ingredient in many of the foods in our supermarkets and our homes.

You can take advantage of the fact that this is a two-part question, because each answer option is actually making two claims: the first is about *whether* the passage accomplishes a certain goal, and the second is about *why* the first claim is true. You can eliminate an option if either part is incorrect, or if the two parts don't agree.

If you already know whether the answer should begin "yes" or "no," then you can easily eliminate two choices. If you aren't sure about the answer to the first question, you can still narrow it down by eliminating a choice if the argument that it offers is untrue, irrelevant, or doesn't actually support the "yes" or "no" answer that it's paired with.

In this case, the question states that the writer's purpose is to explain the health risks associated with sugar consumption. The idea that there are "concerns" over "health impacts" does come up, but there's nothing like an explanation of the health risks—they're only vaguely mentioned in passing. It's pretty clear that this essay doesn't fulfill the goal of explaining health risks, so (F) and (G) are both incorrect because they answer the first question incorrectly. If you aren't so sure, you can still eliminate these choices with a little extra work.

You can tell that (F) is incorrect because the essay never actually claims that "sugar can be very dangerous for certain people," so this can't be the correct answer.

You can also tell that (G) is incorrect, because the number and variety of products containing sugar has no direct relevance to the health risks associated with consuming too much sugar. It's true that the essay explains that sugar is used in a wide variety of food products—but that's irrelevant to the question about health risks, so this can't be the correct answer.

(J) claims that the passage fails to fulfill the stated goal because it "suggests that there are no health risks." If you've read a lot about the health impacts of sugar before or have strong opinions on the subject, then this essay might seem to minimize those risks by mentioning them only in passing—but it certainly doesn't suggest that there are none. It specifically mentions "concerns over the health impacts of the added sugar used in many food products." (J) contradicts the passage, so it can't be the correct answer.

(H) is correct, because the essay does limit itself to discussing the uses of sugar. Even in the sentence that mentions "health impacts," they are mentioned mainly to raise a point about changes in the use of sugar.

Effects of Changes
Part 4

Sometimes it takes many revisions before a piece of writing is just right. Writers often have to think very carefully about the effects their changes will have. **Effects of Changes** questions will test your ability to analyze the likely effects of various changes to a piece of writing. They may ask you to select an option that best describes the likely effect of a proposed change, or to select the option that correctly indicates whether a specific change should be made and why or why not.

Effects of Changes questions will ask you to consider a variety of issues of style, tone, structure, and logic that are discussed in various parts of this book. Whatever the specific prompt, though, the approach that you should take only varies depending on whether you're tackling a two-part question that asks if you should make a change and why, or a one-part question that asks only what the effects of a change would be.

Two-part questions on the ACT are phrased as "yes or no" along with reasons supporting those answers. Consider the following example:

Example

Have you ever wondered why some words in English have the same sound and spelling, even though they mean totally different things? [1] One good example is "rare," which means both "unusual" and "lightly cooked meat." The first meaning comes from the Latin word "rarus," which means "infrequent." The second comes from the Old English word "hrer," which means "lightly boiled." "Rarus" and "hrer" both came to be spelled "rare" later.

[1] At this point, the writer is considering adding the following sentence:

> "Sometimes it's because two similar-sounding words from different languages, with different meanings, both make their way into English, and eventually end up sounding and being spelled the same."

Given that this is true, should the writer make this addition?

A. Yes, because it answers the question posed by the sentence before it, ensuring a logical order.

B. Yes, because otherwise the paragraph would have no topic sentence.

C. No, because the paragraph is about English, not words from other languages.

D. No, because it fails to provide any examples of what it describes.

In this case, (A) is the right answer; the first sentence asks a question, and the suggested addition answers it. The result is a more logical structure. (B) does give the right answer about adding the sentence, but gives a bad reason for that addition—there is a topic sentence even without the addition.

(C) is not the best choice because the paragraph discusses, in part, how words from other languages can become English words. (D) also offers a poor reason for deletion. While the sentence in question does not provide any examples, the following sentence does.

Consider the following example of an Effects of Changes question:

Example

If you want to bake an apple pie from scratch, you should begin by getting the right ingredients. Fortunately, it's a short list, and your local grocery store should carry all of the necessary ingredients: flour, butter, sugar (white and brown), Granny Smith apples, salt, and shortening. You will also need a pie plate, mixing bowls, a rolling pin, a set of measuring spoons, and—of course—an oven. You should plan to spend about an hour working on the pie, another hour baking it, and another hour waiting for it to cool—so if you want to eat pie for dessert, you should begin working on the pie well before dinner. Baking a pie can be a big commitment of time, but once you taste the results I think you will agree that it's worth it!

This paragraph is written primarily in the second person (*you, your*). If this paragraph were revised so that the second-person pronouns were replaced with the third-person pronouns *one* and *one's*, the essay would primarily:

F. lose a sense of close, personal connection between the reader and the writer.

G. lose a sense of addressing the audience appropriate to its purpose of providing directions.

H. gain the neutral, formal tone appropriate to the purpose of this paragraph.

J. gain a broader sense of truth and applicability by using a more universal pronoun.

This question asks you about a change to the passage, but doesn't ask you to decide whether that change should be made. Instead, it only asks you to select the choice that best describes the effect the change *would* have if it *were* made. First, imagine what the passage would be like if the change were made. Mentally plug the proposed change into the passage. Here's the first sentence of that paragraph with the proposed change:

If one wants to bake an apple pie from scratch, one should begin by getting the right ingredients.

Next, consider each answer option in terms of that change, and decide whether it accurately describes the effect of the change on the passage. Eliminate any answer choice that makes a false or irrelevant claim about what the passage was like before the change, what it would be like after, or what the difference would be.

In this case, (F) is incorrect because it states that the passage would "lose" a sense of "close, personal connection" that it never had to begin with. The original directions directly address the reader, but they read like they could be from a cookbook or cooking blog—not like something from a love letter. Since this isn't a feature of the original passage, it's not something that can be lost when you make a change.

(H) is incorrect because it claims that a formal tone would be "appropriate to the purpose of this paragraph." This paragraph just provides partial directions for baking a pie. There's no reason to believe that directions for baking a pie should have a "neutral, formal tone." Furthermore, the final sentence emphatically expresses the writer's opinion that baking a pie is worth it—even using an exclamation mark. That sentence alone creates a pretty informal tone, even if you change the pronouns—so even if a formal tone were appropriate, merely changing the pronouns wouldn't actually accomplish that goal.

(J) isn't the best answer mainly because it's vague and somewhat irrelevant. "One" is technically a more "universal" pronoun that "you," in the sense that it can refer to a broader range of things, but "you" can refer to any person who is actually reading the text. The original passage is not particularly narrow in its "sense of truth and applicability," and we are free to imagine that its directions could be just as true for us as for any number of other readers. You could make the argument that (J) is kind of a true statement, but that would be a stretch—and it's certainly not the primary effect that the change would have.

(G) is the best answer, because it accurately describes the primary effect of the change. Directions very often use the second person voice, because writers know that when they address you directly you will pay closer attention. You may even have noticed that we do this all over this book.

Writing Strategy Practice Questions ✗

Part 5

Alan Turing

[1]

[1] Alan Turing was the father of theoretical computer science. ☐1 [2] The Turing "machine" was a logical and mathematical description of how to use very simple steps to compute anything that could be computed, using a simple hypothetical machine.

1. Given that all of the following statements are true, which one provides the most relevant information at this point in the essay?

   A. He devised the idea of a machine, called a Turing machine, which was a theoretical forerunner to today's computers.

   B. Though he was long forgotten, his name is now well-known, thanks to a movie starring Benedict Cumberbatch.

   C. Turing was British and he studied at Cambridge.

   D. Turing was a computer scienctist who helped to break Nazi codes during the Second World War.

☐2 [3] The hypothetical machine that Turing described would use a strip of tape with symbols on it, a "head" that can scan those symbols, and a few decision rules input by its user to perform

2. The writer is considering deleting the following phrase from the preceding sentence:

   "to compute anything that could be computed,"

   If the writer were to make this deletion, the essay would primarily lose:

   F. information that distracts from the main purpose of the passage.

   G. an example of how modern computers improve upon the idea of a Turing machine.

   H. evidence for the claim that Turing was the father of theoretical computer science.

   J. information that explains the purpose and function of the Turing machine.

calculations. ☐3 [4] Any machine that can follow the rules he outlined for performing calculations

can be called a Turing machine, though it's best

$\overline{4}$

to use the materials he suggested.

4

[5] Turing machines are so simple they can actually be built without any electronic components. [6] Such machines are called mechanical Turing machines because they rely exclusively on mechanical components and motion to make their calculations. [7] That means that anything a modern computer can calculate can also be calculated by a machine with no electronic components. ☐5 ☐6

3. At this point, the writer is considering adding the following true statement:

> It was the very simplicity of Turing's hypothetical machine that made some "experts" scoff.

Should the writer add this sentence here?

A. Yes, because it provides important background information about the reception Turing's theory received.

B. Yes, because it shows how competitive the field of theoretical computer science was at the time.

C. No, because it distracts the reader from the main point of this paragraph.

D. No, because it does not provide specific information about Turing's critics.

4. At this point, the writer would like to provide the information that the design of the Turing machine is flexible. Given that all the choices are true, which one best accomplishes this purpose?

F. NO CHANGE

G. whether or not it uses exactly the same parts.

H. provided that the parts are assembled correctly.

J. which is a very important feature of Turing machines.

5. The writer is considering deleting the last sentence of the first paragraph of the essay. If the writer were to make this deletion, the essay would primarily lose a statement that:

A. introduces the organization of the next three paragraphs.

B. summarizes points made earlier in that paragraph.

C. provides a significant detail that sets up the information in the next paragraph.

D. creates a humorous tone in the essay.

[2]

[1] Of course, mechanical Turing machines work relatively slowly: it can take one or two seconds for a mechanical Turing machine to calculate a single step of its instructions,

while most modern computers run through
$$\overline{}$$
$$7$$
billions of steps of instructions each second.
$$\overline{}$$
$$7$$
[2] So, while mechanical Turing machines can *theoretically* calculate anything that a modern computer can calculate, they aren't a practical

alternative to modern computers. $\boxed{8}$

6. The writer has decided to divide the first paragraph into two. The best place to add the new paragraph break would be at the beginning of Sentence:

   F. 3, because it would indicate that the essay is now going to focus on how Turing managed to build his theoretical machine.

   G. 4, because it would signal the essay's shift in emphasis from the components of Turing's machine to the function of the machine.

   H. 5, because it would signal that the essay is now going to address the simplicity of Turing's theoretical machine.

   J. 7, because it would signal the essay's shift from Turing's theoretical invention to the actuality of modern computers.

7. At this point in the essay, the writer wants to show that mechanical Turing machines are not a practical alternative to modern computers. Given that all the choices are true, which one best conveys this message?

   A. NO CHANGE

   B. which is faster than many people can calculate by hand.

   C. and it can be powered by a motor or even a hand-crank.

   D. but depending on its design it may perform calculations at a slower or faster pace.

8. The writer is considering adding the following true statement to this paragraph:

   > Mechanical Turing machines are generally built as projects by hobbyists.

   Should the sentence be added to this paragraph, and if so, where should it be placed?

   F. Yes, before sentence 1.

   G. Yes, after sentence 1.

   H. Yes, after sentence 2.

   J. The sentence should NOT be added.

[3]

[1] Even a person can be a Turing machine.

9 [2] Given a strip of paper, a pencil with an eraser, and a simple program for addition, anyone can add the numbers 2 and 3 together in as few as

15 steps. 10 [3] That's not very efficient, but there's one important thing to keep in mind: that person doesn't have to know how to do math in

9. At this point, the writer is considering adding the following true statement:

> The term "calculator" actually used to be a job title.

Should the writer make this addition here?

A. Yes, because it supports the main point of the paragraph by providing a real-world example.

B. Yes, because it explains the relevance of the ideas in the paragraph to the main idea of the essay.

C. No, because it undermines the paragraph's point by providing contradictory information.

D. No, because it distracts from the paragraph's point by adding irrelevant information.

10. The writer is considering deleting the preceding sentence from this essay. The sentence should NOT be deleted because it:

F. specifically describes the program a person must follow to simulate a Turing machine.

G. explains in general terms how a person can simulate a Turing machine.

H. introduces the key idea that a Turing machine doesn't have to understand its operations.

J. reinforces the idea that Turing machines are a slow and impractical alternative to modern computers.

order to get the correct answer. [11] [4] He doesn't even have to know what math is, or what he's trying to accomplish—he just has to follow the steps in the

program. [12]

[4]

Turing machines can calculate any problem that can be calculated without understanding or even knowing the problem they're trying to solve. That's why they can be so simple, and that's what ultimately makes them so

powerful. [13] [14] [15]

11. The writer is considering deleting the following phrase from the preceding sentence:

> That's not very efficient, but

If the writers makes this deletion, the essay will primarily lose:

A. an unnecessary qualification that confuses the writer's point.

B. supporting evidence for the previous claim that mechanical Turing machines are significantly slower than modern computers.

C. a qualification that acknowledges a flaw in calculating like a Turing machine and sets up a contrast with an advantage.

D. information suggesting that adding according to the rules of a Turing machine may be less efficient than regular arithmetic.

12. If the writer were to delete sentence 4, the essay would primarily lose details that:

F. emphasize the key idea that Turing machines can compute a problem without understanding it.

G. suggest that people should consider using Turing machine rules for math, because they are easier than arithmetic.

H. imply that machines are better at calculating than people because they are more likely to follow a program.

J. needlessly repeat information from the previous sentence.

13. Upon reviewing this essay and realizing that some information has been left out, the writer composes the following sentence, incorporating that information:

> Some mechanical Turing machines don't even have motors: they are hand-cranked calculators.

The most logical and effective place to add this sentence would be after the last sentence in Paragraph:

A. 1.

B. 2.

C. 3.

D. 4.

14. Suppose the writer's goal had been to write an essay that briefly provides a general introduction to the idea of a Turing machine. Would this essay fulfill the writer's goal?

    F. Yes, because the essay provides detailed information about the rules used by a Turing machine.

    G. Yes, because the essay provides some information about various aspects of Turing machines.

    H. No, because the essay would only make sense to readers who are already somewhat familiar with Turing machines.

    J. No, because the essay limits itself to discussing Turing machines only as an example of Alan Turing's work.

15. Suppose the writer's goal had been to write an essay that briefly explained the life and career of Alan Turing. Would this essay fulfill the writer's goal?

    A. Yes, because the essay shares details about Turing's career, such as his development of a hypothetical machine.

    B. Yes, because the essay provides ample biographical detail about Turing.

    C. No, because the essay primarily focuses on the Turing machine rather than on Turing as the father of theoretical computer science.

    D. No, because the essay indicates that Turing's work was not as advanced as today's computers.

Section 6
Organization

Organization questions will ask you to consider the order of elements in a passage and the transitions between them. They ask about the order of phrases within sentences, sentences within paragraphs, and paragraphs within passages. They also ask you to select the transitional words and phrases that correctly express the most logical relationships among sentences, ideas, and paragraphs, and to select sentences that correctly introduce, conclude, or signal transitions within paragraphs.

Organization questions come in a variety of styles. In this section, we'll review the four main kinds of Organization questions that you'll see on the exam, and talk about how to approach each type of question. In this section, we'll review:

- Order
- Coherence of Ideas
- Opening, Transitional, and Closing Statements
- Logical Relationships

Organization questions often require you to read a whole paragraph or even the whole passage before selecting your answer, so be sure to keep the full context in mind when answering them.

There are 11 Organization questions on each English Test, so they make up about 15% of the English Test.

Order
Part 1

The arrangement of words and clauses within sentences is referred to as "syntax." On the English Test, you will sometimes be asked to choose between different ways of ordering the parts of sentences in order to clearly express ideas. Effective use of syntax means ordering the elements of a sentence in a clear and straightforward manner.

Order questions are similar to Misplaced Modifier questions, because they relate to the placement of elements within a sentence. Misplaced Modifier questions deal specifically with modifiers that are placed next to the wrong object, while Order questions deal with more general problems. It might be clear in a sentence what the subject is, what the action is, and what all of the modifiers modify—but if those elements are in an unusual order, it can still be an awkward sentence.

Consider the following example:

Example

Dancing on the table is what we almost felt like doing that night, while we ate our pizzas, that a jazz band played.

A. NO CHANGE

B. The night that a jazz band played while we ate our pizzas was when we almost felt like dancing on the table.

C. A jazz band played, and while we ate our pizzas we felt like dancing, almost, on the table that night.

D. That night, a jazz band played while we ate our pizzas, and we almost felt like dancing on the table.

The incorrect choices don't sound quite right, though they aren't obviously grammatically incorrect. These sentences just order the words in awkward ways that introduce a variety of problems. Some of them use the passive voice to accommodate the oddly ordered words, while others use parenthetical elements to clarify ideas that could be expressed clearly without them.

Usually, it's best to place the subject before the verb, the object after the verb, and any modifiers directly next to the element that they modify. A modifier that applies to the whole sentence should be placed at the beginning or end of the sentence, not in the middle. It's also generally better to use the active voice, so that the grammatical subject is the same as the one doing the action.

The incorrect answers make a mess of the sentence's various clauses and phrases, causing some confusing and silly results. The ordering of phrases in (A) creates an awkward, passive construction. "We" refers to the people doing the action in the sentence, but "dancing on the table" is the subject of this passive-voice sentence. This is clunky, slightly confusing, and less concise than an active construction could be. The order of phrases in (B) likewise forces the writer to use an awkward passive construction, since "night," the noun that is placed ahead of the verb, is the grammatical subject but not the person or thing doing the action. (C) uses a clunky word order, creating an awkward effect. "Almost" is awkwardly placed as a parenthetical phrase interrupting the middle of the sentence.

(D) is the best choice, because it logically arranges the parts of the sentence in a neat order. The structure of the sentence is clear, and it is easy to understand what the writer is trying to express.

Questions about Order can also look like this:

Example	
By October 14th, the puppeteer had finished; she had used nearly 5,000 pieces of drinking straws <u>building the new puppet</u> and enough wire to stretch 100 miles.	The best placement for the underlined phrase would be: **F.** where it is now. **G.** before the word *By* (revising the capitalization accordingly). **H.** after the word *finished.* **J.** After the word *used* (placing commas around the underlined phrase).

(F) is not the best answer because the underlined phrase clearly describes her whole project, not just the part on which she used straws. (G) is not the best option because placing the phrase "building the new puppet" at the beginning of the sentence would place the object of the verb before its subject, in a modifier phrase. That's an illogical and confusing word order. (J) is incorrect because it is not necessary to turn the phrase into a parenthetical phrase; doing so creates an awkward and confusing structure.

The best answer is (H) because the phrase "building the new puppet" logically describes what the puppeteer had finished doing. In this position, the phrase serves to describe what the puppeteer had finished.

Coherence of Ideas
Part 2

Coherence of Ideas questions will ask about moving a sentence from one place to another within a paragraph, ask where a new sentence should be added in a paragraph, or even ask about rearranging paragraphs within a passage as a whole. These sentences express ideas, and you need to make sure that they are placed so that they **cohere**: stick together and form a logical whole. Ideas that are disordered can make incoherent paragraphs that are difficult to interpret.

Consider the following example of a Coherence of Ideas question:

Example

[1] The Crystal Palace Dinosaurs, unveiled in London in 1854, were the first dinosaur sculptures ever made. [2] The story of their construction is chock-full of Victorian eccentricity and earnest—albeit somewhat inaccurate—science. [3] Designed and built by Benjamin Waterhouse Hawkins, with scientific advice from the paleontologist Sir Richard Owen, the sculptures were commissioned to populate two artificial lakes in Crystal Palace Park. [4] The public reacted enthusiastically, and Hawkins even famously held a New Year's banquet inside the mould of his huge *Iguanodon* sculpture. [5] A bone now known to belong to the *Iguanodon*'s spiked thumb was depicted on its nose, like a horn! [6] While the models captured London's imagination, it must be said that they were not quite perfect. [7] Mistakes aside, Owen and Hawkins' pioneering exhibit inspired many more museum displays around the world.

For the sake of logic and coherence of this paragraph, Sentence 5 should be placed:

A. where it is now.
B. after Sentence 3.
C. after Sentence 6.
D. after Sentence 7.

It's true that in (A), the remark about the *Iguanodon*'s spiked thumb immediately follows another mention of the *Iguanodon* model, namely a banquet held inside the mould. Yet the two sentences are not connected by signal words or internal references; the remark about the horn is a non-sequitur. (B) is more obviously wrong, as it creates a real sense of disorder. (D) is not the best choice because Sentence 7 refers to the mistake in Sentence 5 as though it has already been stated—indicating that Sentence 5 should come before Sentence 7, not after it. Sentence 7 also already provides a logical conclusion to the passage, while Sentence 5 does not, so placing Sentence 5 after Sentence 7 would create confusion.

The best choice is (C) because Sentence 6 uses "While" to signal a transition to the idea that the models were not perfect, and Sentence 7 refers to the "mistakes" but shifts the focus to the concluding idea that the exhibit was an inspiration for others. The perfect place for a specific example of one of the mistakes is between the sentence that introduces that idea and the sentence that shifts the focus away from it. Because Sentence 5 gives the example of the *Iguanodon* horn error, this sentence fits best between Sentence 6 and Sentence 7.

There are three important kinds of clues that you should use to help you order sentences correctly and make coherent paragraphs:

1. **Signal words**: if a sentence contains a signal word that expresses a specific type of relationship to another sentence, it should always be adjacent to—and should usually follow—the sentence to which it is related.
2. **References**: references within sentences to other information in a passage can be a big clue about where the sentence belongs. Sentences that refer to ideas that haven't been introduced yet should be moved so that they follow the sentences that introduce them; sentences that introduce ideas should be moved so that they come before sentences that refer to them.
3. **Purpose**: the purpose of a sentence isn't always clear when you're reading it out of context, but when the purpose is clear it's usually a very good clue about where the sentence belongs. Sentences that are designed to introduce the main idea of a paragraph usually come first, or near the beginning. Sentences that provide supporting information usually come in the middle. Sentences that provide a conclusion, or summarize the paragraph, usually come at the end.

Some questions on the ACT will also ask about the placement of paragraphs within a passage. Consider the following example:

<table>
<tr><td>Example</td></tr>
</table>

[1]

Shoes and boots should be good-looking, durable, comfortable, and versatile—they'll go with everything in your capsule collection.

[2]

Because outerwear should last for a number of seasons, find a coat that is a classic style like a trench, a peacoat, or a fitted, long down coat.

[3]

To build a good wardrobe, start with a "capsule collection" of classic pieces that will form the foundation for a number of different looks. These items would include such articles as basic tank tops and loose tops; a white button-front shirt; stylish jeans, trousers, and skirts; dresses for day and evening; a fitted blazer and one embellished jacket; plus shoes and outerwear.

For the sake of logic and coherence of this paragraph, Paragraph 3 should be placed:

F. where it is now.
G. before Paragraph 1.
H. after Paragraph 1.
J. after Paragraph 4.

[4]

Keep in mind that the materials matter. Find the best quality basics you can afford because otherwise you're just going to look a mess and regret having made the purchase in the first place.

Signal words, references, and purpose allow you to figure out the proper order of sentences within a paragraph because paragraphs have a structure. Passages also have a structure, and the same clues can help you figure out the proper order of paragraphs within a passage.

(G) is the best option because the purpose of Paragraph 3 is to introduce the main idea of the passage as a whole. This is evident because it introduces the idea of a "capsule collection," and paragraphs 1 and 2 provide specific examples of items to add to such a collection and guidance on how to select appropriate items. (F) is not the best answer because Paragraph 1 references information that will logically follow the information in Paragraph 3. (H) is not the best choice because both Paragraph 1 and Paragraph 2 support the ideas introduced in Paragraph 3 so placing the paragraph between them creates confusion. (J) is not the best answer because Paragraph 4 provides the logical conclusion to this passage.

Opening, Transitional, and Closing Statements
Part 3

Writers often choose to begin a passage with a sentence that introduces some of the ideas that will be discussed. An introductory sentence doesn't necessarily spell out the whole main idea. It might just provide some basic facts that prepare the reader to understand the main idea. Sometimes, a writer might even ask a question as an introductory sentence, so that they can answer that question in the rest of the passage.

As the writer moves through the passage, they will need to shift focus between different ideas. To accomplish that, they will use transitional sentences. A typical transitional sentence will bridge two specific ideas by explaining their relationship. Sometimes, a transitional sentence creates a smooth transition at a place where the broader focus of the passage is shifting from one general idea to another.

Finally, writers usually end a passage on a strong concluding sentence. An effective concluding sentence ties together the ideas in the passage, usually by offering a summary of the key ideas and the conclusion of the writer's argument.

Consider the following example:

Example

[2]

The first person to show me the comic potential of slowing things down, or speeding them up, was my friend Andy. He told me that he and his roommates loved to watch the animated show *King of the Hill* at either too fast or too slow a speed. He gave me a demonstration; it was hilarious! On my own, I messed around with the playing speed of *He-Man*, *The Simpsons*, and *Hey Arnold!* These cartoon experiments were a source of endless chortles.

[3]

In much the same way, the fun never ends when you change the speed that you play your music. For instance, if you slow down a Chipmunks album, the vocalists sound like three middle-aged men singing over a sludgy, syrupy-slow backing track. If you speed up a Tribe Called Quest album, the beat sounds like something from a UK garage song. At parties, I like to play vinyl records at the wrong speed all the time, to the delight (I presume) of everyone present.

Which choice is the effective first sentence of Paragraph 3?

A. NO CHANGE
B. Modern record players usually have a setting for two speeds: one for 45 rpm, and one for 33 rpm.
C. The Chipmunks were created in 1958, by Ross Bagdasarian, Sr.
D. The members of A Tribe Called Quest are named Q-Tip, Phife Dawg, Ali Shaheed Muhammad, and Jarobi.

The best choice here is (A), as it most effectively bridges the ideas about the effects of changing the playing speeds of animated shows in Paragraph 2 with the idea that this technique can also be used on vinyl records, which is explored further in Paragraph 3. (B) doesn't work as a transition between paragraphs because it doesn't provide a bridge between the ideas about changing the playing speeds of animated shows and records; it merely introduces a peripheral fact about records without providing context for that information. (C) likewise does not provide a bridge because this sentence only introduces a peripheral fact about The Chipmunks without providing context. (D) is an incorrect choice because the information about the members of A Tribe Called Quest does not build a bridge between the two ideas.

Logical Relationships
Part 4

Logical Relationships questions will ask you to choose a signal word or phrase that expresses the most logical relationship or transition between two or more sentences in a passage. Signal words and phrases express the relationship between two or more pieces of information. The chart below provides a handy guide to some common signal words and phrases.

Type of Signal Word or Phrase	Examples
Examples introduce a specific piece of information to support a more general point.	For example, much like, specifically, for instance
Continuations introduce additional information that supports points made in earlier examples, or that continue a description of a series of events.	Moreover, also, additionally, similarly, furthermore, next
Changes introduce a contrasting piece of information or signal a shift in emphasis within a text.	While, in spite of, yet, however, although
Conclusions introduce the last event or piece of information in a text, or conclude an argument.	As a result, finally, therefore, consequently, hence

On the ACT, you'll be asked to replace signal words and phrases that express the wrong logical relationship between sentences, or to identify an answer choice that would not be an acceptable alternative to an underlined word or phrase. You need to consider the ideas in linked sentences, and decide what sort of logical relationship those ideas have.

Here's an example of a Logical Relationships question like those you'll see on the ACT:

Example

The tannins that naturally occur in tea leaves most likely developed to ward off herbivores. The bitter, astringent flavor of the tannins deters animals that might otherwise eat the foliage of a tea bush. Likewise, that same bitter flavor is one of the reasons that humans grow and harvest tea for consumption.

    F. NO CHANGE
    G. Meanwhile
    H. Moreover
    J. However

First, consider the ideas that are being expressed *before* the underlined word, and compare them to the ideas expressed *after* the underlined word. In this case, (J) is the best answer because "however" signals that what follows is a contrast to the information that came before the signal word—the bitter tannins deter animals but make the tea seem delicious to humans. (F) is not the best answer because "likewise" incorrectly signals a continuation of the undesirable character of the tannins. (G) is not the best choice because "meanwhile" only signals that something occurs at the same time, and does not signal a contrasting idea that tannins make tea tasty for humans. (H) is not the best answer because "moreover" also signals a continuation of the point about tannins' tendency to ward off herbivores.

Organization Practice Questions
Part 5

Passage 1

[1]

Picnic is a word with an unclear origin.
_____
                1

To have a picnic, my pal Henry suggested that
_____
                      2
we bike last year to the ferry terminal, and my
_____
                    2
friends and I planned to take a ferry to an island.
_____
                  2
I hadn't ridden a bike since I was a teenager,

and I didn't have one of my own, but Henry said

he had plenty of bicycles for me to choose from.

[2]

Only, the road wasn't quite open:

streetcars run back and forth along Queen Street

constantly. With a bank of parked cars to my

right and a clanging streetcar to my left, I hardly

had room to breathe! I'd like to tell you that I

bravely stayed on the road all the way to our

destination, but the truth is that I got off my bike

and walked on the sidewalk. However, I didn't
                                   _____
                                       3
let that one bad experience stop me—today I

maneuver through traffic with ease.

1. Which choice is the most effective first sentence of Paragraph 1?

   A. NO CHANGE
   B. Bicycles come in many shapes and sizes.
   C. Nowadays I love biking in the city, but it wasn't always that way.
   D. It's nice to borrow things from your friends.

2. F. NO CHANGE
   G. Last year, my friends and I planned to take a ferry to an island to have a picnic, and my pal Henry suggested that we bike to the ferry terminal.
   H. My friends, last year, and my pal Henry and I, planned to take a ferry to an island to have a picnic and suggested that we bike to the ferry terminal.
   J. I, to have a picnic, and my friends, planned to take a ferry to an island last year, and Henry, my pal, suggested that we bike to the ferry terminal

3. A. NO CHANGE
   B. Consequently,
   C. Additionally,
   D. Also,

[3]

When I got to his house, I saw a motley
collection of ancient bikes lashed to his front
fence. I picked out a heavy white creature that
looked to be about forty years old, and Henry
warned me not to try shifting gears. Meanwhile,
                                          4
After a few wobbly (and very wide) turns up
and down the street, we were ready for the open
road. 5

Passage 2

[1]

Most singers can produce just one note at
a time. Likewise, the throat singers of Tuva, a
                      6
Siberian region north of Mongolia, are able to
sing two or more notes at once. They achieve
this through a method called overtone singing,
which produces hauntingly beautiful music. 7

4. **F.** NO CHANGE
   G. Conversely,
   H. Therefore,
   J. OMIT the underlined portion

5. For the sake of the logic and coherence of
   the passage, Paragraph 2 should be placed:

   A. Where it is now.
   B. Before Paragraph 1.
   C. After Paragraph 3.
   D. OMIT the paragraph.

6. **F.** NO CHANGE
   G. Furthermore,
   H. Thus,
   J. However,

7. Given that all of the following sentences are
   true, which one, if added here, would offer
   the best transition from Paragraph 1 to
   Paragraph 2?

   A. Tuva is now a part of modern-day
   Russia, but was once an independent
   state.
   B. Beatboxing is another example of
   complex music made only with the
   mouth.
   C. An American country musician named
   Arthur Miles independently developed
   a similar technique in the 1920s.
   D. Despite its phenomenal effects, no
   instruments are needed for overtone
   singing—only the human body.

[2]

Overtone singers create two separate resonance chambers by carefully shaping their lips, teeth, throat, and tongues. This is the key to producing multiple tones. A high, clear, whistling and a deep growling are the range of resulting sounds, and Tuvan singing, throat singing, has four distinct forms, depending on the particular style. These tones mimic the natural sounds of wind and water on the steppes.

[3]

Tuvan throat singers traditionally perform at archery competitions, horse races, wrestling matches, banquets, and ceremonies. However, increasing interest from around the world has also brought Tuvan throat singers to far-flung venues. Kongar-ol Ondar, for example, the great singer, many times performed for a new audience on American television, bringing this remarkable multi-toned music.

8. **F.** NO CHANGE
   G. From a high, clear whistling, to a deep growling, depending on the particular style of throat singing, the resulting sounds can range, and Tuvan singing has four distinct forms.
   H. Depending on the particular style of throat singing—Tuvan singing has four distinct forms—the resulting sounds can range from a high, clear whistling to a deep growling.
   J. Tuvan singing has four distinct forms, depending on the particular style, and the resulting sounds can range from a high, clear whistling to a deep growling of throat singing.

9. **A.** NO CHANGE
   B. Correspondingly,
   C. As such,
   D. For this reason,

10. **F.** NO CHANGE
    G. On American television, for example, this remarkable multi-toned music, many times performed by Kongar-ol Ondar, was brought to a new audience by the great singer.
    H. For example, the great singer Kongar-ol Ondar performed many times on American television, bringing this remarkable, multi-toned music to a new audience.
    J. Many times, performed on American television for example, this remarkable multi-toned music was brought to a new audience by Kongar-ol Ondar, the great singer.

Passage 3

[1]

Approximately 200,000 people every year
injure the anterior cruciate ligament, or ACL,
which runs diagonally through the middle of the
knee. Tearing or rupturing an ACL is one of the
most common injuries among athletes and over
half the people who sustain this injury end up
having surgery.

[2]

12 [1] In 1917 the British surgeon Dr.
Groves performed the first complete ACL
reconstruction surgery. [2] He harvested a portion
of another tendon and used ivory screws to attach
the band to the femur and tibia. [3] This was the
usual procedure until the 1960s, when a doctor in
Arkansas tried routing the patellar tendon that
attaches to the tibia though the knee and
attaching it to the femur. [4] In 1903, a new
technique of replacing the ligament with silk
braids was attempted in Germany; however, this
technique was not successful. 13

[3]

The ACL runs diagonally through the
middle of the knee, providing rotational stability
and preventing the tibia from sliding in front of
the femur. Of the four ligaments in the knee, the

11. **A.** NO CHANGE
    B. Each year, approximately 200,000 people injure the anterior cruciate ligament, or ACL, which runs diagonally through the middle of the knee.
    C. The anterior cruciate ligament, or ACL, which runs diagonally through the middle of the knee is injured by approximately 200,000 people annually.
    D. Each year an ACL injury happens to approximately 200,000 people annually.

12. Which of the following sentences should the writer add to the beginning of Paragraph 2 to create the clearest and most logical transition from Paragraph 1?
    F. It's important to do appropriate exercises after the injury to avoid losing muscle strength and endurance.
    G. A torn or ruptured ACL is not to be taken lightly, as the injury requires a surgical repair.
    H. ACL repair surgeries have a long history, beginning in 1895 when a miner's torn ACL was stitched back together.
    J. An injury to the ACL can effectively end the career of a promising young athlete.

13. For the sake of logic and coherence of this paragraph, Sentence 4 should be placed:
    A. where it is now.
    B. before Sentence 1.
    C. before Sentence 2.
    D. before Sentence 3.

ACL is the weakest. Otherwise, it is the weakest
⎯⎯⎯⎯⎯⎯⎯⎯
14
ligament in the body: it doesn't take much to

partially tear or even completely sever the ACL

These types of injuries can be debilitating and

extremely painful. However, surgery to repair

ACL injuries can be very effective.

[4]

Today the most common ACL repair is

the "Clancy procedure," named for Dr. William

Clancy, in which a tendon is harvested from the

hamstring that is attached to the femur and tibia

and pulled through the middle of the knee.

Recently, however, doctors at Boston Children's

Hospital in Boston have been experimenting with

a new way to fix the ACL called bridge-

enhancement ACL repair. It involves using a

sponge placed between the ligament's severed

ends to act as a bridge that helps the ligament

grow back together. Preliminary results seem

promising, but only time will tell if this technique

will become the new standard for repairing the

ACL. [15]

14. **F.** NO CHANGE
    G. In fact,
    H. Although
    J. Therefore,

Question 15 asks about the preceding
passage as a whole.

15. For the sake of logic and coherence,
Paragraph 3 should be placed:

    A. where it is now.
    B. before Paragraph 1.
    C. after Paragraph 1.
    D. after Paragraph 4.

Section 7
Style

Style questions will ask you to improve portions of the passage that may be grammatically correct, but contain wordy, awkward, or redundant phrases, or are inconsistent with the style and tone of the passage as a whole.

In this section, we'll review:

- Tone
- Clarity
- Economy

Style questions can be tricky, because they look similar to Grammar and Usage questions but don't necessarily break any English rules. If you're moving too quickly, you might glance at the question, realize the underlined portion doesn't contain any formal errors, select (A) or (F), and move on without fully considering all your answer choices because you don't think anything needs to be corrected. That can cost you points!

Always read all the options, and don't assume that no change should be made just because the underlined portion is technically correct. Remember that your task on a multiple-choice test is always to pick the best answer: if both the underlined portion and your answer choices are grammatically correct, your task is to pick the option that best fits the style and tone of the passage as a whole and sounds best in context.

Style questions come in a variety of specific styles and subtypes. In this section, we'll review the three main kinds of style questions that you'll see on the exam and talk about how to approach each type of question.

There are 12 Style questions on each English Test, so they make up about 16% of the English Test.

Tone
Part 1

Tone relates to the way that a passage feels, or how it is supposed to feel. On the English Test, most Tone questions will focus on the differences between formal and informal tone. Tone questions often have no stated question, so a good technique is to ask yourself, "which answer option fits with the rest of the passage?"

You should consider what the writer sounds like in other parts of the passage, and choose the answer that continues the writer's tone. Here's an example of a typical Tone question you'll find on the English Test:

Example

The seventeenth-century English poet and philosopher Margaret Cavendish participated in many debates in the emerging discipline of natural science. Her 1666 book, *The Blazing World*, is often considered one of the earliest examples of the genre we now call "science fiction." It's pretty great.

A. NO CHANGE

B. It is a cool book, full of wacky creatures like "Fish-men."

C. This book is fantastic.

D. OMIT the underlined portion.

The passage is mostly formal and academic; its tone fits with the relating of factual information. Given this tone, "It's pretty great" feels out of place so (A) must be incorrect. (B), with its informal word choices, is also inappropriate. (C), while slightly more formal, still diverges from the formal tone in the rest of the passage. In this case, none of the suggested alternatives are good choices. The right answer must be (D), which omits the sentence altogether.

A lot of the differences between formal and informal tone have to be picked up over time, but there are a few common clues that you can look out for to identify informal tone.

Slang is major clue: slang is language that people use in their everyday speech that has an informal meaning that is different from the dictionary definitions of the words. Words like "cool" and "awesome" are often used informally to mean "good," or "very good." Slang phrases are always informal, and on the ACT that's *usually* not cool. Occasionally, a passage will have a sufficiently informal tone to include some informal language when the alternatives are very different in tone from the passage as a whole. More often, you will need to select options that avoid informal language.

Intensifiers are a kind of adverb used to increase the emphasis on another adverb or adjective, and they are another signal of informal tone. These include words like "pretty," "really," and "super" in phrases like "pretty great," "really angry," and "super strong." Formal writing usually doesn't usually need intensifiers because it doesn't often call for intense language. When intense language is called for, formal writing uses stronger adjectives rather than adding intensifiers to adjectives. For example, a writer who needs to describe someone as being "really angry" but wants to use a more formal tone would use a stronger word like "furious."

It is occasionally appropriate to use intensifiers in formal writing, but in those cases a writer will almost always use only one intensifier. Even in informal writing, extra intensifiers are usually not called for. If you see an option with two intensifiers, like "really, really angry," then it's almost certainly not correct.

Clarity
Part 2

Mark Twain once claimed, "The difference between the right word and the wrong word is the difference between lightning and a lightning bug." In other words, **clarity** matters. Clarity questions will ask you to replace vague or unclear language that does not fully express the writer's meaning. All of your options will be the same part of speech, and any of them would make a complete and grammatical sentence, but only one will clearly express the correct idea.

Connotations and Denotations

ACT Clarity questions often bring together words that have very similar **denotations**, or literal meanings, but quite different **connotations**, or implicit, unstated meanings. Sometimes they will have a prompt that asks about a word choice, but sometimes they will simply underline a word and provide possible alternatives.

In either case, they will try to trick you into selecting a word with a literal meaning that's very close to what needs to be expressed, but with connotations that are not right for the sentence in question. Sentences with errors of this kind will still be somewhat understandable—they just won't say exactly what they mean to.

Consider the following example:

Example

Prakruti was a mischievous child, who enjoyed

fooling her friends with clever practical jokes.

Which of the following alternatives to the underlined portion would be the LEAST acceptable?

F. tricking

G. outwitting

H. conning

J. pranking

All of the choices denote deception, and technically mean similar things in this sentence.

But while "conning" denotes deception, it has a negative connotation. "Tricking," "outwitting," and "pranking" can all connote lighthearted fun—but "conning" would suggest that Prakruti is victimizing her friends. That's not very nice, and it's not an appropriate connotation in this context.

The ACT won't just give you words that have the wrong connotations: sometimes, they'll also give you words that just don't *quite* mean what a sentence is trying to say. In other words, they have denotations that are close to what is intended—but not quite right.

When you encounter these Clarity questions on the ACT, your best bet is to compare each word's subtler shades of meaning. Sometimes it will be very obvious that one or two words don't fit. Having eliminated them, compare the others, and assess what effect each one has on the sentence. Let's consider another example:

Example

The pieces of rock salt are ground down into small grains. After that, they are packaged and doled out for sale across the country.

    A. NO CHANGE
    B. distributed
    C. spread
    D. scattered

"Doled out" means something like "handed out," but also has the connotation of charity—which doesn't match the context of "for sale," so you can eliminate (A). You can also eliminate (D), "scattered," because it has a clear connotation of random and unplanned activity that doesn't fit in this context.

It's not immediately obvious that you can eliminate either (B) or (C), so you have to consider their impact on the sentence: "spread" has geographical or geometric implications—it means to increase the area of something. However, "distributed" has very specific commercial connotations. Distribution is the process by which products are sent out from a central supplier to different customers and vendors, and that strongly matches the process being described in this sentence—a process that moves from the creation of a product from raw materials to its sale in stores. (B) is therefore a stronger choice that (C).

If you're having trouble with Clarity questions, then work on expanding your vocabulary. When you come across a new word on a test, you can also try to work out its meaning based on its roots. Refer to the common word roots discussed in the Reading chapter, and go online for extra vocabulary lists.

 For additional resources, please visit **ivyglobal.com/study**.

Economy

Part 3

Strong writing is **concise**: it doesn't use more words than needed. Economy questions on the English Test will require you to consider whether a writer has expressed his ideas without being redundant or wordy. When answering an Economy question, consider whether the underlined words improve the sentence or add necessary information. If not, you should pick the shortest option that effectively expresses the key idea.

Consider the following example:

Example

While many people think of peas as
 	
vegetables, <u>peas are actually, in fact, legumes.</u>   **F.** NO CHANGE
           G. the reality is that peas are actually legumes.
           H. legumes are actually what peas are.
           J. peas are actually legumes.

Beginner writers sometimes think that sentences with more words sound more sophisticated. However, less is often more in good prose writing. In the example above, (F), (G) and (H) just use too many words. The phrases "in fact" and "the reality is that" don't add anything to (F) or (G). They are **empty phrases**, phrases that take up space without adding meaning or that can easily be rewritten as a shorter phrase or a single word.

(H) is wrong for a couple of reasons. You might recognize that this choice is incorrect because it shifts to the passive voice. Not only does it shift voice mid-sentence, but it does so in a way that makes the sentence needlessly wordy. Phrases and sentences are usually less concise in the passive voice than they would be in the active voice: that's one of the reasons you should avoid it.

(J) is a simple, effective, and clear sentence, so it is the best choice.

Always carefully consider the meaning of all of the words in a sentence and keep an eye out for redundant phrases. A great number of ACT Economy questions will ask you to eliminate redundancies.

Consider the following example:

Example	
Novice drivers <u>who don't have much experience driving are more likely to be involved in</u> car accidents.	**A.** NO CHANGE **B.** who don't have much experience driving cars are more likely to be involved in **C.** are more likely to be involved in crashes and **D.** are more likely to be involved in

In (A) "novice" means lacking experience, so "who don't have much experience driving" is unnecessary. (B) is even longer, and creates a redundancy with the phrases "driving cars" and "car accidents." (C) fixes the redundancy around "novice drivers," but introduces a new one with "crashes and car accidents." (D) is the least redundant option, so it is the best choice.

There's a fun vocab word for this sort of redundancy: a phrase or sentence that expresses the same idea twice using different words is called a **tautology**.

Sometimes a tautology takes the form of two modifiers that mean the same thing and have the same object, as in "the fast, quick goose." In that phrase, "fast" and "quick" mean the same thing and both describe the same goose. Other times, the definition of a noun or verb implies something that is expressed twice when you add a modifier, as in "morning sunrise." Sunrise always happens in the morning, so the modifier "morning" doesn't add anything that "sunrise" doesn't already imply.

Tautology can be used intentionally to create certain effects. The sentence "we, hushed and noiseless, watched the morning sunrise" definitely feels richer than "we silently watched the sunrise." However, when you come across questions on the ACT that include several repetitious options and a very concise choice, the most concise choice is usually correct.

Below are some examples of redundant phrases and sentences compared to more concise versions. Notice how only one instance of a repeated idea is eliminated, so that the concise version still has all of the meaning of the redundant version but in fewer words.

Redundant	Concise
Suddenly, the price dropped precipitously.	The price dropped precipitously.
A novel new idea	A novel idea
Bears hibernate in caves when they are hibernating.	Bears hibernate in caves.

She writes funny stories that are humorous in nature.	She writes funny stories.
The musicians drew large crowds and many people came to see them play.	The musicians drew large crowds.
Steady and reliable work	Steady work
Teaches and instructs	Teaches
Winners and the victorious	Winners
A coin collection of rare and uncommon coins	A collection of rare coins
Succinct and concise language	Succinct language

Style Practice Questions ⚡

Part 4

The döner kebab is a Turkish dish, said to have been plotted in Bursa in the 19th century. The name "döner kebab" translates to "rotating roast," and that name is a reference to the way it's cooked: meat, typically lamb or beef, is grilled in a gargantuan chunk on a vertical rotisserie spit, shaved off, and served either on a platter or a pita. What's especially striking about the döner kebab is the many national variations it has inspired, each with its own individual name: in Arabic-speaking countries, it's called a shawarma; in Greece, it's a gyro; in Mexico, it's known as tacos al pastor; and an Eastern Canadian rendition is called a donair.

The word "shawarma" comes from the Turkish word "çevirme," or "turning"; just like "döner," it refers to the way the meat is cooked. Shawarma is produced from beef, chicken, or lamb.

1. **A.** NO CHANGE
    B. coined
    C. hatched
    (D) invented

2. **F.** NO CHANGE
    G. that name being a reference to
    (H) and refers to
    J. and the name is referring to

3. **A.** NO CHANGE
    B. big lunk
    (C) large cone
    D. super-big hunk

4. **F.** NO CHANGE
    G. specific
    H. particular
    (J) OMIT the underlined portion.

5. **A.** NO CHANGE
    B. model
    C. edition
    (D) version

6. **F.** NO CHANGE
    G. fashioned
    H. fabricated
    (J) made

It's often served with a tasteful sesame
sauce, called tahini, and pickled turnips, which
add color and texture. The Greek "gyro"
similarly gets its name from a word meaning
"turn." Often made from pork, Greek gyros are
typically served with tomatoes, onions, and a
yogurt-based cucumber sauce that is known by
its Greek name, tzatziki.

Lebanese immigrants brought the vertical
rotisserie to Mexico in the early 20th century,
and instituted a new döner-like dish called tacos
al pastor. Literally "shepherd-style," probably
because they were once made with lamb, tacos
al pastor are now made from pork. They are
served up upon small tortillas, with pineapple,
cilantro, and green onions. The Canadian donair
also pairs sweet and savory flavors. It originated
in the Atlantic province of Nova Scotia in the
1970s, in Peter Gamoulakos's restaurant.
Gamoulakos devised a sweet sauce of

evaporated milk, sugar, and garlic. He spilled
it over shaved beef, tomatoes, and onions,
and wrapped it in a pita. It remains a very
popular late-night food to this day, and now

7. **A.** NO CHANGE
   B. a flavorful
   C. an appropriate
   D. an elegant

8. **F.** NO CHANGE
   G. Greek gyros are typically served with tomatoes, onions, and a Greek yogurt-based cucumber sauce that is called tzatziki.
   H. gyros, typically served with tomatoes and onions, feature a classic Greek sauce made of yogurt and cucumbers; the Greeks call this sauce tzatziki.
   J. gyros are typically served with tomatoes, onions, and the yogurt-based cucumber sauce called tzatziki.

9. **A.** NO CHANGE
   B. enacted
   C. inspired
   D. commissioned

10. **F.** NO CHANGE
    G. on
    H. upon the surface of
    J. on top of

11. **A.** NO CHANGE
    B. where Peter Gamoulakos formulated the dish in his restaurant.
    C. having originally been produced in Peter Gamoulakos's restaurant.
    D. in Peter Gamoulakos's restaurant in the Canadian Province of Nova Scotia.

12. **F.** NO CHANGE
    G. poured
    H. plopped
    J. thronged

you can get it all over.
13

The döner story shows how a simple
14
idea—meat cooked on a vertical rotisserie—can

make its way around the world, take on the

characteristics of local cuisines, acquire new

names, and break yummy new culinary ground.
15

13. A. NO CHANGE
     B. it may be supped even in that
         metropolis, Toronto.
     C. lots and lots of people eat them at very
         late or early hours.
     D. it has spread to other provinces and
         countries.

14. F. NO CHANGE
     G. plain
     H. normal
     J. bald

15. A. NO CHANGE
     B. delicious
     C. very nice
     D. ambrosial

Math
Chapter 3

Section 1
Approaching the Math Test

The ACT Math Test tests your ability to understand and apply math theory to solve a diverse array of problems. These concepts and skills provide the foundations for the math you will learn in college and use in everyday life. The ACT groups these concepts into six major areas on the Math Test:

- Pre-Algebra
- Elementary Algebra
- Intermediate Algebra
- Coordinate Geometry
- Plane Geometry
- Trigonometry

In this chapter, we will review all of the topics that you may see on the Math Test. We will also practice strategies for solving different types of questions and for tackling difficult or unfamiliar problems. But first, let's take a look at the format of the Math Test.

The Basics
Part 1

The Math Test is one continuous section with 60 questions. You have 60 minutes to complete the section, or an average of 1 minute per question. You can use your calculator for all of the Math Test.

This might not seem like a lot of time, but reviewing and practicing the concepts in this chapter will help you apply your knowledge quickly and efficiently on test day! We'll talk about time management and other test-taking strategies in Part 2 of this section.

By the Numbers

There are six main content areas covered by the Math Test. Here is a breakdown of the topics and number of questions in each content area:

Content Area	Topics Covered	Number of Questions
Pre-Algebra	Foundational concepts essential to algebra, such as number properties, the manipulation of fractions, factoring, and probability	14
Elementary Algebra	Solving single linear and quadratic equations, and manipulating higher order expressions	10
Intermediate Algebra	Advanced concepts in algebra, including inequalities, systems of equations, matrices, and complex numbers	9
Coordinate Geometry	Graphing algebraic functions, as well as points and basic shapes in the standard (x,y) plane	9
Plane Geometry	Using the properties of angles, lines, and shapes in two and three dimensions to solve problems	14
Trigonometry	Solving problems that require you to calculate, apply, and graph trigonometric ratios of sine, cosine, tangent, secant, cosecant, and cotangent	4
	Total	60

Focus topics

Note that the number of questions in any given area may vary, but this provides a good estimate of what you will most likely see on the Math Test. Sections 2–7 cover the topics in each of these content areas in depth. Fundamental math skills that apply to all of these topics are covered online.

 For a fundamental review, visit **ivyglobal.com/study**.

Questions

The Math Test consists of multiple choice questions, each with five answer options. Each test contains two **problem sets**, which are two to four questions that are based on the same given information. These problem sets usually occur around the midpoint of the Math Test.

Questions on the Math Test are ordered by difficulty, which means that the test tends to emphasize Pre-Algebra and Elementary Algebra questions towards the beginning, Intermediate Algebra, Coordinate and Plane Geometry towards the middle, and Trigonometry towards the end of the test. While what you may perceive as difficult may vary, the ACT tends to define subject difficulty in this manner.

Some of the questions are written solely in text, while for others the equations will be given to you directly. You will also see graphs, charts, and diagrams in some of the problems and answer choices. Math Test questions require you to apply reasoning and critical thinking skills in order to analyze situations, create mathematical models, and find relevant solutions.

Scoring

Each question is worth one point and there is no penalty for guessing. The number of points you receive on each section contributes to your raw score, which is scaled to give you your final math score from 1–36.

The six content areas mentioned before are divided into three scoring categories for the Math Test: Pre- and Elementary Algebra (24 questions), Intermediate Algebra and Coordinate Geometry (18 questions), and Plane Geometry and Trigonometry (18 questions). While these categories will be included as subscores for all ACT tests taken before September of 2016, schools will mostly pay attention to your overall score. However, looking at these categories may help you to identify the areas that need further study as you prepare for the Math Test.

In the next section, we'll discuss the different question types on the Math Test and learn strategies for approaching and solving each type of question. The rest of the chapter provides an in-depth review of the topics covered on the Math Test. To practice applying your knowledge, make sure to do the practice exercises for each section. Let's get started!

Plan Your Approach
Part 2

Know the Directions

You will be given directions and reference information at the beginning of the Math Test. The directions contain important information about the types of questions you will see and how much time you have to complete them. Make sure to read the directions before starting the problems so you know what to expect in each section.

The "Directions" section at the beginning of each math section will look similar to the one below. This section lets you know that you may use a calculator. It also gives you some definitions of mathematical terminology and information about the figures you will see and use on the test.

Mathematics Test
60 Minutes—60 Questions

DIRECTIONS: For each problem, solve for the correct answer, select your choice, and fill in the corresponding bubble on your answer document.

Some problems may take a longer time to solve, but do not take too much time on any single problem. Solve the easier questions first, then return to the harder questions in the remaining time for this test.

A calculator is allowed on this test. While you may be able to solve some problems without a calculator, you are allowed to use a calculator

for all of the problems on this test.

Note: Unless otherwise directed, all of the following statements are considered correct.

1. All drawn figures are NOT necessarily drawn to scale.
2. All geometric figures are in a plane.
3. The word *line*, when used, is the same as a straight line.
4. The word *average*, when used, is the same as arithmetic mean.

Notice that this section doesn't have any formulas or mathematical content. There are fundamental math concepts that you need to know for the test; a review of these concepts is posted online.

For a fundamental review, visit **ivyglobal.com/study**.

If a question requires a more complex formula, it will be included as part of the question.

Use Your Calculator

You can use a calculator for all questions on the Math Test. Most math problems on the ACT can be solved without a calculator, but your calculator can help you save time and avoid errors.

You must provide your own calculator. A scientific or graphing calculator is recommended. While some calculators with keypads, styluses, touchscreens, internet access, cellular access, or power cords may be used after some modifications, generally it is best to avoid these kinds of calculators. Calculators with built-in or downloaded computer algebra system functionality are prohibited. Finally, your calculator can't make noise, and you can't use a laptop, tablet, or phone as a calculator.

Make sure to practice using the calculator that you plan to bring to the ACT so you are familiar with it. Before the test, make sure your calculator is working properly and has fresh batteries. Also, bring a spare set of batteries or a back-up calculator.

Don't rely too much on your calculator when you take the test. Most problems can be solved without a calculator, and with some problems using a calculator can slow you down. When you start a problem:

- Look at its answer choices, think about how you will solve it, and consider whether you need to use a calculator.
- Look for ways to simplify the problem that will make the calculation easier, such as factoring.
- Write down calculations and scratch work in the test booklet.

These steps will help you avoid calculator errors and make it easier to check your work. If you find yourself doing complicated or tedious calculations, there is likely a simpler method to find the answer.

Use Figures

While figures in the Math Test are not always drawn to scale, they are mostly accurate. Moreover, you can always double-check a drawn figure with the information given to you in the question. If needed, you can redraw the figure. Features like right angles and parallel and perpendicular lines will be defined if they are needed to solve the question. Charts, graphs, and figures in the standard (x,y) coordinate plane will always be accurate.

Some figures may not show all of the lines that you need to solve the problem. In these cases, you should add any necessary lines as accurately as possible:

What is the area of quadrilateral *ABCD*, shown in the standard (*x*,*y*) plane below?

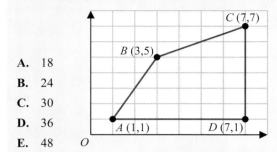

A. 18

B. 24

C. 30

D. 36

E. 48

Since quadrilateral *ABCD* is irregular, you cannot easily find the area. However, if you draw a line between *B* and *D*, you will have two triangles whose areas you can calculate:

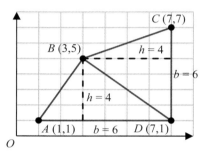

Define the base of triangle *ABD* to be $\overline{AD}$ and the base of triangle *BCD* to be $\overline{CD}$. The height of each triangle is the line segment from the base to the opposite vertex, perpendicular to the base. The bases and heights are labeled in the diagram.

We can use the formula $A = \frac{1}{2}bh$ to find the areas of each of these triangles. The area of triangle *ABD* is $\frac{1}{2}(6)(4) = 12$, and the area of triangle *BCD* is $\frac{1}{2}(6)(4) = 12$. Therefore, the area of quadrilateral *ABCD* is 24, which is (B).

As you learned in Chapter 1, it is often useful to draw a diagram if a figure is not provided for a geometry problem. Figures may also be helpful for solving other types of problems. You might draw a number line, graph, or quick sketch of a situation. Keep your diagrams simple and accurate.

Pay Attention to Units and Variables

When choosing an answer, double check that it is in the correct units. The answer may have different units than the given data. Circle or underline any units given in the problem and the units of the answer. Problems involving units will almost always have answer choices that are correct for different units:

The chart below shows the amount of time Jenny spent on homework in one week. On average, how many minutes per day did Jenny spend on homework?

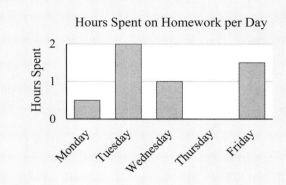

F.   1

G.   1.25

H.   1.5

J.   60

K.   75

Notice that the units of the graph are hours, but the answer must be in minutes. First, find the average number of hours Jenny spends on homework per day. We take the average by adding together the hours for each day and then dividing by the number of days:

$$\frac{0.5 + 2 + 1 + 0 + 1.5}{5} = 1$$

Jenny spends an average of 1 hour per day on homework, but you need to convert this into minutes. There are 60 minutes in 1 hour, so (J) is correct.

Pace Yourself

Remember that you will be answering questions under a time limit, and you need to leave yourself enough time to attempt every question on the test. One way to save time during the test is to be familiar with the format and instructions before the test day.

Since there are 60 questions on the Math Test and you have 60 minutes for the section, you should aim for a maximum of 1 minute per question. As detailed in the Key Strategies section of this book, plan to spend less time on the early questions so that you have enough time for the more challenging ones at the end of the section.

Finally, remember that every question is worth the same number of points. If you get stuck on any problem, make a guess and return to that question if you have time at the end. You don't lose points for guessing, so you should never leave a question blank. In Part 3, we'll talk about some strategies for guessing efficiently on the ACT Math Test.

Math Strategies
Part 3

In Chapter 1, we reviewed general strategies that you can use on all parts of the ACT, such as Pencil on Paper, Predicting, Plugging in Options, and Process of Elimination. In Part 1 of this chapter, we reviewed general strategies that will help you master the Math Test as a whole.

Once you have mastered these strategies, you'll be ready to review the math concepts on the exam. All of these concepts are covered in Sections 2–7 of this chapter. If you feel comfortable with some or all of the material, you may find it useful to first solve the example practice problems in the content of each section in order to determine which topics you should review.

We will now review a process and specific tactics that apply to the Math Test questions. This process will help you use your time and resources to answer questions quickly, and will reduce your chance of making mistakes.

Read the Question Carefully

Read through the whole question. Don't assume you understand the question just by reading the first few words! Reading the whole question will help you avoid making assumptions that can lead to careless errors.

If you see unfamiliar or difficult-looking material, stay calm and keep reading until the end of the question. There might be more information in the question that will help you figure out the solution. If you still think a question is too difficult after you have finished reading the whole thing, you should make your best guess, circle it in your question booklet, and come back to it if you have time.

Identify What the Question is Asking

Ask yourself, "What is the question asking me to solve?" This is especially important for word problems. Sometimes the wording of a question can be confusing, so make it simpler by summarizing in your own words what the question is asking for. Focus on the meanings of the key words you have underlined. In Math Test questions, make sure to pay special attention to the final one or two sentences of the question to determine what you are being asked:

A window is an isosceles triangle with a width of 10. If the window has a height of 12, what is the perimeter of the window?

A. 4

B. 24

C. 36

D. 40

E. 48

In our example question, you are being asked to find the perimeter of the triangle. Put this in your own words: the perimeter is the length of the outline of the triangle.

Draw a Chart or Diagram

Sometimes, it's necessary to draw, re-draw, or label a chart or a diagram. Charts and diagrams are great tools to help you visualize the problem and organize your information, as you saw with the Pencil on Paper strategy in Chapter 1. In our example question, you might try drawing a quick sketch of a triangle. Fill in any information given in the question:

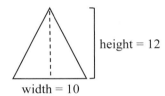

Stop and Strategize

Because of the time constraints, Math Test problems may tempt you to start solving them right away. Often, however, this approach will result in wasted time, as you discover important pieces of information later in the question that you may have initially neglected. Before you dive into a question, take a few moments to come up with a strategy.

Think about all of the information provided in the question and how it is related. Think about where you have seen this type of question before, and what methods you have used to solve similar types of questions. If there is a formula you know that could help, write it down.

Here's a strategy you could use to solve the example question:

- You know: width = 10, height = 12
- You want: the perimeter of the whole triangle
- Your strategy: find the length of one side of the triangle, and then use a formula that relates to an isosceles triangle's perimeter:

$$\text{perimeter} = (\text{width}) + (2 \times \text{side})$$

Notice that the dotted line in your drawing cuts the triangle in two. In this case, because it is an isosceles triangle, the line creates two identical right angle triangles, each with a base (width) of 5. You could use the Pythagorean Theorem to solve for the remaining side, but a shorter way would be to notice that 5 and 12 are two sides of the special triangle with side ratios of 5:12:13. The missing length is therefore 13.

We can now plug in the values and solve:

$$\text{perimeter} = (10) + (2 \times 13) = 10 + 26 = 36$$

Is our solution one of the answer choices? It is indeed! The answer is (C).

Remember, Math Test questions are not designed to take a long time. Here are some possible shortcuts you can use when coming up with your strategy:

- Look at the answer options: they'll tell you what kind of math to do, and how far to solve.
- Look for simple visual patterns.
- Avoid using your calculator: estimate, factor, and simplify whenever possible.
- Plug in: Use your own values, making sure they're representative of what the question is asking for (positive, negative, odd, even), and that they're easy to work with.
- Backsolve: As discussed in our Strategies section at the beginning of this book, start on (C) or (H), the middle value, and plug it in to the expression.

How and When to Check Your Answer

When you solve a problem, you want to avoid "feel-good work." This is work that you don't have to do, but you do it because it makes you feel good. While it is very important to be confident, it's also important to be efficient with your time. If you can solve a problem by eyeballing it or estimating, don't continue to show every single step.

"Feel-good work" can also happen when you're checking your answers. You want to briefly look over every question that took time to solve, and ensure you didn't make any errors. If you have time left at the end of the test, you should review only those questions that you circled because you found them difficult, or circled as a part of your Pick & Skip strategy. You don't want to review every single question or do all the work for any question again.

Instead, try to use a different process to find the answer to avoid making the same mistake twice. Write out your calculations when solving complicated problems to make it easier to find your mistakes. Remember to always guess on problems that you cannot solve.

Finally, check that you bubbled in the answer on your answer sheet correctly. It would be a shame to have solved the question correctly and not get credit!

Formulas

Part 4

Here are some formulas you should memorize before the test. The rest of the Math chapter will explain what these mean and when to use them.

Pre-Algebra	
Probability of A = $\dfrac{\text{\# of ways A can occur}}{\text{\# of all possible events}}$	Mean = $\dfrac{\text{sum of all values in a set}}{\text{total number of terms in a set}}$
Median = middle value of a set	Mode = most frequent value in a set
Combinations of n objects taken r at a time = $\dfrac{n!}{r!(n-r)!}$	$P(A \cap B) = P(A) \times P(B)$
Permutations of n objects taken r at a time = $\dfrac{n!}{(n-r)!}$	$P(A \cup B) = P(A) + P(B) - P(A \cap B)$
	$P(not\,A) = 1 - P(A)$

Absolute Value		
If $\lvert a \rvert = b$ then $a = b$ or $a = -b$	If $\lvert a \rvert < b$ then $-b < a < b$	If $\lvert a \rvert > b$ then $a > b$ or $a < -b$

Exponents and Logs				
$\log_a b = c$, where $a^c = b$	$x^m x^n = x^{m+n}$	$(xy)^m = x^m y^m$	$(x^m)^n = x^{mn}$	$\sqrt{x} \times \sqrt{y} = \sqrt{(xy)}$
	$\dfrac{x^m}{x^n} = x^{m-n}$	$x^{-m} = \dfrac{1}{x^m}$	$\sqrt[n]{x^m} = x^{\frac{m}{n}}$	$\sqrt[n]{\sqrt[m]{x}} = \sqrt[nm]{x}$

Factoring and Sequences			
Quadratic Formula	Difference of Squares	Arithmetic Sequence	Geometric Sequence
$x = \dfrac{-b \pm \sqrt{b^2 - 4ac}}{2a}$	$a^2 - b^2 = (a+b)(a-b)$	$a_n = a_1 + d(n-1)$	$a_n = a_1(r)^{n-1}$

Coordinate Geometry	
$d = \sqrt{(x_2 - x_1)^2 + (y_2 - y_1)^2}$ (think: $a^2 + b^2 = c^2$)	For $y = mx + b$, $m = \dfrac{\text{rise}}{\text{run}} = \dfrac{y_2 - y_1}{x_2 - x_1}$
For a parabola with a vertex (h,k), $y = ax^2 + bx + c$, and $h = \dfrac{-b}{2a}$. Plug in for k.	If z is perpendicular to y, $m_z = -\dfrac{1}{m_y}$
For a circle with a center of (h, k), $(x - h)^2 + (y - k)^2 = r^2$	If z is parallel to y, $m_z = m_y$

Plane Geometry			
Special Triangles	**Regular Prisms**		**Circles**

Special Triangles	Regular Prisms		Circles
30°-60°-90° $1:\sqrt{3}:2$ 45°-45°-90° $1:1:\sqrt{2}$ 12:13:5	**Rectangular** $V = lwh$	**Cylinder** $V = \pi r^2 h$	$\dfrac{x°}{360°} = \dfrac{\text{arc length}}{\text{circumference}} = \dfrac{\text{sector area}}{\text{circle area}}$
	Triangular $V = \dfrac{1}{2}bhl$		$\dfrac{x°}{360°} = \dfrac{\text{arc length}}{2\pi r} = \dfrac{\text{sector area}}{\pi r^2}$

Trigonometry			
General Form of a Sine (or Cosine) Wave:	$y = a \cdot \sin\left[k\left(x - d\right)\right] + c$ where a is the amplitude, c is the vertical shift, d is the horizontal shift, and the period is $\dfrac{2\pi}{k}$		
$\sin\theta = \dfrac{O}{H}$	$\cos\theta = \dfrac{A}{H}$	$\tan\theta = \dfrac{O}{A}$	$\sin^2\theta + \cos^2\theta = 1$
$\csc\theta = \dfrac{H}{O}$	$\sec\theta = \dfrac{H}{A}$	$\cot\theta = \dfrac{A}{O}$	$180° = \pi$ radians

Complex Numbers, Matrices, and Vectors			
$i = \sqrt{-1}$	**Unit Vectors** $\mathbf{i} = \langle 1, 0\rangle \qquad \mathbf{j} = \langle 0, 1\rangle$		$\begin{bmatrix} a & b \\ c & d \end{bmatrix} \pm \begin{bmatrix} e & f \\ g & h \end{bmatrix} = \begin{bmatrix} a \pm e & b \pm f \\ c \pm g & d \pm h \end{bmatrix}$
$\begin{bmatrix} a & b \end{bmatrix} \times \begin{bmatrix} c \\ d \end{bmatrix} = \begin{bmatrix} ac + bd \end{bmatrix}$		$\begin{bmatrix} a \\ b \end{bmatrix} \times \begin{bmatrix} c & d \end{bmatrix} = \begin{bmatrix} ac & ad \\ bc & bd \end{bmatrix}$	$k\begin{bmatrix} a & b \\ c & d \end{bmatrix} = \begin{bmatrix} ka & kb \\ kc & kd \end{bmatrix}$
Unique diagonals (in a given polygon) $= \dfrac{\text{\# of vertices} \times (\text{\# of vertices} - 3)}{2}$			

Given on Math Test		
Law of Sines	**Law of Cosines**	**Compound Interest**
$\dfrac{\sin(\angle A)}{a} = \dfrac{\sin(\angle B)}{b} = \dfrac{\sin(\angle C)}{c}$	$a^2 = b^2 + c^2 - 2bc \times \cos(\angle A)$	$\text{Final} = P\left(1\dfrac{r}{n}\right)^{nt}$
Volume of a Sphere	**Volume of a Pyramid**	**Volume of a Cone**
$V = \dfrac{4}{3}\pi r^3$	$V = \dfrac{1}{3}lwh$	$V = \dfrac{1}{3}\pi r^2 h$

Section 2
Pre-Algebra

Numbers and their properties are an integral part of analytical thinking and are foundational to all math problems on the ACT. Pre-Algebra makes up around 14, or 23%, of the Math Test's 60 questions.

This section will cover key aspects of numbers and will show you how to manipulate them in order to answer ACT questions quickly and correctly. This section includes:

- Number Properties
- Factors and Multiples
- Counting and Probability
- Variables
- Mean, Median, and Mode
- Numbers in Tables and Graphs

We will refresh your understanding of basic math principles and demonstrate how to solve related ACT-style questions while outlining key principles that you need to know. Let's get started!

Number Properties
Part 1

The ACT will test your knowledge of basic concepts in unusual ways. This section will cover ACT problems that make use of the basic properties of fractions, percentages, exponents, and absolute values.

Fractions

The ACT frequently uses fractions as a part of their questions and occasionally asks questions that only use fractions and nothing else. A fraction can be thought of as another way to represent division: $\frac{1}{3}$ means that you divide 1 by 3. The number on top, 1, is the **numerator,** and the number on the bottom, 3, is the **denominator**.

Many ACT problems will require you to convert fractions to a **common denominator** in order to combine, compare, add, or subtract them.

Example
$\frac{5}{8} - \frac{1}{3} = ?$
A. $\frac{4}{8}$
B. $\frac{4}{3}$
C. $\frac{5}{12}$
D. $\frac{7}{24}$
E. $\frac{9}{24}$

First, convert each fraction so that they have a common denominator:

$$\frac{5}{8} = \frac{5 \times 3}{8 \times 3} = \frac{15}{24}$$

$$\frac{1}{3} = \frac{1 \times 8}{3 \times 8} = \frac{8}{24}$$

Next, subtract the numerators:

$$\frac{15}{24} - \frac{8}{24} = \frac{7}{24}$$

The answer is (D).

Converting fractions is also important when working with **mixed numbers**, or numbers written as an integer and a fraction. In order to convert a mixed number to a fraction, follow these steps:

1. Multiply the integer by the denominator of the fraction.
2. Add the numerator of the fraction to the product from the first step to get the new numerator. The denominator stays the same.

For example:

$$1\frac{1}{3} = \frac{(1 \times 3) + 1}{3} = \frac{4}{3}$$

On the ACT, you will also need to know how to divide and multiply fractions.

Example

Of 600 people who are going to the zoo, $\frac{2}{3}$ are going to see the lion, and $\frac{1}{2}$ of those will also buy snow cones. How many people are going to see the lion and buy snow cones?

F. 200
G. 300
H. 400
J. 500
K. 600

To solve this, you first need to figure out how many people are going to see the lion and are also going to buy snow cones. The people who are going to see the lion are $\frac{2}{3}$ of the total, and those who are going to buy snow cones are $\frac{1}{2}$ of that, so you can multiply the fractions together to find how many people are going to see the lion and also are going to buy a snow cone:

$$\frac{2}{3} \times \frac{1}{2} = \frac{2 \times 1}{3 \times 2} = \frac{2}{6} = \frac{1}{3}$$

In order to multiply fractions, multiply the numerators and the denominators separately. In this case, you can also simplify the fraction by dividing both the numerator and the denominator by 2. You have found that $\frac{1}{3}$ of the people are both going to see the lion and buying snow cones. The Math Test will always ask you to represent fractions in their lowest form. A fraction is in its **lowest form** when the numerator and denominator have no common factors.

Multiply the total number of people by $\frac{1}{3}$ to find the actual number of people who are seeing the lion and buying snow cones: $\frac{1}{3} \times 600 = 200$, or (F).

To divide fractions, multiply the first fraction by the reciprocal of the second fraction. The **reciprocal** of a fraction is the fraction created when you flip the original numerator and denominator, for example, the reciprocal of $\frac{1}{3}$ is $\frac{3}{1}$ or 3:

$$\frac{\frac{1}{3}}{\frac{1}{3}} = \frac{1}{3} \times \frac{3}{1} = \frac{3}{3} = 1$$

Since both the numerator and the denominator of the fractions are the same, the result is equal to 1.

Percentages

Percent literally means "per one hundred" and is often represented by the % symbol. Integers and decimals can be transformed to percent form by multiplying them by 100 and then writing their result as percent or %.

$$3 = 3 \times 100 \text{ percent} = 300\%$$

$$0.3475 = 0.3475 \times 100 \text{ percent} = 34.75\%$$

A fraction can be converted to a percent by multiplying both the denominator and numerator by a number that results in a denominator of 100. The numerators in these examples are the percent:

$$\frac{3}{4} = \frac{3 \times 25}{4 \times 25} = \frac{75}{100} = 75\%$$

$$\frac{1}{5} = \frac{1 \times 20}{5 \times 20} = \frac{20}{100} = 20\%$$

You will often encounter problems involving percentage increase and decrease, in terms of the price or quantity of something:

The table below shows the monthly sales for three items at a small department store in Jacksonville. Which of the following is closest to the percent decrease in sales of pants from February to March at the department store?

A. 60%
B. 54%
C. 46%
D. 30%
E.   9%

Product	Month		
	January	February	March
Shoes	110	100	160
Pants	90	130	70
Ties	400	450	600

To calculate a percent change, you need to remember the following formula:

$$\frac{\text{second} - \text{first}}{\text{first}} \times 100 = \text{percent change}$$

If you read the table, you can easily see that sales of pants decreased from 130 to 70, or by 60, between February and March, so:

$$\frac{\text{second} - \text{first}}{\text{first}} = \frac{-60}{130} = \frac{-0.46}{1} \times 100 \text{ or } -46 \text{ percent}$$

A change by a negative number is the same thing as a decrease. You have therefore calculated that the decrease of sales of 60 pants is equal to a decrease of 46 percent of the original sales. The correct answer is 46%, or (C).

Absolute Value

The **absolute value** of a number is the magnitude of its distance away from 0 on a number line. Two vertical bars around a number or quantity indicate absolute value.

$|6 - 9| = ?$

F. −3
G. 0
H. 3
J. 6
K. 9

Whenever possible, you should try to evaluate the expression inside the absolute value brackets before dealing with the absolute value itself:

$$\left|6-9\right| = \left|-3\right|$$

You need to evaluate the absolute value of –3, meaning that you need to figure the distance from –3 to 0. Put these values on a number line, and the problem becomes a simple counting question:

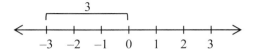

As you can see, –3 is a distance of 3 units from 0 on the number line:

$$\left|-3\right| = 3$$

The answer is (H).

Once you understand the number line approach, you can use the following shortcuts for absolute value:

- The absolute value of a number that is positive or 0 is simply the number itself: $\left|5\right| = 5$, $\left|0\right| = 0$
- The absolute value of a negative number is the number multiplied by –1: $\left|-10\right| = 10$

As you may have noticed, the absolute value of a number is always positive or 0. Any number will either be a positive distance from 0, or it will be equal to 0.

Factors and Multiples
Part 2

A number is **divisible** by another number if the result of division is an **integer**. Integers are numbers with no decimal values, whose properties are covered in greater detail in the online ACT Fundamental Review.

For a fundamental review, visit **ivyglobal.com/study**.

For instance, 12 is divisible by 3 because $12 \div 3 = 4$ with nothing left over. Because 12 is divisible by 3, you can say that 3 is a **factor** of 12. Because 3 multiplied by a whole number is 12, you can say that 12 is a **multiple** of 3. Sometimes a number is not divisible:

Example

Herve needs to purchase 600 pounds of rice for his kitchen, and his store's wholesaler sells only 45 pound bags. If the wholesaler cannot split up its bags, what is the minimum number of bags that Herve must purchase in order to have 600 pounds of rice?

A. 14
B. 13
C. 12
D. 11
E. 10

To solve this problem, you need determine the number of bags that will give you at least 600 pounds of rice. Since each bag weighs 45 pounds, you need to divide 600 by 45 to see how many bags you will need:

$$\frac{600}{45} = \frac{131}{3} \sim 13.33$$

Because there is a decimal, 45 is not a factor of 600, and 600 is not a multiple of 45. Since Herve can't buy partial bags, the minimum number of bags that he would need to purchase in order to get 600 pounds of rice is 14 bags. (A) is the correct answer choice.

Here are some quick ways to test whether one number is divisible by another:

Divisibility Rules		
Divisible by ...	When ...	Example
2	The last digit is divisible by 2 (the number is even)	4028 is divisible by 2 because 8 is divisible by 2.
3	The sum of the digits is divisible by 3	465 is divisible by 3 because 4 + 6 + 5 = 15, which is divisible by 3.
4	The number formed by the last two digits is divisible by 4	340 is divisible by 4 because 40 is divisible by 4.
5	The last digit is 0 or 5	750 is divisible by 5 because it ends in 0.
6	The number is even and the sum of the digits is divisible by 3	1044 is divisible by 6 because it is even and 1 + 0 + 4 + 4 = 9, which is divisible by 3.
7	The number is divisible by 7 – there is no easy rule for this	7, 14, 21, 28…77, 84, 91 are all divisible by 7.
8	The number formed by the last three digits is divisible by 8	1024 is divisible by 8 because 024 is 24, which is divisible by 8.
9	The sum of the digits is divisible by 9	1296 is divisible by 9 because 1 + 2 + 9 + 6 = 18, which is divisible by 9.
10	The last digit is 0	3390 is divisible by 10 because it ends in 0.

Prime and Composite Numbers

A **prime** number is an integer that has only two factors: itself and 1. A prime number is not divisible by any other integer. 1 is not a prime number, because it only has one factor: 1, itself! The only even prime number is 2.

Example
How many prime numbers are there between 65 and 85?

F. 2

G. 3

H. 4

J. 5

K. 6

All even numbers are divisible by 2, so they are not prime numbers. You can easily eliminate those, leaving you with:

$$67, 69, 71, 73, 75, 77, 79, 81, 83$$

Of these, you can eliminate 69 and 81 because they are divisible by 3, 75 because it is divisible by 5, and 77 because it is divisible by 7. 69, 81, 75, and 77 are **composite** numbers. Composite numbers are not prime numbers because they are divisible by three or more integers.

The remaining numbers in the question are 67, 71, 73, 79, and 83. To test if they're prime numbers, you only need to divide them by the primes up to the approximate value of their square root. For example, the square root of 67 would be approximately 8 (since the square root of 64 is 8), so you'd divide 67 by 2, 3, 5, and 7. None leave an integer, so 67 is prime. Your answer is 5, so (J) is correct.

Greatest Common Factor and Least Common Multiple

The **greatest common factor (GCF)** of two integers is the largest integer that is a factor of both integers. The **least common multiple (LCM)** of two integers is the smallest integer that is a multiple of both integers. The Math Test may ask you to find the GCF and/or the LCM of a set of numbers, as seen in the example problem below:

Example
If x is the greatest common factor of 84 and 144, and y is the least common multiple of 84 and 144, then $y - x = ?$

A.   12
B.   84
C.   144
D.   996
E.   1,008

To find the GCF and LCM, you start by finding the prime factors of each number. Check out the Fundamental Review to refresh how to find prime factors. The prime factors of 84 are (2, 2, 3, 7) and the prime factors of 144 are (2, 2, 2, 2, 3, 3). Next, organize these prime factors into a Venn diagram, with the shared factors in the middle sector.

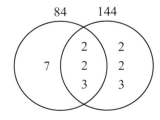

Now that you have organized the prime factors, finding the GCF and the LCM is simple. You can determine the GCF by multiplying all of the shared prime factors—the numbers in the middle section of the Venn diagram.

$$2 \times 2 \times 3 = 12$$

The GCF of 84 and 144, or x, is 12.

To find the LCM, you need to multiply all of the prime factors in the Venn diagram, but be sure to only count the shared factors once:

$$\underbrace{7}_{\substack{\text{factor} \\ \text{of} \\ \text{84 only}}} \times \underbrace{2 \times 2 \times 3}_{\substack{\text{factors} \\ \text{of both numbers}}} \times \underbrace{2 \times 2 \times 3}_{\substack{\text{factors of} \\ \text{144 only}}}$$

The LCM of 84 and 144, or y, is 1008.

To finish solving the example problem, all you need to do is subtract x from y.

$$1008 - 12 = 996$$

(D) is the correct answer.

Counting and Probability
Part 3

Counting

Counting—which you may consider an incredibly simple mathematical concept—is tested fairly often on the Math Test:

Example

Sammy's Sandwich Shop serves 3 types of bread, 5 types of meat, and 2 types of cheese. If a sandwich must consist of a bread, a meat, and a cheese, how many distinct sandwiches can be ordered at Sammy's?

F. 5

G. 6

H. 10

J. 15

K. 30

You could list every possible sandwich, but keeping track of all the options would quickly become difficult. Instead, you can use the following trick:

$$\text{\# of possible combinations} =$$

$$\text{\# of options for Category 1} \times \text{\# of options for Category 2} \times \text{\# of options for Category 3} \ldots$$

In other words, simply multiply the number of options in each category to find the total number of possible combinations. In the example above, you have 3 categories of items: bread, meat, and cheese. So in order to find the number of possible sandwiches, use the formula:

$$\text{\# of possible sandwiches} = \text{\# bread options} \times \text{\# meat options} \times \text{\# cheese options}$$

$$= 3 \times 5 \times 2$$

$$= 30$$

(K) is the correct answer.

Factorial Notation

Before delving into more advanced probability questions, first it is necessary to outline how shorthand notation can be used to express the product of consecutive whole numbers. For example:

$$1 \times 2 \times 3 \times 4 \times 5 \times 6 \times 7 \times 8$$

can also be written as:

$$8!$$

That's not just a really excited number 8—the exclamation mark means **factorial**, a mathematical operator that tells you to multiply the integer by every integer less than it, one by one, all the way to 1.

Note: $0! = 1$

Permutations

Counting permutations is a fancy way of counting outcomes where the order of events matters, like in a race or when arranging objects.

Example
How many different three-digit numbers can you write using the digits 1, 2, and 3, without repeating any digits?
A. 27
B. 9
C. 8
D. 6
E. 3

This question involves permutations because changing the order of the digits creates a distinct outcome. The number 123 is not the same as 213 or 231. Here are all of the permutations involving these three digits:

123	213	312
132	231	321

Thus, there are 6 possible numbers, and (D) is correct.

You can solve this, however, without writing all the possibilities out. Think about it as if you are choosing a digit for each position.

$$\underline{3} \quad \underline{2} \quad \underline{1}$$

Since you are creating a three-digit number, there are three slots. You have three digits to choose from for the first space—but you can't repeat any digits—so that leaves two choices for the second and only one for the final space. Each position acts like its own independent event. To find the total number, you simply multiply each event together as we did before, to get $3 \times 2 \times 1 = 6$.

$3 \times 2 \times 1 \dots$ That looks like a factorial, and it is!

In fact, the number of permutations of n objects is $n!$. Notice that if you have fewer positions than numbers, you run out of space to do the whole factorial.

In the example, if you were only making a one-digit number, it would look like:

$$\underline{3} \times \underline{2} \times \underline{1} = 3$$

The truncated factorial when choosing from n objects with r positions can always be found using the following formula:

$$\frac{n!}{(n-r)!} = \frac{3 \times 2 \times 1}{2 \times 1} = \frac{3!}{2!} = 3$$

This formula may help you quickly solve a Math Test problem, but if it's hard to recall, remember you can always figure it out by drawing slots.

Combinations

When the order doesn't matter, the number of outcomes decreases, since each group you pick can now be arranged in any order. For instance, $\underline{3} \quad \underline{2} \quad \underline{1} \quad \underline{4}$ is the same group as $\underline{1} \quad \underline{2} \quad \underline{3} \quad \underline{4}$. You can rearrange these numbers any way you want, but they will always be the same four numbers. The number of **combinations** is the number of unique sets of numbers, where order does not matter.

Example
Liu, Jose, Marie, Milos and Tom are members of a soccer team. If their coach Mr. Ianine chooses 2 of them to be midfielders, how many combinations are possible?

F. $5!$

G. $\dfrac{5!}{(5!-3!)}$

H. 5×4

J. $\dfrac{5!}{(5!-2!)2}$

K. 5

If you treat this as a permutations problem, you would get the incorrect answer (H):

$$\frac{n!}{(n-r)!} = \frac{5!}{(5-2)!} = \frac{5 \times 4 \times 3 \times 2 \times 1}{3 \times 2 \times 1} = 20$$

Notice that in the question it doesn't matter if the coach chooses Marie and Milos or if he chooses Milos and Marie. By assuming order matters, you over-count.

You would be over-counting by exactly $r!$, which is equal to the number of ways in which you can rearrange the spaces themselves. Rearranging the spaces only gives you a different order, not a new group of numbers. You solve this by dividing by $r!$, which in this example is 2!:

$$\frac{\text{Number of Permutations}}{r!} = \frac{20}{2!} = 10$$

You have calculated that coach can choose two of them in 10 different ways. (J) is correct.

The formula for all combinations is with n objects and r spaces is:

$$\frac{n!}{r!\,(n-r)!}$$

This formula will be the quickest way for you to solve combination problems on the Math Test, especially those with larger values for n and r.

Probability

If you've ever used a weather forecast or looked up the chance that your favorite sports team will win a game, you have used **probability**. Probability describes how likely something is to happen. On the ACT, you will use probability to solve word problems and determine the chance of two events occurring.

The formula to calculate probability is:

$$\text{Probability} = \frac{\text{Number of ways to get a certain outcome}}{\text{Number of possible outcomes}}$$

Probabilities are written as fractions or decimals between 0 and 1, or as percentages between 0% and 100%. The lower the probability, the less likely an event is to occur. The higher the probability, the more likely an event is to occur.

A probability of 0.5, 50%, or $\frac{1}{2}$ means that the outcome in question is equally as likely to occur as to not occur. A probability of 1 or 100% means that an outcome is certain, while a probability of 0 or 0% means that an outcome is impossible.

In a standard deck of cards, there are 4 categories of cards: hearts, clubs, diamonds, and spades. Each of these categories has 13 cards. If a card is randomly chosen, what is the probability that the card will NOT be a heart card?

A. 0

B. $\frac{1}{4}$

C. $\frac{1}{2}$

D. $\frac{3}{4}$

E. 1

In order to answer the example question, you need to convert the word problem into a mathematical expression. The outcome you are interested in is drawing a card that is not a heart:

$$\text{Probability of NOT drawing a heart card} = \frac{\text{number of cards that are } not \text{ hearts}}{\text{total number of cards}}$$

At this point, all you need to do is count. The cards that are *not* hearts are the diamonds, spades, and clubs. There are 13 of each, so there are 13×3 or 39 cards that are *not* hearts. The question also tells you that there are 4 sets of 13, or 52 total cards in a standard deck. Now you can solve the problem:

$$\text{Probability of NOT drawing a heart card} = \frac{\text{cards that are } not \text{ hearts}}{\text{total cards}} = \frac{39}{52} = \frac{3}{4}$$

Alternately, the probability of an event occurring and the probability of that event *not* occurring must add up to 1 or 100%, so you can solve this problem by subtracting the probability of the event occurring from 1:

$$P(not\ A) = 1 - P(A)$$

$$\text{Probability of NOT drawing a heart card} = 1 - \text{Probability of drawing a heart card} = 1 - \frac{1}{4} = \frac{3}{4}$$

The answer is $\frac{3}{4}$, or (D).

Conditional Probability

If there are multiple events whose outcomes do *not* depend on each other, they are called **independent events**. The probability of multiple independent events is simply the product of their separate probabilities. If Event A has a probability of 0.7, and Event B has a probability of 0.2, the probability of both Event A and Event B occurring is:

$$0.7 \times 0.2 = 0.14$$

Events are **dependent** if one event affects the probability of the other event occurring. If two events are dependent, you need to figure out what happens to the probability of the second event after the first one has taken place:

> ### Example
>
> A game involves picking up cards that are red, white, and blue. There are 5 red cards, 5 white cards, and 5 blue cards that are randomly shuffled together and placed facing up on the table. Three players take turns, picking the top card from the deck and putting it into their hand. If 2 red cards have been drawn by the first two players, when it is the third player's turn, what is the probability that her card will also be a red card?
>
> F. $\dfrac{1}{3}$
>
> G. $\dfrac{1}{5}$
>
> H. $\dfrac{2}{15}$
>
> J. $\dfrac{1}{13}$
>
> K. $\dfrac{3}{13}$

The probability of the first player's picking a red card is easy. All you have to do is take 5, the number of red cards, and divide it by the total number of cards, 15. But here you are looking at the probability of picking a card *after* two people have already gone.

The simplest way to look at this is that the number of red cards remaining is $5 - 2$, or 3, since two people already picked them. This also affects the total number of cards remaining in the deck, which is $15 - 2$, or 13. Now that you have dealt with the conditions of the *prior* event, you can concentrate on the *current* event, or the chance of the third person picking the remaining red card:

$$\frac{\text{number of red cards remaining}}{\text{total cards remaining}} = \frac{3}{13}$$

The probability of the third person selecting a red card given that two red cards have already been selected is $\dfrac{3}{13}$, or (K).

Logic and Event Notation

Sometimes you will see questions which use logical words such as "and," "or," and "at least." These can let you know whether you are looking at the overlap of two different sample groups or possible outcomes.

In a class of 20 people, 15 play the piano and 10 play the flute. At least how many students must play both the piano *and* the flute?

A.   0

B.   5

C.   10

D.   15

E.   20

This question is asking for the **intersection** of these groups, denoted in mathematical notation as ∩. Since there are 20 people total, you know that the number of people who play the piano (but not the flute) plus the number of people who play the flute (but not the piano), can be no greater than this number.

You can find the minimum number of people who play both instruments by adding the total for both instruments and then subtracting the total number of people:

$$(\text{Flutists} + \text{Pianists}) - \text{Total} = (10 + 15) - 20 = 5$$

You have found that 5, or (B), is the correct choice.

Another way of thinking about this problem is to visualize the scenario with a Venn diagram.

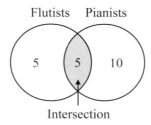

The numbers in the diagram must add up to 20, and the minimum overlap is obvious. In the above example, you can write the number of flutists and pianists as (Flutists ∩ Pianists).

If the question wanted you to find the number of people who played *at least* one instrument, it would then be asking for the **union** of these two groups. This would be denoted as (Flutists ∪ Pianists) and, in this case, is equal to the total number of students. If you draw this on the Venn diagram, it looks like this:

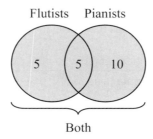

This is true for the union of any two groups, and is written as the equation:

$$(A \cup B) = (A) + (B) - (A \cap B)$$

Note that you need to subtract the intersection of A and B, otherwise you would count the overlap twice! If there are 15 pianists and 10 flutists, and 5 students who are both, then $15 + 10 - 5 = 20$. Intersection refers only to the group of A *and* B, while union is the total elements that belong to A and to B, minus the number that apply to both A and B.

This idea applies to events and probability as well. Remember that the probability of two independent events occurring is the product of their individual probabilities. Using notation:

$$P(A \cap B) = P(A) \times P(B)$$

Therefore, the probability of at least one event occurring can be expressed as:

$$P(A \cup B) = P(A) + P(B) - P(A \cap B)$$
$$P(A \cup B) = P(A) + P(B) - (P(A) \times P(B))$$

Analyzing Two-Way Tables

Conditional probability on the ACT may also be used to analyze two-way tables.

Example

The table below summarizes preference in music for students in the 9th and 10th grades. If a student is randomly chosen from the 9th grade, what is the probability that they prefer pop music?

F. $\dfrac{1}{5}$

G. $\dfrac{2}{9}$

H. $\dfrac{1}{2}$

J. $\dfrac{4}{9}$

K. $\dfrac{5}{9}$

Student Music Preference			
	9th Grade	10th Grade	Total
Classical	50	60	110
Rock	20	30	50
Pop	20	20	40
Total	90	110	200

This example is actually easier than the last one. The trick is that you need to determine your given conditions, in this case "being in 9th grade" and "preferring pop music," and then solve for the whole of that group of people, in this case the students in 9th grade:

$$\frac{\text{number of students in 9}^{\text{th}} \text{ grade who prefer pop music}}{\text{number of students in 9}^{\text{th}} \text{ grade}} = \frac{20}{90} = \frac{2}{9}$$

The number of students in 9th grade who prefer pop music is equal to $\dfrac{2}{9}$, or (G).

Variables
Part 4

A **variable** is a letter that represents an unknown, changing number. The opposite of a variable is a **constant**, which is an unchanging number. A constant can be a number, or it can be represented by a letter.

An algebraic **expression** is a mathematical phrase containing constants, variables, and operations. An algebraic expression is made up of **terms**, which are variables or numbers multiplied together. When a number is right in front of a variable, it means the variable is being multiplied by that number. This number is called the **coefficient**.

$$\text{Coefficient} \longleftarrow \underbrace{9x}_{\text{Term}} \longrightarrow \text{Variable}$$

When a variable does *not* have a written coefficient, it has a coefficient of one. For example, the term x is the same as $1x$.

Any expression with two or more terms is called a **polynomial**. An expression with one term only, like the one above, is called a **monomial**. The expression $4x + 6$ has two terms and is called a **binomial.**

Like Terms

Like terms have the same variable and are raised to the same exponent. For example, $4x$ and $6x$ are like terms. However, $3y$ and $3x$ are not like terms because they contain two different variables.

If you have more than one term, add or subtract the like terms, and leave any remaining terms as they are.

Example
The sum of $A + C + 5$ and $(2A - 6) = ?$
A. $-A + C - 1$
B. $A + C - 1$
C. $3A + C - 11$
D. $3A + C - 1$
E. $3A + C + 11$

The two groups of like terms are A and $2A$, and 5 and -6. Add these like terms together, and leave C as it is. A simple way to organize this is to write an expression with all the terms with variables first, in alphabetical order, and the constants last:

$$A + C + 5 + 2A - 6$$

Group like terms: $(A + 2A) + C + (5 - 6)$

Calculate like terms: $3A + C - 1$, or (D)

Distributive Property

You can simplify expressions by multiplying and dividing, and the distributive property can help you multiply and divide expressions with more than one term. The **distributive property** states that a number multiplies each number in parentheses independently:

$$a(b + c) = ab + ac$$

The distributive property also works for division. To multiply or divide like terms, multiply or divide their coefficients.

Example

$\dfrac{2b + 10z}{2b}$ is equivalent to:

F. $1 + 5z$

G. $1 + \dfrac{5z}{b}$

H. $b + \dfrac{5z}{b}$

J. $2b + 5z$

K. $2b + 20z$

In this example, you need to divide $2b$ by $2b$ and also $10z$ by $2b$ separately:

$$\frac{2b + 10z}{2b} = \frac{2b}{2b} + \frac{10z}{2b} = 1 + \frac{5z}{b}$$

Therefore, your answer is $1 + \dfrac{5z}{b}$, or (G).

Factoring

Factoring is the opposite of distributing. You can factor out numbers or variables from expressions. When **factoring** an expression, find the greatest common factor of all the terms. Then, work backward to take this factor out of your expression.

Example

Which of the following is equal to $5x + 5y - 10$?

A. $x + y$
B. $3(x + y - 1)$
C. $10(x + y - 5)$
D. $5(x + y - 2)$
E. $5(x + y + 2)$

The greatest common factor is 5, so you can factor it out of each term in the expression. Factoring out 5 from $5x$ gives you x, 5 from $5y$ gives you y, and 5 from 10 gives you 2:

$$5x + 5y - 10 = 5(x + y - 2)$$

You have found that $5(x + y - 2)$ is the factored form, and therefore (D) is the correct choice. You can always check that you have factored correctly by distributing (multiplying the expression out) and checking that your answer matches the original expression.

Mean, Median, and Mode
Part 5

The **mean** of a dataset (sometimes called the **arithmetic mean**) is the same as its average. The mean is one measure of the center of a dataset:

$$\text{mean} = \frac{\text{sum of all values in the set}}{\text{total number of terms in the set}}$$

The **median**, or middle of a dataset, is another measure of center. The easiest way to find the median is to list all the terms in numerical order and then locate the middle number. If there is an even number of terms, there is no true middle value. In this case, you should find the mean of the two numbers closest to the middle.

Example

A student received the following scores on 5 exams during the semester: 81, 81, 77, 96, and 65. What is the sum of the mean and the median of this set of exam scores?

F. 80

G. 160

H. 161

J. 162

K. 165

First, you need to calculate the mean of the set of exam scores:

$$\frac{81 + 81 + 77 + 96 + 65}{5} = 80$$

Next, you should order the list of scores to find the median:

$$65, 77, \text{\textcircled{81}}\ 81, 96$$

Finally, simply add the 2 values:

$$80 + 81 = 161$$

Therefore, the answer is (H).

The **mode** is most common value in a dataset. It is rarely tested on the ACT. In order to find the mode, simply count the number of times each value appears in a dataset. The mode of the dataset above is also 81, because 81 appears twice in the set, and no other number appears more than once.

On the Math Test, you may need to get an average from values which are given different importance. To calculate the average in this case, you need the **weighted average**, or the average resulting from the multiplication of each component by a number indicating its value or importance.

Example

A man receives 10 coins. If 4 are quarters, 3 are dollars, and 3 are dimes, what is the average value of 1 of his 10 coins?

A. $0.10

B. $0.43

C. $0.68

D. $1.35

E. $4.30

The easiest way to solve this is to first group each of the equaled weighted values together. Luckily the question already does this, so all you have to do is take the number of coins in each group and multiply it by the value for the group:

$$\text{Value of all quarters: } 4 \times 0.25 = 1.00$$

$$\text{Value of all dollars: } 3 \times 1.00 = 3.00$$

$$\text{Value of all dimes: } 3 \times 0.10 = 0.30$$

Add them together to find the total value of all the coins, and divide by the number of coins:

$$\frac{1.00 + 3.00 + 0.30}{10} = \frac{4.30}{10} = 0.43$$

You have determined that the weighted average of this group of coins is $0.43, or (B).

Questions on the ACT may also give you a probability table that looks kind of like your final table of grades for a class, and ask for the **expected value**.

Grade	Weight
80	0.5
60	0.3
70	0.2

This is the same thing as calculating your weighted average. All you need to do is multiply each value by each percent weight (in this case out of a total of 1), and then add the results together to calculate the weighted average. The average is $(80 \times 0.5) + (60 \times 0.3) + (70 \times 0.2) = 72$, which is higher than it would have been if these three grades were weighted equally.

Numbers in Graphs
Part 6

One way to make data, trends, and measures of spread easy to see is to display them as a table or graph. When you see a question with a chart or graph, examine it carefully to make sure you understand it. In a brief glance, try to identify its purpose, what it measures, and its units. Aside from tables, which you've already seen how to assess, the most common graphs on the ACT Math Test are pictographs, bar graphs, line graphs, circle graphs, and histograms.

Pictograph

A **pictograph** represents data as relevant images. Each image represents a certain chunk of data, indicated by the Key. A pictograph isn't very accurate, but it's ideal when data can be rounded. In the pictograph here, you can clearly see that Sweet Cheeses sold the most burgers last week.

Example

The pictograph below shows the number of burgers sold last week by 4 restaurants, to the nearest 500 burgers. Based on the table below, how many more burgers were sold by Burger Prince than by Patty O'Beef's?

Restaurant	Burgers Sold
Burger Prince	🍔🍔🍔🍔
Free the Cows	🍔🍔
Sweet Cheeses	🍔🍔🍔🍔🍔◖
Patty O'Beef's	🍔🍔◖

🍔 = 1,000 burgers

F. 3,500
G. 3,000
H. 2,000
J. 1,500
K. 500

To solve this question, count the number of burger symbols in the Burger Prince section, which is 4, so Burger Prince sold 4,000 burgers. Next, count the number of burgers Patty O'Beef's sold, which is 2,500. Subtract 2,500 from 4,000 to get (J).

Bar Graph

Like a pictograph, a **bar graph** also compares sizes of data. A bar graph represents data along two axes using vertical or horizontal bars. Bars of different lengths help compare the sizes of different categories of data.

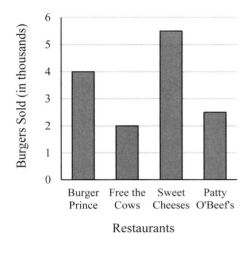

The horizontal axis (the *x*-axis) displays the different restaurants. The vertical axis (the *y*-axis) displays what is being measured: burgers sold. Here, the *y*-axis is in units of 1,000. Pay attention to this information; Burger Prince sold 4,000 burgers, not 4.

The ACT likes to rearrange the layout of graphs. Sometimes, you will see a bar graph on its side, with "Burgers Sold" on the horizontal axis, so the bars move from left to right instead of from bottom to top (like the pictograph to the left). Either way, the graph represents the same thing.

Circle Graph

A **circle graph** compares different sections of data as fractions of a whole. The circle represents the total amount, and differently sized sections of the circle represent parts of the total amount.

Example

Based on the circle graph below, what percentage of the burgers sold by all 4 restaurants was sold by Burger Prince, to the nearest percent?

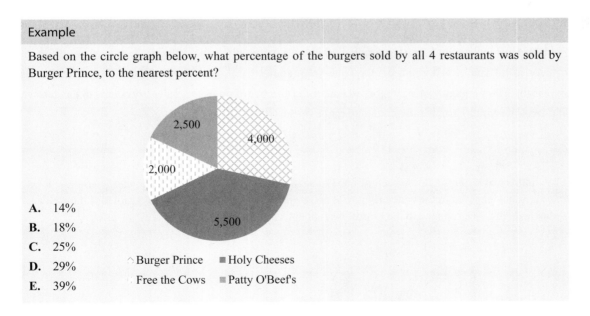

A. 14%
B. 18%
C. 25%
D. 29%
E. 39%

The fastest way to do this problem is to estimate the sizes of the sections. If the whole circle is 100%, then each section is a fraction of 100. Burger Prince's section is just over a quarter of the circle, so the percentage of burgers sold by Burger Prince must be just over 25%, which is (D).

Line Graph

A **line graph** uses a line or several lines to represent changes in amounts, usually over time. Like bar graphs, line graphs also represent data along two axes. The x-axis displays different dates or time periods, and the y-axis displays the amounts being measured.

Example

The line graph below shows the number of burgers sold each week, over a three-week period, by Free the Cows. If the trend continues, how many burgers will Free the Cows sell in the fourth week?

F.   0
G.   1,250
H.   2,000
J.   2,500
K.   4,000

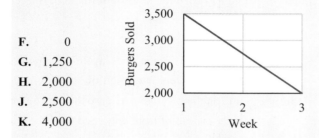

You don't know the exact number of burgers sold in Week 4, but if the trend continues, you can **extrapolate** that the number of burgers sold will be less than 2,000. You can eliminate (H), (J), and (K). You can see that each week, the number of burgers sold decreases by about 750, so (F) is incorrect, and your answer is (G). This question can also be solved by finding the slope of the line, a concept that we will cover in Section 5, Coordinate Geometry.

Histogram

A **histogram** looks a lot like a bar graph, but where a bar graph displays the different sizes of different categories of data, a histogram displays the **frequencies** of one category of data. This difference is important. The frequency of a category of data is the number of times that category occurs in the dataset, and it allows you to graphically calculate range, mean, median, and mode.

Example

The number of burgers sold by each of the 37 restaurants in the Puget Sound area was determined for a study as shown in the figure on the right. If A is the mean of the data, O is the mode, and M is the median, what is $A + M - O$, rounded to the nearest whole number?

A.   2,946
B.   3,495
C.   5,605
D.   8,605
E.   11,605

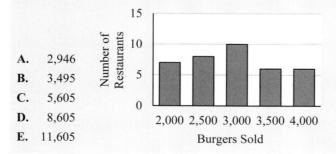

To find A, the mean of the data, you must divide the total number of burgers sold by the total number of restaurants who sold them. You can calculate the total number of burgers sold by multiplying each bar by the value of its group and adding all these values together: $7 \times 2,000 + 8 \times 2,500 \ldots + 6 \times 4,000 = 109,000$. By dividing this number by the number of restaurants (37), you can find the mean: approximately 2,946 burgers were sold per restaurant.

To find the mode, O, look at the category with the highest frequency, or the highest bar: 3000. The median, M, is also easy to find. Since there are 37 restaurants in the set, then the middle is at the 19th restaurant. Simply count up until you find the 19th restaurant. The 2,000 category has 7, and the 2,500 category has 8, so that's 15 restaurants. The 3,000 category has 10, so that's 25 restaurants. Since the 19th restaurant is found in this category, the median is 3,000. Therefore, since $A = 2,946$, $M = 3,000$, and $O = 3,000$, $A + M - O = 2,946 + 3,000 - 3,000 = 2,946$, or (A).

Pre-Algebra Practice Questions

Part 7

1. A city planner is trying to determine the minimum distance between 3 counties, A, B, and C. One residence needs at least half a square mile of land. The graphic below shows approximately how many residences there are in each of the 3 counties.

County A	🏠🏠🏠
County B	🏠🏠🏠
County C	🏠🏠🏠🏠🏠🏠

If each house represents 100 residences, how many square miles of land does county A need?

A. 50
B. 100
C. 125
D. 350
E. 600

2. $|-4(5) + 7| = ?$

F. −13
G. 5
H. 13
J. 33
K. 35

3. What is the sum of 154, 784, and 324, rounded to the nearest tens?

A. 1,200
B. 1,260
C. 1,262
D. 1,270
E. 1,300

Use the following information to answer questions 4-5.

A researcher polled 90 vehicle owners about the type and age of their vehicles. The researcher's results are shown in the table below.

Type of Vehicle	Year of Vehicle	
	2000–2009	2010–2016
Car	20	10
Truck	20	30
SUV	5	5

4. How many of the polled vehicle owners indicated that they owned a truck whose year was from 2010–2016?

F. 10
G. 15
H. 20
J. 30
K. 90

5. A vehicle owner is randomly selected from the 90 vehicle owners in the researcher's poll. What is the probability that this person owns an SUV?

A. $\frac{5}{9}$
B. $\frac{4}{9}$
C. $\frac{3}{9}$
D. $\frac{2}{9}$
E. $\frac{1}{9}$

6. Which of the following numbers has factors, excluding 1 and the number itself, that are ONLY prime numbers?

    F.   26

    G.   60

    H.   120

    J.   126

    K.   140

7. Given the following set of data, what is the difference between the mean and the median?

$$8, 11, 22, 23, 98$$

    A.   10.4

    B.   18

    C.   22

    D.   26.3

    E.   32.4

8. What is the lowest common multiple of 16, 8, and 12?

    F.   36

    G.   48

    H.   96

    J.   1,536

    K.   23,040

9. Christina has 1,560 pieces of candy that she wants to give equally to her friends. She is trying to decide how many of her friends she should give candy to. Which of the following number of friends would NOT allow her to equally distribute her candy?

    A.   3

    B.   5

    C.   7

    D.   10

    E.   13

10. Suppose that x is an odd number. Which of the following will yield an even number?

    F. $2x + 1$

    G. $2x - 1$

    H. $3x$

    J. x^2

    K. $x^2 - 1$

11. Hamburger buns are sold in packages of 6, and patties are sold in packages of 4. Tyler is hosting a party, and he has invited 28 people. If he assumes that all the guests are coming and that each guest will consume at least 2 hamburgers, how many packages of buns must he buy?

    A.   5

    B.   6

    C.   8

    D.   9

    E.   10

12. What is the sum of the following fractions:

$$\frac{1}{6}, \frac{1}{2}, \frac{1}{5}?$$

    F. $\dfrac{12}{60}$

    G. $\dfrac{13}{60}$

    H. $\dfrac{3}{15}$

    J. $\dfrac{13}{15}$

    K. $\dfrac{3}{13}$

13. A teacher had her students write down the amount of time it took them to complete a question. The results of her class of 25 students are found below.

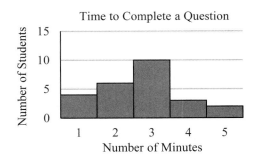

What percentage of her students wrote that they took 4 minutes to complete the problem?

    A.   40%

    B.   24%

    C.   16%

    D.   12%

    E.   8%

14. Carla has drawn up the budget for her first month of college. The chart below shows her expenditures on books, meals, rent, and entertainment.

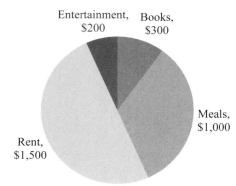

In the second month of college, she decided to spend $400 on entertainment. What is the percent increase of Carla's spending on entertainment from the first to the second month of her college semester?

F.　5%

G.　10%

H.　25%

J.　50%

K.　100%

15. A stone has 5 uneven faces, each painted with 1 unique number from 3 to 7. No number is repeated. A researcher rolls the stone, averaging the numbers she receives over thousands of rolls. Based on the probability distribution in the table, to the nearest tenth of a number, what is the average expected value that the researcher will roll?

Number Rolled	Probability
3	0.1
4	0.2
5	0.1
6	0.4
7	0.2

A.　2.5

B.　2.7

C.　5.0

D.　5.4

E.　6.2

16. How many different ways can the letters in the word LILAC be arranged?

F. $\dfrac{5!}{3!2}$

G. $\dfrac{5!}{2!}$

H. $\dfrac{5!}{3!}$

J. $5!$

K. 5^5

17. The same value, x, is both the mean and the median of a set of data. Two values, a and b, are added to the set of data. a is 25 less than x, and b is 100 greater than x. Given this information, which of the following is true?

A.　The mean and median are unchanged.

B.　Both the mean and median increase.

C.　Both the mean and median decrease.

D.　The mean is now greater than the median.

E.　The median is now greater than the mean.

18. Let P(D) and P(V) denote the probability of two independent events. Which of the following equations denotes the probability of both D and V happening?

F. $P(D \cap V) = P(D) + P(V)$

G. $P(D \cap V) = P(D) \cdot P(V)$

H. $P(D \cap V) = \dfrac{P(D) \cdot P(V)}{P(D) + P(V)}$

J. $P(D \cap V) = P(D) + P(V) - (P(D) \cdot P(V))$

K. $P(D \cap V) = P(D) + P(V) - 1$

19. If $|13 - 2x| = 3$, $x = ?$

    A.   5 or 8

    B.   −5 or −8

    C.   −5 or 8

    D.   5 or −8

    E.   5

20. James decides to run 12 miles. If he runs the first 6 miles in 36 minutes, and takes 54 minutes for the next 6 miles, what is his average speed for the entire run, in miles per hour?

    F.   5

    G.   6

    H.   7

    J.   8

    K.   9

Section 3
Elementary Algebra

On the ACT Math Test, Elementary Algebra questions test your ability to understand expressions involving multiple variables, such as linear and quadratic equations. This content builds upon the Pre-Algebra concepts that you learned in the previous section of this book and includes:

- Linear Expressions and Equations
- Properties of Exponents and Square Roots
- Higher-Order Expressions and Equations
- Quadratic Equations

In addition to being tested directly, the key ideas covered in this section form the foundation for most of the other questions on the Math Test. Typically, Elementary Algebra makes up 10 of the questions on the Math section, or about 17%.

Linear Expressions and Equations

Part 1

An algebraic **equation** tells you that two expressions are equal to each other. For example, you can use an equation to say that $9x$ is equal to 36:

$$9x = 36$$

Often on the Math Test, you will be asked to solve algebraic equations. If you are asked to "solve for x," you need to find a value for x that makes the equation true. For the equation above, you may know right away that $x = 4$ because $9 \times 4 = 36$. For more complicated algebraic equations, you may not be able to figure out the answer in your head. You will need to use a method to manipulate the equation and solve for the unknown variable.

Your goal is always to **isolate** your variable—to get it by itself on one side of the equation. To do this, you can work backwards to "undo" all of the operations that are being performed on your variable until you can get it by itself.

There's one important rule to remember when working with equations: whatever you do to one side of the equation, you must also do to the other! If you violate this rule, the two sides of your equation will no longer be equal.

Example
If $5a - 7 = 2a - 1$, what is the value for a?
A. 1
B. 2
C. 3
D. 4
E. 5

First, get all of your variables on one side of the equation by subtracting $2a$ from each side and combining like terms:

$$5a - 2a - 7 = 2a - 2a - 1$$
$$3a - 7 = -1$$

Then, undo the subtraction by adding 7 to each side:

$$3a - 7 + 7 = -1 + 7$$

$$3a = 6$$

Finally, undo the multiplication by dividing each side by 3:

$$\frac{3a}{3} = \frac{6}{3}$$

$$a = 2, \text{ and (B) is correct.}$$

To test if you got the right answer, you can plug your solution back into the original equation:

$$5a - 7 = 2a - 1$$

$$5 \times 2 - 7 = 2 \times 2 - 1$$

$$10 - 7 = 4 - 1$$

$$3 = 3$$

Some equations will look much more complicated than the ones above. Don't let this scare you! You will always use the same process for solving linear equations with one variable. Work carefully through each step. Get your variable on one side and then undo the operations.

Example

If $\dfrac{5(x + 7)}{4} = \dfrac{100 - 5x}{5}$, then $x = ?$

F. 45

G. 35

H. 25

J. 15

K. 5

You can see there are a lot of operations in this equation. You need to get the variable x on one side, but you'll have to do some other operations first. First, multiply both sides by 5 and then both sides by 4 to undo the division:

$$\frac{5(x + 7)}{4} = \frac{100 - 5x}{5}$$

$$(5 \times 5)(x + 7) = 4(100 - 5x)$$

Next, use the distributive property that you learned about in the Pre-Algebra section:

$$25(x + 7) = 4(100 - 5x)$$

$$25x + 175 = 400 - 20x$$

Elementary Algebra

Then, undo the operations to get your variable on one side of the equation and your constant on the other side:

$$25x + 175 + 20x = 400 - 20x + 20x$$

$$45x + 175 = 400$$

$$45x + 175 - 175 = 400 - 175$$

$$45x = 225$$

Finally, divide by 45 on both sides to solve for x.

$$\frac{45x}{45} = \frac{225}{45}$$

$$x = 5$$

You have found that $x = 5$, so (K) is the correct answer.

Math Dictionary

Many questions on the Math Test will require that you translate words into mathematical expressions or equations. The following chart shows some quick ways of translating plain English into the language of mathematics:

Word/Phrase	Translation	Symbol
is, was, has, will be	Equals	=
more, total, increased by, exceeds, gained, older, farther, greater, sum	Addition	+
less, decreased, lost, younger, fewer, difference	Subtraction	−
of, product, times, each	Multiplication	×
for, per, out of, quotient	Division	÷
what, how much, a number	unknown variable	x, y, n, etc.
at least	greater than or equal to	≥
at most	less than or equal to	≤

Example

7 less than 4 times a number is equivalent to 11 more than twice the same number. What is the value of the number?

A. 9
B. 8
C. 7
D. 6
E. 5

First, write this as an algebraic expression using your translation chart. If you let your unknown number be n, then "four times a number" means $4n$, and "seven less" means you need to subtract 7. This expression equals:

$$4n - 7$$

The question then states that the above expression is equivalent to a second expression. Following the same procedure that you used for the first half of the question, you know that "twice the same number" means $2 \times$, and "eleven more" means that you need to add 11. From this, you have:

$$4n - 7 = 2n + 11$$

By combining like terms you deduce that $2n = 18$. Therefore, $n = 9$, and (A) is correct.

Basic Inequalities

You might have noticed that the first table of the section had two unusual symbols, $\geq$ and $\leq$, for "at least" and "at most." These symbols belong to a mathematical statement called an **inequality**, which compares two quantities that are not the same. The ACT frequently works with inequalities, which can be represented with these symbols:

Inequality Symbols	
$>$	greater than
$<$	less than
$\geq$	greater than or equal to
$\leq$	less than or equal to

An algebraic inequality states that a certain algebraic expression is greater than or less than another quantity. For example, $x < 3$ means "an unknown quantity, x, is less than 3." There are many possible solutions for this inequality. The variable x may equal 1, 2, 0.5, –4, –6, 0, or any other number that is less than and not equal to three.

To solve a more complex inequality, treat it like an equation—manipulate the inequality to isolate your variable. You'll end up with a range of solutions that can satisfy the inequality.

Example

If $4x \geq 24$, what are all the possible values for x?

F. $x \leq 24$

G. $x < 6$

H. $x > 6$

J. $x \geq 6$

K. $x \geq 20$

The first thing you need to do is to isolate your variable by dividing both sides by 4:

$$\frac{4x}{4} \geq \frac{24}{4}$$

$$x \geq 6$$

If $4x$ is greater than or equal to 24, then x can be any value greater than or equal to 6. (J) is correct.

The ACT also uses number lines and circles to represent inequalities. A shaded segment on a number line represents all of the possible solutions for the inequality. Circles show whether numbers at the end of a line segment are part of the solution set. If a circle is shaded in completely, it means the number is included in the solution set: it is a possible solution for the inequality $\geq$ or $\leq$. If a circle is unshaded, it means the number is excluded from the solution set: it is not a possible solution for an inequality represented by $>$ or $<$.

For example, the number line below shows the possible solutions for $x > 1$:

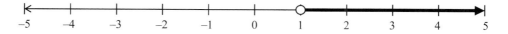

All numbers greater than 1 are possible solutions for this inequality, so a shaded line extends to the right of 1. The number 1 is not a possible solution for this inequality, so there is an unshaded circle over the number 1.

Example

Which of the following number lines represents the inequality $x \leq -4$?

A.

B.

C.

D.

E.

The first step to tackling this problem is identifying the inequality symbol. This question asks for values less than or equal to -4. Because it is less than -4, the line should extend to the left of -4. Since $x = -4$ is also included in the set of answers, a closed circle should be placed over -4. (A) is the correct option.

Properties of Exponents and Square Roots
Part 2

In the previous section, you looked at linear expressions and equations. Many Math Test questions also deal with higher-order expressions that make use of exponents:

$$\text{Base} \longrightarrow 2^3 \longleftarrow \text{Exponent}$$

The **exponent** (3 in this case) is a superscripted number that tells you how many times to multiply the **base** (2 in this case) by itself. In this example:

$$2^3 = 2 \times 2 \times 2 = 8$$

For the purposes of the Math Test, you should also memorize the following facts:

- A number with "no" exponent has an implied exponent of 1: $6 = 6^1$
- Zero raised to a power is always equal to zero: $0^3 = 0 \times 0 \times 0 = 0$
- Any number raised to a power of zero is equal to 1: $15^0 = 1$

A **root** is the opposite of an exponent. A root is indicated by a **radical** placed over a **radicand**. The **degree** of a root is indicated by a superscripted number to the left of the radical.

$$\text{Degree} \longrightarrow \sqrt[4]{16} \longleftarrow \text{Radical}$$
$$\uparrow$$
$$\text{Radicand}$$

A root tells you that the radicand is the product of some unknown number multiplied by itself a certain number of times. The degree tells you how many times the unknown number is multiplied by itself to produce the radicand. In the example above, the unknown number is 2:

$$\sqrt[4]{16} = 2$$

because $2 \times 2 \times 2 \times 2 = 16$

You can see that $2 \times 2 \times 2 \times 2$ is the same as 2^4. This demonstrates how roots are the opposite of exponents.

Often, you will see a root with no written degree. In this case, a degree of 2 is implied, and the root is called a **square root**. The square root of a number is the opposite of the square of a number:

$$\sqrt{9} = 3 \text{ because } 3^2 = 9$$

In addition to being directly tested in ACT questions, exponents are also a handy way to simplify expressions, to factor, and to do mental math. **Exponent laws** are rules for manipulating exponents. Here is a table with all the exponent laws that you should memorize and practice:

With different bases	$(xy)^m = x^m y^m$ $\left(\dfrac{x}{y}\right)^m = \dfrac{x^m}{y^m}$
With the same base	$x^m x^n = x^{m+n}$ $\dfrac{x^m}{x^n} = x^{m-n}$ $(x^m)^n = x^{mn}$
With radicals and rationals	$\sqrt[n]{x} = x^{\frac{1}{n}}$ $\sqrt[n]{x^m} = x^{\frac{m}{n}}$ $\sqrt[m]{x^m} = x^{\frac{m}{m}} = x^1 = x$ $x^{-1} = \dfrac{1}{x}$ $\sqrt{x} \times \sqrt{y} = \sqrt{(xy)}$ $\sqrt[n]{\sqrt[m]{x}} = \sqrt[nm]{x}$

Take a look at an example that combines several exponent laws:

Example

$\dfrac{\sqrt[3]{\dfrac{11^6}{(11^2 \times 11^1)}}}{11^{-1}}$ is equivalent to:

F. $\dfrac{1}{121}$

G. $\dfrac{1}{11}$

H. 11

J. 121

K. 1331

This problem looks a lot more difficult than it is. Use order of operations and work on the numbers in brackets inside the radical first:

$$(11^2 \times 11^1)$$

Recall the exponent rule about multiplying exponents with the same base—you must add the exponents:

$$(11^2 \times 11^1) = 11^3$$

Now you have $\dfrac{\sqrt[3]{\dfrac{11^6}{11^3}}}{11^{-1}}$.

Still working with the numbers under the radical, you know that when you divide exponents with the same base, you subtract the exponents, so:

$$\frac{11^6}{11^3} = 11^{6-3} = 11^3$$

If possible, avoid using your calculator, so leave the value of 11^3 as an exponent for now:

$$\frac{\sqrt[3]{11^3}}{11^{-1}}$$

When you have an exponent inside a radical, you divide the exponent by the degree of the root. In the example problem, since the exponent and the radical are both 3, you are simply left with the base:

$$\sqrt[3]{11^3} = 11^{\frac{3}{3}} = 11^1 = 11$$

You have now simplified the original expression to $\dfrac{11}{11^{-1}}$.

There is one final step of simplification. A number with a negative exponent is equal to 1 divided by the number with the exponent. Therefore:

$$\frac{11}{11^{-1}} = \frac{11}{\frac{1}{11}} = 11 \times 11 = 11^2 = 121$$

The answer is 121, or (J).

Higher-Order Expressions and Equations
Part 3

Now that you have learned exponent rules and how to apply them to basic operations, you can solve any ACT math problem that uses higher-order expressions. Their properties are similar to linear expressions. The only thing that changes with higher-order expressions is that now you have to also keep track of the exponent value of your terms.

Example

What is the value of $4p^3 + 6p^2 - 8p + 11$ minus $3p^3 - 2p^2 + 12p - 3$?

A. $7p^6 + 4p^4 + 4p^2 + 7$

B. $7p^3 + 4p^2 + 4p + 7$

C. $p^3 + 8p^2 - 20p + 14$

D. $p^3 + 4p^2 - 20p + 8$

E. 8

First, you need to combine the like terms. In this case, you are subtracting one expression from the other, so you need to remember to subtract the *whole* expression. Using parentheses is a good way to keep track of this:

$$4p^3 + 6p^2 - 8p + 11 - (3p^3 - 2p^2 + 12p - 3)$$

Then, distribute the negative sign across the parentheses:

$$4p^3 + 6p^2 - 8p + 11 - 3p^3 + 2p^2 - 12p + 3$$

Next, you're ready to combine like terms for your result. When adding and subtracting higher order terms, you need to treat each term with a different exponent as a *separate* term, even if they have the same base. In this case, the terms containing p^3 can only be combined with other p^3 terms, the terms containing p^2 can only be combined with other p^2 terms, etc. Organizing these like terms gives you:

$$4p^3 - 3p^3 + 6p^2 + 2p^2 - 8p - 12p + 11 + 3 =$$
$$p^3 + 8p^2 - 20p + 14$$

$p^3 + 8p^2 - 20p + 14$ is the answer, and (C) is correct.

Multiplying Polynomials

When you multiply polynomials, you will need to use the distributive property, covered in the Pre-Algebra section:

Using the distributive property, you can rewrite the expression like this:

$$2x \times x + 2x \times 3$$

Then, simplify to get your solution:

$$2x^2 + 6x$$

(J) is the correct choice.

When you're multiplying more than one polynomial with multiple terms, the idea is the same: use the distributive property and simplify. You just have to make sure you've multiplied every term in one polynomial by every term in the other.

Luckily, for multiplying two binomials, there's an easy way to keep everything straight. The **FOIL method** tells you to multiply the **F**irst terms, the **O**uter terms, the **I**nner terms, and the **L**ast terms. Always remember to combine like terms when you've finished.

$$(x + 3)(2x + 5)$$

The FOIL method makes this simple. Multiply together the *first* terms in the parentheses (x and $2x$), then the *outer* terms (x and 5), then the *inner* terms (3 and $2x$), and finally the *last* terms (3 and 5):

$$(x \times 2x) + (x \times 5) + (3 \times 2x) + (3 \times 5)$$

Then, simplify and combine like terms:

$$2x^2 + 5x + 6x + 15$$

$$2x^2 + 11x + 15$$

Dividing Polynomials

To divide polynomials, you can think of it as factoring the numerator by the denominator. Factoring variables, like factoring numerals, which you learned about in Pre-Algebra, involves finding a common term across all the terms of the polynomial. In the case of division, this common term is often found in the denominator:

Example

For all nonzero values of x, $\dfrac{2x^3 + 4x^2 - 6x}{2x} = ?$

A. $x + 2x - 3$

B. $x + 2x^2 - 3$

C. $x^2 + 2x - 3$

D. $x^3 + 2x^2 - 3$

E. $x^3 + 2x^2 - 3x$

This operation is asking you to divide each term of the polynomial by $2x$. Remember that dividing two expressions with the same base means you *divide* the coefficients and *subtract* the exponents:

$$\frac{2}{2}x^{3-1} + \frac{4}{2}x^{2-1} - \frac{6}{2}x^{1-1}$$

Carry out that arithmetic, and simplify the coefficients where you can:

$$x^2 + 2x - 3$$

The correct answer is (C). Don't worry if the number you're dividing the coefficients by isn't a common factor. It's fine to leave coefficients as fractions in lowest terms.

Quadratic Equations
Part 4

Now that you have reviewed higher-order expressions and factoring, you can focus on quadratic equations. **Quadratic equations** are equations whose highest order variable is raised to the second degree. Here is an example:

$$x^2 + 10x + 21 = 0$$

Equations like this appear often on the ACT Math Test, sometimes in a word problem:

Example

Josh drops a water balloon from the top of a tree in his backyard. The height h of the balloon at time t is given by $h = -t^2 - t + 20$. How many seconds does it take for the balloon to fall to the ground?

F.   0

G.   4

H.   5

J.   9

K.   20

To solve quadratic equations, use what you have learned about factoring polynomials. First, you need to make one side of equation equal to zero. In the example problem, this is easy. The question asks you to find t when the balloon hits the ground—in other words, when $h = 0$:

$$0 = -t^2 - t + 20$$

If neither side of the equation is already zero, be sure to collect all non-zero terms on one side of the equation in order to get zero on the other side. Now you can factor the right side. In section 4 we cover quadratic factoring in greater detail. In this simpler example, a quadratic that has a second-order coefficient of 1, all you need to do is to find two numbers whose sum is equal to its first-order coefficient and whose product is equal to its constant:

$$0 = -t^2 - t + 20$$
$$0 = -(t^2 + t - 20)$$
$$0 = -(t + 5)(t - 4)$$

On the right side, you now have two factors that have a product of zero. For two numbers to have a product of zero, at least one of them has to be equal to zero. In this equation, there are two ways for that to be true:

$$t + 5 = 0 \text{ or } t - 4 = 0$$

$$t = -5 \text{ or } t = 4$$

Therefore, this quadratic equation has two possible solutions: $t = -5$ or $t = 4$. These values are known as the **roots** of the equation.

However, you are not quite finished. Which one of your solutions makes sense in this context? Clearly, the time when the balloon hits the ground cannot be negative, so you can discard $t = -5$. This is an **extraneous solution**: it works mathematically but does not make logical sense. The useful solution to the problem is $t = 4$, or (G), so the balloon hits the ground 4 seconds after being dropped.

Difference of Squares

In some cases, there is no first-order term, so you may find it difficult to factor in the usual way:

Example

What is the solution of the equation $\dfrac{(x^2 - 16)}{(x - 4)} = 0$?

F. −16

G. −4

H. 0

J. 4

K. 16

While this may seem challenging at first, if you recognize that the expression in the numerator is a **difference of squares**, or simply one square (x^2) minus another square (16), factoring becomes quite simple. The expression $x^2 - 16$ is an example of a difference of squares:

$$x^2 - 16 = x^2 - 4^2$$

To factor a difference of squares, remember the following formula:

$$a^2 - b^2 = (a + b)(a - b)$$

Because you know that 16 is equal to 4^2, apply the difference of squares formula, with $a = x$ and $b = 4$:

$$x^2 - 16 = (x + 4)(x - 4)$$

Put this back into the equation in the question, and simplify your expression:

$$\frac{(x + 4)(x - 4)}{(x - 4)} = 0$$

$$x + 4 = 0$$

$$x = -4$$

The answer to the question is (G).

Elementary Algebra Practice Questions

Part 5

1. How many solutions does the following equation have?

$$0 = 7x + 9$$

   A. None
   B. One
   C. Two
   D. Three
   E. Infinitely many

2. $(x - 3)(x + 7) = ?$

   F. $x^2 - 4x - 21$
   G. $x^2 + 4x - 21$
   H. $x^2 + 4x + 21$
   J. $x^2 + 10x - 21$
   K. $x^2 + 10x + 21$

3. The height, h, in meters, of a ball thrown into the air after t seconds is given by the equation $h = -3t^2 + 10t + 15$. What is the height of the ball, in meters, after 3 seconds?

   A. 9
   B. 12
   C. 18
   D. 28
   E. 72

4. Lola has a lemonade stand, for which she needs paper cups and lemonade. Each paper cup costs \$0.10 to buy, and each cup of lemonade costs \$0.50 to make. Lola decides to sell each cup of lemonade for \$1. If x represents the number of cups of lemonade that she sells, which of the following expressions represents Lola's profits?

   F. $-1.5x$
   G. $-0.6x$
   H. $0.4x$
   J. $0.6x$
   K. $1.6x$

5. When $x = 4$, what is the value of $x^3 - 14$?

   A. -2
   B. 0
   C. 16
   D. 50
   E. 88

6. Which of the following is equivalent to $\left(3a^2 + 7ab^3 - 11a^2\right) - \left(2ab^3 - 6c^4\right)$?

   F. $-8a^2 + 9ab^3 - 6c^4$
   G. $-8a^2 + 9ab^3 + 6c^4$
   H. $-8a^2 + 5ab^3 + 6c^4$
   J. $-8a^2 + 5ab^3 - 6c^4$
   K. $-14a^2 + 5ab^3 - 6c^4$

7. $y = x^2 + 10x - 3$ and $x = \frac{1}{2} - b$. If $b = \frac{3}{2}$, $y = ?$

   A. 6
   B. -1
   C. -6
   D. -8
   E. -12

8. An electrician charges a flat fee of $114 for her services, plus an additional $30 for every hour that she works. If the electrician charges $204, how many hours did she work?

F. 2
G. 3
H. 4
J. 5
K. 6

11. Jerry operates a Ferris wheel at a carnival. For the first 5 minutes on the ride, he charges visitors a flat fee of $8. For the remaining ride time, he calculates the square root of the number of minutes and multiplies that by $3. If a visitor rides for 30 minutes, how much should Jerry charge?

A. $3
B. $8
C. $23
D. $83
E. $90

9. $11x^2 + 3y^3 - 2\left(6x^2 - \dfrac{1}{4}y^3\right) = ?$

A. $-x^2 + \dfrac{7}{2}y^3$

B. $-x^2 + \dfrac{5}{2}y^3$

C. $-x^2 + 2y^3$

D. $x^2 + \dfrac{7}{2}y^3$

E. $-12x^2 + \dfrac{7}{2}y^3$

Use the following information to answer questions 12-13.

Robbie is a sales assistant who is paid $10.25 for every hour he works and receives a commission equal to 4% of his total sales. His monthly sales reports are shown in the table below.

Robbie's Monthly Sales Report		
	Hours Worked	Total Sales (in dollars)
September	80	2,000
October	90	3,000

10. Marcia and Tyler both work at a clothing store. During one shift, Marcia sells $11 + x$ shirts, $5 - x$ pants, and $6 + 2x$ jackets. Tyler sells $16 - x$ shirts and $2x$ jackets. If a shirt sells for s dollars, a pair of pants for p dollars, and a jacket for j dollars, what is the value of all the clothing that Marcia and Tyler sell?

F. $(27 + 2x)s + (5 - x)p + (6 + 4x)j$

G. $(27 + 2x)s + (5 - x)p + (6 + 2x)j$

H. $27s + (5 + x)p + (6 + 4x)j$

J. $27s + (5 - x)p + (6 + 2x)j$

K. $27s + (5 - x)p + (6 + 4x)j$

12. In September, Robbie was given a sales bonus of $300 in addition to his regular salary and commission. Which of the following expressions represents his total earnings for September, where h is the total number of hours worked and t is the total sales?

F. $10.25h + 4t + 300$
G. $0.04h + 10.25t + 300$
H. $10.25h + 0.04t - 300$
J. $10.25h + 0.04t + 300$
K. $10.25h + t + 300$

13. Robbie worked 100 hours in November and his total sales were 10% greater than they were in October. If he is given a bonus of $400 for his work in November, how many total dollars would Robbie make that month?

    A. 1,557

    B. 1,545

    C. 1,425

    D. 1,157

    E. 1,025

14. For all x, $(9x^2 - 64) = $?

    F. $(3x - 8)(x - 8)$

    G. $(3x - 8)(3x - 8)$

    H. $(3x - 8)(3x + 8)$

    J. $(3x + 8)(8x - 8)$

    K. $(3x + 8)(8x + 8)$

15. Which of the following number lines represents the solution set of the inequality $2x - 7 > 3$?

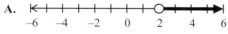

16. If $n = -3$, what is the value of $\dfrac{(n^3 - n)}{(n + 1)}$?

    F. -15

    G. -12

    H. 10

    J. 12

    K. 15

17. A local gym collects data about its pricing model. It currently offers a $295 yearly pass and has 403 customers. The company finds that for every $5 decrease in yearly pass price, it gains 3 customers. If x is the number of times the price was decreased, which of the following equations best represents the gym's total revenue, r?

    A. $(295 + 5x)(403 - 3x) = r$

    B. $(295 - 5x)(403 + 3x) = r$

    C. $(295 + 5x)(403 + 3x) = r$

    D. $(403 - 5x)(295 + 3x) = r$

    E. $(403 - 295x)(5 + 3x) = r$

18. If $b = \dfrac{n^2 + 6n + 9}{n - 3}$, what is a possible value for n if b is 0?

    F. 6

    G. 3

    H. 0

    J. 1

    K. -3

19. Which of the following best represents the number line below?

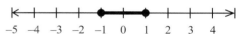

    A. $|x| \le 1$

    B. $|x| \ge 1$

    C. $x \ge 1$

    D. $x \le 1$

    E. No equation can represent this line.

20. Karen works at a cell phone accessories store in a mall. There are 3 items that the store carries: cell phone cases for $15 each, cell phone charms for $4 each, and screen protectors for $7 each. At the end of one day, Karen has sold half as many charms as screen protectors, and twice as many cell phone cases as screen protectors. If Karen sold 10 charms, how much money did she make that day?

    F. $70

    G. $140

    H. $180

    J. $600

    K. $780

Section 4
Intermediate Algebra

In this section you will learn about more complex applications of algebra, which frequently occur in the second half of the Math Test. This section covers the following:

- Units, Ratios, Rates, and Proportions
- Factoring Complex Quadratic Equations
- Inequalities and Quadratic Equations
- Systems of Equations and Inequalities
- Functions
- Advanced Algebra

Intermediate Algebra represents 9 of the 60 questions on the Math Test, or about 15%. While some of this material looks challenging, once you understand the rules and principles behind these questions, you will discover that solving these questions is just a matter of practice!

Units, Ratios, Rates, and Proportions
Part 1

Units, proportions, and ratios are frequently used in multi-step questions on the Math Test. Keeping these steps organized will help you both save time and avoid simple mistakes.

Units

Units describe quantities. You know that the length of a day is not simply "24"—it's "24 hours." Units like miles, feet, and meters are units of distance. Seconds, days, and years are units of time. Dollars and cents are units of currency. A dozen is a unit that refers to a group of 12 things.

For the Math Test, you need to memorize the conversions between these units of time:

Time
Second
Minute: 60 seconds
Hour: 60 minutes

There are two systems of units frequently used to measure mass, length, and volume. The **imperial system** is widely used in the United States. In questions, these units are usually accompanied by their conversion values. You should, however, memorize the conversion between feet and inches.

Weight	Length	Volume
Ounce	Inch	Cup
Pound: 16 ounces	Foot: 12 inches	Pint: 2 cups
Ton: 2000 pounds	Yard: 3 feet	Quart: 2 pints
		Gallon: 4 quarts

The **metric system** is commonly used internationally and in the scientific community. This system also appears frequently on the Math Test. In the metric system, mass is measured in grams (g), length is measured in meters (m), and volume is measured in liters (L).

The metric system uses prefixes to indicate multiples of 10. These prefixes can be combined with any of the units (grams, meters, or liters). Each prefix has a short form that is combined with the unit abbreviation. The following table summarizes the metric system:

Factor	1,000	100	10	0.1	0.01	0.001
Prefix	Kilo	Hecto	Deca	Deci	Centi	Milli
Short Form	K	h	D	d	c	m

A kilogram (kg) is 1,000 grams, a centimeter (cm) is 0.01 meters, and a milliliter (mL) is 0.001 liters. The Math Test will most likely give you these conversions when they are required, but make sure to familiarize yourself with the conversions between "kilo," "centi," and "milli."

Unit Conversions

Some problems will require you to convert between different units.

Example

The speed of sound in air is 768 miles per hour. Approximately how many feet will a sound wave travel in 1 second?

(Note: There are 5,280 feet in 1 mile.)

A.   0.21
B.   1,126
C.   3,600
D.   67,584
E.   4,055,040

First, set up a ratio between the two units so that the numerator and the denominator are equal. Since 1 mile = 5,280 feet, the ratio of feet to miles is:

$$\frac{5,280 \text{ feet}}{1 \text{ mile}}$$

This can also be written as a ratio of miles to feet:

$$\frac{5,280 \text{ feet}}{1 \text{ mile}} = \frac{1 \text{ mile}}{5,280 \text{ feet}}$$

The ratio between two units is called a **conversion factor**. Conversion factors provide two ways of looking at the same relationship. In this case, you can either have miles or feet as the denominator, but the number of feet per mile or miles per foot will always remain the same.

To convert a measurement into a different value, multiply it by the conversion factor with the desired units on top and the current units on the bottom. When you multiply a measurement by a conversion factor, the old units cancel out in the numerator and denominator. You are left with the new units:

$$\frac{768 \cancel{\text{ miles}}}{1 \text{ hour}} \times \frac{5{,}280 \text{ feet}}{1 \cancel{\text{ mile}}} = \frac{4{,}055{,}040 \text{ feet}}{1 \text{ hour}}$$

Always check that the units cancel out correctly. You should be able to cancel out all units in the conversion except for the units of the answer.

Now, you are ready to convert from hours to seconds. Follow the same process as before, but keep in mind that this conversion requires two steps: hours to minutes, and minutes to seconds. In the final step, be sure to reduce the fraction so you know how many feet the wave traveled in 1 second, not 3,600 seconds:

$$\frac{4{,}055{,}040 \text{ feet}}{1 \cancel{\text{ hour}}} \times \frac{1 \cancel{\text{ hour}}}{60 \cancel{\text{ minutes}}} \times \frac{1 \cancel{\text{ minute}}}{60 \text{ seconds}} = \frac{4{,}055{,}040 \text{ feet}}{3{,}600 \text{ seconds}} = \frac{1{,}126 \text{ feet}}{1 \text{ second}}$$

The distance traveled is 1,126 feet, or (B).

Ratios, Rates, and Proportions

Ratios, rates, and proportions compare numbers or express how numbers are related. **Ratios** compare two numbers with the same kind of unit, such as distance. For example, there are 3 feet in 1 yard, or in a bag of 8 marbles, there are 3 green marbles for every yellow marble. They are typically written with a colon, so "3 green marbles for every yellow marble" would look like 3:1.

Rates relate two numbers with different kinds of units. Rates are often **rates of change**, where one unit is changing over time. For example, Jan can run 4 laps in 3 minutes. **Proportions** compare two ratios.

Example

A cartographer is charting the distance in miles between two cities on a large map. Every 3 miles of distance is represented by 7 inches on the map. What is the distance, in inches, on a map displaying two cities that are separated by 27 miles?

F. 10
G. 21
H. 42
J. 49
K. 63

This is a proportion question. You must compare the ratio of 3:7 (miles:inches) with the ratio of 27:x (miles:inches)—where x is the number of inches that you don't know. Notice that the "miles" quantity and the "inches" quantity are in the same position. This is crucial to solving proportions. You can ask yourself, "What do I do to 3 miles to get 27 miles?" The answer is "Multiply by 9." Since the relationship expressed by a ratio always stays the same, and the relationship expressed by a proportion also always stays the same, you must multiply 7 inches by 9 to get x. The answer is 63 inches, or (K).

Algebraically, you can write these ratios as fractions and solve by cross-multiplying:

$$\frac{7}{3} = \frac{x}{27}$$

$$\frac{7}{3} \times 27 = x$$

$$63 = x$$

This isn't a bad way to solve proportions, but when you're converting ratios to fractions, you want to be careful. Ratios, such as the marbles example above, often represent the relationship between two parts of a whole, whereas fractions represent the relationship between a part and a whole.

Example

Mary-Jo collects skipping stones. She counts her skipping stones and finds that, for every 3 black stones, she has 2 brown stones. Assuming she has no other colors of stones, what fraction of her stones is black?

A. $\dfrac{2}{5}$

B. $\dfrac{3}{5}$

C. $\dfrac{2}{3}$

D. $\dfrac{1}{2}$

E. $\dfrac{3}{2}$

Because the ratio 3:2 represents parts of a whole, which is the number of stones Mary-Jo has in total, you must add them to find the whole: $3 + 2 = 5$. Therefore, the fraction of all her stones that is black is $\dfrac{3}{5}$, or (B).

Factoring Complex Quadratic Equations
Part 2

In Elementary Algebra, you solved quadratic expressions in the form $ax^2 + bx + c$, where a was equal to 1. How do you solve a quadratic where there is a different coefficient in front of the first term, x^2?

First, take a look and see if you can simply factor a out:

$$4x^2 + 24x + 32 = 4(x^2 + 6x + 8)$$

But, if you can't factor out a quadratic's coefficient, then you need to add a few variables, m, n, p and q. Think of the expression as:

$$ax^2 + bx + c = (px + m)(qx + n)$$

If you use FOIL on this expression, you will see that you need a few things to happen in order for this equation to work:

1. $p \times q = a$
2. $m \times n = c$
3. $(p \times n) + (m \times q) = b$

Example

$3x^2 - 5x - 2$ is equivalent to which of the following?

F. $3(x + 1)(x - 2)$
G. $(3x + 1)(x - 2)$
H. $(3x - 1)(x + 2)$
J. $(3x - 1)(x - 2)$
K. $(x + 1)(3x - 2)$

---

p and q will multiply to 3 so their values must be 1 and 3. (If a is negative, remember to first factor -1 out of the expression.) Therefore, you know the two binomials will look something like this:

$$3x^2 - 5x - 2 = (3x + m)(x + n)$$

To find m and n, you need values that will multiply to -2. There are two sets of possible values: -2 and 1 or -1 and 2. Which of these values should you pick so that $(3 \times n) + (m \times 1) = -5$? The only option is -2 and 1, because $(3 \times -2) + (1 \times 1) = -5$. Therefore, the two binomials must be $(3x + 1)(x - 2)$, so the correct answer is (G).

The Quadratic Formula

While all quadratic Math Test questions can be factored, you may find it faster to use the Quadratic Formula to solve challenging quadratic equations. The **Quadratic Formula** states that if you have a quadratic equation in the form:

$$ax^2 + bx + c = 0$$

you can solve for x using this formula:

$$x = \frac{-b \pm \sqrt{b^2 - 4ac}}{2a}$$

A quadratic equation will always have zero, one, or two roots, and you can use the discriminant of the Quadratic Formula to figure out how many it has. The square root term in the Quadratic Formula is called the **discriminant** and looks like this by itself:

$$b^2 - 4ac$$

Example

What is a possible value for x in the equation $x^2 + x + 2 = 0$?

A. −2 or 1
B. −1 or 2
C. −2
D. 1
E. There is no solution for x.

This looks like an easy question, but if you try to solve it, you will quickly get frustrated! Using the quadratic discriminant formula, however, is fast. $b = 1$, $a = 1$, and $c = 2$. You can plug them in:

$$1^2 - 4(1)(2) = -7$$

But wait! Remember that the quadratic formula takes the square root of the discriminant. Since $\sqrt{-7}$ is not possible, you have determined that there is no real solution. (E) is the correct answer.

Here is a table that outlines the possible values for the discriminant and what they mean:

Value of Discriminant	Number of Solutions
$b^2 - 4ac < 0$	0
$b^2 - 4ac = 0$	1
$b^2 - 4ac > 0$	2

Inequalities and Quadratic Equations
Part 3

You were introduced to inequalities in the Elementary Algebra section of this book. The following part will show you how to manipulate and solve inequalities involving algebraic expressions.

Rules for Inequalities

You can add or subtract the same number from both sides of an inequality and the inequality symbol will stay the same; it will be **preserved**. Multiplying or dividing both sides of an inequality by a positive number also preserves the inequality, but multiplying or dividing by a negative number *reverses* the inequality—you have to flip the direction of the inequality sign.

Example

$1 \geq -2x$ is equal to which of the following inequalities?

F. $\quad -2 \geq x$

G. $\quad -\dfrac{1}{2} \leq x$

H. $\quad -\dfrac{1}{2} \geq x$

J. $\quad \dfrac{1}{2} \leq x$

K. $\quad \dfrac{1}{2} \geq x$

Since you are looking for x, you need to divide the inequality by -2. Also, since you are dividing by a negative number, you must flip the inequality sign:

$$\frac{1}{-2} \geq -\frac{2x}{-2}$$

$$-\frac{1}{2} \leq x$$

You have found that x is greater than or equal to $-\dfrac{1}{2}$, and the correct answer is (G).

Inequalities with Two Variables

Sometimes, you will see an inequality that has two different variables in it, such as $y < -4x - 5$. You will not be able to find an exact number for x or y without more information. You can, however, solve for x in terms of y, as you would with an equation:

What is x in terms of y, if $y < -4x - 5$?

A. $x < \dfrac{y+5}{-4}$

B. $x < \dfrac{y+5}{4}$

C. $x > \dfrac{y+5}{-4}$

D. $x > \dfrac{y+5}{4}$

E. $x < -4x - 5$

To solve for x in terms of y, add 5 to both sides, then divide by -4 and reverse the inequality sign:

$$y < -4x - 5$$
$$y + 5 < -4x - 5 + 5$$
$$\frac{y+5}{-4} > \frac{-4x}{-4}$$
$$\frac{y+5}{-4} > x$$

That's it! The answer is $x < \dfrac{y+5}{-4}$, or (A).

Quadratic Inequalities

The Math Test sometimes combines quadratic equations with inequalities. In this case, you want to solve the quadratic expression first and then take care of the inequality:

Which of the following values of x satisfy the inequality $5x^2 + 15x < -10$?

F. 2

G. 1

H. -1

J. -1.5

K. -2

First, gather all like terms to one side of the equation, with zero on the other side. For now, consider the inequality as a regular quadratic equation equal to zero:

$$5x^2 + 15x < -10$$

$$5x^2 + 15x + 10 < -10 + 10$$

$$5x^2 + 15x + 10 < 0$$

Did you notice that every term in the quadratic expression has a common factor of 5? That means you can also pull 5 out of the entire expression:

$$5x^2 + 15x + 10 = 5(x^2 + 3x + 2)$$

Next, factor the quadratic expression. You're looking for two numbers that have a product of 2 and a sum of 3. The numbers 1 and 2 fit those requirements:

$$5(x^2 + 3x + 2) = 5(x + 1)(x + 2) = 0$$

You now know that if x is equal to -1 or -2, then the quadratic expression is equal to zero.

The last piece of the question is the right-hand portion of the inequality, < 0. The two factors of the quadratic equation may be either positive, negative or equal to zero depending on the value of x. You are looking for a value less than zero, so you need to find a value of x for when one of the factors is positive and one is negative. The question answer choices are summarized in the table below:

Value for x	$(x + 1)$	$(x + 2)$	Result	Value
−2	−	0	0	Equal to zero
−1.5	−	+	−	Less than zero
−1	0	+	0	Equal to zero
1	+	+	+	Greater than zero
2	+	+	+	Greater than zero

Since a value of -1.5 for x is the only choice that gives you a negative value, (D) is the answer. You can also check this by plugging -1.5 back into your original inequality:

$$5(-1.5)^2 + 15(-1.5) + 10 < 0$$

$$-1.25 < 0$$

Note that in some cases, it may be simpler and quicker to pick a number from the answer choice and plug it in to solve the equation.

Systems of Equations and Inequalities
Part 4

In this part you will learn how to combine several equations or inequalities in order to solve for a value or a range of values of a single variable. Questions with systems of equations and inequalities test your ability to solve a problem using several steps.

Systems of Equations

A **system of equations** is a group of equations that share like terms. On the Math Test, you often have to create and evaluate your own equations from a word problem. If you have two equations with two variables, you can always find a solution for both variables, provided a solution exists.

Example
A theater sold a total of 100 tickets in 2 ticket groups. Student tickets sell for $5 each, and adult tickets sell for $15 each. The sum of the adult ticket sales was equal to the sum of the theater's student ticket sales. How many adult tickets were sold?   **A.** 5   **B.** 10   **C.** 15   **D.** 20   **E.** 25

First, you need to create your equations. You know that there are two ticket groups, adults and students; you can use a for adults and s for students. You also know that there are a total of 100 tickets, so:

$$a + s = 100$$

The question also tells us that the revenue from student tickets equals the revenue from adult tickets:

$$\$5 \times s = \$15 \times a$$

You can use substitution or elimination to solve systems of equations. To use **substitution**, choose a variable to isolate in either equation. Since you're looking for a, you need to eliminate s by finding its value in one equation. Start by isolating s in that first equation, since it's the easiest:

$$a + s = 100$$
$$s = 100 - a$$

You can substitute this value of s into the second equation and then solve for a, which yields (E).

$$\$5 \times (100 - a) = \$15 \times a$$

$$\$500 - \$5a = \$15a$$

$$\$500 = \$20a$$

$$25 = a$$

Elimination allows you to cancel variables by adding or subtracting the two equations. In the example, since you are looking for a, you need to change the first equation so that the coefficient of s is the same in both equations. In this case, multiply both sides of the equation by 5.

$$5(a + s) = 5(100)$$

$$5a + 5s = 500$$

Next, reorder the second equation so that a and s are on the same side and divide both by $\$1$:

$$\$5 \times s = \$15 \times a$$

$$-\$15 \times a + \$5 \times s = 0$$

$$-15a + 5s = 0$$

Finally, subtract the second equation from the first equation:

$$5a + 5s = 500$$
$$\underline{-(-15a + 5s = 0)}$$
$$20a = 500$$
$$a = 25$$

Again, you calculated that there are 25 adult tickets, and that (E) is correct.

How do you know when to use substitution and when to use elimination? If one of the equations involves variables without coefficients (like $x + y = 3$) or could be easily simplified by dividing (like $2x + 2y = 8$), then substitution may be easier. If you choose elimination, just remember that you may need to first transform equations in order to solve for your desired variable.

Systems of Inequalities

On the Math Test, you may also see systems of inequalities. These are often represented as two sides of one inequality. In this case, you may be asked to solve for values of x that satisfy both sides.

Example

Which of the following inequalities represents all values of x for $3 \geq -4x + 1 > -1$?

F. $-1 \leq 2x$

G. $-2 \geq 2x$

H. $-2 \leq 2x < -1$

J. $-1 \leq 2x < 1$

K. $-1 \geq 2x > 1$

First, isolate x by subtracting 1 from both sides of the inequality:

$$3 \geq -4x + 1 > -1$$
$$2 \geq -4x > -2$$

Next, since the answer choices don't include $4x$, undo the multiplication by dividing both sides by -2. Remember to reverse the inequality sign because you are dividing by a negative number!

$$2 \geq -4x > -2$$
$$-1 \leq 2x < 1$$

You have found your result: $-1 \leq 2x < 1$, or answer (J).

Absolute Value Inequalities

The Math Test occasionally uses inequalities in combination with absolute value:

Example

If $\left| x - 3 \right| \geq 3$, what is a possible value for x?

A. -1

B. 1

C. 2

D. 4

E. 5

The first thing you need to do is to solve for the absolute value expression on the left side. Unless there is an extraneous solution, you will always have two inequalities based on an absolute value inequality. The first can be found by simply taking off the absolute value bars and treating the expression like a regular inequality:

$$|x-3| \geq 3$$
$$x-3 \geq 3$$
$$x \geq 6$$

The second involves taking off the absolute value bars and multiplying the side opposite the absolute value expression by -1. Don't forget to flip the inequality!

$$x-3 \geq 3$$
$$x-3 \leq 3 \times (-1)$$
$$x-3 \leq -3$$
$$x \leq 0$$

You know that x must be larger than or equal to 6 *or* smaller than or equal to 0. Therefore, -1, or (A), is the correct answer.

Functions
Part 5

A **function** shows how an "input" value is transformed into an "output" value. The input, x, will produce an output, $f(x)$, according to the rules of the function. The notation $f(x)$ is read as "f of x." Functions are most often referred to by f, but you may also see other letters such as g, h, or A. A function is different from an equation or an expression. In order for an equation to be a function, each input can only produce one output. If an input produces more than one output, the equation is *not* a function:

Equations and their y-outputs			
x-input	$y = 2x - 3$	$y = x^2 - 4x + 3$	$y^2 = 9 - x^2$
2	1	-1	$\sqrt{13}$ and $-\sqrt{13}$
1	-1	0	$\sqrt{10}$ and $-\sqrt{10}$
0	-3	3	3 and -3
-1	-5	8	$2\sqrt{2}$ and $-2\sqrt{2}$

In this table the first two equations are functions, but the third is not, because there is more than one value of y for each value of x.

Because $y = 2x - 3$ is a function, it can be written as $f(x) = 2x - 3$. The function $f(x) = 2x - 3$ means that for any input, x, the function assigns it the output $2x - 3$. This is how you **evaluate** a function—just replace the variable in the function with the given input value and solve:

If $x = 2$, then:

$$f(2) = 2(2) - 3$$
$$f(2) = 1$$

If $x = a + b$, then:

$$f(a + b) = 2(a + b) - 3$$
$$f(a + b) = 2a + 2b - 3$$

Example

If $f(x) = x^2 + 5x - 11$, what is the value of $f(3)$?

F. -17
G.   3
H.   13
J.   10
K.   35

The question tells you to find the value of $f(x)$ when $x = 3$. So, just substitute and evaluate.

$$f(x) = (3)^2 + 5(3) - 11$$
$$f(x) = 9 + 15 - 11$$
$$f(x) = 13$$

The correct answer is 13, or (H).

Composite Functions

On the Math Test, you might see functions combined through a notation like $f(g(x))$. This notation means that you need to use the output of $g(x)$ as the input of $f(x)$. You would read this as "f of g of x."

Example

If $f(x) = \dfrac{x^2 - 7}{x}$ and $g(x) = \sqrt{x}$, what is the value of $f(g(9))$?

A. $-\dfrac{1}{3}$

B. $\dfrac{2}{3}$

C. 1

D. $\dfrac{3}{2}$

E. $\dfrac{74}{9}$

Don't be intimidated if the functions look complicated! It's simply a matter of substituting values into functions in the correct order. Start by working from the inside out. First, find $g(9)$. Then, use that answer and plug it into $f(x)$:

$$g(9) = \sqrt{9}$$
$$g(9) = 3$$
$$f(3) = \frac{3^2 - 7}{3}$$
$$f(3) = \frac{2}{3}$$

$\dfrac{2}{3}$, or (B), is the correct answer.

There are many other things to learn about functions, such as how to graph and transform them. These topics are covered in the book's Coordinate Geometry section, the next section of this chapter.

Advanced Algebra

Part 6

The math principles covered in this part occur less frequently on the Math Test and are generally more conceptually complex than the rest of the Algebra sections. While they may appear challenging, these concepts have clear steps that you can follow to quickly find the correct answer.

Strange Symbols

The ACT may present questions that have **strange symbols**, such as @ or #, which don't normally indicate a mathematical function. These questions can be solved with simple pattern recognition.

Example

Geoffrey creates a function that requires two inputs, a and b, such that the output is determined by the function $a \nabla b = \dfrac{a^b + b}{2a}$. What is the value of the output of the function $2 \nabla 3$?

F. $\dfrac{11}{4}$

G. $\dfrac{9}{4}$

H. 2

J. $\dfrac{11}{6}$

K. $\dfrac{4}{3}$

There is a clear pattern here. If you look at the function and at what information the question gives you, you will see that:

$$a \nabla b = 2 \nabla 3$$

Notice that a and 2 are in the same position, and that b and 3 are in the same position. Therefore $a = 2$ and $b = 3$—these are your inputs. You can now substitute 2 and 3 for a and b, respectively. You can see that the correct answer is (F):

$$a \nabla b = \frac{a^b + b}{2a}$$

$$2 \nabla 3 = \frac{2^3 + 3}{2(2)}$$

$$= \frac{8 + 3}{4}$$

$$= \frac{11}{4}$$

Not so bad, after all! Those arbitrary strange symbols can be reduced to patterns. The same is true for *all* mathematics. For example, why does "+" indicate addition? It's simply a convention we accept.

Strange symbols, therefore, aren't just non-mathematical symbols. The ACT will sometimes give you complicated equations—like trigonometric identities or matrix determinants—and expect you to solve them. You never have to know *what they mean*; all you have to know is *how to plug numbers into the correct places*.

The following sections on logarithms, sequences, matrices, and complex numbers reveal more odd conventions in math. It's strange that writing the letters "log" should indicate the opposite of an exponent, but when you think about it, it's no stranger than the fact that making a number tiny and putting it at the top right corner of another number indicates an exponent.

Logarithms

Logarithms are the inverse of exponents. The logarithm of a number is the power to which a fixed value, the **base**, must be raised to yield that number. The logarithm function is written as "log":

$$\log_a b = c$$

In this formula, a is the base of the logarithm. This expression tells you that a must be raised to the power of c to yield b as the result. In other words:

$$a^c = b$$

You should always rewrite logarithms as exponents on the ACT. When using actual numbers, this relationship is slightly clearer:

$$\log_2 8 = 3 \text{ because } 2^3 = 8$$

If a logarithm is written without a base, you can assume that the base is 10.

Even when dealing with more complex logarithms, such as the one below, be sure to start by rewriting the logarithm in exponent form.

Start by writing the first two expressions in exponent form:

$$\log_c u = r \rightarrow c^r = u$$

$$\log_c v = s \rightarrow c^s = v$$

Now you can tackle the question itself by plugging in the known values of u and v:

$$\log_c \left(\frac{u}{v}\right)^{-5} \rightarrow \log_c \left(\frac{c^r}{c^s}\right)^{-5}$$

Use the rules of exponents from the previous chapter to simplify the expression:

$$\log_c \left(\frac{c^r}{c^s}\right)^{-5} = \log_c (c^{r-s})^{-5} = \log_c \left(c^{-5(r-s)}\right)$$

To what power would you raise c to yield $c^{-5(r-s)}$? Alternatively, recall that logarithms and exponents are inverse functions, so when they have the same base, they can cancel out. At this point, the answer is simple:

$$\log_c c^{-5(r-s)} = -5(r-s)$$

(C) is the correct answer.

Sequences

A **sequence** is an ordered list of numbers that follows a specific pattern. An **arithmetic sequence** is generated by *adding* a constant from one term to the next. The number that is added is called the **common difference** between terms, and it can be either negative or positive. Take a look at the set of numbers: $\{1, 4, 7, 10, 13, \ldots\}$. Here, the number 3 is added to each consecutive term. The common difference is 3. If a_1 is the first term of an arithmetic sequence, and d is the common difference between terms, then you can find the nth **term**, the term you are looking for in the sequence, by using the formula:

$$a_n = a_1 + d(n - 1)$$

In a **geometric sequence**, the next term is generated by *multiplying* the previous term by a constant. The number by which the previous term is multiplied is called the **common ratio** between terms, and it can be less than 1. Take a look at the set of numbers: {1000, 100, 10, 1, ...}. Here each term is divided by 10 to create the next term. The common ratio is $\frac{1}{10}$. If a_1 is the first term of a geometric sequence, and r is the common ratio between terms, then you can find the nth term in the sequence by using the formula:

$$a_n = a_1(r)^{n-1}$$

If you are asked to find the sum or average of a certain number of terms in a sequence on the Math Test, it is easiest to write out the terms of the sequence and to look for patterns rather than using a formula.

Example

Bonny collects rings. On Monday, she buys 2 rings. Each subsequent day, she buys 4 more rings than she bought on the previous day. After 14 days of collecting rings, how many rings does Bonny have?

F. 28
G. 54
H. 392
J. 756
K. 1,512

The first step to solving this problem is to list the number of rings Bonny buys on each of the first 14 days, using the formula for an arithmetic sequence with $a_1 = 2$ and $d = 4$:

Day	1	2	3	4	5	6	7	8	9	10	11	12	13	14
# Rings	2	6	10	14	18	22	26	30	34	38	42	46	50	54

You could try to add all these up, but this approach takes a lot of time and it's easy to make calculation errors. A better approach is to look for patterns in the sequence. You should notice that the ring totals from Day 1 and Day 14 add up to 56, as do the ring totals from Day 2 and Day 13, and so on. There are 7 pairs of days, and each pair adds up to 56, so:

$$\text{total rings} = 7 \times 56 = 392$$

Bonny buys 392 rings in the first 14 days, so (H) is the correct answer.

Matrices

A **matrix** is an ordered arrangement of numbers. Matrices can be complex, but the Math Test only requires you to know a few things about them, and will only give you one matrix question, if any.

Matrices are displayed as rectangles of numbers and they are enclosed by brackets. Each number in a matrix is called an **entry** or an **element**. Matrices are named after their **dimensions**, which means the numbers of rows and columns they have. Matrix A has 1 row and 3 columns, so it is a 1×3 matrix:

$$A = [1 \quad -2 \quad 0]$$

Matrices can be added and subtracted only by matrices that have the *same dimensions*. You can't add or subtract matrices and constants or matrices with different dimensions. When two matrices that have the same dimensions are added or subtracted, you simply add or subtract each entry at each position.

For example, $\begin{bmatrix} 1 & -5 \\ 8 & 0 \end{bmatrix} + \begin{bmatrix} 6 & -2 \\ 1 & 7 \end{bmatrix} = \begin{bmatrix} 1+6 & -5+(-2) \\ 8+1 & 0+7 \end{bmatrix} = \begin{bmatrix} 7 & -7 \\ 9 & 7 \end{bmatrix}$.

On the Math Test, most matrix questions will involve multiplication. This can happen in two ways. The first is **scalar multiplication**, which involves multiplying a matrix by a constant. To multiply a matrix by a constant, simply multiply each entry in the matrix by that constant. You are left with a matrix of

the same dimensions, so $\begin{bmatrix} -1 \\ 0 \\ 9 \end{bmatrix} \times 4 = \begin{bmatrix} -1 \times 4 \\ 0 \times 4 \\ 9 \times 4 \end{bmatrix} = \begin{bmatrix} -4 \\ 0 \\ 36 \end{bmatrix}$.

The second way is **matrix multiplication**, which is the multiplication of a matrix by another matrix. Matrix multiplication is only possible if the number of columns of the first matrix is equal to the number of rows of the second. The resulting matrix will have the same number of rows as the first matrix and the same number of columns of the second.

Example

$\begin{bmatrix} 1 \\ 5 \\ -1 \end{bmatrix} \times [2 \quad 3 \quad 0] = ?$

A. $\begin{bmatrix} 2 & 3 & 0 \\ 10 & 15 & 0 \\ -2 & -3 & 0 \end{bmatrix}$

B. $\begin{bmatrix} 2 & 10 & -1 \\ 3 & 15 & -3 \\ 0 & 0 & 0 \end{bmatrix}$

C. $[11 \quad 15 \quad 0]$

D. $[25]$

E. The matrices cannot be multiplied.

First, check to see that the matrices can be multiplied. The first is a 3 × 1 matrix, and the second is a 1 × 3 matrix. Since the number of columns of the first, 1, is equal to the number of rows of the second, 1, they can be multiplied. Second, check to see what the dimensions of the resultant matrix will be. The first matrix has 3 rows and the second has 3 columns, so their product will be a 3 × 3 matrix.

When multiplying a matrix, you must multiply the rows of the first by the columns of the second, one entry at a time. The process is shown below, and yields (A) as the answer:

$$\begin{bmatrix} 1 \times 2 & 1 \times 3 & 1 \times 0 \\ 5 \times 2 & 5 \times 3 & 5 \times 0 \\ -1 \times 2 & -1 \times 3 & -1 \times 0 \end{bmatrix} = \begin{bmatrix} 2 & 3 & 0 \\ 10 & 15 & 0 \\ -2 & -3 & 0 \end{bmatrix}$$

Note that if the order of these matrices were reversed—$\begin{bmatrix} 2 & 3 & 0 \end{bmatrix} \times \begin{bmatrix} 1 \\ 5 \\ -1 \end{bmatrix}$—the resultant matrix would be a 1 × 1 matrix, because there is one row in the first matrix and one column in the second. If you multiply the rows of the first by the columns of the second, the process would look something like this: $\begin{bmatrix} 1 \times 2 + 5 \times 3 + -1 \times 0 \end{bmatrix} = \begin{bmatrix} 17 \end{bmatrix}$.

Complex Numbers

Normally, it is impossible to take the square root of a negative number. However, sometimes it's helpful to "imagine" that you can take the square root of a negative number and use this in your calculations. You can do this by introducing the unit i, which is equal to the square root of -1: $i = \sqrt{-1}$.

This number does not exist in the set of real numbers, so it's called an **imaginary number**. In equations and calculations that involve imaginary numbers, you can use i as a placeholder for $\sqrt{-1}$. The ACT will always provide the equation for i, as shown above, or a variant of it (such as $i^2 = -1$).

You know that $i^2 = -1$, but what about i^3, or i^{322}? You can figure out any exponential value for i using the following values:

Exponential Values of i				
$i^0 = 1$	$i^1 = i$	$i^2 = -1$	$i^3 = -i$	$i^4 = 1$

You will notice that the values of i^0 and i^4 are the same. This is also true for the values of i^1 and i^5. In fact, there are only four values possible for i raised to an exponent: 1, i, -1, and $-i$; these values always repeat in a pattern of four and need to be memorized. Using this pattern, you can determine the value of i raised to any other power.

$i^{5345} = ?$

F. -1

G. $-i$

H. 1

J. i

K.   This value cannot be determined.

You know that i repeats in groups of four. All you need to do, therefore, is to divide the exponent by 4:

$$\frac{5345}{4} = 1336.25$$

Since any integer in this resulting number is a multiple of 4, all you need to worry about is the decimal, in this case 0.25 or $\frac{1}{4}$. Since i repeats itself every 4 integers, this is like saying that you are on the *first* of the cycle (1 of 4) of i exponents, i^1. In the example, therefore:

$$i^{5345} = i^1 = i$$

The answer is (J).

The Math Test may also ask you to evaluate i with another numeral. A **complex number** is the sum of a real number and an imaginary number. Complex numbers are written in the form $a + bi$, where a and b are real numbers, and i is imaginary. You may be expected to simplify an expression with complex numbers in it by adding, subtracting, and multiplying.

Example

In the complex numbers, where $i^2 = -1$, simplify $\dfrac{i}{2 + 3i}$.

A. $\dfrac{1}{5}$

B. $\dfrac{i}{2} + \dfrac{1}{3}$

C. $\dfrac{3 + 2i}{13}$

D. $\dfrac{-3 + 2i}{13}$

E. $\dfrac{3 - 2i}{5}$

First, when the ACT asks you to simplify an expression that is a fraction, you should know to remove radicals and complex numbers from the denominator. Remember that you can substitute i^2 with -1.

In this expression, the best way to get i^2 in the denominator is to multiply by an expression that will make the denominator a difference of squares. Don't forget to multiply both the numerator and the denominator by this same expression, so as not to change the *value* of the expression. In this case, you multiply by $2 - 3i$ in the numerator and denominator:

$$\frac{i}{2 + 3i} \times \frac{2 - 3i}{2 - 3i} = \frac{2i - 3i^2}{4 - 9i^2}$$

Now, you can substitute all the i^2 with -1:

$$\frac{2i - 3i^2}{4 - 9i^2} = \frac{2i - 3(-1)}{4 - 9(-1)} = \frac{2i + 3}{4 + 9} = \frac{2i + 3}{13}$$

This calculation gives you (C).

Intermediate Algebra Practice Questions

Part 7

1. For which value of x is $3x - 4 = -\frac{1}{2}x$?

    A. $-\frac{8}{7}$

    B. $\frac{7}{8}$

    C. 1

    D. $\frac{8}{7}$

    E. $\frac{8}{5}$

2. Which of the following is a solution of the quadratic equation $x^2 + 6x - 7$?

    F. -7

    G. -6

    H. -1

    J. 7

    K. 6

3. What is the 21st term in the following sequence?

$$11, 8, 5, 2, -1\ldots$$

    A. -46

    B. -49

    C. -52

    D. -55

    E. -58

4. Suppose r is equal to x^2, q is equal to $12x$, and y is equal to rq. If the value of x is halved, what happens to the value of y?

    F. It decreases by factor $\frac{1}{12}$

    G. It decreases by factor $\frac{1}{8}$

    H. It decreases by factor $\frac{1}{6}$

    J. It decreases by factor $\frac{1}{4}$

    K. It decreases by factor $\frac{1}{2}$

5. Which of the following number lines shows the set of solutions for the inequalities $2x \leq 8$ and $x > 1$?

    A.

    B.

    C.

    D.

    E.

6. $2x^2 - x - 1 = ?$

    F. $(x + 1)(2x - 1)$

    G. $(2x - 1)(2x + 1)$

    H. $(2x + 1)(x - 1)$

    J. $(2x - 1)(x - 1)$

    K. $(2x + 1)(x + 1)$

7. If x is a real number and $7x + 7 = x^2 + 2x + 1$, which if the following is a possible value for x?

   A. -1
   B. 0
   C. 1
   D. 2
   E. 7

8. Let $y = x + 1$, and $y = |x - 7|$. Which of the following is the value of x?

   F. -4
   G. 0
   H. 1
   J. 3
   K. 6

9. A tank of water is being filled. The volume of water in the tank as a function of time is shown in the graph below. A distinct event occurs at time T which changes the rate of water pouring into the tank. Which of the following could be the event at T?

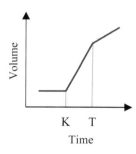

   I. The water begins to drain out of the tank.
   II. The rate of water pouring into the tank increases.
   III. The rate of water pouring into the tank decreases.

   A. I
   B. I and II
   C. I and III
   D. II and III
   E. I, II, and III

10. There are 62 students in a class. The ratio of boys to girls is 14:17. How many boys are there in the class?

    F. 14
    G. 20
    H. 24
    J. 28
    K. 34

Use the following information to answer questions 11-12.

A lumber mill takes tons of raw wood, w, chips it, and puts together blocks of pressed boards, b, according to the formula $b(w) = \sqrt{20 + 2w}$.

11. The manager wishes to produce 10 blocks of pressed boards per hour. How many tons of raw wood does she need to use per hour?

    A. 5
    B. 10
    C. 20
    D. 40
    E. 100

12. The manager finds a more efficient system of producing boards, which follows the formula $b(w) = w$. If she is able to transport and process raw wood in her mill at a rate of 8 tons per hour, how many more blocks of pressed boards will she be able to produce in 5 hours using her new formula rather than her old one?

    F. 10
    G. 15
    H. 20
    J. 30
    K. 100

13. If $\log_2 128 = x$, what is the value of x?

    A. 6
    B. 7
    C. 8
    D. 9
    E. 64

14. If $f(x) = x^2 - 4x + 4$ and $g(x) = x^2 + 5x - 14$, what is the value of $\dfrac{f(x)}{g(x)}$?

F. $(x - 2)$

G. $(x + 2)$

H. $(x + 7)$

J. $\dfrac{x - 2}{x + 7}$

K. $\dfrac{x + 7}{x - 2}$

15. If $i^2 = -1$, $i^{356} = ?$

A. $\sqrt{-1}$

B. -1

C. $-\sqrt{-1}$

D. 1

E. 0

16. Lucy decides to collect aluminum cans for exchange at the store. On the first day of the month, she has 2 cans. Every day following the first, Lucy collects twice the number of cans that she found the previous day. How many cans has she collected by the end of the 5th day?

F. 8

G. 16

H. 32

J. 62

K. 64

17. $\begin{bmatrix} 7 & 0 & 3 \end{bmatrix} \times \begin{bmatrix} 2 \\ 2 \\ 7 \end{bmatrix} = ?$

A. $[21]$

B. $[35]$

C. $[9 \quad 2 \quad 10]$

D. $[14 \quad 0 \quad 21]$

E. $\begin{bmatrix} 14 \\ 0 \\ 21 \end{bmatrix}$

18. Euler's equation states that if you cut the surface of a sphere into faces, edges, and vertices, where F is the number of faces, E is the number of edges, and V is the number of vertices, then $V - E + F = 2$. If a sphere is cut so that it has 6 edges and the same number of faces as vertices, how many faces does it have?

F. 2

G. 4

H. 6

J. 8

K. 10

19. If $n > m$ and $\log_6 6^{\frac{n}{m}} = p$, then which of the following statements *must* be true?

A. $p > 1$

B. $p < 1$

C. $p < m$

D. $p > m$

E. $p > n$

20. If $i^2 = -1$, which of the following expressions is equivalent to $\dfrac{(i + a)(i - a)}{i^3 - ia^2}$?

F. $-i$

G. i

H. $i - a$

J. $-a$

K. a

Section 5
Coordinate Geometry

In this section, you will learn about what the Math Test usually calls "the standard (x,y) coordinate plane," as well as many formulas, shortcuts, and tips. This section builds upon the concepts you learned in the previous sections and includes:

- The Standard (x,y) Coordinate Plane
- Graphing Linear Equations and Functions
- Graphing Quadratic Functions and Systems
- Graphing Discontinuous and Piecewise Functions
- Shapes in the (x,y) Coordinate Plane
- Transformations
- Vectors

Coordinate Geometry makes up about 15% of the Math Test, which is approximately 9 questions. This section incorporates most of the math you've learned in the previous three algebra sections and builds upon the graphical analysis introduced in Pre-Algebra. It also provides a brief glimpse into concepts later discussed in Plane Geometry.

The Standard (*x,y*) Coordinate Plane
Part 1

From algebra to geometry to trigonometry, the Math Test may require you to use coordinate planes in your analyses and calculations. You can review the basic definition and explanation of the coordinate plane in the online ACT Fundamental Review. Four terms you should know are:

- **Plane:** A flat, two-dimensional surface that extends infinitely, both horizontally and vertically
- **Origin:** The fixed point (0,0) from which all coordinates are measured
- **Axis:** A fixed line of reference in a plane—the *x*-axis extends horizontally in both directions from the origin, and the *y*-axis extends vertically in both directions from the origin
- **Ordered pair:** A pair of numbers used to locate a point on a coordinate plane—the first number indicates how far to move horizontally, and the second number indicates how far to move vertically from the origin

In this section you will learn fundamental principles of the standard (*x,y*) coordinate plane that you can apply to all coordinate problems.

 For a fundamental review, visit **ivyglobal.com/study**.

Distance in the Coordinate Plane

The Math Test frequently asks you to find the distance between two points in the coordinate plane. If the two points share an *x*-coordinate or a *y*-coordinate, this process is very easy:

- If the two points have the same *x*-coordinate, calculate the difference between the points' *y*-coordinates. The distance between (1,3) and (1,−2) is $3 - (-2) = 5$.
- If the two points have the same *y*-coordinate, calculate the difference between the points' *x*-coordinates. The distance between (−7,3) and (1,3) is $-7 - 1 = -8$, but since distance is always positive, this is 8.

For most Math Test problems using distance, however, the two points will have neither the same *x*- nor *y*-coordinates. You'll need to use the **distance formula**, which tells you how to calculate the distance *d* between any two points with coordinates (x_1,y_1) and (x_2,y_2). Make sure to memorize this formula:

$$d = \sqrt{(x_2 - x_1)^2 + (y_2 - y_1)^2}$$

What is the distance in the standard (x,y) coordinate plane between the points $(7,10)$ and $(5,-7)$?

A.   0

B.   2

C.   17

D. $\sqrt{293}$

E.   293

Because you are squaring the difference between the two points, the order in which you subtract the numbers does not matter. Just be consistent throughout the problem. You could designate $(7,10)$ as (x_1,y_1) and $(5,-7)$ as (x_2,y_2) and then plug in these values to the distance formula:

$$d = \sqrt{(x_2 - x_1)^2 + (y_2 - y_1)^2}$$
$$= \sqrt{(5-7)^2 + ((-7)-10)^2}$$
$$= \sqrt{(-2)^2 + (-17)^2}$$
$$= \sqrt{4 + 289}$$
$$= \sqrt{293}$$

The correct answer is (D).

Lines in the Standard (x,y) Coordinate Plane

A **line** is a straight, one-dimensional object with infinite length but no width. Using any two points, you can draw a line. The simplest line $y = x$, for example, can be graphed according to the following table and graph:

y = x	
x-value	y-value
−2	−2
−1	−1
0	0
1	1
2	2

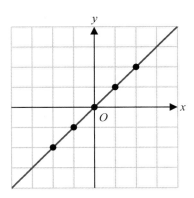

As you can see, this line passes through the origin O, $(0,0)$. If a point is part of a line, it lies on the line. In the figure above, for example, you could say that $(-4,-4)$ and $(2,2)$ lie on the line.

It is possible to describe a line with only two quantities:

- The **slope** of a line (represented by the letter m) describes how steeply it is going upwards or downwards.
- The **y-intercept** of a line (represented by the letter b) describes the y-coordinate of the point where the line intersects the y-axis.

You can think of the slope of a line as the rate of change between two points on the line. To calculate the slope of a line, you only need to know the coordinates of two points. If you divide the difference in y-coordinate between the two points (the **rise**) by the difference in x-coordinate between the two points (the **run**), you will get the slope:

$$m = \frac{\text{rise}}{\text{run}} = \frac{y_2 - y_1}{x_2 - x_1}$$

Again, the order of the two points does not matter, as long as you are consistent.

Example

If m is the slope and b is the y-intercept of the line graphed on the standard (x,y) coordinate plane below, what is the value of mb?

F. $-\dfrac{28}{9}$

G. $-\dfrac{7}{9}$

H. 0

J. 4

K. 9

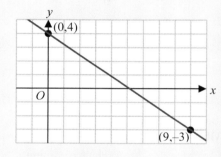

You've been given two points on the line, and one of them is the point where the line intersects the y-axis. You have all the information you need to solve the problem.

First, find the y-intercept. Since the y-coordinate of the intersection point is 4, you know that $b = 4$.

Next, find the slope. Use the rise-over-run slope formula:

$$m = \frac{\text{rise}}{\text{run}} = \frac{y_2 - y_1}{x_2 - x_1} = \frac{(-3) - 4}{9 - 0} = \frac{-7}{9} = -\frac{7}{9}$$

Now that you know m and b, you can multiply them:

$$m \times b = \left(-\frac{7}{9}\right) \times 4 = -\frac{28}{9}$$

The answer is (F).

Here are a couple key facts about slope that you need to know for the Math Test:

- A line pointing upwards from left to right means that y increases as x increases. The line's slope is positive:

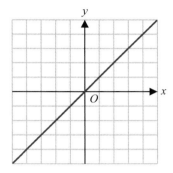

- A line pointing downwards from left to right means that y decreases as x increases. The line's slope is negative:

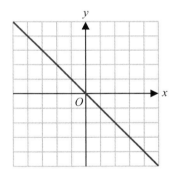

- The steeper a line is, the faster y is changing as x changes, so the slope will be more positive or more negative:

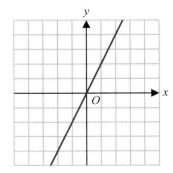

A **horizontal line** has a slope of zero:

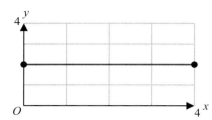

$$m = \frac{\text{rise}}{\text{run}} = \frac{0}{3} = 0$$

For this line, the slope is zero because when x changes, y does not change at all. This line will always have the same y-coordinate.

A **vertical line** has an undefined slope:

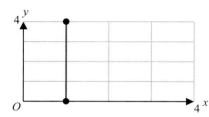

$$m = \frac{\text{rise}}{\text{run}} = \frac{3}{0} = \text{undefined}$$

The slope of this line is undefined because it is impossible to divide by zero. This line will always have the same x-coordinate.

Non-vertical **parallel lines** have equal slopes.

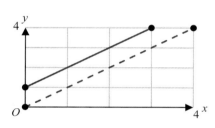

Parallel lines never intersect. Therefore, two lines that are parallel must always have the exact same steepness. They both need to be changing at the same rate.

In the graph on the left, both lines have a slope of $m = 1$. However, the solid line has a y-intercept of $b = 1$, while the dashed line has a y-intercept of $b = 0$.

Non-vertical **perpendicular** lines have slopes whose product is -1.

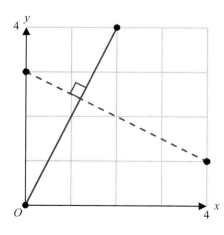

If the slope of a line is m, the slope of the line perpendicular to it will be $-\frac{1}{m}$. One slope is always the negative reciprocal of the other slope in perpendicular lines.

The slope of the dashed line is: $\dfrac{\text{rise}}{\text{run}} = -\dfrac{2}{4} = -\dfrac{1}{2}$.

The slope of the solid line is: $\dfrac{\text{rise}}{\text{run}} = \dfrac{4}{2} = 2$.

The product of these two slopes is: $-\dfrac{1}{2} \times 2 = -1$.

Line P has a slope of $-\dfrac{1}{5}$. Line Q passes through the points $(k,7)$ and $(-1,-3)$. If Line P and Line Q are perpendicular, what is the value of k?

A. −1

B. 0

C. 1

D. 3

E. 5

First, you need to figure out the slope of Line Q. You know that Line P has a slope of $-\dfrac{1}{5}$, and that Line Q is perpendicular to Line P. You know, therefore, that the product of Line P's slope and Line Q's slope is −1. Write out this equation with m standing for Line Q's slope:

$$-\frac{1}{5} \times m = -1$$

Now, you can solve for m:

$$-5 \times \left(-\frac{1}{5} \times m\right) = -1 \times -5$$

$$m = 5$$

So Line Q has a slope of 5. You can now plug this into the slope formula to find the value of k:

$$m = \frac{\text{rise}}{\text{run}} = \frac{y_2 - y_1}{x_2 - x_1}$$

$$5 = \frac{y_2 - y_1}{x_2 - x_1}$$

Using the coordinates in the two points given, you can plug in 7 for y_1, −3 for y_2, k for x_1, and −1 for x_2:

$$5 = \frac{y_2 - y_1}{x_2 - x_1}$$

$$5 = \frac{-3 - 7}{-1 - k}$$

$$5(-1 - k) = -10$$

$$-1 - k = -2$$

$$k = 1$$

The value of k is 1. (C) is correct.

Graphing Linear Equations and Functions
Part 2

For the Math Test, you will only be expected to graph equations or functions with two variables. If there are more than two variables and you are expected to graph them, you will be able to simplify the equation or expression to two variables.

In the algebra sections of this book, you learned about equations and functions involving two variables. Because you will never have more than one value of y for each value of x, all linear equations on the ACT are functions as well. The most common equation form for a line is called **slope-intercept form**:

$$y = mx + b$$

In function notation, this is represented as:

$$f(x) = mx + b$$

This is a very powerful tool, especially when dealing with more than one line:

Example

Two linear equations are graphed on the standard (x,y) coordinate plane below. At what point do the two lines intersect?

F. $\left(\dfrac{3}{13}, \dfrac{7}{8} \right)$

G. $\left(-\dfrac{3}{16}, \dfrac{7}{8} \right)$

H. $\left(-\dfrac{3}{16}, -\dfrac{7}{8} \right)$

J. $\left(-\dfrac{7}{8}, \dfrac{3}{16} \right)$

K. $(-1 , 1)$

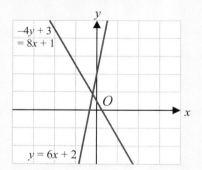

In this problem, you are shown two intersecting lines and are provided with the equations of those lines. How can you use this information to find the point of intersection?

In the Intermediate Algebra section, you learned how to solve problems involving systems of two linear equations. You should remember that those problems usually asked you to find a value of x and a value of y that satisfied both equations. In graphical terms, these values represent the x- and y-coordinates of the **point of intersection** of two lines. Think about it: linear equations represent lines, and finding a point that satisfies both equations is equivalent to finding a point that lies on both lines. This is equivalent to finding the point where the two lines intersect.

So to solve the example problem, you need to solve the system of linear equations using $-4y + 3 = 8x + 1$ and $y = 6x + 2$. You can use either the substitution method or the elimination method. Look back at the Intermediate Algebra section if you need to review the method for solving systems of linear equations. Here's a way to solve it using substitution.

Change Equation 1 to slope-intercept form:

$$-4y + 3 = 8x + 1$$
$$-4y = 8x - 2$$
$$y = -2x + \frac{1}{2}$$

Equation 2 is already in slope-intercept form:

$$y = 6x + 2$$

Equation 1 = Equation 2:

$$-2x + \frac{1}{2} = 6x + 2$$

Solve for x:

$$\frac{1}{2} = 8x + 2$$
$$-\frac{3}{2} = 8x$$
$$-\frac{3}{16} = x$$

Substitute x into either equation to solve for y:

$$y = 6\left(-\frac{3}{16}\right) + 2 = \frac{7}{8}$$

You have found that $x = -\frac{3}{16}$ and $y = \frac{7}{8}$. Therefore, the point of intersection of the two lines is $\left(-\frac{3}{16}, \frac{7}{8}\right)$, and (G) is the correct answer.

A few additional useful facts about the connection between lines and systems of equations:

- If a system of linear equations has **no solution**, then the two lines are parallel and never intersect.
- If a system of linear equations has **infinite solutions**, then the two lines are the same line and intersect at every point.

Graphing Quadratic Functions and Systems
Part 3

As you recall, both quadratic equations and functions are simply expressions with a variable raised to the second power. As with linear expressions, for the purposes of the Math Test, quadratic equations and functions are identical. The equation is represented by:

$$y = ax^2 + bx + c$$

The function is represented by:

$$f(x) = ax^2 + bx + c$$

The type of curve created by graphing quadratic functions or equations is called a parabola. Parabolas can move up or down, be wider or narrower, or flip upside down, but they will always retain this basic shape:

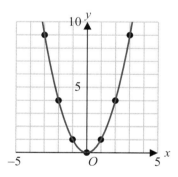

A parabola's x-intercepts are the points where the parabola meets the x-axis. The parabola above has one x-intercept. Parabolas can also have zero or two x-intercepts:

Parabola with zero x-intercepts

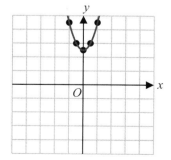

Parabola with two x-intercepts

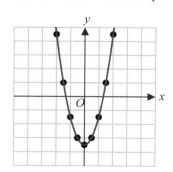

The y-coordinate for any point on the x-axis is always zero, so the coordinates for the x-intercepts are x-values of the quadratic function that will make y equal to 0. These values are also known as the **solutions** or the **roots** of the quadratic equation:

Example

The equation $2x^2 - 2x - 4 = y$ is graphed on the standard (x,y) coordinate plane. Two points, a and b on this curve have y-values of 0. If point a has an x-value of -1, what are the coordinates of point b?

A. $(-1,0)$

B. $(0,0)$

C. $(1,0)$

D. $(2,0)$

E. $(3,0)$

You are looking for the point where the y-value is 0, so you can rewrite the equation:

$$2x^2 - 2x - 4 = 0$$

Now just factor it like any other quadratic equation:

$$2(x^2 - x - 2) = 0$$

Solve for x:

$$2(x^2 - x - 2) = 0$$
$$2(x - 2)(x + 1) = 0$$

So you know that when $y = 0$, $x = -1$ or 2. Since point a has an x-value of -1, then the remaining x-value, where y is equal to 0, must belong to point b. In this case, this is where $x = 2$, so $(2,0)$ is point b. Answer (D) is correct.

You noticed in this example that there were two values of x for each value of y. This is true for all parabolas. The only point on a parabola that has one x-value for a given y-value is the parabola's vertex.

Parabolas are symmetric about a vertical line drawn through their **vertex**, which is the highest or lowest point. To find the x-coordinate h of the vertex (h,k) of any parabola, you can use the following formula, where a is the coefficient of x^2 and b is the coefficient of x:

$$h = \frac{-b}{2a}$$

In the function $f(x) = x^2$, b is equal to zero, so the vertex has the x-coordinate 0. If you plug $x = 0$ into $f(x) = x^2$, you can find the y-coordinate of the vertex: $f(x) = 0^2 = 0$. Therefore, the parabola's vertex is located at $(0,0)$—something that you can see on the graph:

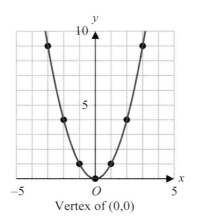

Vertex of (0,0)

What if you wanted to figure out the vertex of the equation $y = x^2 + 4x$? In this case, $b = 4$, so the x-coordinate of the vertex would be $\dfrac{-b}{2a} = \dfrac{-4}{2 \times 1} = -2$. You can plug this x-value into the function to find the y-coordinate: $y = (-2)^2 + 4 \times (-2) = -4$. The vertex of this equation is located at the point $(-2,-4)$. The section on transformations will cover how vertices in quadratic equations and functions can shift.

Graphic Systems of Inequalities

The Math Test may also require you to understand graphs of systems of inequalities. These systems always include other graphs, such as lines, parabolas, or shapes such as circles.

Graphing inequalities is similar to graphing equations. Start by graphing the inequality as if it were an equation. Use a solid line for $\leq$ or $\geq$, and a dashed line for $<$ or $>$. Then, shade in the solution area. For "greater than" inequalities, shade *above* the line. For "less than" inequalities, shade *below* the line.

Take a look at $y \leq \dfrac{1}{2}x + 3$. In order to graph it, rewrite it as: $y = \dfrac{1}{2}x + 3$. Because the inequality uses the symbol $\leq$, you'll want to graph a solid line:

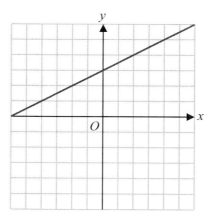

Next, shade in the solution area. "Less than" is shown on the left side, and "greater than" is shown on the right side. The graph on the left side, therefore, represents the inequality $y \le \frac{1}{2}x + 3$.

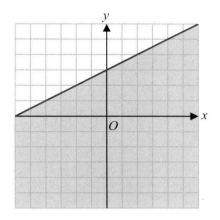
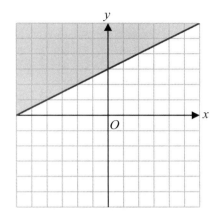

Which of the following systems of inequalities is shown in the standard (x,y) coordinate plane below?

F. $\begin{aligned} y &\ge -3x + 2 \\ y &\ge -x^2 + 1 \end{aligned}$

G. $\begin{aligned} y &\ge -3x + 2 \\ y &\le x^2 + 1 \end{aligned}$

H. $\begin{aligned} y &\le -3x + 2 \\ y &\le x^2 + 1 \end{aligned}$

J. $\begin{aligned} y &\le -3x + 2 \\ y &\ge x^2 + 1 \end{aligned}$

K. $\begin{aligned} y &\le 3x + 2 \\ y &\ge x^2 + 1 \end{aligned}$

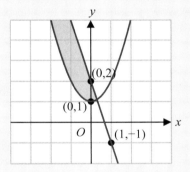

In a lot of ways, this problem looks similar to a system of equations question. The graph shows two functions, one linear and one quadratic, with two points of intersection. However, as you probably noticed, there is also a region of the graph that is shaded. This shaded region represents all the points that satisfy the system of inequalities.

The best way to solve a problem like this is to tackle each inequality separately.

First, take a look at the line. You are given two points, so you can use the skills you learned earlier in this section to derive the equation of the line:

$$m = -3 \text{ and } b = 2$$

$$y \le -3x + 2$$

You now know the equation of the line represented on the graph, but you still need to decide the direction of the inequality sign. Notice that the shaded area lies on and below the line, not above it. This tells you that y is less than or equal to $-3x + 2$. With these more complex questions, it is often worthwhile to eliminate answers as you work. In this case, you can eliminate (K) because you know that the slope of the line is negative. You've figured out one of the two inequalities, so you can eliminate (F) and (G):

$$y \leq -3x + 2$$

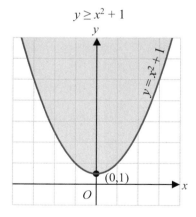

Now you can deal with the parabola. You don't really need to be able to calculate the exact equation of the quadratic. Pay attention to significant features and use the answer choices to guide you. The answer choices include two different quadratics: $y = -x^2 + 1$ and $y = x^2 + 1$. Notice that the parabola on the graph faces upward, so the coefficient in front of the x^2 must be positive. The equation of the quadratic must therefore be $y = x^2 + 1$.

Which direction should the inequality sign face? The shaded area lies on and above the parabola, so y is greater than or equal to $x^2 + 1$.

$$y \geq x^2 + 1$$

Combine the two inequalities:

$$y \leq -3x + 2$$
$$y \geq x^2 + 1$$

(J) is the correct answer.

Graphing Discontinuous and Piecewise Functions

Part 4

Graphs of Discontinuous Functions

So far you have looked at continuous functions, whose graphs have no breaks. The Math Test will also occasionally ask you about **discontinuous functions**, or functions with holes or jumps in their graphs. Two types of discontinuous functions may be tested: asymptotic and piece-wise discontinuities.

The basic idea behind asymptotic discontinuities is that you cannot divide anything by zero. This simple idea applies to algebra and also to graphs of algebraic functions. In rational functions, a value of x that would lead to a division of 0 is called a vertical **asymptote**. You can also think of this as a line that a function approaches, but never actually intersects.

Think of the example $f(x) = \dfrac{1}{x-1}$. In this function, x can never be equal to 1, because then the function would be undefined, but it can get *close* to 1. Take a look at the graph of this function:

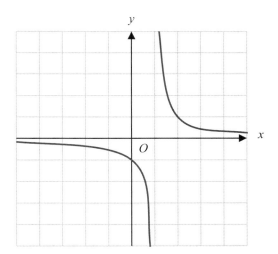

Notice that the function approaches the value of $x = 1$ from either side, but is never able to cross it. From the left side the value of y stretches towards an infinitely large negative number, and from the right side the value of y stretches towards an infinitely large positive number. The asymptote of $f(x) = \dfrac{1}{x-1}$ is therefore $x = 1$. While the Math Test will not ask you about asymptotic discontinuities directly, some of the questions may require that you know that a function is undefined at any point where the denominator is 0.

Piece-wise discontinuities, or functions that are defined by several pieces of functions and domains, are created by defining *x*-coordinate parameters for a series of functions:

Example

Which of the following is the graph of the function $f(x)$ defined below?

$$f(x)=\begin{cases} x-1 \text{ for } x \leq -1 \\ -x^2 - 4 \text{ for } -1 < x \leq 4 \\ -2x + 10 \text{ for } x > 4 \end{cases}$$

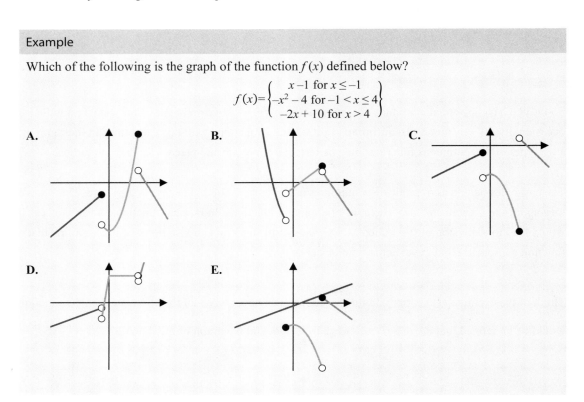

You are given three pieces of a function here: $x - 1$, $-x^2 - 4$, and $-2x + 10$. Take a look at the first one, $f(x) = x - 1$. (A), (C), (D), and (E) all have this function, but only (A), (C), and (D) stop where $x = -1$. Of these three, notice that the circles are closed for two of them and open for one.

An open circle means that there is a **discontinuity**, so the line does not exist at that point. Since the accompanying inequality is that $x \leq -1$ when $f(x) = x - 1$, the circle must be *closed* because the function *does* exist when $x = -1$. This eliminates (D), which has an open circle at $x = -1$.

To pick the right answer, you need to move to $f(x) = -x^2 - 4$, the next piece of the function. You know that $-x^2$ means that the function will contain a downward facing parabola. Without going any further you can eliminate (A), leaving (C) as your answer.

At this point you can continue looking at the other properties and pieces of $f(x)$ in the graph to confirm your choice. You will find that the inequality accompanying $f(x) = -x^2 - 4$ does match the open and closed circles on the graph, and that the following function $f(x) = -2x + 10$ and its inequality $x > 4$ also match what you see on the graph. Your choice is confirmed!

Modeling Using Functions

So far you've seen linear and quadratic functions. Functions can be used as a tool to model real world behavior. It is important to note, however, that the mathematical relationships do not always match exactly what happens in real life.

Recall the **extraneous solution**, introduced in the Elementary Algebra section of this chapter, where an answer that makes sense in an equation does not match what makes sense in reality. Whenever you are solving a word problem, always make sure to check whether the numerical solution makes sense in the context of the question.

Example

Use the following information to answer questions 1-2.

A ball is thrown upward by a person, as shown in the graph below. The height of a ball at t seconds is given by the function $h(t) = -5t^2 + 15t + 1.6$, where h is the height in meters and t is the time in seconds.

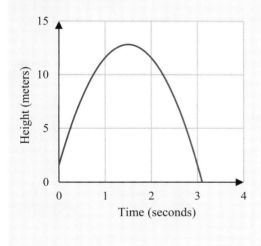

1. For which of the following values of t is the ball NOT in the air?

   F. 1
   G. 2
   H. 2.5
   J. 3
   K. 4

2. A tall cannon is built to mimic the person throwing the ball. After the cannon is ignited, however, the ball takes one second to leave the cannon, so the function's input changes from t to $t + 1$, where t is measured as the time when the ball leaves the cannon. How much height does the ball gain, in meters, between 0 and 0.5 seconds?

   A. 0
   B. 1.25
   C. 10
   D. 11.6
   E. 21.6

To start answering this question, you should first understand what the equation means in the situation presented. In this example, $h(t)$ represents height with respect to t, which represents time. The question asks for which value of t, or at how many seconds, the ball is NOT in the air.

The easiest way to solve this question is to simply look at the graph. You can see that any value a little longer than 3 seconds shows a value below 0. Because you can't have a negative value for height in this case, you can interpret this as meaning that the ball has returned to the ground.

Further, you can **extrapolate**, or use the graph, to predict results that are not part of the information given to you to determine that any time greater than a little longer than 3 seconds will *also* be a time when the ball is on the ground. The only choice that works is (K), or 4 seconds. Remember, you can always plug this value back into your function to double check, too.

To solve question 2, you need to change $h(t)$ to $h(t+1)$, and then solve for $t = 0.5$ and $t = 0$:

$$h(t) = -5t^2 + 15t + 1.6$$

$$h(t+1) = -5(t+1)^2 + 15(t+1) + 1.6$$

$$h(t+1) = -5(t^2 + 2t + 1) + 15t + 15 + 1.6$$

$$h(t+1) = -5t^2 + 5t + 11.6$$

Now solving for $t = 0.5$:

$$-5(0.5^2) + 5(0.5) + 11.6$$

$$-1.25 + 2.5 + 11.6 = 12.85$$

You can easily find that at $t = 0$, $h(t+1) = 11.6$. Now that you have both of these:

$$12.85 - 11.6 = 1.25$$

You know that from 0 to 0.5 seconds the ball's height has increased by 1.25 meters, so (B) is correct.

Another type of question that the Math Test may include is interpreting the rate of change of a function in particular intervals. To explain this, look at the following example.

Example

Monica is driving from Seattle to Vancouver. The graph below shows the distance traveled at every hour of her journey. The graph of her journey can be divided into three parts. What is the order of events of her journey?

    I.   Monica stops briefly.
   II.   Monica drives quickly.
  III.   Monica drives slowly.

F. I, II, III
G. I, III, II
H. II, III, I
J. II, I, III
K. III, I, II

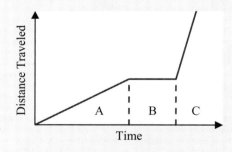

First, start by putting together the function and the real life situation. The function represents the distance that Monica has travelled each hour. If Monica drives quickly, that means she has travelled more miles in a set amount of time, and so the slope of the line is steeper $\left(\text{recall that speed} = \dfrac{\text{distance}}{\text{time}}\right)$. Similarly, if Monica drives slowly, the slope of the line is less steep. If Monica is not driving, she is not moving regardless of how much time passes, and so the slope of the line is 0, or the line is horizontal.

In the graph, you can see that section A is not as steep as section C, and that section B is horizontal. Knowing this, all you have to do is match the situation to the slopes of the line. In section B Monica is not moving. The most likely explanation for this is I. Since C is steeper than A, you know that Monica was driving faster in C. So, C corresponds with II and A with III.

The correct answer is (K).

Shapes in the (*x,y*) Coordinate Plane
Part 5

Coordinate Geometry questions require that you know basic properties of triangles, rectangles, and circles in order to determine points of these shapes in the (*x,y*) plane. You need to know specific details, like the number of sides in basic shapes, and the characteristics of angles specific to triangles and rectangles.

For triangles, make sure that you know what the terms *scalene*, *equilateral*, *isosceles*, and *right* mean. Because right triangles are involved in trigonometry, they will be covered in more detail in the Trigonometry section of this chapter. For rectangles, you need to be familiar with *parallelograms*, *squares*, *trapezoids*, and their properties. Circle questions may refer to *diameter*, *radius*, or *circumference*, so familiarize yourself with these terms.

If you need a review of any of these concepts, make sure to take a look at our online ACT Math review.

 For a fundamental review, visit **ivyglobal.com/study**.

Most of the time, Coordinate Geometry questions involving shapes will contain both the shape and a line or curve:

Example

In the standard (*x,y*) coordinate plane below, three lines, *l*, *m*, and *n*, form an isosceles triangle. If the first line, *m*, is defined by the equation $y = 2x - 4$ and intersects with line *n* at (2,0), what is the equation of line *n*?

A. $y = 2x + 4$

B. $y = -2x + 4$

C. $y = -2x - 4$

D. $y = 2$

E. $y = -2$

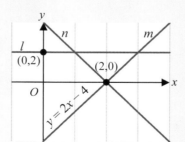

You know that an isosceles triangle has two equal sides. You are looking for the slope of the line *n*. Next, you need to find out which of the two sides of the triangle are equal.

First look at the top of the triangle. You can see that the top of the triangle is formed by the line *l*. Reading the graph, you can see that line *l* passes through (0,2) and intersects with line *m* at the *x*-value of 3. Plugging 3 into line m, you can determine that the y-coordinate of that intersection is 2. This means that line l passes through (0,2) and (3,2).

By reading the graph, you also know that this intersects line n at the x-value of 1. Since line l has a slope of zero, this intersection is found at the coordinate (1,2). This also means that the side length of l is 2. Working with line m you know that the length of its side, from (2,0) to (3,2), is greater than 2. You could use the distance formula here to confirm this, but it is not necessary in this case and would take up too much time on the test.

Since the side of the triangle formed by m is greater than 2, it is not equal to the side of the triangle formed by line l. Therefore, the sides formed by m and n are equal. The side formed by line n is defined by the points (2,0) and (1,2), so you can find its slope by calculating the rise over run between these two points:

$$\frac{\text{rise}}{\text{run}} = \frac{2-0}{1-2} = -2$$

Now that you have the slope, all you need to do is plug it into a point on the line of that side of the triangle to get the line's equation. You can pick (1,2):

$$-2x + b = y$$
$$-2(1) + b = 2$$
$$b = 4$$

Finally, with the slope and the y-intercept value of b, you can write the equation out fully as $-2x + 4 = y$, and (B) is the correct answer.

But what if you have no equations in the question? Sometimes, the ACT may give you a problem that involves only shapes in the (x,y) coordinate plane and expect you to use their properties and coordinates to solve the problem:

Example

A rectangle has vertices A (0,0), B (0,4), C (g,h), and D (j,k). A circle inscribed in the rectangle has a center L(2,2), as shown in the standard (x,y) coordinate plane below. What is the value of $\dfrac{j+k}{g+h}$?

F. $-\dfrac{1}{2}$

G. 1

H. 0

J. $\dfrac{1}{2}$

K. The value is undefined.

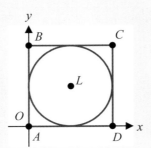

Since you aren't given x- and y-axis labels, you need to figure out the distance between the points in order to determine their coordinates. You know that the center of the circle, L, is at (2,2). You also know that the rectangle's side from A (0,0) to B (0,4) touches the circle's side, so label the diagram:

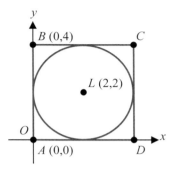

You can see that this circle is bordered by $\overline{AB}$, a vertical line where $x = 0$. The distance from (2,2) to the point that touches with $\overline{AB}$, where $x = 0$, is simply 2. You have found the circle's radius.

You know that the distance from L to *any point* on the circle is exactly its radius, 2. In fact, because of this, any rectangle with a circle inscribed in it must be a square. Since the rectangle is a square, you know that $\overline{AB} = \overline{BC} = \overline{CD} = \overline{DA}$. Since the distances of all of these sides are equal and form a square, you can fill out all of the remaining coordinates:

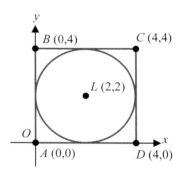

The x-coordinates for the points C and D are equal and are 4 greater than the x-values for the points B and A:

$$g = j = 0 + 4 = 4$$

Similarly, the y-coordinates of B and C are equal and are 4 greater than the y-values for the points D and A:

$$h = 4$$

$$k = 0$$

So the coordinates for C and D are:

$$C\,(g,h) = C\,(4,4)$$

$$D\,(j,k) = D\,(4,0)$$

$$\frac{j+k}{g+h} = \frac{4+0}{4+4} = \frac{1}{2}$$

The answer is $\dfrac{1}{2}$, or (J).

Graphing Circles

In the last example, you saw how different shapes can be incorporated in (x,y) coordinate space, but there is one last piece of information that comes up occasionally on the Math Test. Circles are the only shape that the ACT will expect you to know as an equation. The equation for circles is:

$$(x - h)^2 + (y - k)^2 = r^2$$

In this equation, h is the x-coordinate and k is y-coordinate of the circle's center. r is the circle's radius. For example, a circle with a center of $(-2,1)$ and a radius of 4 would have the following equation:

$$(x - h)^2 + (y - k)^2 = r^2$$

$$(x - (-2))^2 + (y - 1)^2 = 4^2$$

$$(x + 2)^2 + (y - 1)^2 = 16$$

The ACT may ask you to interpret any form of this equation:

Example

$(9,0)$ lies on the circumference of a circle on the (x,y) coordinate plane. The circle's center is located at $(5,a)$ and it has a radius of 5. What is a possible value for the circle's radius divided by a?

A. $-\dfrac{5}{3}$

B. $-\dfrac{5}{4}$

C. $\dfrac{5}{4}$

D. $\dfrac{5}{2}$

E. 5

First, you should write out the equation for the circle in the question:

$$(9 - 5)^2 + (0 - a)^2 = 5^2$$

Now all you need to do is solve:

$$(9 - 5)^2 + (0 - a)^2 = 5^2$$

$$4^2 + (-a)^2 = 5^2$$

$$16 + a^2 = 25$$

$$a^2 = 9$$

$$a = \pm 3$$

The answer is either $\dfrac{5}{3}$ or $-\dfrac{5}{3}$. Since $-\dfrac{5}{3}$ is the only answer that appears in the answer options, (A) is correct.

Transformations
Part 6

Transformations in the (x, y) coordinate plane involve altering an equation or function by moving it, changing its slope, or both. In this section, we will use function notation for all examples, but you can substitute y for $f(x)$ in all of these cases, and it will give you the same result as an equation. Note that whether it is $f(x)$ or $f(x + a)$, they can both be substituted for y. This section will show both the equations and the functions for all of the possible transformations.

If you start with the function $f(x) = ax$, you can shift the function vertically b units by adding b to the right side of the equation or function:

$$f(x) = ax + b$$

If b is positive, the function shifts b units up. If b is negative, the graphs shift b units down.

The graphs below show the function $f(x) = 2x$ and the same function shifted 3 units up:

$$f(x) = 2x \qquad\qquad\qquad f(x) = 2x + 3$$

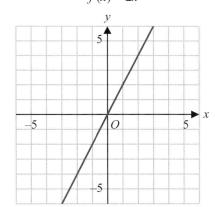
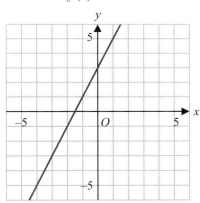

If you start with the function $f(x) = ax$, you can shift the function horizontally b units by taking the function of $x + b$. If you are asked to do this to an equation, treat it like a function, and make sure to multiply your coefficient a by b as well:

$$f(x + b) = a(x + b)$$

If b is a positive value, the function shifts b units to the left. If b is a negative value, the function shifts b units to the right.

The graphs below show the function $f(x) = 2x$ and the same function shifted 1 unit to the left:

$f(x) = 2x$

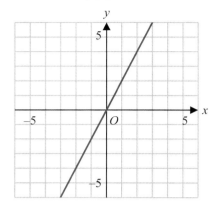

$f(x + 1) = 2(x + 1)$

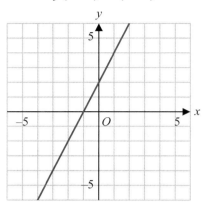

If you start with the function $f(x) = ax$, you can stretch the function by multiplying it by b:

$$b \times f(x) = b \times ax$$

This means the slope of the line is multiplied by b.

The graphs below show the function $f(x) = 2x$ and the same function stretched by a factor of 3:

$f(x) = 2x$

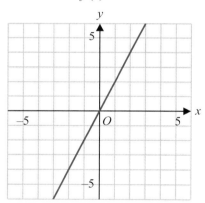

$3f(x) = 3 \times 2x$

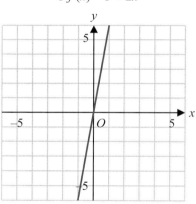

To reflect a function about the x-axis, multiply the whole function by -1.

The graphs below show the function $f(x) = \frac{1}{2}x + 1$ and the same function reflected about the x-axis:

$$f(x) = \frac{1}{2}x + 1$$

$$-f(x) = -\left(\frac{1}{2}x + 1\right)$$

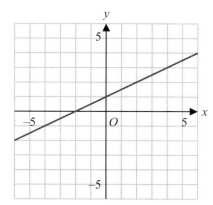
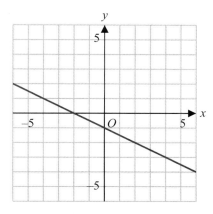

To reflect a function about the y-axis, take the function of $-x$.

The graphs below show the function $f(x) = \frac{1}{2}x + 1$ and the same function reflected about the y-axis:

$$f(x) = \frac{1}{2}x + 1$$

$$f(-x) = -\frac{1}{2}x + 1$$

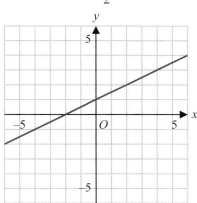
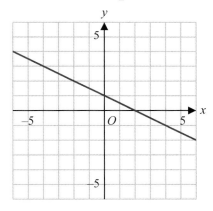

Transformations of Quadratic Functions

As with linear functions, this section will treat quadratic equations and functions as the same. Adding a constant to a quadratic function moves its vertex up or down. Adding a positive constant moves the vertex up, and adding a negative constant moves the vertex down. If you add 5 to the function $f(x) = x^2$, you'll shift the vertex of the parabola up by 5 units. If you subtract 7, you'll shift the vertex of the parabola down by 7 units:

$$f(x) = x^2 + 5$$

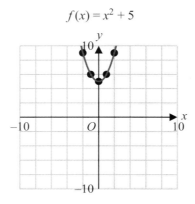

$$f(x) = x^2 - 7$$

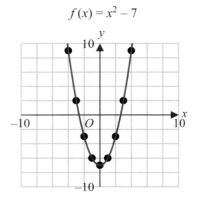

Instead of being located at (0,0), the vertex of the function $f(x) = x^2 + 5$ is located at (0,5). The vertex of the function $f(x) = x^2 - 7$ is located at (0,–7).

Shifting a parabola left or right works in the same way as shifting linear functions left or right. Remember that if you add a number to x in $f(x)$, you need to replace every x with x plus that number. Adding a positive number shifts the parabola's vertex to the left, and adding a negative number shifts the parabola's vertex to the right. If you take the function of $(x + 2)$, you'll shift the vertex of the parabola left by 2 units. If you take the function of $(x - 1)$, you'll shift the vertex of the parabola right by 1 unit:

$$f(x) = (x + 2)^2$$

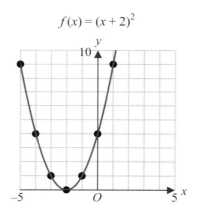

$$f(x) = (x - 1)^2$$

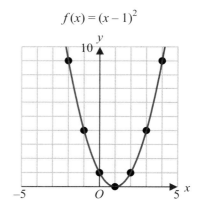

If you are dealing with an equation instead of a function, treat it the same and don't forget to add the number to the x *under* the exponent sign!

The vertex of the function $f(x) = (x + 2)^2$ is located at (–2,0). The vertex of the function $f(x) = (x - 1)^2$ is located at (1,0).

Just like with linear functions, if you start with $f(x) = ax^2$, you can "stretch" a quadratic function by multiplying the value of a by b: $b \times f(x) = b \times ax^2$. If b is bigger than 1, you'll end up with a narrower parabola. If b is a fraction between 0 and 1, you'll end up with a wider parabola. For example, the function $f(x) = 2x^2$ is compressed so it is narrower, and the function $f(x) = \frac{1}{2}x^2$ is stretched so it is wider:

$$f(x) = 2x^2 \qquad\qquad f(x) = x^2 \qquad\qquad f(x) = \frac{1}{2}x^2$$

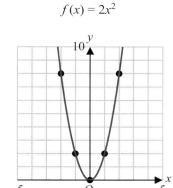 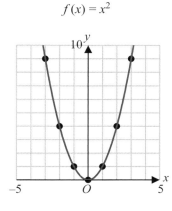 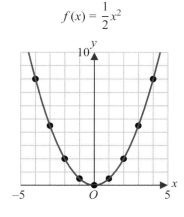

Finally, what about a negative constant? If *a* is equal to a negative number, an increase in distance of *x* from the parabola's vertex results in a decrease of value for *y*; basically, the parabola flips upside down. In other words, it's reflected about the *x*-axis:

$$f(x) = -x^2$$

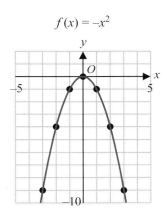

Transformations of Shapes

The Math Test may also ask you to transform shapes in the (x,y) coordinate plane. For triangles, rectangles, and any other polygons, this will only ever mean a reflection about the *x*- or *y*-axis, a rotation, or a shift. First take a look at reflections:

Example

A rectangle, *ABCD*, is reflected across the *y*-axis to become *A'B'C'D'* in the standard (x,y) coordinate plane. *A* becomes *A'*, *B* becomes *B'*, *C* becomes *C'*, and *D* becomes *D'*. The coordinates of *C* are (f,g). What are the coordinates of *C'*?

F. $(-f,-g)$

G. $(-f, g)$

H. $(f,-g)$

J. (f, g)

K. The coordinate cannot be determined with the information given.

First, it is important to see that each of the points of the rectangle become new points, so no points of the rectangle are touching the y-axis. Next, especially since there is no figure in this question, it is useful to draw the shape the easiest way possible (here, we've imagined it all in the top right quadrant):

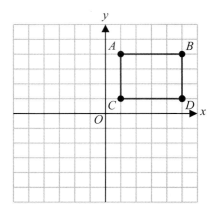

From here reflect the shape across the y-axis:

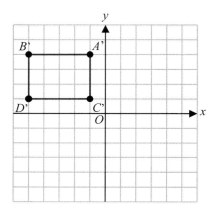

Reflecting across the y-axis, you see that y remains constant, while x becomes the negative value of itself:

$$y' = y$$

$$x' = -x$$

For this reason, C (f,g) becomes C' $(-f,g)$, and (G) is correct.

The Math Test may ask you transform the equation of a circle by moving the center of the circle on the *x*- or *y*-axis.

A circle is drawn on the (x,y) coordinate plane with the equation of $r^2 = (x - a)^2 + (y - b)^2$ and has a center located at $(0,0)$. The circle is redrawn on the (x,y) coordinate plane so that its new center is at $(3,-4)$, and *a* becomes *a'* and *b* becomes *b'*. What is the value of $\dfrac{a'}{b'}$?

A. $-\dfrac{4}{3}$

B. $-\dfrac{3}{4}$

C. 0

D. $\dfrac{3}{4}$

E. $\dfrac{4}{3}$

The circle's center is moving to the left 4 and up 3. Very simply, in the equation of a circle, *a* is the *x* coordinate of its center and *b* is the *y* coordinate of its center. *a'* is therefore 3 and *b'* is therefore −4. The answer is $-\dfrac{3}{4}$, so (B) is correct.

Vectors
Part 7

The Math Test will have one or two questions on **vectors**. These are essentially line segments that have a direction, and can be represented in the standard (x,y) coordinate space.

Properties of Vectors

Vectors are mathematical objects that have both **magnitude**, or the length of the vector, and **direction**, or where the vector is pointing. Vectors can be represented in the standard (x,y) coordinate space as a line segment, with an arrowhead indicting the direction of the vector. Here is what a vector looks like:

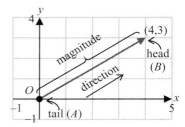

The vector above can be referred to as either $\vec{r}$ or **r**. Since the vector above has labelled endpoints, it can also be referred to as $\overrightarrow{AB}$. The magnitude of the vector is referred to as $\|r\|$; note that magnitude is calculated using the distance formula, which you learned about at the beginning of this chapter.

A few facts about vectors:

- If two vectors have the same magnitude and direction, they are identical.
- If a vector has the same magnitude but has the opposite direction, it is the negative vector of the original.
- Vectors have direction. The regular lines that you have been working with so far do not.

At the beginning of the Coordinate Geometry section, you learned about distance. The x-axis and y-axis distances for a vector segment are shown by using a special kind of bracket $\langle x,y \rangle$. In our example, the distances of the vector would simply be $\langle 4,3 \rangle$, because the tail end of the vector begins at $(0,0)$, and the head ends at $(4,3)$.

These x and y components are also called **unit vectors**, which are defined as vectors with magnitudes of 1 that point in the direction of their respective axes. The horizontal (x-axis) component corresponds to the unit vector *i* and the vertical (*y*-axis) component corresponds to the unit vector *j*. While vectors can also be represented in many dimensions, the Math Test will only ask for two.

In order to perform operations with vectors, it's easiest to break them up into their *x*- and *y*-components. The component form of a vector is written as the sum of the *i* and *j* unit vectors. Take a look again at our example:

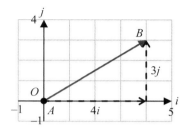

As you can see, the vector in the example, $\vec{r}$, can be broken into two unit vectors: $4i$ and $3j$. Remember, the Math Test may also represent this component form as $\vec{r} = \langle 4,3 \rangle$.

Now that you know what the unit vectors of the example are, you can find the magnitude of the vector. You find the magnitude by calculating the length of the vector's line. To do this, you can treat the vector as a line and use the distance formula introduced earlier. Here, the two points are (0,0) and (3,4):

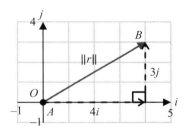

Therefore, using the distance formula:

$$||r|| = \sqrt{(4-0)^2 + (3-0)^2}$$

$$||r|| = \sqrt{16+9}$$

$$||r|| = \sqrt{25}$$

$$||r|| = 5$$

The magnitude of $\vec{r}$, $||r||$, is 5.

Operations on Vectors

The Math Test may also ask you to multiply vectors by a constant; this is called **scalar multiplication of vectors**. To do this, break up the vector into its unit components and multiply each component by the constant. From the previous example, $4\vec{r}$, or multiplying $\vec{r}$ by 4, is calculated as follows:

$$4\vec{r} = 4(4i + 3j)$$
$$4\vec{r} = 16i + 12j$$

The resulting vector would look like this:

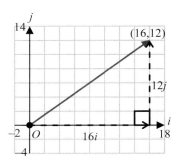

You can also add and subtract vectors:

Example

Vectors $\overrightarrow{QR}$ and $\overrightarrow{ST}$ are shown in the standard (x,y) coordinate plane below. Which of the following is the unit vector notation of the vector $\overrightarrow{QR} + \overrightarrow{ST}$?

F. $9i + 6j$

G. $9i - 6j$

H. $6i + 9j$

J. $i + 2j$

K. $8i + 7j$

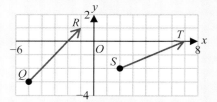

Since you are given a diagram, all you have to do is count the vertical and horizontal lines to determine the vectors' component forms. If you add each vector's component forms onto the diagram, it looks like this:

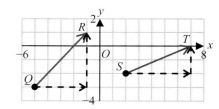

You can see that in component form, $\overrightarrow{QR} = 4i + 4j$ and $\overrightarrow{ST} = 5i + 2j$.

Now all you have to do is add like terms together, just like any other algebra problem:

$$\overrightarrow{QR} + \overrightarrow{ST} = (4i + 4j) + (5i + 2j)$$
$$\overrightarrow{QR} + \overrightarrow{ST} = 9i + 6j$$

(F) is the correct answer.

When adding or subtracting vectors, it may help to visualize the addition or subtraction. When adding or subtracting vectors, the vectors must touch head to tail. When subtracting vectors, flip the direction of the vector you are subtracting and then add them like usual, as shown below:

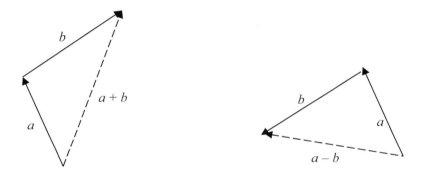

This rule is especially important because vectors have direction, in addition to magnitude.

Coordinate Geometry Practice Questions

Part 8

1. The point K is translated down 5 units and then reflected across the x axis in the standard (x,y) coordinate plane, creating the point L as shown below. What were the coordinates of point K?

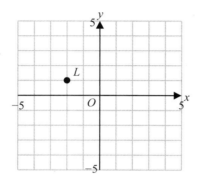

    A. $(-6,-2)$
    B. $(-2,-7)$
    C. $(-2,-4)$
    D. $(-2, 4)$
    E. $(-2, 6)$

2. In the standard (x,y) coordinate plane, what is the distance between point B (7,3) and point F (2,10)?

    F. $\sqrt{74}$
    G. $\sqrt{111}$
    H. 12
    J. $9\sqrt{2}$
    K. $5\sqrt{10}$

3. What is the slope of the line below, graphed in the standard (x,y) coordinate plane?

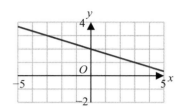

    A. $-\dfrac{1}{3}$
    B. $-\dfrac{1}{2}$
    C. -2
    D. -3
    E. $\dfrac{1}{3}$

4. Which of the following equations represents the line shown in the standard (x,y) plane below?

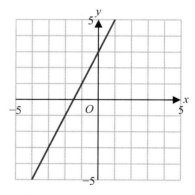

    F. $y = 3x$
    G. $y = 2x$
    H. $y = 3x + 2$
    J. $y = 2x + 3$
    K. $y = 2x - 3$

5. The equation of a line in the standard (x,y) coordinate plane is $y = 5x - 3$. Which of the following two points, when connected, would produce a line with a slope that is steeper than that of line y?

A. (0,2) and (4,2)

B. (6,3) and (4,2)

C. (0,0) and (3,4)

D. (−2,4) and (−1,10)

E. (−6,7) and (−4,8)

Use the following information to answer questions 7-8.

Line l is graphed in the standard the standard (x,y) coordinate plane below.

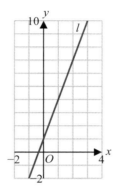

7. Line b is parallel to the line l in the standard (x,y) coordinate plane. What is the slope of line b?

A. −3

B. $-\dfrac{1}{3}$

C. $\dfrac{3}{8}$

D. 3

E. $\dfrac{8}{3}$

6. The vertices of a square are (1,1), (−3,1), (−3,−3), and (1,−3) in the standard (x,y) coordinate plane. When the square is graphed, what percent of its total area, rounded to the nearest percent, lies in quadrant II?

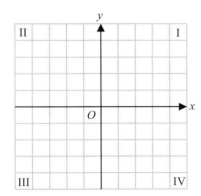

F. 6%

G. 15%

H. 19%

J. 32%

K. 56%

8. If line k is perpendicular to line l and has a y-intercept of 2, what is the equation of line k?

F. $y = 3x + 1$

G. $y = 3x + 2$

H. $y = \dfrac{1}{3}x + 2$

J. $y = -\dfrac{1}{3}x + 2$

K. $y = -\dfrac{1}{3}x + 1$

9. The vertices of a triangle are A (1,0), B (4,1), and C (2,5) in the standard (x,y) coordinate plane. Of the three line segments that make up the triangle, one line is the steepest. Which line segment has the steepest slope?

A. $\overline{AB}$

B. $\overline{AC}$

C. $\overline{BC}$

D. $\overline{AC}$ and $\overline{BC}$ have the same slope

E. $\overline{AC}$ and $\overline{AB}$ have the same slope

10. The equations of two perpendicular lines in the standard (x,y) coordinate plane are shown below. What is the value of m?

$$y = \frac{1}{2}x - 7$$

$$y = mx + 10$$

F. -7

G. -2

H. $-\dfrac{1}{2}$

J. $\dfrac{1}{2}$

K. 2

11. Three parabolas are graphed in the standard (x,y) coordinate plane, shown below. These three parabolas $F(x)$, $H(x)$, and $G(x)$ are each modeled on the function $p(x) = a(x - b)^2$, where the value of a changes to create these three distinct parabolas. If F, H, and G, are the values of a in $F(x)$, $H(x)$, and $G(x)$, respectively, what is the relationship between F, H, and G?

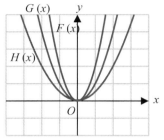

A. $F > G > H$

B. $F > H > G$

C. $H > G > F$

D. $H > F > G$

E. $G > F > G$

12. In the standard (x,y) coordinate plane there exists a line b, where b must pass through the point (2,3) and b has a slope of 7. What is the y-intercept of line b?

F. -19

G. -11

H. -7

J. -5

K. 0

13. The component forms of vectors $\mathbf{q}$ and $\mathbf{r}$ are given by $\mathbf{q} = \langle 2,4 \rangle$ and $\mathbf{r} = \langle -1,5 \rangle$. If $-\mathbf{q} + 2\mathbf{r} + \mathbf{s} = 0$, what is the component form of $\mathbf{s}$?

A. $\langle -4, 6 \rangle$

B. $\langle -1,-9 \rangle$

C. $\langle 0,-14 \rangle$

D. $\langle 4,-6 \rangle$

E. $\langle 3,-1 \rangle$

14. Points A, B, C, D, E, and F are labeled in the standard (x,y) coordinate plane below. Which two points, when joined to form a line segment, will be perpendicular to the line $y = 2x - 1$ shown in the figure below?

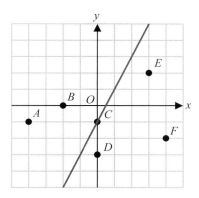

- **F.** A and B
- **G.** B and C
- **H.** C and D
- **J.** D and F
- **K.** E and F

15. A circle is drawn in the standard (x,y) coordinate plane, with a radius of 5 and a center at the origin $(0,0)$. The center of the circle was moved such that the equation of the circle is now $(x - 4)^2 + (y + 2)^2 = 25$. How was the circle transformed on the coordinate plane?

- **A.** 4 units right
- **B.** 4 units right, 2 units up
- **C.** 4 units right, 2 units down
- **D.** 4 units left, 2 units right
- **E.** 4 units left, 2 units down

16. In the function $f(x) = (x + a)^2 + b$, a and b are both positive integers. Which of the following is the correct graph of $f(x)$ in the standard (x,y) coordinate plane?

F.

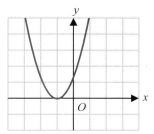

G.

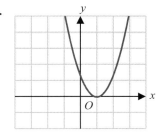

H.

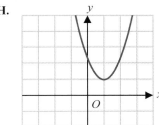

J.

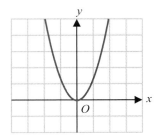

K.

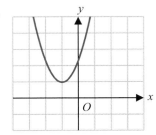

17. Vectors $\overrightarrow{QR}$ and $\overrightarrow{ST}$ are shown in the standard (x,y) coordinate plane below. Which of the following is the unit vector notation of the vector $\overrightarrow{QR} + \overrightarrow{ST}$?

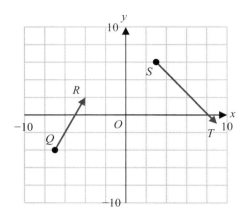

A. $-4i$

B. $-3i - \quad j$

C. $-3i + 13j$

D. $9i - \quad j$

E. $3i - \quad j$

18. The distance traveled by a particle from its starting position is recorded on the graph below. A certain order of 3 of the following 5 actions describes the movement of the particle. Which order is it?

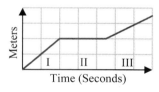

I. the particle moves at 1m/s

II. the particle moves at 4m/s

III. the particle moves at $\dfrac{3}{5}$ m/s

IV. the particle moves at $\dfrac{5}{4}$ m/s

V. the particle is stationary

F. I, V, II

G. I, V, III

H. I, V, IV

J. II, V, I

K. II, V, III

19. $f(x)$ is graphed in the standard (x,y) coordinate plane, as shown below. Which of the following functions is NOT represented by this graph?

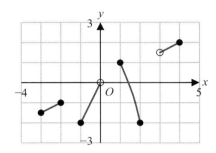

A. $y = -x^2 + 2,\ 1 \le x \le 2$

B. $y = \dfrac{1}{2x},\ -3 \le x \le -2$

C. $y = 2x,\ -1 \le x < 0$

D. $y = x,\ x = 0$

E. All of these functions are correct for the graph shown

20. Which of the following correctly represents the shaded region below?

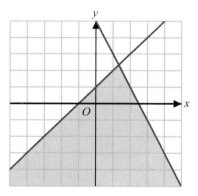

F. $y \ge x + 1$ and $y \ge -2x + 5$

G. $y \le x + 1$ and $y \ge -2x + 5$

H. $y \ge x + 1$ and $y \le -2x + 5$

J. $y \le x + 1$ and $y \le -2x + 5$

K. $y < x + 1$ and $y < -2x + 5$

Section 6
Plane Geometry

In this section, you will review the fundamentals of the lines, angles, and shapes that compose the Plane Geometry portion of the Math Test. As usual, you will have to use concepts learned in previous sections to solve Plane Geometry questions. In addition, you will learn the following new concepts:

- Angles and Lines
- Triangles
- Polygons
- Irregular Polygons
- Circles
- Basic three-dimensional (3D) shapes

Plane Geometry makes up about 23% of the Math Test, or around 14 questions. Plane Geometry questions often incorporate aspects of Coordinate Geometry, so it's important to have a good understanding of both of these sections and how they relate to one another. As with most questions on the Math Test, Plane Geometry questions will require general arithmetic and algebra skills.

Angles and Lines
Part 1

Lines

As you learned in the Coordinate Geometry chapter, a line is a straight, one-dimensional object with infinite length but no width. Using any two points, you can draw a line. For example, between the points A and B below, you can draw the line $\overleftrightarrow{AB}$—the double-headed arrow symbol denotes a line.

A line segment is a portion of a line with a finite length. The two ends of a line segment are called endpoints. For instance, in the figure below, the points A and B are the endpoints of the line segment $\overline{AB}$, denoted by the bar. The midpoint of a line segment is the point that divides the segment into two equal parts:

Point M is the midpoint of $\overline{AB}$. Therefore, $\overline{AM} = \overline{BM}$, and A, B, and M are **collinear**—they're on the same line.

Example

Points E and F lie on $\overline{DG}$ as shown below. The length of $\overline{DG}$ is 80 units. $\overline{DF}$ is 42 units long, and $\overline{EG}$ is 65 units long. How many units long, if it can be determined, is $\overline{EF}$?

A. 15
B. 27
C. 38
D. 53
E. Cannot be determined from the given information.

The total line length is 80, but you're given overlapping segment lengths of 42 and 65, which add to 107. To find the missing segment length, simply find the overlapping length, which is $107 - 80 = 27$. The answer is (B).

Angles

An **angle** is formed when two lines or line segments intersect. Angles are usually measured in degrees from 0° to 360°, and are classified according to their degree measurements:

Name	Description	Diagram
Acute	Less than 90°	
Right	90°	
Obtuse	Between 90° and 180°	
Straight	180°	
Reflex	Between 180° and 360°	
Circle	360°	

Groups of angles can also be classified according to their degree measurements.

Name	Description	Diagram
Complementary	Angles add up to 90°	55° 35°
Supplementary	Angles add up to 180°	135° 45°
Congruent	Angles are equal	60° 60°

Usually, an angle is named by three points: a point on one of the lines that forms the angle, followed by the point at the vertex of the angle, followed by a point on the other line that forms the angle. In the diagram below, ∠*ABC* is shown.

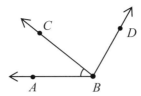

An angle can also be named by the point at its vertex, as in the triangle below, where ∠*B* is shown.

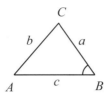

An angle is **bisected** if a line divides it into two congruent angles.

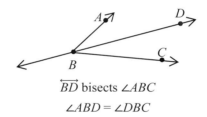

$\overrightarrow{BD}$ bisects ∠*ABC*

∠*ABD* = ∠*DBC*

If two or more lines intersect, they form pairs of **opposite** angles, which are congruent.

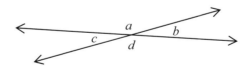

Opposite angles: *a* = *d* and *b* = *c*

If two parallel lines are intersected by a third line, called a **transversal**, they form eight angles. These angles have a number of useful properties:

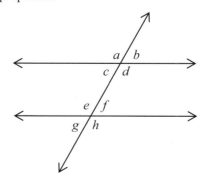

Name	Relationship	Example
Corresponding angles	Congruent	$a = e, b = f, c = g$, and $d = h$
Alternate interior angles	Congruent	$c = f, d = e$
Alternate exterior angles	Congruent	$a = h, b = g$
Same-side interior angles	Supplementary	$c + e = 180°$ and $d + f = 180°$

Example

In the figure shown below, points A, U, X, and B are collinear. Points C, V, X, and D are collinear. Line $\overleftrightarrow{CD}$ bisects angle $\angle AXY$. Which of the following statements is NOT justifiable from the given information?

F. The measure of $\angle AXC$ is 45°.

G. The measure of $\angle UVX$ is 45°.

H. $\overleftrightarrow{UV}$ is parallel to $\overleftrightarrow{WY}$.

J. $\overline{AU}$ is congruent to $\overline{XB}$.

K. $\angle WXD$ is congruent to $\angle VXY$.

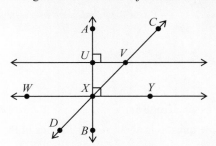

First of all, you should remember that figures are not necessarily drawn to scale. This means that any answer you choose should be justified using math and not estimation.

From the figure, you can see that $\overleftrightarrow{AB}$ intersects both $\overleftrightarrow{UV}$ and $\overleftrightarrow{WY}$ at 90°. Since the transversal intersects both lines at the same angle, you know that $\overleftrightarrow{UV}$ and $\overleftrightarrow{WY}$ are parallel, and (H) is true.

You can also see that if $\overleftrightarrow{CD}$ bisects $\angle AXY$, and $\angle AXY$ is a 90° angle, then the two resulting angles must each be half of 90°. Therefore, $\angle UXV$ and $\angle VXY$ are both 45°. Since $\angle AXC$ is just another name for $\angle UXV$, (F) is also true.

Since $\angle AXC$ and $\angle VXY$ are complementary angles, and $\angle AXC$ is 45°, then $\angle VXY$ must also be 45°. You also know that $\angle UVX$ and $\angle VXY$ are alternate interior angles, since they are formed through the intersection of $\overleftrightarrow{CD}$ with $\overleftrightarrow{UV}$ and $\overleftrightarrow{WY}$, and $\overleftrightarrow{UV}$ and $\overleftrightarrow{WY}$ are parallel. Since $\angle VXY$ is 45°, this means that $\angle UVX$ is also 45°. Therefore, (G) is true.

Finally, you can see that the three lines that intersect at point X form pairs of opposite angles. Therefore, $\angle VXY = \angle WXD$, which means that (K) is also true.

You're left with (J), the correct answer, which states that the line segments $\overline{AU}$ and $\overline{XB}$ are congruent. While they certainly *look* congruent, there's no way to be sure.

Triangles
Part 2

Before proceeding, make sure that you understand a triangle's basic properties, such as its area and perimeter, as well as the properties of equilateral, isosceles, and scalene triangles. These fundamental properties are the building blocks of many Math Test problems in geometry. Basic properties and types of triangles can be reviewed in the online ACT Fundamental Review.

 For a fundamental review, visit **ivyglobal.com/study**.

Right Triangles

Right triangles, triangles where one angle measures 90°, are extremely common on the Math Test. You can expect to see multiple questions about right triangles in the context of Plane Geometry, Coordinate Geometry, and Trigonometry. For more advanced principles of right triangles, see the Trigonometry section of this book.

The side of the right triangle opposite the 90° angle is called the **hypotenuse**. It is always the longest side of the triangle, since it's opposite the largest angle.

If you know the two sides of a right triangle, you can use a special equation called the **Pythagorean Theorem** to find the third side.

Pythagorean Theorem

If a, b, and c are the side lengths of the three sides of a right triangle, with c being the length of the hypotenuse, the following relationship is always true:

$$a^2 + b^2 = c^2$$

You can see the Pythagorean Theorem in action in the example problem below:

The hypotenuse of the right triangle △JMC shown below is 26 centimeters. The ratio of the length of $\overline{JM}$ to the length of $\overline{MC}$ is 12:5. What is the length of $\overline{MC}$?

A. 5

B. 12

C. 10

D. 24

E. 25

This problem combines ratios with the Pythagorean Theorem. Ratios are common in triangle problems, so make sure you're comfortable with them.

To solve this problem, write out what you know in equation form.

The ratio of the length $\overline{JM}$ to the length of $\overline{MC}$ is 12:5. This means that $\dfrac{a}{b} = \dfrac{12}{5}$, where a is the length of $\overline{JM}$ and b is the length of $\overline{MC}$.

Using the Pythagorean Theorem, you know that $a^2 + b^2 = 26^2$, because the length of the hypotenuse (c) is 26 centimeters.

Now you have two equations and two unknowns (a and b). Use the substitution method to solve:

$$\frac{a}{b} = \frac{12}{5}$$

$$a = \frac{12b}{5}$$

Now plug in this expression for a into the second equation and solve for b:

$$\left(\frac{12b}{5}\right)^2 + b^2 = 26^2$$

$$\frac{144b^2}{25} + b^2 = 676$$

$$\frac{144b^2}{25} + \frac{25b^2}{25} = 676$$

$$\frac{144b^2 + 25b^2}{25} = 676$$

$$169b^2 = 16{,}900$$

$$b^2 = 100$$
$$b = 10$$

So b, the length of $\overline{MC}$, is 10. (C) is the correct answer.

Pythagorean Triples

There are a few types of right triangles that have whole-number side ratios. These **Pythagorean triples** are important to memorize. Being familiar with them will help you save precious time.

- **3-4-5 right triangle**: In this type of triangle, the sides satisfy a 3:4:5 ratio. Expect to see various multiples of this ratio on the test, such as 6:8:10 or 12:16:20.

- **5-12-13 right triangle**: In this type of triangle, the sides satisfy a 5:12:13 ratio.

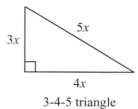

3-4-5 triangle

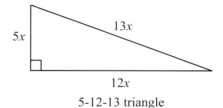

5-12-13 triangle

Example

Two walls, A and B, are built in a flat field. The walls are supported by beams that attach to the top of the walls and in the field away from the walls at the same angle. The support beam for wall A is attached to the ground 12 meters away from the wall. Wall B is 28 meters tall and its support beam is attached in the ground 21 meters away. What is the length of the support beam that holds up wall A?

F. 3
G. 6
H. 9
J. 20
K. 35

First, sketch a diagram of these two walls:

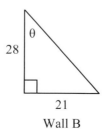

Wall B

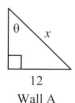

Wall A

You have sketched an approximation of the two walls. Notice that since the field is flat, each wall, its support beam, and the ground create a right triangle. Furthermore, these two triangles are similar because the angles of the two support beams are the same. Since you have most of the measurements for wall B, look to see if you can simplify and find any pattern with its two sides. Notice that 28 and 21 both have factors of 7, so it could be redrawn as:

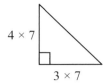

Two of the triangle's sides factor to 3 × 7 and 4 × 7. Because it is a right triangle you know that the other side must therefore factor to 5 × 7. You have determined that the triangle is a 3-4-5 Pythagorean triple. Since the triangle made by the beam in wall A is a similar triangle to the triangle made by the beam in wall B, you know that it must also be a 3-4-5 triangle, with its smallest side created by the ground.

Now you can solve for x. First, factor 3 out of 12, which gives you 4. Next, multiply 5 by the factor that you found, 4: 5 × 4 = 20. You have determined that the length of the beam supporting wall A is 20 meters and (J) is the correct choice.

Special Right Triangles

Besides the Pythagorean triples, there are two other special triangles that you should be familiar with. These triangles have common angle measures that will show up often on the Math Test:

- 30-60-90: These triangles have a 30° angle and a 60° angle in addition to a right angle. The ratio of sides is always $1:\sqrt{3}:2$.
- 45-45-90: These triangles have two 45° angles in addition to a right angle. The ratio of sides is always $1:1:\sqrt{2}$.

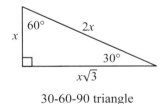

30-60-90 triangle

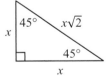

45-45-90 triangle

Polygons
Part 3

A polygon is a closed figure composed of straight line segments. Triangles, which you just reviewed, are the simplest type of polygon, with three sides. Polygons are divided into two general categories: regular polygons and irregular polygons.

Regular Polygons

A regular polygon is a polygon whose side lengths are all congruent, or equal, and whose interior angles are also all congruent. Here a few common examples of regular polygons:

- A **square** is a regular **quadrilateral** (4-sided shape), with 4 equal sides and interior angles each measuring 90°.
- A regular **pentagon** has 5 equal sides and interior angles each measuring 108°.
- A regular **hexagon** has 6 equal sides and interior angles each measuring 120°.

Area and Perimeter

The Math Test will sometimes ask you to determine the area or perimeter of a regular polygon. This will be very similar to solving area and perimeter problems for triangles.

Recall that:

- The **perimeter** of a shape is the sum of the length of its sides.
- The **area** of a shape is the measure of the space enclosed by a figure.

Example

What is the perimeter, in centimeters, of a regular pentagon with sides measuring 7 centimeters each?

A.   7

B.   35

C.   42

D.   49

E.   70

Keep an eye out for clues like "regular" in the question stem, which will give you additional information about the polygon that can help you solve the problem. Remember that for regular polygons, all side lengths are equal. Therefore, to determine the perimeter of this regular pentagon, all you have to do is to multiply the side length by the number of sides:

$$5 \times 7 = 35$$

(B) is the correct answer.

Scale Factors

Sometimes, the Math Test will ask you to use scale factors to determine the magnitude of a size change. A **scale factor** is simply a number that multiplies some quantity. For example, for the following two equations:

$$y = x$$
$$y = Cx$$

C is the **scale factor** of the equation. This same principle can also be applied to polygons. The Math Test will occasionally contain questions that require you to use scale factors to solve them:

Example

Square *ABCD* has a side length of 5 cm. Square *WXYZ* has a side length twice as large as that of *ABCD*. What is the ratio of the area of square *ABCD* to the area of square *WXYZ*?

F. 1:2

G. 1:4

H. 2:5

J. 2:1

K. 3:2

Since square *ABCD* has a side length of 5 cm, and square *WXYZ* has a side length double that (or 10 cm), you know that the scale factor between the side lengths here is 2. Does this mean that the scale factor between the two areas is also 2? Not quite! To solve this problem, first calculate the area of each square.

$$A = s^2$$
$$\text{Area of } ABCD = 5^2 = 25$$
$$\text{Area of } WXYZ = 10^2 = 100$$

The ratio of the area of square *ABCD* to the area of *WXYZ* is thus 25:100, which simplifies to 1:4, so the answer is (G).

Diagonals

Diagonals are the straight lines that join two opposite, non-adjacent vertices of a shape. The Math Test may also test a special kind of diagonal, called a **line of symmetry**, which is a diagonal that perfectly cuts a shape in two. Because they are rarely tested, lines of symmetry are covered in the online ACT Fundamental Review.

 For a fundamental review, visit **ivyglobal.com/study**.

A more common Math Test problem may ask you to calculate how many diagonals can be formed in a given regular polygon:

Example

What is the largest number of distinct diagonals that can be drawn in the regular hexagon below?

A. 4
B. 6
C. 9
D. 12
E. 18

To answer this question, you could count the number of diagonals formed at each corner, and add them at the end. However, there's a trick to this sort of problem that may be helpful to memorize: note that in a hexagon, there are 6 vertices. You can form 3 diagonals from each vertex (since you cannot form a diagonal to adjacent vertices).

However, you cannot just multiply 6 by 3 in order to arrive at your answer, because then you would be counting some diagonals twice! To avoid this problem, divide the product by 2, which will get rid of all of those double-counted diagonals:

$$\frac{6 \times 3}{2} = 9$$

So, the answer is (C).

This trick works for a regular polygon of any number of sides. Take an octagon, for example. From one vertex of an octagon, you know you can draw $8 - 3 = 5$ diagonals (as you cannot draw a diagonal to adjacent sides, or to the original vertex). Multiply this by the number of vertices, and you get $8 \times 5 = 40$. Finally, divide this by 2 to find the number of diagonals you can draw in an octagon: 20.

Special Area Questions

You will encounter other types of area questions on regular polygons, too. Some of these may require you to break up a larger area into smaller units, or to solve word problems that involve a number of different polygons.

One important note to keep in mind for word problems: real-world measurements are often imprecise, but make sure that you use the level of precision required by the question. For example, make sure that you do not round too early and then use these less precise figures in your calculations.

Example

The rectangle below is divided into one large square A measuring x centimeters on each side, seven long rectangles B that measure x centimeters on one side and y centimeters on another, and six small squares C that measure y centimeters on each side. What is the total area, in square centimeters, of the rectangle?

F. $2x + 7xy + 6y$

G. $4x + 13y$

H. $2x^2 + 6y^2$

J. $x^2 + 6xy + 7y^2$

K. $x^2 + 7xy + 6y^2$

A		B	B	B	B	B	B
B		C	C	C	C	C	C

While this problem may seem complicated at first, it is actually quite simple when you break it down into its different steps. All you need to do is to add the area of the different interior squares and rectangles to come up with the area of the whole. Remember that there is one large square A, seven long rectangles B, and six small squares C, as noted in the question stem.

$$\text{Area of } A + 7(\text{Area of } B) + 6(\text{Area of } C)$$

You know that the area of a square is the square of one side length. The area of A, a square with side length x, is thus x^2. The area of C, a square with a side length y, is y^2. Since rectangle B has one side length of x and one side length of y, its area is simply xy.

Now, plug in these values:

$$x^2 + 7xy + 6y^2$$

Therefore, (K) is correct.

You may see different variations of all of these question types on regular polygons on the Math Test, but if you apply these simple principles, you will have no trouble tackling them.

Irregular Polygons
Part 4

Not all polygons you see on the Math Test will be regular polygons. You may also encounter irregular polygons, or polygons that do not have equivalent side lengths or interior angle measures. But don't be intimidated by these questions! You've actually already encountered some irregular polygons. In the final example from the last section, you worked with both squares and rectangles—and rectangles are one example of an irregular polygon.

Here are a few other examples of what irregular polygons may look like:

Parallelograms, the second example from the left, and trapezoids, the third example from the left, are two simple irregular polygons that are covered in greater detail in the online ACT Fundamental Review. Make sure that you understand how to calculate their perimeters and areas as they frequently come up on the Math Test.

 For a fundamental review, visit **ivyglobal.com/study**.

Area and Perimeter

Determining the perimeter of an irregular polygon is similar to determining the perimeter of a regular polygon: you will need to add up the lengths of the sides. However, unlike with regular polygons, the side lengths of irregular polygons may all be different, so pay special attention to the figures. Determining the area of an irregular polygon will often require you to break the polygon into smaller, more recognizable polygons, then find the area of each polygon and add them together.

What is the area of the figure shown below, in square inches?

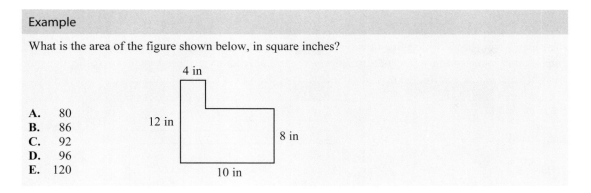

A. 80
B. 86
C. 92
D. 96
E. 120

To answer this problem, break the image down into two smaller rectangles by drawing a horizontal line between them.

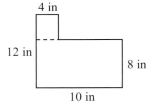

Find the area of the top rectangle and the area of the bottom rectangle, and then add them together.

You can see from the figure that one side of the top rectangle measures 4 inches. The other side measures $12 - 8 = 4$ inches as well (calculate this by taking the given long side, 12 inches, and subtracting it by the distance cut off by the drawn-in line, equal to 8 inches). The area is thus $4 \times 4 = 16$ square inches.

The bottom rectangle has one side measuring 10 inches, and another side measuring 8 inches. The area is thus $10 \times 8 = 80$ square inches.

The total area can therefore be calculated: $16 + 80 = 96$ square inches, or (D).

The Math Test will also sometimes present slightly more complicated area and perimeter problems, such as problems that ask you to compute the perimeter of a simple geometric figure where not all side lengths are given. Don't worry, though! Your approach to these will be very similar; it is just a matter of breaking the problems down into manageable steps. You will always be able to find the information you need in the question or figures, even if it takes you an additional step to locate it.

Missing Side Lengths

On the Math Test, you will also sometimes need to calculate the length of a line segment based on the lengths of other line segments in the polygon. To tackle these problems, often you will only need to use simple arithmetic to determine the missing values.

The map below shows the location of two offices in a town. If the offices lie on a parallel line to the line represented by the bottom of the map, what is the distance, in centimeters, between the two offices on the map? (Note: On the scale of the map, the dimensions of the offices are negligible.)

F. $8\frac{5}{18}$

G. 9

H. $9\frac{1}{3}$

J. $15\frac{7}{15}$

K. $23\frac{1}{18}$

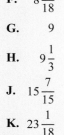

$15\frac{2}{3}$ cm

$3\frac{2}{9}$ cm $4\frac{1}{6}$ cm

bottom of the map

Even though you are not explicitly given the length between the two buildings, you can calculate it using simple arithmetic. Since you are given the length of the longer side of the rectangle, you know that the distance from the edge to each of the buildings, plus the distance between the two buildings, is equivalent to this value. In other words:

Distance from left edge of map to left building + Distance between buildings +

Distance from right edge of map to right building = $15\frac{2}{3}$

Plug in your values and solve.

$$3\frac{2}{9} + \text{Distance between buildings} + 4\frac{1}{6} = 15\frac{2}{3}$$

$$\text{Distance between buildings} = 15\frac{2}{3} - 3\frac{2}{9} - 4\frac{1}{6}$$

$$\text{Distance between buildings} = 15\frac{12}{18} - 3\frac{4}{18} - 4\frac{3}{18}$$

$$\text{Distance between buildings} = 8\frac{5}{18} \text{ centimeters}$$

You have found the answer, $8\frac{5}{18}$, or (F).

Circles

Part 5

Circles are very important to the Math Test. They come up in many questions, from Algebra to Probability. Make sure that you understand properties such as a circle's radius, diameter, and how to apply them to calculate the circle's circumference and area before you proceed. As with triangles and polygons, the fundamental properties of circles are included in the online ACT Fundamental Review.

 For a fundamental review, visit **ivyglobal.com/study**.

Chords

A chord is a line segment that connects two different points on the circumference of a circle.

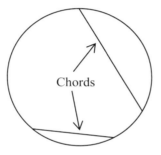

Chords

There's only one fact about chords that you need to memorize: the shortest line from the center of a circle to a chord is always found at the midpoint of the chord as it is perpendicular to the chord. If you remember this fact, chord problems are really just applications of other concepts in geometry:

Example

Chord A is drawn in a circle, as shown below. The shortest distance from the center of the circle to Chord A is marked on the diagram. All units on the diagram are in meters. What is the length of the chord, in meters?

A. 2
B. 3
C. 4
D. 8
E. 16

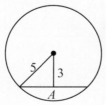

Since the distance from the center of the circle to the chord is 3 meters, you know that the 3-meter line segment is perpendicular to the chord.

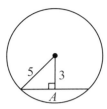

By drawing in that right angle, you can now see that you have a right triangle, with the radius as the hypotenuse. Using your knowledge of Pythagorean triples, you know that the half of the chord that's part of the triangle has a length of 4 meters.

This means that the full length of the chord is 8 meters, or (D).

Arcs and Sectors

An **arc** is a portion on the circumference of a circle between two radii that are separated by an angle (in the figure below, the angle is x). **Arc length** is the measure of distance along an arc. The area of the region bounded by the arc and the two radii is called a **sector**. Sectors are essential to circle graphs, so the Math Test will often ask about arcs and sectors in questions with circle graphs. It's important to know that an arc can be represented by its corresponding angle: for example, "a 30° arc." But an arc can also be represented by its arc length, so that very same 30° arc might be 7 meters long.

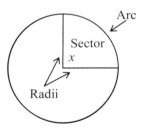

The key to solving problems involving angles and circles is ratios. The ratio of the arc angle to the total angle of the circle is equal to the ratio of the arc length to the total circumference of the circle, and equal to the ratio of the sector area to the total area of the circle:

$$\frac{x°}{360°} = \frac{\text{arc length}}{\text{circumference}} = \frac{\text{sector area}}{\text{circle area}}$$

$$\frac{x°}{360°} = \frac{\text{arc length}}{2\pi r} = \frac{\text{sector area}}{\pi r^2}$$

Shayna's Sandwich Shop sells 4 kinds of sandwiches: turkey, ham, BLT, and grilled cheese. On Monday, the shop sells 84 sandwiches. The number of each sandwich type sold is shown in the circle graph below. To the nearest degree, what is the angle measure of the BLT sector?

F.   21°
G.   60°
H.   84°
J.   90°
K.   100°

In this case, you can't calculate the actual area of the sector or of the entire circle. However, since you know the proportion of the circle's area consisting of the BLT sector, you don't need to know the actual measurements.

Out of 84 sandwiches sold, 21 were BLTs. This means that the fraction of the circle's total area consisting of the BLT sector is $\frac{21}{84}$, or $\frac{1}{4}$.

Since you know that the angle of a full circle is 360°, you can set up the proportions to finish the problem:

$$\frac{\text{Sector Area}}{\text{Circle Area}} = \frac{x°}{360°}$$

$$\frac{1}{4} = \frac{x°}{360°}$$

$$x° = 360° \times \frac{1}{4}$$

$$= 90°$$

The angle of the BLT sector is 90°, or (J).

Circumscribed and Inscribed Figures

Sometimes, polygons and circles will be combined on the Math Test. In these sorts of problems, one shape will often be **inscribed** in the other—the inscribed figure is drawn inside of the outer figure so that its boundaries touch, but do not intersect with, the outer figure. You could also say that the outer figure is **circumscribed** about the inner figure. The two phrases are equivalent.

There aren't any specific formulae you need to memorize to tackle problems with inscribed figures. If you see inscribed figures, remember that you already have all the knowledge you need to answer the question. Try out the following example:

A square is circumscribed about a circle of 12-inch diameter, as shown below. What is the perimeter of the square, in inches?

A. 12

B. 24

C. 12π

D. 36

E. 48

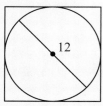

To answer this question correctly, you need to somehow connect the dimensions of the circle with the dimensions of the square.

Try drawing the diameter of the circle as a horizontal instead of diagonal line. When you do this, you should see that the diameter of the circle is equivalent to the length of one side of the square. Therefore, the side length of the square is 12 inches.

To find the perimeter of the square, simply multiply the side length by 4.

$$12 \text{ in} \times 4 = 48 \text{ in}$$

(E) is the correct answer.

Three-Dimensional Shapes
Part 6

The Math Test devotes several questions to three-dimensional geometry. So far, we've only discussed one- and two-dimensional geometry—shapes with only length, or with only length and width. Three-dimensional (3D) geometry involves shapes with length, width, and height (or depth).

A 3D shape can be called a **solid**. Some solids that the Math Test may test are spheres, cones, prisms, and cylinders. All solids have **faces**, which are its exterior surfaces. Many 3D shapes also have **edges**, the lines where faces intersect, and **vertices**, the points where edges intersect (singular: vertex).

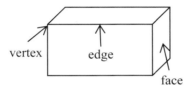

All solids also have a **volume**, which is the space contained inside them, and a **surface area**, which is the sum of the areas of its faces.

Prisms

A **prism** is a solid with two congruent polygons as its bases. The bases are joined by perpendicular rectangles. Prisms are named for the shape of their bases. The volume of a prism is equal to the area of one of its congruent bases multiplied by the length of its rectangular side. The surface area of the prism is equal to the sum of the areas of its faces. You don't need to remember exact equations for each prism if you can remember these facts and the areas of simple shapes, given online in our online ACT Fundamental Review.

For a fundamental review, visit **ivyglobal.com/study**.

Here are two sample prisms you are likely to encounter on the Math Test, along with the formulas for calculating their volumes and surface areas. The first is a **rectangular prism,** and the second is an isoceles **triangular prism.**

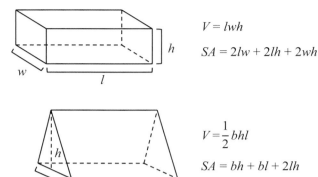

$$V = lwh$$

$$SA = 2lw + 2lh + 2wh$$

$$V = \frac{1}{2}bhl$$

$$SA = bh + bl + 2lh$$

A **cube** is a special case of a rectangular prism—all of its sides are the same length.

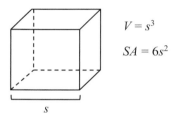

$$V = s^3$$

$$SA = 6s^2$$

The Math Test will ask you about basic properties of these solids—their volumes, surface areas, number of faces, number of edges. But it will also ask you questions that require several steps to solve—diagonals, inscriptions and circumscriptions, and dividing a surface area or volume into equal parts. These questions are a synthesis of information you've already learned in the Algebra sections, and the information you've just learned here.

Example

The shaded region is a triangular prism with isosceles triangle bases. This prism is inscribed in a cube so that four of its edges align with four of the cube's edges and its fifth edge bisects the topmost face of the cube. The edge length of the cube is 10 feet. What is the volume, to the nearest cubic foot, of the unshaded regions?

F.   250 ft³
G.   500 ft³
H.   750 ft³
J.   1,000 ft³
K.   1,250 ft³

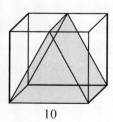

10

There are a few ways to approach this question. You could subtract the volume of the prism from the volume of the cube. You could also find the volume of one of the unshaded regions and multiply it by two, since you know that if the top edge of the prism bisects the cube, these edges must be equal.

However, the best way to solve this problem is to recognize that because this triangular prism bisects the top of the cube, the sum of the volumes of the unshaded regions will be equal to the volume of the triangular prism.

Its height, base, and length are equal to the cube's edge length, so the volume of the triangular prism is equal to the area of its base multiplied by its length:

$$\frac{1}{2}bhl = \frac{1}{2}(10)(10)(10) = 500 \text{ ft}^3$$

Therefore, the answer is (G).

3D Shapes with Circles

A **cylinder** is like a prism because it is composed of two congruent circles (its bases) connected by a perpendicular curved surface. The Math Test will only give you cylinders where the height makes a right angle with the bases.

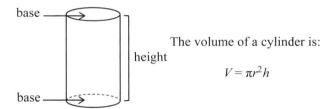

The volume of a cylinder is:

$$V = \pi r^2 h$$

You can see that a cylinder has 3 faces, 2 edges, and no vertices. Two of its faces are equal circles, and the area of a circle is πr^2, so the area of two circles is $2\pi r^2$. The other face is that "perpendicular curved surface"—and it turns out that this is a rectangle. The area of a rectangle is $l \times w$, but what are the length and width of this rectangle?

If you "unfold" a cylinder, you can see that the length of the rectangle is equal to the circumference of the circular base. The width of the rectangle, therefore, is the height of the cylinder. So the area of the rectangle becomes circumference × height, which is equal to $2\pi rh$.

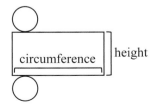

Adding the areas of these three faces together gives you the equation for the surface area, *SA*, of a cylinder:

$$SA = 2\pi r^2 + 2\pi rh$$

A **sphere** is like a 3D circle: the surface of the sphere is a collection of points that are all the same distance away from the center. As in a circle, the line segment drawn from the center to a point on the sphere's surface is called the sphere's **radius**, and all radii of a sphere are equal in length. A sphere has one face, but no edges or vertices.

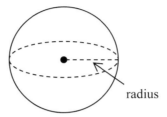

The volume, *V*, of a sphere is expressed by the following equation, where *r* is the radius.

$$V = \frac{4}{3}\pi r^3$$

You don't have to memorize this because the it will almost always be given in the question, but it's helpful to familiarize yourself with it. The Math Test won't ask you about the surface area of a sphere.

A **cone** is the last 3D shape that involves a circle that you may see on the Math Test. A cone is a collection of straight lines that move from the circumference of a circle to a single point, which looks like a triangle set up on a circle. A cone therefore has two faces, one edge, and one vertex.

The **height** is the perpendicular distance from the base to the vertex. A **radius** of the base is the radius of the circle. A **slant height** is the distance from the vertex to a point on the circumference.

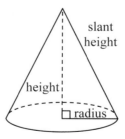

As you can see in the figure, a single slant height, a single radius, and the height form a triangle. This example is a right triangle, which means it's a right cone; this is the most common type of cone the Math Test will ask you for (if it asks you for any).

The volume of a cone is expressed by the following equation, where V is the volume, r is the radius, and h is the height. Again, you don't have to memorize it, but make sure that you are comfortable using the formula. The Math Test won't ask you about the surface area of a cone.

$$V = \frac{1}{3}\pi r^2 h$$

Notice that this equation is similar to the equation of a cylinder—a cone with the same height and base as a cylinder will have $\frac{1}{3}$ the volume of the cylinder.

Example

A sphere and a cylinder have the same volume. If the radius of both solids is 3 units, what is the surface area of the cylinder?

A. 18π
B. 24π
C. 36π
D. 42π
E. 48π

The Math Test is unlikely to give you a question involving both of these 3D shapes, and also to give you a question without also telling you the formulas for their volumes and surface areas, if necessary. But it's a good way to test your skills, so give it a try!

You know from the question that the volumes and radii of both the sphere and the cylinder are equal. You can set up this equation:

$$\text{volume of sphere} = \text{volume of cylinder}$$

$$\frac{4}{3}\pi r^3 = \pi r^2 h$$

You can see that you can cancel π and r^2 from both sides of the equation:

$$\frac{4}{3}r = h$$

You also know that the radii are equal to 3 units. Substitute 3 in for r in the equation, and then cancel out 3 from the left side, since it appears in both the numerator and the denominator:

$$\frac{4}{3}(3) = h$$

$$\frac{4}{\cancel{3}}(\cancel{3}) = h$$

$$4 = h$$

Therefore, the height of the cylinder is 4. Now you can plug this value and the value of r into the surface area equation:

$$SA = 2\pi r^2 + 2\pi rh$$
$$= 2\pi(3)^2 + 2\pi(3)(4)$$
$$= 18\pi + 24\pi$$
$$= 42\pi$$

Remember to treat terms with π in them as like terms, and don't do anything to π that you wouldn't do to a variable such as x. Your answer is (D).

Plane Geometry Practice Questions
Part 7

1. Triangles $\triangle ABC$ and $\triangle ACD$ are congruent. If the measure of $\angle ADC$ is 30°, what is the measure of $\angle BCD$?

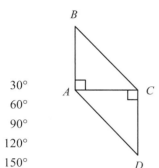

   A. 30°
   B. 60°
   C. 90°
   D. 120°
   E. 150°

2. The perimeter of a rectangular park is 1,200 meters. One of its longer sides is 350 meters long. What is the area, in square meters, of the park?

   F. 350,000
   G. 297,500
   H. 175,000
   J. 87,500
   K. 250

3. In the figure shown below, each pair of intersecting line segments meets at a right angle, and all the lengths are given in millimeters. What is the perimeter, in millimeters, of the figure?

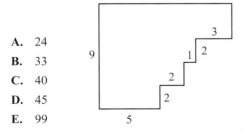

   A. 24
   B. 33
   C. 40
   D. 45
   E. 99

4. In the figure below, $\overline{AD}$ and $\overline{EG}$ are parallel. To the nearest whole number, what is the value of x?

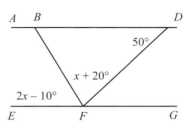

   F. 13°
   G. 33°
   H. 40°
   J. 60°
   K. 130°

5. It takes Rafael 2 hours to walk across his garden, which is a perfect circle. If he walks at the same speed, how long would it take Rafael, to the nearest minute, to walk around the circumference of his garden?

   (Note: You may use 3.14 as an approximation of π.)

   A. 3 hr 9 min
   B. 6 hr 17 min
   C. 6 hr 28 min
   D. 12 hr 34 min
   E. 12 hr 56 min

6. In the figure below, $\overline{AB}$ and $\overline{CD}$ are parallel to each other, and are also perpendicular to $\overline{AC}$. Triangle $\triangle BCD$ is an isosceles triangle with two equal legs $\overline{BC}$ and $\overline{BD}$. Which of the following pairs of angles are NOT congruent?

F. $\angle ABC$ and $\angle BCD$
G. $\angle ABC$ and $\angle BDC$
H. $\angle BCD$ and $\angle BDC$
J. $\angle ACD$ and $\angle CAB$
K. $\angle ACB$ and $\angle BDC$

7. In a 4-inch-by-6-inch rectangular picture of a basketball net, the basketball net is 3 inches tall. If that picture is magnified into a rectangular poster that measures 12 inches by 18 inches, how tall, in feet, will the basketball net in the poster be?

(Note: There are 12 inches in a foot.)

A. $\dfrac{1}{4}$

B. $\dfrac{1}{2}$

C. $\dfrac{3}{4}$

D. 1

E. 9

8. Points E and F lie on $\overline{DG}$ as shown below. The length of $\overline{DG}$ is 50 units. $\overline{DF}$ is 26 units long, and $\overline{EG}$ is 32 units long. How many units long, if it can be determined, is $\overline{EF}$?

F. 6
G. 8
H. 18
J. 24
K. Cannot be determined from the given information.

9. An equilateral triangle shares one edge with a square. If the area of the square is 64 square units, what is the perimeter, in units, of the triangle?

A. 12
B. 24
C. 48
D. 96
E. 192

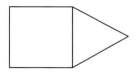

10. A pennant is a right triangle with measurements in inches, as shown below. To the nearest tenth of an inch, what is the value of x?

F. 3.0
G. 5.2
H. 9.0
J. 13.5
K. 27.0

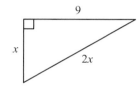

11. Zoë builds a garden for her beans in the corner of her yard. The garden is an isosceles right triangle, and its longest side is 20 feet. What is the area of the garden?

A. 100
B. 200
C. $100\sqrt{2}$
D. $200\sqrt{2}$
E. Cannot be determined from the given information.

12. The two triangles shown below are similar. What is the perimeter of the larger triangle?

F. 17
G. 21
H. 30
J. 44
K. 51

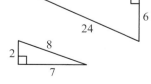

13. Three spherical balloons A, B, and C have volumes such that the volume of B is twice the volume of A, and the volume of A is one third the volume of C. If the radius of B is 10 centimeters, what is the radius of C, to the nearest tenth of a centimeter?

(Note: The volume of a sphere is equal to $V = \frac{4}{3}\pi r^3$)

A. 7.9
B. 11.4
C. 14.4
D. 15.0
E. 18.5

14. A man has a rectangular pizza with sides 5 inches by 12 inches. If he cuts it in half along its diagonal, what is the length, in inches, of the cut he has made?

F. 5
G. 8
H. 12
J. 13
K. 26

15. A line of symmetry is a line that divides a figure into congruent parts that are mirror images of each other. The trapezoid shown below has one line of symmetry:

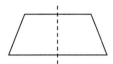

Which of the regular polygons (A and B) shown below has more lines of symmetry, and by how many?

A. A; 5.
B. A; 3.
C. A; 2.
D. B; 1.
E. Neither; A and B have the same number of lines of symmetry.

16. The 3 squares shown below each have an area of 361 meters squared. They overlap each other so that point E is in the center of square $ABCD$, point C is in the center of square $EFGH$, and point G is in the center of square $CJKL$. What is the perimeter, in meters, of the resulting shape?

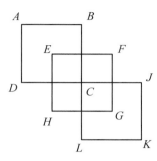

F. 152
G. 190
H. 228
J. 722
K. 1,083

17. What is the area, in square units, of the parallelogram shown below?

A. 65
B. 100
C. 240
D. 260
E. 300

18. The circle below has a radius of 10 units. If the shaded sector represents 20% of the area of the circle, what is the arc angle, a?

F. 20°
G. 36°
H. 63°
J. 72°
K. 80°

19. A regular hexagon, which is made up of 6 congruent equilateral triangles, has edges that are 4 units long. What is the area of the hexagon, in square units?

A. $6\sqrt{3}$

B. $12\sqrt{3}$

C. 24

D. $24\sqrt{3}$

E. $48\sqrt{3}$

20.

A cardboard box is 30 inches by 40 inches by 6 inches, as shown below. A store has shelves that are 42 inches high, 48 inches long, and that protrude 32 inches from the wall. What is the maximum number of boxes the store can fit on one shelf if all the boxes must face the same way, and no part of the boxes can extend past the shelf?

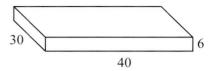

F. 5

G. 6

H. 7

J. 8

K. 9

Section 7
Trigonometry

Trigonometry is a portion of the Math Test that covers relationships between the angles and sides of triangles. In this section, you will learn about the fundamental concepts of trigonometry. This section includes many new concepts that you may not have encountered before:

- Trigonometric ratios
- Radians and Quadrants
- Trigonometric Identities
- Graphs of Trigonometric Functions

Trigonometry is the smallest portion of the Math Test, making up 7% of the test, or about 4 questions. Because there are so few trigonometry questions, you likely won't see all the topics discussed in this section. A basic understanding of the trigonometric ratios should be your main focus.

Before getting started with this section, make sure you have a good understanding of the concepts covered in Coordinate Geometry and Plane Geometry, especially those relating to triangles.

Trigonometric Ratios
Part 1

In trigonometry, the relationships between sides and angles of right triangles can be written as ratios. The following table displays the three primary ratios, where θ is the angle measure marked in the diagram. A great mnemonic for these three ratios is SOHCAHTOA:

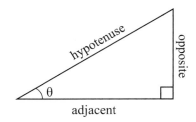

Trigonometric Ratio	Function	Ratio of Sides	SOHCAHTOA
Sine	$\sin \theta$	$\dfrac{\text{opposite}}{\text{hypotenuse}}$	$\sin = \dfrac{O}{H}$
Cosine	$\cos \theta$	$\dfrac{\text{adjacent}}{\text{hypotenuse}}$	$\cos = \dfrac{A}{H}$
Tangent	$\tan \theta$	$\dfrac{\text{opposite}}{\text{adjacent}}$	$\tan = \dfrac{O}{A}$

It's important to remember that these functions represent *ratios*, which means that the side lengths change in proportion to each other and to the angle measure. Notice that tangent can also be expressed as sine divided by cosine:

$$\frac{\sin \theta}{\cos \theta} = \frac{\dfrac{\text{opposite}}{\text{hypotenuse}}}{\dfrac{\text{adjacent}}{\text{hypotenuse}}}$$

$$\frac{\sin \theta}{\cos \theta} = \frac{\text{opposite}}{\text{hypotenuse}} \times \frac{\text{hypotenuse}}{\text{adjacent}}$$

$$\frac{\sin \theta}{\cos \theta} = \frac{\text{opposite}}{\text{adjacent}} = \tan \theta$$

In right triangle $\triangle ABC$ shown below, c has length 14 meters. The cosine of $\angle A$ is $\frac{3}{5}$. To the nearest tenth of a meter, how many meters long is a?

A. 3.0
B. 4.0
C. 8.4
D. 11.2
E. 14.0

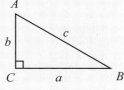

You know from the definition of cosine $\left(\text{cosine} = \dfrac{\text{adjacent}}{\text{hypotenuse}}\right)$ that the ratio of the side adjacent to $\angle A$ and the hypotenuse is 3:5. Plugging in the names of the sides of the triangle above, this tells you that $\dfrac{b}{c} = \dfrac{3}{5}$. You may recognize from the Plane Geometry section that this is a special triangle, a 3-4-5 triangle, and so side a would be the "4" side. This is the side length the question is asking for, but be careful here—a is not exactly 4.0 meters long. It's only that the *ratio* of a:c is 4:5. After all, we already know that the hypotenuse, c, is not 5.0 meters.

You know that a:c = 4:5, and you know that c is 14 meters long. You can set up a simple proportion:

$$\frac{4}{5} = \frac{a}{c}$$

$$\frac{4}{5} = \frac{a}{14}$$

$$\frac{4 \times 14}{5} = a$$

$$\frac{56}{5} = a$$

$$11.2 = a$$

The answer is (D).

For the Math Test, it's also important to know the **reciprocal functions** for each of the trigonometric functions. These each have their own names, and can be found by flipping the ratio upside-down:

Function	Reciprocal	Reciprocal Function	Ratio of Sides	SOHCAHTOA
$\sin \theta$	cosecant	$\csc \theta$	$\dfrac{\text{hypotenuse}}{\text{opposite}}$	$\csc = \dfrac{H}{O}$
$\cos \theta$	secant	$\sec \theta$	$\dfrac{\text{hypotenuse}}{\text{adjacent}}$	$\sec = \dfrac{H}{A}$
$\tan \theta$	cotangent	$\cot \theta$	$\dfrac{\text{adjacent}}{\text{opposite}}$	$\cot = \dfrac{A}{O}$

It's important not to confuse cosecant and secant. Despite the *co-* prefixes, *co*secant is the reciprocal of sine, whereas secant is the reciprocal of *co*sine.

Radians and Quadrants
Part 2

So far, we have been measuring angles with degrees. Angles can also be measured in another unit called **radians**, which measure an angle as a part of a circle. Radians are expressed in terms of π.

There are 2π radians in a circle, or in a full rotation. Since both 2π radians and 360° are equal to a full rotation, $360° = 2\pi$ radians. You can divide both sides by 2 to get the following equation:

$$180° = \pi \text{ radians}$$

You can use this equation to convert between degrees and radians. Some common degree angles translated into radians are:

$30° = \dfrac{\pi}{6}$	$45° = \dfrac{\pi}{4}$	$60° = \dfrac{\pi}{3}$	$90° = \dfrac{\pi}{2}$

The Math Test may also test you on **quadrants**. A quadrant is one quarter of the (x,y) coordinate plane. Each quadrant is also a 90° $\left(\text{or } \dfrac{\pi}{2} \text{ radians}\right)$ range of angles, and any angle that falls within a specific range is in that specific quadrant. Quadrants are labeled in Roman numerals counterclockwise from 0° on the figure below. They play an important role in trigonometry, where they indicate the positive or negative sign of the trigonometric functions of any angle appearing in any quadrants.

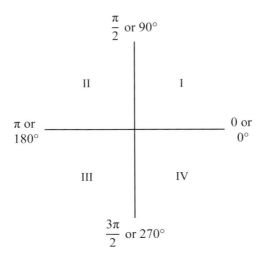

The Math Test is far more likely to ask you about quadrants than about the unit circle itself (see our online ACT Fundamental Review for more information). A handy way to remember the signs of the trigonometric functions in each of the quadrants is the **CAST rule**. CAST stands for Cos, All, Sin, Tan, and it tells you which function is positive, given an angle that lies in a certain quadrant. The following table and figure show where the functions are positive and negative:

Quadrant	Range	Positive Function	Negative Functions
I	$0 < \theta < \dfrac{\pi}{2}$	all	none
II	$\dfrac{\pi}{2} < \theta < \pi$	sin	cos, tan
III	$\pi < \theta < \dfrac{3\pi}{2}$	tan	sin, cos
IV	$\dfrac{3\pi}{2} < \theta < 2\pi$	cos	sin, tan

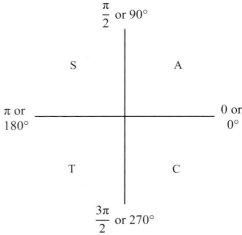

The 0° or 0 radian line is also the 2π line, and can be called either. The following example shows how the reciprocal functions follow the same pattern as the functions to which they are the reciprocal.

Example

If $\cos \theta = \dfrac{-3}{5}$, and $\dfrac{\pi}{2} < \theta < \pi$, then $\cot \theta = ?$

F. $\dfrac{3}{4}$

G. $\dfrac{4}{3}$

H. $-\dfrac{3}{4}$

J. $-\dfrac{4}{3}$

K. $\dfrac{5}{3}$

First, $\dfrac{\pi}{2} < \theta < \pi$ tells you that angle θ lies in the second quadrant. You're asked to find $\cot \theta$, and you know from CAST that in the second quadrant, only sine is positive. Therefore, $\tan \theta$ is negative, and so is $\cot \theta$. You can immediately eliminate (F), (G), and (K).

Now you need to remember SOHCAHTOA, or sketch the triangle in question. If $\cos \theta = \dfrac{-3}{5}$, and $\cos \theta = \dfrac{\text{adjacent}}{\text{hypotenuse}}$, then the side adjacent to angle θ is 3 units long, and the hypotenuse is 5 units long.

You can tell that this is a special triangle again, which means the other side, the side opposite angle θ, is 4 units long. From SOHCAHTOA, you know that $\tan \theta = \dfrac{\text{opposite}}{\text{adjacent}}$, and therefore its reciprocal is $\cot \theta = \dfrac{\text{adjacent}}{\text{opposite}} = \dfrac{3}{4}$. You know that the answer has to be negative, so it's (H).

The other way to solve this problem is to draw the triangle:

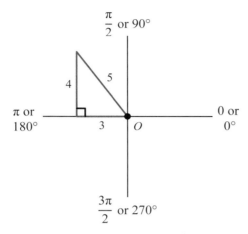

If you can picture the triangle in your head, however, you may not need to draw it out. This will save time on the test.

Applying CAST

When you work with quadrants, it's important to remember reference angles. A **reference angle** is the smallest angle that can be made with the hypotenuse and the x-axis. It makes a larger angle easier to deal with.

For example, the angle θ below has a reference angle of α:

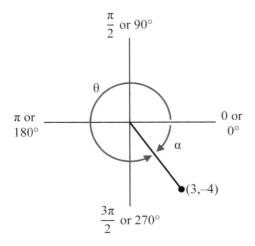

If you're asked for any of the trigonometric functions of angle θ, you can simply translate the large angle into its reference angle, then apply the CAST rule. In the triangle made with the point (–3,4) and the x-axis, the horizontal leg is 3, the vertical leg is 4, and the hypotenuse is 5. This triangle is also in the fourth quadrant, where only cosine is positive.

So in this example, –sin α is the same as sin θ, –tan α is the same as tan θ, and cos α is the same as cos θ. You can test this out by plugging in two numbers for θ and α. In this case, the reference angle and the actual angle add up to 360°, but this is not always true.

The ACT may also ask you about coterminal angles. **Coterminal angles** share the same point and hypotenuse, and have the same trigonometric ratios, but their angle measures differ by 360° or 2π. This happens because trigonometric functions are periodic, which you'll learn about in Part 4. Every time you rotate once around the circle and end up at the same hypotenuse, you have a coterminal angle. In the diagram below, angle θ and angle β are coterminal. Angle β, as you can see, rotates one full revolution more than angle θ, but ends at the same point. Therefore, sin θ = sin β, cos θ = cos β, and tan θ = tan β.

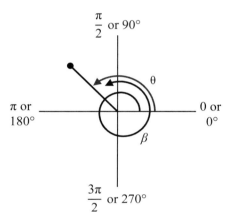

Here's a Math Test example:

<hr>

Example

What are the values of θ, between $\frac{\pi}{2}$ and 3π, when sin θ = 0?

A. $\frac{2\pi}{3}$ and π

B. $\frac{2\pi}{3}$ and 2π

C. π and 2π

D. π and $\frac{5\pi}{2}$

E. π, $\frac{3\pi}{2}$, 2π, and $\frac{5\pi}{2}$

Using CAST you know that sin θ turns from negative to positive twice, between quadrants I and II and also between quadrants III and IV. Because it is positive in one quadrant and negative in the other, you know that *on the border between* these two quadrants sin θ must equal zero. Dividing 2π radians by 2, you can determine that these occur every π radians.

You are dealing with a range between $\dfrac{\pi}{2}$ and 3π. Because the CAST circle starts again every 2π radians, you know that sin (3π) = sin (π). Careful! The question asked you to find the values *between* $\dfrac{\pi}{2}$ and 3π, so you need to exclude both $\dfrac{\pi}{2}$ and 3π as possibilities.

You are therefore left with π and 2π as the only other possibilities, and (C) is correct.

Trigonometric Identities
Part 3

If you've taken a trigonometry class, you probably learned about **trigonometric identities**: ways to write certain trigonometric functions in terms of other trigonometric functions. Using and rearranging these identities can often simplify a problem.

On the Math Test, there is only one trigonometric identity that you need to memorize:

$$\sin^2 \theta + \cos^2 \theta = 1$$

Example

Which of the following expressions is equivalent to $\dfrac{1 - \sin^2 x}{\cos^2 x} - 1$?

F. -1

G. 0

H. 1

J. $\cos^2 x$

K. $\sin x$

Often, the Math Test won't present a trigonometric identity in its most common, recognizable form. In this example, you should recognize that $\sin^2 \theta + \cos^2 \theta = 1$ can be rewritten as $\cos^2 \theta = 1 - \sin^2 \theta$ or $\sin^2 \theta = 1 - \cos^2 \theta$.

To solve the problem, you can start by replacing $1 - \sin^2 x$ with $\cos^2 x$.

$$= \frac{1 - \sin^2 x}{\cos^2 x} - 1$$

$$= \frac{\cos^2 x}{\cos^2 x} - 1$$

$$= 1 - 1$$

$$= 0$$

(G) is the correct answer.

More complicated trigonometric relationships—law of cosines and law of sines—may appear on the Math Exam. In these cases, you will be given the relevant formulae. All you need to do is plug in the relevant numbers, just like in the strange symbols section in Intermediate Algebra, Section 4 of this chapter.

In $\triangle ABC$ shown below, the measure of $\angle A$ is 51°, the measure of $\angle B$ is 37°, and $\overline{BC}$ is 12 inches long. Which of the following is an expression for the length, in inches, of $\overline{AC}$?

(Note: The law of sines states that, for any triangle, the ratios of the sines of the interior angles to the lengths of the sides opposite those angles are equal.)

A. $\dfrac{12 \sin 37°}{\sin 51°}$

B. $\dfrac{12 \cos 37°}{\cos 51°}$

C. $\dfrac{12 \sin 37°}{\sin 37°}$

D. $\dfrac{12 \sin 37°}{\sin 72°}$

E. $\dfrac{12 \sin 72°}{\sin 51°}$

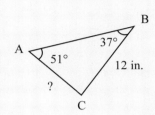

Since the triangle in this problem isn't a right triangle, you can't use the usual trigonometry techniques you've seen so far. But the "Note" gives you all the additional information you need.

The "Note" tells you that the ratio of the sines of the interior angles to the lengths of the opposite sides are equal. You are given two interior angles and one side, so you can set up the following proportion, substituting the variable x for the unknown side length:

$$\frac{x}{\sin 37°} = \frac{12}{\sin 51°}$$

Now solve for x:

$$x = \frac{12 \sin 37°}{\sin 51°}$$

(A) is the correct answer.

Trigonometric Functions
Part 4

Sine, cosine, and tangent can all be represented as functions. They all have the general forms: $y = a \sin (b (x + c)) + d$, which you can also think of as a function, $f(x) = a \sin (b (x + c)) + d$, where:

- a = vertical expansion
- b = horizontal expansion
- c = translation left/right
- d = translation up/down
- x = angle

Note that any trigonometric function could replace the function sin, used in this explanation.

You should recall the effects of changing the constants a, b, c, and d on the output of the function from Coordinate Geometry. The constants a and d change the function vertically, and the constants b and c change the function horizontally. Just like in Coordinate Geometry, b and c do the reverse of what you might expect. For example, adding c means you shift the function to the *left*, whereas adding d means the function simply moves up.

Trigonometric functions are **periodic functions**, which means that the function has the same output value at regular intervals. The length of this interval is called the **period**. When the value of b changes, the period of the function changes according to this equation:

$$\text{period} = \frac{2\pi}{b}$$

Therefore, when b increases, the period becomes smaller and the function repeats more frequently. When b decreases, the period becomes larger and the function repeats less frequently.

Periodic functions can either be even or odd. If you reflect a periodic function across the y-axis and it remains identical, then it is an **even** function. If you reflect a periodic function across the y-axis and it results in the negative value of the original function, then it is an **odd** function.

Algebraically this means that $f(x) = f(-x)$ for even functions, and that $f(-x) = -f(x)$ for odd functions. Take a look at the "Trigonometric Functions" table, following the definition of amplitude, for examples of even and odd periodic functions.

The **amplitude** of a trigonometric function is the distance from its mean position to its maximum height or minimum depth. The mean position will typically be the *x*-axis on the Math Test. Amplitude is modeled by this equation:

$$\text{amplitude} = |a|$$

Therefore, as the absolute value of *a* increases, amplitude increases, and as the absolute value of *a* decreases, amplitude decreases. The following diagram shows what period and amplitude look like on the graph of a sine function:

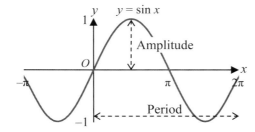

Below is a summary of the major characteristics of each trigonometric function on the Math Test.

Trigonometric Functions		
Function	Graph	Characteristics
sin(*x*)	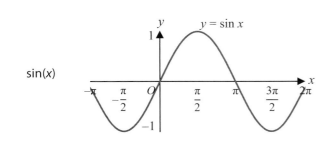	• sin(*x*) is an odd function, because $-\sin(x) = \sin(-x)$ • When $x = 0$, $\sin(x) = 0$ • The period of the function is 2π • sin(*x*) intersects the *x*-axis at every π (i.e. π, 2π, 3π…) • $\sin\left(\dfrac{\pi}{2}\right) = 1$ • $\sin\left(\dfrac{3\pi}{2}\right) = -1$
cos(*x*)	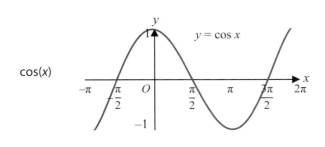	• cos(*x*) is an even function, because $\cos(x) = \cos(-x)$ • When $x = 0$, $\cos(x) = 1$ • The period of the function is 2π • cos(*x*) intersects the *x*-axis two times per period, with a cycle of π beginning at $\dfrac{\pi}{2}$ i.e. $\left(\dfrac{\pi}{2}, \dfrac{3\pi}{2}, \dfrac{5\pi}{2}…\right)$ • $\cos(0) = 1$ • $\cos(\pi) = -1$

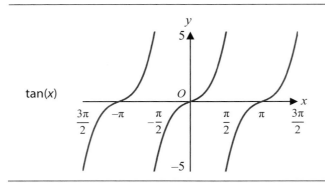

- tan(x) is neither an even nor odd
- When $x = 0$, $\tan(x) = 0$
- The period of $\tan(x)$ is π
- $\tan(x)$ intersects the x-axis at every π (i.e. π, 2π, 3π...)
- $\tan(x)$ has asymptotes at every $\dfrac{\pi}{2}$ $\left(\text{i.e. } \dfrac{\pi}{2}, \dfrac{3\pi}{2}, \dfrac{5\pi}{2}\cdots\right)$

You will also need to understand translations with respect to trigonometric functions:

Example

The functions $y = \sin(2x)$ and $y = \sin(2x - g) + h$, for constants g and h, are graphed below. Which of the following statements about g and h must be true?

F. $\left|h\right| = \left|g\right|$

G. $\left|h\right| > \left|g\right|$

H. $\left|h\right| < \left|g\right|$

J. $\dfrac{g}{h} = 1$

K. $\dfrac{h}{g} = 1$

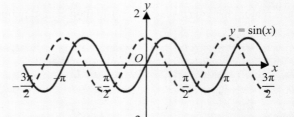

When evaluating transformations on trigonometric graphs, think backwards to what the original graph looks like. You know that the graph of $\sin(x)$ intersects the origin $(0,0)$. The translated graph does not intersect the origin, so there must be a horizontal shift. Therefore, g is nonzero. The translated graph is also not translated vertically—it didn't move up or down—so you know that the value of h is 0. Therefore, (F), (J), and (K) are incorrect. Since the value of h is 0 and the value of g is nonzero, then the absolute value of g must be greater than the absolute value of h. The correct answer is (H).

Trigonometry Practice Questions
Part 5

1. Right triangle $\triangle HJC$ is shown below, with side lengths as indicated. What is the tangent of $\angle C$?

A. $\dfrac{5}{8}$

B. $\dfrac{8}{5}$

C. $\dfrac{5}{17}$

D. $\dfrac{8}{17}$

E. $\dfrac{17}{8}$

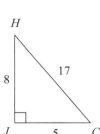

3. If $\sin \theta = \dfrac{5}{13}$ and $\cos \theta = \dfrac{12}{13}$, what is the value of $\cot (\theta)$?

A. $\dfrac{5}{13}$

B. $\dfrac{12}{13}$

C. $\dfrac{5}{12}$

D. $\dfrac{12}{5}$

E. $\dfrac{13}{5}$

2. A vertical flagpole is placed in the ground and casts a shadow along the ground, as shown below. At 3:00 pm, the sun makes an angle of $x°$ with the flagpole. At 5:00 pm, the sun is lower in the sky, and it makes an angle of $y°$ with the flagpole, where $y > x$. Which of the following statements *must* be true?

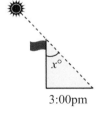
3:00pm

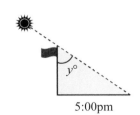
5:00pm

F. $x + y = 90$

G. $x + y = 180$

H. $\sin x = \sin y$

J. $\tan x < \tan y$

K. $\cos x < \cos y$

4. Which of the following is the graph of $y = 2 \sin x$?

F.

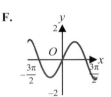

J.

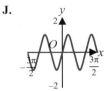

G.

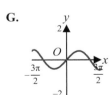

K.

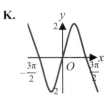

H.

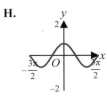

5. The hypotenuse of right triangle $\triangle XYZ$ shown below is 847 meters long. The cosine of $\angle Z$ is $\dfrac{3}{7}$. How many meters long is $\overline{YZ}$, to the nearest tenth of a meter?

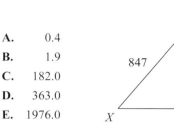

A. 0.4
B. 1.9
C. 182.0
D. 363.0
E. 1976.0

6. If $\tan \theta = 0.35$, which of the following statements must be false?

   I. $0 < \theta < \dfrac{\pi}{2}$

   II. $\dfrac{\pi}{2} < \theta < \pi$

   III. $\pi < \theta < \dfrac{3\pi}{2}$

F. I only
G. II only
H. III only
J. I and III
K. I, II, and III

7. Jessica wants to hang a painting on her wall. Her ladder is 8 feet long, and she wants to hang the painting at a height of $4\sqrt{3}$ feet. What angle, in degrees, should the ladder make with the ground?

A. 15
B. 30
C. 45
D. 60
E. 90

8. For the function graphed below on the standard (x,y) coordinate plane, the frequency f is defined as the number of complete cycles made in an interval of 2π radians. What is the value of f?

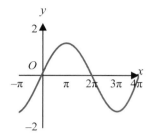

F. 0

G. $\dfrac{\pi}{4}$

H. $\dfrac{1}{2}$

J. 1

K. 2

9. If $\tan C = \dfrac{m}{n}$, $m < 0$, $n < 0$, and $\pi < C < \dfrac{3\pi}{2}$, then what is $\sin C$?

A. $\dfrac{m}{n}$

B. $\dfrac{n}{m}$

C. 1

D. $\dfrac{m}{\sqrt{m^2 + n^2}}$

E. $-\dfrac{m}{\sqrt{m^2 + n^2}}$

10. Kevin's house is situated near two trees, as shown in the diagram below. One of the trees is 127 feet from the house, and the other tree is 245 feet from the house. The angle between the trees, as measured from the house, is 22°. To the nearest foot, what is the distance between the two trees?

(Note: For a triangle with sides of length a, b, and c opposite angles $\angle A$, $\angle B$, and $\angle C$, respectively, the law of sines states $\dfrac{\sin \angle A}{a} = \dfrac{\sin \angle B}{b} = \dfrac{\sin \angle C}{c}$ and the law of cosines states $c^2 = a^2 + b^2 - 2ab \cos \angle C$.)

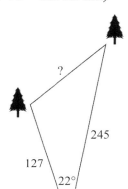

F. 127
G. 136
H. 245
J. 372
K. 508

11. A trigonometric function with the equation $y = A \sin B(x + C)$, where A, B, and C are real numbers, is graphed in the standard (x,y) coordinate plane below. Which of the following could NOT be the value of C?

A. $-\pi$

B. $-\dfrac{\pi}{2}$

C. 0

D. $\dfrac{\pi}{2}$

E. π

Use the following information to answer questions 12-13.

Sophia is cutting down a tree. The trunk of the tree has a diameter of 28 centimeters. In order to cut down the tree, Sophia cuts a triangular piece out of the trunk, as shown below. Her horizontal cut h and her diagonal cut d, measured in centimeters, form an angle θ.

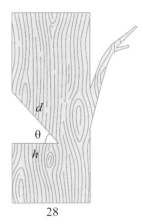

28

12. Which of the following expressions gives the value of θ?

F. $\sin \theta = \dfrac{d}{h}$

G. $\sin \theta = \dfrac{h}{d}$

H. $\cos \theta = \dfrac{d}{h}$

J. $\cos \theta = \dfrac{h}{d}$

K. $\tan \theta = \dfrac{h}{d}$

13. If $h = 12$ and $d = \sqrt{288}$, what is the measurement of θ, in degrees?

A. 30
B. 40
C. 42
D. 45
E. 50

14. Which of the following expressions is equivalent to $\dfrac{(\cos x + \sin x)^2}{1 + 2(\cos x)(\sin x)}$?

F. $\dfrac{\cos^2 x}{1 + 2(\cos x)(\sin x)}$

G. $\dfrac{\sin^2 x}{1 + 2(\cos x)(\sin x)}$

H. $\dfrac{1}{1 + 2(\cos x)(\sin x)}$

J. 1

K. 0

15. What is $\sin \dfrac{\pi}{3}$, given that $\sin(2\theta) = 2(\sin \theta)(\cos \theta)$?

$\left(\text{Note: } \sin \dfrac{\pi}{6} = \dfrac{1}{2} \text{ and } \cos \dfrac{\pi}{6} = \dfrac{\sqrt{3}}{2}.\right)$

A. $-\dfrac{1}{2}$

B. 0

C. $\dfrac{1}{2}$

D. $\dfrac{\sqrt{3}}{2}$

E. $\dfrac{\sqrt{3} - 1}{2}$

16. For any right triangle, $(\cos A)(\csc B)$ is equivalent to:

F. 0

G. 1

H. $\dfrac{b}{c}$

J. $\dfrac{c}{b}$

K. $\dfrac{b^2}{c^2}$

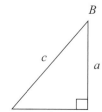

17. If $\sin x$ has a positive value, which of the following quantities must also be positive?

A. $\cos x$

B. $\tan x$

C. $\sec x$

D. $\csc x$

E. $\cot x$

18. Which of the following expressions is equivalent to $\dfrac{\sin x + \sin(-x)}{2} - 1$?

(Note: $\sin(-x) = -\sin x$.)

F. $\sin x - 1$

G. $\sin^2 x - 1$

H. 1

J. 0

K. -1

19. The graphs of $y = \cos x$ and $y = r \cos(sx)$, for constants r and s, are shown in the standard (x,y) coordinate plane below. Which of the following statements about r and s is true?

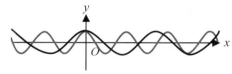

A. $r < 0$ and $s < 0$

B. $r < 0$ and $s = 0$

C. $r = 0$ and $s \ne 0$

D. $r = 0$ and $s = 0$

E. $r > 0$ and $s \ne 0$

20. The rectangular prism shown below has a length of 7 inches, a width of 4 inches, and a height of 3 inches. A diagonal is drawn on the smaller side of the prism. What is the value of the cosine of θ, the angle formed by the diagonal and the base of the prism?

F. $\dfrac{4}{5}$

G. $\dfrac{3}{5}$

H. $\dfrac{4}{3}$

J. $\dfrac{3}{4}$

K. $\dfrac{5}{4}$

Reading
Chapter 4

Section 1
Approaching the Reading Test

The ACT Reading Test is a test of advanced reading comprehension. You will be presented with a variety of reading passages and asked questions about each one. While the passages and questions will be new every time, the structure of the ACT Reading Test will always be the same. By learning about it now, you can make sure you won't encounter any surprises on test day!

The following section will cover:

- The Basics
- Reading a Passage
- Question Strategies
- Additional Resources

The Basics
Part 1

You will have 35 minutes to complete the ACT Reading Test, which is composed of three individual passages and one passage pair. Each passage or pair will be between 700 and 900 words, or about one and a half pages. Each passage or pair of passages will have 10 questions, for a total of 40 questions.

ACT Reading Test by the Numbers

- 35 minutes to complete section
- Three single passages and one passage pair
- 700–900 words per passage or pair for a total of 2800–3600 words
- 10 questions per passage or pair for a total of 40 questions

Scoring

Each question is worth one point.

The number of questions you answer correctly will be scaled to give you a Reading Test score from 1–36.

All passages on the ACT Reading Test will come from previously published sources, and may represent a variety of tones and styles. The passages will contain all of the information you need to answer the related questions; you will never need to rely on any prior knowledge about the material. The following chart shows the specific passage types that you will see on each Reading Test.

Order doesn't matter, switch it up.

Passage Breakdown

Passage Type	Topics and Passage Sources
Prose Fiction	A literary narrative based on passages from short stories, novels, memoirs, and personal essays
Social Science	Topics based on articles and essays taken from disciplines such as anthropology, archaeology, biography, business, economics, education, geography, history, political science, psychology, and sociology
Humanities	Subject matter drawn from essays, including memoirs and personal essays, from content areas including architecture, art, dance, ethics, film, language, literary criticism, music, philosophy, radio, television, and theater
Natural Science	Subjects in the natural sciences, including anatomy, astronomy, biology, botany, chemistry, ecology, geology, medicine, meteorology, microbiology, natural history, physiology, physics, technology, and zoology

The passages will always be presented in the above order. They are not presented in order of difficulty. If you know that you consistently perform better on certain types of passages than on others, you can choose to read the passages out of order, tackling the ones you are most comfortable with first. Remember the importance of Pacing strategies when working through the test!

Questions

The questions associated with the passages will assess whether or not you understand information and ideas in the text, and are able to analyze the author's argument and methods. When you encounter a passage pair, you will also be tested on your ability to synthesize, compare, and contrast information from the two passages.

The questions will generally not be presented in a consistent order, either in terms of question types or in terms of difficulty. You'll notice that every question will have a **question stem**, that is, the text of the question itself that appears before the four answer choices. Questions may be about structure, main ideas, the author's method, and more. You may also be asked specific questions about the meaning of a particular word or phrase, or about details or specific lines referenced in the question.

The rest of this chapter will introduce you to all of these concepts in more detail, and will teach you strategies for approaching the passages and correctly answering questions. Reading comprehension is something you can improve with practice; take your time to work through all of the lessons and exercises in this chapter and you will see yourself getting better!

Additional Resources

We have many additional online resources that will help you improve your reading and vocabulary.

The ACT's Reading Test will require you to understand and occasionally identify the meanings of various words in context. Understanding this vocabulary will help you not only on test day, but also in your future studies as you continue to engage with academic and other high-level writing.

One way to improve your vocabulary is to learn about word parts. Roots carry the basic meaning of a word, prefixes come before roots and alter their meaning, and suffixes come after roots and alter either their meaning or their part of speech. Because English is related to French, German, Spanish, Latin, and Greek, many of these word parts will look familiar if you know one of these languages. We have included lists that contain some of the most common English roots, prefixes, and suffixes in our supplementary materials online.

Further, you can improve your reading speed and comprehension by reading material that challenges you every day. You can find a reading list organized by grade and subject matter, also in our supplementary materials online.

You won't be asked about your knowledge of individual words on test day, but rather will need to understand words used in context. Thus, while we provide some additional vocabulary words online, don't spend hours memorizing long lists of vocabulary words! Instead, focus on building your vocabulary naturally through reading and reviewing the common roots, prefixes, and suffixes, which will help improve your passage comprehension and help you choose the best answers on the ACT Reading Test.

 For additional resources, please visit **ivyglobal.com/study**.

Reading a Passage
Part 2

You will encounter different types of passages on the ACT Reading Test, just as you encounter various types of content in your everyday reading. While we will explore how to tackle different kinds of passages later in this section, the basic strategy for reading a passage will remain the same regardless of its content.

What Makes the ACT Different?

The ACT requires a different kind of reading than what you may do in your everyday life. Normally when you read, you are focused on the content of the text, rather than on how an author has organized her writing, or why she chose certain words.

However, the techniques, evidence, and structure an author uses are all things you are likely to be asked about on the ACT Reading Test. Thus, when you read ACT passages, you need to understand their content and also *how* and *why* the author organized that content in a certain way.

Questions on the ACT Reading Test will go beyond basic comprehension to test how different parts of a passage relate to each other, the implications behind a passage's ideas, and meanings of words or phrases in a passage. Questions will also test you on the author's point of view and purpose in parts of a passage or a passage as a whole. If you are already looking for these things as you read, answering the questions will be faster and easier!

Plan Your Approach

1. **Read one at a time.** Read only one passage or pair at a time, and try to answer all the related questions before moving on to the next passage. Switching between passages will make it harder to recall what you have read.

2. **Read the passage introductions.** Read the blurb above each passage. These can include details about the passage such as its author, date, topic, and other important information to help you understand the passage.

3. **Pick and Skip.** As you learned in Chapter 1, you are free to answer questions in the order that works best for you. The reading passages are not presented in order of difficulty, so you may choose to read passages that you are best at first.

   After practicing with some practice questions and practice tests, you can determine the types of passages for which you get the best scores. For instance, if you find that you consistently score best on Humanities passages, you can always skip to that passage first when answering questions. If you do this, be sure to bubble in your answers on the correct part of your answer sheet!

4. **Read the whole passage**. You may have heard that you can avoid reading the full passage by reading just the lines each question asks about. However, not all questions will have line references, and some questions will require you to understand the passage as a whole. You will answer questions more accurately when you read the entire passage first.

One exception to this rule is if the five-minute warning has been called or you do not have time to read another passage. In those cases, you may look for a question that gives you a line reference, read that portion of the passage, and attempt the question.

Again, pay attention to your pacing. Make sure to give yourself time to *read* the passage and not just skim it! You need to understand the passage to accurately answer questions. A good guideline is to split your time almost equally between reading a passage and answering its questions, devoting a bit more time to the questions. Remember that you have 35 minutes for the Reading Test. The time constraint is tight, but manageable, and the more you practice, the better you will be at getting through passages comfortably. Refer back to the 5 Ps in Chapter 1 for more on Pacing.

Mark Up the Passage

On the ACT, you know you will be tested on the content you read, so you want to understand it as you go, rather than trying to make sense of ideas only once you reach the questions. As you learned in Chapter 1, you can achieve this by using the Pencil on Paper strategy. This will help you to be an **active reader**, by encouraging you to interact with the passages while reading them, to find and understand the information you will be tested on.

The best way to be an active reader is to use your pencil to **mark up** the passage as you read by underlining text, and adding your own notes and symbols to highlight what is important. The goals of marking up the passage are to help you stay focused, understand what you read, and make it easier to find key ideas in the passage when you refer back to it.

Use your pencil to circle or underline two to three **main ideas** per paragraph. Main ideas are those that relate to the **5 Ws:** "who," "what," "where," "when," and "why."

Let's look at the first few paragraphs from a reading passage and see how it might look if we mark it up using these strategies:

Social Science: This passage is adapted from the article "Paid Sick Days and Physicians at Work: Ancient Egyptians Had State-Supported Health Care" by Anne Austin (©2015 by Anne Austin).

We might think of state-supported health care as an innovation of the 20th century, but it's a much older tradition than that. In fact, texts from a village dating back
5   to Egypt's New Kingdom period, about 3,100–3,600 years ago, suggest that in ancient Egypt there was a state-supported health care network designed to ensure that workers making the king's tomb were
10 productive.

The village of Deir el-Medina was built for the workmen who made the royal tombs during the New Kingdom (1550–1070 BCE). During this period, kings were buried in the
15 Valley of the Kings in a series of rock-cut tombs, not the enormous pyramids of the past.

The village was purposely built close enough to the royal tomb to ensure that workers could hike there on a weekly basis.
20 These workmen were not what we normally picture when we think about the men who built and decorated ancient Egyptian royal tombs—they were highly skilled craftsmen. The workmen at Deir el-Medina were given
25 a variety of amenities afforded only to those with the craftsmanship and knowledge necessary to work on something as important as the royal tomb. The village was allotted extra support: the Egyptian state
30 paid them monthly wages in the form of grain and provided them with housing and servants to assist with tasks like washing laundry, grinding grain, and porting water. Their families lived with them in the village,
35 and their wives and children could also benefit from these provisions from the state.

Let's see how these key words helped us locate the 5 Ws for this passage:

1.   **Who** is involved in this passage?
     - Skilled craftsmen working on the royal tombs

2.   **What** is being discussed in this passage?
     - State-supported health care for workers

3.   **Where** are the events in the passage taking place?
     - The village of Deir el-Medina in ancient Egypt

4.   **When** are the events in the passage taking place?
     - The royal tombs were built during 1550–1070 BCE
     - The passage is written in the present tense and in modern English, and because the copyright dates from 2015, we can assume the discovery of the historical texts was fairly recent.

5.   **Why** is the information in this passage important?
     - The information we underlined in the first paragraph shows a surprising revelation—state-sponsored health care is an old idea. The workers of Deir el-Medina are an interesting historical example of this phenomenon.

Though it can be tempting, don't go overboard with your active reading! If you mark up your entire passage nothing will stand out as important, and you won't be able to find anything. Too much underlining can also slow you down. You may find that the more you practice, the less you need to mark up your passage in order to understand it. With practice, you will find a personal balance of active reading that works for you.

Exercise on Marking Up a Passage

Now that you've seen how to mark up a text, practice marking up the rest of the Egyptian health care passage below. This passage contains a lot of information, but not all of it contributes to the main ideas of the paragraph. Remember to stay focused on the 5 Ws! When you are finished, compare your work with the sample marked-up version of this passage in the answer key at the end of the book.

Social Science: This passage is adapted from the article "Paid Sick Days and Physicians at Work: Ancient Egyptians Had State-Supported Health Care" by Anne Austin (©2015 by Anne Austin).

We might think of state-supported health care as an innovation of the 20th century, but it's a much older tradition than that. In fact, texts from a village dating back
5 to Egypt's New Kingdom period, about 3,100–3,600 years ago, suggest that in ancient Egypt there was a state-supported health care network designed to ensure that workers making the king's tomb were
10 productive.

The village of Deir el-Medina was built for the workmen who made the royal tombs during the New Kingdom (1550–1070 BCE). During this period, kings were buried in the
15 Valley of the Kings in a series of rock-cut tombs, not the enormous pyramids of the past. The village was purposely built close enough to the royal tomb to ensure that workers could hike there on a weekly basis. These
20 workmen were not what we normally picture when we think about the men who built and decorated ancient Egyptian royal tombs— they were highly skilled craftsmen. The workmen at Deir el-Medina were given a
25 variety of amenities afforded only to those with the craftsmanship and knowledge necessary to work on something as important as the royal tomb. The village was allotted extra support: the Egyptian state
30 paid them monthly wages in the form of

grain and provided them with housing and servants to assist with tasks like washing laundry, grinding grain, and porting water. Their families lived with them in the village,
35 and their wives and children could also benefit from these provisions from the state.

Among these texts are numerous daily records detailing when and why individual workmen were absent from work. Nearly
40 one-third of these absences occur when a workman was too sick to work. Yet, monthly ration distributions from Deir el-Medina are consistent enough to indicate that these workmen were paid even if they were out
45 sick for several days. These texts also identify a workman on the crew designated as the _swnw_, physician. The physician was given an assistant and both were allotted days off to prepare medicine and take care of
50 colleagues. The Egyptian state even gave the physician extra rations as payment for his services to the community of Deir el-Medina.

This physician would have most likely treated the workmen with remedies and
55 incantations found in his medical papyrus. About a dozen extensive medical papyri have been identified from ancient Egypt, including one set from Deir el-Medina. These texts were a kind of reference book for
60 the ancient Egyptian medical practitioner, listing individual treatments for a variety of ailments. The longest of these, Papyrus Ebers, contains over 800 treatments covering anything from eye problems to digestive

disorders. Just like today, some of these ancient Egyptian medical treatments required expensive and rare ingredients that limited who could actually afford to be treated, but the most frequent ingredients found in these texts tended to be common household items like honey and grease. One text from Deir el-Medina indicates that the state rationed out common ingredients to a few men in the workforce so that they could be shared among the workers.

Despite paid sick leave, medical rations, and a state-supported physician, it is clear that in some cases the workmen were actually working through their illnesses. For example, in one text, the workman Merysekhmet attempted to go to work after being sick. The text tells us that he descended to the King's Tomb on two consecutive days, but was unable to work. He then hiked back to the village of Deir el-Medina where he stayed for the next ten days until he was able to work again. Though short, these hikes were steep: the trip from Deir el-Medina to the royal tomb involved an ascent greater than climbing to the top of the Great Pyramid. Merysekhmet's movements across the Theban valleys were likely at the expense of his own health. This suggests that sick days and medical care were not magnanimous gestures of the Egyptian state, but were rather calculated health care provisions designed to ensure that men like Merysekhmet were healthy enough to work.

In cases where these provisions from the state were not enough, the residents of Deir el-Medina turned to each other. Personal letters from the site indicate that family members were expected to take care of each other by providing clothing and food, especially when a relative was sick. These documents show us that caretaking was a reciprocal relationship between direct family members, regardless of gender or age. Children were expected to take care of both parents just as parents were expected to take care of all of their children. When family members neglected these responsibilities, there were financial and social consequences. In her will, the villager Naunakhte indicates that even though she was a dedicated mother to all of her children, four of them abandoned her in her old age. She admonishes them and disinherits them from her will, punishing them financially, but also shaming them in a public document made in front of the most senior members of the Deir el-Medina community.

This shows us that health care at Deir el-Medina was a system with overlying networks of care provided through the state and the community. While workmen counted on the state for paid sick leave, a physician, and even medical ingredients, they were equally dependent on their loved ones for the care necessary to thrive in ancient Egypt.

Summarize

Another good way to be an active reader is to **summarize** as you read. Summarizing helps ensure that you understand what you read, and that you stay focused throughout the passage rather than "zoning out." This way you can avoid the dreaded feeling of finishing a passage and wondering what you just read!

Summarizing also makes long passages easier to manage. Breaking passages up into smaller pieces to analyze is easier than trying to make sense of the entire passage all at the end.

As you read, make a summary after each paragraph. Use the words you have underlined to help you. Your summaries should be short and snappy and cover only main ideas, not details or specific examples. Try to keep your summaries three to six words long, like a newspaper headline. Summarize in your own words; doing so helps you to understand the paragraph, and remember key information.

At the end of the passage you can combine these short summaries to come up with a brief summary of the entire passage. After you're comfortable with this strategy and are ready to start doing practice tests, you can choose to make your summaries in your head to save time, rather than writing them down.

Let's refer back to our passage about Egyptian health care and see how we could summarize the main ideas in the second paragraph.

Example

> The village of Deir el-Medina was built for the workmen who made the royal tombs during the New Kingdom (1550–1070 BCE).
> During this period, kings were buried in the
> 15 Valley of the Kings in a series of rock-cut tombs, not the enormous pyramids of the past. The village was purposely built close enough to the royal tomb to ensure that workers could hike there on a weekly basis.
> 20 These workmen were not what we normally picture when we think about the men who built and decorated ancient Egyptian royal tombs—they were highly skilled craftsmen.
>
> The workmen at Deir el-Medina were given a
> 25 variety of amenities afforded only to those with the craftsmanship and knowledge necessary to work on something as important as the royal tomb. The village was allotted extra support: the Egyptian state paid them
> 30 monthly wages in the form of grain and provided them with housing and servants to assist with tasks like washing laundry, grinding grain, and porting water. Their families lived with them in the village, and
> 35 their wives and children could also benefit from these provisions from the state.

While there is a lot of information in this paragraph, the most important idea is about how the workers at Deir el-Medina were treated. The village itself was built for the workers in a convenient location, and they were provided extra support for non-work activities. To capture this we might write something as simple as "Workers supported by state." You might also choose to abbreviate proper names mentioned in a passage, so another summary for this paragraph might read "DeM workers supported."

Exercise on Summarizing

Now that you've seen how to make a good summary, you can practice with the rest of the Egyptian worker passage. Remember to keep your summaries short! The first three paragraphs have summaries. Write your own summaries for paragraphs three through seven, and compare them to the answer key at the end of this book.

Social Science: This passage is adapted from the article "Paid Sick Days and Physicians at Work: Ancient Egyptians Had State-Supported Health Care" by Anne Austin (©2015 by Anne Austin).

(1) State health care old idea
> We might think of state-supported health care as an innovation of the 20th century, but it's a much older tradition than that. In fact, texts from a village dating back
> 5 to Egypt's New Kingdom period, about 3,100–3,600 years ago, suggest that in ancient Egypt there was a state-supported health care network designed to ensure that workers making the king's tomb were
> 10 productive.

(1 fr cc

> The village of Deir el-Medina was built for the workmen who made the royal tombs during the New Kingdom (1550–1070 BCE). During this period, kings were buried in the
> 15 Valley of the Kings in a series of rock-cut tombs, not the enormous pyramids of the past.

(2 or pa

The village was purposely built close enough to the royal tomb to ensure that workers could hike there on a weekly basis. These workmen were not what we normally picture when we think about the men who built and decorated ancient Egyptian royal tombs—they were highly skilled craftsmen. The workmen at Deir el-Medina were given a variety of amenities afforded only to those with the craftsmanship and knowledge necessary to work on something as important as the royal tomb. The village was allotted extra support: the Egyptian state paid them monthly wages in the form of grain and provided them with housing and servants to assist with tasks like washing laundry, grinding grain, and porting water. Their families lived with them in the village, and their wives and children could also benefit from these provisions from the state.

Among these texts are numerous daily records detailing when and why individual workmen were absent from work. Nearly one-third of these absences occur when a workman was too sick to work. Yet, monthly ration distributions from Deir el-Medina are consistent enough to indicate that these workmen were paid even if they were out sick for several days. These texts also identify a workman on the crew designated as the *swnw*, physician. The physician was given an assistant and both were allotted days off to prepare medicine and take care of colleagues. The Egyptian state even gave the physician extra rations as payment for his services to the community of Deir el-Medina.

This physician would have most likely treated the workmen with remedies and incantations found in his medical papyrus. About a dozen extensive medical papyri have been identified from ancient Egypt, including one set from Deir el-Medina. These texts were a kind of reference book for the ancient Egyptian medical practitioner, listing individual treatments for a variety of ailments. The longest of these, Papyrus Ebers, contains over 800 treatments covering anything from eye problems to digestive disorders. Just like today, some of these

ancient Egyptian medical treatments required expensive and rare ingredients that limited who could actually afford to be treated, but the most frequent ingredients found in these texts tended to be common household items like honey and grease. One text from Deir el-Medina indicates that the state rationed out common ingredients to a few men in the workforce so that they could be shared among the workers.

Despite paid sick leave, medical rations, and a state-supported physician, it is clear that in some cases the workmen were actually working through their illnesses. For example, in one text, the workman Merysekhmet attempted to go to work after being sick. The text tells us that he descended to the King's Tomb on two consecutive days, but was unable to work. He then hiked back to the village of Deir el-Medina where he stayed for the next ten days until he was able to work again. Though short, these hikes were steep: the trip from Deir el-Medina to the royal tomb involved an ascent greater than climbing to the top of the Great Pyramid. Merysekhmet's movements across the Theban valleys were likely at the expense of his own health. This suggests that sick days and medical care were not magnanimous gestures of the Egyptian state, but were rather calculated health care provisions designed to ensure that men like Merysekhmet were healthy enough to work.

In cases where these provisions from the state were not enough, the residents of Deir el-Medina turned to each other. Personal letters from the site indicate that family members were expected to take care of each other by providing clothing and food, especially when a relative was sick. These documents show us that caretaking was a reciprocal relationship between direct family members, regardless of gender or age. Children were expected to take care of both parents just as parents were expected to take care of all of their children. When family members neglected these responsibilities, there were financial and social consequences. In her will, the villager Naunakhte indicates

[Handwritten margin notes:]
DeM workers supported
(3)
physician treated workmen (4)
(4) Cont. from prev. column
w/ home remedies like honey & grease.
Some workers continued w/ out care. (5)
Family is expected to take care of one another. (6)

People could be financially punished.

(6)... Continued

115 that even though she was a dedicated mother to all of her children, four of them abandoned her in her old age. She admonishes them and disinherits them from her will, punishing them financially, but also shaming them in a
120 public document made in front of the most senior members of the Deir el-Medina community.

This shows us that health care at Deir el-Medina was a system with overlying
125 networks of care provided through the state and the community. While workmen counted on the state for paid sick leave, a physician, and even medical ingredients, they were equally dependent on their loved ones for the
130 care necessary to thrive in ancient Egypt.

(7)

Paid sick leave & family care were just as important.

Question Strategies
Part 3

Now that you've learned how to approach ACT passages and have read about types of passages you'll see, let's learn more about the questions. In this part, you will learn general strategies for approaching questions, such as referring back to the passage and eliminating clearly wrong answer choices. Later on, you'll get to strategies for specific question types.

You can answer every question on the ACT Reading Test with information from the passage. Don't answer the questions using outside knowledge or opinions. Applying all the strategies you learned for understanding passages is the first step to answering questions quickly and correctly. Make sure you're comfortable with the strategies from earlier in this chapter, and then keep reading for more approaches to help you conquer reading questions.

Reading and Answering the Questions

When you approach a question, read the question stem fully, making sure you understand what exactly it is asking you to identify about the passage.

Most questions will ask you for something that is correct based on the passage or information given. For example, consider these question stems:

"The author states that Mars' atmosphere is…"
"According to the passage, which of the following choices reflects Brontë's early life?"

Make sure to watch out for EXCEPT and NOT questions. Some questions will be phrased to ask you to select the answer choice that is incorrect based on the passage or information given; examples of this format include question stems such as:

"In the passage, all of the following are associated with escalators EXCEPT…"
"Which of the following are NOT mentioned by the passage as a factor in the main character's decision to move cities?"

These questions will always be clearly marked by the word "EXCEPT" or "NOT" appearing in the question stem in capital letters. Still, watch for them closely, and remember when you see them that you are looking for the one answer choice that is incorrect; the three wrong answer choices will actually be true based on information from the passage!

Most questions on the ACT will test your understanding of information explicitly stated in the passage. Some questions will require making **inferences**. Inferences are conclusions that you can draw by combining information from different parts of the passage, or by reading between the lines to make deductions about things that are implied, but not stated directly in the text. Inferences are not guesses; they are still always based on information from the passage.

For now, just be aware that inferences figure in some questions on the ACT. We will get to more about inferences, particularly for question types that feature inferences more prominently, when we reach the sections on strategies for specific question types.

Refer Back to the Passage

For every question, the correct answer will either be based on something stated explicitly in the passage, or on something that can be inferred by reading between the lines of the text.

Take advantage of the fact that on the ACT Reading Test, you can refer back to the material you are being asked about! Don't answer the questions by memory alone, and don't rely on your own knowledge or opinion of the subject, which might lead you to the wrong answer. Instead, look back at the passage. You should always be able to support your answer choice with specific lines or words in the text, even if none are specified in the question.

Some questions use **specific references** to indicate which part of the passage they are asking you about, such as a line or a certain paragraph. When you are given a line reference, always return to the passage to review that line, as well as two to three lines before and after the one you are asked about. When you are given a paragraph reference, always return to the passage to read or skim that paragraph. This helps you understand the context of the question, and find clues there that will help you choose the correct answer.

Let's see how this works with a line reference question for a sample passage.

Example

Social Science: The following is an excerpt adapted from the article "How the First 'Horse Race' Poll Changed American Political History" by Edwin Amenta (©2015 by Edwin Amenta).

In the spring of 1935, President Franklin D. Roosevelt was worried about his reelection. He was especially concerned about Louisiana Senator Huey Long. Long
5 and his organization were garnering media attention—"Candidate Long" appeared on the April 1 cover of *Time*. Though a Democrat, Long planned to run against Roosevelt as an independent, and was ready
10 for a long game.

In April 1935, Democratic National Committee chief and Roosevelt campaign manager James Farley called on Emil Hurja, who had done some in-house polling for
15 Farley in the 1934 congressional election cycle to ascertain Long's potential as a spoiler. Hurja was a private stock analyst who was a self-taught pollster and used sampling principles to adjust the unscientific
20 surveys taken by popular magazines.

Hurja devised sample ballot postcards asking whom the public would support in the upcoming election: President Roosevelt, an unnamed "Republican Candidate," or Senator Long.

Once the ballots were in, the results were shocking. Hurja's estimates gave Roosevelt 49% of the popular vote, with the unnamed Republican at 43% and Long at 7%. Roosevelt's team feared that a swing of a few percentage points away from Roosevelt would flip tossup states like Iowa and Minnesota—and the election.

But the first horse race poll's premises were faulty, and its results dubious. Not naming a specific candidate inflated the Republican's totals. Worse, by using a very primitive "likely voter" model, Hurja completely discounted the ballots of recipients of relief programs such as welfare, who were numerous and sharply in favor of Roosevelt, whereas richer Americans opposed him. Moreover, experience has since shown that third-party candidates do much better in polls than in elections.

Had all that been taken into account, the results would have indicated an easy Roosevelt victory. Indeed, that is what Farley was predicting and what happened.

The author mentions that "'Candidate Long' appeared on the April 1 cover of *Time*" (lines 6–7) to suggest that:

A. *Time* predicted that Long would win the election.

B. Long was planning to run against Roosevelt for the Democratic nomination.

C. Roosevelt's team had used a faulty polling method.

D. Long was gaining prominence as a potential presidential contender.

You may not remember this line from the passage, but if you refer back to the text, you can easily answer this question.

If you read the lines referenced and skim the two lines above and below it, you learn Roosevelt was worried about competing against Huey Long in the presidential election, and that Long was ready for a "long game" in his fight to win. These lines, and the mention of Long appearing on *Time* magazine's cover, suggest that Long was starting to be seen as a strong contender for the presidency. Only answer choice (D) matches the passage, and is the correct answer.

Notice that even though you are asked about lines 6–7, it is the surrounding lines that provide you with the context needed to understand the purpose of this reference, and thus choose the correct answer.

The other answer choices are all wrong for different reasons. Recall the wrong answer types from the Process of Elimination strategy in Chapter 1. (A) is an irrelevant answer choice; while it may be possible, there is no evidence in the passage to support it. (B) contradicts the passage, as the first paragraph states that Long was planning to run as an independent; it is therefore a confused content answer choice. (C) is true of the passage, but the directed line about Long on the cover of *Time* does not have to do with Roosevelt's team's faulty polling strategy; it is therefore an out-of-scope answer choice.

When you answer questions that do not provide line references, you should still refer back to the passage. Look at the information mentioned in the question stem, and try to find parts of the passage related to that information. If you have marked up your passage, you will likely know where to find the evidence you need. If a question asks you something general about the passage, you can refer back to the summaries you made while reading and to any notes you made in the margins.

Selecting Your Answers

Now that you have learned how to effectively read passages and questions, you are ready to tackle some different techniques for answering questions. Make sure to always refer back to the passage when selecting your answer choices!

Prediction

One of the best ways to answer reading questions is by **predicting** your answer before reading the choices. Once you read a question, try to come up with your own response. How would you put the answer in your own words? You can cover up the answer choices as you think of your phrasing for the answer. While this technique is simple, it has huge benefits when used consistently.

Once you have come up with your answer, check the choices: does any one stick out to you as a good match? This strategy will help you avoid the temptation of picking a wrong, tricky answer choice.

Let's practice using this technique with a question from a passage excerpt.

Example

Humanities: The following is an excerpt adapted from writer Andy Martin's personal essay "The Man with No Plot: How I Watched Lee Child Write a Jack Reacher Novel" (©2015 by Andy Martin).

Nobody really believes him when he says it. But Lee Child is fundamentally clueless when he starts writing. He really is. He has no idea what he is doing or where he
5   is going. And the odd thing is he likes it that way. The question is: Why? I mean, most of us like to have some kind of idea where we are heading, roughly, a hypothesis at least to guide us, even if we are not sticking
10   maps on the wall. Whereas he, in contrast, embraces the feeling of just falling off a cliff into the void and relying on some kind of miraculous soft landing.

When I had this idea of writing a book
15   about a novelist working on a story from beginning to end, Lee Child was the first writer I thought of. He has always struck me as a blessed (and I don't mean by that successful) and exemplary incarnation of
20   what Borges called "the spirit of literature." He is, more than anyone I can think of, a pure writer, with a degree zero style. Maybe sub-zero. He doesn't plan. He doesn't premeditate. He loves to be spontaneous. I
25   noticed this right away when he immediately agreed to meet about my book, and then added nonchalantly about his own book, "I have no plot and no title. Nothing."

When I got there, on September 1 of last
30   year, to his apartment on the Upper West Side of Manhattan, overlooking Central Park, all he had was sublime confidence. And a title, which he had come up with the night before: Make Me. He just liked the sound of it.

The primary purpose of the passage is to:

Let's pause at the question stem. Based on your summaries and marking of the passage, what do you think it was trying to do? The excerpt explains how Lee Child, unlike most other writers, goes into writing his literary works without a plan. It then discusses the author of the passage's visit to Child, and how Child had spontaneously come up with a title for his new work.

We might summarize that as "explaining Lee Child's unique writing strategy." Now let's look for an answer choice that matches our prediction.

Does one answer choice jump out at you right away? (G) matches almost exactly what you predicted! The other options can be ruled out: (F) is out-of-scope, since the narrator's relationship to Lee Child is not the main purpose of the passage. (H) is confused, as the passage actually notes that Lee Chld does not rely on planning, while (J) is irrelevant.

Doing the mental work of answering the question in your own words pays off when you can make your choice and gain a point so quickly.

Process of Elimination

If you are unsure of an answer, you may want to use the **Process of Elimination,** which you learned about in Chapter 1. Because there is only one correct answer for each question, it is helpful to eliminate the choices you know are wrong. Consider every answer option as you work through questions, knocking out obviously wrong answers and leaving everything else "open" before going back to choose the correct answer.

Make sure you only eliminate answer choices you are certain are wrong—either because they are directly contradicted by the passage, or because there is no information in the passage to support them. After you eliminate these clearly wrong answer choices, you can focus on choosing the correct answer choice. Next, eliminate tempting answer choices that misconstrue or incorrectly attribute information in the passage. You can eliminate answers by crossing them out in your test booklet.

Let's put this to use with a sample passage and question.

Prose Fiction: The following is an excerpt adapted from a story called "Chemistry of Sacrifice" by Craig Bernardini, about his mother's life as a first-generation immigrant in America (©2016 by Craig Bernardini).

Eighteen years before, my mother stopped practicing medicine. She had conceded that raising children and working at the hospital were not compatible, at least
5 with the devotion she believed each deserved. Now, children fled or fleeing the nest, she studied to go back.

She was sitting outside my high school in our old yellow Firebird, the car that
10 we shared. A big, heavy clothbound medical textbook lay open on her lap. Instead of reading, she did a simple arithmetic problem over and over in her head: twenty-seven plus twenty-seven, the age at which she arrived
15 in the United States plus the number of years she has resided here. She thinks: *After this year, I will have been* here *longer than I was* there. *After this year, I will be more of* this, *less of* that. From motherland to adopted
20 one, mother tongue to second language. That year, at some unforeseeable moment, she would have moved far enough from the fulcrum upon which her life balanced to tilt it irredeemably toward the *yanqui.* That
25 year, she would have felt the pull of time like a riptide.

I imagined her taking our car and driving through the swamps of Colombia, the cordillera of the Andes, the steppes of
30 Bolivia—south, ever south, until she can smell the dry, hot plains of her native Santa Fe. And then south again, into the pampas,

the battalions of cattle, south, until she sees the tip of another obelisk pointing over a
35 mythic Argentinian skyline. Home.

But no. She pulled on her driving gloves, her suit and cap rolled in a towel on the back seat, drives one, two, maybe three exits before doing a one-eighty across the
40 grass median. She goes to the Y. Running in circles, biking in place, swimming laps, caught in medicine, marriage, family, each enfolded inside the other, all the chemistry of sacrifice. And so the year passes,
45 mornings at the Y, just like the one before, just like the one after.

Ten years later, my mother was sworn in as a U.S. citizen. On that day, she pledged to put first the U.S., a country that in her
50 heart had always been second. But so it had been all her life, putting second things first, sacrifice, every step of the way. By the time she raised her right hand in that stadium full of smiling Americans-to-be, she had already
55 been a *yanqui* for a decade.

According to the passage, at the time of the story, the narrator's mother:

A. is embarking immediately upon a move to her native Argentina.

B. is happy to live in the U.S. and has made a clean break from Argentina.

C. has made the choice to live in the U.S. but is also attached to Argentina.

D. plans to live five more years in the U.S. before returning to Argentina.

The answer choices deal with the narrator's mother's decisions and feelings about her living situation. Refer back to the passage, and look for information about the narrator's mother's living situation and feelings about where she lives.

(A) misconstrues a part of the passage, where the narrator envisions his mother driving immediately to Argentina. This is just an imagined event, so you can knock (A) out. (B) is incorrect, as the passage characterizes the mother as conflicted, rather than happy, about her life in the U.S.. The mother also has not made a clean break from Argentina, as the narrator implies that his mother has lingering feelings about Argentina, calling it her "Home" in line 35.

(C) matches the passage, so we can keep it open for now. (D) contradicts the passage, as the narrator suggests that his mother continues to live in the U.S. for the next ten years, and did not move back to Argentina after five years. You can knock it out, and choose (C) as your correct response.

The Process of Elimination cannot always help you knock out all the wrong answers, but it is helpful to have fewer answer choices to consider. Be sure to use it whenever you get stuck!

One Correct Choice

Remember that every question has only one correct answer. For many questions it will be clear that only one answer relates to the passage, as the others are irrelevant, either containing information not mentioned in the passage, or contradicting information given in the passage.

However, other questions may have more than one answer option that could potentially be true. Remember you are looking for the **one correct choice**, which means the answer that most directly and completely answers the question and is supported by the passage. The best way to ensure that you select the correct answer choice is to make sure you can find a word, line, or selection of lines in the text that supports your answer.

Here is another example question from the "Chemistry of Sacrifice" passage used above:

Example
The passage most strongly suggests that the narrator's mother:

F.   never regarded her children as a priority.
G.   remained in the U.S. without ever seeking citizenship.
H.   gave up her career at one point to focus on her family.
J.   has lost her ability to speak her mother tongue.

First, use the Process of Elimination to knock out any answer choices you know are wrong. Both (F) and (G) contradict the passage, so you can eliminate them.

(H) and (J) do not contradict the passage, so you can now consider each one more closely. Which answer choice has more support from the passage?

While (J) doesn't contradict the passage, and may even be tempting because of the mention of moving from "mother tongue to second language" in line 20, there is nothing in the text to indicate that the narrator's mother has outright forgotten her mother tongue. Remember, you cannot make assumptions or use outside information to answer questions. You must find support for your answers in the passage itself.

On the other hand, you can find specific evidence to support (H). The first paragraph talks about how the narrator's mother gave up the practice of medicine in order to devote more time to her children. So while (J) could potentially be true, (H) can be proven true by the passage, and is therefore the one correct choice for this question.

What should you do if it seems that you can support two separate answer choices with information from the passage? First, make sure that the evidence supports the answer choice in the way you think it does. Remember, confused content answer choices may use the same words as the passage, but in a way that means something different than the original text, or connects information in an incorrect way.

Second, for questions that ask what you can infer about the passage by reading between the lines, be sure to look for the most likely, or most plausible, conclusion you can reach. Try to make as few leaps as possible. If your answer choice requires making a lot of assumptions, or relies on information not found in the text, it is likely incorrect. Avoid using outside knowledge and stick to what is on the page.

Finally, if you really can't decide between options, it's okay to make your best guess and move on.

Answer Questions in Order

The most efficient way to answer the questions for a specific passage is to answer them in order. As you learned in Chapter 1, if you are unsure of the answer to any one question, you can mark it in your test booklet, bubble in your best guess, and come back to it later if you have time.

Approaching the Reading Test Practice Questions

Part 4

Active Reading

Consider how you will approach the passage and questions below. Use the active reading techniques you learned earlier in this chapter, by marking up the passage and making paragraph summaries.

Natural Science: This passage is adapted from the article "Sunscreen or Camouflage? Why So Many Animals Have Dark Backs and Pale Bellies" by Julie Harris and Olivier Penacchio (©2015 by Julie Harris and Olivier Penacchio).

The animal kingdom contains a huge diversity of color patterns, from the near-perfect camouflage of the cuttlefish to the extravagant displays of birds of paradise.
5 Evolution has shaped this diversity, but exactly which selective pressures are at work is still controversial.

While some theories propose that such patterns evolved specifically for camouflage,
10 other theories link them to things like attracting mates, regulating body temperature, and giving off warning signals.

One common pattern of animal coloration that has been the subject of this kind of debate
15 is called countershading. Found across air, land, and water on many different animals—from tigers to tuna—it refers to a darker skin or fur on the surface of the animal's body that faces the sun, and a lighter color on their
20 underside.

Countershading has typically been considered beneficial for protection against ultraviolet light. This is because the dark color of the skin or fur is due to melanin, a
25 pigment that strongly dissipates potentially damaging ultraviolet radiation. A dark body color also often helps animals to gain more heat from sunlight.

Yet it has also long been suggested that this
30 pattern of coloration evolved to enhance visual camouflage. This goes back to one of the oldest theories in the evolution of camouflage, originally put forward in the late 19th and early 20th centuries by the British
35 evolutionary biologist Sir Edward Bagnall Poulton and the American artist and naturalist Abbott Thayer. They suggested that shading might counteract the effects of light and make animals harder to see.

1. Which of the following animals is NOT mentioned as utilizing countershading?

   A. Tigers
   B. Toads
   C. Tuna
   D. All of the above animals use countershading.

2. The purpose of the third paragraph (lines 13–20) is to:

   F. introduce a concept.
   G. tell a story.
   H. provide counterevidence.
   J. state a thesis.

3. The passage indicates that countershading may serve all of the following purposes EXCEPT:

   A. visual camouflage.
   B. protection against ultraviolet light.
   C. intimidating potential prey.
   D. the acquisition of heat from the sun.

4. The authors indicate that evolution:

F. works independently of any changes in camouflage.

G. is spurred on by rapid changes in coloration and camouflage.

H. plays a role in the development of camouflage that is not fully understood.

J. halts the development of countershading in most animals.

5. The authors most likely use the phrase "from the near-perfect camouflage of the cuttlefish to the extravagant displays of birds of paradise" (lines 2−4) in order to:

A. prove that the animal kingdom has animals of many sizes.

B. illustrate a typical rivalry between animal species.

C. demonstrate the range of animal species' color patterning.

D. give examples of other animals that use countershading.

Selecting Your Answers

Use the active reading strategies you learned as you read this passage.

Social Science: This passage is adapted from the article "Leaning In At Work and At Home: Why Workplace Policies Matter" by David S. Pedulla and Sarah Thebaud (©2015 by David S. Pedulla and Sarah Thebaud).

The latter part of the twentieth century saw a dramatic increase in women's participation in the workforce as well as a rise in ideological support for women's
5 employment in the United States. However, women still comprise only a small fraction of elite leadership positions in government and business. And they still do the lion's share of the housework and caregiving. In other words,
10 the "gender revolution" appears to have stalled.

What accounts for this stalled progress toward gender equality in the workplace and at home? A piece of the answer may lie in workplace policies and practices that
15 continue to limit men's and women's ability to establish equal relationships at home. Our recent research casts new light on the large disconnect between workplace policies and the ideals that individuals hold about how to
20 balance work and family life.

Childcare costs are high, hours are increasingly long or inflexible, and only a lucky minority of workers has access to paid family leave. Politicians and the general
25 public have started to pay close attention to this set of issues. President Obama recently announced that all federal employees would have access to six weeks of paid leave to care for a new child. In his recent State of the
30 Union address, he also emphasized the importance of access to childcare.

This thinking is not taking place in a vacuum. Recent scholarship by Kathleen Gerson, for example, shows that many
35 young, unmarried men and women ideally prefer egalitarian relationships where both partners contribute equally to earning, housework, and caregiving. However, many of the individuals that Gerson interviewed
40 doubted that this egalitarian vision would be attainable due to the long hours required for a successful career and the long hours required to raise a child. When considering this reality, many favored a "fallback plan"
45 that was more in keeping with traditional gender roles. For example, men's fallback plans were largely for a relationship in which they would be the primary breadwinner.

50 Gerson's insights, as well as other research in this area, point to the idea that work-family preferences develop largely in response to the limited set of options that workplaces currently offer. It is also
55 possible, however, that the lack of equality at work and at home results from deep-seated, ingrained beliefs about men, women, caregiving, and earning.

To date, it has been challenging to
60 separate out the extent to which preferences for employment and caregiving are produced by social conditions (such as unsupportive workplace policies) versus individuals' deeply held beliefs about what roles men and
65 women should play.

Think about the primary purpose of this passage, and try to put it in your own words. Here, the author appears to be trying to highlight issues surrounding the division of workplace and childcare duties, including relevant policies. Next, if you can, analyze the individual parts of the passage and try to figure out why the authors included certain bits of information. For example, in lines 26–31, the authors mention President Obama's new initiatives as an example of how politicians have started trying to address these issues.

For the following questions:

- Use Prediction by answering the questions in your own words first, before looking at the given options. If you need to, use your hand or pencil to cover up the choices.
- Note which answers you can eliminate using the Process of Elimination, and why you know they are wrong.
- Note why the answer you selected is the best one, using words and lines from the passage to support your answer choice.

1. The authors suggest that the "gender revolution" has stalled in part because:

   A. government's laws have not kept pace with social change.

   B. men refuse to do their fair share of housework.

   C. more pressing economic concerns have distracted women.

   D. women still have not achieved equal leadership roles.

2. As used in lines 32–33, the phrase "in a vacuum" most nearly means:

   F. in isolation.

   G. in the mind only.

   H. in the home.

   J. in laboratories.

3. The passage indicates that partners often come to adopt a "fallback plan":

   A. reluctantly.

   B. enthusiastically.

   C. indifferently.

   D. angrily.

Full-Length Practice

For the full-length passages that follow, use all the strategies you learned in this section about approaching passages and answering questions. Think about what strategies you might use if you cannot answer a question. Read questions fully, try to answer the questions in order, watch for EXCEPT and NOT questions, and be aware of the potential for making inferences. And, refer back to the passage for all questions to look for relevant information, including questions with specific line or paragraph references.

Natural Science: This passage is adapted from the essay "Tracking American Eels on the Open Sea to Crack the Mystery of Their Migration" by Julian Dodson and Martin Castonguay (©2015 by Julian Dodson and Martin Castonguay).

It's been one of biology's greatest mysteries: How do American eels travel many hundreds of miles from the rivers and estuaries they live in as juveniles to their
5 open-ocean birthing, or spawning, grounds? Their rearing habitat stretches from Southern Greenland to the Gulf of Mexico and the Caribbean Sea, but somehow they make it all the way to the Sargasso Sea,
10 south of Bermuda, to reproduce.

To throw light on this persistent question, we tracked the movements of adult American eels with satellite tags, to recreate their migratory routes. This is the first
15 observation of American eels migrating in the open ocean to their spawning grounds and represents an important step in understanding the eels' migration patterns and orientation mechanisms.

20 Our study subjects were 38 wild-caught eels equipped with satellite tags, 28 of which successfully transmitted data to satellites. We released the eels along the coast of Nova Scotia, Canada. The tags continuously
25 recorded water temperature, depth, and light levels; we programmed them to come apart from the eels during migration, float to the surface, and send their data—including location—to orbiting satellites. Based on the
30 tags' reports, we reconstructed the migratory routes of individual eels.

We identified two distinct migratory phases. Following their release over the Nova Scotian Shelf, all eels immediately headed
35 southeast toward the edge of the continental shelf. During this first stage of the migration, eels generally showed daily vertical migrations: spending time in shallow waters at night and bottom waters during the day.

40 Further, during this first stage, the eels appear to rely on gradients associated with temperature and salt levels. Temperature and salt gradients increase from the coast to open waters and may have guided eels to the edge
45 of the continental shelf away from the coast immediately after their release. The eels then moved mainly eastward along the edge of the Scotian shelf, departing the shelf where the waters of the Gulf of St. Lawrence flow
50 into the Atlantic Ocean.

The second phase of the marine migration occurs in deep (more than 2,000 meters in depth), salty oceanic waters. The eels, tracked all the way to the Sargasso Sea,
55 showed a relatively sudden change in direction, heading south to the spawning site in a generally straight line. They performed marked daily vertical migrations, staying in shallow depths at night and deeper depths
60 during the day.

We don't know the orientation and navigation cues that eels relied on in this second phase. Gradients in salt levels and temperature might play a role, but these
65 horizontal gradients are weak. And, these eels have never before experienced this migratory trajectory. Though they hatched in the Sargasso Sea, as larvae they were shaped like leaves and drifted north with the currents on
70 the Gulf Stream before eventually peeling off to search for estuaries and fresh waters, heading as far as Greenland. So, although they've been to the Sargasso Sea before, it wasn't as adults, and they certainly weren't
75 actively navigating their route.

Considering the speed and direction of this second and last phase of the eels' track to the Sargasso Sea, it seems likely that they use some kind of inherited bidimensional
80 map based on the earth's geomagnetic field. The sensitivity of eels to the geomagnetic field has been known for a long time, and previous studies have shown that they have a magnetic compass that they can use for
85 orientation.

The extensive vertical migrations we observed in the North Atlantic Ocean are part of the behavior of many eel species. The reason for the daily nature of these
90 migrations is associated with a compromise between two biological functions: the use of deep, dark waters to avoid eel predators and the need to occupy warmer, shallow waters to use energy efficiently during the long
95 migration.

There is no doubt that eels must deal with formidable predators during their migration. Our research team has previously reported heavy predation on eels by
100 Porbeagle sharks in the Gulf of St Lawrence and in the North Atlantic Ocean. Such predation is easily detected by satellite tags because Porbeagle sharks have warm guts; when our tagged eels get eaten, the tags
105 record the warm temperature inside these predators—a noticeable jump over the normal ocean temperature.

For the moment, we can only speculate about the orientation mechanisms used by
110 eels. Is the Olympic-style performance of one eel typical of all eels entering deep oceanic waters? Do variations in the earth's magnetic field influence the migratory patterns of eels? How does eel behavior
115 change once the spawning grounds have been reached and spawning begins? The American eel still has many secrets to reveal. We're continuing to satellite-tag open-ocean-migrating eels to unravel more of
120 their mysteries.

1. According to the authors, the study they conducted on American eels' migration from their habitats to their spawning grounds is:

   A. the latest in a long line of similar studies.
   B. a follow-up to a previous study performed by the authors.
   C. part of a cluster of similar studies.
   D. the first of its kind.

2. The authors suggest that they find the migration pattern of American eels to be:

   F. majestic and elegant.
   G. lengthy and inefficient.
   H. curious and impressive.
   J. mundane and regimented.

3. It can be reasonably inferred from the passage that the term "vertical migrations" (lines 37–38) refers to:

   A. the journey from the northern to the southern hemisphere.
   B. movement from one depth of water to another depth.
   C. travel while in an upright position.
   D. migration south for the winter.

4. The correct sequence of directions for American eels' adult migration is:

   F. southeast, east, and then south.
   G. east, south, and then southeast.
   H. southeast, east, and then north.
   J. east, north, and then northeast.

5. Which of the following do the authors cite as evidence that horizontal gradients of temperature and salt probably do not significantly influence American eels' second phase of migration?

A. American eels become physically exhausted in this second phase.

B. Horizontal gradients are not substantial in the area where the eels are during the second phase.

C. Vertical gradients interfere with horizontal gradients in this second phase.

D. American eels rely primarily on cues from ocean currents in the second phase.

6. In the context of the passage, the term *peeling off* (line 70) most nearly means:

F. shedding.

G. dispersing.

H. aging.

J. sounding.

7. The authors suggest all of the following about American eels' bidimensional map EXCEPT that it:

A. relies on geomagnetic fields.

B. is inherited.

C. involves use of an internal compass.

D. can detect predators.

8. The authors assert that American eels' vertical migrations throughout their journey are associated with the:

F. need to balance safety and energy use.

G. repulsion of geomagnetic fields.

H. necessity of engaging in physical exercise.

J. biological need to prey on other fish.

9. According to the passage, the authors were able to measure predation by Porbeagle sharks on American eels by means of:

A. the fluorescent tags on Porbeagle sharks.

B. observing Porbeagle sharks in the wild.

C. the satellite tags on American eels.

D. comparing the numbers of eels at different points on their migration path.

10. The purpose of the questions in the final paragraph (lines 108–120) of the passage is to:

F. note further possible areas of research about eel migration.

G. suggest that some secrets about eels will never be solved.

H. summarize the main questions answered by the passage.

J. outline the key inquiries of an earlier study.

Humanities: This passage is adapted from the article "Absorbed in Translation: The Art—and Fun—of Literary Translation" by Juliet Winters Carpenter (©2015 by Juliet Winters Carpenter).

I recently stumbled upon a post that describes the process of literary translation as "soul-crushing." That's news to me, and I've been engaged in literary translation for the
5 better part of four decades now. How would I describe it? "Humbling," yes. "All-consuming," definitely. But above all, "the most fun imaginable."

Some may figure that literary translators
10 are a dying breed, like quill pen makers, and assume that computers will eventually take over the job. Don't hold your breath. Machine translation has a role to play—and no doubt an increasing one—but it is doomed
15 to be literal, to merely skim the surface. Enter "Don't hold your breath" into Google Translate and you'll get an injunction to not stop breathing. A human touch is needed to understand layers of meaning in context and
20 to create something pleasurable to read.

Yet the process is humbling, primarily because as a translator, you are constantly made aware of your limitations: there are all the events or interactions described in the
25 original text that you know nothing about, or have never experienced. Or you long to reproduce the wit, rhythm, and beauty of the original, but, for a host of reasons, have to settle for less. I also find that humility is a
30 practical necessity. When the original makes little sense, often the first impulse is to blame the author. Humility allows you to see the original text in a new light—to appreciate it for what it is, rather than what you may think
35 it's supposed to be. If you approach a confusing sentence with the assumption that you're missing something, you're usually right. So my first rule would be: assume you are wrong, not the author.
40

I've collaborated with Japanese author Minae Mizumura on translating two of her books, including *The Fall of Language in the Age of English*. *The Fall of Language* was first translated by Mari Yoshihara, a
45 professor at the University of Hawaii.

Mizumura then asked me to review the entire book with her—to incorporate changes she made to render the text more accessible
50 and relevant to non-Japanese readers. The book explores the importance of national literature and warns against the unchecked proliferation of English, lamenting that not only nuances, but also "truths"—accessible
55 only in other languages—are in danger of being lost. Translating such a book into English may seem perverse, but it underscores the point that in our age, ideas can spread only if they're communicated in
60 English.

Over the course of two books, Mizumura and I have worked out a routine. First, I spend however long is needed to write a draft. Usually I translate alone—most often
65 between the hours of 9 p.m. and 3 a.m. Once the draft is finished Mizumura and I will review it separately, making tentative changes and formulating questions. Then we get together and spend hours discussing,
70 probing, researching, and reshaping. At the end of the day, I go home and review what we accomplished (once, before a deadline, our "day" concluded at 5 a.m.). When our brains start to go numb with exhaustion, we meet
75 every other day, rather than daily. The number of drafts varies, but every little improvement, every step closer to the outcome she and I both envision, makes the process one of unfolding joy—all the more so
80 when translating a major author such as Mizumura.

The process of rewriting involves focusing on the author's main point (or the character's emotion) and ensuring these are
85 conveyed as originally intended. It's like bringing a musical score to life: you pay attention to tempo, dynamics, and phrasing, and above all you seek to end up with not a collection of notes but music. If a turn of
90 speech doesn't work well in English, it's better to alter or omit it. And unlike Lydia Davis—who recently translated Flaubert's *Madame Bovary*—I could consult the author. Much power is entrusted to the translator; tact
95 and discretion are a must. Likewise, respect for the voice and vision of the author, living

or dead, is paramount. And getting a
sentence or a bit of dialogue to sound right—
so right that it seems inevitable—is deeply
100 satisfying, even exhilarating. Now, I ask
you, what's soul-crushing about any of that?

11. It can reasonably be inferred from the
passage that the author thinks *The Fall of
Language in the Age of English*:

    A. should not have been translated into
English, since the book claims that the
English language obscures the truth.

    B. is worth making accessible to all
audiences, even though some material
may be lost in translation.

    C. is not accessible or relevant for most
non-Japanese readers, making the
translation a purely academic exercise.

    D. represents an important moment in the
development of Hawaiian national
literature.

12. As it is used in line 57, the word *perverse*
most nearly means:

    F. disgusting.

    G. immoral.

    H. stubborn.

    J. contradictory.

13. The author most likely places the word "day"
in quotation marks in line 73 in order to:

    A. sarcastically indicate that the amount of
time she worked on that occasion was
actually much shorter than a full day.

    B. introduce to the reader an unusual
insider's term for a professional editing
session.

    C. acknowledge that in reality she worked
much longer than a typical working day.

    D. remind readers that the translator and
author worked in different time zones.

14. According to the passage, Minae Mizumura is:

    F. the author's colleague at the University
of Hawaii.

    G. a translator of Japanese novels into
English.

    H. a distinguished Japanese author.

    J. the editor of a series of mid-18th
century novels.

15. The author asserts that machine translation
is:

    A. increasingly important but insufficient.

    B. increasingly important and pleasurable.

    C. increasingly unimportant and too literal.

    D. completely unimportant and inaccurate.

16. In lines 17–18, the author mentions the
phrase "you'll get an injunction to not stop
breathing" in order to suggest that:

    F. some phrases are protected by copyright
law and thus cannot be translated.

    G. Google Translate accurately translates
expressions into other languages.

    H. machine translation misses the more
subtle meanings of phrases.

    J. public health announcements are
becoming more common online.

17. The author states that she typically translates:

    A. alone, starting at 5 a.m.

    B. alone, starting at 9 p.m.

    C. with the original author, for as long as
necessary.

    D. with the original author, beginning at 9
a.m.

18. It can be most reasonably inferred that the
author compares translation to "bringing a
musical score to life" in lines 85–89 in order
to:

    F. remind readers of the similarly soul-
crushing power of classical music.

    G. emphasize the crucial influence of
music theory on *The Fall of Language
in the Age of English*.

    H. further demonstrate how working with
Minae Mizumura was a process she
sometimes dreaded.

    J. demonstrate the importance of
maintaining meaning and unity in a
translated text.

19. The passage characterizes the translator's relationship to the author as all of the following EXCEPT:

    A. truly respectful.

    B. exhausting due to their differing personalities.

    C. highly collaborative.

    D. dependent upon frequent consultation.

20. The author associates humility with everything EXCEPT:

    F. learning from past failures.

    G. settling for less than you wanted.

    H. seeing a text in a new light.

    J. accepting your limitations.

Section 2
Passage Types

Now that we've outlined the basic strategies for reading ACT passages, let's talk about the types of passages you'll see.

As you learned earlier in this Chapter, there are four passages in the Reading Test. These passages fall into four categories: one passage will be Prose Fiction, one will be Social Science, one will be Humanities, and one will be Natural Science.

There will also be one passage pair per set which will consist of two shorter, paired passages instead of the standard longer passage.

In this section we're going to highlight some important elements that you'll want to keep an eye out for in each type of passage, and explain how to apply active reading strategies to each one. Then, you'll have you a chance to practice your skills. We will cover the following topics here:

- Prose Fiction Passages
- Social Science Passages
- Humanities Passages
- Natural Science Passages
- Paired Passages

Prose Fiction Passages
Part 1

There is one Prose Fiction or Literary Narrative passage in the Reading section of the ACT (we will refer to these as Prose Fiction passages in the rest of this Chapter). This passage will usually be an excerpt from a recently published novel or short story, and will appear first on the Reading Test. It's unlikely that you'll encounter anything that was published before the twentieth century. Prose Fiction will generally not be presented as passage pairs.

Prose Fiction passages will usually tell a story, or describe a scene, object, or character—often with an underlying message that is implied rather than stated directly. With Prose Fiction passages, your goals are to follow the details of what is being described, to look for any underlying messages in the passage, and to pay attention to how the author uses language and literary techniques to convey these messages. The tips that follow will help you put Pencil on Paper and use your active reading skills to accomplish these goals.

You won't be tested on your knowledge about specific works, but you will need to be comfortable reading various types of literature. To help you practice, go online to see our reading list with recommended literature sources listed by grade.

 For additional resources, please visit **ivyglobal.com/study**.

Important Information in Prose Fiction Passages

As we mentioned in Section 1, you should pay special attention to important information in a passage as you're reading it. Determining which information is the most important will depend largely on what type of passage you're reading.

For Prose passages you may want to think about the narrator, setting, characters, and tone. Many of the questions on the ACT will ask you to locate important information from the text, so it is essential to understand the order of events in the passage, and the relationships between different characters and elements in the story.

Also important for Prose Fiction passages is the ability to use implicit reasoning in order to come up with logical inferences based on information in the passage. In other words, you should be able to use the details given to draw additional conclusions about the characters, events, and themes of the story.

For example, a story about two sisters may never explicitly mention their mother, but based on the conversation or events in the story, you may be able to draw conclusions about her. If the two sisters are worried about their curfew and mention that they hope that it is their father that is home, it might be possible to infer that their mother is quite strict.

When answering these questions, make sure that your inferences are always based on evidence in the text. You should be able to support any additional conclusions you make with specific lines from the passage.

Characterization

The people in stories, plays, and novels are characters. **Characterization** is the process the author uses to give the reader new information about the characters.

Writers can use a number of techniques for characterization, including description, dialogue, and action.

Paying attention to how the author uses these techniques will help you to answer questions about characters and their relationships, and about the author's purpose. Keep an eye out for characterization, and pay attention to how it shapes individual characters, their relationships to one another, and their role in the story.

Let's look at an excerpt from the story "Walking." Take a look at the following portion, when the narrator goes into the headmaster's office.

Example

Prose Fiction: The following is an excerpt from "Walking" by Ray Daniels, a short story about a former teacher (©2014 by Ray Daniels).

The headmaster escorted me to his office. He was much taller than I realized, and sitting in his office that day, I understood for the first time how tall he must have always
5 seemed to my students sitting in that same chair. As I watched his chin bob up and down, I noticed his head was disproportionately small compared to his shoulders. The more he talked and nodded and told me he
10 understood my extenuating circumstances, the smaller his head became, so that by the time I stood up and made for the door, his head was barely the size of a green apple, perhaps a small, cold plum, though his tie
15 was still magnificent, impeccably knotted into a double Windsor.

Now, take a look at the following question:

The narrator's attitude towards the headmaster is one of:

A. unsettled interest.
B. marked disdain.
C. intense fear.
D. staunch admiration.

How would you go about answering this question? The passage does not directly state that the narrator is interested, disdainful, afraid, or admiring. Instead, it is important to pay attention to the different characterization techniques employed by the author in order to draw a conclusion.

Here, the narrator examines the headmaster's height, watches his "chin bob up and down," and seems mesmerized by the size of the headmaster's head, comparing it to a "green apple" and then a "small, cold plum." The narrator's attitude toward the headmaster seems interested and somewhat uncertain, given the peculiar observations she makes about the headmaster's appearance. Thus, (A) is the correct answer.

The narrator shows no evidence of disdain, meaning contempt or scorn, so (B) can be ruled out. Though the narrator seems somewhat in awe of the headmaster's height, there is not enough in the passage to suggest the narrator feels fear (C) or admiration (D), so these choices can be eliminated as well.

As you continue to read and practice with a variety of sources, you'll become an expert at recognizing these techniques.

The Structure of a Prose Fiction Passage

As you read the passage, you should pay attention to how it's structured, meaning the focus of different parts of the passage and how they fit together.

Some Prose Fiction passages will be mostly **narrative**, which means that they focus on telling a story. A narrative passage describes events that happen in a certain order. Others will be mostly **descriptive**, which means that they focus on describing an important person, place, or thing in detail. For example, the excerpt of "Walking" above, showing the narrator observing the headmaster, is mostly descriptive.

Many of the passages you encounter will mix some narrative and descriptive elements. In these passages, the two kinds of elements are usually intended to support one another. Descriptive elements in a narrative passage often provide additional details about an important figure in the story, while narrative elements in a descriptive passage often help characterize the subject that the passage is describing.

Social Science Passages
Part 2

Social Science passages will always appear as the second passage in a set. They may be one single passage or a set of two shorter, paired passages. These passages will probably come from a magazine, newspaper, or non-fiction book, and will be from a contemporary source. The Social Sciences include fields like economics, psychology, political science, linguistics, and history.

You won't be tested on your knowledge of these particular fields, but you will be required to read and decipher information from these fields, including any technical language. Check out our reading list online for some recommended reading in the social sciences, which will help familiarize you with this type of writing.

 For additional resources, please visit **ivyglobal.com/study**.

Important Information in Social Science Passages

Social science passages may provide a general overview of a particular topic, but will most often discuss a specific new discovery or trend within a field. Authors may present new items in a neutral manner, or they may discuss the items' limitations or benefits. Your goal when working through Social Science passages is to identify the main topic, locate key evidence, and understand any arguments or claims the author is trying to make. Take this short example:

Example

Social Science: This passage is adapted from the article "AI is Different Because It Lets Machines Weld the Emotional With the Physical" by Peter McOwan (©2014 by Peter McOwan).

The challenge for an artificial intelligence that attempts to write literature is the processing of language and semantics. While sophisticated systems like Apple's
5 Siri or Microsoft's Cortana can react to basic spoken phrases, the ambiguity of meaning in language is difficult for a machine to learn. Add to this the use of figures of speech, metaphor, and other cultural references, not
10 to mention the characters, their speech and relationships, and a coherent well-paced story arc with the branching narrative twists and turns that are needed in a good novel, and we are arguably still some way from the
15 first best-selling book totally written by a machine.

According to the passage, the writing of literature by artificial intelligence machines is

F. surprisingly imminent.
G. persistently challenging.
H. often successful.
J. increasingly common.

When answering this question, make sure you understand not only the details in the excerpt, but also the main point of the passage. You might want to come up with your own answer first using the Predicting strategy discussed in Chapter 1. Here, the author uses words like "challenge" and "difficult" in reference to artificial intelligence machines writing literature, so (G) is the best answer.

All of these challenges make it unlikely that literature written by machines is imminent, meaning "about to happen," so (F) can be eliminated. (H) is directly contradicted by the last sentence of the passage, which says that machines struggle to produce the narrative and stylistic hallmarks of literature, and we are still some way from a best-selling book being written by a machine. This suggests that machines are not successful at writing literature. (J) is not supported by the passage, which doesn't discuss how often artificial intelligence machines are tasked with writing literature.

Make sure to practice with similar passages in order to help you get the hang of these types of texts and questions!

Humanities Passages
Part 3

Next up in the ACT is the Humanities passage. This will always be the third passage out of four. Humanities passage topics include art, literary criticism, music, film, and architecture. Occasionally, Humanities passages may be presented as a personal memoir or essay. Other times, they will involve discussions about a specific topic in the arts.

This category could also include passage pairs, where one author responds directly to another, two authors write on similar themes, or two different pieces from one author are presented.

The more you practice, the more you'll get a feel for these passages and the questions associated with them. Check out our reading list online for some recommended material to help you practice.

 For additional resources, please visit **ivyglobal.com/study**.

Important Information in Humanities Passages

Humanities passages may use rhetorical techniques like metaphor or simile more often than Science passages, and may have a less neutral tone if presented as a personal essay or memoir. In Humanities passages, it is also important to pay attention to the main topics, and any arguments, that the author is presenting. What evidence does the author use to support her claims? Also consider how different parts of the passage, including key details and events, relate to one another. Don't forget to use the Pencil on Paper strategy to help you note down these key facts.

FACT: I'm tired

Take this short example:

Humanities: This passage is adapted from the article "Martin Luther King Jr. in Dialogue With the Ancient Greeks" by Timothy Joseph (©2016 by Timothy Joseph).

Martin Luther King Jr.'s medium for enacting his teaching, civil disobedience, was informed by the Greeks—or, rather, one Greek in particular. Three times in his 1963
5 "Letter from Birmingham Jail," King evokes Socrates (469–399 BCE), the philosopher who famously made the public streets and squares of Athens his classroom. King's letter is addressed to fellow clergymen who had
10 discouraged his practice of nonviolent resistance, on the grounds that it was "unwise and untimely" and could incite civil disturbances. In making the case for the importance of civil disobedience, King
15 introduces Socrates as one of its early practitioners.

Based on the passage, it can be inferred that Martin Luther King Jr. used which of the following strategies to argue in favor of civil disobedience?

A. Appeals to historical authority figures
B. Reference to philosophical treatises
C. Championing of his past successes
D. Condemnation of opponents' character

When answering this question, use the details given in the passage to make an inference about Martin Luther King Jr.'s strategies. Martin Luther King addressed clergymen who had discouraged nonviolent resistance by making reference to the philosopher Socrates, so (A) is most appropriate.

Though Socrates was a philosopher, the excerpt does not mention King referencing any treatises, meaning comprehensive texts, so (B) can be eliminated. (C) and (D) are incorrect because King is not mentioned as either referencing past successes or assailing his opponents' character.

Natural Science Passages

Part 4

The final passage in the ACT Reading Test is a Natural Science passage. The Natural Science passages you encounter on the ACT will usually come from magazines, newspapers, or non-fiction books on popular science. Natural Science passages will almost always be from contemporary sources, which means they address current scientific topics. Natural Science passages may include topics from physics, biology, astronomy, chemistry, or similar fields.

You won't be tested on your knowledge of science, but you will have to be comfortable reading passages that use scientific language. Check out our reading list online for some recommended reading in science, which will help familiarize you with this type of writing.

For additional resources, please visit **ivyglobal.com/study**.

Important Information in Natural Science Passages

With Natural Science passages, your goal is to identify the main topic or argument, and understand how the additional information and evidence provided explains the topic or supports the argument. The tips that follow will help you to accomplish this goal.

Natural Science passages will focus on communicating specific facts about scientific issues. You need to pay special attention to data and experimental evidence, or any specific experiments discussed. Sometimes details about an experiment may be offered as supporting evidence, and other times an experiment may be the main subject of the passage. Keep in mind that experiments measure whether a change in one thing causes a change in another—and what kind of change occurs—to see if a cause and effect can be determined.

Below is an example. Read the passage, paying special attention to the elements we have discussed:

Example

Natural Science: This passage is adapted from the article "Europa" by Corwin Henville (©2015 by Ivy Global).

Europa, a moon of Jupiter, is the place where we are most likely to find extraterrestrial life in our own solar system. Liquid water is widely considered to be one
5 of the most important preconditions for life, and there are likely vast oceans of liquid water beneath Europa's surface. Certain organic chemicals are also considered necessary precursors for life, and we have
10 reason to believe that natural processes on Europa's surface create them in abundance.

Given that sunlight is the main source of energy for life on Earth, it may seem that
15 Europa's thick icy crust, which prevents any sunlight from reaching the ocean, would make life on the moon impossible. But there is an alternative source of energy on Europa: tidal flexing, a process in which gravitational
20 tugs cause Europa's oceans to slosh about, generating heat and energy.

With its suitable environment, and sources of the chemicals and energy necessary for life, it would be more
25 surprising to find that Europa was barren than to discover life beneath its crust.

The first paragraph begins with a clear thesis statement. It proceeds to offer a couple pieces of supporting evidence. The second paragraph then raises a counterclaim, but only for the purpose of refuting it. Finally, the third paragraph summarizes the evidence and restates the thesis.

Now review the following question.

The passage indicates that Europa is the place in our solar system most likely to contain life in part because it:

F. is nearest to the sun.
G. contains an essential resource.
H. has a thick, icy crust.
J. warmed significantly over the years.

Look at the information in the passage. Which answer choice is supported by the text? You can use the Process of Elimination to help you tackle this question.

Here, only (G) is supported by the text, as the author mentions that Europa contains water, an essential resource to support life. The passage does not indicate that Europa is nearest to the sun (F) or that it has warmed significantly over the years (J). Though Europa does have a thick, icy crust (H), the passage does not suggest that this feature makes it more likely to host life.

As you can see, it is important not only to locate details in the passage, but to see how they are being used to support the author's argument. You can continue practicing these skills with the practice questions at the end of this section.

Paired Passages
Part 5

One of the four sets of questions on the ACT Reading Test may be about a set of two short passages, rather than one long one. These passages will usually be Social Science, Humanities, or Natural Science pairs.

Although different from single passages, these paired passages can be treated in some ways as a single passage. Combined, the two passages in the pair are about the same length as a single regular passage, have the same number of questions as a single regular passage, and—most importantly—are worth *the same number of points* as a single regular passage.

Each passage pair will be about the same general subject. The passages might agree with one another, or they might disagree. They might just explore different aspects of the same subject, without directly agreeing or disagreeing with one another at all. They may also be two separate short pieces by the same author on a similar topic.

You should treat each of the two short passages the same way that you treat other passages of that type. However, you will also need to pay attention to the relationship between the two passages when approaching pairs.

Look for Similarities and Differences

Passage pairs always have some similarities. There will also always be some differences between them. Look for similarities and differences in:

- **Main Ideas:** Pay attention to the main ideas in each passage, and consider how they compare. Do they agree? Disagree? Are they talking about *exactly* the same thing, or only related things?

- **Purpose:** Look for differences in the purpose of the passages. Is one author trying only to provide information about the subject, while the other is expressing an opinion?

- **Claims:** Pay attention to what the authors claim is true. See which claims the authors seem to agree about, which ones they disagree about, and which ones are addressed by only one author.

- **Style and Tone:** Pay attention to how the passages are alike or different in style and tone. Do they both contain dry exposition? Is one an exciting story about a museum exhibition, while the other is a more scholarly review of that same exhibition?

- **Focus:** Even if the passages are about the same main topic, they might focus on slightly different aspects of that topic. It might be that both passages are about tax policy, but one focuses on the effects of tax policy on the government's ability to raise revenues while the other focuses on the effects of tax policy on individuals and businesses.

Summarizing Paired Passages

When summarizing paired passages, start by jotting down summaries of each passage in the pair as you read them—just as you would with regular passages. Then, consider the relationship between the two passages, and think of a quick summary about how they relate to one another.

This summary won't usually be as simple as "Authors 1 and 2 agree" or "Authors 1 and 2 disagree." If that's all that comes to mind, you might want to think for a moment longer; there's usually something subtler going on. Consider the elements that are most different and most similar between the two passages, regarding purpose, style and tone, and focus, and make a note about them.

Finding Repeated Ideas

To figure out the relationship between two passages, pay attention to information that appears in both. Remember the Pencil on Paper strategy mentioned in Chapter 1 and earlier in this chapter—you want to make sure you engage with and interact with the text. Mark up the passage and add your own notes to emphasize key information.

In addition to your usual notes and markings on passages, you can note ideas or important words in the second passage that are repeated from the first passage. You can also note any contrasts or opposites that you find as you read the second passage. This will help you easily find these lines if you are asked about any of these concepts.

Let's see how this works with an example of two short passage excerpts:

Example

Passage A is adapted from the article "Beyond Recycling: Solving E-Waste Problems Must Include Designers and Consumers" by Josh Lepawsky (©2015 by Josh Lepawsky). Passage B is adapted from the article "Our Thirst for New Gadgets Has Created a Vast Empire of Electronic Waste" by Ian Williams (©2016 by Ian Williams).

Passage A

E-waste is usually narrowly defined as a byproduct of consumption. Serious proposals to reduce e-waste must address how electronics are manufactured in the first
5   place. Some ways to do that include <u>designing electronics that are more durable, repairable, and recyclable</u>. Doing so would increase the likelihood that the energy and materials in electronics would be conserved
10 through longer use and that their components

Design better electronics to reduce waste

and materials could be recovered once discarded.

To date, efforts to reduce e-waste focus on recycling. In the <u>U.S.</u>, a growing number
15 of states have <u>enacted electronics take-back legislation</u>. These laws have <u>shifted the cost of recycling electronics to consumers</u>.

Le shi rec cos coi

Passage B

Technological improvements mean that the phones, tablets, computers, and other
20 electric devices we find so essential are cheaper and more powerful than ever. But this means we upgrade them sooner and they quickly become unwanted or obsolete, and are thrown away. The <u>huge amounts of waste</u>
25 electrical and electronic equipment—

Qu up ma e-v lar wo issi

WEEE, or e-waste—that result is quickly becoming a <u>major worldwide environmental, economic, and health problem</u>.

With the <u>world's population</u> expected
30 to grow to nine billion by 2050, and a <u>corresponding leap in the amount of waste</u>

electronics that we consume and discard, we urgently need to get a grip on this problem and <u>introduce proper laws, regulations, and</u>
35 <u>procedures</u> that will ensure that electronic waste is safely dealt with.

} Regulation urgently needed

Passages A and B show the main ideas marked up using the 5 Ws (who, what, where, when, and why), and passage summaries are also shown at the sides. What do the mark-ups and passage summaries tell us? Passage A shows that designing electronics in certain ways can reduce e-waste, and that legislation has moved the cost of recycling electronics to consumers. Passage B conveys that the trend of upgrading electronics quickly has led to large amounts of e-waste worldwide, and argues that laws and policies must address growing waste.

Notice that some ideas in the first paragraph of Passage A overlap with ideas from Passage B. We've underlined these overlapping ideas with a wavy line. Passage A mentions "electronics take-back legislation" that some states have adopted that puts the cost of recycling on consumers. Passage B also mentions the need for additional regulation in order to address the e-waste problem. The mention of government regulation by both passage authors is a key fact to note here.

By noting how the passages overlap, you can see how they fit together. You can tell that the author of Passage A is more focused on U.S. regulations of e-waste and the cost to consumers, while Passage B is more focused on the global impact and potential regulation of e-waste. Both authors, however, appear interested in how to solve this growing problem.

Approaching the Questions

The questions following each paired passage will follow the same format. First, you will be asked a few questions about the first passage. Next, you will be asked a couple of questions focusing exclusively on the second passage. You can answer these questions in the same way as you would for a single, unpaired passage. It is easiest to read Passage A and answer the associated questions, and then move on to Passage B and its questions.

Finally, you will be asked a handful of questions about both passages, which will require you to consider elements from both passages at once. This can mean comparing the information from the passages, as well as their structure, tone, or way of making an argument. It may also mean teasing out main ideas from both passages, or thinking of how the author of one passage might respond to the other.

To answer these final questions, look for the element you are asked about in each individual passage first. For example, if you are asked about bird flight patterns, identify what each passage says about that topic.

If you are asked about something more general, like tone, use your notes and summaries to determine the tone of each passage first. Then you can combine or compare these ideas to find your answer.

Let's see how this works with a question about the e-waste passage excerpts from above. Read the longer excerpts of the passages below and mark up the repeated and contrasting ideas. Then attempt the question that follows.

Example

Passage A is adapted from the article "Beyond Recycling: Solving E-Waste Problems Must Include Designers and Consumers" by Josh Lepawsky (©2015 by Josh Lepawsky). Passage B is adapted from the article "Our Thirst for New Gadgets Has Created a Vast Empire of Electronic Waste" by Ian Williams (©2016 by Ian Williams).

Passage A

E-waste is usually narrowly defined as a byproduct of consumption. Serious proposals to reduce e-waste must address how electronics are manufactured in the
5   first place. Some ways to do that include designing electronics that are more durable, repairable, and recyclable. Doing so would increase the likelihood that the energy and materials in electronics would be conserved
10 through longer use and that their components and materials could be recovered once discarded.

To date, efforts to reduce e-waste focus on recycling. In the US, a growing number
15 of states have enacted electronics take-back legislation. These laws have shifted the cost of recycling electronics to consumers.

This is perhaps not a bad thing— arguably, people who consume a particular
20 commodity should share some responsibility for its end-of-life management. Yet, until electronics manufacturers feel the sting or are able to differentiate themselves in the marketplace on more than just their
25 recycling credentials, they have little or no incentive to modify how their products are designed and made.

An even more concerning development is that electronics manufacturers are
30 challenging established US legal doctrine to attempt to make it illegal for consumers to

open, modify, or repair their own electronic equipment. For example, the printer manufacturer Lexmark won a key case in
35 2003 that made it illegal for other firms to refill and sell used toner and ink cartridges from Lexmark's printers. These moves by manufacturers have sparked a growing consumer movement to protect the right to
40 repair in law.

However, it is still possible to bring a version of fair trade—now used with coffee and other goods to improve workers' conditions—to the exchange and processing
45 of discarded electronics. When it comes to reducing waste from electronics, it is time to experiment with change in how these technologies are produced, consumed, and discarded.

Passage B

50 Technological improvements mean that the phones, tablets, computers, and other electric devices we find so essential are cheaper and more powerful than ever. But this means we upgrade them sooner and
55 they quickly become unwanted or obsolete, and are thrown away. The huge amounts of waste electrical and electronic equipment— WEEE, or e-waste—that results is quickly becoming a major worldwide environmental,
60 economic, and health problem.

A recent report by the European Union-funded Countering WEEE Illegal Trade project found that only just over a third of Europe's e-waste ended up in official
65 collection and recycling programs. The rest, amounting to over 6m tons a year, was either exported (1.5m tons), recycled in ways that fell outside the law (3.15m tons),

scavenged (750,000 tons), or simply thrown away (750,000 tons). Considering the vast quantities of e-waste produced worldwide, where this waste ends up is a serious concern. Considering the energy and materials-intensive process of manufacturing it in the first place, so is the impact on the world's natural resources and environment.

Electronic waste was at first just dumped in landfill sites. But the danger of the highly toxic elements in e-waste escaping landfill sites—into the water, for example—meant that tighter controls were needed. Problems related to e-waste disposal in developing countries are worse, and already cause significant environmental and health problems. The open burning of plastics, widespread general dumping, and malpractices associated with improper dismantling and treatment of e-waste as observed in countries such as China, India, and Nigeria can result in serious health consequences.

Places such as Guiyu in China and Agbogbloshie in Ghana have become notorious for their unregulated, heavily polluted, sweatshop-dominated, digital dumps. Metals do not degrade in the environment and so can accumulate, contaminating the soil and groundwater, bioaccumulating in the creatures living in them.

With the world's population expected to grow to nine billion by 2050, and a corresponding leap in the amount of waste electronics that we consume and discard, we urgently need to get a grip on this problem and introduce proper laws, regulations, and procedures that will ensure that electronic waste is safely dealt with.

Both Passage A and Passage B highlight how the issue of e-waste:

A. requires additional government regulations to solve.

B. is complicated by companies trying to prevent consumers from repairing their own devices.

C. has the most devastating consequences on the global environment.

D. will only grow as the worldwide population skyrockets.

To answer this question, you can refer back to the things you underlined and noted in the passages. Pay particular attention to ideas that overlap between the two passages. This can help you select the correct answer choice, (A), as the final paragraphs of each passage discuss the necessity of government regulations to solve the e-waste issue.

You can use Process of Elimination to knock out incorrect answer choices. For this question, answers are incorrect if they mention something only mentioned in Passage A or Passage B, or something that is not mentioned in either passage.

You can therefore eliminate (B), as only Passage A discusses companies attempting to block consumers from repairing their own devices. (C) and (D) are both incorrect, as the environment and growing population are only touched on in Passage B.

Passage Types Practice Questions

Part 6

Prose Fiction Passage

Below is an example passage. Read the passage, paying special attention to the elements we have discussed, such as characterization, and then answer the accompanying practice questions.

Prose Fiction: The following is an excerpt of a story called "Exit Strategy" by Ivan Vladislavić, which follows a woman's thoughts and experiences at her company (©2015 by Ivan Vladislavić).

The corporate storyteller is having a bad day. She badly needs a story for the quarterly meeting of the board, a parable to open proceedings and set the tone. But the story
5 will not write itself. She's spent the morning in her office on the 11th floor peering at the monitor, occasionally typing a line and deleting it, or standing at the window, looking down into the square. She doesn't
10 like the view and so the force with which it draws her to the window is all the more irritating. The square is a paved rectangle, to be precise, enclosed in a shopping mall and surrounded by restaurant terraces. She sees
15 an arrangement of rooftops suggesting office parks, housing complexes and parking garages, and streets nearly devoid of life. No one walks around here if they can help it.

While she's been musing, the monitor
20 has gone to sleep. In its inky depths she sees the outline of her head, a darker blot with a spiky crown. A face surfaces in the milk of her memory just as her own surfaced in the ink of the screen. There's a plot there
25 somewhere. Who's that again? A friend of a friend. Dumisane. Yes, it comes back to her. She begins to type, but then shakes her head and walks to get a coffee.

1. The main character is described as a "corporate storyteller" (line 1) because she:

   A. has a second job as a creative writer.

   B. is the most experienced worker at the corporation.

   C. is required to tell stories as part of her job.

   D. works in advertisement at her company.

2. Details in the passage suggest that the view outside of the main character's building is:

   F. crowded and full of life.

   G. manicured and representative of the city.

   H. lush and heavily decorated.

   J. dismal and deserted.

3. It is reasonable to infer from the passage that the main character had been hoping, after remembering Dumisane, to:

   A. write a story about Dumisane to use later.

   B. invite Dumisane to join the company.

   C. reconnect with the friend who introduced her to Dumisane.

   D. meet Dumisane for coffee.

Social Science Passage

Below is an example passage. Read the passage, paying special attention to the elements we have discussed, such as the author's attitude toward the topic, and then answer the accompanying practice questions.

Social Science: This passage is adapted from the article "We found only one-third of published psychology research is reliable—now what?" by Elizabeth Glibert and Nina Strohminger (©2015 by Elizabeth Gilbert and Nina Strohminger).

The ability to repeat a study and find the same results twice is a prerequisite for building scientific knowledge. Replication allows us to ensure empirical findings are
5 reliable and refines our understanding of when a finding occurs. It may surprise you to learn, then, that scientists do not often conduct—much less publish—attempted replications of existing studies.

10 Journals prefer to publish novel, cutting-edge research. And professional advancement is determined by making new discoveries, not painstakingly confirming claims that are already on the books. As one of our colleagues
15 recently put it, "Running replications is fine for other people, but I have better ways to spend my precious time."

Once a paper appears in a peer-reviewed journal, it acquires a kind of magical,
20 unassailable authority. News outlets, and sometimes even scientists themselves, will cite these findings without a trace of skepticism. Such unquestioning confidence in new studies is likely undeserved, or at least
25 premature.

A small but vocal contingent of researchers—addressing fields ranging from physics to medicine to economics—has maintained that many, perhaps most,
30 published studies are wrong. But how bad is this problem, exactly? And what features make a study more or less likely to turn out to be true?

Publishing together as the Open Science
35 Collaboration and coordinated by social psychologist Brian Nosek from the Center for Open Science, research teams from around the world each ran a replication of a study published in three top psychology
40 journals—*Psychological Science; Journal of Personality and Social Psychology*; and *Journal of Experimental Psychology: Learning, Memory, and Cognition*. To ensure the replication was as exact as
45 possible, research teams obtained study materials from the original authors, and worked closely with these authors whenever they could.

Almost all of the original published
50 studies (97%) had statistically significant results. This is as you'd expect—while many experiments fail to uncover meaningful results, scientists tend only to publish the ones that do.

55 What we found is that when these 100 studies were run by other researchers, however, only 36% reached statistical significance. This number is alarmingly low. Put another way, only around one-third of the
60 rerun studies came out with the same results that were found the first time around. That rate is especially low when you consider that, once published, findings tend to be held as gospel.

65 The bad news doesn't end there. Even when the new study found evidence for the existence of the original finding, the magnitude of the effect was much smaller—half the size of the original, on average.

70 Although perfect replicability in published papers is an unrealistic goal, current replication rates are unacceptably low. The first step, as they say, is admitting you have a problem. What scientists and the
75 public now choose to do with this information remains to be seen, but our collective response will guide the course of future scientific progress.

1. The author's tone in the passage can best be described as:

   A. relaxed.
   B. concerned.
   C. passionate.
   D. amused.

2. As used in line 10, the word "novel" most nearly means:

   F. new.
   G. narrative.
   H. unusual.
   J. readable.

3. In comparison to the original studies, the replicated studies yielded results that were:

   A. more consistent than the results in the original studies.
   B. not as strong as the results in the original studies.
   C. less scientifically accepted than the results in the original studies.
   D. more widely publicized than the results in the original studies.

Humanities Passage

Below is an example passage. Read the passage, paying special attention to the elements we have discussed, such as the evidence the author uses to support his point, and then answer the accompanying practice questions.

Humanities: The following is an excerpt from the essay "Archiving New Media Art: Nola Farman's Lift Project" by Ted Snell, about Farman's elevator-simulating art project (©2014 by Ted Snell).

In 1983, artist Nola Farman embarked on a two-year examination of the physical and psychological experience of elevator travel. As Perth boomed and glass and
5 concrete towers transformed St Georges Terrace into a replica of every other international city, traveling vertically through a building, suspended on a steel cable and trapped in a contrived relationship
10 with strangers, became an everyday occurrence.

No one else discussed it or thought about it as an audio-visual experience or examined its impact on our psyche. Farman
15 did. Over a period of two years of intensive research, prototyping, fabricating, and refining, Farman, with her technical collaborator Michael Brown, recreated an elevator environment. Complete with fully
20 automatic steel doors and computer-controlled operations, spectators experienced a 12-minute audio-visual program in the elevator, which she called "The Lift."

This was the early 80s, and
25 developments in computer-based, immersive, and interactive works were emerging in the U.S. and Europe through the work of Nam June Paik, Paul Sermon, Jeffrey Shaw, Roy Ascott, and Ken Rinaldo. Farman, through
30 her insight, diligence, and openness, was at that cutting edge. The project generated an intellectual buzz that attracted many artists and engineers, tech-heads, architects, and scientists.

35 On the top floor of Ed Jane's Fremantle Furniture Factory in an old warehouse in the port city's heart, Farman ushered visitors into a sealed enclosure, swathed in plastic sheeting, to experience The Lift. The Lift
40 was a metaphor for the unconscious and structured experiences the audience shared when elevator traveling. Images and sounds recreated the upward movement of elevators as The Lift stopped at each floor while other
45 images examined fears associated with elevator travel.

1. According to the passage, Farman's way of thinking about elevators is unique because compared to most people, Farman:

   A. made a habit of talking to strangers in elevators.
   (B) contemplated the effect of elevators on the human mind.
   C. considered the impact of elevators in small cities.
   D. denounced elevators as dangerous technological burdens.

2. The author's mention of "that cutting edge" (line 31) most likely refers to:

   F. advancements in sculptural art in the U.S.
   (G) growing innovation in interactive artworks.
   H. technological developments of elevators.
   J. intellectual excitement among art critics.

3. The passage says that "The Lift" featured all of the following EXCEPT:

   A. a closed-off space.
   B. sounds mimicking those of elevators in motion.
   (C) reflective tiles.
   D. images associated with fears about elevators.

Natural Science Passage

Below is an example passage. Read the passage, paying special attention to the elements we have discussed, such as experimental evidence, and then answer the accompanying practice questions.

Natural Science: This passage is adapted from the article "Explainer: Is It Really OK to Eat Food That's Fallen on the Floor?" by Paul Dawson (©2015 by Paul Dawson).

When you drop a piece of food on the floor, is it really OK to eat if you pick it up within five seconds? This urban food myth contends that if food spends just a few
5 seconds on the floor, dirt and germs won't have much of a chance to contaminate it. Research in my lab has focused on how food and food contact surfaces become contaminated, and we've done some work on
10 this particular piece of wisdom. So what does science tell us about what a few moments on the floor means for the safety of your food?

In 2007, my lab at Clemson University published a study—the only peer-reviewed
15 journal paper on this topic—in the *Journal of Applied Microbiology*. We wanted to know if the length of time food is in contact with a contaminated surface affected the rate of transfer of bacteria to the food. To find out,
20 we inoculated squares of tile, carpet, or wood with Salmonella. Five minutes after that, we placed either bologna or bread on the surface for five, 30, or 60 seconds, and then measured the amount of bacteria transferred
25 to the food. We repeated this exact protocol after the bacteria had been on the surface for two, four, eight, and 24 hours.

We found that the amount of bacteria transferred to either kind of food didn't
30 depend much on how long the food was in contact with the contaminated surface— whether for a few seconds or for a whole minute. The overall amount of bacteria on the surface mattered more, and this decreased
35 over time after the initial inoculation. It looks like what's at issue is less how long your food languishes on the floor and much more how infested with bacteria that patch of floor happens to be.

40   We also found that the kind of surface made a difference as well. Carpets, for instance, seem to be slightly better places to drop your food than wood or tile. When
45 carpet was inoculated with Salmonella, less than 1% of the bacteria were transferred. But when the food was in contact with tile or wood, 48%–70% of bacteria transferred.

    So the next time you consider eating dropped food, the odds are in your favor that
50 you can eat that morsel and not get sick. But in the rare chance that there is a microorganism that can make you sick on the exact spot where the food dropped, you can be fairly sure the bug is on the food you are
55 about to put in your mouth. Research, and common sense, tell us that the best thing to do is to keep your hands, utensils, and other surfaces clean.

1. According to the study discussed in the passage, which of the following most affected the amount of bacteria transferred to food?

  A. Whether the surface was wood or tile

  B. Number of seconds the food was in contact with the surface

  C. Type of food in contact with the surface

  (D) Amount of bacteria initially on the surface

2. The primary purpose of the passage is to:

  (F) discuss research that sheds light on a common myth.

  G. argue for greater care in food safety laws.

  H. highlight a study showing the dangers of Salmonella.

  J. outline best practices for avoiding food contamination.

3. The results of the study indicate that food dropped on the floor:

  A. can be eaten safely if picked up before 10 seconds has passed.

  (B) is most likely not going to become contaminated with dangerous bacteria.

  C. faces a 48–70% chance of becoming infected with Salmonella.

  (D) is almost never safe to eat due to bacterial risks.

Paired Passages

Below is an example passage. Read the passage, paying special attention to the elements we have discussed, such as repeated or contrasted ideas between the two passages. Then answer the accompanying practice questions. In this practice set, the three questions ask you to compare or combine information from the pair. Remember that for the paired passage on the ACT Reading section, you will answer several questions about each short passage first, and then a couple of questions comparing the two short passages.

Passage A is adapted from the article "Egg Colors Make Cuckoos Masters of Disguise" by William Feeney (©2014 by William Feeney). Passage B is adapted from the article "Cuckoos Beat Competition by Laying 'Cryptic' Eggs" by William Feeney (©2014 by William Feeney).

Passage A

    Cuckoos are notorious cheats. Instead of building a nest, incubating their eggs, and raising their chicks, they lay their eggs in the nests of other birds and leave the task of
5 raising their offspring to the unsuspecting host. Their eggs are usually the first to hatch in a nest. Then, before it even opens its eyes, the newly hatched cuckoo chick heaves its unrelated siblings out of the nest, leaving it
10 to monopolize the attention of its foster parents.

    Not surprisingly, hosts defend themselves against parasitism by cuckoos. Hosts can aggressively attack adult cuckoos
15 to stop them from getting into their nest in the first place, and they can learn to

recognize and attack cuckoos by watching the response of other birds.

It does not stop there. If the cuckoo gets
20 around these initial defenses, hosts can reject odd-looking eggs or chicks from their nest. In turn, cuckoo eggs or chicks that resemble those of their hosts are less likely to be rejected. So, through evolutionary time,
25 cuckoo eggs and chicks have evolved to resemble those of their hosts, in some cases to a startling degree.

The interactions between cuckoos and their hosts are classic examples of a "co-
30 evolutionary" arms race. When cuckoos face the problem of having multiple host species in their immediate vicinity that have eggs that vary in color, they deal with the situation in different ways. For example, it has
35 previously been shown that individual female cuckoos can also evolve to lay eggs of different colors to match those of their hosts (egg evolutionary races), or, they can lay dark eggs that, in dark nests, are hard for
40 the hosts to detect and reject. Alternatively, cuckoos could lay an "average" egg, that is not a perfect match of the eggs of any host species, but is a pretty good match of most.

Passage B

Cuckoos aren't the kind of parents
45 you'd want. They never raise their young ones, leaving that job to other birds. They achieve this by laying their eggs in other expectant birds' nests, who treat them as their own and take on parenting duties.

50 Cuckoos are not alone. A whole class of species, called brood parasites, trick other animals into taking on parenting duties. This can be achieved in many ways. Some brood parasites remove a host egg before replacing
60 it with their own. The parasitic chicks can kill the host chicks upon hatching, and the host is left to raise an unrelated chick.

Such behavior is costly for the hosts, whose nests these alien young ones will
65 leave never to come back and, some times, even negatively affect the hosts' future generations. This is why natural selection

favors hosts that are better able to defend themselves against brood parasitism.

70 Some cuckoos lay cryptic eggs, which are dark in color and don't resemble the host's eggs. Instead they are hidden in dark domed nests, where it is hoped that the host won't find them.

75 But this may have another advantage, because when a few cuckoos try to trick the same host nest, they do so by selectively removing competing cuckoo eggs before laying their own. In such cases, well-hidden
80 dark eggs may help evade other cuckoos' gaze.

This suggests that cuckoos are simultaneously locked in two very specific arms races: one between species and another
85 within species (other cuckoos).

Brood parasites, such as cuckoos, are really useful for understanding how interactions between species can affect their evolution in the natural world. They may
90 also be useful for understanding how interactions within a species can drive evolutionary change.

1. Which of the following evolutionary pressures does Passage B, but not Passage A, discuss?

   A. Pressure of cuckoos on hosts
   B. Pressure of hosts on cuckoos
   C. Pressure of non-cuckoo brood parasites on cuckoos
   D. Pressure of cuckoos on other cuckoos

2. Which of the following evolutionary changes would the author of both passages likely NOT expect to find?

   F. Cuckoo eggs develop to take on the color of the eggs of other bird species around them.
   G. Cuckoo birds develop the ability to lay different-sized eggs.
   H. Cuckoo eggs develop a colorful outer layer that is visually appealing and distinguishes them from other eggs.
   J. Other birds living near cuckoo birds develop the ability to lay eggs with a distinctive scent.

3. Passage A and Passage B are different in that Passage B:

A. discusses a broader phenomenon, while Passage A focuses on one specific example of that phenomenon.

B. uses more technical language, while Passage A focuses only on delivering an anecdote.

C. focuses on an experimental scientific study, while Passage A discusses background research.

D. takes a more negative view toward cuckoos, while Passage A is more neutral toward them.

Section 3
Details and Implicit Meaning

Introduction

In this and the following sections, you will learn about the specific question types you will see on the ACT. Each passage's questions will be unique, as they will ask about specific information from that passage. However, the general types of questions you will be asked will be repeated on every test. Learning about them now means that the questions you'll encounter on test day won't be entirely new to you—it will be like you have seen them before!

These question types fall under several categories, and will require you to understand and analyze passages in different ways. In the following sections, we will cover the following question categories:

- Details and Implicit Meaning
- Generalizations and Main Ideas
- Author's Voice and Method
- Meanings of Words and Phrases in Context
- Relationships: Comparative Relationships, Cause-Effect Relationships, and Sequences of Events

To make the question types more clear, we sometimes describe them differently than the ACT does. However, rest assured that all question types are covered!

We'll describe each question type and the strategies for answering them, followed by practice exercises so you can try questions on your own. At the end of each section you will have a chance to apply what you've learned to practice passages.

This section will cover both Details questions and Implicit Meaning questions. Let's get started!

Details

Part 1

Details questions ask you about something stated more or less directly in the passage, in a specific line or paragraph. To answer these questions, you will need to refer back to the text and read closely to understand what the author wrote. Use Process of Elimination to knock out any answers that contradict what the author wrote, or any answers that are not directly stated in the passage. You are looking for ideas the author has stated explicitly, which can be clearly found in the text.

Some Details questions may require a slight inference; questions that ask for significant inferences are called Implicit Meaning questions, and will be explained later in this section. Details questions are also different from Generalizations and Main Ideas questions, which we will discuss next, in that the correct answer for a Details question will not ask you to combine information from several paragraphs. Again, the answer to a Details question can be found in a specific line or paragraph.

Here are some ways that Details questions might be phrased:

- According to the author…
- As described in the passage…
- The author suggests that…
- The passage states that…

Let's have a look at a sample passage excerpt and see how a Details question about that passage would work.

Example

Humanities: The following excerpt is adapted from Henry Adams' article "What Happened to the Blockbuster Art Exhibition?" (©2014 by Henry Adams).

A blockbuster art exhibition can double the annual attendance of an art museum and pull in significant amounts of money. Bring Vermeer's *The Girl with a Pearl Earring* to
5 the Frick Collection in New York and there will be a line of people snaking around the block. But there are signs that the blockbuster game is no longer what it was.

It's a telling indicator that the
10 Metropolitan Museum of Art in New York doesn't have a major traveling show this holiday season. Rising costs, the growing difficulty of securing loans, and a lack of curating talent have made the blockbuster
15 exhibition a hazardous enterprise.

The modern museum blockbuster was largely a development of the 1960s. Two figures of the time—the Met's Thomas Hoving and the National Gallery's J. Carter

20 Brown—played a large role in the phenomenon. Notably, both were young: Hoving was just thirty-six in 1967 when he became director of the Metropolitan, and Brown only thirty-four in 1969 when he 25 became director of the National Gallery. Their intense rivalry spurred exhibitions of financial and visual extravagance; they injected vitality into institutions that had until then been widely regarded as stuffy and 30 backwards-looking.

Hoving took the lead, although his first ventures were surprisingly modest by modern standards. The first of them, grandly titled *In the Presence of Kings*, was a rather 35 haphazard assortment of paintings, sculptures, coins, furniture, crossbows, and other bric-a-brac from the Metropolitan Museum's own collection, all possessing some sort of tenuous link to royal ownership. 40 For all its flimsiness, the show was a smash success.

Carter Brown took note, and managed to grab most of the credit for the blockbuster that remains an icon of the genre: 1976's 45 *King Tut*. The exhibition, which featured the

treasures of the Pharaoh Tutankhamen's tomb, opened with much fanfare at the National Gallery. It then made stops at museums across the United States, including 50 the Metropolitan, drawing an astonishing eight million visitors.

1. According to the author, Carter Brown's *King Tut* exhibition opened at which of the following venues?

    A. The National Gallery
    B. The Frick Collection
    C. The Metropolitan Museum of Art
    D. The Museum of Fine Arts

2. The passage states that prior to Thomas Hoving's and Carter Brown's work, institutions that housed art exhibitions were seen as:

    F. exciting and vibrant.
    G. conformist and outdated.
    H. costly and inefficient.
    J. varied and innovative.

The answer to Question 1 can be found in the fifth and final paragraph of this excerpt. Zero in on this paragraph by noting that you are looking for details about Carter Brown's *King Tut* exhibition, which is mentioned in this paragraph. The paragraph states that Brown's *King Tut* exhibition opened at the National Gallery, making (A) the correct answer.

"The Frick Collection," (B), is mentioned in the passage in the first paragraph, but is not mentioned in relation to Carter Brown's work or his *King Tut* exhibition, and is thus incorrect. "The Museum of Fine Arts," (D), is not mentioned at all in the passage, let alone in relation to Carter Brown, and is therefore also incorrect.

(C) is also incorrect, as "The Metropolitan" did house the exhibition, but only during a subsequent stop. This is a confused content answer choice, which you learned about in Chapter 1, and uses a common trick on the ACT: an answer choice may include information that relates to the topic in the question stem (here, the *King Tut* exhibition), and even accurately describe an aspect of the topic (a venue where the *King Tut* exhibition visited) while still not accurately answering the specific question about the topic in the question stem. This question asks not for just any venue the *King Tut* exhibition visited, but specifically a venue where the exhibition opened.

To answer Question 2, look through the passage to see where it mentions what art exhibition institutions were like before Thomas Hoving and Carter Brown. The third paragraph says that Hoving and Brown "injected vitality into institutions that had until then been widely regarded as stuffy and backwards-looking" (lines 28–30).

Choose the answer choice that restates or reflects this detail. (G) restates this detail by saying that these institutions before Hoving and Brown were seen as "conformist," which is similar to the passage word "stuffy," and "outdated," which is similar to "backwards-looking." Thus, (G) "conformist and outdated" is the correct answer.

You should know that this is a common way of phrasing Details questions on the ACT; the test makers will use synonyms of words found in the passage so that the correct answer has the same meaning but does not use the exact same vocabulary as is found in the passage. Keep this in mind for future questions!

(F), (H), and (J) do not reflect what the passage says about these institutions, and are all incorrect. (F) and (J) are more representative of the style of exhibit put on by Hoving and Brown, and so are incorrect. (F) and (J) represent another common answer choice trick. These answer choices accurately describe *something* in the passage (here, exhibits by Hoving and Brown). However, because they do not accurately describe the item indicated by the question stem (the state of these institutions before Hoving and Brown), they are ultimately wrong answers. This is typical of the confused content answer choice you learned about in the Process of Elimination Strategy in Chapter 1.

The passage does not talk about the cost to support exhibitions prior to Hoving and Brown, so (H) is also incorrect.

Details questions, as you can see, are fairly straightforward. Some, such as question 1, have answers that are easy to find word for word in the passage, based on cues in the question stem. A larger portion of Details questions are like question 2 and take a bit more time and effort to answer by translating information in the passage into appropriate synonyms or paraphrases. These questions are still directed by the question stem and are associated with clearly stated information in a particular line or paragraph in the passage.

Remember that with Details questions, you are looking for the correct answer based on explicit information in a particular part of the passage, either using the same words as the passage, or very similar but adapted language. Incorrect answers may associate the wrong information from the paragraph with the question, pertain to other parts of the passage, contradict the passage, or have no evidence in the passage.

Implicit Meaning
Part 2

Implicit Meaning questions are questions that ask you to extend or interpret the information in a passage. They will not require outside knowledge, but may ask for an inference, request a conclusion, or encourage you to apply an idea from the passage to a new concept. However, it is still vital to understand the explicit information and larger ideas in a passage. It is by combining these pieces of information that you will be able to make reasonable deductions from what is on the page.

Inferring from Information

The first type of Implicit Meaning question often asks for an inference. An inference is a conclusion you make by combining information from different parts of the passage, or "reading between the lines" to make deductions about things not stated directly. Inference questions often have "inferred" in the question stem.

Here are some ways that inference questions might be phrased:

- It can reasonably be inferred from the passage that…
- It is reasonable to infer that…
- It can be inferred that…
- According to the passage…
- Based on the passage…

When you see the word "infer" in the question stem, recognize that you will have to make a reasonable deduction from information or general ideas in the passage. Let's take a look at how an inference question might appear.

Example

Natural Science: This passage is adapted from the article "Fluorescent Proteins Light Up Science By Making the Invisible Visible" by Marc Zimmer (©2015 by Marc Zimmer).

When you look up at the blue sky, where are the stars that you see at night? They're there, but we can't see them. A firefly flitting across a field is invisible to us
5 during the day, but at night we can easily spot its flashes. Similarly, proteins, viruses, parasites, and bacteria inside living cells can't be seen by the naked eye under normal conditions. But a technique using a
10 fluorescent protein can light up cells' molecular machinations like a microscopic flashlight.

The first fluorescent protein found in

nature comes from the crystal jellyfish,
15 *Aequorea victoria*, where it is responsible for the green light emitted by its photo organs. It's called green fluorescent protein (GFP). Fluorescent proteins absorb light with short wavelengths, such as blue light, 20 and immediately return it with a different color light that has a longer wavelength, such as green. In *Aequorea victoria*, a protein named aequorin produces blue light, which GFP converts into the green light emitted by 25 the jellyfish's photo organs.

Now, take a look at the following question:

Example

It can reasonably be inferred from the passage that the crystal jellyfish *Aequorea victoria*:

A. can't be seen by the naked eye except when the fluorescent proteins are active.

B. uses its special emissions of light in order to hunt smaller prey.

C. flashes its fluorescence intermittently in order to conserve energy.

D. has natural fluorescent proteins that function without any outside intervention.

The correct answer is (D), as it is an inference that is directly supported by the passage. The passage states that "the first fluorescent protein found in nature comes from the crystal jellyfish" (lines 13−14). Thus, it can be inferred that, unlike techniques mentioned in the paragraph above that involve artificially using fluorescent proteins to light up cells, the crystal jellyfish has natural fluorescent proteins.

(A) is incorrect, because although the passage notes that fluorescent protein from the crystal jellyfish is used to make items like viruses and bacteria visible to the naked eye, it does not suggest that this protein serves the same purpose in the jellyfish itself. Neither (B) nor (C) is supported by the passage, as there is no evidence that the crystal jellyfish uses fluorescent proteins to hunt, nor that it tries to conserve energy in this way.

Correct inferences are ones that are reasonable to make from the passage; they will ask you to think about the given information from a different perspective, or combine pieces of information that are already there. Remember that when making inferences, you should not have to make assumptions, or stretch the passage too far. (A), (B), and (C) are all incorrect because they make unreasonable assumptions or rely on unsupported ideas that have no evidence in the passage. You can use the Process of Elimination to help you rule out any answer choices that contain these errors.

Drawing a Conclusion

Similar to asking you for direct inferences, Implicit Meaning questions will sometimes also ask you to draw larger conclusions from the passage. Drawing conclusions from passages can be similar to answering a Generalization question, but will require a bit more analysis of how ideas in the passage connect.

The following are some ways that conclusion questions might be phrased:

- The passage implies that for researchers, the biggest obstacle to learning more about the new squid species is the…
- According to the passage, Rachel Carson's work was most closely aligned with…

Below is an example of this kind of Implicit Meaning question, where you have to draw a conclusion by connecting ideas in the passage.

Example

Social Science: This passage is adapted from the article "Why We Should Still Be Reading *Democracy in America*" by John Keane (©2015 by John Keane).

Alexis de Tocqueville's four-volume Democracy in America (1835–1840) is commonly said to be among the greatest works of 19th-century political writing. Its
5 daring conjectures, elegant prose, formidable length, and narrative complexity certainly make it a masterpiece, yet exactly those qualities have together ensured, through time, that opinions greatly differ
10 about the roots of its greatness.

Some observers cautiously mine the text for its fresh insights on such perennial themes as liberty of the press, the tyranny of the majority, and civil society; or they focus
15 on such topics as why it is that modern democracies are vulnerable to "commercial panics" and why they simultaneously value equality, reduce the threat of revolution, and grow complacent. Some readers of the text
20 treat its author as a "classical liberal" who loved parliamentary government and loathed the extremes of democracy. More often, the text is treated as a brilliant grand commentary on the decisive historical
25 significance for old Europe of the rise of the new American republic, which was soon to become a world empire.

How should we make sense of these conflicting interpretations? Each arguably
30 suffers serious flaws, but at the outset it's important to recognize that the act of reading past texts is always an exercise in selection. There are no "true" and "faithful" readings of what others have written.

35 Readers like to say that they have "really grasped" the intended meanings of dead authors, whose texts belong to a context, but "full disclosure" of that kind is forbidden to the living. Hemmed in by
40 language and horizons of time and space, reading is always a stylizing of past reality. Just as walking is a pale imitation of dancing, and dancing an exaggerated form of walking, so interpretations frame past
45 realities. They are acts of narration. Acts of reading past texts are always time- and space-bound interpretations and, as one of my teachers, Hans-Georg Gadamer, liked to remark, all such interpretations of past texts
50 turn out to be misinterpretations.

Now, take a look at the following question:

According to the passage, Alexis de Tocqueville's *Democracy in America*:

F. has diminished in reputation over time.
G. is best understood as having multiple interpretations.
H. criticizes the emerging American republic.
J. is a contradictory and often flawed text.

(G) is the correct answer, because the passage implies (but does not explicitly state) that *Democracy in America* should be understood to have multiple interpretations. The passage implies this by giving the different views of *Democracy in America* in the second paragraph, and then, in the third and fourth paragraphs, talking about how readings of texts are always interpretations, and interpretations are always numerous. Thus, you can conclude that the author of the passage implies that *Democracy in America* is best recognized as having multiple interpretations.

(F) is incorrect as there is no evidence in the passage to support the idea that the reputation of *Democracy in America* has diminished over time. (H) is similarly incorrect as there is no evidence to support the idea that the work is critical of America; indeed, the passage seems to indicate the opposite. (J) can also be eliminated, as the passage is talking about the conflicting interpretations of *Democracy in America*, and not suggesting that the text itself is contradictory (or flawed).

Notice that to draw conclusions, you may have to connect ideas from different parts of the passage, and apply an idea from one part of the passage to another. Avoid answer choices that make unsupported assumptions or connections, and choose the answer choice that reflects a reasonable and supported deduction.

Applying or Supporting an Idea

The final type of Implicit Meaning question you will encounter will require applying information from the passage to hypothetical scenarios or proposed ideas not in the passage. These questions may stand out and seem quite eccentric, but they are straightforward if you understand the ideas of the passage! They may or may not use the terms "inferred" or "according to the passage," but always require forming a new conclusion or making new connections from information given in the passage.

Here are some of the ways that these questions might be phrased:

- According to the passage, the comic book with which of the following opening lines would grab the most attention?

- Which of the following findings, if true, would best support the idea that the piano once was "a stoic, percussive instrument" (lines 21–22)?
- Based on the passage, which of the following statements, if true, would most WEAKEN the hypothesis made by the researchers of the bog willow study?

You'll see that these questions have a lot of variety in terms of the type of example or scenario they propose. Some will look for hypothetical examples that demonstrate an idea in the passage, in the form of hypothetical newspaper headlines, book titles, showcase taglines, etc. Some questions may ask for a hypothetical piece of evidence or research finding that supports an idea. Many will ask you to find simply a statement of opinion that props up one of the main ideas or arguments of the passage.

Returning to the passage by John Keane on Alexis de Tocqueville's *Democracy in America*, let's study one of these Applying or Supporting an Idea questions.

Example

Which of the following would support the author's ideas about the interpretations of past texts?

A. A professor's assessment of a text is universally accepted as the best interpretation of the author's ideas.
B. An obscure interpretation of a text is found to be exactly in line with the author's original intentions.
C. An elderly author disagrees strongly with the recent interpretations of her first novel.
D. A historian discovers new information about an author's life that helps clarify the meaning of her most famous work.

(C) is the correct answer; it is the most plausible, given that the author emphasizes that interpretations of texts do not always match up with the author's original intentions or goals. The hypothetical statement of (C)—that an author may disagree with later interpretations of her own work—would support the passage's ideas.

(A) is incorrect because the author indicates that interpretations are "acts of narration" (line 45), which opposes the idea that there is one "best interpretation" of an author's ideas. (B) is incorrect for the same reason; given that the author emphasizes that interpretations are formed by their own historical time and biases, it is unlikely that he would agree that an interpretation would be exactly in line with the author's original intentions.

(D) is similarly against the spirit of the passage, which discusses how context affects the interpretation of texts, not their content when first written, and makes perfect interpretation impossible.

Understanding the main ideas of the passage will help you to apply them to hypothetical scenarios. Make sure you're clear about the ideas in the text that the question refers to, then read through the answer choices and choose the one that best supports or applies the passage's ideas.

Details and Implicit Meaning Practice Questions

Part 3

Here is a practice passage excerpt with three Details questions. Use what you have just learned about this category to answer these questions. Refer back to the passage to find the correct information to answer them, and remember that some Details questions require more work than others.

Prose Fiction: The following excerpt is adapted from the story "Civil Twilight" by Timothy Hedges, which follows a bus driver on his route (©2013 by Timothy Hedges).

He didn't mind the Woodward route—"The Cruise," his fellow drivers called it. "The Fade to Black" North to Troy, the ritzy mall—the Somerset *Collection*—then back

5 into the warzone of twenty-first-century Detroit. Augie settled into his seat, his legs squeezing beneath the giant steering wheel, and waited.

He scanned his shivering passengers,
10 bundled-up souls who'd gotten on in Birmingham to escape the cold even though they knew the bus was not yet heading in the direction they needed to go. He figured he had a few Twelve Milers, a couple of Tens.
15 Momentarily, he knew, they'd be joined by a troop of people wearing janitorial jumpsuits and Sbarro aprons under their winter coats. They'd settle in for the sixty-minute ride to Seven Mile, the fairgrounds, Highland Park.

20 "It's freezing, man," yelled the kid in the back. "You wanna close the door? When we gonna move?" If the heater had been working, Augie would never have heard the complaint. Noise from the back row would
25 have been swallowed by the gushing roar of the booster fans. He raised his eyes to the mirror again and held up three fingers to signify the minutes until departure. He

pushed a button, and the doors rattled shut.
30 He scratched his thigh through two layers of pants, pulled at the sleeves of his ribbed military-style sweater. He flexed his hands on the wheel, fingertips wiggling at the ends of his leather fingerless gloves.

35 A fist pounded on the glass door, and Augie's head jerked forward. A string of riders stood on the curb. One by one, each swiped a card or fed crumpled bills into the machine before claiming seats near the back.

40 When Augie had started as a driver, when he'd had more responsibility—such as counting change—he'd talked more. Now he just stared forward and let the money machine rattle and hum. Periodically he'd
45 push a button to release the tray of coins into the lockbox, and, every time, the crashing noise reminded Augie of a slot machine.

As soon as the clock blinked 4:20, Augie pulled the bus into traffic and headed
50 west toward Woodward. Over his right shoulder, one of the women started to sing softly. Her voice had the timbre of a stringed instrument, Augie thought. A cello, maybe. It was bound to make him sleepy as he
55 headed toward the setting sun, so until he turned south on Woodward, he recited in his head the fifty U.S. states and their capitals, a trick he'd learned from his father, Mayo, a colorful map forming in his head.

1. According to the passage, what do other drivers call the Woodward route?

   (A) "The Cruise"
   B. "The Warzone"
   C. "The Somerset Collection"
   D. "The Fade to Black"

2. The passage indicates that the bus driver responds to the kid's demand by:

   F. retorting angrily.
   (G) signaling the time until they start moving.
   H. turning on the heaters.
   J. ignoring the kid completely.

3. The author states that the bus driver found the singing woman's voice reminded him of:

   A. his father, Mayo.
   B. a colorful map.
   C. the clinking sound of money.
   (D) a musical instrument.

Now that you have learned how to make inferences, draw conclusions, and apply and support ideas, it is time to practice some questions. Pay attention to the ideas of the passage, and remember that in the questions, you will have to return to the passage and read between the lines in order to come up with the correct answer.

Prose Fiction: This passage is adapted from the short story "Medora" by Sonja Copenbarger (©2012 by Sonja Copenbarger).

Somebody put the baby in Medora's lap, and a crowd of people gathered at her elbows, as if she might forget—after six babies, nineteen grandchildren, and a horde
5 of great-grandchildren—as if she might forget how to hold a baby. She leaned back to let the baby roll in, the round head coming to rest on her shoulder, her right arm drawn across the small body. The eyelids were still
10 thick and red with the sleep of the womb, the head warped from the pressure of birth.

"Granny," said one of the fluttering crowd, "this is your first great-great-granddaughter. She's named Medora, for
15 you."

Medora held the baby for a while, and people took pictures. Then the mother—her great-granddaughter Anne—took the little Medora away, and most of the young people
20 left, taking most of the children. They would come back later, with birthday cake. Anne stayed, putting the baby in a complicated stroller that looked as if it could fly to the moon.

25 "My mom's gone to get your cake," Anne said. "With one hundred and six candles."

"I don't feel a day over ninety." Medora had made the same joke on her birthday ever
30 since she turned eighty, and Anne laughed respectfully, as they all did. This was one of the advantages of being old.

"What's the first thing you remember?" Anne asked. A week didn't go by without
35 somebody asking this: that was a disadvantage.

"The day of the big dinosaur hunt," Medora said, and Anne laughed again, with the same dutiful respect; but it was a lie. The
40 first thing Medora remembered was the day she was named.

It was summer, a brown summer, the sky blazing blue every day, with thunderstorms that turned the air inside out.
45 The road was so hot, the air boiled and shook. There was a line of purple in the air, like the brightest color in their rooster's throat. The purple line thickened into a tall blue smudge, and the smudge wobbled,
50 twisted, came nearer without apparently

moving, and suddenly a man stood on the road, just outside the gate. He wore a gray suit and gray shoes, and his hair was the same gray, smooth and rich, like a leather cap.

55 "I need to know your name," he said. A hot, soft smell came off him: peaches brown with rot, a smell full of wasps. "I need to know who you are," he said.

Baby slammed the gate. She wished that 60 she hadn't broken the latch, but it was too late now. She backed away from the gate and dropped a handful of chickenfeed at her feet, while the biddies gathered around her in a fluttering noisy mass, and their rooster rushed 65 at them, enraged.

The broken gate swung away from the gray man's hand, and he came into the yard. "I'm the census taker," he said. "I need to take everybody's name. Is this the Lake 70 family home?"

Baby shook her head. Another big sister came out of the house, flapping her skirt at the hens. "Baby, they'll kill each other if you don't spread the feed," she scolded.

75 "Mrs. Lake," the gray man said. Baby wrinkled her nose at the smell of hot fruit.

"No. I'm Annie. Mama's inside."

"Miss Lake, I'm the census taker. I need to know how many people live here, and their 80 names and ages."

And big sister Annie stood there and told the gray man their names, everybody's name from old Grampa Buford down to the smallest big sister Tommie, "and this is the 85 baby," Annie finished.

"I need her real name."

"We just call her Baby. We've run out of girl names."

1. The passage implies that Baby is:

   A. Medora's great-granddaughter.
   B. Medora's new child.
   C. one of Medora's older sisters.
   D. Medora's childhood name.

2. It is reasonable to infer that the crowd of people around Medora consists of:

   F. Medora's family.
   G. curious townspeople.
   H. all of Medora's sisters.
   J. the children in the village.

3. Based on the passage, Medora feels that:

   A. people treat her differently due to her age, in both positive and negative ways.
   B. as she has aged she has lost the respect of her family, especially of the newest generations.
   C. her younger family members do not trust her, given that they are closer with her sisters.
   D. many of her daughters have moved too far to maintain a close relationship with her.

4. Which of the following is most likely true, based on the information in the passage?

   F. Medora learned early on to fear the government.
   G. Medora grew up in extreme poverty.
   H. Medora is the youngest sister of many.
   J. Medora married a chicken farmer.

Section 4
Generalizations and Main Ideas

There are several types of questions on the ACT Reading Test that require you to identify central ideas within the text. These questions may ask you to make generalizations by combining information from different parts of the text, summarize single paragraphs, or identify the main idea of the passage as a whole. In this section we'll cover:

- Generalizations
- Combining Information Across Paragraphs
- Summarizing a Single Paragraph
- Main Ideas

Be sure you are using the active reading and summarizing strategies discussed in Section 1 as you read each passage. Summarizing paragraphs as you read will make these question types much easier!

Generalizations
Part 1

Combining Information Across Paragraphs

Generalization questions will ask you about larger ideas or implications of the passage. Most Generalization questions will require you to combine clues from different parts of the text to understand what the author is suggesting. So, when answering questions that ask about a general idea in the passage, skim through relevant paragraphs and think about what conclusion you can draw by putting them together.

Combining information across paragraphs may seem like a tough task, but if you pay attention to the central ideas of the paragraphs as you read the passage, it will be manageable!

Here are some common ways Generalization questions might be phrased:

- According to the passage…
- As described in the passage…
- Details in the passage suggest…

Let's look at a passage excerpt to see how these Generalization questions work.

Example

Social Science: This passage is adapted from the article "How Studying the Old Drawings and Writings of Kids Can Change Our View of History" by Karen Sánchez-Eppler (©2016 by Karen Sánchez-Eppler).

Only recently have historians begun studying the history of childhood. It's part of an important strand of historical scholarship that, since the middle of the 20th
5 century, has attempted to look at history "from the bottom up." This sort of approach studies history not only through the lens of the rich and powerful, but also through the lens of everyday life, which includes the
10 perspectives of people excluded from power, like women, slaves, and immigrants. These "bottom up" historians have stressed the importance of using materials produced by the people they study—not just the things
15 said, for example, by men about women, or by masters about their slaves.

While historians of childhood have mostly continued to rely on sources produced by adults, I've plumbed the
20 archives of childhood to find and use things made by children, particularly the writings and drawings produced by 19th-century American children. The first challenge is locating these documents. There are plenty
25 of child drawings, copybooks, letters, diaries, school essays, and marginal doodles in library collections. But most of this stuff isn't catalogued in a way that identifies it as child-made. Generally, it got into libraries as
30 part of family collections: think the nieces

and nephews of Emily Dickinson (who made a scrapbook of holiday cards), or the children of industrialists like Leland Stanford Jr., the son of the railroad magnate, whose parents preserved his childhood letters and his many drawings of sailboats after he died at 15. For this reason, it's easiest to find writing and drawings by children who grew up to be important adults or were related to a famous adult. At the other extreme, collections from orphanages, reformatories, or schools often contain some things produced by children. (I have, however, found some items made by children born into ordinary families, saved for their own sake.)

The second challenge is figuring out how to interpret the documents. Take eight-year-old Mary Ware Allen, the daughter of a minister in Northborough, Massachusetts. She wrote the following in an 1827 diary entry:

[Nov.] 7th

It snowed hard all day. We began to study geography this evening. Mama played on the guitar and we marched around the table.

[Nov.] 9th

Nothing in particular happened a most beautiful day.

The passage may be brief, but there's a lot of ripe material for a social historian: there's the use of guitars in middle-class households, and the nature of play in the early 19th century. The diary entry shows how involved adults were in the play of children, and how children might not have needed to be bought toys—traits of play that would change a great deal over the course of the 19th century. Other historical details include how weather impacts household activities, the age when a girl might study geography, and the timing of such study in a family's day. But Mary Ware Allen's diary also invites us to imagine other viewpoints, and to understand the childhood sense of self that thinks what matters in a day is the march around a table.

As it is presented in the passage, the author's historical research is most concerned with:

A. the libraries of the rich and powerful, especially the Stanfords.

B. the children of famous adults, as remembered by their families.

C. the everyday activities of American children, in their own words.

D. the ways that children play, specifically in the mid-20th century.

(C) is the best generalization of the author's research interests, and is thus the correct answer. Notice that it is helpful to look around the passage for information on the author's historical research to answer this question.

In the second paragraph, the author mentions looking at children's "drawings, copybooks, letters, diaries, school essays, and marginal doodles" (lines 25–26) to get a sense of children's activities. She also gives a case study of Mary Ware Allen's account of her playing with a guitar and marching around a table, and discusses in the final paragraph how Allen's diary was helpful in making conclusions about children's day-to-day experiences in the 19th century. These details can be combined to correctly choose (C), and to eliminate the wrong answer choices.

Notice that the wrong answers draw on minor details or misinterpretations of the passage. (A) is incorrect because the author mentions that she also tries to find information about ordinary children, not just very privileged ones like Leland Stanford Jr. (B) is wrong for the same reason. (D) is a confused content answer that aims to trick you; it's true that the author studies the ways that children used to play, but the time period she is interested in is the 19th century, not the 20th.

Summarizing a Single Paragraph

Now that you've seen an example of a Generalization question that asks you to combine information from several paragraphs, let's look at Generalization questions that ask for a summary of all or part of a single paragraph. This will require you to paraphrase certain lines from the text—in other words, to provide a short, clear restatement of what you have read.

The techniques you learned about summarizing in Section 1 of this Chapter will help you to paraphrase concisely and accurately, so review that section for guidance. Don't forget to use the Pencil on Paper strategy to help you keep track of key ideas in the passage.

Make sure your answer contains ideas discussed within the paragraph in question rather than elsewhere in the passage, and make sure it highlights the true focus of the paragraph—not merely a detail.

Here are some ways that Generalization questions concerned with summarizing a single paragraph might be phrased:

- In the seventh paragraph, the author is portraying…
- The main point of the second paragraph is to…
- According to the fifth paragraph…

Let's take a look back at the passage excerpt we just saw, and try out one of these Generalization questions.

Example

The main point of the last paragraph is that Mary Ware Allen's diary entry:
- **F.** reveals that playing music in homes was popular in the early nineteenth century.
- **G.** offers a wealth of information for historians despite its brevity.
- **H.** shows that she had a childlike worldview, caring only for marching.
- **J.** indicates that on days with good weather, children stayed indoors.

You can determine that (G) is the best answer because the author dedicates most of the paragraph to listing all of the ways in which the "brief" entry offers "a lot of ripe material" for historians (lines 61–62).

(F) provides an answer that is true based on the description of Mary Ware Allen's diary, but is not mentioned in the last paragraph and does not encompass the main point of this paragraph. (H) makes an inaccurate generalization about the point of the last paragraph, as Allen's childlike view of the world is only noted briefly. (J) is not supported, as staying indoors is not mentioned in the final paragraph, which only quickly notes that weather can affect activities.

To answer these types of questions, you have to distill the information in the paragraph of interest into one line. Eliminate any answers that do not summarize the key idea or ideas of the paragraph, are irrelevant to the paragraph, or contradict the passage as a whole.

Main Ideas
Part 2

Main Idea questions are similar to Generalization questions, in that they ask you for information central to the text, and will require you to combine information from many parts of the passage. However, Main Idea questions are different in that they ask you about the one central idea that is the focus of the text. To answer these questions, review the paragraph summaries you created to come up with an overall summary, or to help you spot recurring themes in the passage you can put into your own words. Then, look for the answer choice that best matches your prediction.

You can also use Process of Elimination to knock out incorrect answer choices. Check each option to be sure it meets the following two criteria: (1) it is true according to the passage, and (2) it deals with most of the passage.

Making sure your answer is true according to the passage helps you knock out answer choices that mention new information or go beyond the passage. For example, just because a passage suggests that a new technology is a good idea does not mean that the author believes it is the best solution to a problem, unless that is directly stated in the text. Be wary of answer choices that include stronger opinions than the passage itself.

Making sure you are considering information from the majority of the passage helps you focus on the big picture, rather than on isolated details. Just because something is mentioned in the passage does not necessarily mean it is a main idea! Look for ideas that are mentioned multiple times or are discussed in-depth across multiple lines and paragraphs.

Here are some ways that Main Idea questions might be phrased:

- The main idea of the passage is that…
- The central idea of the hypothesis proposed by the authors is that…
- Which of the following is NOT an accurate description of the passage?

With this information in mind, let's look at a Main Idea question:

Natural Science: This passage is adapted from the article "Antibiotic Resistance Doesn't Just Make Bacteria Harder to Kill—It Can Actually Make Them Stronger" by Gerald Pier and David Skurnik (©2015 by Gerald Pier and David Skurnik).

Antibiotics are wonderful drugs for treating bacterial infections. Unfortunately, disease-causing bacteria can become resistant to antibiotics that are meant to kill
5 them. This is called selective pressure—the bacteria that are susceptible to the drug are killed, but the ones that withstand the antibiotic survive and proliferate. This process results in the emergence of
10 antibiotic-resistant strains. Once a bacterial strain is resistant to several different antibiotics, it has become a multi-drug-resistant (MDR) microbe. When there are virtually no antibiotics available to treat an
15 infected patient, a microbe is said to be "pan-resistant." These strains are becoming more and more common in hospitals and in the community at large. You might have heard of some of them: for instance, *methicillin-*
20 *resistant Staphylococcus aureus* (MRSA), *vancomycin-resistant Enterococci* (VRE), and *carbapenem-resistant Enterobacteriaceae* (CRE). Bacteria can become drug-resistant in two ways—resistance can be natural,
25 meaning that the genes conferring resistance are already present in the bacterial chromosome, or they can be acquired through mutation or by picking up antibiotic-resistance genes from other
30 microbes.

It is now possible to use new DNA-sequencing technologies to take a closer look at how antibiotic resistance can make some bacteria weaker or stronger. In a new
35 study, we found that—contrary to conventional wisdom around antibiotics—resistance can actually make some bacteria fitter and even more virulent. For decades, an established dogma in the field of
40 infectious diseases has been the so-called "fitness cost of antibiotic resistance." We

believed there was a trade-off for bacteria between antibiotic resistance and how well they could carry out their regular tasks of
45 living. The idea is that while antibiotic-resistant strains cause infections that are more difficult to treat, they are also less hardy. Either they are less able to survive within an infected host or they're less
50 virulent, causing less severe infection, with a reduced ability to be passed along to another human. And we know that this picture is true for some bacteria. Both *Mycobacterium tuberculosis* (which causes
55 tuberculosis) and *Mycobacterium leprae* (which causes leprosy) can become resistant to the drug rifampicin, which is one of the main antibiotics used to treat these diseases.

For M. tuberculosis and *M. leprae*,
60 resistance to *rifampicin* comes thanks to a mutation in one gene. The mutation buys the bacteria the ability to fend off antibiotics, but it interferes with their normal cell physiology and the factors that make them
65 virulent. As we'd expect, resistance comes with a clear fitness cost in this case. But what if resistance actually makes some bacteria stronger and deadlier? Our team used DNA sequencing techniques to tease apart the
70 relationship between antibiotic resistance and fitness cost in infections in laboratory animals. It turns out that for some bacteria, drug resistance actually makes them fitter.

The main point of the passage is that:

A. MRSA, VRE, and CRE are the most common types of antibiotic-resistant bacteria.

B. the authors' study has proven the "fitness cost of antibiotic resistance" theory.

C. rifampicin mutates upon contact with *M. leprae*, proving its ineffectiveness as an antibiotic.

D. new research challenges the idea that developing drug resistance always makes bacteria weaker.

The passage contains many informative details about antibiotic-resistant drugs, and describes the established theory about their decreased virulence. However, these details all serve as background for the new scientific discovery, making (D) the best choice.

(A) is relevant to the passage, as the first paragraph mentions MRSA, VRE, and CRE as antibiotic-resistant bacteria; however, this is not the main point of the passage, and it would be a stretch to say definitively that these are the most common strains of antibiotic-resistant bacteria.

(B) is tricky, because the passage does discuss research that argues for the "fitness cost of antibiotic resistance theory," which is the theory that bacteria become weaker through antibiotic resistance. However, the authors' study has not proven this theory—in fact, the authors' study challenges the idea that developing drug resistance always makes bacteria weaker.

In (C), the relationship of rifampicin to *M. leprae* is reversed; it's actually *M. leprae* that mutates when they make contact. In any case, the relationship between *M. leprae* and rifampicin comes from a supporting detail in the passage, and doesn't capture the main idea.

For Main Idea questions, be on the lookout for wrong answer choices that fixate on isolated details but miss the larger point of the passage, misconstrue the main idea of the passage, or directly contradict any information in the passage. You are looking for an answer choice that correctly combines information in the passage and states the key idea of the passage.

Generalizations and Main Ideas Practice Questions
Part 3

Review the techniques we discussed in Section 1, and mark up and make summaries for this passage excerpt. Then, answer the Generalization and Main Idea questions using the strategies you just learned. Pay attention to the central ideas of each paragraph, and the central idea of the text as a whole. Doing this will prepare you to answer all types of Generalization and Main Idea questions.

Humanities: This passage is adapted from the essay "Gustave and Emma" by Margot Livesay (©2016 by Margot Livesey).

Emma Bovary would surely never have behaved as she did if she had read the novel that bears her name, but Charles Bovary, such is his feeling for her, might have. Or so it
5　seems to me upon rereading the novel they share. Much has shifted in my own life during the decades since I first met them, and much has shifted in the novel. The rooms are the same but the views from the windows vastly
10　altered. Windows are important to Emma. Over and over she is depicted at windows, looking out, longing. Sometimes she sees a man she loves—Charles, Leon, Rodolphe, Leon again—but mostly what meets her gaze
15　is the boredom of her father's farm or the dreary village of Tostes, or the, initially, more promising town of Yonville. One of the great scenes in the novel, the courtship between Rodolphe and Emma, is set at a window in
20　the town hall where they sit looking down on the agricultural fair. I, too, as I first read these pages, was looking out of windows, longing.

I had only just begun to write. I had no concept of reading as a writer, or even—how
25　strange this now seems—of learning from the novels I loved and admired. On this first reading I gave myself over to Emma's ardors and despairs, and entirely failed to notice how expertly Flaubert structures the novel, how
30　deftly he moves the reader from one point of view to the next, how conscious he is of imagery and patterns, how cunningly he foreshadows the main events, and how, despite the admonitions of friends, he cannot resist romantic flourishes.
35　The first time Charles visits Emma's father's farm, for example, his horse, which plods along obligingly for the rest of the novel, shies in melodramatic fashion.

Not only did I not understand how the novel
40　worked its magic, I also knew little about its author and why we might consider him our first modern novelist. I knew he was French, that the novel had been published in the 1850s, that Henry James had called him a novelist's
45　novelist. I knew some of the sweeping claims he had made: "A writer should be in his work as God is in the physical universe—everywhere present and nowhere visible." "The only truth in the world is a well-made sentence." "Art
50　requires a priestly devotion." (And in his own case, I would add, family money.) But I knew almost nothing about his life and how he had come to write such a magnificent "first" novel. Nor did I know the degree to which the novel
55　was the fruit of his devoted friendship with Louis Bouilhet, a poet and playwright. Bouilhet visited Flaubert almost every weekend to pore over the week's pages, usually no more than four or five, and suggest cuts, additions, and
60　revisions. He encouraged the writer to give the novel the beauty and density one would normally find in a poem.

1. The main point of the passage is that:

   A. Flaubert was the first modern novelist, according to fellow novelist Henry James.

   B. the author's perception of her friends, Charles and Emma, has shifted over the years.

   C. Flaubert's book inspired the author to write her own novel about an agricultural fair.

   (D) the author's knowledge of and attitude toward Flaubert's novel have grown since her first reading.

2. As it is presented in the passage, Flaubert's book is:

   F. melodramatic and clumsily structured.

   (G) poetic and masterfully constructed.

   H. occasionally romantic but often rather dreary.

   J. the product of a stimulating friendship with Charles Bovary.

3. The main point of the second paragraph is that:

   (A) the narrator was at first so captivated by the book that she did not think about Flaubert's choices as a writer.

   B. Flaubert was stubborn and never paid attention to his friends' words of advice or instruction.

   C. it is impossible to learn anything by reading other writers.

   D. looking back after many years, the author now finds Flaubert's book very strange and difficult to follow.

4. As he is presented in the passage, Louis Bouilhet is best described as:

   F. a meddlesome editor.

   G. a minor playwright.

   (H) a dedicated friend.

   J. a forgiving husband.

Section 5
Author's Voice and Method

Passages on the ACT Reading Test will use a variety of techniques, devices, and language to communicate ideas to the reader. Questions that test understanding of these techniques are called Author's Voice and Author's Method. This section will cover the types of questions you will be asked under these categories and how to answer them. You will find:

- Author's Voice
- Author's Method
- Analyzing the Purpose of a Whole Passage
- Analyzing the Purpose of a Part
- Identifying Evidence

First, you'll learn how to identify the point of view and attitude of an author. Next, you'll learn how to decipher the purpose of a passage, as well as the purpose of individual sections, details, and phrases within passages. There will be examples of these questions for you to learn from along the way, and a practice passage excerpt at the end of the section where you will put together everything you've learned about Author's Voice and Method questions.

Author's Voice
Part 1

Author's Voice questions will ask you questions related to point of view. They will most often ask you to describe the point of view or attitude of the author. This may involve determining what the author's attitude is toward a specific subject, or describing how the author approaches writing the text overall.

These questions can sometimes be similar to questions about tone, which you will learn about later in this section. They may also ask you to determine the sort of person that would tell the story or write the passage.

Here are some ways Author's Voice questions might be phrased:

- The author's attitude toward the subject of the passage can best be characterized as…
- Which of the following best characterizes the attitude…
- It can reasonably be inferred from the passage that the author believes that Washington was…
- The passage is best described as being told from the point of view of someone who is…

Although most of these questions ask you to identify the point of view of the passage's author, some will ask for the point of view of a character or person introduced in the passage. As we work through this section, we will refer to finding the "author's point of view," but keep in mind that questions can ask about the point of view of other people in the text. You may need to assess how an author or character feels about another person or item in the passage, or about the subject of the passage as a whole.

One good place to find the author's point of view is through certain adjectives she may use. Adjectives can be simple and descriptive, such as "the sky is blue," or can demonstrate how we feel about something, such as "Brussels sprouts are delicious." When you see adjectives like the latter that convey an opinion in the text, and they are not attributed to another person or character in the passage, you can infer that they represent the point of view of the author.

After considering the adjectives that the author has used, your next task is to characterize the author's point of view about the subject in your own words. Use the Predicting strategy to try and come up with an answer before reviewing the choices. To identify point of view, pay attention to whether the view is positive, negative, or neutral, and then try to narrow it down further.

For instance, if an author seems to view a new medical treatment positively, can you define this view more precisely, perhaps as exciting, promising, or merely interesting? Or, if a passage is profiling a musical, and the author has a negative view of a particular actor's performance, think about whether the words he uses suggest that he sees it as boring, offensive, amateur, or something else.

There may be passages with very few strong adjectives or statements by the author that indicate her opinion. In that case, do not make assumptions that go beyond what is stated in the passage. Be wary of answer choices that state the author's opinion too strongly, or use absolute language like "best" or "worst" that doesn't fit with the passage.

Let's look at an Author's Voice question to see how this works:

Example

Prose Fiction: This passage is adapted from the short story "Gray Gumbo" by Ron Carlson (©2013 by Ron Carlson).

The clay flat at Locomotive Springs on the desolate northern tip of the Great Salt Lake is made of gray gumbo, a clay in which only dog sage will grow, and bitter-leaved
5 weed, which is a dun green and ugly and which no animal can eat. A million of these tenacious plants spread to every horizon and create a breathtaking eye trick that makes you worry that you may have landed on the
10 vacuum planet, a world of clay and bush and sky and nothing for miles on every side.

The desolation is multiplied by the fact that you can only get to the springs on one road, twenty miles of gravel in and the same
15 twenty miles of gravel out. Gray gumbo is always wet, even in August, and the dirt track to the springs is also always wet, because it is nothing more than a strip of land with clay bladed up to look like a real road. When it
20 rains, as it started to rain early on the October morning that we were hunting ducks, the clay turns to a gray grease that is a remarkable element in its similarity to lard. The first turn your tires make on the wet clay road clogs
25 every tread regardless of the clever manufacture of the grooves, and all four tires

become ridiculous greasy cylinders, throwing clay and picking it up at the same speed. The roadways there are all gouged
30 gorgeously with the grand fishtailing sweeps of the last vehicle to pass, as well as great dramatic slashes of mud down onto the flat where vehicles for decades have slid off the road.

35 Marcus and I had driven out before dawn to catch the first flights of mallards as they came through, and in the first light we had had some shooting, taking just four birds, and we were lucky enough to find
40 them all. If you dropped one over the water, there was no way to cross. We talked about that a great deal walking out where the green weeds grew tall between the path bank and the water, and how we would shoot
45 judiciously when they swung west and when they swung north, but what we did when the first flocks winged heavily past was we stood and just shot and the four birds we took from the three flights fell luckily where we
50 could claim them. It was luck.

We'd given it until midmorning, when the rain stopped, and then we'd walked back to the old maroon station wagon.

Now, take a look at the following question:

The narrator indicates that he views the clay flat at Locomotive Springs as:

A. welcoming.
B. popular.
C. bleak.
D. fearsome.

The narrator describes the isolation and desolation of the clay flat at Locomotive Springs, saying that arriving there feels like being on a different "planet" (line 10) and that streaks of mud have caused other cars to slide off the road. He also describes the area where the clay flat is located as "desolate" (line 2). "Bleak" (C) is most appropriate, as "bleak" means dreary and unwelcoming.

(A) can be eliminated, as the isolation and desolation the narrator conveys suggest an environment that is opposite to "welcoming." As the narrator focuses on isolation, "popular" (B) is incorrect as well. Though the flat is described as desolate and uninviting, "fearsome" (D) is too strong a word, as the narrator does not indicate fear toward the setting.

Notice how paying attention to the narrator's adjectives and description help you to identify his point of view. When answering point of view questions, refer back to the passage and look for these aspects, think of how you would describe the point of view in your own words, and choose the answer that best matches this description.

Author's Voice questions may test how certain words or lines shape the tone of a part of the passage, or the tone of the passage overall. Tone questions are similar to the more common Author's Voice questions that ask for point of view. **Tone** refers to the feeling or attitude the author demonstrates in his writing. You can determine the tone of a passage by paying attention to the words the author uses, and to how you feel as you read the passage.

When you answer a Tone question, use the Predicting strategy again. First think back to your impression of the passage, or the section you are asked about. How did it make you feel? Think of your own word to describe the tone of the text. If you cannot think of a specific word, try to think more generally about the tone. Was it strong or neutral? Positive or negative? Happy or sad? Then, compare your prediction to the answer choices.

Here are some ways Author's Voice questions concerning tone might be phrased:

- Viewed in the context of the passage, the words *light-hearted*, *diversion*, and *airy* are most likely intended by the author to convey a tone of...
- The language of the third paragraph is most likely intended to convey a sense of...

Let's take a look at a Tone question. Here's another excerpt from a personal essay about Lee Child that we saw before in Section 1.

Example

Humanities: The following is an excerpt adapted from writer Andy Martin's personal essay "The Man With No Plot: How I Watched Lee Child Write a Jack Reacher Novel" (©2015 by Andy Martin).

When Lee Child sat down to write the first sentence of his book, all he had in his head was a scene. He had no idea who the characters are, why they are doing this, or
5 who the big guy is either, other than that his name is Keever.

So he wrote the following sentence: "Moving a guy as big as Keever wasn't easy." I was looking over his shoulder, but I
10 was about a couple of yards or so behind him, perched on a couch, so I had to peer hard at the screen. All I could make out was the "-ing." It was enough for me. Good start, I thought: participle, verb, action. I had to
15 know more. But he didn't know more, at this point. We discussed the first couple of pages, when they popped up out of his printer. He knew it had to be third-person. No dialogue, but he tried to capture
20 something of the vernacular in a Flaubertian style indirect libre. And Reacher, when he gets off the train in the small town of Mother's Rest, in the midst of "nothingness," has absolutely no idea what
25 is going on.

Which was exactly how Lee Child felt. For the next few months I looked on with a degree of anxiety. Maybe he would never finish this one. The whole project looked
30 doomed. Reacher was wandering around this small town, trying to work out mainly why it was even called Mother's Rest. Child didn't even know that Keever was a dead man at this point. He couldn't even figure out what
35 the crime was, let alone solve it.

Now, take a look at the following question:

The language of the second and third paragraphs is most likely intended to convey a sense of:

F. hostility.
G. anticipation.
H. serenity.
J. danger.

To answer this question, pay attention to the author's language. The second paragraph shows the author of the passage peering over Child's shoulder, suggesting intent interest in Child's spontaneous writing process. In the third paragraph, the author of the passage notes his "anxiety" (line 28) about Child's writing, and says with a mix of exaggeration and sincerity that Child's project "looked doomed" (line 29–30). These clues about the author's actions and words suggest a tone of "anticipation," so (G) is the correct answer.

You can use Process of Elimination to eliminate answer choices that clearly do not match the tone of the directed paragraphs. (F), "hostility," is incorrect because there is nothing in the passage to suggest that the author dislikes Child or Child's work. (H), "serenity," is the opposite of the correct tone, as the words used suggest worry rather than calm, and is thus also incorrect. Finally, (J), "danger," is incorrect because although the passage has a tone that is anxious and anticipatory, it does not imply through its language that there is anything risky or dangerous about the situation.

Author's Method
Part 2

Just like all texts you read, the passages on the ACT Reading Test were written from a specific point of view and for a specific reason. Author's Method questions ask you about the purpose of passages. They will ask you to identify the purpose of either an entire passage or specific lines or paragraphs. To answer these questions you need to determine what the author was trying to achieve with her writing.

Analyzing the Purpose of a Whole Passage

Some Author's Method questions ask you to identify the purpose of the entire passage. Here are some ways these questions might be phrased:

- The author's purpose in writing this passage is most likely to…
- The passage as a whole can primarily be characterized as the narrator's…

For questions that ask you about the purpose of the passage as a whole, you will want to choose a "big-picture" answer. Ask yourself why the passage was written. Was it to persuade the reader of something, to argue against a previously held idea, or simply to introduce a new concept? Use the Prediction strategy to describe the goal of the passage in your own words before looking at the answer choices.

This is also a good time to think back to the summaries you made while reading, or to review what important ideas you underlined in the passage. If you used the Pencil on Paper strategy to mark up passages as you read, this will be much easier.

Here's an example of an Author's Method question on the purpose of the passage:

Example

Social Science: This passage is adapted from the article "Evolution of Moral Outrage: I'll Punish Your Bad Behavior to Make Me Look Good" by Jillian Jordan (©2016 by Jillian Jordan).

What makes human morality unique? One important answer is that we care when other people are harmed. While many animals retaliate when directly mistreated,
5 humans also get outraged at transgressions against others. And this outrage drives us to protest injustice, boycott companies, blow whistles, and cut ties with unethical friends and colleagues.

10 Scientists refer to these behaviors as third-party punishment, and they have long been a mystery from the perspective of evolution and rational self-interest. Why should people invest time, effort, and
15 resources in punishing—even when they

---

haven't been harmed directly? While it's clear that our punishment is motivated by moral outrage, that raises the question of why we developed a psychology of outrage in the first place.

One theory is that people punish to benefit society. Social sanctions from peers can deter misbehavior, just as legal punishment does. To take an example from daily life, if Ted decides to criticize his coworker Dan for going on Facebook during work, Dan and others will be less likely to slack off, and the company will be more productive. Perhaps, then, Ted punishes Dan to promote a successful workplace. However, this logic can fall prey to the "free-rider problem": everyone wants to be at a successful company, but nobody wants to sacrifice for it. If Ted punishes Dan, Dan might exclude him from his upcoming party. Why should Ted take this hit? One reason individuals might benefit from punishing is via rewards for deterring misbehavior: Ted's boss might reward him for promoting company productivity by criticizing Dan.

In a recent *Nature* paper, my colleagues and I provide evidence for a different theory of individual benefits of punishment—one that can operate in conjunction with the rewarding process described above. We argue that individuals who punish can boost their reputations by signaling that they can be trusted. If Ted punishes Dan for going on Facebook, his other coworker, Charlotte, might trust that he won't slack off if assigned to an important project.

Now, take a look at the following question:

The primary purpose of the passage is to:

A. question the morality of anger and outrage and encourage readers to assess their own behavior.

B. argue that common punishment schemes do not take into account evolutionary predispositions.

C. elaborate on difficult workplace politics that have their origins in humans' competitive nature.

D. discuss the possible reasons behind an interesting evolutionary development.

When answering this question, think about why the passage was written. What was the author's purpose in creating this passage? Try to come up with your own answer before looking at the answer choices.

Here, you might say that the purpose of the passage is, for example, to explain how moral outrage developed among humans, as encapsulated by the author's question in lines 13–16. (D) is closest to this and is the correct answer, as the passage discusses the phenomenon of moral outrage, and possible evolutionary reasons behind it.

(A) is incorrect because the passage discusses the evolution of moral outrage, instead of questioning the morality of outrage. (B) is incorrect because the passage is informative rather than persuasive, and the author does not make any arguments about punishments. (C) is incorrect because, though the author mentions workplace scenarios of moral outrage, the passage is not focused on workplace politics, and does not connect them to humans' competitive nature.

Analyzing the Purpose of a Part

Other Author's Method questions will ask you to identify the purpose of a certain part of a passage. These questions may ask for the purpose of a specific paragraph, the purpose of a certain detail, or the purpose of a particular line or phrase.

These Author's Method questions that ask for the purpose of a part of a passage may or may not use line references. What they all have in common is that they will ask you to determine the reason the author included the part.

As with questions about the purpose of a passage, consider what the author was trying to achieve with the given lines. Do the details provide evidence, offer examples, or indicate a point of view? How do they support an idea in the passage? Try to come up with your own answer before looking at the various choices.

Here are some ways these questions might be phrased:

- The main purpose of the statement in lines 63–64 is to…
- The main function of the second paragraph (lines 32–38) in relation to the passage as a whole is to…
- The author of Passage 2 refers to the novel *War and Peace* primarily to suggest that…
- The author refers to "the life of an academic" primarily to…
- The details in lines 18–23 primarily serve to suggest the…

Let's return to the Prose Fiction passage from earlier in this section, "Gray Gumbo" by Ron Carlson, to look at some questions that ask for the purpose of a part of the passage.

Example

Prose Fiction: This passage is adapted from the short story "Gray Gumbo" by Ron Carlson (©2013 by Ron Carlson).

The clay flat at Locomotive Springs on the desolate northern tip of the Great Salt Lake is made of gray gumbo, a clay in which only dog sage will grow, and bitter-leaved

5 weed, which is a dun green and ugly and which no animal can eat. A million of these tenacious plants spread to every horizon and create a breathtaking eye trick that makes you worry that you may have landed on the

10 vacuum planet, a world of clay and bush and sky and nothing for miles on every side.

The desolation is multiplied by the fact that you can only get to the springs on one road, twenty miles of gravel in and the same

15 twenty miles of gravel out. Gray gumbo is always wet, even in August, and the dirt track to the springs is also always wet, because it is nothing more than a strip of land with clay bladed up to look like a real road.

20 When it rains, as it started to rain early on the October morning that we were hunting ducks, the clay turns to a gray grease that is a remarkable element in its similarity to lard. The first turn your tires make on the wet clay

25 road clogs every tread regardless of the clever manufacture of the grooves, and all four tires become ridiculous greasy cylinders, throwing clay and picking it up at the same speed, applying for a purchase that

---

30 will never come. The roadways there are all gouged gorgeously with the grand fishtailing sweeps of the last vehicle to pass, as well as great dramatic slashes of mud down onto the flat where vehicles for decades have slid off 35 the road.

Marcus and I had driven out before dawn to catch the first flights of mallards as they came through, and in the first light we had had some shooting, taking just four 40 birds, and we were lucky enough to find them all. If you dropped one over the water, there was no way to cross. We talked about that a great deal walking out where the green weeds grew tall between the path bank and 45 the water, and how we would shoot judiciously when they swung west and when they swung north, but what we did when the first flocks winged heavily past was we stood and just shot and the four birds we took 50 from the three flights fell luckily where we could claim them. It was luck.

We'd given it until midmorning, when the rain stopped, and then we'd walked back to the old maroon station wagon.

Now, take a look at the following questions:

The second paragraph in the passage serves primarily to:

F. highlight the danger and isolation of the road to the clay flat.

G. describe the gray gumbo that is the natural habitat of the birds.

H. detail the men's journey out to Locomotive Springs.

J. show the variable and unpredictable weather of that part of the world.

The narrator states in lines 49–51 that "the four birds we took from the three flights fell luckily where we could claim them. It was luck." in order to emphasize:

A. the fact that it was their first time out hunting.

B. the meticulous attention with which the men completed their task.

C. the random good fortune that followed the men's carelessness.

D. the serendipity of the men hitting their target on every shot.

When answering the above questions, think about what the author was trying to achieve in each section. For Question 1, the correct answer is (F). The given paragraph notes the desolation and emptiness of the road, as well as its danger. It mentions the "fishtailing sweeps" that past cars have made, cars that "slid off the road." Thus, (F) is the best answer.

(G) is incorrect because, although gray gumbo is described, the passage doesn't indicate that gray gumbo is the natural habitat of the birds. (H) is similarly incorrect because the paragraph is focused generally on the description of the setting, not specifically on the men's journey out. Though the paragraph mentions rain, it does not indicate that the weather is unpredictable in that setting, so (J) is also incorrect.

For Question 2, the correct answer is (C). The narrator indicates that if a bird is shot over the water, there is no way to fetch the body out. So, the narrator states, one must take care when shooting birds. Despite this, he and his companion "just" shoot carelessly when they encounter the birds, and luckily "drop" the birds only in places they can reach. The narrator repeats "luckily" and "luck" in order to emphasize this fact, so (C) is correct.

The narrator does not suggest it is his first time hunting (A), especially given his knowledge of the process and the terrain. (B) is exactly opposite of the carelessness the men exhibit; though they discuss shooting carefully, they do not follow through on this. (D) is incorrect because the narrator does not indicate that every shot connected with a bird.

As you can see, understanding the general purpose and arc of the passage will help you analyze the purpose of specific details as well. However, make sure to focus *only* on that particular section when coming up with your answer—don't be distracted by choices that give broader answers about the author's purpose if the question is only asking about a specific section or limited lines.

Identifying Evidence

We're now going to talk about a type of purpose question that asks you for evidence. These questions will still require you to think about the purpose of certain sections of the passage or of the passage as a whole. However, they will not ask you to identify the purpose, but rather will give you the purpose in the question stem and ask you to identify evidence used to support this purpose.

Evidence is information used to support an argument or idea. When you understand the larger arguments and ideas in a passage, it will be easier to identify the examples and details that prop up those ideas.

Here are some ways these Evidence questions might be phrased:

- Which of the following details is used in the passage to indicate that the soccer player was satisfied with her contract?
- Without the last paragraph, the passage would contain no specific examples of…

Here is a passage excerpt and Evidence question, using a passage we saw in the Section 1.

Example

Social Science: The following is an excerpt adapted from the article "How the First 'Horse Race' Poll Changed American Political History" by Edwin Amenta (©2015 by Edwin Amenta).

In the spring of 1935, President Franklin D. Roosevelt was worried about his reelection. He was especially concerned about Louisiana Senator Huey Long. Long
5 and his organization were garnering media attention—"Candidate Long" appeared on the April 1 cover of *Time*. Though a Democrat, Long planned to run against Roosevelt as an independent, and was ready
10 for a long game.

In April 1935, Democratic National Committee chief and Roosevelt campaign manager James Farley called on Emil Hurja, who had done some in-house polling for
15 Farley in the 1934 congressional election cycle to ascertain Long's potential as a spoiler. Hurja was a private stock analyst who was a self-taught pollster and used sampling principles to adjust the unscientific
20 surveys taken by popular magazines.

Hurja devised sample ballot postcards asking whom the public would support in the upcoming election: President Roosevelt, an

unnamed "Republican Candidate," or
25 Senator Long.

Once the ballots were in, the results were shocking. Hurja's estimates gave Roosevelt 49% of the popular vote, with the unnamed Republican at 43% and Long at
30 7%. Roosevelt's team feared that a swing of a few percentage points away from Roosevelt would flip tossup states like Iowa and Minnesota—and the election.

But the first horse race poll's premises
35 were faulty, and its results dubious. Not naming a specific candidate inflated the Republican's totals. Worse, by using a very primitive "likely voter" model, Hurja completely discounted the ballots of
40 recipients of relief programs such as welfare, who were numerous and sharply in favor of Roosevelt, whereas richer Americans opposed him. Moreover, experience has since shown that third-party candidates do
45 much better in polls than in elections.

Had all that been taken into account, the results would have indicated an easy Roosevelt victory. Indeed, that is what Farley was predicting and what happened.

Now, take a look at the following question:

Which of the following details about the first horse race poll is NOT used in the passage to indicate that the poll's premises and results were questionable?

F. The use of the "likely voter" model
G. The underestimation of third party candidates' election performance
H. The appearance of two Republican names on the ballot
J. The overlooking of the ballots of relief program recipients

The question asks you to consider what evidence supports the idea that the first horse race poll was faulty. It specifically asks you to choose which of the answer choices is *not* a piece of evidence used this way. Remember to look out for these Except and Not questions, which we discussed in the Question Strategies part of Section 1. To answer, rule out the answer choices that are used as evidence to prove that the poll was faulty, and choose the only answer that does not supply evidence.

Glance through the passage to see where the author asserts and supports his assertion that the poll was deficient. The author makes the argument that the poll was faulty in the fifth paragraph (lines 34–45). Here, you can see that the author cites the use of the "likely voter" model as evidence for the suspiciousness of the poll (F), along with the underestimation of votes for third party candidates on election day (G), and the ignoring of relief-recipients' ballots (J).

The only choice left is (H), and indeed, the author never refers to two Republican names on the poll ballots, let alone uses such a piece of information as evidence against the trustworthiness of the poll.

This question, among others, can effectively be solved using Process of Elimination. Note also that the evidence for the argument referenced in the question stem could be found in a single paragraph—this often happens, although in other Evidence questions, you will have to combine information from several paragraphs in order to answer.

Author's Voice and Method Practice Questions

Part 3

Review the techniques we discussed in Section 1, and mark up and make summaries for this passage excerpt. Then review the Author's Voice and Author's Method strategies you just learned, including staying alert to words that indicate point of view and tone, and keeping track of the purpose of the passage as a whole and of individual paragraphs. When you're done reviewing, answer the questions for the passage below.

Natural Science: This passage is adapted from the article "The Mysterious Biomechanics of Riding—and Balancing—a Bicycle" by Stephen Cain (©2016 by Stephen Cain).

Humans have been riding bicycle-like machines for close to 200 years, beginning with the Draisine or "velocipede" in 1817.
While riding and balancing a bicycle can
5 seem simple and effortless, the actual control process used by a human rider is still somewhat of a mystery. Using mathematical equations, researchers have explained how a bicycle without a rider can balance itself and
10 have identified the bicycle design features critical for that to happen. However, the stability—that is, the ability to remain balanced—of a bicycle with a rider is more difficult to quantify and describe
15 mathematically, especially since rider ability can vary widely. My colleagues and I brought expert and novice riders into the lab to investigate whether they use different balancing techniques.

20 A big part of balancing a bicycle has to do with controlling the center of mass of the rider-bicycle system. The center of mass is the point at which all the mass (person plus bicycle) can be considered to be
25 concentrated. During straight riding, the rider must always keep that center of mass over the wheels, or what's called the base of support—an imaginary polygon that connects the two tire contacts with the

30 ground. Bicycle riders can use two main balancing strategies: steering, and body movement relative to the bike. Steering is critical for maintaining balance and allows the bicycle to move to bring the base of support
35 back under the center of mass. Imagine balancing a broomstick on one hand—steering a bicycle is equivalent to the hand motions required to keep the broomstick balanced. Steering input can be provided by the rider
40 directly via handlebars (steering torque) or through the self-stability of the bicycle, which arises because the steer and roll of a bicycle are coupled; a bicycle leaned to its side (roll) will cause a change in its steer angle.

45 Body movements relative to the bicycle— like leaning left and right—have a smaller effect than steering, but allow a rider to make balance corrections by shifting the center of mass side to side relative to the bicycle and base of support.
50 Steering is absolutely necessary to balance a bicycle, whereas body movements are not; there is no specific combination of the two to ensure balance. The basic strategy to balance a bicycle, as noted by Karl von Drais (inventor of the
55 Draisine), is to steer into the undesired fall.

Despite our work and that of others in the field, there is still much to be learned about how humans ride and balance bicycles. Most research, including ours, has been limited to
60 straight line riding, which only makes up a fraction of a typical bicycle ride. Ideally, we

would like to identify the measurements that quantify the balance performance, control strategy, and fall risk of a rider in the real
65 world.

With such measurements, we could identify riders at high risk of falling, explore the extent to which bicycle design can reduce fall risk and increase balance performance,
70 and develop the mathematical equations that describe riders of different skill levels.

1. The primary purpose of the passage is to:

    A. highlight the physics and mathematics behind the concept of balance.

    B. discuss research on the mechanisms behind balancing a bicycle.

    C. present findings on the underappreciated field of bicycle design.

    D. suggest that novice riders balance better instinctively through steering.

2. The author mentions balancing a broomstick on one hand in lines 36–38 in order to:

    F. detail a personal anecdote.

    G. provide a supporting metaphor.

    H. offer a counterexample.

    J. transition to a new topic.

3. The author includes lines 7–11 in order to:

    A. contrast an explainable phenomenon with a more mysterious one.

    B. set out the area of research the rest of the passage will discuss.

    C. suggest that bicycle manufacturers should alter the basis of their design.

    D. indicate the painstaking research behind bicycle development and manufacturing.

4. The final paragraph indicates that the author feels that research on how humans ride bicycles is:

    F. often biased.

    G. mostly futile.

    H. still incomplete.

    J. rarely practical.

Section 6
Meanings of Words and Phrases

Some passages will include one or more Meanings of Words and Phrases questions. Meanings of Words and Phrases questions can be quite varied; some ask for what a phrase refers to, some ask for how a phrase helps explain a larger idea, and some ask for an answer that matches the meaning of a word or short phrase as it is used in the passage. In this section we'll cover the following question types:

- Precise Meaning of a Word or Phrase in Context
- Most Likely Means
- Explain a Concept
- Term Refers To…
- Uses a Term Because…

With all of these questions, the word or phrase of interest will be quoted in the question stem. Be sure to refer back to the passage, find the phrase, and read around it, before answering the question. Pay attention to how the question asks you to interpret the term.

Precise Meaning of a Word or Phrase in Context
Part 1

Some Meanings of Words and Phrases questions will give you a word or phrase from the passage and ask you to select the answer choice that could best replace it. Here are common ways that these questions are phrased:

- As it is used in line 9, the word *critical* most nearly means…
- As it is used in line 19, the phrase *get in* most nearly means…
- As it is used in line 30, the word *domain* can reasonably be said to mean all of the following EXCEPT…

Several answer choices may be valid synonyms of the word or phrase you are asked about, but only one will make sense in the original sentence. Therefore, make sure to read the full sentence in which the word or phrase appears. You can also read a few lines above and below to help you understand the context. Look out for tempting but incorrect answer choices—other words may work in the sentence, but don't convey the exact same meaning or have the same connotation.

As you learned in Section 1, it is helpful to think for yourself when answering questions by predicting an answer before looking at the answer options. You should use this approach for Meanings of Words and Phrases questions. Refer back to the passage, and try thinking of a suitable word or phrase to replace the one you are asked about.

Let's take a look at a Meanings of Words and Phrases question that asks for a synonym of the word as it's used in context.

Example

Prose Fiction: This passage is adapted from the short story "The Ditchrider" by Joe Wilkins (©2015 by Joe Wilkins).

Squatted down on his great haunches, Glen Ryan, the ditchrider, fingers the hairy green leaves, the tight buds erupting into waxy purple stars. Knapweed. And a mess of
5 it. He's supposed to open the headgate tomorrow, let folks start irrigating, but you can't risk knapweed riding the water all down the valley, pouring into fields—at least that's what the ditchrider's manual says.
10 He'll have to burn it out. Burn the whole length of the county ditch.

Glen blows a shot of air out his nose. Takes off his ball cap and wipes at the wide expanse of his sweating forehead. A dry

15 wind purls down the hills, bending the grass. Glen says to himself, just under his breath, "We'll have to burn it out."

Glen places his right foot just past a scraggly sagebrush, and the step holds, gives
20 him back his weight, save a little dust cloud puffing from beneath his boot. He walks on. Though it has only been six weeks since the ditch board retired Drease and made Glen the Musselshell County ditchrider, he thinks
25 he's been doing a good job. He's checked the flow rate at the dam daily and oiled the headgate twice, repaired a half-dozen snowmelt washouts east of here, walked the length of the county ditch twice.

30 When he was up for the job, Art Kincheloe took him aside and told him the board knew he was strong and a hard worker, but they worried about his creativity, his thinking on things. Glen allowed that he
35 hadn't gotten the best grades in school, but he swore to Art that he'd study the manual every night and ride the ditch every day. Art looked him in the eye and shook his hand, then said, "You do that, son, and I'll speak
40 for you at the next meeting." Art did. And even if he has to burn the length of the ditch, Glen's determined to prove they made the right choice for ditchrider.

As it is used in lines 39–40, the phrase *speak for* means:

A. talk over.

B. support.

C. replace.

D. talk to.

Here, Art tells Glen that if he works hard as promised, Art will "speak for" him at the next meeting, implying that he will support him despite his reservations about Glen's creativity and grades. Thus, (B) is the correct choice. (A) is incorrect as it implies a disrespect contrary to the spirit of the line. (C) is incorrect as Art here is talking about supporting Glen's bid for a position, not about replacing him for a position. (D) is also incorrect because Art is talking about addressing a group of people at the meeting, not about addressing Glen.

As you learned in Chapter 1, you can test each answer choice by plugging it back into the original sentence to see which choice works best in context. Remember that the correct answer must provide nearly the same meaning as the original word. Compare your choice to the original sentence and ensure it matches the context of the lines above and below in order to be sure of your answer.

If you weren't sure of your answer for the example question above, you could try plugging each answer choice into the original sentence to see which one makes sense:

X   I'll talk over you at the next meeting …

✓   I'll support you at the next meeting …

X   I'll replace you at the next meeting …

X   I'll talk to you at the next meeting …

Only answer choice (B) makes sense when you plug it into the original sentence, so you know (B) must be the correct answer.

Most Likely Means
Part 2

Another common Meanings of Words and Phrases question is the question type that will ask you to explain something about a term, or consider a term as it is used in context in order to explain a related or larger idea. Here are common ways that these questions are phrased:

- When the author says that she is "hoping things will settle down" (line 23), she most likely means that she…
- In the context of the passage as a whole, it is most reasonable to infer that the phrase "the press secretaries were out of one door and into another" means…
- When the author claims that the house shows *principle*, he most likely means that its architect…
- What does the author suggest in lines 56–57 when he says that starfish "are resilient in different waters"?

Pay close attention to the phrase or word, and read around it to understand the meaning or idea that the question stem asks for. Let's take a look at another question from "The Ditchrider" passage. Read the question, look back at the passage, and then look for the best answer choice.

Example

When the author states that the buds are "erupting into waxy purple stars" (lines 3–4), he most likely means that the buds are:

- **F.** gushing water from the runoff of the ditches.
- **G.** exploding under the extreme heat of the fire.
- **H.** disintegrating under the pressure of Glen's fingers.
- **J.** growing from buds into fully formed flowers.

First, find where in the passage this phrase occurs:

Squatted down on his great haunches, Glen Ryan, the ditchrider, fingers the hairy green leaves, the tight buds erupting into waxy purple stars. Knapweed. And a mess of
5 it. He's supposed to open the headgate tomorrow, let folks start irrigating, but you can't risk knapweed riding the water all down the valley, pouring into fields—at least that's what the ditchrider's manual says.
10 He'll have to burn it out. Burn the whole length of the county ditch.

Here, the phrase "erupting into waxy purple stars" is used to indicate that the buds are transforming into purple flowers as they grow, so (J) is the best answer. The description after this phrase of "Knapweed. And a mess of it" (lines 4–5) confirms that the narrator was referring to growth of a plant, along with the reference to green leaves in line 3.

(F) is incorrect as the passage does not mention water gushing onto the flowers. As "erupting" is used metaphorically, the given phrase does not mean that the buds are "exploding under the extreme heat of the fire" (G), especially as Glen has not set any fire yet. (H) is also incorrect; though Glen is touching the flowers, the passage gives no indication that they are disintegrating under his touch.

For these questions, which commonly have "means" or "most likely means" at the ends of their question stems, try to understand the ideas around the phrase. Reading before and after the phrase "erupting into waxy purple stars" helps you to understand what it means—a blooming of flowers on weeds, in the context of the story's character examining a ditch. With these Most Likely Means questions, you will go beyond simply translating the phrase's meaning and explain the larger context or ideas that are created by the phrase.

Explain a Concept
Part 3

Another type of Meanings of Words and Phrases question asks you to explain a concept referenced in the passage. We call these Explain a Concept questions. They may ask you how the author views a certain quoted phrase or topic, or what a quoted term means in the passage. These questions will commonly offer explanatory choices rather than direct substitutions. Sometimes, especially if the concept is central to the passage, these types of questions might reference the given term as it is used in various points of the passage.

Here are some ways that Explain a Concept questions might be phrased:

- The author sees his "important milestone" to be…
- In the context of the passage, *the common frog* is a name for…

Now, let's look at an example of an Explain a Concept question.

Example

Humanities: This passage is adapted from the article "Everything New is Old Again: The Pink Sculpture and the Debate Over Public Art" by Darryl Lauster (©2015 by Darryl Lauster).

The latest front in the battle over public art is taking place in Queens, New York, where Councilman Jimmy Van Bramer, responding to angry constituents, has drafted
5 a bill to allow more public input on commissions funded through the city's "Percent for Art" initiative. The outcry was directed at Ohad Meromi's "Sunbather," an abstract figuration embellished in bright
10 pink that has been selected for installation in Long Island City.

As always, some of the dissent is fueled by the cost of the project, approximated at $515,000. But while money is an easy and
15 frequently misunderstood target for such complaints, the sculpture's color in this instance seems to attract the most critics.

"Looks like someone's used bubblegum!" read an online comment.

20 In her essay "Looking Around: Where We Are, Where We Could Be," the renowned scholar Lucy Lippard defined public art as an "accessible work of any kind that cares about, challenges, involves, and
25 consults the audience for or with whom it was made, respecting community and environment." Encoded into her definition is the very dichotomy that has created tension between artists and the public for millennia.
30 How does one simultaneously consult and challenge? In a democracy, public space is the terrain reserved for the open exchange and dissection of political ideas. And it can be argued that one's politics drives one's
35 aesthetics. So is it possible to present a work to a narrow-minded public that reacts with gut-level outcry to any departure from previously formed sensibilities?

Why do we react so reflexively to the unfamiliar? On one hand, it may be a symptom of an era where we increasingly demand instant gratification. Politicians ask us to declare ourselves for or against issues the second we hear of them. Our televised media presents us news in four-minute segments. Overworked already, we seek simple, immediate answers.

Great artists seek to begin conversations by dissecting the world around us. Great art presents itself to the world as a polite intruder, sneaking into our public space and calling for attention. Once constructed, it demands one meets it on its level. And as viewers, we are called to encounter it, forsaking ethnocentrism, our biases, and our baggage. There's no need for a new definition of public art. Rather, it's time for the public to reaffirm the way art challenges us—how it asks us to see our communities and ourselves in new ways.

The author sees "public art" (lines 1-2 and 57) to be:

A. any artwork that intrudes on public life.
B. displayed artwork that can create a public dialogue.
C. art commissioned by the government for public consumption.
D. artwork that is made by people who are not professional artists.

(B) is correct; the author quotes scholar Lucy Lippard, whose definition provides a clue. Lippard defines public art as "accessible work of any kind that cares about, challenges, involves, and consults the audience for or with whom it was made, respecting community and environment." Based on this and the way that the author talks about public art elsewhere in the passage, it can be concluded that the author is talking about artwork that can challenge its viewers and create a public conversation due to its display in an accessible, potentially prominent public space.

(A) is too specific, as the author is not focused on intrusive art in the passage. (C) is incorrect as it focuses the definition of public art on government commission, which is not a connection made by the author. (D) is also incorrect because the passage does not say public art is made by people who are not professional artists.

In these types of questions, it is important to understand the main ideas of the passage as a whole in order to see how the given concept functions in the passage. Make sure to refer to every instance of the phrase or term cited in order to get a fuller picture of how that particular concept is used.

Term Refers To...
Part 4

Some questions may also ask you what a term in the passage refers to. These will be similar to the Most Likely Means question type, but instead of offering a direct substitution, the answer choices will instead offer potential explanations of the meaning of that term. Term Refers To questions often require you to look further than the directed line—for instance, earlier in the text—to find what the term is referring to in the passage.

Here are some ways that Term Refers To questions might be asked:

- The "modus operandi" mentioned in line 36 most directly refers to what the author sees as...
- It can be reasonably inferred that, as it is used in line 80, the term *free thinker* refers not only to activists but also to...
- When the author says "the boiling point" (lines 12–13), she is most likely referring to...
- The term *brisk*, as it is used in line 72, refers to which of the following?

Here is an example of this type of question for the passage we just saw, "Everything New is Old Again: The Pink Sculpture and the Debate Over Public Art" by Darryl Lauster.

Example

The term *dissent*, as it is used in line 12, refers to which of the following?

F. The public's disapproval of the artwork
G. The city board's dismissal of artistic plans
H. The artist's cultural rebellion in his work
J. The councilman's objection to a bill

Let's look back at where the term "dissent" is used in the passage:

The latest front in the battle over public art is taking place in Queens, New York, where Councilman Jimmy Van Bramer, responding to angry constituents, has drafted
5 a bill to allow more public input on commissions funded through the city's "Percent for Art" initiative. The outcry was directed at Ohad Meromi's "Sunbather," an abstract figuration embellished in bright
10 pink that has been selected for installation in Long Island City.

As always, some of the dissent is fueled by the cost of the project, approximated at $515,000. But while money is an easy and
15 frequently misunderstood target for such complaints, the sculpture's color in this instance seems to attract the most critics. "Looks like someone's used bubblegum!" read an online comment.

Here, "dissent" is used in reference to the "outcry" of "angry constituents" at the installation of the controversial statue in Queens. Thus, (F) is most appropriate, as the dissenting party here is the public. (G) is incorrect as the passage does not mention a city board voting on the artistic plans. (H) is incorrect as the dissent is not referring to the artist's vision or intent. (J) is also incorrect as the councilman mentioned was fighting to allow for more public input on art with the creation of his own bill, not objecting to any bill.

As you can see, the answer choices in this type of question offer potential meanings for "dissent" in the form of explanatory phrases. Here, you are not looking for a direct substitution for "dissent," but rather what dissent means *in this particular passage*. After reading the passage and referring back to it, you know that "dissent" refers to the earlier mention of the public's upset over the statue. The answer choices all reference specific people or items within the passage, and it is your job to figure out to which of these items the term actually refers.

Uses a Term Because…
Part 5

Some Meanings of Words and Phrases questions will ask why the author uses a term, and will commonly include "because" in the question stem. These questions are similar in some ways to the Author's Method questions that ask you for the purpose of a certain part of a passage—particularly, those that ask for the purpose of a certain phrase in the passage. These Meanings of Words and Phrases "because" questions, though, will require you to look for an answer choice that explains the ideas associated with the given term.

Let's look at some ways that Uses a Term Because questions are phrased:

- The author calls slow cookers "improbable" (line 63) because…
- The author uses the term "recycled or retired" (line 15) to indicate that…
- The author most likely uses the statement in lines 45–48 because…

We can now look at an example of this sort of Meanings of Words and Phrases question, still working from "Everything New is Old Again: The Pink Sculpture and the Debate Over Public Art" by Darryl Lauster.

Example

The author most likely calls some of the public "narrow-minded" in line 36 because they:

A. don't understand the pricing of high-end sculptures.
B. cannot appreciate public artwork.
C. disapprove of work that challenges conventions.
D. can appreciate television shows but not visual art forms.

Again, let's look back to the passage to see where the term occurred. Then, we can understand why it was used.

20 In her essay "Looking Around: Where We Are, Where We Could Be," the renowned scholar Lucy Lippard defined public art as an "accessible work of any kind that cares about, challenges, involves, and 25 consults the audience for or with whom it was made, respecting community and environment." Encoded into her definition is the very dichotomy that has created tension between artists and the public for millennia.

30 How does one simultaneously consult and challenge? In a democracy, public space is the terrain reserved for the open exchange and dissection of political ideas. And it can be argued that one's politics drives one's

35 aesthetics. So is it possible to present a work
to a narrow-minded public that reacts with
gut-level outcry to any departure from
previously formed sensibilities?

(C) is the best answer because the author mentions that the public reacts with a "gut-level outcry to any departure from previously formed sensibilities," (lines 37–38) indicating that the public reacts negatively to anything that challenges previous ideas of what is normal.

(A) is incorrect because, though the author mentions price as one reason for outcry against public sculptures, the author does not make any arguments about pricing scales. (B) is too extreme; the author does not make the argument that the public does not appreciate art at all. (D) is incorrect because the author is not making any arguments in the passage about the appreciation of one art form over another.

Answering this question requires thinking about why the author used the given phrase. Why does the author say that the public is "narrow-minded"? Looking for the idea that "narrow-minded" is describing will help you fill in the answer, which is that the public disapproves of work that goes against conventions.

Meanings of Words and Phrases Practice Questions

Part 6

Review the techniques we discussed in Section 1, and mark up and make summaries for this passage excerpt. Then, answer the Meanings of Words and Phrases questions using the strategies you just learned. Refer back to the passage and re-read around the directed lines. Pay attention to the question stem and be ready to choose a synonym for a word as it's used in context, identify why a word or phrase is used, explain a concept, or apply your learning about any of the other question types discussed above.

Social Science: This passage is adapted from the article "Providing Support for Community College Education is Not a New Idea" by Christopher P. Loss (©2015 by Christopher P. Loss).

The public community college model traces its origins to Illinois and the founding of Joliet Junior College, southwest of Chicago, in 1901. Slow but steady growth
5 ensued over the next several decades, particularly in the western United States, as local leaders and pedagogues sought ways to provide their burgeoning populations with low-cost education options. Typically this
10 meant supplementing the local high school with a smattering of vocational and college preparatory classes, or re-purposing existing teacher-training institutes into two-year "people's colleges."

15 Boosters championed the model primarily as a gateway for poor or underprepared students to ready themselves for transfer to a four-year college. The reality was something different, however. During
20 the economic crisis of the 1930s, the aims of these institutions irrevocably shifted to workforce training in "semiprofessional" fields such as stenography, typing, and bookkeeping—whatever vocational fields
25 were then in shortest supply. President Franklin D. Roosevelt's New Deal contributed directly to this reframing.

Economist Rexford Tugwell, a leading member of FDR's "brain trust," promoted
30 adult retraining as a key weapon in the government's fight against the Great Depression, believing that an educated workforce would be more creative, dynamic, and socially cohesive. Harry Hopkins'
35 Works Progress Administration and Harold Ickes' Public Works Administration, meanwhile, helped fund and staff campus construction projects, such as libraries and classroom buildings. And, finally, the
40 enactment of the George-Deen Act of 1936 authorized the distribution of federal funds to community colleges that agreed to use those funds for the provision of vocational coursework of "less than college grade."

45 The New Deal was but a rehearsal for the real revolution in community colleges that followed World War II. Once again, federal action played a vital role. The 1944 GI Bill of Rights provided veterans with
50 generous educational subsidies that boosted attendance at all institutions, including the country's 500 community colleges, where accommodating older students had become a core mission.

55 Demobilization of the military not only pushed enrollment up, it also resulted in the issuing of new equipment; surplus tools and machinery became available from sources

such as decommissioned federally-run national defense training centers. This was especially true in California, a state that became ground zero of the burgeoning defense industry and home to the most vibrant community college system anywhere.

The agility of community colleges in the face of unprecedented demand and a booming postwar economy was not lost on policymakers. In 1947 the release of Higher Education for American Democracy, a report commissioned by President Harry Truman, whose own education ended after a single term at a Kansas City area business college, brought national attention to the bustling two-year arena. The Truman Report, as the six-volume study was more commonly known, declared that "the time has come to make education through the fourteenth grade available in the same way that high school education is now available."

1. The term *reframing*, as it is used in line 27, refers to which of the following?

   A. The New Deal's investment in the building and development of two-year institutions

   B. The development of two-year vocational institutions into broader four-year colleges

   C. The shift of the focus of two-year colleges to preparing students for job fields in need of labor

   D. The changing of workforce training from peacetime to wartime jobs

2. The author calls the New Deal a "rehearsal" in line 45 because:

   F. it did not accomplish its major initiatives.

   G. the greatest changes in two-year institutions came later.

   H. the deal repeated a great many policies from the early 1900s.

   J. it preceded a second New Deal that vastly altered college education.

3. As it is used in line 10, the word "supplementing" means:

   A. swelling.

   B. intensifying.

   C. increasing.

   D. augmenting.

4. The author refers to the "agility" of community colleges in line 66 most likely because these colleges:

   F. offered a variety of courses to soldiers who were going off to war.

   G. were able to nimbly meet demand in the face of sudden changes.

   H. emphasized physical fitness as one of their graduation criteria.

   J. were able to offer education despite disruptions caused by the war.

Section 7
Relationships

Some questions will ask you to describe the ways parts of the passage relate to one another. They may ask you to compare two items in a passage, to understand a cause-effect relationship, or to order a series of events. Answering these questions may require combining information across paragraphs, or understanding information in just one paragraph. In this section we'll cover the following question types:

- Comparative Relationships
- Comparative Relationships and Paired Passages
- Cause-Effect Relationships
- Sequence of Events

In all of these questions, you will have to understand the relationship that is being referenced, and either identify an aspect of that relationship, or summarize it. Use the summaries you jotted down using the Pencil on Paper strategy to help you keep track of the different parts of the passage.

Comparative Relationships
Part 1

Comparative Relationship questions will ask you to compare or contrast individuals, events, or ideas in a passage. These relationships may be explicitly stated, or may be implied and require you to read between the lines.

Here are some ways that Comparative Relationship questions might be phrased:

- The author indicates that, in comparison to individuals, traditional organizations have tended to be...
- Which of the following choices best describes the difference between Shakespeare's comedies and his dramas?

To answer these questions, consider which two elements in the passage you are asked about and put the relationship between them into your own words. Identifying the elements ensures that you know what you are looking for, and Predicting will help you be precise when selecting your answer.

To figure out the relationship between elements, look back to the passage. Where are the people or ideas mentioned, and what is said about them? How would you compare these two elements—how are they similar, and how are they different? You can also refer back to any important parts of the passage you marked up, or to the summaries you made for each paragraph.

Let's look at an example of a Comparative Relationship question:

Example

Natural Science: This passage is adapted from the article "Fluorescent Proteins Light Up Science by Making the Invisible Visible" by Marc Zimmer (©2015 by Marc Zimmer).

The first fluorescent protein found in nature comes from the crystal jellyfish, *Aequorea victoria*, where it is responsible for the green light emitted by its photo
5   organs. It's called green fluorescent protein (GFP). We don't know why these jellyfish have this lit-up feature.

Fluorescent proteins absorb light with short wavelengths, such as blue light, and

10   immediately return it with a different color light that has a longer wavelength, such as green. In *Aequorea victoria*, a protein named aequorin produces blue light, which GFP converts into the green light emitted by the
15   jellyfish's photo organs. This visibility under standard conditions is extremely rare; most other organisms have fluorescent proteins that are only visible if they are illuminated by external blue light sources.

20   After the green fluorescent jellyfish protein, many other fluorescent proteins

have been both found in nature and created in the lab. We now have a spectrum of fluorescent colors available to us that make previously invisible biological structures and processes visible in blazing fluorescent glory. Many new applications reliant on these colors are being published on a regular basis.

CaMPARI is one new technique, short for calcium-modulated photoactivatable ratiometric integrator. By exploiting the fact that calcium concentrations change when nerve cells send signals, CaMPARI is able to light up all the neurons that have fired in a living organism. The technique is based on a fluorescent protein called EOS, which changes its fluorescence from green to red. In fruit flies, zebrafish, and mice, CaMPARI-genetically-modified neurons fluoresce red if they are active and green if they are less active.

Before CaMPARI, all the fluorescent calcium indicators available temporarily lit up when the neuron fired. They couldn't record the firing history of neurons or indicate whether a neuron had fired in the past. According to Loren Looger, one of the researchers who worked on the development of CaMPARI, "The most enabling thing about this technology may be that you don't have to have your organism under a microscope during your experiment. So we can now visualize neural activity in fly larvae crawling on a plate or fish swimming in a dish."

The passage states that the advantage of CaMPARI, as compared to older fluorescence methods, is that CaMPARI:

A. lights up temporarily, while the older methods lit up constantly.

B. allows researchers to use a microscope, while the older methods did not.

C. records the full firing history of neurons, while the older methods did not.

D. shows active neurons using green fluorescence, but the older methods used red.

This question asks you to identify the relationship between CaMPARI and the older fluorescence methods. The passage states that before CaMPARI, the available methods didn't show the firing history of neurons (lines 46–47), suggesting that, by contrast, CaMPARI does show the firing history of neurons (lines 35–37). This makes (C) the best answer.

(A) is incorrect, as it was actually the older methods that lit up temporarily (lines 44–46). (B) is incorrect because Looger explicitly praises CaMPARI for not requiring a microscope (lines 53–54). (D) aims to trick you, as green and red fluorescence are mentioned in the passage. However, these colors are specific to CaMPARI and the passage never states what color the older methods used, so (D) can be ruled out.

In this passage, the comparative relationship between the methods is stated quite explicitly, and the information you need is localized in one paragraph. Remember that you may also be tested on implicit comparative relationships, and have to synthesize information across several paragraphs.

Comparative Relationships and Paired Passages

Part 2

You'll recall from the Paired Passages part in Section 2 that most passage pair questions ask about just one or the other short passage, and can thus be treated like questions for single passages. However, the questions that ask about both short passages are a bit different. These questions can be thought of as Comparative Relationship questions of a sort—although instead of asking you to compare two elements of a single passage, they will ask you to compare elements between two passages!

For Comparative Relationships questions that compare two short passages of a passage pair, you will be asked about similarities or differences between the passages. You might also be asked about how one short passage applies to the other, or how the author of one of the short passages responds to something the author of the other short passage has written. You can apply the same strategy discussed earlier to these question types: note similarities and differences and refer back to any information you jotted down using the Pencil on Paper strategy.

Let's look at two example questions from a paired passage:

Example

Natural Science: Passage A is adapted from the article "Move Over Exoplanets, Exomoons May Harbor Life Too" by Andrew Norton (©2014 by Andrew Norton). Passage B is adapted from the article "Eying Exomoons in the Search for E.T." by Bryan Gaensler (©2016 by Bryan Gaensler).

Passage A

An exomoon is simply a moon that orbits an exoplanet—any planet that orbits a star other than our sun. Although more than 1,000 exoplanets have been
[5] discovered since the first one was found in 1995, only a handful of those are thought to be habitable, at least by life as we know it. New research shows that exomoons, too, could provide habitable
[10] environments. Although we have yet to find exomoons, we have good reasons to believe that there should be many, even more than exoplanets.

Perhaps the most habitable planet found
[15] to date is the recently announced Kepler-186f. This is one of five exoplanets discovered by NASA's Kepler satellite, all orbiting a small, faint, red dwarf star, 500 light years away in the constellation of
[20] Cygnus.

Kepler-186f is an Earth-sized planet that orbits its star in only 130 days and is about as distant from its star as Mercury is from the Sun. But, because the red dwarf is
[25] much dimmer than the Sun, Kepler-186f receives only about one-third of the energy that the Earth does. As a result, Kepler-186f lies at the outer edge of its star's "habitable zone." This is the hypothetical region of
[30] space surrounding a star in which liquid water may conceivably exist on the surface of any exoplanets.

In our own solar system, Venus lies too close to the Sun and is too hot. Mars lies too far from the Sun and is too cold. But Earth, of course, lies within the critical "Goldilocks zone," where the temperature is just right.

Simply residing in the habitable zone, though, is no guarantee that an exoplanet has water oceans. The climate of a planet is much more complicated than we can capture with a simple calculation based on the distance of a planet from a star. We know that Mars probably had running water on its surface in the past, but now it is a frozen desert. Earth, meanwhile, was probably in a completely frozen "snowball" state about 650 million years ago.

Passage B

There are now around 1,600 confirmed exoplanets, and the ones we know about are just a tiny fraction of the more than 100 billion exoplanets we now believe are spread throughout our galaxy. While the golden age of exoplanets has barely begun, an exciting additional chapter is also taking shape: the hunt for exomoons.

Exoplanets are exciting because they're a path to answering one of the grandest questions of all: "Are we alone?" As we find more exoplanets, we eagerly ask whether life could exist there, and whether this planet is anything like Earth. However, so far we've yet to find an exact match to Earth, nor can we yet really know for sure whether any exoplanet, Earth-like or otherwise, hosts life.

There are several reasons why exomoons may be the key to finding life elsewhere in the universe.

First, life on Earth may not have happened at all without our own moon. The Earth's axis is tilted by 23.5 degrees relative to its motion around the sun. This tilt gives us seasons, and because this tilt is relatively small, seasons on Earth are mild: most places never get impossibly hot or unbearably cold. One thing that has been crucial for life is that this tilt has stayed almost the same, varying only by a couple of degrees, for millions of years. What has kept the Earth so steady? The gravity of our moon.

In contrast, Mars' two tiny moons have negligible gravity. Without a stabilizing influence, Mars has gradually tumbled back and forth, its tilt ranging between 0 and 60 degrees over millions of years. Extreme changes in climate have resulted. Any Martian life that ever existed would have found the need to continually adapt very challenging. Without our moon, the Earth, too, would likely have been subject to chaotic climate conditions, rather than the relative certainty of seasons that stretches back deep into the fossil record.

Also, the gravity of the moon may support life by producing the Earth's tides. Billions of years ago, the ebb and flow of the oceans produced an alternating cycle of high and low salt content on ancient rocky shores. This recurring cycle could have enabled the unique chemical processes needed to generate the first DNA-like molecules.

As we continue to hunt for another Earth out there, it seems likely that a twin of Earth without a moon would not look familiar. Finding exomoons is a key part of finding somewhere like here.

1. The author of Passage A and the author of Passage B most likely agree on which of the following statements?

F. Exomoons are the first bodies in space, other than Earth, that host life on them.

G. We can hypothesize about but will never find a planet that contains life other than Earth.

H. The prospect of finding life, that resembles life as we know it, is exciting.

J. Exomoons could be important to finding life beyond Earth.

2. Which of the following is discussed by Passage B, but not by Passage A?
   A. The conditions of a specific discovered exoplanet
   B. The relationship between a planet's temperature and conditions that may support life
   C. The association of the tilt of a planet to its temperature
   D. The influence of distance from a parent star on a planet's temperature

To answer Question 1, think about what is common between the two passages. Then, read through the answer choices and choose the one that reflects a statement on which the authors of the two passages would agree.

(J) is the correct choice, as both authors would agree that exomoons could be important to finding life beyond Earth. The first paragraph of Passage A says that both exoplanets and exomoons "could provide habitable environments" (lines 1–13). Passage B says, "exomoons may be the key to finding life elsewhere in the universe" (lines 70–71).

(F) is incorrect because neither passage indicates that life has been found outside of Earth. (G) is extreme, and incorrect because neither passage asserts that we will never find life on a planet other than Earth. (H) is incorrect because only Passage B shows clear excitement about the possibility of finding other life, as shown in the statements: "Exoplanets are exciting because they're a path to answering one of the grandest questions of all: 'Are we alone?' As we find more exoplanets, we eagerly ask whether life could exist there…" (lines 60–63). Passage A does not show this enthusiasm.

When answering Question 2, you'll want to focus on aspects of the two passages that are different. Then you can correctly identify items that are discussed by Passage B, and not Passage A. (C) is the correct answer, because Passage B discusses how the tilt of a planet can influence its temperature in the fourth and fifth paragraphs, while Passage A does not.

(A) is incorrect because Passage A, but not Passage B, discusses the conditions of a specific discovered exoplanet, that is, Kepler-186f. (B) is incorrect because the relationship between a planet's temperature and conditions that may support life is discussed by both passages, just in different ways. (D) is incorrect because only Passage A, and not Passage B, discusses the influence of distance from a parent star on a planet's temperature; remember, Passage B's discussion of temperature is centered around the subject of tilt, not distance from parent star.

Notice that to answer these questions, you had to think about the similarities and differences between the two short passages. It is helpful to be comfortable with comparing the main ideas of the passages, and it is always good to refer back to the pair to answer questions, especially questions about specific information in the passages.

Remember to pay attention to whether the question is asking about something in Passage A but not Passage B, Passage B but not Passage A, both Passage A and Passage B, or neither passage. Eliminate answer choices that refer to the wrong passage, or misconstrue information about either or both passages.

Cause-Effect Relationships
Part 3

You may also encounter Cause-Effect Relationship questions. These questions ask you to think about a cause-effect relationship in the passage, where one thing directly causes another. They may ask you to characterize the cause-effect relationship, or to identify either the cause or the effect.

Here are some ways that Cause-Effect Relationship questions could be phrased:

- Based on the passage, chemically strengthening glass causes…
- The author states that the phenomenon of groupthink is a result of…

Pay attention to the language of the question stem to ensure that you correctly identify what you need to find about the given cause-effect relationship. For instance, if the question stem says "chemically strengthening glass causes…" you are looking for what chemically strengthening glass leads to—that is, the effect of chemically strengthening glass. Conversely, if the question says that "groupthink is a result of…" you know groupthink is the effect, so you will choose the answer choice that identifies its cause.

Below is an example of a Cause-Effect Relationship question:

Example

Prose Fiction: This passage is adapted from the story "Telref" by Edward McPherson (©2014 by Edward McPherson).

The Telephone Reference Service was established by the New York Public Library in 1968, back when a dedicated call center seemed cutting edge, and most of the
5 inquiries came from secretaries trying to sound out a word their boss had used in dictation. Lately, of course, the department had been shrinking. Through the years, the number remained the last-ditch resource
10 for fact-checkers, journalists, recluses, and writers, their own personal oracle available five days a week, nine hours a day, just dial ASKNYPL. You no longer had to be a trained librarian, just a person with time
15 on your hands and modest powers of research. The real librarians looked down on them as glorified receptionists.

Still, even with the Internet, Sam fielded about a hundred calls a day. Most
20 were silly: Where is Jimmy Hoffa? What's my wife's birthday? And so there had to be rules: no medical advice, crossword clues, interpretation of dreams, or helping with homework. Recently, management had
25 instituted a "no philosophical speculation" rule, but that one was largely ignored.

Sitting in their cramped office off the main floor, the operators had five minutes to dedicate to each question, which was meant
30 to rein in the researchers more than the callers. Sam would have been happy to lose an afternoon tracking down a rare

Bolivian mushroom, or the number of manholes in Cleveland. The callers wanted
35 answers, pure and simple; Sam's job was to cut through the extra stuff. If he couldn't settle the request, he had to pass on the name of someone who could. Five minutes and on to the next. Question, answer,
40 question, answer—the hours passed quickly.

Every morning Sam walked up Fifth Avenue to mount the sweeping steps of the main branch, flanked by the twin marble
45 lions, Patience and Fortitude, which he first recognized from *Ghostbusters*. He also worked in a mausoleum, with the collected bones of Astor, of Lenox, of Carnegie. It

fit his sense of living in a city where
50 everything eventually was plowed under to make room for everything else.

Based on the evidence in the passage, the library's Telephone Reference Service has most likely shrunk because:

F. the operators receive too many silly or irrelevant questions.

G. the service operators provide is no longer cutting edge in the Internet age.

H. there are not enough trained librarians to keep it running.

J. the library is going to be demolished to make room for a mausoleum.

In this question, the effect is the shrinking of the Telephone Reference Service. Your task is to identify the cause of the shrinking. The best choice is (G), for two reasons. First, the phrase, "back when a dedicated call center seemed cutting edge" (lines 3-4) strongly suggests that the call center is no longer cutting edge. Second, the remark that the Telephone Reference Service still has business "even with the Internet" (line 18) acknowledges that the Internet is a significant competitor for what the Telephone Reference Service does—which is answer people's questions.

(F) is incorrect; while the operators do receive a number of silly questions, the passage doesn't suggest that this is the cause of the shrinking of the Telephone Reference Service. (H) is also incorrect, as the passage does not assert that there are not enough trained librarians to keep the Service running. In fact, the passage says that people who are not trained librarians are now working for the Service. The Service no longer requires its employees to be trained librarians *because* it is shrinking, not the other way around.

(J) is also wrong, as Sam's thoughts about mausoleums and "everything [being] plowed under" (line 50) are metaphors, not literal statements, and there is no mention of the library being demolished.

Here, the answer could be found by looking back to the passage for information about the Telephone Reference Service shrinking, and then more specifically the cause of this shrinking. Sometimes the cause-effect relationship will be very obvious; other times, as in this question, you'll have to do a bit of digging to identify the relationship. Be careful not to confuse the causes and effects of events in the passage, as some wrong answers may try to trap you by presenting the wrong causality.

Sequence of Events
Part 4

The final relationship questions we will discuss are Sequence of Events questions. Sequence of Events questions are concerned with the order of events, as they are explicitly stated or implied by the passage. Many of these questions will ask you to outline a series of events in the passage, or simply ask you to identify an element of the passage that occurred before or after another element in the passage.

Sequence of Events questions may also ask you to think about ordering the events of the passage with time that is not explicitly mentioned by the passage—for instance, some questions will ask for the age or position of a character at the time that the passage is set. For these questions, look out for lines, often at the beginning of the passage, that reveal the sequence of the passage's events within a larger time scale.

The following are sample Sequence of Events question stems:

- The author's statement in lines 29–31 implies that the tax law was instituted after…
- At the time of the story, the narrator is…
- Which of the following choices correctly describes the order in which the declarations were instated?

Let's take a look at a Sequence of Events question from the passage "Telref" by Edward McPherson, just seen in the previous part.

Example

Considering the information given in the passage, which of the following most accurately describes when the story takes place?

A. In 1968, during the creation of the Telephone Reference Service
B. After 1968, after the release of the film *Ghostbusters*, but before the invention of the Internet
C. After 1968, after the release of the film *Ghostbusters*, and after the invention of the Internet
D. During the lifetimes of Astor, Lenox, and Carnegie

The best answer to this question is (C), and you don't need to be a history or pop-culture whiz to figure it out! At the beginning of the passage, the events of 1968 are described as being in the past, as the time "back when a dedicated call center seemed cutting edge" (lines 3–4). The film *Ghostbusters* must also have been released already, because Sam thinks about it when he sees the library.

Finally, you can tell that the Internet exists at the time the narrative takes place from the phrase "even with the Internet" (line 19). Therefore, the story takes place after 1968, after the release of the film *Ghostbusters*, and after the invention of the Internet (C).

You can eliminate (A) because the narrator refers to 1968 as having already happened. (B) is incorrect because of the remark, "even with the Internet" (line 19), which indicates the passage takes place after and not before the invention of the Internet. (D) might seem like a tricky choice if you don't know anything about Astor, Lenox, or Carnegie. However, the narrator describes Sam working amidst their "collected bones"—not normally a way you'd talk about living people!

This example shows how you can answer a Sequence of Events question without needing any prior knowledge of the topics in the passage, or of historical events or figures. Don't be intimidated by references you aren't familiar with! Using internal evidence from the passage, you can always determine the right answer. Simply look for information in the passage that outlines the sequence of events referenced in the question stem or suggested by the answer choices.

Relationships Practice Questions
Part 5

Now that you have learned about Comparative Relationship questions, Cause-Effect Relationship questions, and Sequence of Events questions, it's time to practice answering these questions on your own.

For Comparative Relationships, remember to pay attention to the relationships between elements that are compared or contrasted, and when it comes to Cause-Effect relationships, remember to be clear about which element is the cause and which is the effect. Finally, for Sequence of Events questions, glance through the passage to see if you can order the events, and keep in mind that you may have to account for events you can infer occur before or after the events in the passage.

Humanities: This passage is adapted from the article "The Blue Humanities" by John R. Gillis (©2013 by John R. Gillis).

Beginning in the late eighteenth century, people began to come back to the sea in search for a quality they felt to be missing in the new industrial environment: that something called
5 wilderness. The desire for an experience of untamed nature originated in the eighteenth century among a small group of European thinkers, for whom the awesome power of the sea, as witnessed from the safety of land, was
10 emotionally and mentally thought-provoking. In 1712, Joseph Addison wrote of the "agreeable Horror" evoked by storms: "Of all Objects that I have ever seen, there is none which affects imagination so much as the Sea
15 or Ocean." Edmund Burke also preferred the sea to the land as a medicine and energizer for mind and soul. No one knew this better than Jules Verne, who wrote: "The human mind delights in grand visions of supernatural
20 beings. And the sea is their very best medium, the only environment in which such giants . . . can be produced and developed."

Dreams and nightmares that had previously been projected on terrestrial
25 landscapes were now invested in seascapes. Even as the oceans became an object of science, they produced new myths. The notion of Atlantis, the submerged continent, was revived by a modern world anxious about its
30 own survival. The sea moved to the center of western collective consciousness. A modern writer, Jonathan Raban, has called it the most variable of all symbols because it is "not a verifiable object . . . it is, rather, the supremely
35 liquid and volatile element, shaping itself newly for every writer and every generation." It became a symbol of eternity, a comfort to those who, having lost their faith in divine assurance of everlasting life, came to see in its
40 apparently timeless flows evidence of nature's immortality and a promise of life everlasting. For Joseph Conrad, who despised what had happened to land in the industrial age, the sea was the only viable alternative.

45 The sea became a mirror that landlubbers used to reflect on their own condition. Even as actual involvement with the sea decreased, its symbolic presence increased. "We have a fine sea," declared Charles Dickens, echoing fellow
50 European thinkers, "wholesome for all people; profitable for the body, profitable for the mind." In America as well, there developed what was "essentially a coastal, sea-consciousness culture with a developing literary tradition
55 anchored in romantic impulses."

But the sea also operated on a more personal level, as a metaphor for life. In an era when everything seemed to be in a state of becoming, it represented the flow of life in
60 ways that the land could not. "Here," wrote J.

G. Francis of the seaside, "better, we think, than in any inland scenery, man can muse and meditate." The flood tide was a reminder of childhood and youth, the ebb tide of old age,
65 while the horizon "tells of a steadfast future, an unchangeable eternity."

1. The passage indicates that artists and writers became especially interested in the sea:

    A. as the land became more industrialized.

    B. before industrial economies formed.

    C. in the sixteenth century.

    D. only recently, as a result of global warming.

2. Compared to attitudes in European countries, American attitudes toward the ocean were:

    F. totally different.

    G. very similar.

    H. more hostile.

    J. less hostile.

3. The author implies that the modern world's anxieties about its own survival caused:

    A. the oceans to become an object of science.

    B. Joseph Conrad to prefer the sea to the land.

    C. renewed interest in the idea of Atlantis.

    D. the production and development of giants.

Science

Chapter 5

Section 1
Approaching the Science Test

The Science Test is similar to the Reading Test, with the addition of some simple Math concepts and a collection of scientific graphics. This section will cover the format, content, and tactics you'll need to deal with every aspect of the Science Test. By the time you're done reading it, you'll have the knowledge and strategies necessary to get a great score.

This section will cover the following:

- Passage Types
- Question Types
- Variables and Relationships
- General Strategy

About the Science Test

The Science Test is the last section of the ACT, which means that there's a good chance test fatigue will set in. You may be tired, bored, or inattentive, and your score may suffer if you don't have strategies to combat these things (see the Key Strategies chapter).

The Science Test is also different from anything you've seen before. It's not like a high school science test, where you've reviewed the material and practiced beforehand; it's unfamiliar, and this is one of the single biggest sources of stress and low scores. It's not like "real" science either—it doesn't reward innovation, critical thinking, or imagination.

Instead, the Science Test rewards pattern recognition, matching, and attention to detail. The passages contain information, and the questions ask you to find it. Simple concepts—direct and inverse relationships, controls and other variables—are presented in odd and complicated ways. The passages are often hard to read, filled with unfamiliar terminology, complex figures, repetition, and symbols. This section will help you sort it all out.

The Science Test expects you to call upon outside scientific knowledge in four or fewer questions. Brushing up on your first two years of high school science is more than enough to prepare you for these few questions. The rest of the questions can be answered based entirely on the passage.

The Science Test by the Numbers

- 35 minutes to complete test
- 40 questions per test
- 6 passages per test
- 6–7 questions per passage
- 5 minutes 50 seconds per passage

All this information can be distilled into one important Pacing checkpoint: when you finish Passage III and all its questions, 15–18 minutes should have elapsed. Where your checkpoint falls in that range will depend on how you feel and on what passages you've completed.

If the passages you completed were simpler or were primarily Data Representation passages, your checkpoint may be closer to 15 minutes. If the first three passages were dense or included a Conflicting Viewpoints passage, your checkpoint may be closer to 18 minutes. After enough practice, you'll know exactly what your personal checkpoint should be, and you won't have to check your watch at the end of every passage. The checkpoint will indicate your pace and tell you if you have to speed up or slow down.

Passage Types
Part 1

There are three **passage types:** Data Representation, Research Summaries, and Conflicting Viewpoints. The following table explains the passage types:

Passage Type	Content	Passages per Test	Word Count	Questions per Test	Figures per Passage	Goal
Data Representation	Definitions, manipulated data in figures	2	≥100	12	2–6	Interpret and analyze data
Research Summaries	Experimental design, raw data	3	≥250	21	2–4	Understand the scientific method and analyze results
Conflicting Viewpoints	2–4 contrasting hypotheses	1	≥300	7	0–1	Evaluate different claims about the same topic

The Science Test covers five general **areas of science**: biology, physics, chemistry, space science, and earth science. The passages often involve topics that are slightly outside the scope of core high school curricula, and you aren't expected to have previous experience with these fields (e.g. plate tectonics, stars and the universe, taxonomy). Almost everything you're asked about will be taken directly from the passage.

However, as previously mentioned, a few questions per test will ask about basic scientific definitions (e.g. cell membrane, Newton's laws, calorie). These questions cannot be answered by referencing the passage, but only by knowing your first two years of high school science. See Section 3, Part 9, and the online glossary for a quick review of important concepts and terms.

For additional resources, please visit **ivyglobal.com/study**.

The six passages aren't presented in any standard order of passage type, area of science, or difficulty. There is no reason to skip passages or plan an approach to them—doing passages in order is the best method. You'll see how to approach each passage type in Section 2.

Question Types
Part 2

Within a passage, the questions tend to move from simple to complex. Even so, it can be a good idea to Pick and Skip questions—especially if they ask about more than one piece of information. Saving those questions for the end of the passage can be helpful because it will allow you to synthesize information you found while answering the other more narrowly focused questions.

There are five **question types**: Understanding, Analysis, Synthesis, Experimental Design, and Knowledge. These are *not* official ACT question types, but rather classifications based on analyses of the ACT and its test specifications. Being familiar with *how* the ACT asks questions is a good tool to use in your approach to the test. The following table explains each question type:

Question Type	Approximate Number per Test	Purpose
Understanding	9	Identify trends, statistics, and claims
Analysis	10	Fit new data into a figure or text (interpolate, extrapolate, infer claims, evaluate claims), transform or evaluate a figure or text
Synthesis	11	Compare and contrast multiple figures or texts, use multiple figures or texts to evaluate claims or data
Experimental Design	6	Identify, manipulate, and evaluate variables, equipment, design flaws, and research intent
Knowledge	4	Define terms, provide information not given in the passage

You can see from the table that the Science Test expects you to do a lot of identifying, evaluating, and defining. These words may make it *seem* like the Science Test requires you to carefully read the passage word by word, to understand it fully, and then to approach the questions. However, as you saw in the Reading Test, this is not necessarily true. You'll see how to approach each question type in Section 3, except for the Knowledge questions, which you can find information about in Section 3, Part 9, and the online glossary.

When you answer Science Test questions, it's also a good idea to remember the Wrong Answer Types from the Key Strategies section. Like Reading, the Science Test uses a formulaic approach to wrong answers. The three types—irrelevant, out-of-scope, and confused content—will often appear.

Variables and Relationships
Part 3

The main things to note on the Science Test are **variables**. A variable is a measured quantity or quality, and must be closely controlled and monitored in order for an experiment to be accurate. An **independent variable** is changed in the experiment in order to produce a change in the dependent variable. As you might guess, changes in the **dependent variable** *depend on* changes in the independent variable.

Example

Four plates of bacteria were grown in an incubator at 37°C for 24 hrs, then massed. 10 mL of a different concentration of soap was added to each plate, and the plates were placed back in the incubator at 37°C for 24 hrs, then massed. The results are shown in Table 1 below.

Table 1		
Concentration of Soap (%)	Initial Mass (mg)	Final Mass (mg)
0	112	112
10	134	123
20	98	82
50	107	64

In this example, the mass of bacteria *depends* on the concentration of the soap. Therefore, the mass of bacteria is the dependent variable, and the concentration of the soap is the independent variable.

The researchers also have several **constants**, which are factors that should have no effect on the variables between separate trials: incubation temperature, incubation time, and volume of soap. Another type of constant is a **control**, a trial in which nothing is expected to happen, which is used to eliminate external effects and to determine exactly what caused the observed changes. In this example, the control is the first plate, which had 10 mL of 0% soap added to it.

Variables have different **relationships** with each other. Two relationships are at the core of the Science Test. A **direct relationship** is when a change in the independent variable causes the *same* type of change in the dependent variable. An **inverse relationship** is when a change in the independent variable causes the *opposite* type of change in the dependent variable. Here, the relationship is inverse: as soap concentration increases, bacterial mass decreases. You can write this as "↑SC = ↓BM." As on the Math Test, make sure you use letters that accurately represent variables in order to avoid confusion!

Each passage is designed to disguise the core relationships under investigation and distract you from discovering them. Don't be fooled—look for relationships.

General Strategy

The Science Test is diverse. Its passages require slightly different approaches, especially the Conflicting Viewpoints passage. Special techniques and strategies will be introduced in the following sections. For now, familiarize yourself with the following general strategy for approaching the Science Test, along with a few smaller tips and tricks.

As you know, the Science Test contains a bunch of complex jargon and a small amount of must-have material. You *do not* want to read the whole passage before answering questions, or skip to the questions without reading the passage. These are common approaches, but they'll make you feel overwhelmed. Instead, skim only the figures, so you know *where information is located*, and then move on to the questions.

Your **general strategy** will be explained below. It will be helpful to have these pages on hand to guide you through your first few practice passages. After you've implemented these tactics effectively, try to do questions on your own without the book.

This strategy requires a lot of practice. It's somewhat counterintuitive, because it requires you not to be a critically minded student, but a locating and sorting machine. Start by clustering information in the passage, then extracting information from questions, then using all that information in order to identify the answers to your questions. Alternate between the questions and the passage with increasing scrutiny and specificity.

3D Skim the Passage

The 3 Ds are details, differences, and definitions. You should circle, underline, or otherwise annotate them in order to highlight the *location* of information, and to preserve your working memory.

Details are found in figures and tables. You should always read these first, and once you do, if you feel you have a good understanding of where information is located, you can skip differences and definitions and start reading the questions.

Important details are often found in axis labels, Figure Keys, and Figure Notes. The ACT will manipulate axes and table increments and start- and end-points to trick you, so never assume that an axis starts at zero or increases linearly, or even increases at all. Circle or underline any deviations from your expectations. Other important details to annotate are maximums and minimums, trends in graphs, increases or decreases in tables, and experimental set-ups.

If you're reading a Research Summaries or Conflicting Viewpoints passage, you'll want to pay attention to **differences** between experiments or arguments. Differences can even help you on Data Representation passages. Often, differences can be found in the column titles of tables of raw data. Sometimes, they may be found in the experimental design, explained in the text above the tables or figures. In Conflicting Viewpoints passages, note differences in interpretations of the same facts or events. Noting differences can be a fast way to familiarize yourself with both details and definitions.

Definitions are the least important of the 3 Ds. They're only necessary to look for if you're totally unsure of what a word means. Even so, you should try to ignore unfamiliar words. If you want to be certain, you can find them in the introductory part of each passage, and they're almost always italicized.

Read a Question

After your brief **3D Skim**, you want to start reading a question. If you're working through a Conflicting Viewpoints passage, however, you want to read the passage more carefully than just a 3D Skim—you'll see what to do when you read Section 2, Part 5, Conflicting Viewpoints.

If you're working on one of the other passage types, do one question at a time and try to quickly organize the information given by the question. To organize given information, *pause briefly* after each piece of information to give your memory a second to absorb it. You can also draw a dot or slash on the page to help break up a confusing or wordy question.

When you read a question, focus on important words and phrases. How do you know what's important? It's easy—whatever matches the 3 Ds you skimmed for earlier. If that's not enough to understand a question, pay attention to the relationships that it asks about. If a question asks about a relationship, you can rewrite it using arrows and letters as variables, like you saw above. You can also scan the answers for the 3 Ds you annotated in the passage, to help indicate where information pertinent to answering the question is located.

Example

Suppose a large volume of *trichloroethane*, a known carcinogen and pollutant, / is released into the atmosphere by a factory adjacent to Site 3. / The biodiversity index of Site 3 will most likely:

A. increase, because air quality is likely to increase.
B. increase, because air quality is likely to decrease.
C. decrease, because air quality is likely to increase.
D. decrease, because air quality is likely to decrease.

You added slashes to separate given information and make it easier to read, and circled your goal. The repetition of the phrase "air quality" in the answer options also indicated that air quality is an important part of answering this question. You would know from the passage that as air quality decreases, the biodiversity index decreases. You can write this as a relationship by writing $\downarrow$AQ = $\downarrow$BI.

You know from the question that a pollutant is added to the air; you might know from your science classes that pollutants decrease air quality, but the passage would probably tell you. Therefore, ↑P = ↓AQ = ↓BI. The answer is (D).

Refer Back to the Passage

Now that you've read the question, you should **refer back** to the relevant part of the passage to answer it. The Science Test will deliberately mislead your memory, so it's dangerous to rely on it alone. It's also dangerous to answer questions based solely on your science background or your logical reasoning ability. Your background and logic can help you, but the passage is far more important.

Combine the given information and goals from the question and answers with the annotations you made during your 3D Skim to quickly locate the part of the passage that's relevant to answering the question. Synonyms for the important words you found during your 3D Skim can also be useful in locating information, as can things that are *easy to spot* without intent reading: don't look for common words, but look for italics, numbers, capital letters, line breaks, brackets and em dashes, units, and double letters (gg, mm).

Next, verify that this information is what the question actually asks about. Questions can point you in the wrong direction with irrelevant or incomplete information. Don't be fooled if a question says "According to Figure 1" but then also mentions a detail only found in Figure 2—you'll have to look at both figures in this case.

Read the relevant information—this is *not a skim.* During your 3D Skim, you only wanted to know where information was. Now, when you refer back to the passage, you want to *understand* information.

To help with your understanding, you can ignore repetitive phrases and jargon and focus on processes and sequences, along with core details and main verbs. You can also use slashes when reading the question, as shown in the previous example, to separate discrete pieces of given information. Make sure to stop reading when you've found the answer and move on to the next question.

If referring back to the passage doesn't give you the exact answer, then use the Prediction strategy. Even if it's vague, or a hunch, making a prediction can help by telling you which answer options are wrong and which are more likely to be correct. Always *estimate* numerical answers, too; since no calculators are allowed, the calculations won't be too complex or exact for you to do in your head.

Process of Elimination

Now that you've marked up the passage, read the question, and referred back to the passage to find the answer or make a prediction, you're ready to answer the question. If at some point in this process you have found the answer, you should move on to the next question. If it's a more complex question, however, you might need to use **Process of Elimination**.

There are two important features of Science Test questions that make Process of Elimination easier. One is the fact that the answers are often very similar to each other, with only one or two words that are different. The other is the fact that the answers are often in parts, as you saw in the example above.

Trust your eyes to read more than one answer choice at a time. If the answer choices are identical except for a word or two, then it's a waste of time to read each answer choice in its entirety. You can use **chunking** to make this reading easier. Simply *read the answers vertically*, comparing their parallel parts to find the differences between them.

If part of the answer is wrong, the whole answer is wrong. This is called **piecewise elimination**, and it works well with chunking and predicting. Don't continue to read an answer choice that has an incorrect part—nothing can make up for an incorrect part, and you can't rationalize it away. Move on to the next option. Check out the example you've just seen, but this time try chunking and piecewise elimination.

Example

Suppose a large volume of *trichloroethane*, a known carcinogen and pollutant, is released into the atmosphere by a factory adjacent to Site 3. The biodiversity index of Site 3 will most likely:

A. increase, because air quality is likely to increase.
B. increase, because air quality is likely to decrease.
C. decrease, because air quality is likely to increase.
D. decrease, because air quality is likely to decrease.

You can vertically read the first and last words, and know that the middle chunk of each answer choice is identical. Often, first and last words are good places to look for differences between answer choices. You know that the addition of a pollutant means air quality must decrease, so answers (A) and (C) are incorrect. Of (B) and (D), you know that biodiversity will decrease if air quality does, so (D) is correct.

After you've made your choice, glance over the eliminated options quickly to ensure you didn't miss anything. If you can't find an answer for what feels like a long time, Pick and Skip. Circle the question and start the next one. Sometimes, answering other questions will give you enough information to return and answer your skipped question, because every time you answer a question, you are likely to return and read a part of the passage again.

If you skip a question, make sure you return to it before moving on to the next passage. It will be time-consuming and difficult to get back into a passage if you return to a question at the end of the entire Science Test.

Section 2
Passage Types

This section will show you how to approach the different passage types on the Science Test. As you know, there are three passage types on each Science Test. These passages will cover five areas of science, most of which will involve concepts you've learned about in your science classes. You don't have to memorize these three types or any scientific facts in order to master these passages, but knowing what you're likely to see on the ACT will help prepare you and boost your confidence. The three passage types are:

- Data Representation
- Research Summaries
- Conflicting Viewpoints

The passages differ based on their frequency, word count, density, figures, and how they present data. In general, they will include tables and figures that present raw and manipulated data, and text that will give background information on the figures, on the processes used to attain the results presented in the figures, or on different models and arguments. Sometimes, a passage won't have a figure at all—if it doesn't, it's most likely a Conflicting Viewpoints passage.

The passages also differ based on what questions they ask. The five (unofficial) question types are explained more in Section 3. For now, have a look at the following section, read through the explanations, and try the practice questions!

Data Representation
Part 1

Data Representation passages require you to understand and analyze scientific figures, trends, and relationships. These passages primarily represent experimental data in technical, often over-complicated figures, which may include bar graphs, line graphs, scatter plots, and large tables.

Data Representations are different from Research Summaries and Conflicting Viewpoints in that the passages are much briefer and the figures tend to be much more complex, similar to those in scientific journals. They do not include design protocols but may include a lot of jargon and a few definitions. They may ask an occasional question that requires you to understand where the presented data came from, or to select an answer based not on the passage, but on your scientific knowledge.

There will usually be two Data Representation passages per test, and each passage will have six questions associated with it. If you can successfully navigate their strange figures—a quick review of Chapter 3, Section 1 might help—then they can be your quickest and easiest Science Test passages. But if you look at the wrong data, or get bogged down in trying to discern some kind of deeper meaning—beware!

Remember that Science passages, and perhaps Data Representations most of all, reward attention to detail. Data Representations focus on recognizing where numbers fit into given trends. Skimming them is an exercise in *locating* details, and *not* in understanding them. Remember the expression *location, location, location*—or use the handy graphic below. You don't need to suspend your critical thinking skills, but they do need to take a backseat to your visual pattern recognition and word- and number-matching skills.

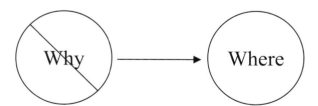

During your 3D Skim, mentioned in Section 1, the most important D is details. Circle axis labels and Figure Keys and Notes. Glance at increments and units, and circle anything out of the ordinary, such as axes that don't start at zero, axes that decrease, and axes that increase non-linearly.

The following Data Representation example displays the data of experiments conducted on the refraction of light. The notes in the margins will point out the characteristics mentioned above and in the Approaching the Science Test section.

As light passes through the boundary between two different media, it may *refract* (bend). In two media, the ratio of the angle of incidence (θ_i) and the angle of refraction (θ_R) is equal to the inverse of the ratio of the *refractive indices*, which are the factors by which the speed of light decreases in different media. Air has a refractive index of 1. Figure 1 shows the angle of incidence in air and the angles of refraction for mercury, water, and polystyrene at 20°C. Figures 2 and 3 show the refractive indices for various wavelengths and temperatures of the three different media.

Don't read this introductory passage. Remember: it's only useful if you have a question that asks you for information that isn't in the figures. When a question refers you to this text, or asks you about a figure that you found difficult to read, pay attention to those sentences that explain the figures. Here, those are the last two sentences.

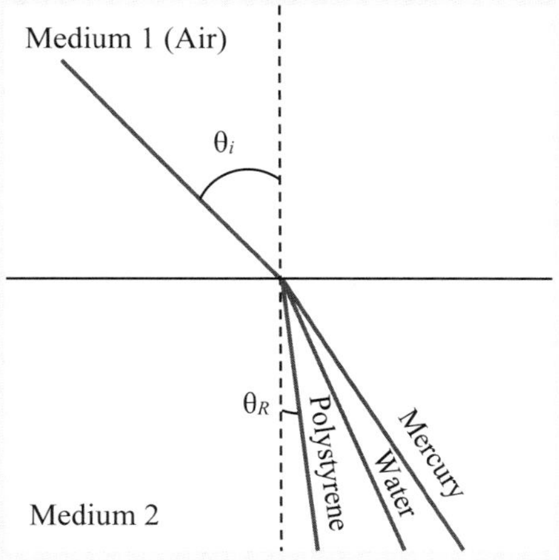

Figure 1

(Note:) All light has a wavelength of 500 nm.

This is where your eyes should go first in your 3D Skim. This figure is strange. It's not a graph—there are no units on the axes. You could glance at the passage to tell you that it's about the refraction of light, or you could continue without knowing. Make sure you circle the "Note" at the bottom (circling the word "Note" is enough for you to know the location). And pay attention to the weird symbols (θ) on the figure. They could be defined in the passage, but you don't have to know that until you reach a question that asks you about it.

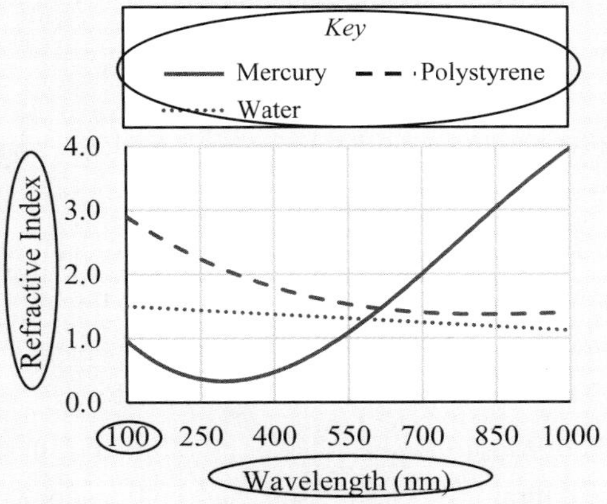

Figure 2

(Note:) All light has a temperature of 20°C.

This figure is complex. Circle the Key. Circle both axis labels ("Refractive Index" and "Wavelength"). Note where the axes start and end, and how they increase: the y-axis goes up by 1.0, and the x-axis goes up by 150 nm. What's an "nm"? Doesn't matter. What does matter is that the x-axis doesn't start on 0—therefore, you should circle 100. Finally, circle the "Note."

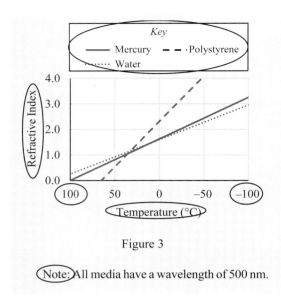

Key

— Mercury   – – Polystyrene

····· Water

Figure 3

Note: All media have a wavelength of 500 nm.

This figure looks a little more normal. Circle the Key again—note that it mentions the same three variables seen in Figures 1 and 2. The y-axis label is the same as the one in Figure 2, but circle it again. The x-axis label is "Temperature,"—that's new, so circle it. Now, look at the axes themselves. The y-axis is the same as Figure 2, but the x-axis is confusing. Temperature decreases as you move to the right. Circle the endpoints to cement this idea. Because this graph is reversed, make a mental note that the trend lines are backward. You could also write a relationship on your page, like this: ↑T = ↓R|. This means "as Temperature goes up, Refractive Index goes down." It's a fast way to get at the heart of the matter—the simple relationship. Finally, circle the "Note."

Example

According to Figure 2, as the wavelength of light increased from 400 nm to 1000 nm, the refractive index of mercury:

A. decreased only.

B. increased only.

C. decreased, then increased.

D. varied, but with no clear trend.

First, note *what* the question asks you. To summarize, it asks you to describe the trend in mercury's refractive index as the wavelength of light increases from 400 nm to 1000 nm. Second, note *where* the question refers you: Figure 2.

Now, refer back to Figure 2. You circled 100 on the *x*-axis, so you are aware that this axis doesn't start at 0. However, the question does *not* ask you for the trend from 100 nm to 1000 nm. Always verify what the question asks you. In this case, it may be most helpful to circle "400" in the question.

There is always a danger of forgetting what the question asks you as you refer back to the passage. Circling key terms in the question—in this case "400" and "mercury"—will prevent that information from slipping away from you. Now that you're sure what the question is asking you for, you can read mercury's trend line between 400 and 1000 on the *x*-axis. There's a clear trend, which makes (D) incorrect. And the trend is increasing. The correct answer is (B).

(A) is tempting if you missed that the question was asking about mercury, because both other lines in Figure 2 (water and polystyrene) are decreasing. (C) is tempting if you missed that the question was asking from 400 nm to 1000 nm, not from 100 nm to 1000 nm.

Based on Figure 3, if the refractive index of water was measured to be 4.0 using light with a wavelength of 500 nm, its temperature would most likely have been closest to which of the following?

F.   175°C
G.   75°C
H.   –75°C
J.   –175°C

Pause after any given information and mark it. There's a lot in this question: water, 4.0, 500 nm, temperature. The answers are all in degrees Celsius. Now, note where the question refers you: Figure 3.

When you refer back to Figure 3, you notice that the "500 nm" information is irrelevant. It's distracting because it sounds important, but the Note, which you circled, tells you that it's true for the whole figure. This is often the case with Notes on the Science Test. They specify a condition that holds true for the whole figure, but they can be very distracting in questions, because they make the question sound like it's asking for something else entirely, or a figure other than the one it references.

You also notice that water never reaches a refractive index of 4.0. Rather, the graph ends when water's refractive index is a little more than 3.0. This question is therefore asking you to extrapolate—to extend the graph.

You can do this in two ways. One, you can extend water's trend line up and to the right, eyeballing the x-value (temperature) where it hits a refractive index of 4.0. Two, you can estimate that when water's refractive index was 2.0, its temperature was about –25°C, and when its refractive index was 3.0, its temperature was about –100°C. This means, roughly, that for every 75°C *decrease* in temperature, the refractive index increases by 1.0. Your best guess in this instance would be around –175°C, so (J) is the correct answer. On the Science Test, estimation is usually enough to find the right answer.

If you think that this is an *increase* of 75°C, you'll incorrectly choose (H). If you miss the negative signs on this odd x-axis, you'll incorrectly choose (F) or (G).

According to Figure 3, at which of the following temperatures are the refractive indices of mercury and polystyrene equivalent?

A.   50°C
B.   40°C
C.   20°C
D.   0°C

Again, the question asks about Figure 3. You just spent time there in the last question, so it's fresh. You can use this to your advantage: don't repeat circles, and don't waste extra time reviewing a figure you've already reviewed.

If refractive indices are equal, then the lines should intersect. Don't calculate anything—no slopes, no intercepts. You can see that the lines for water and mercury intersect at a point slightly less than 50°C, which would be (B).

(A) is tempting if you overgeneralize or too broadly estimate. The Science Test rewards attention to detail, and it won't penalize good estimation, but it will penalize poor attempts to estimate. It's a good idea to estimate using ranges—to find the highest and lowest reasonable estimations—because point estimations may be too precise. (C) is wrong because it's the temperature at which mercury and water have equal refractive indices.

Example

At 20°C and 200 nm, what is the order of the three media from highest to lowest refractive index?

F.   Mercury, polystyrene, water
G.   Water, polystyrene, mercury
H.   Polystyrene, water, mercury
J.   Polystyrene, mercury, water

This question doesn't reference a figure, which means that it might refer to the passage or to all figures. However, it mentions a temperature of 20°C and a wavelength of 200 nm. Figures 1 and 3 only use light at 500 nm, so you know you have to look at Figure 2.

Find the 200 nm mark on the *x*-axis. It's unlabeled, but you can see that the increments on the *x*-axis are 150 nm, so it's between 100 nm and 250 nm. Carefully draw a vertical line up so that it intersects all three trend lines. This will allow you to map out which medium has the highest refractive index at this point. Because the *y*-axis is standard—it increases linearly, in increments of 1.0—the medium with the highest trend line is also the medium with the highest refractive index. From highest to lowest, that's polystyrene, water, and mercury, or (H).

(F) is incorrect because it reflects Figure 1, and Figure 2 at 600 nm and above. Similarly, (G) reflects Figure 3 between, roughly, 50°C and 100°C. (J) is the most tempting incorrect answer because it's the closest in order, but it's only true for a narrow range of wavelengths from about 500 nm to 550 nm.

Polystyrene is a polymer, a chain of repeating molecular units bonded together. If the behavior of water is characteristic of liquids in general, and the behavior of polystyrene is characteristic of polymers in general, one would most likely make which of the following conclusions about the effect of temperature on the refractive indices of both polymers and liquids?

A. As temperature increases, the refractive indices of both polymers and liquids increase.

B. As temperature increases, the refractive indices of both polymers and liquids decrease.

C. As temperature increases, the refractive indices of polymers increase, and the refractive indices of liquids decrease.

D. As temperature increases, the refractive indices of polymers decrease, and the refractive indices of liquids increase.

This question is wordy. It's the type of question that, when you read it, you want to pause and let your memory absorb given information. A good rule of thumb is that if the question is three lines or longer, you should pause, add slashes after given information, and circle your goal.

The first sentence, it turns out, is irrelevant. This is factual information, but the question only asks for the relationship between temperature and refractive indices for polystyrene and all polymers, and for water and all liquids. The second sentence tells you that, for the purpose of the question, polystyrene = all polymers, and water = all liquids.

You know from your 3D Skim that Figure 3 represents the relationship between temperature and refractive index. Refer back to Figure 3. You've circled the *x*-axis for a reason: it decreases. All the trend lines *look* like they have a positive slope, but because the *x*-axis is decreasing, they all actually represent an inverse relationship. Note also that the trend lines of both polystyrene and water move in roughly the same direction, which means that (C) and (D) are incorrect.

(B) is the correct answer. If you write the relationship on the graph, ↑T = ↓RI, then you won't be confused. (A) is the exact opposite of the correct answer, and it's only tempting if you haven't circled the axes or written down the relationship.

Example

Suppose an unknown medium had a greater angle of refraction than mercury in Figure 1. Compared with the speed of light in mercury, the speed of light in the unknown medium was:

F. higher, because the unknown medium has a higher refractive index than mercury.

G. higher, because the unknown medium has a lower refractive index than mercury.

H. lower, because the unknown medium has a higher refractive index than mercury.

J. lower, because the unknown medium has a lower refractive index than mercury.

"Speed of light" wasn't graphed on any figure, so you must refer back to the passage to determine what it means. Rather than reading the whole passage, search specifically for those words only, and read the surrounding sentence. The passage says, "the *refractive indices*, which are the factors by which the speed of light decreases in different media." The larger the refractive index, the greater the decrease in the speed of light: $\uparrow$RI = $\downarrow$SL.

Now that you know this relationship, you need to find out how the refractive index relates to the angle of refraction. In the passage, the sentence before the one you just read says, "In two media, the ratio of the *angle of incidence* and the *angle of refraction* are equal to the inverse of the ratio of the *refractive indices*." This tells you that the ratios have an inverse relationship: $\uparrow$AR = $\downarrow$RI.

Combine these two inverse relationships: $\uparrow$AR = $\downarrow$RI = $\uparrow$SL. Be careful here. If an unknown medium had a higher angle of refraction than mercury, it had a lower refractive index and a higher speed of light, so (G) is correct.

To find the correct answer, use chunking and piecewise elimination. Look at the first words and the middle words: higher, higher, lower, lower, etc. You can eliminate (H) and (J) immediately, because "lower" at the start is incorrect, and then you can eliminate (F) as you *read vertically* through the second column of parallel words.

The wrong answers all depend on your mixing up these relationships, or mixing up the step where you need to combine the two relationships. If you were confused by the use of the word "ratio" in the passage, you could have used the figures. In Figure 1, mercury has the greatest angle of refraction, followed by water, and then polystyrene.

Data Representation Practice Questions
Part 2

Passage I

Fossil evidence shows that two lineages of African saber-toothed cats, *Homotherium ethiopicum* and *Homotherium hadarensis*, existed in Africa until their extinction approximately 12,000 years ago. Fossils show that the body size of African saber-toothed cats declined before their extinction. Ankle-bone fossils of African saber-toothed cats were dated using radiocarbon years (years determined by the proportion of radioactive carbon to non-radioactive carbon in a fossil), as shown in Figure 1. Figure 2 shows the number of discovered ankle bones of African saber-toothed cats against the lengths of these ankle bones. Figure 3 shows the length and width of the ankle bones for the species *H. ethiopicum* and *H. hadarensis*.

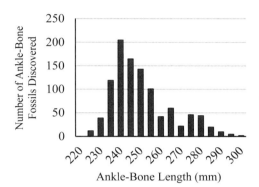

Figure 2

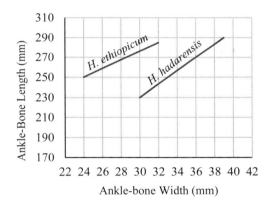

Figure 3

Data adapted from Open I, Weinstock J. Weinstock et al., "Evolution, Systematics, and Phylogeography of Pleistocene Horses in the New World: A Molecular Perspective." ©2015 from PLoS Bio. 10.1371/journal.pbio.0030241

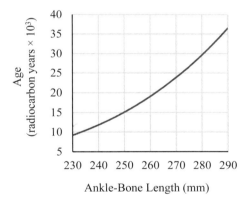

Figure 1

1. According to Figure 1, fossils of African saber-toothed cats dated 12,000 radiocarbon years ago had an ankle-bone length closest to which of the following?

   A.   220 mm
   B.   230 mm
   C.   240 mm
   D.   250 mm

2. According to Figure 1, if the trend in ankle-bone length had continued, the ankle-bone length of fossils of African saber-toothed cats dated 40,000 years ago would most likely be:

   F.   less than 290 mm.
   G.   between 290 mm and 330 mm.
   H.   between 330 mm and 370 mm.
   J.   more than 370 mm.

3. Based on Figure 2, the number of ankle-bone fossils found that were approximately 225 mm was closest to which of the following?

   A.   20
   B.   40
   C.   80
   D.   100

4. Which of the following would most likely be the average width of the most commonly discovered ankle bones?

   F.   28 mm
   G.   30 mm
   H.   32 mm
   J.   34 mm

5. Which of the following statements best describes the trend of ankle-bone length in African saber-toothed cats?

   A.   Ankle-bone length increased over time.
   B.   Ankle-bone length decreased over time.
   C.   Ankle-bone length remained stable over time.
   D.   Ankle-bone length varied with no general trend over time.

6. A scientist discovers an ankle bone with a width of 38 mm. Approximately how old, in radiocarbon years, is the ankle bone?

   F. 28×10^3
   G. 30×10^3
   H. 32×10^3
   J. 34×10^3

Passage II

Lyme disease is an infectious disease that causes a circular rash, joint swelling, and headaches. It is caused by the bacteria *Borrelia burgdorferi*, which is only carried by ticks and mammals. Because ticks feed on mammalian blood, an infected tick can release the bacteria into an uninfected mammal's blood, and an uninfected tick can absorb the bacteria from an infected mammal's blood, as shown with a mouse in Figure 1.

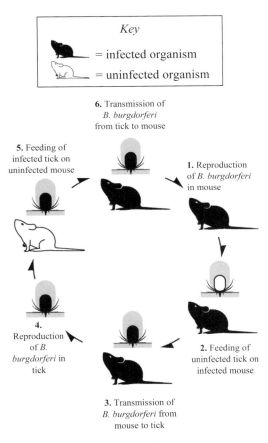

Figure 1

B. burgdorferi has evolved three proteins that allow it to survive and reproduce in many different hosts. It requires all three proteins to survive in any host. Figure 2 shows the concentrations of these proteins—OspC, BpaB, and Erp—in an infected tick and an infected mouse. Figure 3 shows the rate of production of these three proteins at various temperatures.

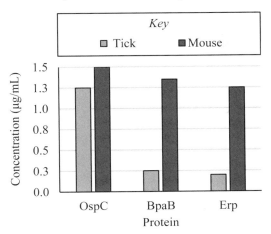

Figure 2

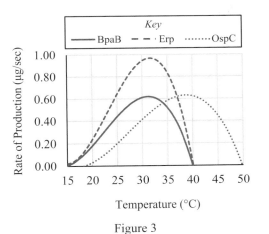

Figure 3

All figures adapted from Jutras et al., Department of Microbiology, Yale University, 2015.

7. According to Figure 2, if an infected tick feeds on an infected mouse, which of the following *B. burgdorferi* proteins is present in the greatest concentration in both tick and mouse?

	Tick	Mouse
(A)	OspC	OspC
B.	BpaB	OspC
C.	Erp	BpaB
D.	Erp	Erp

8. Based on Figure 1, in which stage is the concentration of Erp the *lowest* in the tick?

   (F) Stage 2
   G. Stage 3
   H. Stage 4
   J. Stage 5

9. Based on Figure 3, at what temperature are the concentrations of the OspC and BpaB proteins equivalent?

   A. 0°C
   B. 25°C
   C. 26°C
   (D) 34°C

10. Assuming that the rate of production of a protein and its concentration are directly related, the internal temperature of ticks is most likely:

    F. less than 25°C.
    G. between 25°C and 30°C.
    H. between 30°C and 35°C.
    (J) greater than 35°C.

11. A *fever* is the sustained elevation of internal temperature. Mammalian immune systems use fevers to decrease the rate of production of the proteins of infecting organisms, leading to the death of the infecting organisms. If a certain mammalian fever involves a temperature of 45°C, will the fever kill *B. burgdorferi*?

    A. Yes, because the OspC protein is not produced at temperatures greater than 50°C.
    (B) Yes, because the Erp and BpaB proteins are not produced at temperatures greater than 40°C.
    C. No, because the OspC protein is not produced at temperatures greater than 50°C.
    D. No, because the Erp and BpaB proteins are not produced at temperatures greater than 40°C.

12. A *green anole* is a lizard found in the southeastern United States. The internal temperature of the green anole is between 15°C and 25°C. A scientist observes a green anole with a circular rash and joint swelling, and hypothesizes that the anole is infected by *B. burgdorferi*. Are the data presented consistent with this hypothesis?

    F. Yes, because a circular rash and joint swelling are symptoms of *B. burgdorferi* infection.
    G. Yes, because *B. burgdorferi* infection is widespread in the southeastern United States.
    H. No, because *B. burgdorferi* proteins are not produced at temperatures less than 25°C.
    (J) No, because *B. burgdorferi* is carried by ticks and mammals only, and the green anole is a reptile.

Passage III

Water can exist in three states: solid, liquid, and gas. The state of water changes depending on environmental conditions. The *freezing point* is the temperature at which water changes from liquid to solid, or vice versa, at a certain pressure. The *boiling point* is the temperature at which water changes from liquid to gas, or vice versa, at a certain pressure.

Figure 1 is a *heating curve,* which shows how the temperature of water changes with heat input at a given pressure. The freezing and boiling points are marked. Figure 2 shows the relationship between temperature, pressure, and phase.

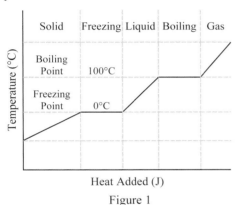

Figure 1

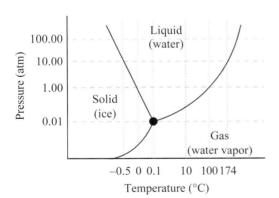

Figure 2

The freezing and boiling points of water can be changed by the presence of ions such as table salt (NaCl). Table 1 shows the effect of dissolving various amounts of table salt in 1 L of water at a pressure of 1 atm.

Table 1		
Mass of salt dissolved (g)	Freezing point (°C)	Boiling point (°C)
0	0.0000	100.0000
1	−0.0318	100.0089
2	−0.0637	100.0178
3	−0.0955	100.0267
4	−0.1273	100.0356
5	−0.1591	100.0445
6	−0.1910	100.0534

13. Based on the data in Table 1, as the amount of salt dissolved in water increased, how did the freezing point and boiling point of water vary?

	Freezing Point	Boiling Point
A.	Increased	Increased
B.	Increased	Decreased
C.	Decreased	Increased
D.	Decreased	Decreased

14. At the surface of the Dead Sea, the pressure is approximately 1.05 atm. The boiling point of water at the Dead Sea will most likely be:

   F. less than 0°C.
   G. between 0°C and 10°C.
   H. between 10°C and 100°C.
   J. greater than 100°C.

15. According to Figure 2, under what conditions can water undergo a direct phase transition from a solid to a gas, without passing through the liquid stage?

    A. Temperatures below 0.1°C and any pressure.

    B. Pressures below 0.01 atm and any temperature.

    C. Temperatures above 0.1°C and pressures below 0.01 atm.

    D. Temperatures below 0.1°C and pressures below 0.01 atm.

16. A scientist states that, as energy is added to water, its temperature changes at a uniform rate. Do the data represented in Figure 1 support this hypothesis?

    F. No; the slope of the line in Figure 1 is negative and constant.

    G. No; the slope of the line in Figure 1 varies as heat is added.

    H. Yes; the slope of the line in Figure 1 is positive and constant.

    J. Yes; the slope of the line in Figure 1 varies as heat is added.

17. If 8 g of salt were dissolved in 1 L of water at 1 atm of pressure, the boiling point of the water would most likely be:

    A. 100.0580°C.

    B. 100.0623°C.

    C. 100.0712°C.

    D. 100.0922°C.

18. Which of the following graphs shows the heating curve of water at 10 atm of pressure?

F.
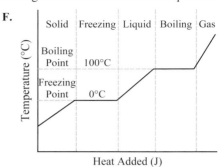

G.
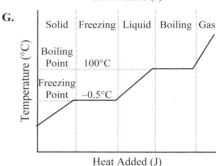

H.
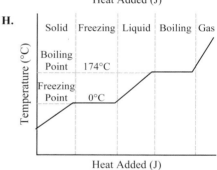

J.
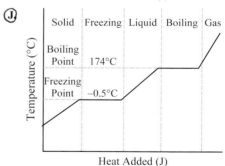

Research Summaries
Part 3

Research Summaries passages require you to understand experimental design and equipment, method and procedure, implications and flaws, and results, which are usually presented in tables and graphs. They have simpler graphics than Data Representation passages, and they're wordier. As with Data Representation passages, you can usually skim the graphs for *details*—variables and trends—and then get started on the questions.

There are three Research Summaries per Science Test. Each has seven questions associated with it. Each presents one or more Experiments, Studies, or Activities that examine related variables and are conducted by scientists, researchers, or students.

Because these experiments are related to each other, Research Summaries will often repeat themselves. The text explaining each experiment will often be parallel, if not identical, and the graphs may have the same axes. This means that during your 3D Skim, the most important D is not details as it was in the last section, but *differences*. You want to note what variables are being tested in each experiment, how they are changed, and how they and their effects compare and contrast.

Before you take a look at the example passage, it might be worthwhile to review the **scientific method**. This is part of what Research Summaries test, and what makes them different from the other passages. If you've taken any science courses and done any experiments, then you're somewhat familiar with the scientific method:

1. Develop a *question*
2. Generate a *hypothesis* (an educated guess to answer the question)
3. *Design* an experiment to test the hypothesis
4. *Conduct* the experiment
5. Assess the *results* of the experiment

The purpose of the scientific method is to develop, test, and extend or overturn theories about how the world works. Often, only one small aspect of a complex phenomenon is examined, such as a simple direct or inverse relationship between two variables. The most important steps for Research Summaries are 3, 4, and 5.

The following Research Summaries example shows the results of three different experiments on the physics of springs. The notes in the margins will point out characteristics that are typical of this passage format. You should use the Pencil on Paper technique to mark up the passage.

Students studied the extensions of springs in response to added force in order to investigate Hooke's Law, which states that the extension of a spring is directly proportional to the force exerted on the spring.

Experiment 1

To calculate the force exerted by various masses, students multiplied each mass by an approximate value of the acceleration due to Earth's gravity, 9.8 m/sec². The results of their calculations are recorded in Table 1.

Table 1	
Mass (g)	Force (N)
10	0.098
20	0.196
50	0.490
100	0.980
500	4.900
1000	9.800

Experiment 2

Students attached the end of a copper spring to a clamp stand. They attached the other end of the spring to a pointer, and attached the pointer to a mass hanger, from which they hung various masses, as shown in Diagram 1. The students stood a centimeter ruler behind the spring-pointer-mass assembly. When they added a mass to the mass hanger, the spring stretched, which caused the position of the pointer on the ruler behind it to change. The position was recorded, and the procedure was repeated with 6 different masses (Trials 2-7). In Trial 1, the force on the spring by the pointer was assumed to be 0. The results are recorded in Table 2.

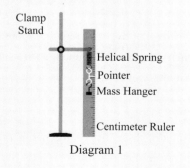

Clamp Stand

Helical Spring
Pointer
Mass Hanger

Centimeter Ruler

Diagram 1

Each Research Summaries passage starts with a statement explaining the purpose of the experiments. Don't read this unless you need the third D— definitions. This section frames the rest of the passage and defines terms, but rarely includes vital information.

Each experiment will begin with a description of the experimental design. Because Research Summaries passages usually contain at least one question on experimental design, you should skim this passage and underline major details of the procedure. Do not spend a lot of time reading this thoroughly, but be prepared to return to it later.

Tables are the most common type of graphic in Research Summaries. During your 3D Skim, focus mainly on the headings of each row or column so that you know which variables are included in the table. Circle headings, labels, and units—and also any Keys or Notes (though there are none here).

If an experimental setup is complex, it will often be illustrated in a diagram. Always skip the text and skim the diagram first. If you need more information for a question, then read the text.

Repeated trials are common in Research Summaries. This is where you'll find information about differences between experiments. Circle or underline these differences so that you know what is being changed between trials.

Diagrams are meant to help you visualize the experiment. Spend a few seconds familiarizing yourself with any diagrams, and supplement them with the text if needed.

Table 2			
Trial	Force on hanger (N)	Ruler reading (cm)	Extension (cm)
1	0.000	8.2	0.0
2	0.098	9.8	1.6
3	0.196	11.4	3.2
4	0.490	16.2	8.0
5	0.980	24.2	16.0
6	1.960	40.2	32.0
7	9.800	168.2	160.0

Experiment 3

Students used the same equipment as in Experiment 2 to test the relationship between force, extension, and type of spring material. They used 3 springs—steel, iron, and aluminum—and tested each spring with 4 forces. The results are recorded in Table 3.

Table 3				
Trial	Metal	Force on hanger (N)	Ruler reading (cm)	Extension (cm)
8	Steel	0.000	5.1	0.0
9		0.098	5.5	0.4
10		0.196	5.9	0.8
11		0.490	7.1	2.0
12	Iron	0.000	8.6	0.0
13		0.098	9.7	1.1
14		0.196	10.9	2.3
15		0.490	14.1	5.5
16	Aluminum	0.000	7.4	0.0
17		0.098	9.7	2.3
18		0.196	12.7	5.3
19		0.490	71.8	64.4

Sometimes, tables contain more than two variables. Even in such tables, though, many questions will only require you to look at two variables. When looking back to answer a question, cover irrelevant columns with your hand so you don't get confused.

Sometimes, you will be asked to identify independent and dependent variables. Circle them. You may want to mark these on the table—force is the independent variable, while the ruler reading and extension are dependent variables.

Many procedures will be repeated between experiments. If you understood the experiment from skimming the diagram or from skimming the text the first time, you do not need to spend much time reading the next one closely. Just be aware of the differences between them.

Example

The force calculated in Experiment 1 is equivalent to which of the following quantities?

A. Acceleration

B. Momentum

C. Magnetism

D. Weight

This is one of those fairly rare questions that tests your scientific knowledge. As long as you know some basic physics, it's easy to answer.

The question asks for another name for the force from Experiment 1. The question is best answered by looking at the text. A quick glance tells you what you need to know: the force in Table 1 is a mass multiplied by a constant, the acceleration of gravity.

Now look at the answer options: (C) can be eliminated because it is irrelevant. (A) is tempting because it contains the word "acceleration," but if you think carefully, you will realize that a mass multiplied by an acceleration could not yield another acceleration. So eliminate (A) as well. (B) and (D) both have something to do with mass. But if you think back to physics class, you will remember that momentum is a property of moving objects, and the masses in Experiment 1 are not moving. So go ahead and eliminate (B) as well. You are left with (D), which is correct. Weight is the force exerted by a mass due to gravity.

Example

Based on the results of Experiment 2, as the amount of force added to the spring increased, the extension of the spring:

F. increased only.
G. decreased only.
H. increased, then decreased.
J. varied, with no apparent trend.

This question requires to you understand the results of Experiment 2. Because it refers to results and not to experimental design, you can ignore the text from Experiment 2. Focus on Table 2 as you refer back to the passage.

The relevant variables here are force and extension. You want to look at the second and fourth columns, labeled "Force on hanger" and "Extension." As you move down the table, you can see that the force increases. Now look at the "Extension" column. Those values also increase as you move down the table. There is a clear trend here.

(F) is clearly correct. (G) is the opposite of what happens. (H) might be tempting because it does say that extension increases, but it also says that the trend reverses at some point. The extension increases all the way down the table, so (H) is incorrect. And finally, (J) is incorrect because you can see a clear trend and not random variation.

If E is Extension, F is Force, R_0 is the Ruler reading at no force, and R_F is the Ruler reading at a given force, which of the following is the correct equation for calculating Extension?

A. $E = F \times R_F$

B. $E = R_F - R_0$

C. $E = R_0 - R_F$

D. $E = \dfrac{R_F}{F}$

This question is a bit difficult because it does not direct you to any particular experiment. Both Experiments 2 and 3 deal with the spring and ruler setup, so you can look at either one.

You know that Force and Extension are related, and you also know that Ruler readings and Extension are related. Perhaps the easiest way to tackle this problem is by Plugging in Options—simply guess and check. Take a look at Trials 1 and 2 from Experiment 2, for example. Trial 1 tells you that when F is 0, E is also 0. You can immediately eliminate (D), since this equation is undefined when F is 0.

Next, look at Trial 2. In this Trial, $R_F = 9.8$. Without a calculator, you can do mental math to estimate $F \times R_F$ (0.098×9.8), which will be less than 1. E, meanwhile, is 1.6. Therefore, (A) is incorrect.

Try (B), with $R_F = 9.8$ and $R_0 = 8.2$ (from Trial 1). Since E is positive, (C), $8.2 - 9.8 = -1.6$, cannot be correct. (B) is correct. You can confirm this by calculating $9.8 - 8.2 = 1.6$.

Example

Based on the results of Experiment 3, which of the following graphs best represents the relationship between force and extension for the aluminum spring?

F.
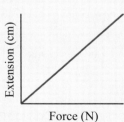

G.
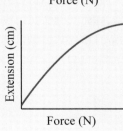

H.
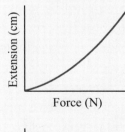

J.
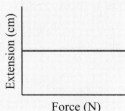

This question requires to you understand the results of Experiment 3. Like Question 2, it refers to results and not to experimental design. You can ignore the text from Experiment 3. Focus on Table 3. The question asks about the aluminum spring, so ignore the rows labeled "Steel" and "Iron." This leaves you with Trials 16–19.

You need to visually represent the relationship between two variables from the table: Force and Extension. Look only at those two columns. Clearly, as Force increases, so does Extension—or $\uparrow F = \uparrow E$. You need to look for a line with a positive slope. You can immediately eliminate (J), because a horizontal line has a slope of zero.

(F), (G), and (H) all have a positive slope, so now you need to figure out the rate at which Extension increases with increasing Force. From Trial 17 to Trial 18, the Force increases twofold and the Extension increases slightly more than twofold. From Trial 18 to Trial 19, the Force increases by a little more than twofold, but the Extension increases by a factor of approximately 12. Clearly, the slope of the curve should increase as the Force increases. The relationship is not linear, so you can eliminate (F). You can also eliminate (G), which shows the slope decreasing as Force increases. This leaves (H), an exponential growth curve.

Example

Suppose the students add the 100 g mass to the steel spring in Experiment 3. Which of the following would be the extension of the spring?

A. 2.4 cm
B. 4.0 cm
C. 7.5 cm
D. 13.1 cm

As usual, you should start by referring back to where the question directs you: the "Steel" rows of Table 3, which contains the results of Experiment 3. The word "suppose" is a clue here. The question is not asking you to find a piece of data in Table 3, but rather to predict where a new piece of data should go. However, you should notice that Table 3 relates force and extension, but not mass. This means that you need to look at Table 1 as well, which relates mass and force. As you can see, a mass of 100 g corresponds to a force of 0.980 N.

Now you can look back to Table 3. As you predicted, there is no data point for 0.980 N. So, you need to determine the relationship between force and extension. Clearly, extension increases as force increases. From Trial 9 to Trial 10, force and extension both double. From Trial 10 to Trial 11, both force and extension increase by a factor of 2.5. Since the relationship seems roughly constant, you can assume that it is linear.

Now you need to fit 0.980 N into the pattern. You should notice that 0.980 N is twice as large as 0.490 N. The extension should be twice as large as well. The extension for 0.490 N is 2.0 cm, so the extension for 0.980 N should be 4.0 cm. The correct answer is (B).

Example

Based on Tables 2 and 3, what is the order of the springs in terms of their extension in response to added force, from the spring that extended the most to the spring that extended the least?

F.   Aluminum, iron, steel, copper
G.   Aluminum, copper, iron, steel
H.   Copper, aluminum, iron, steel
J.   Steel, iron, copper, aluminum

Just by reading the question, you know that you need to synthesize information from two different sources. When you first look at Table 2, it might not be obvious what material the spring from Experiment 2 is made of, but a brief skim of the text tells you that the spring is copper. Meanwhile, Table 3 contains the data for the steel, iron, and aluminum.

You need to order the spring materials with regard to their response to force. The best approach here is to choose a certain force and examine the extension of each spring. Obviously, 0.0 N will not work, since none of the springs extend at all.

Try the next force: 0.098 N. Table 2 tells you that copper spring has an extension of 1.6 cm. Table 3 tells you that steel spring extends 0.4 cm, the iron spring extends 1.1 cm, and the aluminum spring extends 2.3 cm. Now, all you have to do is place the springs in order. Be careful to put the spring with the largest extension first and the spring with the smallest extension last. The correct order is aluminum (2.3 cm), copper (1.6 cm), iron (1.1 cm), and finally steel (0.4 cm). The correct answer is therefore (G).

Be wary of (J), which is the reverse order. To help your brain separate similar answer options, try chunking and piecewise elimination. Aluminum must be the first spring listed, so (H) and (J) are wrong. Copper must be next, so (F) is wrong. You're left with (G), and you haven't even read past two words of each answer option!

Example

In Trials 1, 8, 12, and 16, the students assumed that the pointer:

A.   had no mass.
B.   had no extension.
C.   had no length.
D.   had no hook.

This question requires a little searching because it asks about the experimental design. The answers to these sorts of questions are generally found in the text and not in the tables. Since the trials referenced in the question refer to Experiments 2 and 3, you can ignore Experiment 1 for now.

If you annotated the passage during your 3D Skim, you may have noticed that, for Trial 1 in Experiment 2, "the force on the spring by the pointer was assumed to be 0." This is an important hint. Trial 1, like Trials 8, 12, and 16, involved no hanging mass. These trials served only to find the original position of the spring under no other forces. The information in Tables 2 and 3 confirms this: the "Force on hanger" for Trials 1, 8, 12, and 16 is 0.

Now you know that the students assumed the pointer exerted no force. But this is not one of the answer options. However, you should remember from Experiment 1 that a mass exerts a force due to the acceleration of gravity. If the pointer is assumed to exert no force, then it must be assumed to have no mass. (A) is correct.

(B) might be tempting, since the extension in Trials 1, 8, 12, and 16 is, in fact, 0. But this is an experimental measurement, not an assumption made by the students. Diagram 1 clearly refutes (C) because the pointer has a definite length. And finally, (D) is irrelevant (although the passage is about Hooke's Law).

Research Summaries Practice Questions

Part 4

Passage I

A series of experiments was conducted to test the hypothesis that air pollution affects *fertility*—the ability to become pregnant—in brown rats (*Rattus norvegicus*). In the wild, these rats are often exposed to carbon monoxide (CO) in areas with heavy automobile traffic and sulfur dioxide (SO_2) in areas near power plants.

Experiment 1

Four groups of female rats, with 50 rats in each group, were mated with the same male rat. Two of the groups were fed a high-protein diet, while the other two groups were fed a low-protein diet. One group in each diet category was exposed to clean air, and the other was exposed to air contaminated with 55 parts per million of CO. After two weeks, the number of females that became pregnant was recorded. The results are shown in Table 1.

Table 1		
Diet	Air	# Pregnant Rats
Low-protein	Clean air	32
	CO-polluted air	18
High-protein	Clean air	49
	CO-polluted air	48

Experiment 2

The researchers repeated the experiment, but used SO_2 instead of CO as a pollutant. The air was contaminated at 55 parts per million. The results are shown in Table 2.

Table 2		
Diet	Air	# Pregnant Rats
Low-protein	Clean air	31
	SO_2-polluted air	8
High-protein	Clean air	48
	SO_2-polluted air	49

Experimental design adapted from United States Department of Agriculture, Program in Wildlife and Fisheries Science, 2001.

1. In Experiments 1 and 2, groups of rats were exposed to clean air most likely in order to allow the scientists to:

   A. test the level of pollutants in clean air.
   B. examine the effects of protein on rat behavior.
   C. measure the baseline fertility of rats.
   D. compare the chemical structure of CO and SO_2.

2. Which of the following conclusions is most consistent with the data in Table 1?

   F. CO exposure increases the fertility of rats.
   G. A low-protein diet increases the fertility of rats.
   H. A high-protein diet helps protect rat fertility from the negative effects of CO exposure.
   J. A high-protein diet, combined with CO exposure, has the greatest negative effect on rat fertility.

3. Which of the following combinations of factors had the largest negative effect on rat fertility?

   (A) Low protein diet and SO_2 polluted air
   B. Low protein diet and CO polluted air
   C. High protein diet and SO_2 polluted air
   D. High protein diet and CO polluted air

4. In past studies on rat fertility, ozone (O_3) has been shown to be more toxic than CO but less toxic than SO_2. Suppose that researchers repeated the experimental procedure using groups of rats that were exposed to 55 parts per million O_3. Which of the following graphs best shows the comparison between the fertility of rats on a low-protein diet after exposure to CO, SO_2, or O_3?

   F.
   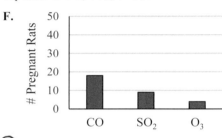

   (G)
   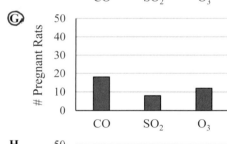

   H.
   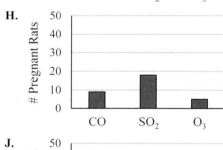

   J.
   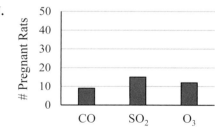

5. As a logical follow-up study to Experiments 1 and 2, the researchers would most likely study:

   (A) the fertility of wild rats living in areas with heavy automobile traffic.
   B. the fertility of wild rats living in areas near solar power stations.
   C. the fertility of wild rats living in areas with very clean air.
   D. the fertility of wild rats living in areas with heavy precipitation.

6. Which of the following was a dependent variable in both Experiment 1 and Experiment 2?

   F. Amount of protein in diet
   G. Amount of CO pollution
   H. Amount of SO_2 pollution
   (J) Number of pregnant rats

7. According to the results of Experiment 2, for the rats fed a low-protein diet, exposure to SO_2 pollution decreased the number of pregnant rats by a factor of:

   (A) 4
   B. 3
   C. 2
   D. $\frac{3}{4}$

Passage II

Porosity is the measure of empty space in a material, such as a rock. Higher porosity allows more fluid to be absorbed by rocks and also increases the speed at which fluid flows through rock. Students conducted two experiments to investigate the porosity of various rock types.

Experiment 1

The students poured 100 mL of water into each of 5 glass beakers. In each beaker, they placed a spherical piece of rock with a radius of 20 mm. The spheres were granite, limestone, basalt, shale, and sandstone. The students covered the beakers in aluminum foil and left the spheres in the water for 30 minutes to allow them to absorb water. After the allotted time, the students removed the spheres and measured the volume of water remaining in each beaker. The results are shown in Table 1, along with the density of each rock type.

Table 1		
Rock type	Density (mg/m^3)	Volume of water remaining in beaker (mL)
Granite	2.64	93
Limestone	2.55	90
Basalt	2.99	96
Shale	2.40	89
Sandstone	2.35	87

Experiment 2

The students cut a hole in the bottom of a plastic bottle and placed a short length of tubing in the hole. They then placed a cylindrical slab of granite—2 mm high and equal in circumference to the bottle—near the bottom of the bottle. The students poured 10 mL of water on top of the granite slab and waited 72 hrs, measuring the total volume of fluid that flowed through the slab at 6-hr intervals. The experimental setup is shown in Diagram 1. This procedure was repeated for the four other rock types listed above. The volume of water collected every 6 hrs during each trial is shown in Figure 1.

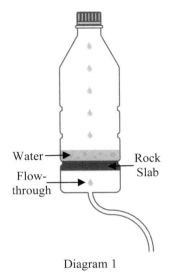

Diagram 1

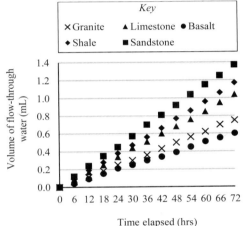

Figure 1

8. In Experiment 1, the students most likely covered the beakers in aluminum foil in order to:

F. maximize possibility of contamination.

G. prevent evaporation of the water.

H. increase the rate of water absorption.

J. decrease the flow rate of the water.

9. In Experiment 2, if the students had allowed the trials to run for 78 hrs, the total volume of water that flowed through the granite slab would most likely have been:

A. less than 0.6 mL.

B. between 0.6 mL and 0.8 mL.

C. between 0.8 mL and 1.0 mL.

D. greater than 1.0 mL.

10. According to Table 1, as the density of rock increases, the porosity of the rock:

   F. decreases only.

   G. decreases, then increases.

   H. increases, then decreases.

   J. increases only.

11. A student finds a sphere of gabbro, which has a density of 3.03 mg/m^3, in her backyard. If she replicated Experiment 1 using the gabbro, the amount of water left in the beaker after 30 minutes would most likely have been:

   A. 90 mL.

   B. 93 mL.

   C. 99 mL.

   D. 101 mL.

12. One of the students knows only that the higher the porosity of a rock, the more water it can absorb. The student concludes that rocks with higher porosity therefore force water to travel through them more slowly. Do the results of Experiments 1 and 2 support this conclusion?

   F. No; the rocks that absorbed more water in Experiment 1 allowed water to flow through more quickly in Experiment 2.

   G. No; the rocks that absorbed more water in Experiment 1 allowed water to flow through more slowly in Experiment 2.

   H. Yes; the rocks that absorbed more water in Experiment 1 allowed water to flow through more quickly in Experiment 2.

   J. Yes; the rocks that absorbed more water in Experiment 1 allowed water to flow through more slowly in Experiment 2.

13. After finishing Experiment 2, one of the students noticed that the rock slabs had not been sized correctly, and that a small amount of water could flow around the slabs instead of through them. How did this affect the results shown in Figure 1?

   A. It decreased the measured rate of water flow through the slabs.

   B. It increased the measured rate of water flow through the slabs.

   C. It changed the measured rate of water flow through the slabs with no consistent pattern.

   D. It did not affect the measured rate of water flow through the slabs.

14. One of the students repeats Experiment 2 using an unknown variety of rock. After 72 hours, 0.8 mL of water have flown through the slab. Which of the following is the best approximation of the density of the unknown rock, in mg/m^3?

   F. 2.55

   G. 2.56

   H. 2.63

   J. 2.65

Passage III

In physical chemistry, gas laws describe the relationships between the volume, temperature, and density (the mass per unit of volume) of a gas. Students conducted two experiments to investigate these relationships for four gases: carbon dioxide (CO_2), oxygen (O_2), nitrogen (N_2), and argon (Ar).

(Note: Equal volumes of all gases, under the same conditions, contain the same number of molecules.)

Experiment 1

For each of the four gases, the students filled a syringe with approximately 50 mL of the gas at 27°C (approximately room temperature), recording the exact volume. They then filled a beaker with 200 mL of water and placed the syringes in the beaker so that they were fully submerged. A thermometer was also placed in the water, as shown in Diagram 1.

The beaker was first placed in a bath of dry ice. As the water cooled, the temperature of the water and the volume of each gas were recorded. The beaker was then removed from the dry ice and placed in a warm water bath. As the water warmed, the temperature of the water and volume of each gas were recorded. The results of this experiment are shown in Table 1.

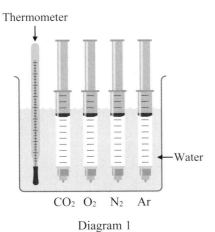

Diagram 1

Table 1				
Temperature (°C)	Gas volume (mL)			
	CO_2	O_2	N_2	Ar
−13	43.4	43.1	43.3	43.3
7	46.7	46.5	46.6	46.6
27	50.2	49.9	50.1	50.0
47	53.4	53.2	53.3	53.2
67	57.0	56.9	56.9	56.5

Experiment 2

At room temperature, the students measured the mass of an empty syringe. They then filled the syringe with various volumes of each of the four gases and measured the mass of the syringe and gas together. The results of this experiment are shown in Table 2.

Mass of empty syringe = 100.00 g

Table 2		
Gas	Volume (mL)	Mass of gas + syringe (g)
CO_2	25	100.05
	50	100.10
	75	100.15
	100	100.20
O_2	25	100.03
	50	100.06
	75	100.09
	100	100.12
N_2	25	100.02
	50	100.04
	75	100.06
	100	100.08
Ar	25	100.04
	50	100.08
	75	100.12
	100	100.16

$$\frac{03}{25}$$

$$\frac{.02}{25}$$

$$\frac{04}{25}$$

15. According to the results of Experiment 1, as the temperature of argon gas increases, its volume:

   A. decreases only.
   B. increases only.
   C. decreases, then increases.
   D. increases, then decreases.

16. One of the students concludes that all four gases exhibit an identical response to changes in temperature. Do the results of Experiment 1 support this conclusion?

   F. No; as the temperature changes, the volumes of the gases change by different amounts.
   G. No; as the temperature changes, the volumes of the gases change by the same amount.
   H. Yes; as the temperature changes, the volumes of the gases change by different amounts.
   J. Yes; as the temperature changes, the volumes of the gases change by the same amount.

17. After recording their measurements from Experiment 2, the students decide to calculate the mass of the gas alone for each volume of each type of gas. Which of the following operations should they perform?

   A. Add the mass of the syringe to the mass of the gas and syringe together.
   B. Multiply the mass of the syringe and the mass of the syringe and gas together.
   C. Subtract the mass of the syringe and gas together from the mass of the syringe.
   D. Subtract the mass of the syringe from the mass of the syringe and gas together.

18. In Experiment 2, if the students had measured the mass of 150 mL of nitrogen gas, the mass of the gas and syringe together would most likely have been:

   F. 0.12 g.
   G. 100.10 g.
   H. 100.12 g.
   J. 100.14 g.

19. The *density* of a gas is defined as the mass of the gas per unit of volume. Based on the results of Experiment 2, which of the four gases examined has the *lowest* density?

   A. Carbon dioxide
   B. Oxygen
   C. Nitrogen
   D. Argon

20. One of the students finds a sample of methane in the laboratory. Using the same syringe from Experiment 2, she measures the mass of 50 mL of methane and the syringe together as 100.03 g. She then used the same sample of methane to repeat Experiment 1. The volume occupied by the methane at 67°C is most likely closest to:

   F. 50.0 mL.
   G. 53.2 mL.
   H. 56.8 mL.
   J. 60.0 mL.

21. At different temperatures, nitrogen can exist as a gas, a liquid, or a solid. In all three states, the nitrogen molecules are constantly in motion, and the temperature is a measure of the average speed of the molecules. Which of the following correctly orders, from slowest to fastest, the three states of nitrogen in terms of the average speed of the molecules?

   A. Solid, liquid, gas
   B. Solid, gas, liquid
   C. Liquid, gas, solid
   D. Gas, liquid, solid

Conflicting Viewpoints
Part 5

Conflicting Viewpoints passages offer two or more perspectives on a particular scientific phenomenon. These viewpoints are sometimes Hypotheses, and other times are perspectives presented by Scientists or Students. In order to answer the questions presented after the passage, you'll need to understand each argument individually, locate the differences and similarities between the arguments, and assess the validity of each argument based on new information presented in the questions.

Unlike Research Summaries and Data Representation passages, Conflicting Viewpoints passages do not include descriptions of experimental design or empirical data. They are composed mainly of text and are also typically the longest of all the passages. You will encounter only one Conflicting Viewpoints passage per exam, and it will have seven questions associated with it.

Of the three passage types on the Science Test, only the Conflicting Viewpoints format requires reading. The best strategy to use for Conflicting Viewpoints is the same strategy you use for the Passage Pairs on the Reading Test. First, read Scientist 1's viewpoint and answer the questions that mention *only* Scientist 1. Then, read Scientist 2's viewpoint and answer the questions that mention *only* Scientist 2. Finally, answer the questions that mention *both* scientists, and the questions that don't mention either, but refer to the introductory text only.

Because the viewpoints often use similar words, this strategy will help you remember which one says what. It is a great way to organize and understand all the densely packed information you are given. It's also a great way to avoid wrong answer options that refer to Scientist 2 in a question about Scientist 1—you haven't read Scientist 2 yet, so these answer options will stand out as obviously wrong.

However, there are two warnings. One, this strategy works best for passages with only *two* viewpoints, and is less effective for passages with more than two viewpoints (though it can still be useful). Two, this strategy requires a fast Pick-and-Skip; be sure to pay attention to which question numbers you're bubbling in! You don't want to bubble in the wrong question, and you don't want to waste time erasing.

When you read a viewpoint, be sure to follow the 3 Ds. Circle a word or phrase that indicates the main argument. You can think of each viewpoint as "The _____ View," where the blank is the argument, such as "The Proteins View." Underline details, which are assertions and evidence. If the viewpoint discusses a relationship, rewrite it as a relation with letters (variables) and arrows. As always, move as quickly as possible through the passage and try to spend the bulk of your time on the questions.

Below you will find a Conflicting Viewpoints sample passage on biological altruism and example questions. The following example will walk you through how to best annotate the passage and the best approach to answering the questions.

Altruism is the phenomenon of one of more organisms acting in a selfless manner. An altruistic organism helps other members of its group at its own expense. For example, upon seeing a leopard, a vervet monkey might howl in order to attract the predator, thereby allowing the rest of the troop to escape. Two scientists debate the evolution of altruism by *natural selection*, which is the process whereby organisms that are better adapted to their environment will survive longer and produce more offspring.

Like the other passage types, Conflicting Viewpoints passages start with background information. If the concept being discussed is particularly complex, the introductory material may be fairly substantial.

As with the other passages, it's not essential for you to read this information first. However, you know that there will be definitions here—the italicized words—so if you stumble across words you don't understand in the viewpoints, this would be the place to look. Since they're italicized, they're essentially already marked, so there's no need to circle them.

Scientist A

Altruism evolved as a result of natural selection acting on the level of genes. Because genes affect physical traits and can be inherited by offspring, genetic differences are the only driving force of natural selection. An individual organism will behave selflessly only in order to benefit genetically similar individuals, such as siblings or offspring. For example, altruistic behavior evolved in vervet monkeys because members of a troop are closely related and therefore share many genes. When a vervet monkey howls to draw the attention of the leopard, there is a good chance that it will increase the chances of its own genes being passed on through surviving family members.

Typically, a viewpoint begins with a broad topic sentence that clearly states how it differs from the other viewpoint(s). This is where you'll find the main argument, and a word you can circle to help you remember what it is. Here, it's "genes." Therefore, Scientist A is "The Genes View."

Strong words like "only" or "always" tend to highlight differences between viewpoints. These differences are usually black-and-white. Subtlety is not common.

If you are having trouble understanding the meanings of all these long, scientific words, break the sentences down and try to rewrite it as a relationship. Basically, this says that altruism only occurs in the case of genetically similar individuals. You could write this relationship in the margin: $\uparrow A = \uparrow GS$. Because writing and note-taking will eat away your time, make sure you are fast about it; use few markings, and use the shortest symbols that you can understand. Nobody else needs to read this—it's for your benefit only.

Scientist B

Altruism evolved as a result of natural selection acting on the level of groups of organisms. Although heritable genetic differences do affect physical traits and play a role in driving natural selection, the differential success of groups can also be a factor in this process. An individual organism will behave selflessly in order to increase the reproductive success of the group as a whole, regardless of the relatedness of its members. When a vervet

Make sure you're looking at the right viewpoint when answering each question. The Science Test typically uses numbers or letters to distinguish between viewpoints.

Scientist B is "The Groups View."

Words like "although" can indicate that the differing viewpoints agree on a certain issue. Be sure to recognize the common ground.

monkey howls to draw the attention of the leopard, the troop as a whole benefits. Groups with members that behave altruistically will be more successful than groups with members that behave selfishly.

Just like with Scientist A, you can rephrase this central idea in terms of a relationship: ↑A = ↑Groups, for example.

Example

Which of the following generalizations about altruism is consistent with Scientist A's viewpoint?

F. Altruism is unlikely to exist in groups that consist of unrelated organisms.

G. Altruism is unlikely to exist in groups that consist of related organisms.

H. Altruism is unlikely to exist in any group of organisms.

J. Altruism is likely to exist in all groups of organisms.

Following the one-by-one strategy mentioned in the introduction, you would approach this question after reading only Scientist A. This question asks you for Scientist A's main idea. You know from your rephrase (Scientist A is "The Genes View") and your relation (↑A = ↑GS, where A stands for Altruism and GS stands for Genetically Similar) that Scientist A thinks that altruism exists only in genetically similar groups.

Therefore, Scientist A's main point is that genetic similarity drives the evolution of altruism in nature. In fact, Scientist A says that altruism only evolved in vervet monkeys because of genetic relatedness. Starting with the first answer choice, you can immediately see that (F) is consistent with Scientist A's viewpoint. Without genetic relatedness, altruism would not evolve.

In order to confirm that the other answers are incorrect, glance through them quickly. (G) is the opposite of what Scientist A says. (H) and (J) are clearly wrong, since Scientist A neither denies the existence of altruism altogether nor believes that it is universal.

If you were unsure about what Scientist A said, don't worry. You can make excellent guesses on the ACT based solely on the number of times words and their synonyms repeat. This is a good tactic to use when you refer back to the passage—look for words repeated in the question, answer, and passage. Often, the correct answer choice will be the one that repeats the most words that the passage repeated. This "repeated words" approach requires a different type of thinking than the standard "understanding the passage" approach. It also requires caution—don't be duped just because you recognize a word or two.

You need to look not for meaning, but for word shapes and repetition. Scientist A says the words offspring, siblings, genetically similar individuals, closely related, share many genes, own genes, and family members. Scientist A also says altruism and selfless. (F) and (G) repeat these words the most. Remember to use chunking to make your Process of Elimination easier—a closer look at the answers will reveal that (G) is the opposite of what the scientist says and (F) is correct.

On that note, pay special attention—in both approaches—to words that change the viewpoint or the answer. These are words like "however," "although," "despite," "neither," "not," and "but."

Scientist B's view differs from Scientist A's view in that only Scientist B would predict that, in a colony of bacteria:

A. if individuals are genetically identical, they would share resources.

B. if individuals are genetically diverse, they would share resources.

C. if individuals are genetically identical, they would not interact.

D. if individuals are genetically diverse, they would not interact.

Since this question asks about both scientists' viewpoints, this would be a question to skip at first. After you finish answering all the questions that ask only about Scientist A, you'd read Scientist B and answer all the questions that ask only about Scientist B. This question would be the first one you answered next.

In order to answer the question, you need to understand Scientist B's viewpoint, but you also need to evaluate the potential effect of new information. Scientist B says that altruism can exist in situations where it benefits the group, regardless of the relatedness of its members.

A quick glance at the answers reveals that they're almost identical. This can make the answers hard to keep straight. To make this easier on yourself, use chunking and piecewise elimination. The differences between the answer options are "identical" / "diverse," and "share resources" / "not interact."

(A) doesn't contradict Scientist B's viewpoint. After all, Scientist B doesn't say that altruism can *only* evolve in groups of unrelated individuals. But Scientist A would also agree with (A), so this answer choice does not show how the two differ.

(B) describes a situation that perfectly matches Scientist B's viewpoint. It is also the opposite of what Scientist A hypothesizes. Therefore, (B) is correct.

As usual, take a quick look through the remaining options to make sure you can eliminate them. (C) is irrelevant to Scientist B's viewpoint since it deals with genetically identical individuals. (D) refers to a situation that Scientist B does not discuss, so it's incorrect.

Both scientists would most likely agree with which of the following statements?

F. Genetic differences do not play a role in driving natural selection.

G. The differential success of groups plays a role in driving natural selection.

H. Altruism evolved as a result of natural selection.

J. Vervet monkeys do not exhibit altruistic behavior.

This question requires you to synthesize information from *both* scientists' viewpoints. This would be one of the last questions you'd answer. Be careful to choose an option that is clearly stated in both viewpoints—use piecewise elimination here.

(F) contradicts both scientists' viewpoints since both scientists say that genetic differences play at least some role in natural selection. Scientist B would agree with (G), but Scientist A believes that natural selection acts on genes, not groups. (H) seems like a good candidate. Both scientists are discussing the evolution of altruism via natural selection, so this option is certainly correct. (J) contradicts both scientists' viewpoints and is clearly incorrect.

Example

Honeybees live in extremely altruistic social groups in which most of the individuals do not reproduce. Instead, they spend their energy caring for the queen, who is the only individual that will pass on her genetic information. In regard to honeybees, Scientist A would most likely predict that:

A. honeybees have very few natural predators.
B. honeybee offspring are genetically identical to their parents.
C. groups of honeybees are highly genetically diverse.
D. groups of honeybees are highly genetically similar.

This question introduces new information and asks you to make a prediction based on Scientist A's viewpoint. You can ignore Scientist B for now.

The question describes a group of animals in which the majority of individuals make significant sacrifices. Scientist A says that altruism evolves in groups of closely related individuals. Look through the answers to see if any of them express this idea.

(A) is irrelevant. (B) seems feasible, but it's out-of-scope. It's too specific: Scientist A says nothing about individuals being genetically identical, only that altruism occurs when individuals are genetically *similar*, or closely related. (C) is the opposite of what Scientist A would say, since individuals in genetically diverse groups would not be closely related. (D) is the best option, since genetically similar individuals would be closely related.

Example

Packs of wolves are composed of individuals who are not closely related. If an adult female dies, her infant cubs are cared for by the rest of the group. How would this discovery most likely affect the scientists' viewpoints, if at all?

	Scientist A	Scientist B
F.	Strengthen	Strengthen
G.	Strengthen	Weaken
H.	Weaken	Weaken
J.	Weaken	Strengthen

This question asks you to understand the new information presented and apply it to both viewpoints. If you don't use the one-by-one strategy, you'll find that questions that ask about both viewpoints can require a lot of searching back through the text. However, with this strategy, you've already done all the questions that ask about each Scientist, so you've read and referred back to the text several times, and you have a better understanding of it.

First, read the new information carefully. Since the wolves care for orphaned cubs, they seem to be acting in an altruistic manner. You also know that they are not closely related.

Scientist A predicts that altruism will only exist in groups of closely related individuals. The wolf example seems to provide evidence against this viewpoint. The new information weakens Scientist A's argument. Therefore, you can eliminate (F) and (G).

Scientist B, on the other hand, predicts that altruism will exist in groups of unrelated individuals. The wolf example provides evidence supporting this viewpoint. Therefore, you can eliminate (H). (J) is the correct answer.

Example

A marine biologist discovers that dolphins often assist a sick or injured member of the group, even though the healthy dolphins spend valuable energy in doing so. Which, if either, of the scientists would consider this an act of altruism?

A. Scientist A only
B. Scientist B only
C. Both Scientist A and Scientist B
D. Neither Scientist A nor Scientist B

This question is fairly similar to the previous one. You need to apply new information to both viewpoints. But instead of evaluating the effect of the information on each of the viewpoints, you need to imagine what each scientist might say about the new discovery.

The question asks about a fairly basic definition: What is altruism? While the scientists disagree on many points, they do not actually differ on the definition of altruism, which was explained in the introductory paragraph. In fact, they both discuss the behavior of vervet monkeys as an example of altruism. Therefore, the scientists will likely agree on what they consider an act of altruism. You can eliminate (A) and (B).

Since the dolphins help other members of their group at their own expense, they seem to fit the definition of altruistic organisms put forth in the passage. The dolphin example is very similar to the vervet monkey example, and both Scientist A and Scientist B would consider this an act of altruism. (C) is correct. (D) is a confused content answer; it's the opposite of the correct answer.

Example

Genes are composed of which of the following classes of molecules?

F. Nucleic acids

G. Proteins

H. Lipids

J. Steroids

This question requires some outside knowledge. There are no hints in the passage that will help you find the answer. Check out Section 3, Part 9, and our online glossary to refresh your memory on what the Science Test may expect you to know outside of what's given on a passage.

You should remember the answer from your high school biology class. Genetic information is contained in nucleic acids such as DNA and RNA, so (F) is correct. Proteins, lipids, and steroids form many of the structures of the cell, but they do not carry genetic information. (G), (H), and (J) are therefore incorrect.

Conflicting Viewpoints Practice Questions

Part 6

Passage I

Scientists discuss two possible causes of the extinction during the Cretaceous-Tertiary (KT) period 65 million years ago, in which 75% of all species became extinct.

Scientist 1

The KT extinction was caused by an asteroid impact. The asteroid struck the earth in Mexico, where a 150 km crater exists today. The impact of the asteroid released dust that blocked the sun's light for years, darkening the earth and drastically cooling its atmosphere, which killed most species. This relatively fast extinction is shown by a sudden decrease in fossilized species.

Iridium, a rare metal on Earth's surface, is found primarily in asteroids and planet cores. In the layer of Earth's crust dated to the KT period, the concentration of iridium is nearly 1000 times its concentration in other layers. This suggests that an asteroid impact deposited iridium during the KT period. Pieces of melted rock (*impact ejecta*) and fracture patterns (*shocked quartz)* are found throughout this layer, and indicate the presence of a large impact.

Scientist 2

The KT extinction was caused by prolonged global volcanic activity. Evidence can be found in India, where *lava flows* (regions of ancient lava) cover over 200,000 square miles. Over a period of 500,000 years, dust and ash from the erupting volcanoes trapped sunlight and heated the earth. Plants died and, without them, herbivores and carnivores soon followed. This relatively slow extinction is shown by a gradual decrease in fossilized species.

Iridium, a rare metal on Earth's surface, is found primarily in planet cores and asteroids. In the layer of Earth's crust dated to the KT period, the concentration of iridium is nearly 1000 times its concentration in other layers. This suggests that this iridium was ejected from the Earth's core by a volcanic eruption. Finally, shocked quartz in this layer also indicates a great explosion.

1. Scientist 1 mentions the crater in Mexico that exists today because the crater provides evidence of:

   A. an asteroid impact in the past.
   B. increased greenhouse gases.
   C. shocked quartz.
   D. fossilized plants.

2. According to Scientist 2, which of the following statements best explains why carnivores went extinct?

   F. Carnivores were burned by lava.
   G. Carnivores were burned by trapped sunlight.
   H. Carnivores had no food source after herbivores and plants went extinct.
   J. Carnivores received heavy metal poisoning from high levels of iridium.

3. Based on the fossil record, a third scientist hypothesizes that competition for scarce resources over millennia caused the KT extinction. This hypothesis is most consistent with the viewpoint(s) on fossilized species of:

   A. Scientist 1 only.
   B. Scientist 2 only.
   C. both Scientists 1 and 2.
   D. neither Scientist 1 nor Scientist 2.

4. Based on the viewpoint of Scientist 1, which of the following best explains the presence of the lava flows in India?

F. The impact of the asteroid triggered volcanic activity in one isolated region.

G. The impact of the asteroid triggered prolonged volcanic activity all over the world.

H. The volcanic activity in one isolated region triggered the impact of the asteroid.

J. The lava flows triggered volcanic activity all over the world.

5. Industrial smog blocks sunlight and is produced today in large quantities by human activity. Scientist 1 would most likely predict that, if these particles continued to be produced, the effect would be:

A. a decrease in the current number of fossilized species.

B. an increase in the current number of fossilized species.

C. a decrease in the temperature of the Earth's atmosphere.

D. an increase in the temperature of the Earth's atmosphere.

6. What piece of evidence found in the layer of Earth's crust dated to the KT period does Scientist 1 mention that Scientist 2 does NOT?

F. Iridium levels

G. Shocked quartz

H. A decrease in fossilized species

J. Impact ejecta

7. Another mass extinction event occurred during the Permian-Triassic (PT) period 250 million years ago. The layer of Earth's crust dated to the PT period has high levels of iridium and shocked quartz. This data is consistent with the viewpoint(s) of:

A. Scientist 1 only.

B. Scientist 2 only.

C. both Scientists 1 and 2.

D. neither Scientist 1 nor Scientist 2.

Passage II

A *virus* is an infective agent that consists of genetic information surrounded by a *membrane*. The membrane of a virus is composed of proteins and lipids, and its genetic information is in the form of RNA or DNA.

A virus lacks the necessary proteins to reproduce on its own. However, it can reproduce through the *lytic cycle*, which is when a dormant virion attaches to a host cell, penetrates it, and becomes an active virus. The active virus releases its RNA or DNA, which instruct the host cell's proteins to produce and assemble viral particles. These new *virions* (inactive viruses) leave the host cell to infect other cells.

All living things reproduce and evolve. Because viruses cannot reproduce on their own, and because of their unknown *phylogenetic history*—the history of their evolution through diversification—their status as living is evaluated in the following 3 hypotheses.

Hypothesis 1

Viruses began as parasitic *prokaryotes*, single-celled organisms with a single membrane around their genetic material. The prokaryotes that used their hosts' proteins to reproduce outcompeted the other prokaryotes, which needed more time and energy to make proteins. Viruses descended from living prokaryotes, and once reproduced on their own, so they too are alive.

Hypothesis 2

Viruses began as pieces of membranes and genetic material shed from multicellular organisms. They are no more alive than pieces of RNA, DNA, or proteins, because they are unable to reproduce on their own. They appear to have evolved, but this is only because they have retained the complex phylogenetic history of the multicellular organisms from which they were shed.

Hypothesis 3

Virions began when genetic material and proteins combined, and have remained the same since. Active viruses and prokaryotes, which are the first living organisms, evolved from virions, and multicellular organisms later evolved from prokaryotes. Lytic cycle stages therefore determine whether a virus is living: a virion is not, but a virus is.

8. Which hypothesis, if any, asserts that viruses descended from prokaryotes?

   F. Hypothesis 1
   G. Hypothesis 2
   H. Hypothesis 3
   J. None of the hypotheses

9. Which hypotheses assert that viruses have *not* diversified over time?

   A. Hypothesis 1 only
   B. Hypothesis 2 only
   C. Hypotheses 2 and 3
   D. Hypotheses 1, 2, and 3

10. According to the passage and the 3 hypotheses, both prokaryotes and viruses:

    F. have genetic material that is composed of only RNA.
    G. have genetic material that is composed of only DNA.
    H. have a second membrane around their genetic material.
    J. have a single membrane around their genetic material.

11. A *cladogram* depicts the phylogenetic history of organisms over time. Each branch represents the evolution of a new species. Based on Hypothesis 3, which of the following cladograms best depicts the phylogenetic history of viruses?

A.

prokaryotes
active viruses

B.

multicellular organisms
active viruses

C.

virions
prokaryotes
active viruses
multicellular organisms

(D)

virions
active viruses
prokaryotes
multicellular organisms

time

12. The recently discovered *mimivirus* is unlike other viruses because it is much larger than many bacteria and it contains the proteins necessary for reproduction. Which hypothesis, if any, is most weakened by the discovery of the mimivirus?

F. Hypothesis 1
(G) Hypothesis 2
H. Hypothesis 3
J. None of the hypotheses

13. According to Hypothesis 2, which of the following treatments would be most effective against a viral infection?

A. A treatment used to eradicate living cells.
(B) A treatment used to destroy RNA, DNA, or proteins.
C. A treatment used to amplify the Lytic Cycle.
D. A treatment used to halt the growth of parasitic prokaryotes.

14. Algae are single-celled organisms that produce energy from sunlight via photosynthesis. Scientists hypothesize that algae gained this ability by absorbing photosynthetic prokaryotes. Which of the following organelles in the cells of algae most likely originated from a prokaryotic cell?

(F) Chloroplast
G. Mitochondria
H. Vacuoles
J. Centrosomes

Passage III

The temperature of the planet has steadily increased in a process referred to as *global warming*. The graph below shows the average global temperature and the average levels of atmospheric carbon dioxide gas (CO_2) over the past 400,000 years.

Two students debate the causes and effects of global warming based on this graph.

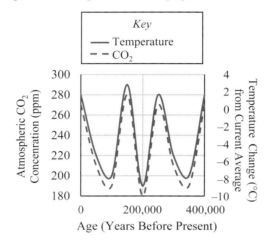

Figure 1

Student 1

Global warming has not been caused by human activity. It is one part of a historical pattern of random fluctuations in the temperature of the Earth's atmosphere. As the graph shows, the average temperature of the atmosphere has increased and decreased, sometimes by very large amounts, during the last 400,000 years. The recent increase in temperature, while large in magnitude, spans only a few hundred years. There is no evidence that the planet is warming consistently over time. Furthermore, historical peaks in atmospheric temperature reached levels similar to those observed recently on at least three other occasions.

Atmospheric CO_2 levels appear to be directly correlated with temperature. This is due to the fact that when the temperature of the planet increases, the metabolism of plants slows. Plants take in CO_2 from the air as part of their metabolism. So as their metabolic activity decreases, atmospheric CO_2 levels increase.

Student 2

Global warming has been caused by human activity. Although the graph shows a historical pattern of fluctuations in the temperature of the Earth's atmosphere, the current trend corresponds to the beginning of the Industrial Age. The average temperature of the atmosphere is currently approaching unprecedented levels and shows no signs of decreasing. The fact that the recent increase in temperature spans only a few hundred years and is also very large in magnitude is especially worrisome, since such abrupt changes have often proven very destructive to the Earth's inhabitants.

Atmospheric CO_2 levels appear to be directly correlated with temperature. This is due to the fact that CO_2 is a *greenhouse gas*, which prevents reflected sunlight from escaping into space. Human industry, particularly the burning of fossil fuels such as oil and coal, has caused the recent increase in CO_2 levels. This, in turn, has caused the recent trend of planetary warming.

15. Which of the students, if either, would agree that increases in atmospheric CO_2 levels has caused the corresponding increase in temperature?

   A. Student 1 only
   B. Student 2 only
   C. Both Student 1 and Student 2
   D. Neither Student 1 nor Student 2

16. According to Student 1's interpretation of the graph, the current average temperature of the atmosphere:

   F. has never been matched by historical levels.
   G. has been matched only once by historical levels.
   H. has been matched multiple times by historical levels.
   J. has been far exceeded by historical levels.

17. Which of the following predictions would Student 1 most likely make about the next 100,000 years of climate data?

   A. Temperature and CO_2 levels will continue to increase over the entire period.

   B. Temperature and CO_2 levels will decrease over the entire period.

   C. Temperature will increase over the entire period, while CO_2 levels will decrease.

   (D) Both temperature and CO_2 levels will fluctuate over the entire period.

18. As part of their metabolism, plants produce oxygen. Student 1 would most likely predict that increasing global temperatures:

   (E) decrease the levels of atmospheric oxygen.

   G. increase the levels of atmospheric oxygen.

   H. have no effect on the levels of atmospheric oxygen.

   J. eliminate all atmospheric oxygen.

19. Student 2 develops a plan for humans to reduce the burning of fossil fuels by 50% over the next 20 years. Based on Student 1's viewpoint, this plan would most likely:

   A. reduce the rate of global temperature increase.

   B. increase the rate of global temperature increase.

   (C) have no effect on the current rate of global temperature increase.

   D. reverse the current trend and cause a global temperature decrease.

20. A climate scientist produces a model, shown below, of temperature and CO_2 levels for the past 1000 years. What effect, if any, does this model have on the strength of the students' viewpoints regarding the correlation between temperature and CO_2 levels?

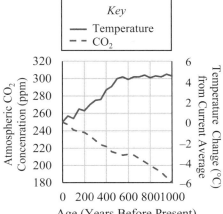

	Student 1	Student 2
F.	Strengthen	Strengthen
G.	Strengthen	Weaken
H.	Weaken	Strengthen
(J)	Weaken	Weaken

21. Gas molecules that consist of a single element from the periodic table do not act as greenhouse gases. Which of the following gas molecules found in the Earth's atmosphere will not act as greenhouse gases?

   I. Argon (Ar)

   II. Nitrogen (N_2)

   III. Water vapor (H_2O)

   (A) I only

   B. II only

   (C) I and II

   D. I, II, and III

Section 3
Question Types

In the following section, you will explore the different question types on the Science Test. Remember that these are *unofficial* question types. They're a good way to classify the ACT, but they aren't the words the ACT uses to describe its questions—you'll see what words they use below. You'll learn some specific tactics, and then you'll have a chance to practice these tactics.

As you saw in Section 1, each passage presents information in different ways, but our five question types will be repeated on every Science Test, and on almost every passage. You don't have to memorize much; simply knowing how the ACT works can really help your test-taking.

The ACT categorizes the Science Test into three question types: Interpretation of Data; Scientific Investigation; and Evaluation of Models, Inferences, and Experimental Results. However, within each type, the ACT tests very different skills. For example, Interpretation of Data questions may ask you to identify trends, to understand the scientific method, or to recall basic scientific terminology. But, respectively, these require distinct tactics: *understanding* figures, evaluating *experimental design*, and simply *knowing terms*. To make everything easier, we use the following five question types:

- Understanding
- Analysis
- Synthesis
- Experimental Design
- Knowledge

Understanding, Analysis, Synthesis, and Knowledge questions can be found on all three passage types. Experimental Design questions will be found primarily on Research Summaries passages. Additional information can be found in our online glossary.

 For additional resources, please visit **ivyglobal.com/study**.

Understanding Questions
Part 1

Understanding questions ask you to perform basic tasks: identify trends, statistics, and claims. The ACT defines these tasks in these ways:

- find one or more pieces of data in a single data presentation
- find one or more pieces of information in the text
- find implications and assumptions in a conceptual model
- perform basic calculations
- determine mathematical relationships

These tasks involve information that is usually presented simply and directly, and mathematics that can be done in your head through estimation (averages, maximums, etc.). While each passage will refer to its own studies, scientists, variables, and units, here are some ways that Understanding questions might be phrased:

- According to Figure 1, which of the following …
- Which hypothesis, if any, asserts that …
- The number was closest to which of the following …
- Based on Figure 1, the average over the past several years was closest to which of the following …

There are approximately nine Understanding questions per Science Test, or nearly 23% of the Test. They tend to be the first questions on any given passage, because they're the simplest. Take a look at a sample Data Representation passage and see how some Understanding questions about that passage would work.

A *white dwarf* is a small star formed from the center of a massive star when the massive star ejects its outer layers—a *supernova*. A white dwarf can then accumulate these outer layers, thus adding mass to itself. When it reaches a mass of 1.4 M_{sun} (1.4 times the mass of the Sun), a white dwarf will explode in a white dwarf supernova. Figure 1 compares the luminosity of white dwarf supernovae to massive star supernovae. As the figure shows, white dwarf supernovae emit a constant amount of luminosity, and thus allow researchers to measure vast distances using the following equation:

$$\text{apparent brightness} = \frac{\text{luminosity}}{4\pi \times \text{distance}^2}$$

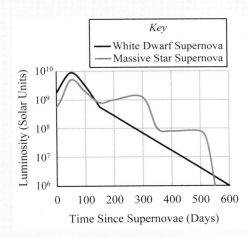

Figure 1

Data and figure adapted from Jeffrey Bennett et al., *The Cosmic Perspective*. ©2010 Addison Wesley.

1. According to Figure 1, the luminosity of a 500-day-old massive star supernova will be closest to which of the following?

   A. 10^6 solar units
   B. 10^7 solar units
   C. 10^8 solar units
   D. 10^9 solar units

2. Researchers would use which of the following equations to calculate the distance between Earth and a white dwarf supernova?

   F. $\text{distance} = \sqrt{\dfrac{\text{luminosity}}{4\pi \times \text{apparent brightness}}}$

   G. $\text{distance} = \dfrac{\text{luminosity}}{4\pi \times \text{apparent brightness}}$

   H. $\text{distance} = \sqrt{\dfrac{4\pi \times \text{luminosity}}{\text{apparent brightness}}}$

   J. $\text{distance} = \sqrt{\dfrac{4\pi \times \text{apparent brightness}}{\text{luminosity}}}$

3. According to Figure 1, as the time since a supernova increases, the luminosity of a white dwarf supernova:

   A. decreases only.
   B. increases, then decreases.
   C. varies, but with an increasing trend.
   D. varies, but with no clear trend.

4. During which of the following times since the massive star supernova was the *decrease* in its luminosity the greatest?

   F. 0 to 100 days
   G. 200 to 300 days
   H. 400 to 500 days
   J. 500 to 600 days

First, you know from reading the General Strategies part in the Approaching the Science section that you do *not* need to read the text, unless a question asks you about it. The questions will tell you what to do; they'll orient you. So, the first thing you do is look for the 3 Ds. That means that you'll primarily look at the Figure—its Key, axes, units, and trends.

Incorrect answers to Understanding questions usually involve looking at the wrong Figure or wrong part of the text. They don't involve the Wrong Answer Types (such as "out of scope"), introduced in the Key Strategies section. Sometimes, they can involve misinterpreting a figure, which is common if you haven't looked at the Key, axes, units, and trends closely enough. Always double-check that you're looking at the right part of the right figure by comparing the words, numbers, and units in the question and the answer options to those in the figure when you're referring back to the passage.

Question 1 asks you to find a point on the graph. Normally, Data Representation passages will have more than one figure, so it's important to read the correct figure. Here, this question is made easier because there's only one figure to choose from, and the question also tells you where to look. This is typical for Understanding questions—they'll tell you which figure, table, or viewpoint to refer back to. If they don't, you can refer back to the text of the passage itself.

The question asks you for the luminosity of a 500-day-old massive star supernova. Find the 500-day mark on the x-axis, and then find the corresponding luminosity value according to the gray curve (you know the gray curve is for massive star supernovae from reading the Key). You can use the Pencil on Paper strategy and trace the line on the figure itself, as shown below:

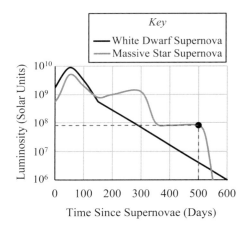

You can see that the luminosity of a massive star supernova after 500 days will be closest to 10^8 solar units, or (C).

Question 2 asks you to rearrange the equation given in the passage. This requires some algebra skills. See Chapter 3 to refresh your memory. Essentially, you are rearranging the equation to find distance, so you need to reverse the order of operations:

$$\text{apparent brightness} = \frac{\text{luminosity}}{4\pi \times \text{distance}^2}$$

$$\text{apparent brightness} \times 4\pi \times \text{distance}^2 = \text{luminosity}$$

$$\text{distance}^2 = \frac{\text{luminosity}}{\text{apparent brightness} \times 4\pi}$$

$$distance = \sqrt{\dfrac{luminosity}{4\pi \times apparent\ brightness}}$$

The answer is (F).

Question 3 asks you to understand the trend in Figure 1. This is a detail you've already looked for during your 3D Skim. You may have circled the peaks of the curves, or the downward slope. In any case, referring back to Figure 1 will tell you that the white dwarf supernova luminosity increases then decreases over time, or (B). Again, make sure you look at the black line, not the gray line, using the Key. When you refer back to the graph to make your Prediction, don't try to oversimplify things. Even though the overall trend of the graph is downward, or decreasing, there *is* a slight increase first, between 0 and 100 days. Don't rule this out for the sake of estimation.

Finally, Question 4 presents several time ranges and asks you for which one of them was the *decrease* in luminosity for the massive star supernova the greatest. The massive star supernova line is the gray line, so make sure you only look at that.

There are two ways to solve this question: (1) you can look at Figure 1 and find the region with the greatest decrease; (2) you can look at the four answer choices, find each one on the graph, and compare them to each other. Option (1) is a good start, but often these questions will *not* present as an answer option the region with the greatest decrease in the figure. They are in fact asking you to use option (2).

Simply find each time period on the *x*-axis, and find the corresponding change in the gray line:

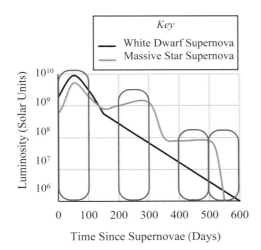

For the times given in (F), the luminosity increases, so (F) is wrong. The luminosity also increases over the times given in (G), so it's wrong too. In (H), the luminosity decreases, but not as much as in (J), so (J) is correct.

Understanding Practice Questions
Part 2

As temperature increases, oils are converted into volatile free fatty acids (VFFAs) and short chain fatty acids (SCFAs). These volatile compounds degrade rapidly in the air, producing soot and smoke. The temperature at which the smoke becomes visible, which occurs when more than 50% of the oil has been converted into VFFAs and SCFAs, is called the *smoke point* of the oil or fat. The smoke point of an oil determines the maximum temperature at which it can be used in cooking. Figure 1 shows the percent of six oils converted into VFFAs and SCFAs as temperature increases. Figure 2 shows the percent of olive oil, reused several times, converted to VFFAs and SCFAs as temperature increases.

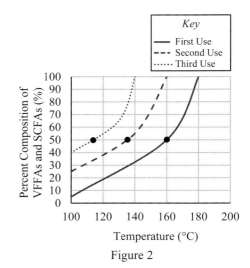

Figure 2

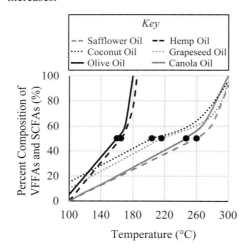

Figure 1

1. Based on Figure 1, which of the following oils has the lowest smoke point?

   A. Safflower oil

   B. Hemp oil

   C. Coconut oil

   D. Grapeseed oil

2. Based on Figure 2, approximately what percent of olive oil is converted to VFFAs and SCFAs at a temperature of 120°C during its second use?

   F. 18%

   G. 32%

   H. 38%

   J. 52%

3. Based on Figure 1, at what temperature are the percent compositions of VFFAs and SCFAs equal for grapeseed oil and canola oil?

   A. 100°C

   B. 200°C

   C. 220°C

   D. 270°C

4. Based on Figure 2, as olive oil is reused, the temperature of its smoke point:

   F. increases only.

   G. decreases only.

   H. increases, then decreases.

   J. decreases, then increases.

5. Based on Figure 1, compared to the change in percent concentration of VFFAs and SCFAs as temperature increases *before* the smoke point of an oil, the change in percent concentration of VFFAs and SCFAs *after* the smoke point of an oil is:

   A. linear, whereas the change before the smoke point is exponential.

   B. exponential, whereas the change before the smoke point is linear.

   C. positive, whereas the change before the smoke point is negative.

   D. negative, whereas the change before the smoke point is positive.

Analysis Questions
Part 3

Analysis questions ask you to fit a piece of data or a claim into a figure or a part of the text, and to infer or evaluate a piece of data or a claim using a figure or a part of the text. They do not involve more than one figure, more than one part of text, or combinations of the two. The ACT defines these tasks in these ways:

- create a graph or figure based on information in the passage
- interpolate and extrapolate data from a figure
- apply mathematical relationships
- predict the results of an additional trial or measurement in an experiment
- use new information to make a prediction
- evaluate a claim using a single data presentation, model, or part of text
- evaluate whether new information supports or contradicts a hypothesis or conclusion
- identify strengths and weaknesses of models in relation to new information

These tasks are not always presented directly, but require you to use your 3D Skim and the strategies in the Approaching the Science Test section to locate the relevant pieces of information. Here are some ways that Analysis questions might be phrased:

- Which of the following statements best describes …
- Scientist 1's viewpoint would be weakened by …
- How would the variable differ from that described in Scientist 1's viewpoint if …
- The results of Study 2 suggest that which of the following factors most affects …
- Which of the following graphs best illustrates the relationship between …
- According to Figure 1, what is the order of the …
- Based on Figure 1, the results of Experiment 1 are best modeled by which of the following equations …
- Suppose that the model presented by Student 1 is correct …
- Is the hypothesis about this relationship supported by the results of Experiment 1 …

There are approximately ten Analysis questions per Science Test, or 25% of the Test. Take a look at a sample Data Representation passage and see how some Analysis questions about that passage would work.

Cones in human eyes are responsible for color vision. There are three types of cones—ρ, β, and γ—and each is responsible for seeing a different color. Colorblindness is caused by damaged ρ cones, which have a more variable and lower sensitivity to light than healthy ρ cones, as shown in Figure 1.

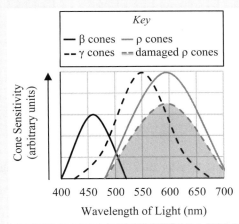

Figure 1

Damaged ρ cones are caused by mutations on a part of the X chromosome. Females have two X chromosomes, one inherited from each parent. If a female inherits a mutation on one of her X chromosomes, the other healthy X chromosome will compensate for it, and she will be unaffected by colorblindness—though she will be a *carrier*. A female is only affected by colorblindness if *both* her X chromosomes have the mutation on them. Males exhibit colorblindness more frequently because they have one X and one Y chromosome. A male inherits his X chromosome from his mother and his Y chromosome from his father. He will therefore be colorblind if his mother is affected, and he may be colorblind if his mother is a carrier. Figure 2 shows four generations of a family with a history of colorblindness.

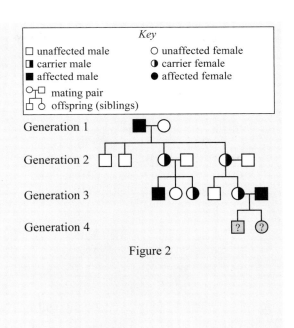

Figure 2

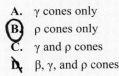

1. Visible light can be categorized into three colors. Blue light has a wavelength between 400 and 500 nm, green light has a wavelength between 500 and 600 nm, and red light has a wavelength between 600 and 700 nm. Which cone(s) would be most responsible for seeing red light?

    A. γ cones only
    B. ρ cones only
    C. γ and ρ cones
    D. β, γ, and ρ cones

2. A patient discovers that her ρ cones have the same maximum sensitivity to light as her β cones. According to Figure 1, the patient most likely has:

    F. damaged β cones.
    G. damaged ρ cones.
    H. healthy β cones.
    J. healthy ρ cones.

3. Based on Figure 2, the chance that the female sibling in Generation 4 is affected by colorblindness is:

A. greater than the chance that the male sibling in Generation 4 is affected by colorblindness.

B. less than the chance that the male sibling in Generation 4 is affected by colorblindness.

C. the same as the chance that the male sibling in Generation 4 is affected by colorblindness.

D. dependent on the chance that the male sibling in Generation 4 is affected by colorblindness.

4. A scientist claims that of the two carrier females in Generation 2, both received the mutation on the X chromosome from their father. Is Figure 2 consistent with this claim?

F. Yes, because the father in Generation 1 is affected by colorblindness, and the mother is not a carrier or affected.

G. Yes, because the mother in Generation 1 is affected by colorblindness, and the father is not a carrier or affected.

H. No, because the father in Generation 1 is affected by colorblindness, and the mother is not a carrier or affected.

J. No, because the mother in Generation 1 is affected by colorblindness, and the father is not a carrier or affected.

Answering Analysis questions correctly will involve looking at the correct locations in the passage, whether the correct figure or the correct part of the text. Answering Analysis questions incorrectly will therefore involve misinterpreting the question, looking at the wrong location in the figures or text, or reading the answers too quickly and missing important differences between them. Incorrect answer options may also involve the Wrong Answer Types, introduced in the Key Strategies section.

Always mark up the passage with your Pencil on Paper, then read the question carefully (note its keywords if it's a long question), refer back to the passage, and make a Prediction. If your prediction can't get you the right answer on its own, then use it along with the Wrong Answer Types and the chunking method to help with Process of Elimination. The chunking method becomes especially important in Analysis questions, where the answers are often wordy and long.

Question 1 provides information about visible light. It tells you that different ranges of wavelengths correspond roughly to different colors. Blue light is 400–500 nm, green is 500–600 nm, and red is 600–700 nm. The question then asks you which cone is most responsible for seeing red light. This is *interpolation*—finding data *inside* the graph. Extrapolation is finding data *outside* the graph.

You can map the range of wavelengths for red light onto Figure 1 and see which cone(s) fit(s) in this range.

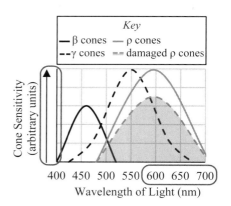

You can see that the ρ cones are most sensitive to this range of wavelengths, (B). The passage confirms this answer choice: "There are three types of cones—ρ, γ, and β—and each is responsible for seeing a different color." Although γ cones have some sensitivity to this range of wavelengths of light, they don't have much sensitivity—certainly not as much as ρ cones, and so answers (A), (C), and (D) are incorrect. One of the key words in the question, therefore, is *most*.

Question 2 gives you some information about a patient. If her ρ cones have the same maximum sensitivity to light as her β cones, then their curves on the graph must be equivalent. You can see that if the patient's ρ cones are only as sensitive as her β cones, then they fall within the range labeled "damaged ρ cones." Therefore, the answer is (G).

Question 3 is tricky. At first, it sounds like it's asking you to do some complicated mathematics. But Science questions don't ask you to do overly complicated math. You can glance at the answer options to help orient yourself, and using chunking, you'd see that the answers are all the same with the exception of the first few words: greater than, less than, the same as, dependent on. The question is therefore comparing the female sibling to the male sibling in Generation 4.

At this point, using only Figure 2 will not give you enough information to answer the question. You should read the text explaining the figure to understand the relationships. The text explains the X chromosomes and their inheritance in males and females. Males have an X and a Y chromosome and are colorblind if their X chromosome has the mutation on it. The male in Generation 4, therefore, has a 50% chance of being colorblind. He will receive his Y chromosome from his father, and his X chromosome from his mother. His mother is a carrier, so one of her X chromosomes is affected and one is not.

Females have two X chromosomes, and both must have the mutation for the female to be colorblind. The female in Generation 4 will receive an X chromosome from her father, who is colorblind. Therefore, the X chromosome she receives from her father has the mutation for colorblindness on it. She will receive her other X chromosome from her mother, who is a carrier. Therefore, she has a 50% chance of receiving a mutated X chromosome from her mother. Her chance of being colorblind is the same as her brother's, so the answer is (C).

Question 4 presents the claim of a scientist and asks you to evaluate whether Figure 2 is consistent with the claim. It points you to the two female carriers in Generation 2, and states that they received their mutated X chromosome from their father. You must therefore evaluate Generation 1. The father is affected by colorblindness, which means his X chromosome has the mutation on it. The mother is unaffected and she's not a carrier. Therefore, her X chromosomes do not have a mutation. The answer is therefore Yes. You can eliminate (H) and (J) via piecewise elimination. Next, you should read the reasons that make (F) and (G) different. You can see that (F) matches the data, but (G) is the exact opposite. Therefore, (F) is correct.

Analysis Practice Questions

Part 4

Some students conducted experiments to test the effect of mass, material, and angle of incline on the velocity of an object by releasing objects of different masses down inclined planes at different angles and made of different materials.

Study 1

A student placed smooth steel cubes of different masses at the top of a polished wooden inclined plane with an angle of 45° to the horizontal (represented by Θ in Diagram 1 below). The student released one cube and pressed a stopwatch, stopping the watch when the cube reached the bottom of the incline, and then repeated the same procedure for four more cubes. The results are recorded in Table 1.

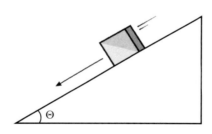

Diagram 1

Table 1	
Mass (g)	Time (sec)
100	4.10
200	3.85
500	3.10
1000	1.85
1500	0.60

Study 2

Another student placed a smooth steel cube with a mass of 200 g at the top of several polished wooden inclined planes. Each plane had a different angle to the horizontal. The student released the cube on one plane and pressed a stopwatch, stopping the watch when the cube reached the bottom of the incline. The procedure was repeated for four more inclines. The results are recorded in Table 2.

Table 2	
Angle	Time (sec)
45°	3.85
50°	3.70
55°	3.55
60°	3.40
65°	3.25

Study 3

Another student placed a smooth steel cube with a mass of 200 g at the top of several inclined planes, each with an angle of 45° to the horizontal. Each plane was made of a different material. The same procedure was used as in Study 1 and Study 2, and the results are recorded in Table 3.

Table 3	
Material	Time (sec)
Wood	3.85
Wool	6.20
Steel	3.20
Glass	2.70

1. In Study 1, if a smooth steel cube with a mass of 750 g had been tested, the time it took to travel down the inclined plane would have been closest to:

   A. 3.10 sec.
   B. 2.50 sec.
   C. 1.90 sec.
   D. 0.80 sec.

2. According to the results of Study 2, if a smooth steel cube with a mass of 200 g had traveled down a polished wooden inclined plane with an angle of 75° to the horizontal, its time of travel would be:

   F. less than 3.25 sec.
   G. between 3.25 sec and 3.40 sec.
   H. between 3.40 sec and 3.55 sec.
   J. greater than 3.55 sec.

3. Suppose a student repeats Study 1 with a glass cube on a smooth steel inclined plane. The student finds that the times it takes different masses of the new cube to reach the bottom of the inclined plane are uniformly 1.15 seconds less than the times it took different masses of the smooth steel cube to reach the bottom of the polished wood inclined plane. Are these results consistent with the results of Study 3?

   A. No; Study 3 indicates that a steel surface on a glass surface allows for faster movement than a steel surface on a wood surface does.
   B. No; Study 3 indicates that a steel surface on a glass surface allows for slower movement than a steel surface on a wood surface does.
   C. Yes; Study 3 indicates that a steel surface on a glass surface allows for faster movement than a steel surface on a wood surface does.
   D. Yes; Study 3 indicates that a steel surface on a glass surface allows for slower movement than a steel surface on a wood surface does.

4. An inclined plane made of concrete was also tested in Study 3, and the time it took the smooth steel cube to reach the bottom was 4.40 sec. Which of the following correctly lists the materials of the inclined planes in *decreasing* order of time it took the cube to reach the bottom?

   F. Wool, concrete, wood, steel, glass
   G. Wool, wood, concrete, steel, glass
   H. Glass, steel, wood, concrete, wool
   J. Steel, glass, concrete, wood, wool

5. Which of the following figures is consistent with the results of Study 1?

   A.
   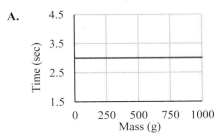

   B.
   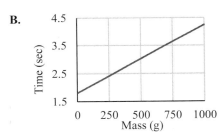

   C.
   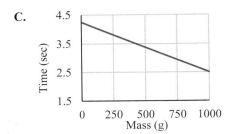

   D.
   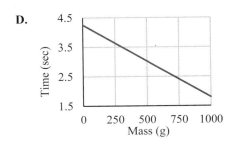

Synthesis Questions
Part 5

Synthesis questions ask you to perform complex tasks: compare and contrast multiple figures, parts of the text, or both, and use multiple figures or parts of the text to evaluate claims or data. Synthesis questions do everything that Analysis questions do, except, instead of referring to only one place in the passage, they refer to multiple places. The ACT defines these tasks in these ways:

- find one or more pieces of data in multiple data presentations
- compare and contrast information from multiple data presentations
- identify similarities and differences between experiments or between conceptual models
- evaluate a claim using multiple data presentations, models, or texts

These tasks involve finding information in one place in the passage, and using that information in another place in the passage. You will have to use definitions from the text in the context of a figure, data from one figure in the context of another, methods from one experiment in another, or evaluate ideas in one model using ideas in another.

These tasks are not presented simply and directly, but require you to use your 3D Skim and the strategies in the Approaching the Science Test section to locate several pieces of information, complex information, and information that's given indirectly. Here are some ways that Synthesis questions might be phrased:

- Which of the following phrases best describes the major point of difference between …
- The results of the two experiments support the conclusion that …
- Which of the following models is most consistent with this observation and the results of the experiments …
- One way Experiment 1 was different from Experiment 2 was that in Experiment 1 …
- According to Tables 1 and 2, as the variable increased, the other variable most likely …
- The variable in Figure 2 corresponds to which of the following points on Figure 3 …

There are approximately eleven Synthesis questions per Science Test, or nearly 28% of the Test. The ACT has moved from asking more Analysis questions to asking more Synthesis questions. They tend to be the last questions on any given passage, because they require the most steps to solve. Take a look at a sample Data Representation passage and see how some Synthesis questions about that passage would work.

When an organism is buried shortly after its death in an area inhospitable to life, it cannot be consumed, and its parts will be preserved as *fossils*. Fossils are remains or impressions of an organism in rock. Their age is determined by two methods. Figure 1 shows a map with four sites where fossils were found on Seymour Island, and Figure 2 shows a cross-section of the Earth at each site. These figures detail the *superposition* method, which states that fossils found in older rocks will therefore be older.

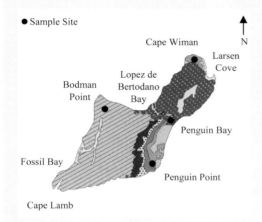

Figure 1

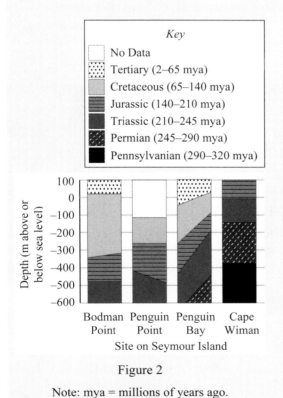

Figure 2

Note: mya = millions of years ago.

Figure 3 shows the *potassium-argon* method. Half of the potassium in an organism will decay into argon over a period of 1.3 billion years, called *half-life*. The age of a fossil is determined by measuring the proportion of its argon atoms and comparing it to the proportion of its potassium atoms.

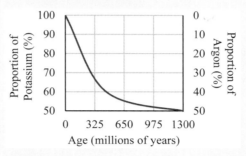

Figure 3

1. The potassium-argon method differs from the superposition method in that only the potassium-argon method measures the:

   A. chemical composition of the fossil.
   B. age of the fossil.
   C. chemical composition of the rock containing the fossil.
   D. age of the rock containing the fossil.

2. On Seymour Island, the oldest fossils were most likely found in the:

   F. northeast.
   G. northwest.
   H. southeast.
   J. southwest.

3. A scientist discovers a fossil containing a potassium-to-argon ratio of 90% to 10%. The fossil was most likely from which of the following periods?

A. Pennsylvanian

B. Permian

C. Triassic

D Cretaceous

4. A scientist claims that as the depth of a fossil increased, the proportion of argon contained in that fossil increased. Is the data presented in Figures 2 and 3 consistent with this claim?

F. Yes, because fossils found at greater depths were found in younger rock, which has a greater proportion of potassium than older rock.

G. Yes, because fossils found at greater depths were found in older rock, which has a greater proportion of argon than younger rock.

H. No, because fossils found at greater depths were found in younger rock, which has a greater proportion of potassium than older rock.

J. No, because fossils found at greater depths were found in older rock, which has a greater proportion of argon than younger rock.

Incorrect answers to Synthesis questions may involve looking at the wrong Figures or wrong parts of the text, or misinterpreting them, especially if you haven't looked for the 3 Ds and mapped out the locations of the pertinent details. They may also involve the Wrong Answer Types, introduced in the Key Strategies section. Always mark up the passage using the Pencil on Paper strategy, then read the question carefully, refer back to the passage, and make a Prediction. If your prediction can't get you the right answer on its own, then use it along with the Wrong Answer Types and the chunking method to help with Process of Elimination.

Question 1 asks you to compare the potassium-argon method with the superposition method. Be sure to pay attention to the syntax of the question. Using short forms, PA for potassium-argon and S for superposition, it says "PA differs from S because only PA …" You can rephrase this slightly: "What does PA do that S doesn't?"

Both of these methods are italicized in the passage, so you would've noted that they're important definitions. The question also doesn't refer to any figures, so your first instinct should be to glance at the text. You can then read these definitions to know that the answer is (A). If you're familiar with chemistry, you may have guessed this from their names alone, but it's a good idea to refer back to the passage and make a prediction anyway. Be wary of (B)—it's incorrect because *both* the methods do it.

Question 2 mentions Seymour Island and the age of fossils. All the answer options are a direction on the island. Therefore, you must refer to Figures 1 and 2. The Key and Note in Figure 2 tell you that the oldest fossils are from the Pennsylvanian period, 290–320 million years ago. This time only corresponds to one sample site, the deepest part of Cape Wiman. On Figure 1, Cape Wiman is on the northeast point of Seymour Island. The answer is (F).

Question 3 presents a fossil discovery and asks you to find what period it came from. The discovery is a fossil containing 90% potassium and 10% argon, which means you have to look at Figure 3. 90% potassium and 10% argon mean the same thing, according to the graph. Use the correct *y*-axis (90% on the potassium axis) to find the corresponding age on the *x*-axis:

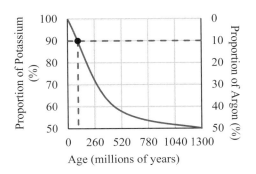

A 90% to 10% ratio indicates an age between 0 and 260 million years. The *x*-value falls closer to the 0 mark than to the halfway mark, so a reasonable guess would be that the fossil is less than 130 million years old. This age corresponds to the Cretaceous period, so the answer is (D). None of the other answers would satisfy these criteria, since they're all 260 million years ago and earlier.

Question 4 mentions two trends: increasing depth of fossils and increasing proportion of argon. Depth points you to Figure 2, where you can see that at each site, older fossils are found at lower depths. From Figure 3, you can see from the second *y*-axis, labeled "Proportion of Argon (%)," that as the proportion of argon increases, the age of the fossil increases as well. You know that increasing depth = increasing age = increasing argon. Therefore, increasing depth = increasing argon.

You can use chunking to match this prediction to the answers. First, the answer is Yes, so you can eliminate (H) and (J). Second, of the Yes answers, you can evaluate the reasons. (F) says deeper rock holds younger fossils, which is false; therefore, the answer is (G).

Synthesis Practice Questions
Part 6

Over the past 200 years, the temperature of the Earth has exponentially increased through a process many scientists call global warming. Global warming has an effect on all ecosystems by destroying and creating habitats, and by causing temperatures which exceed the heat tolerance of different organisms, leading to their adaptation, migration, or extinction.

One organism influenced by global warming is the polar bear (*Ursus maritimus*). Polar bears typically reside in or near the Arctic Circle, but have recently been spotted far outside their natural habitat. Two scientists discuss the appearance of polar bears outside their natural habitat and its relation to global warming.

Scientist 1

Polar bears primarily prey on seals that live in the Arctic Ocean. Polar bears can swim for extended periods of time, but they need dry ground where they can rest and breathe. Typically, polar bears have used sea ice to rest and breathe while they hunt seals, but global warming has caused sea ice in the Arctic Ocean to melt. Without sea ice, polar bears cannot hunt seals, and lose their primary food source. They migrate southward, away from the Ocean and melting ice, in search of more food.

Scientist 2

Over thousands of years, polar bears have evolved translucent fur, which scatters and reflects visible light. This gives their fur the appearance of being white, which helps to camouflage them when they hunt for their prey in snow and ice. However, global warming has melted the snow and ice in much of the bears' habitats. Against the new habitat of grass and brush, the polar bears' white-looking fur is bright and obvious. No longer camouflaged, the bears are unable to successfully hunt their prey. They migrate northward in search of whiter habitats in which to hunt.

1. Latitude is a measurement of location relative to the equator (0°) and the poles (90°). The Arctic Circle begins at approximately 66°N. If a family of polar bears was discovered just north of Saskatoon, Canada, a city located at 52°N, what would be the effect of this discovery on the views of the two scientists?

	Scientist 1	Scientist 2
A.	Strengthen	Strengthen
B.	Strengthen	Weaken
C.	Weaken	Weaken
D.	Weaken	Strengthen

2. Which of the following figures is consistent with the claims of *both* scientists?

F.

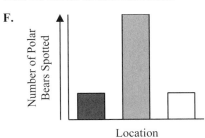

G.

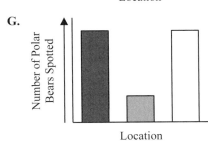

H.

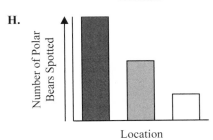

J.

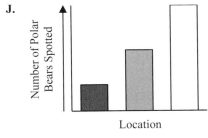

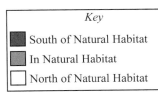

Key
■ South of Natural Habitat
▨ In Natural Habitat
□ North of Natural Habitat

3. Scientist 2's argument implies that Scientist 1's argument would be *weakened* by which of the following observations?

    A. Melting snow and ice north of the Arctic Circle

    B. The presence of seals north of the Arctic Circle

    C. The white fur of polar bears

    D. The northward migration of polar bears

4. Which of the following statements about polar bears is consistent with the views of both scientists?

    F. Polar bears migrate primarily because of melting sea ice.

    G. Polar bears migrate primarily because of their lack of camouflage.

    H. Polar bears have been affected by global warming.

    J. Polar bears have not been affected by global warming.

5. Suppose a third scientist conducts a study to determine the relative fitness of polar bears, and concludes that the longer a polar bear is able to rest while swimming, the more likely it is to capture food and therefore to reproduce. This study supports the view of which scientists, if any?

    A. Scientist 1 only

    B. Scientist 2 only

    C. Both Scientists 1 and 2

    D. Neither Scientist 1 nor Scientist 2

Experimental Design
Part 7

Experimental Design questions ask you about the scientific method, highlighting *how* and *why* researchers carried out a particular study or set of studies. These questions are unlike Understanding, Analysis, and Synthesis questions because they do not usually ask you to analyze experimental results. Instead, Experimental Design questions focus on the experiments themselves—usually the text, but sometimes also diagrams of equipment. The ACT defines these tasks as follows:

- understand experimental tools, methods, and controls
- determine the conditions that would produce certain results
- determine an alternate method for testing a hypothesis
- understand precision and accuracy issues
- predict the effects of modifying the design or methods of an experiment
- determine which additional trial or experiment could be performed to enhance or evaluate experimental results

As you probably guessed, Experimental Design questions typically appear on Research Summaries passages. As with the other question types, you need to understand what is being presented in the figures. However, you may also need to refer to the text—including the "Notes"—and the diagrams to gain a deeper comprehension of hypotheses, methods, and variables. You may even be asked to expand or improve upon the experiments that were performed.

Usually, Experimental Design questions are presented in a straightforward manner. Experimental Design questions also often require understanding of the scientific method and different types of variables. This information can all be found in Section 2, Part 3, Research Summaries.

Sometimes, Experimental Design questions will refer to more than one piece of information, like a Synthesis question. Use the skills and information you've learned and the strategies from the Approaching the Science Test section. Refer to the text as needed, and be wary of misleading answer choices.

Here are some phrases you might see in Experimental Design questions:

- Which of the following variables was controlled in the design of Study 1 …
- In Study 1, the variable was used to study the …
- Which of the following is a weakness of the design of Study 1 …
- Suppose the researchers wanted to determine …
- Which of the following experiments should be performed …
- Why was the study designed so that …

There are approximately six Experimental Design questions per Science Test, or around 15% of the Test. Have a look at the following sample Research Summaries passage and the accompanying Experimental Design questions.

A **fluid** is a substance that has no set shape and deforms under external pressure. Students performed two experiments to study how fluids move through small orifices.

Experiment 1

The students cut plastic bottles into cylinders of identical diameter and various heights ranging from 10 cm to 100 cm. In each cylinder, exactly 1 cm from the bottom of the cylinder, they cut a circular hole 2 cm in diameter, as shown in Diagram 1. The holes were temporarily plugged with rubber stoppers.

Each cylinder was completely filled with water and placed over a beaker. The rubber stoppers were removed, allowing the water to flow out of the hole and into the beaker. Using a stopwatch, the students measured exactly 30 seconds. After 30 seconds, the stoppers were placed in the holes, and the volume of water that had flowed out of the cylinders (the *flow-through*) was measured. Using these measurements, the students calculated the flow rate of the water, in cm³/sec. All results are shown in Table 1.

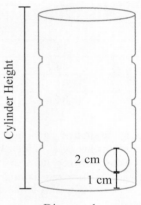

Diagram 1

Table 1		
Height of cylinder (cm)	Flow-through volume (cm³)	Flow rate (cm³/sec)
10	7.01	0.234
20	9.90	0.330
30	12.12	0.404
40	14.02	0.467
50	15.65	0.522
60	17.15	0.572
70	18.52	0.617
80	19.80	0.661
90	21.00	0.699
100	22.14	0.738

Experiment 2

The students constructed six plastic cylinders, all with height 80 cm, using the same method as used in Experiment 1. In each cylinder, 1 cm from the bottom of the cylinder, they cut a circular hole. The holes varied in diameter from 0.5 cm to 3.0 cm. The holes were temporarily plugged with a rubber stopper.

The students repeated the water flow procedure from Experiment 1, measuring the flow-through volume and flow rate for each hole size. All results are shown in Table 2.

Table 2		
Hole diameter (cm)	Flow-through volume (cm^3)	Flow rate (cm^3/sec)
0.5	1.24	0.041
1.0	4.95	0.165
1.5	11.16	0.372
2.0	19.80	0.662
2.5	31.01	1.034
3.0	44.64	1.488

1. Suppose the students' goal in performing the experiments was to determine the relationship between the density of the fluid and the flow rate through a small orifice. Do Experiments 1 and 2 achieve this goal?

   (A) No; the same fluid was used in all trials.

   B. No; fluids of different densities were compared between trials.

   C. Yes; the same fluid was used in all trials.

   D. Yes; fluids of different densities were compared between trials.

2. In Experiments 1 and 2, the students plugged the holes with rubber stoppers most likely in order to:

   F. increase the mass of the cylinder.

   G. increase the flow rate of the water.

   (H) prevent the water from flowing prior to starting the stopwatch.

   J. measure the amount of water that flowed out of the cylinder.

3. Which of the following was the independent variable in Experiment 2?

   A. Height of cylinder

   (B) Diameter of hole

   C. Flow-through volume

   D. Flow rate

4. After completing Experiment 1, one of the students noticed that some of the flow-through had splashed out of the collection beaker and onto the laboratory bench. Compared to the actual volume of flow-through, the volume measured by the students was most likely:

   (F) lower.

   G. higher.

   H. equal.

   J. lower for some of the trials and higher for others.

Question 1 asks you about the goal of the study as a whole. When you see the phrase "Suppose that …", you know that the question is going to introduce a bit of new information. In this case, the question brings in the idea of experimental purpose, which wasn't discussed in depth in the passage. You should also take note of the variables the question asks about: fluid density and flow rate. Just by looking at the tables, which you should have done at first glance, you already know which variables are being studied in Experiments 1 and 2: cylinder height, hole diameter, flow-through volume, and flow rate. Fluid density was never mentioned. In fact, if you skim the text, you will see that water was used in all trials. Combined, these observations tell you that (A) is the correct answer.

Question 2 asks about the purpose of the rubber stoppers. If you only looked at the figures your first time through the passage, as was suggested in the Approaching the Science Test section, then you may not be familiar with the rubber stoppers. What's more, Diagram 1, which shows the experimental setup, doesn't include a rubber stopper. This means that you need to skim the text and look for your key phrase. Experiment 1 tells you that the stoppers were inserted before the cylinders were filled with water and then removed as the timing began, "allowing the water to flow out of the hole and into the beaker." Looking at the answer choices, (H) is clearly the best choice. If the stoppers hadn't been used, the water would have started flowing out of the cylinders before the students were ready to start the stopwatch.

Question 3 asks about the independent variable in Experiment 2. If you look at Section 1, Part 3, you will know that the independent variable is the factor altered by the researchers in order to measure its effect on other quantities. Often, though not always, the independent variable is displayed in the leftmost column of a table, or on the x-axis of a graph. In the case of Experiment 2, you could make an educated guess that "Hole diameter" is the independent variable. If you have time, skim the text. In Experiment 2, the students cut holes of various sizes to measure the effect on flow rate. This confirms your hunch. "Hole diameter" is the independent variable, so (B) is correct. If you're not careful, you might be tempted to choose (A), which is the independent variable from Experiment 1.

Question 4 asks about a potential source of error in Experiment 1. From the diagram and the explanation of the experimental methodology, you know that the students are allowing water to flow out of the cylinder for 30 seconds. You know they are collecting this water in a beaker. Normally, all the water would go in the beaker—that's the *actual* volume of water. However, in this case, some of the water does *not* go in the beaker. The students measure only the water that goes in the beaker. Therefore, they will measure *less* water than the actual amount of water that flowed out of the cylinder. The answer is (F).

Experimental Design Practice Questions
Part 8

Students conducted a flame test—they exposed different strips of metal to the flame of a Bunsen burner—to determine the colors of different metal ions. Color is produced from a metal exposed to flame because the electrons orbiting the metallic nucleus jump between different *orbital levels* (areas in which electrons orbit the nucleus). Orbital levels are separated by energy: levels that are farther from the nucleus have higher levels of energy. When an electron jumps between orbital levels, it releases the energy difference between the levels as electromagnetic radiation, and the wavelength of this radiation is often within the visible spectrum.

Study 1

Students placed a Bunsen burner on the base of a retort stand. They attached a titanium clamp to the retort stand at a fixed height above the Bunsen burner. The Bunsen burner was ignited and set to produce a flame of medium intensity, as shown in Diagram 1. Strips of known metals, each with a mass of 100 mg, were placed separately in the clamp for 30 seconds each, measured using a stopwatch. The colors they produced when exposed to the flame were recorded in Table 1.

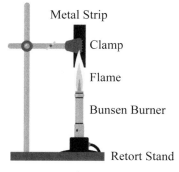

Diagram 1

Table 1	
Metal	Color
Lithium (Li)	Red
Sodium (Na)	Yellow
Potassium (K)	Pink
Barium (Ba)	Pale green
Copper (Cu)	Blue-green

Study 2

The students repeated Study 1 with the same experimental set-up, but recorded the time at which each metal first exhibited its color in Table 2.

Table 2	
Metal	Time to Color's Appearance (sec)
Li	4.05
Na	5.80
K	9.65
Ba	12.40
Cu	16.30

Study 3

In order to test the composition of four 100 mg strips of unknown metals, students repeated Study 1. They recorded the colors that appeared, and the times at which the colors appeared, in Table 3.

Table 3				
Unknown Metal	First Color	Time to First Color (sec)	Second Color	Time to Second Color (sec)
U1	Red	4.20	Light Red	10.05
U2	Green	12.60	Blue-green	16.25
U3	Orange	4.95	None	None
U4	Gray-white	20.10	None	None

1. Which of the following variables was *least* precisely controlled throughout all three studies?

   A. Mass of the metals

   B. Time the metals were exposed to flame

   C. Height of the clamp on the retort stand

   D. Temperature of the flame

2. Which of the following procedures should be performed to determine the metal(s) present in U4?

   F. Repeat Study 1 using metals that were not originally tested.

   G. Repeat Study 2 using metals that were not originally tested.

   H. Repeat Studies 1 and 2 using metals that were not originally tested.

   J. Repeat Studies 1 and 2 using only the metals that were originally tested.

3. Suppose that the clamp attached to the retort stand was composed of copper. Students would have most likely concluded that, in Study 3:

   A. the Bunsen burner produced a flame at too high a temperature.

   B. the Bunsen burner produced a flame that did not reach the clamp.

   C. copper was absent from all four unknown metals.

   D. copper was present in all four unknown metals.

4. What was the dependent variable in Study 1?

   F. Mass of metal

   G. Type of metal

   H. Temperature

   J. Color

5. It is most likely that the researchers measured the time it took each color to appear when the metals from Study 1 were exposed to flame in Study 2 in order to:

   A. determine the composition of the unknown metals in Study 3.

   B. determine the composition of the metals in Study 2.

   C. ensure that the colors were appearing after a constant time.

   D. ensure that the colors were the same as those that appeared in Study 1.

Knowledge Questions
Part 9

Knowledge questions are the only questions that do *not* ask you about information given in the passage. They may use an introductory sentence to connect themselves to the passage, but the information to answer them will not be found there. This makes them unlike all the other question types.

It also makes Knowledge questions difficult to prepare for—though not impossible. You won't be able to study specific tactics as you did for the others, but you can review the areas of science below and our online glossary to see what kind of outside information the ACT has required its test-takers to know in the past, and what you may reasonably expect to see.

For additional resources, please visit **ivyglobal.com/study**.

To master Knowledge questions, pay attention in your science classes! Do some extra-curricular reading, and most of all, be alert. If a question and its answer options mention terms that are not present in the passage, it's a Knowledge question. There are usually about four Knowledge questions per test, or about 10% of the test.

Here's a sample Knowledge question, based on the following sample passage excerpt from the Synthesis Questions section:

Figure 3 shows the *potassium-argon* method. Half of the potassium in an organism will decay into argon over a period of 1.3 billion years, called *half-life*. The age of a fossil is determined by measuring the proportion of its argon atoms and comparing it to the proportion of its potassium atoms.

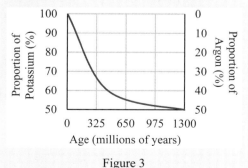

Figure 3

Potassium is a chemical element also used to date human fossils because it is commonly found in human tissue, and the chemical content of the tissue remains essentially the same after fossilization. If all elements used to date human fossils must be elements found in human tissue, which of the following elements could NOT be used to date fossils?

A. Carbon

B. Oxygen

Ⓒ Aluminum

D. Nitrogen

This question essentially asks "what element is not found in human tissue?" You can see from the passage excerpt that these words do not appear in the passage, so you're dealing with a Knowledge question. You know from biology and chemistry what kinds of chemicals are found in living cells, and therefore in human tissue—carbon, oxygen, and hydrogen make up most living tissues and compounds. Aluminum does not, so the answer is (C).

Here's a modified version of the ACT's own list of **areas of science**, which also includes common high school science concepts that may appear on the Science Test. These concepts may or may not appear in the passages or in Knowledge questions, but understanding them will help you be fully prepared for test day.

It's a good idea to familiarize yourself with these concepts if you've never heard of them. If you've heard of them, it's a good idea to refresh your memory.

Areas of Science	
Biology	(a)biotic factors, adaptation, (a)sexual reproduction, (an)aerobic conditions, animal behavior, animal development and growth, biodiversity, biomolecules, body systems, carrying capacity, cellular respiration, climate change, ecology, ecosystems, energy flow, evolution, extinction, genetics, heredity, homeostasis, infection, life cycles, meiosis and mitosis, microbiology, molecular biology, mutation, organelles, organs, origin of life, photosynthesis, plant development and growth, taxonomy
Physics	acceleration, circular motion, conservation of energy, displacement, force and motion, friction, gravity, heat and work, kinetic and potential energy, magnetism, momentum, position, properties of matter and waves, reflection, refraction, sound and light, springs, superposition and interference, vectors, velocity, wavelength
Chemistry	acids and bases, atomic structure, chemical bonding, chromatography, combined gas law, electrical circuits, endo/exothermic reactions, energy curves and catalysts, entropy, equations, equilibrium, intra/intermolecular forces, kinetic molecular theory, Le Chatelier's principle nomenclature, nuclear chemistry, organic chemistry, periodic table and trends, phases of matter, pH scale, properties of solutions, reactions, reduction and oxidation, stoichiometry, titration
Space Science	age of the universe, asteroids, Big Bang, comets, earth's atmosphere, galactic motion, meteors, orbital motion, ozone, planets, solar system, star life cycles, weather and climate
Earth Science	carbon cycle, climate change, earthquakes and volcanoes, earth's resources, erosion, fossils and geological time, geochemical cycles, lakes, oceans, plate tectonics, rivers, rocks and minerals, thermal convection and the core, water cycles

Writing
Chapter 6

Section 1
Approaching the Writing Test

The ACT Writing Test tests your writing and analytical skills, specifically your ability to express judgments by taking a position on an issue. It also tests your skill in reading a short prompt, and planning and writing an essay in response to that prompt. In this section, we'll cover the following topics:

- The Basics
- Essay Scoring
- Strategies for the Writing Test

Unlike the rest of the ACT, the Writing Test is optional. If you take the Writing Test, it will be administered after the four multiple choice tests. While the Writing Test will use a different prompt for each exam, the overall structure of the Writing Test will always be the same. Becoming familiar with the format and scoring of the Writing Test now will help you prepare for test day!

The Basics
Part 1

You will have 40 minutes to complete the Writing Test. You will read a prompt that introduces an issue, read and analyze three perspectives on the issue, and write an essay in which you analyze the given perspectives and develop your own perspective on the issue.

The prompt will be very short: there are only about 200 words that you need to read in each prompt. The prompt provides a general overview and a few specific facts about a topic, and it's followed by three perspectives. The three perspectives will be presented as three short statements expressing valid but distinct perspectives on the topic. The three perspectives will agree on the basic facts presented in the prompt, and you can assume that all factual information presented is true.

You can use your test booklet as scratch paper, and you will be provided with four lined pages on which to write your essay. You should use these lined pages only to write your essay: use the blank space provided in the test booklet for your notes and outlining. You don't need to fill all four lined sheets, but you should strive to use at least two. You're not graded on the amount of space that you fill, but an essay of one page or less is unlikely to express a fully developed analysis.

Top-scoring essays usually include five or six well-organized paragraphs, which are usually about one hundred words long—with body paragraphs generally being a little longer than introductions or conclusions. You don't need to count your words as you write: the word count of your essay doesn't directly affect your score. However, it might be a sign of other problems if you're writing essays that are much shorter than 500–600 words. If you're writing very short essays, then you're probably not addressing multiple perspectives or fully developing your own ideas.

The Writing Test		
Time	40 minutes	~5 to read and outline, ~35 to write and revise
Prompt	1 issue, 3 perspectives	175–190 words
Your Essay	5–6 paragraphs	~600 words

In 2015, the ACT changed the format of the Writing Test. Older materials might contain prompts that just ask you to explain your position on a short question. On the new ACT essay, you must still take a position on an issue, but you'll also be asked to assess the merits of other perspectives and to consider the relationships between them. You can see an example essay prompt on the following page.

Commercials in School

Schools distribute various type of media: textbooks, yearbooks, school newspapers, and TV and radio content. Many of these types of content include advertisements and commercially sponsored content, and some are compulsory. For example, students may be required to watch a school news program at the beginning of each school day, and some of those programs may include commercial content. Including advertisements in school media provides a source of revenue for schools or providers of free content to schools, and is a standard practice in many other forms of media. However, critics argue that it is exploitative to require students to view advertisements, or that promoting commercial content in school media is contrary to the values of education. Is it appropriate for schools to raise revenue by selling advertisements in school media, or to promote free media that includes commercial content—or should schools be ad-free zones?

Read and carefully consider these perspectives. Each suggests a particular way of thinking about commercials in school.

Perspective 1	Perspective 2	Perspective 3
By providing advertisers with the opportunity to share relevant content with students, schools can raise revenues, allowing them to provide better services to students. It's a win-win situation.	Schools exist to provide students with an education, not to sell captive audiences to advertisers. School media has an ethical obligation to be educational—not commercial.	Students have to view ads all the time, so learning how to evaluate them is important. School media should both include ads and encourage students to evaluate them critically.

Essay Task

Write a unified, coherent essay in which you evaluate multiple perspectives on commercials in school. In your essay, be sure to:

- analyze and evaluate the perspectives given
- state and develop your own perspective on the issue
- explain the relationship between your perspective and those given

Your perspective may be in full agreement with any of the others, in partial agreement, or wholly different. Whatever the case, support your ideas with logical reasoning and detailed, persuasive examples.

Planning Your Essay

Your work on these prewriting pages will not be scored.

Use the space below and on the back cover to generate ideas and plan your essay. You may wish to consider the following as you think critically about the task:

Strengths and weaknesses of the three given perspectives

- What insights do they offer, and what do they fail to consider?
- Why might they be persuasive to others, or why might they fail to persuade?

Your own knowledge, experience, and values

- What is your perspective on this issue, and what are its strengths and weaknesses?
- How will you support your perspective in your essay?

If you need more space to plan, please continue on the back of this page.

Essay Scoring
Part 2

The Writing Test is scored differently than the multiple choice sections of the ACT. Instead of being scored by a machine, each essay is evaluated by two or more human graders. Two graders read each student essay, and each scorer assigns a score of 1–6 points each in four domains to obtain scores of 2–12 for each domain. If the graders disagree by more than one point on the score that your essay should receive, a third scorer is asked to resolve the disagreement.

These scores are reported individually, and are also averaged to generate an overall Writing Test score from 2–12. You will also receive a percentile score, which shows how you did in relation to other students who took the test at the same time. If you take the Writing Test, you will also receive an ELA score, which is the average of your Reading, English, and Writing Test scores. The Writing Test section of your score report will look something like this:

		Score	U.S. Rank
Writing		6	51%
	Ideas and Analysis	7	
	Development and Support	5	
	Organization	6	
	Language Use and Conventions	5	
ELA		19	

Below is a breakdown of the four domains the graders will use to evaluate student essays, with an overview of how each relates to the ACT's expectations for that domain:

- Ideas and Analysis: assesses the clarity of your ideas, the effectiveness with which you create a context for analysis, and your engagement with other perspectives.
- Development and Support: assesses the reasoning and evidence that you provide to develop and support your argument.
- Organization: assesses your overall organizational strategy, the unity of your paragraphs and logical progression of your ideas, and your use of transitions.
- Language Use: assesses your word choices, your sentence structure and style, and your adherence to the rules of English grammar.

The scoring rubric is explored in more detail in Section 5 of this chapter.

Surprising Scores on Writing

Because the essays aren't scored by machine, human opinion factors into the scoring process—and opinions tend to vary. That means that scores tend to vary a little bit, and there's no way to be exactly sure what score a given essay will receive in advance.

While it's possible for some students to reliably attain near-perfect scores on multiple choice sections of the ACT with lots of practice, the same is not always possible on the Writing Test, and students who score very highly on multiple choice sections of the exam may find that the scaled score they receive on the essay falls into a lower range.

Don't be discouraged by a low Writing Test score! Because the ACT Writing Test is optional, and because it is generally required only by more competitive schools, the students who take it tend to be more prepared for the exam than the students who take only the required components. That means that the scaling and percentile ranking are both much more competitive on the ACT Writing Test than on the required components of the exam.

Furthermore, in addition to receiving your scores, colleges that receive your ACT score report will also receive an image of the essay that you have written. If an admissions office is otherwise interested in your application, they are able to review your ACT essay along with your application essays and make their own decision about your writing skills. A less-than-perfect Writing Test score is not likely to ruin an otherwise good application.

Strategies for the Writing Test
Part 3

Because the Writing Test has a lot in common with writing assignments you may have received in school, some of the following guidance will be familiar. However, some of our tips are quite specific to what ACT graders are looking for in an essay.

Read the Prompt Efficiently

You might feel obligated to read the whole prompt, but it's not always necessary. For one thing, the "Essay Task" and "Planning the Essay" sections will be the same every time, and if you study that language beforehand then you won't need to read it again on test day.

You can also save valuable time by just seeking out anything in the prompt that's phrased as a question. There may be one or two such questions, and they generally indicate the main ideas and themes of the prompt. If there are no questions, then find the sentence (often the last sentence) that looks most like a central conflict or problem.

Focus on the key information in the prompt, and don't feel pressure to work every part of the prompt into your analysis and essay.

Put your Pencil to Paper

Preparing to write your essay is a very good time to use Pencil on Paper. You can symbolize each argument with letters, if you like, remembering that the three perspectives are often some variation of:

- Perspective 1: A
- Perspective 2: B
- Perspective 3: A+B

In other words, the perspectives often offer two strong, opposed positions and a more nuanced, compromise position. If you don't have time to symbolize the perspectives, you should at least circle keywords and ideas.

As you mark up these keywords, begin to identify each perspective's potential weaknesses and unstated assumptions. Here's an example of a prompt marked up by a student using Pencil on Paper:

Commercials in School

Only exploit if comp — just don't make it comp?

Schools distribute various type of media: textbooks, yearbooks, school <u>newspapers,</u> and TV and radio content. Many of these types of content include advertisements and commercially sponsored content, and some are <u>compulsory</u>. For example, students may be required to watch a school news program at the beginning of each school day, and some of those programs may include commercial content. Including advertisements in school media provides a source of revenue for schools or providers of free content to schools, and is a standard practice in many other forms of media. However, critics argue that it is <u>exploitative</u> to require students to view advertisements, or that promoting commercial content in school media is contrary to the <u>values of education</u>. Is it appropriate for schools to raise revenue by selling

Which values?

advertisements in school media, or to promote free media that includes commercial content—or should schools be ad-free zones? → *Yes!*

Our p... sells a... use ex...

Read and carefully consider these perspectives. Each suggests a particular way of thinking about commercials in school.

Perspective 1	Perspective 2	Perspective 3
By providing advertisers with the <u>opportunity to share</u> relevant content with students, schools can raise revenues, allowing them to provide better services to students. It's a win-win situation.	Schools exist to provide *Seriously?* students with an education, not to sell <u>captive audiences</u> to advertisers. School media has an ethical obligation to be educational--not commercial. *Not realistic!*	Students <u>have to view ads all the time</u>, so learning how to evaluate them is important. *True!* School media should both include ads and encourage students to evaluate them critically.

Misses point: COMPULSORY is not a "win"

Close my v... but n... comp... ads

Write Neatly in the Space Provided

Unlike the other computer-graded sections of the ACT, the Writing Test has to be read by another human being, which makes the legibility of your writing very important. Ensure that your grader sees the greatness of your essay by writing neatly and legibly. Don't use small handwriting to save space: bigger letters are easier to read.

You should write your essay inside the margins of the lined paper provided. Graders will only see what you write inside of the margins, so don't try to pencil in a correction in the margins or scrawl out past the margins.

Even though the graders won't see what you write in the margins, avoid writing notes in the margins of your essay. If you write in the margins, you may make a stray mark that makes your essay more difficult to read and interpret, or that interferes with the scanner that scans your essay for review by graders. Use your test booklet for outlining and notes.

Write a Lot

Filling up as many of the answer pages as you can with a well-organized argument tells your graders that you have taken the time to write a thorough, well-argued essay. You have plenty of space to write; use as much of it as you can in the time available to develop your argument.

Write five or six full paragraphs. Forty minutes is plenty of time to read a sample essay and perspectives, then outline and write an introduction, body paragraphs, and a conclusion. Writing five or six paragraphs will properly break up four pages of writing and make it easier for your graders to follow your argument. Using one long run-on paragraph or many short paragraphs will be difficult to follow, and will affect your Organization score.

Be Explicit

State your argument (which is your opinion about the subject of the author's essay and the perspectives on that issue) as clearly as possible. When you are writing it's easy to think that the main point of your argument is abundantly clear, and the connections between pieces of information are obvious. However, your graders are going to need help following your argument. Make it easy for them by re-emphasizing your main point at the beginning and end of every paragraph, and illustrating the connections between points with transitional words and phrases.

Analyze the Perspectives Skeptically

You've seen the word "analysis" a couple of times already in this chapter. Now might be a good time to work out what, exactly, it means. It was originally a Greek word that meant "a breaking up, a loosening, releasing." So, when you "analyze," you break things apart.

When you analyze the three perspectives, think like a safe-breaker—remember that there are multiple points at which you could break in.

- Analyze at the level of the whole perspective:
    - Question the assumptions of the perspective
    - Question the consequences of the perspective if it were followed through
- Analyze at the level of a sentence in the perspective:
    - Does one of the sentences contradict the others, or seem especially vulnerable to criticism?
- Analyze at the level of the individual words
    - Question the definitions the perspective seems to be using; could there be other definitions that would yield a different result?

On the ACT Writing Test, you should do your best to question everything closely. This habit can take some getting used to. Consider these two brief skits:

Everyday life:

- Q: "Hi, Jenny, how are you?"
- A: "Fine, thanks."

ACT Writing Test:

- Q: "Hi, Jenny, how are you?"
- A: "How do you know my name?"

We don't usually question every assumption and premise of the statements we encounter in daily life, but on the Writing Test it's the best way to develop your position on the given perspectives.

Consider the example prompt we discussed earlier: all of these perspectives include assumptions that you can question and challenge in your analysis.

By providing advertisers with the opportunity to share relevant content with students, schools can raise revenues, allowing them to provide better services to students. It's a win-win situation.	Schools exist to provide students with an education, not to sell captive audiences to advertisers. School media has an ethical obligation to be educational—not commercial.	Students have to view ads all the time, so learning how to evaluate them is important. School media should both include ads and encourage students to evaluate them critically.

Perspective 1 seems to assume that schools will use ad revenues to provide better services. You could challenge that assumption by suggesting governments that decide to raise money for schools through ads in school media might also decide to cut taxes or change their budget priorities, so that schools ultimately end up with the same amount of money from different sources.

Perspective 2 sets up a contrast between "educational" media and "commercial" media. You could challenge the assumption that these are exclusive categories by arguing that having a market for ads in media will actually help to promote the success of the best educational media.

Perspective 3 seems to assume that viewing ads in school media will help students learn how to evaluate them. You could challenge that assumption by suggesting that viewing even more ads than they already do will actually make students so accustomed to advertisements that they can't really view them critically anymore.

These are only a few possibilities: when you read critically, you can find many other angles!

Finally, be on the lookout for absolutes and extremes. An absolute is a claim like, "We always need a strong executive" or "We must never have a strong executive." It's easy to find nuance when you're faced with an absolute; look for alternative explanations, conditions, and exceptions to the claim. You should also avoid absolute claims in your own essay, for exactly the same reason: it makes it look as though you've overlooked nuance and left out qualifications.

Pick your Position Strategically

Your task in the ACT Writing Test is to write a clear, compelling essay. That doesn't necessarily mean truthfully expressing your own opinions. In fact, you might have more success if you take a position that you don't entirely agree with.

When you read any given prompt, you might have a reflexive position on that issue. That is, you might almost automatically know what your position is, even before you start considering how you would support it. However, when you consider how to defend or explain that position, you might draw a blank. Maybe you just can't imagine why you would ever *need* to defend it, because it's so self-evidently correct that there are simply no good counterarguments. That's a red flag.

If you're like most of humanity, you don't always take the most critical look at your own firmly held opinions. When it comes to evaluating ideas that you believe in, you're more likely to consider weak evidence as good evidence and to ignore contradictory evidence—even when it's strong. You're also less likely to be able to acknowledge good counterarguments, or to realize logical flaws in your own argument.

The fact is, it's much, much easier to be logical about ideas and opinions that you don't like or don't care about than it is to be just as logical about your own ideas and opinions. So, when you're coming up with your thesis, consider using a thesis that you don't entirely agree with. That way, when you're building your argument you don't have to wonder if a hypothetical critic would find it persuasive. You can ask yourself "if someone made this argument to me, would *I* think that it was persuasive?"

Revise

It's often said that most of the writing process is rewriting. Pieces of professional writing, and even your student papers in college, may go through several drafts before they're done. Because the ACT is administered under timed conditions, you don't get to go through the process of writing multiple drafts.

However, forty minutes should give you plenty of time to go back and read over your essay after you've finished writing so that you can correct grammatical errors. Graders can penalize you for grammatical or spelling errors, particularly if they make your essay difficult to read. Once you've finished writing, take time to read over your essay and make small corrections and revisions. If there are any mistakes that you know you make frequently, then look for those first.

Keep in mind that you're looking for errors that you can correct in the time available: this is not the time to erase and rewrite a large portion of your essay. Focus on small but potentially confusing errors of grammar, punctuation, and word choice. If you realize that you are unhappy with the order of your paragraphs when you have only two minutes left, you will just need to make peace with that fact and keep reviewing the small things. You're much better off with an imperfectly organized essay than you are with an incomplete one!

Keep these tips in mind as you continue on to the next section, which will walk you through the process of writing the ACT essay in detail.

Section 2

Writing the Essay

There are many ways to write a good essay, and experienced writers use a variety of forms and structures to accomplish various objectives. When you're writing the ACT essay, you have to write a clearly organized essay in a limited amount of time. That means that you will benefit a lot from using a clear, straightforward structure that you have practiced beforehand.

You also need to come up with a clear thesis, and develop it thoughtfully and logically. That means ordering and connecting your ideas in a logical way to make a clear and complete argument. That also means taking note of the weaknesses in your argument, and addressing them. In addition to developing your own thesis, you need to acknowledge other viewpoints—and to do so in a way that demonstrates your understanding of other views.

Essays are made up of a number of component paragraphs. You need to structure those paragraphs well in order to create a well-crafted essay. This section will show you the best way to structure your essay on the ACT.

In this section, we're going to discuss:

- External Structure and Internal Structure
- Drafting your Short Outline
- Writing your Introduction
- Writing your Body Paragraphs
- Writing your Conclusion

External Structure and Internal Structure
Part 1

There are two types of structures that make up your essay. First is the **external** or overall structure. The external structure of your essay is how you arrange your paragraphs in relation to one another. The proper arrangement of your introduction, body paragraphs, and conclusion provides the foundation for your argument. Without it, your graders will not be able to follow your argument and all of your wonderful analysis will be lost.

Below is a map of what the overall structure of your essay should look like, and approximately how much time you should spend on each section. This is probably similar to the format you learned in school. The ACT isn't looking for anything fancy: they want to see a clear and well-organized argument.

Essay Structure
Read and analyze the prompt (2–3 minutes)
Sketch a *brief* outline (2–3 minutes)

* Not all ads wrong—compulsory ads are
* Ads everywhere, but optional—ex: internet
* Some school media required, "captive audience," school ads only ok if optional
* Need money—my paper sells ads
* Conclusion: schools can put ads in optional media, like newspaper.

Write an introduction, 3-4 body paragraphs, and a conclusion (30 minutes)

Introduction (1 paragraph)

In the modern media landscape, advertisements are ever-present. They are present in the media that we consume for information and entertainment, the social media that plays an increasing role in our social lives, and even in our physical environment in the form of billboards and other signs. It's appropriate that advertisements should also be in school media. Our objective should not be to attempt to shelter students from the advertisements that are an inescapable element of media culture, but to take a balanced approach to regulating advertisements in school media.

The desire to shelter students from all advertisements comes from the belief that advertisements are inherently exploiting. It's true that advertisements aim to persuade readers to purchase specific products, and it's easy to confuse these sales with exploitation. However, commerce is about exchanges that are good for both parties. Products like appliances and computers clearly make life better, and people often learn about them through advertisements. Our revulsion to exploitative advertising should not poison the well against all advertising: it should teach us that we have to consider ads critically, not take them at face value.

Nevertheless, while not all ads are exploitative or harmful, we must recognize that a few are. There are some advertisements that exploit our fears or weaknesses in ways that we cannot overcome through critical thought. For example, you may understand that a cigarette advertisement is trying to exploit you by creating the impression that cool and attractive people smoke, but you may still end up feeling like that is true after seeing enough ads. Because some ads exploit our psychology, a critical view is not always enough. However, treating all ads like the worst ads would punish good advertisers along with the bad. Refusing to publish exploiting ads in school media, while publishing good ads, will encourage advertisers to produce good advertisements rather than exploitative advertisements.

Finally, attempting to protect students from all advertising—even if it were the right goal—would simply not be practical. Because advertisements are present in almost every part of a student's life, refusing to allow advertisements in school media would mean giving up a revenue source for schools without significantly changing the amount of advertising that students see. Even during school hours, many students will visit websites, look at social media, or watch YouTube videos that include advertisements. Having advertisements in school media only slightly increases their exposure to ads, while also giving us a source of revenue for schools and an opportunity to have some control over which ads students see.

Because some advertising is good, because we can use school media to promote good advertising, and because there is no practical way to shelter students from all advertising, allowing advertising in school media while insisting that schools exercise control over what ads are published is clearly the most ideal course of action. To shelter students from ads in school would remove a source of revenue for schools, and the school's voice in the conversation about ads, while doing little to affect the amount of advertising that students experience.

Proofread and revise (3–5 minutes)

Next we will address the other type of structure found in your essay: the **internal structure**. This refers to the kinds of information you should include within each paragraph, and how that information should be arranged.

We will walk you through the internal structure of each step in your essay: short outline, introduction, body paragraphs, and conclusion.

Drafting Your Short Outline

Part 2

Your short outline is actually the first thing that you're going to commit to paper. You have to think about all the steps that you will take next: you're planning the entire external structure of your essay. Start by reviewing your notes on the prompt.

Let's have another look at the marked-up essay prompt from Section 1:

Commercials in School

Our pa sells ads—u exampl

Only exploit. if comp— just don't make it compulsory?

Schools distribute various type of media: textbooks, yearbooks, school newspapers, and TV and radio content. Many of these types of content include advertisements and commercially sponsored content, and some are compulsory. For example, students may be required to watch a school news program at the beginning of each school day, and some of those programs may include commercial content. Including advertisements in school media provides a source of revenue for schools or providers of free content to schools, and is a standard practice in many other forms of media. However, critics argue that it is exploitative to require students to view advertisements, or that promoting commercial content in school media is contrary to the values of education. Is it appropriate for schools to raise revenue by selling advertisements in school media, or to promote free media that includes commercial content—or should schools be ad-free zones? → Yes!

Which values

Read and carefully consider these perspectives. Each suggests a particular way of thinking about commercials in school.

Perspective 1	Perspective 2	Perspective 3
By providing advertisers with the opportunity to share relevant content with students, schools can raise revenues, allowing them to provide better services to students. It's a win-win situation.	Schools exist to provide students with an education, not to sell captive audiences to advertisers. School media has an ethical obligation to be educational—not commercial. *Seriously?*	Students have to view ads all the time, so learning how to evaluate them is important. School media should both include ads and encourage students to evaluate them critically. *True!*
Misses point: COMPULSORY is not a "win"	Not realistic!	Closest to my view, but no compulsory ads

Using the notes that you jot on your prompt, you can build your short outline. You should jot down a short statement about your thesis, and the ideas that you will use to support it. Pay attention to the elements that you underlined while you were reading the prompt, but don't feel like you have to try to include all of them. It's okay to use new ideas if they seem better. Here's an example outline based on the prompt above:

* Not all ads wrong—compulsory ads are
* Ads everywhere, but optional—ex: internet
* Some school media required, "captive audience," school ads only ok if optional
* Need money—my paper sells ads
* Conclusion: schools can put ads in optional media, like newspaper.

After jotting down your outline, you might realize that you want to do something slightly different in your essay. For example, the order of ideas in this outline isn't really ideal.

The point that ads are everywhere but that they're optional does set up the point that some school media is not optional by creating a contrast between the ads that you see in the world in general and the ads that you might be required to see in school. However, adding the idea that schools might need money from the ads disrupts a natural transition: the fact that some school media is actually required is really a crucial point, and it might be better to put that right before the conclusion.

Think of how the argument would sound if you ordered it in these different ways:

"Ads are everywhere, but they're optional. However, school ads might not always be optional, and that's not okay. But schools can really benefit from the money for the ads. Schools should put ads only in optional media."

This sounds a little confused—like the writer couldn't make up his mind.

"Schools can really benefit from the money for the ads. And ads are everywhere, but they're optional. However, school ads might not always be optional, and that's not okay. Schools should put ads only in optional media."

That makes more sense. So, should you change the outline? Not much. You aren't turning this part in, so you shouldn't put that much work into it. Just draw a little arrow so that you don't forget your decision when you're writing the essay.

* Not all ads wrong—compulsory ads are
* Ads everywhere, but optional—ex: internet
* Some school media required, "captive audience," school ads only ok if optional
* Need money—my paper sells ads
* Conclusion: schools can put ads in optional media, like newspaper.

And, there you go! You've decided what you're going to write about, and you've organized your ideas. That's all the outline is for, so you're done.

However, there's one more important fact to keep in mind: the outline is intended to be a time-saving organizational strategy. When you plan the structure of your essay in advance, you can save time by sticking to your plan and avoiding costly erasing and rewriting. In some cases, though, students find that they tend to spend too long on outlines, or that they don't get much out of them. Outlines aren't required: if they don't save you time or improve your essay, you don't need to use them.

Writing Your Introduction
Part 3

The introductory paragraph of your essay is the first one that your graders will read and thus sets the tone for the rest of your essay. People often say that "you only get one chance to make a first impression." The same thing applies to your introduction; it's hard to structure a coherent essay if the introduction doesn't make any sense.

The best way to make your introduction clear is to keep it brief and straightforward. Start with one or two sentences relevant to the prompt, to demonstrate that you've read and understood it, and to create a context for your essay.

Next, move directly to your **thesis**, the sentence where you will lay out the argument of your essay. In your thesis, be sure to briefly describe the different supporting arguments you will be making. This will make it easier for your graders to follow your essay as they read. Think of your thesis as a road map for your essay; you don't want your graders taking any wrong turns.

A clear thesis will help your reader understand your intentions, but it will be just as helpful for you as a writer. If your position on an issue is muddled, and you write a confusing thesis as a result, the quality of the following paragraphs will suffer. If your thesis is clear, however, it will be much easier for you to build a strong argument.

Writing Your Body Paragraphs
Part 4

After the introduction comes the meat of your essay: the **body paragraphs**, the three or four paragraphs in the middle of your essay. In your body paragraphs, you will elaborate on the different claims that you mentioned in your thesis statement and link them together to create your overall argument.

Each body paragraph is like a mini-essay, in a way. Each paragraph should start with a **topic sentence**. A topic sentence is like a mini-thesis statement: it states what the rest of the paragraph is going to be about.

Following the topic sentence should be 3–4 **supporting sentences**. These sentences should develop claims about the various perspectives, address complications and qualifications, and support the argument you made in your topic sentence.

Part of your task is to consider the relationship between the three perspectives, so you should place each body paragraph with that relationship in mind. If one perspective offers a combination of the views of the other two, it might be best to discuss it in your last body paragraph—not your first or second.

Finally, following these supporting sentences, you should have a **concluding sentence**. This sentence should summarize the point you have made in your body paragraph so that you leave the reader with a solid foundation for going on to your next point.

It's also important to use **transitions** in your essay. Transitions are words or phrases that link your ideas together. They help your reader follow your argument and keep your writing from seeming choppy. The most common place for transitions is in your topic sentences. In the following sentences, the words in italics are examples of transitions:

- *However*, more funding for school art departments will not just benefit high schoolers.
- Members of the public can *also* enroll in night-time continuing education classes, improving access to art education in the community at large.
- *Furthermore*, the increase in funding will provide more new art teachers with full-time jobs.

Support Your Thesis with Care

You should have good reasons for choosing your essay's supporting arguments; don't just fling them in randomly! Make sure that they genuinely support your thesis. You don't need to try to squeeze in a reference to George Orwell's *1984* just because you know the novel well: select your support for your argument—don't twist your argument to fit a preselected example.

Next, make sure that you're selecting strong forms of evidence.

↑ Best ↑
Specific, Realistic, Hypothetical examples
Unique Personal Anecdotes
Specific, Relevant Facts from History, Literature, Philosophy, and Current Events
Pop Culture References
Banal Personal Anecdotes
General Knowledge and Scientific Facts
Vague "Studies Have Shown …" Claims
Controversial Issues
Statistics
Clichés (e.g., WWII)
Obviously Unrealistic Hypothetical Examples
↓ Worst ↓

The best types of examples include realistic hypotheticals that specifically demonstrate your point, unique and interesting personal anecdotes, and specific, relevant examples from history, literature, or current events.

If you can't think of specific and relevant historical examples, it's acceptable to use examples from pop culture. Your personal anecdotes are also acceptable even when they're not particularly unique, provided that they demonstrate your point.

Avoid simply making the claim that "studies have shown" that your point is true: if you refer to scientific facts or studies, be specific.

Finally, avoid controversial topics. Don't talk about current political figures, contemporary political controversies, or sensitive subjects. Also avoid clichés: WWII is a classic example of a struggle between the forces of good and evil, but it doesn't necessarily fit in every essay.

Having selected strong examples, you also want to make sure that they are clearly connected to your thesis. Explain how your supporting points back up your main argument. If you don't do this, the resulting essay will be fragmented and hard to follow. Consider the following example:

Thesis: The best way to teach computer skills in high school is to require all subjects to include a computing component.

Supporting Argument (Unexplained): It is expensive to train full-time computer-science teachers.

In this example, the writer has provided a supporting argument, but has not explained exactly how it supports the thesis. The effect is a bit like an unfinished game of connect-the-dots; the writer forces the reader to make the connection herself rather than setting it out clearly. The next example is an improvement:

Thesis: The best way to teach computer skills in high school is to require all subjects to include a computing component.

Supporting Argument (Explained): It is expensive to train full-time computer-science teachers. However, providing currently-employed teachers with some computer training would be comparatively inexpensive. This means that incorporating computing into regular classes would allow our schools to teach computer skills to everyone while also saving money.

In this example, the writer has connected the dots. You can now see how addressing the expense of training full-time computer science teachers relates to the thesis.

Build Your Arguments off of One Another

The sequence in which you present your arguments is also important. Have you ever written an essay where you kept finding yourself writing phrases like, "as I will say later" or "as we will see"? If so, you may have arranged your arguments in a less-than-ideal order. The best-developed essays are structured such that each point sets up the next one in an elegant sequence. Less well-developed essays will read a bit like a grocery list: there are lots of ideas there, but their order doesn't really seem to matter.

Try to make sure your body paragraphs form a logical sequence; if a certain claim only makes sense when placed after another, related one, then arrange your paragraphs accordingly. You may even find it helpful to review our guide to the English Test's Organization question type for some examples of out-of-sequence paragraphs.

Complications and Qualifications

The issues you'll be writing about in your ACT Essay are usually quite complicated, and don't always have easy solutions. When you're writing about an issue that has complex shades of grey, your argument will be less thorough if you don't acknowledge those complexities. Adjusting your claim slightly to acknowledge the complexity of an issue is called a qualification or a qualifying statement. Consider these examples:

Claim, No Qualification

There is never a time when cell phones are acceptable in class.

This claim is too absolute. You might think that such absolute claims "sound better" and are therefore more persuasive, but in essays of this kind it's best to take a more nuanced approach. All it takes to refute the claim is one example to the contrary, so they are actually much weaker than more nuanced claims.

Claim, With Qualification

Cell phones are usually a distraction in a classroom setting, especially when the teacher is giving a lecture. Admittedly, there might be some times when cell phones could help students to learn—in a drama class, students could study a video of a famous soliloquy, and chemistry students could film their experiments. However, these moments are comparatively rare.

Here the writer makes a less absolute, more easily defended claim. She acknowledges that there are a few times when students could benefit from having access to cell phones in class, but emphasizes that these are relatively rare occasions. She also uses a more nuanced phrase, "usually a distraction", instead of "never acceptable." The result is a more sophisticated statement, attentive to the complexity of the issue being discussed.

Engaging with Multiple Perspectives

The ACT Writing Test asks you to do more than simply develop your own position. You're also tasked with analyzing other perspectives on the issue (in the three "Perspective" boxes below the prompt) and considering their relationships. This may seem like a lot to do in a limited amount of time, but evaluating these other views is actually part of the process of developing your own view. If you manage your time well, you should be able to complete both parts of the task effectively!

As we discussed in Section 1, "analysis" means "to break apart." If you break down the other perspectives, question their assumptions, and give good reasons in support of your own position, then you're well on your way to an essay that's analytical and persuasive!

Remember that analysis is not the same as simply contradicting a statement. You must not misrepresent a statement, either. Evaluate every perspective honestly, even if you are arguing against it. Here's a simple way to remember to evaluate positions fairly: think in terms of "Yes but…" rather than "Yes/No."

The following examples will explain this concept in detail.

Limited Engagement with Another Perspective

While some argue that the mastery of skills is the best way to assess students in P.E. class, participation is a better way to evaluate P.E. students.

In this example, the writer acknowledges that another perspective exists, but he doesn't analyze it. He just asserts that his own position is better. This is a prime example of "Yes/No" thinking.

Adequate Engagement with Another Perspective

Some argue that the mastery of skills is the best way to assess students in P.E. class. They say that it encourages competition. However, we should question whether a competitive environment is ideal for gym classes; while it might reward some students, it will likely discourage others. If students are given a mark for their enthusiastic participation instead, they will feel more comfortable in class.

This analysis is more detailed. The writer demonstrates "Yes but…" thinking by briefly explaining the reason why some people support the perspective. Next, the writer questions their reasoning, suggesting some possible negative consequences to competitive gym classes.

Critical Engagement with Another Perspective

P.E. teachers commonly evaluate students by testing them on their mastery of athletic skills. It's true that this method rewards athletic students for their achievements. However, this perspective assumes that the goal of gym should be competitive achievement—an assumption worth challenging. Students who receive a low grade in such a competitive environment may become too discouraged to keep trying. Furthermore, current statistics show that Americans are becoming less physically active; if gym classes want to address this problem, they should make it their priority to encourage healthy exercise instead of competition. The best way to do this is by grading students on their enthusiastic participation in activities, not their mastery of skills.

This example shows the next level of critical analysis. The writer once again acknowledges the reason why some people support the other perspective—and even acknowledges that some of the supporting evidence for an opposing view is true. However, she questions their underlying assumptions, and challenges them in two ways. First, she provides an example of a potential negative consequence; second, she provides support for an alternative view. Her analysis demonstrates more detailed "Yes but…" thinking.

Writing your Conclusion
Part 5

The first sentence of your conclusion should rephrase the thesis statement you wrote in your introduction. Don't rewrite it word for word (your graders will notice), but generally restate the ideas presented in the thesis. The purpose of this sentence is to show how you have proven the arguments of your thesis statement.

Following this restatement of purpose, you should try to answer the "so what?" question. Your teachers may have asked you this question before. The point of asking this question is to make you think about the importance or implications of your argument. In other words, why should anyone care about what you've just written? Does it make you think about the issue presented in a different way? Or does it perhaps reveal some flaws in arguments defending a different position on the issue?

When you're satisfied with your conclusion, your essay is done. Congratulations! You should use your remaining time to proofread what you've written, correct errors of grammar and punctuation, and improve any poor word choices.

Practice Prompt
Part 6

Now that we've discussed the step-by-step process of writing your essay, apply what you've learned by writing an essay to the following practice prompt. Clear a space of any distractions, give yourself four sheets of lined paper, sharpen your pencils, and set a 40 minute timer. Make sure that you will have no interruptions, and begin when you're ready.

After you've written your essay, turn to the next section for guidance on estimating your score. If you can, have a trusted reader evaluate your essay and score it for you using the directions in that section.

Finally, there are additional practice prompts at the end of this chapter: continue to practice your essay-writing using these prompts, but remember always to evaluate your work carefully after writing each essay. If you are working on your own, carefully proofread your essay, making note of any errors and considering how you would improve the overall style and organization of your work. If you have someone else reading your essay, ask for and carefully consider their feedback.

You will benefit much more from taking this additional time to consider how you can improve your work before writing the next essay than you would from simply estimating a grade and trying again!

Space Exploration

The Apollo missions to the Moon remain the farthest that human beings have ever been from Earth. Since that time, NASA has sent robotic probes to more distant points in the solar system, and Voyager I—launched in 1977—has even left our solar system. However, humans have never set foot on Mars or attempted to settle permanently on the Moon. The risk and expense of such projects would be considerable, but the Earth's uncertain future makes them an attractive prospect to some. Should there be renewed efforts to explore space?

Read and carefully consider these perspectives. Each suggests a particular way of thinking about space exploration.

Perspective 1	**Perspective 2**	**Perspective 3**
Humanity's future is in space. Government space agencies must have more resources so that they can plan more adventurous projects, including settlements on other planets.	We have too many serious problems on Earth to commit additional resources to exploring space at this time. We shouldn't fund space exploration until those problems have been satisfactorily addressed.	Space exploration is important, but human space exploration is dangerous, expensive, and inefficient. We should continue to send out robotic probes, but not try to settle other planets.

Essay Task

Write a unified, coherent essay in which you evaluate multiple perspectives on space exploration. In your essay, be sure to:

- analyze and evaluate the perspectives given
- state and develop your own perspective on the issue
- explain the relationship between your perspective and those given

Your perspective may be in full agreement with any of the others, in partial agreement, or wholly different. Whatever the case, support your ideas with logical reasoning and detailed, persuasive examples.

Planning Your Essay

Your work on these prewriting pages will not be scored.

Use the space below and on the back cover to generate ideas and plan your essay. You may wish to consider the following as you think critically about the task:

Strengths and weaknesses of the three given perspectives

- What insights do they offer, and what do they fail to consider?
- Why might they be persuasive to others, or why might they fail to persuade?

Your own knowledge, experience, and values

- What is your perspective on this issue, and what are its strengths and weaknesses?
- How will you support your perspective in your essay?

If you need more space to plan, please continue on the back of this page.

Section 3
Scoring Rubric and Sample Essays

The ACT Writing exam is scored on a scale of 2–12. Two scorers read each student's essay, and each scorer assigns a score of 1–6 points in four domains to obtain scores of 2–12 for each domain. These domain scores are reported individually, and their rounded average is taken to create a Writing Score of 2–12. The ACT also calculates a scaled score from 1-36, based off of the Writing Score from 1–12, in order to calculate the ELA sub-score, but this scaled score is not shown on your score report.

This section provides a grading rubric that explains how to score essays for each category, includes a scaling chart to help you find a scaled score for each essay, and shows examples of essays at various score levels accompanied by explanations of how they were scored.

Once you have determined a score for each domain, add up all four of your scores to find a Raw Score for the Writing Test. Refer to the chart on the following pages to find your ELA Scaled Score and Writing Score: the ELA Scaled score, on a scale of 1-36, is a score that you can use to estimate your ELA score by averaging it with your Reading and English scores. The Writing Score, on a scale of 2–12, is the score that will actually be reported on your score report for the Writing Test.

Using the Rubric
Part 1

The rubric in this part serves as a guide for scoring the ACT essay. It is a simplified version of the rubric published by the ACT. You should use either this rubric or the official rubric on the ACT website to evaluate your essays. If you can, avoid scoring your own essays. Instead, you should ask a parent, tutor, or trusted friend to read these directions and score your essays. Actual ACT essays will be scored by two readers, so if you can have two scorers look at your work then it will help you to determine with more confidence what your score on the actual ACT may be.

There are four domains in this rubric (Ideas and Analysis, Development and Support, Organization, and Language Use), and each domain asks you to evaluate a few related aspects of the essay. For example, the rubric relies on your consideration of the overall organizational strategy of the essay, the progression of ideas, and the use of effective transitions between ideas when determining an Organization score. Read the specific descriptions for each domain, and select a score for each domain that best describes the essay that you're evaluating.

If you aren't quite sure how to distinguish between the score levels, refer to the sample essays and score explanations for more information. Examining essays at different score levels and getting a feel for the overall differences is the best way to learn those differences, and—in fact—is exactly what the ACT scorers do. The rubric looks very precise and technical, but in reality the essay is scored by readers who have a lot of experience scoring a large number of essays, and just have a very good feel for the difference between, say, a 5 and a 4.

	Ideas and Analysis	Development and Support
6	Critical engagement with multiple perspectives. Nuanced and precise thesis. Insightful context for analysis.	Ideas are developed in a manner that deepens insight and broadens context. Reasoning is skillfully integrated into an effective, cogent argument. Complications and qualifications are addressed in such a way as to bolster the writer's analysis.
5	Productive engagement with multiple perspectives. Precise thesis. Thoughtful context for analysis.	Ideas are developed in a manner that deepens understanding. Reasoning mostly integrated with clear purpose. Complications and qualifications are addressed in such a way as to enrich the writer's analysis.
4	Adequately engages with multiple perspectives. Clear thesis. Relevant context for analysis.	Ideas are developed in a manner that clarifies their purpose. Reasoning is clear and adequate. Complications and qualifications are addressed in such a way as to extend the writer's analysis.
3	Insufficiently engages with multiple perspectives. Mostly clear thesis. Limited or tangential context for analysis	Ideas are developed in a simplistic or overly general fashion. Reasoning is somewhat repetitious or imprecise. Some qualifications or complications may be raised, but fail to meaningfully extend the writer's analysis.
2	Weak engagement with multiple perspectives. Unclear thesis. Incomplete or irrelevant context for analysis.	Development of ideas is weak, confused, or disjointed. Reasoning is inadequate, illogical, or circular. Few qualifications or complications are addressed.
1	Fails to engage with multiple perspectives. No thesis. No context for analysis.	Ideas are not developed. Reasoning is unclear, incoherent, or largely absent. No qualifications or complications are addressed.
0	Essay is off-topic, illegible, not written in English, or blank.	

	Organization	Language Use
6	Skillful organizational strategy. Unified and logical progression of ideas. Nuanced and precise transitions.	Skillful and precise word choices. Varied and clear sentence structure. Strategic and effective style. Few errors, and errors do not detract from clarity of writing.
5	Productive organizational strategy. Productive progression of ideas. Precise transitions.	Productive word choices. Mostly varied and clear sentence structure. Purposeful and productive style. Some errors, but errors do not detract significantly from clarity of writing.
4	Clear organizational strategy. Clear progression of ideas. Clear transitions.	Adequate word choices. Sometimes varied and clear sentence structure. Appropriate style. Some errors, which may rarely detract from the clarity of writing.
3	Basic organizational strategy. Basic progression of ideas. Mostly clear transitions.	Inadequate word choices. Sentence structure is mostly clear, but not varied. Mostly appropriate tone. Some distracting errors are present, but meaning is mainly clear.
2	Rudimentary organization. Rudimentary, inconsistent progression of ideas. Unclear or confusing transitions.	Weak word choices. Sentence structure is sometimes unclear, and not varied. Inconsistent or inappropriate style. Distracting errors are present, and make some elements of the essay difficult to understand.
1	No clear organization of ideas. No apparent progression of ideas. No effective transitions.	Incomprehensible word choices. Sentence structure is neither varied nor clear. Style is difficult to identify. Pervasive errors make the essay as a whole difficult to understand.
0	Essay is off-topic, illegible, not written in English, or blank.	

Raw Score	ELA Scaled Score	Writing Score	Raw Score	ELA Scaled Score	Writing Score
48	36	12	27	21	7
47	36	12	26	21	7
46	35	12	25	20	6
45	34	11	24	19	6
44	34	11	23	18	6
43	33	11	22	17	6
42	33	11	21	17	5
41	32	10	20	16	5
40	31	10	19	14	5
39	30	10	18	14	5
38	30	10	17	13	4
37	29	9	16	12	4
36	28	9	15	10	4
35	28	9	14	10	4
34	27	9	13	9	3
33	26	8	12	8	3
32	25	8	11	6	3
31	24	8	10	6	3
30	23	8	9	5	2
29	23	7	8	1	2
28	22	7	---	---	---

Sample Essay Prompt
Part 2

Commercials in School

Schools distribute various types of media: textbooks, yearbooks, school newspapers, and TV and radio content. Many of these types of content include advertisements and commercially sponsored content, and some are compulsory. For example, students may be required to watch a school news program at the beginning of each school day, and some of those programs may include commercial content. Including advertisements in school media provides a source of revenue for schools or providers of free content to schools, and is a standard practice in many other forms of media. However, critics argue that it is exploitative to require students to view advertisements, or that promoting commercial content in school media is contrary to the values of education. Is it appropriate for schools to raise revenue by selling advertisements in school media, or to promote free media that includes commercial content—or should schools be ad-free zones?

Read and carefully consider these perspectives. Each suggests a particular way of thinking about commercials in school media.

Perspective 1	Perspective 2	Perspective 3
By providing advertisers with the opportunity to share relevant content with students, schools can raise revenues, allowing them to provide better services to students. It's a win-win situation.	Schools exist to provide students with an education, not to sell captive audiences to advertisers. School media has an ethical obligation to be educational—not commercial.	Students have to view ads all the time, so learning how to evaluate them is important. School media should both include ads and encourage students to evaluate them critically.

Essay Task

Write a unified, coherent essay in which you evaluate multiple perspectives on commercials in school media. In your essay, be sure to:

- analyze and evaluate the perspectives given
- state and develop your own perspective on the issue
- explain the relationship between your perspective and those given

Your perspective may be in full agreement with any of the others, in partial agreement, or wholly different. Whatever the case, support your ideas with logical reasoning and detailed, persuasive examples.

Planning Your Essay

Your work on these prewriting pages will not be scored.

Use the space below and on the back cover to generate ideas and plan your essay. You may wish to consider the following as you think critically about the task:

Strengths and weaknesses of the three given perspectives

- What insights do they offer, and what do they fail to consider?
- Why might they be persuasive to others, or why might they fail to persuade?

Your own knowledge, experience, and values

- What is your perspective on this issue, and what are its strengths and weaknesses?
- How will you support your perspective in your essay?

If you need more space to plan, please continue on the back of this page.

Sample Essays and Score Explanations

Part 3

The following sample essays are written at various score levels, and the accompanying explanations illustrate how readers should evaluate and score essays.

Sample Essay with Domain Scores of 1/1/1/1

> To be honist with you i don't mind commercial even in school i can see the point of not liking them if you think that the students they can't tell the difference between commercial and reality like if I say buy my product thus it will make you smart and so you just do it without even using your own mind then that is wrong. I haven't had that problem but as they say its not a problem until its a problem so maybe some students it would be so you should not have those commercial in school. The problem is as i see it is the students and not the medias that is the problem in general in life today both tv and also the internet at the same time if you can't tell the difference thats a series problem at least in school you know that they are probabaly are at least making sure that they are selling you things that educational or would be help to you in education if you bought them at the same time schools should not have commercial

Ideas and Analysis: 1

The writer fails to clearly state a thesis: it is unclear whether he supports having commercials in school or not. While the writer could be interpreted as expressing several perspectives, they are each expressed as his own perspective at different points in the essay, rather than recognized as separate perspectives on the topic. The writer therefore fails to engage with these alternative perspectives. The writer does begin to approach a broader context by mentioning that "the media is the problem in general," and mentioning "tv and … the internet," but fails to use these ideas as a context for analysis.

Development and Support: 1

The writer makes a series of claims, but fails to develop any individual claim. The writer does employ several words typically associated with reasoning, such as "thus," "so," and "if … then," but uses them to make incoherent connections between independent assertions rather than to show the logical steps of a reasoned argument. While the writer does offer a qualifying statement in "I haven't had that problem but as they say its not a problem until its a problem," this single qualification is insufficient to merit a higher score.

Organization: 1

The writer has not divided up his material into paragraphs, and the essay consists mainly of run-on sentences without any apparent transitions between key ideas or any strategy for organization. This lack of organization contributes to the confusing effect the essay has on the reader.

Language Use: 1

The writing in this essay is so full of errors that it is hard to follow. It lacks capitalization and internal punctuation, and each sentence is a long run-on. The word choices are repetitive, informal, and sometimes difficult to understand.

Sample Essay with Domain Scores of 2/2/2/2

I believe the media is so distracting that we shouldn't have it in school at all. Just think about the celebrities and shows people watch and how it makes it hard to pay attention at school. Watching their phones instead of the teacher as well. Back before internet and TV and phones students were better behaved and even though it is a sacrifice for us not to get to watch the morning announcements show and the kids who take video class will not get to do that for us anymore it will be better if we have old fashioned announcements on the PA and get back to work. Some people think differently but they are really wrong. Just stopping ads isn't enough and allowing any of them is too much.

Think about how much time we are goofing off in computer class. Students waste valuable time on the internet when they should be doing research or projects. This is also a media problem. And I can tell also when the teacher is tired and gives us a movie to watch instead of teaching us. We are sort of being tricked by the movie because everyone gets excited and starts to relax, but do we get tested about movies in science class? no!

When George Washington was a young boy in the USA, he did not have distracting media to stop him from learning and he became a great hero. If there was media at

Valley Forge the soldiers would forget to fight the British because they were playing Candy Crush. And we would not be able to do everything that we have done since then, like inventions, victories and, so on.

In the end, if we watch TV or use computers at school, we are learning less than if we did not. That is why I am advocating an end to computers, TV, phones etc. in the school. Maybe even the yearbook if it divides people like over who gets to be in charge of design and other committees or they put in commercials.

Ideas and Analysis: 2

While it's clear that this essay takes a position, it does not do so with sufficient clarity. The writer makes a very bold claim (all media should be removed from school) without properly defining what she means by "media." Sometimes the writer cites computers as the problem, and at other times she seems to be more concerned by the Internet. The writer should be more precise.

The writer barely analyzes the other perspectives. She simply states that they are wrong, and remarks that "stopping ads isn't enough and allowing any of them is too much."

Development and Support: 2

The writer does use examples to try to support her argument. However, they tend towards the superficial ("Think about how much time we are goofing off in computer class") or the hypothetical ("If there was media at Valley Forge…"). There are also obvious problems with the supporting examples: while it's true that a science class probably won't test students on "movies" as such, it could certainly test them on concepts discussed in educational films.

The writer makes one qualifying statement ("even though it is a sacrifice for us not to get to watch the morning announcements show and the kids who take video class will not get to do that for us anymore") but never expands upon it. In fact, it mostly seems to hurt the argument—the reader may end up sympathizing more with the poor video students.

Organization: 2

This essay does use paragraphs and rudimentary introductory and concluding remarks. However, the lack of clear transition statements makes it hard to trace the progress of the argument. A totally new point ("Maybe even the yearbook…") is also distractingly introduced at the very end.

Language Use: 2

Long sentences without internal punctuation, sentence fragments, and misplaced commas all diminish the effectiveness of the essay.

My position is that we should make some kind of compromise to help fund our schools but also prevent the students from being taken advantage of by ads. It would be wrong if companies selling unhealthy or addictive things had a place in the school, but if a company's product is good for your mind or body than that could be different. I also agree that we would need to teach about how advertising can be dangerous in our Civics class.

Schools definitely need more money for good quality programs and services. Political battles make it hard for us to know if governments will fund schools high or low. On the other hand, companies would be a more reliable source of money. That being said, we need to be careful.

An example of a company that would be appropriate for our school paper or announcements is Rosetta Stone. Their software helps you to learn another language and so is useful for students. However, it is fairly expensive and I have actually been using a free online site to practice French instead. So following my plan, we should include the ads but also make sure that we have class disscussions about the pros and cons of spending so much money when there are free alternatives.

Another good example is Healthy Snaps. They make dried fruit chips that are better for you than candy. But we would need to have a talk in class about healthy eating, and how there is other ways to do that then just by buying special products. You can also make your own dried fruit in the oven, or just eat a fresh apple!

The last example is companies that can teach you a musical instrument, a martial art, or something along those lines. If we limit the ads in school to only examples like my examples and we make sure that we hold good disscussions about them than we can make money for the school without being led astray by the ads.

Ideas and Analysis: 3

This essay takes a more clearly defined position than the previous ones, and it makes some more nuanced gestures ("It would be wrong if companies selling unhealthy or addictive things had a place in the school..."). It doesn't expand on what "unhealthy or addictive things" might be, though—in other words, the writer's attempt to qualify his position is incomplete. The student does not address the other perspectives directly enough, or with sufficient critical attention. He would need to analyze the assumptions of the other perspectives more explicitly to get a higher score.

Development and Support: 3

The second paragraph does offer a relevant point, but without the specificity or context to make it a strong one: "political battles" is much too vague. The subsequent paragraphs do not adequately serve a sequential argument. Rather than developing support for his position, the writer gets bogged down in a consideration of what products might be appropriate to advertise at school. The examples are somewhat repetitious, and unevenly developed. Where the writer does begin to develop specific examples, the writer focuses on how his plan should be implemented rather than developing an argument that supports his position. Remember that the goal of this essay is to give well-developed reasons in support of your position on an issue. A lack of attention to the wider context for the debate also prevents this essay from scoring higher.

Organization: 3

The essay follows a basic paragraph structure, and introduces its position in an identifiable statement. While clear, the essay's transitions are on the simple, unvaried side ("An example...Another good example...The last example"). The conclusion reiterates the introduction almost verbatim, and awkwardly shares space in the paragraph with the writer's final example ("companies that can teach you a musical instrument...").

Language Use: 3

The language of the essay, while simple and a little informal, is clear. The writer's spelling and word choice mistakes (for example, the consistent mixing up of "then" and "than") are noticeable but not overwhelming. Some variations in the length and syntax of the sentences show that this writer is on the right path; however, at times his sentences are too wordy ("I also agree that we would need to teach about how advertising can be dangerous...").

Sample Essay with Domain Scores of 4/4/4/4

Now that media is a part of every day life, it has begun to seep into the schools. A controversy has arisen about this, however; is it appropriate for schools to raise revenue by selling advertisements in school media, or to promote free media that includes commercial content-or should schools be ad-free zones? This is an important question to consider because some schools make students watch news program that teach about current events. I think some ads are fine if they are part of media the schools get for free.

Of course school newspapers and even yearbooks have always sold ads to local businesses and some schools, like mine, even have classes in TV and radio. The controversy arises when schools raise revenue by selling ads in school media. Some people think this is fine because that makes it possible to provide better services for students. For example, the money raised could be used pay for extra stuff like the senior class trip or prom or something like that. So that's a win-win situation and maybe teachers could use the ads as part of a lesson. Others believe that since students are bombarded with ads all the time anyway, using them in school gives the students a great opportunity to develop their critical thinking skills. So, for instance, if an ad is apart of some video that a teacher was using, that would probably be okay because then the teacher could make critical thinking part of that day's lesson. Both of these perspectives contain some valid points about the positive impact of media in schools.

On the other hand, though, when media includes ads for products, there are those who object to this being part of the education system because students are then treated like a captive audience. These people think that schools exist to provide students with an education, not to sell them stuff; they believe it is inethical to bombard students with ads when they should be learning. This is also a valid point, even if those who believe this don't take into account the potential financial benefits for funding extracurricular activities and whatnot.

I personally believe that it's okay to sell adds in yearbooks and school newspapers but there shouldn't be ads like in the cafeteria or something; unless the ad is promoting something like healthy eating, so like a PSA is okay. At the same time, it's probably a good idea to keep school separate from stuff like TV shows and radio shows because those are for entertainment, not learning. For instance, what if a school sold ads for stuff like the latest version of a violent video game; that would make it seem as if (like) the school was endorsing that video game, wouldn't it? Political ads probably shouldn't be allowed in school for that same reason.

The bottom line is that some media does belong in schools because it can be educational and selling ads can help schools pay for extras, while other media should be kept out of the schools. School should, as much as possible, be an ad-free zone.

Ideas and Analysis: 4

The essay shows that the student understands what is expected for this essay. This essay has a clear thesis ("I think some ads are fine if they are part of media the schools get for free.") and the first paragraph provides a context for the student's analysis of what she calls a "controversy." In the body paragraphs, the student examines each of the sample perspectives and points to the strengths and weaknesses of those perspectives.

Development and Support: 4

This student provides evidence of the reasoning she has used to analyze the various perspectives on this issue, and seems to understand the arguments being made in those perspectives. She also does some analysis of how those arguments fail to address the issue completely. Although the last sentence could be seen as contradicting her position, the inclusion of the phrase "as much as possible" saves her from completely undermining the stance she has taken on the issue.

Organization: 4

This essay is well organized with a clear introduction, body paragraphs that address the conflicting points of view on the issue (including her own), and a concise conclusion that addresses ideas that have been explored throughout the essay. The organization is, however, somewhat predictable; exploring the issues on a point-by-point basis might have been more effective than organizing by position on the issue. Transitions between the paragraphs is adequate.

Language Use: 4

The language is adequate, though there are some spelling and word choice errors. The student uses a variety of sentence structures. For most of the essay the tone is appropriately formal, though there are some lapses, including such sentences as, "For example, the money raised could be used pay for extra stuff like the senior class trip or prom or something like that" and the phrase "and whatnot" at the end of the third paragraph.

In a world in which everyone, including students, is exposed to an onslaught of commercials advertising everything from diapers to life insurance, the question about whether media belongs in school seems inevitable. Some people argue that school should be strictly educational, while others say that some media should be allowed-and even encouraged-in schools. In this essay I will explore the issues in this controversy and explain why my own view on this is flexible and encompasses elements of both sides.

The question of media's place in schools, particular the role of advertising, is a complicated one. After all, many schools are actually the source of media in the form of school newspapers, yearbooks, and even the programs for such events as concerts and school plays. In addition, school sports are often supported by local businesses, and that support is acknowledged in print and during announcements at sports events; my school has a thriving TV and radio program that is run by students and some of the shows that are created are paid for by donations from the community, which is always acknowledged. Yet critics would say that these announcements and commercials even in educational materials such as mainstream news programs that are shown in class exploits what they call a "captive audience." Which side is right, and which side is wrong? A look at the some specific points may help us decide.

One argument in this controversy concerns the idea that schools can raise money from allowing advertisers to reach students. The side that is pro-advertisers believes that this is a benefit to the schools because the revenues raised allows them to provide better services to their students. The anti-advertising in schools side claims that schools have an ethical obligation to provide education and nothing but education; they believe that it's unfair to sell products to students who are being forced to watch those ads. While the anti-advertising has a point, the truth is that many schools need the extra money to provide better services, particularly schools in poor neighborhoods that might not get enough money from the government. Therefore, I believe that selling ads in school-sponsored media and even allowing ads in materials that are used in classes is a beneficial thing for many schools.

The second point in this argument concerns the educational opportunities to be found in advertising. Though critics might object on ethical grounds, the truth is exposure to media provides teachers to have students evaluate ads in a critical way. This is, in my opinion, more valuable than protecting students—I thinks students are savvy enough to not buy into the messages in ads, in part because teachers force students to conduct critical evaluation. Education that exists in a vacuum and never addresses real life issues isn't very holistic, after all; students should be given the skills to navigate the world, including media. Besides, not all ads are bad; think about ads for products that can enhance a student's educational experience or even provide information about possible future opportunities. For example, a student who can't afford to pay for college might see an ad for the military and learn that this can lead to valuable workplace skills in the future. If we get the advantage of such valuable educational content as historical documentaries, then being exposed to an ad for a product like toothpaste or school supplies is a small price to pay.

In conclusion, while critics have a few good points about the damage that can be caused by exposing students to commercial content, it seems obvious that schools should not be ad-free zones. Instead, schools should welcome ads as a way to help pay for valuable educational skills activities that may not be available otherwise, and as a valuable tool for helping students navigate in the real world with real life skills. Providing those skills is the ethical thing to do, along with being extremely educational—and that's what school should be about.

Ideas and Analysis: 5

This essay is written in a competent manner. It seems obvious that the student planned his essay well, which allows him to address the various perspectives on the issue while using those perspectives to provide context for his own argument. After introducing his topic, the student states his thesis clearly in relation to the arguments being made by other participants in the discussion. He recognizes and evaluates those arguments and his analysis acknowledges the complexities of those arguments. However, his thesis lacks nuance. He takes the simple position that commercials in school are good. Furthermore, he fails to provide an insightful context for his analysis.

Development and Support: 5

In addition to acknowledging the arguments made by those providing various perspectives, the student provides specific examples and details. This enriches his analysis; however, he fails to use his discussion of qualifications to bolster his own argument. The development of ideas is logical, moving from the general to the specific in a way that shows he understands the reasoning behind each side's perspective while showing evidence of his own reasoning about specific elements of the issue. However, some of his arguments are merely presented as a series, rather than being skillfully integrated into an overarching argument.

Organization: 5

The organization of the essay is clear and transitions between paragraphs are skillful. From the introduction through the body paragraphs to the conclusion, the student maintains focus on the specific issue in the prompt without unnecessary and confusing tangents. He develops his ideas well. However, the essay suffers from a thesis which is introduced too long after the introduction of the essay.

Language Use: 5

The student uses language competently; the sentences are varied and his word choices are precise. His tone throughout is appropriate and there are few grammatical or mechanical errors. There are, however, a number of opportunities for stronger word choices: very colloquial phrases like "and nothing but" could be eliminated, choices like "enough money" could be replaced with stronger choices like "adequate funding," and some choices, like "extremely educational," are too emphatic for this context.

Sample Essay with Domain Scores of 6/6/6/6

<u>In the modern media landscape, advertisements are ever-present.</u> They are present in the media that we consume for information and entertainment, the social media that plays an increasing role in our social lives, and even in our physical environment in the form of billboards and other signs. It's appropriate that advertisements should also be in school media. [Our objective should not be to attempt to shelter students from the advertisements that are an inescapable element of media culture, but to take a balanced approach to regulating advertisements in school media.]

The desire to shelter students from all advertisements comes from the belief that advertisements are inherently exploiting. It's true that advertisements aim to persuade readers to purchase specific products, and it's easy to confuse these sales with exploitation. However, commerce is about exchanges that are good for both parties. Products like appliances and computers clearly make life better, and people often learn about them through advertisements. Our revulsion to exploitative advertising should not poison the well against all advertising: it should teach us that we have to consider ads critically, not take them at face value.

(handwritten margin note:) No, not most popular products. Apple doesn't advertise as much as Geico because word-of-mouth and societal standards are more common.

Nevertheless, while not all ads are exploitative or harmful, we must recognize that a few are. There are some advertisements that exploit our fears or weaknesses in ways that we cannot overcome through critical thought. For example, you may understand that a cigarette advertisement is trying to exploit you by creating the impression that cool and attractive people smoke, but you may still end up feeling like that is true after seeing enough ads. Because some ads exploit our psychology, a critical view is not always enough. However, treating all ads like the worst ads would punish good advertisers along with the bad. Refusing to publish exploiting ads in school media, while publishing good ads, will encourage advertisers to produce good advertisements rather than exploitative advertisements.

Finally, attempting to protect students from all advertising—even if it were the right goal—would simply not be practical. Because advertisements are present in almost every part of a student's life, refusing to allow advertisements in school media would mean giving up a revenue source for schools without significantly changing the amount of advertising that students see. Even during school hours, many students will visit websites, look at social media, or watch YouTube videos that include advertisements. Having advertisements in school media only slightly increases their exposure to ads, while also giving us a source of revenue for schools and an opportunity to have some control over which ads students see.

[Because some advertising is good, because we can use school media to promote good advertising, and because there is no practical way to shelter students from all advertising, allowing advertising in school media while insisting that schools exercise control over what ads are published is clearly the most ideal course of action.] To shelter students from ads in school would remove a source of revenue for schools, and the school's voice in the conversation about ads, while doing little to affect the amount of advertising that students experience.

Ideas and Analysis: 6

The writer effectively introduces the topic by providing a description of "ever-present" advertising in the "modern media landscape" that serves to establish a context for insightful analysis. The writer provides a clear, nuanced thesis: advertisements are an "inseparable element of media culture" that should be allowed in schools with some regulation. In support of this thesis, the writer examines conflicting viewpoints, pointing out and analyzing underlying values and assumptions behind the perspective that no ads should be allowed, and examining tensions between ideas about honest commerce and exploitative advertising.

[Handwritten margin notes:]
No, all adds are just trying to make $$, they don't care about the means.

Yes, one of the only decent points.

Using synonyms & changing the order of the original.

They cover revenue which obviously effects education quality.

Meh, it could zoom out but decent summary

Development and Support: 6

The writer demonstrates insight into the broader context of the issue by addressing the role of advertising in the broader "media culture" and how decisions about advertisements in school should be shaped by that broader context. The writer notes several complications, addressing them in such a way as to bolster her analysis. The acknowledgment that some ads are "exploitative or harmful" is turned into an argument in favor of allowing advertising in school, in order to give schools an opportunity to "encourage advertisers to produce good advertisements." The reasoning is skillful and effective, and clearly integrates supporting arguments to create a cogent argument in support of the writer's thesis.

Organization: 6

The writer skillfully organizes her essay, introducing key ideas and arguments early in the essay while avoiding a repetitive structure. The paragraphs are unified, and proceed in a logical order that supports the development of the writer's argument. The writer makes skillful use of nuanced and precise transitions to clearly demonstrate the relationships between sentences and paragraphs.

Language Use: 6

The essay contains few errors, and uses clear sentences with a variety of structures. The writer makes skillful word choices throughout the essay; choices like "to attempt to shelter students from … an inescapable element of media culture" clearly and effectively contrast an impossible challenge with the "balanced approach" the writer advocates. The writer's choices shape the tone of the essay strategically and effectively, anticipating and minimizing possible counterarguments, and emphasizing the value of the view that the writer advocates.

Section 4
Practice Essay Prompts

Practice writing essays with the prompts on the following pages. Clear your workspace of any distractions, set aside four sheets of lined paper to write on, and allow yourself 40 minutes to work on each prompt.

After writing an essay, carefully review your work according to the rubric or have a trusted reader review it. Look for errors and consider how you would improve your essay before moving on to another prompt.

Animal Testing

In the United States and Canada, more than 100 million animals are used every year in animal testing. Animal testing is used in scientific research, medical training, and drug trials, as well as a host of other commercial applications such as chemical, food, and cosmetic safety testing. Such testing may help develop new treatments for disease and ensure the safety of products that we use every day. However, ethical concerns exist about the harms inflicted on animals in such experiments, and society has long prohibited the harmful treatment of animals in other contexts, such as entertainment. In a society that values the rights of animals, scientific advancement, and consumer safety, how should we think about the conflict between animal rights and animal testing?

Carefully read and consider the following perspectives. These perspectives each suggest a certain way of thinking about animal testing.

Perspective 1	Perspective 2	Perspective 3
The interests of human beings are simply more important than those of non-human animals. If harming some animals provides real benefits to human society then it should be done.	The life of an animal is as valuable as that of a human. Animal testing causes animals to suffer, and sometimes kills them. It is reprehensible. Regardless of alternatives, it should cease.	The knowledge gained from animal testing improves the lives of domesticated animals as well as humans. Animal testing must be limited and controlled, but a total ban would harm both humans and animals.

Essay Task

Write an organized, logical essay in which you evaluate multiple perspectives on the conflict between animal rights and animal testing. In your essay, you should:

- examine and evaluate the perspectives given
- describe and develop your own perspective on the issue
- relate your perspective to those given

Your perspective may be the same as any of the others, similar to them, or entirely different from them. In any case, you should support your perspective and analysis with logical arguments and detailed, persuasive examples.

Planning Your Essay

Your work on these prewriting pages will not be scored.

Use the space below and on the back cover to generate ideas and plan your essay. You may wish to consider the following as you think critically about the task:

Strengths and weaknesses of the three given perspectives

- What insights do they offer, and what do they fail to consider?
- Why might they be persuasive to others, or why might they fail to persuade?

Your own knowledge, experience, and values

- What is your perspective on this issue, and what are its strengths and weaknesses?
- How will you support your perspective in your essay?

If you need more space to plan, please continue on the back of this page.

High School Language Requirements

Some states currently require students to complete one or more classes in a foreign language in order to receive a diploma, and others are considering adopting such a requirement. A second language can improve job prospects, and if more Americans learn foreign languages, U.S. employees might become more competitive in the global economy. However, language requirements imply that languages are not only useful, but are also more useful than elective classes in arts, business skills, health, or other subjects that a student might otherwise take. Is learning a second language important enough that language credits should be required, or should students have the opportunity to decide whether to take language classes or other electives?

Read and carefully consider these perspectives. Each suggests a particular way of thinking about high school language requirements.

Perspective 1	Perspective 2	Perspective 3
Foreign languages are essential in a global economy. If Americans want to remain competitive in the global marketplace, they must require expanded language education.	Students who want foreign language classes may choose them as electives. Forcing all students to take them erodes student choice, and adds no value for students who may only need English.	Foreign language classes should be required only if they do not take the place of electives. If we need to increase requirements, then we should increase school time proportionately.

Essay Task

Write a unified, coherent essay in which you evaluate multiple perspectives on high school language requirements. In your essay, be sure to:

- analyze and evaluate the perspectives given
- state and develop your own perspective on the issue
- explain the relationship between your perspective and those given

Your perspective may be in full agreement with any of the others, in partial agreement, or wholly different. Whatever the case, support your ideas with logical reasoning and detailed, persuasive examples.

Planning Your Essay

Your work on these prewriting pages will not be scored.

Use the space below and on the back cover to generate ideas and plan your essay. You may wish to consider the following as you think critically about the task:

Strengths and weaknesses of the three given perspectives

- What insights do they offer, and what do they fail to consider?
- Why might they be persuasive to others, or why might they fail to persuade?

Your own knowledge, experience, and values

- What is your perspective on this issue, and what are its strengths and weaknesses?
- How will you support your perspective in your essay?

If you need more space to plan, please continue on the back of this page.

Art and Real Life

People have long debated how art—including television, film, and novels—should relate to real life. Some believe that art should try to reflect real life closely. They believe this is the best way for audiences to learn more about themselves, the world, and the lives of other people. Others think that art should be less realistic, and explore worlds of dream, fantasy, and play. They believe this stimulates the imagination, and encourages audiences to think about the world differently. Should art try to resemble life closely, or should it show us things we'd never see in reality?

Read and carefully consider these perspectives. Each suggests a particular way of thinking about the relation of art to life.

Perspective 1	Perspective 2	Perspective 3
Fantastical art is a distraction from reality. Art improves our lives most when it makes us more aware of the beauties, horrors, tragedies, triumphs, and complexities of the real world.	Art is about feeling and experience. It shouldn't be too practical. Leaving behind the constraints of the real world allows us to experience and enjoy new and amazing realities.	If all art were purely realistic, we might lose touch with our imaginations. If all art were purely unrealistic, we might lose sight of important truths. We should honor both kinds of art.

Essay Task

Write a unified, coherent essay in which you evaluate multiple perspectives on the relation of art to life. In your essay, be sure to:

- analyze and evaluate the perspectives given
- state and develop your own perspective on the issue
- explain the relationship between your perspective and those given

Your perspective may be in full agreement with any of the others, in partial agreement, or wholly different. Whatever the case, support your ideas with logical reasoning and detailed, persuasive examples.

Planning Your Essay

Your work on these prewriting pages will not be scored.

Use the space below and on the back cover to generate ideas and plan your essay. You may wish to consider the following as you think critically about the task:

Strengths and weaknesses of the three given perspectives

- What insights do they offer, and what do they fail to consider?
- Why might they be persuasive to others, or why might they fail to persuade?

Your own knowledge, experience, and values

- What is your perspective on this issue, and what are its strengths and weaknesses?
- How will you support your perspective in your essay?

If you need more space to plan, please continue on the back of this page.

"No Pass, No Drive" Policies

More than half of U.S. states require students to be enrolled in school in order to obtain a learner's permit or driver's license before the age of 18, and some even have minimum attendance or GPA requirements. Such policies have been shown to reduce rates of truancy and deter students from dropping out, but they may also further reduce access to job opportunities for students who don't complete high school or are unable to meet academic standards. How should we balance our desire to keep students in school with our desire to extend opportunities to all citizens, including those who do not compete high school?

Read and carefully consider these perspectives. Each suggests a particular way of thinking about "No Pass, No Drive" policies.

Perspective 1	Perspective 2	Perspective 3
Driving is a privilege, not a right. Students have a social obligation to complete school, and it is appropriate to withdraw privileges to encourage them to fulfill that obligation.	High school dropouts and struggling students already face many challenges, and it's not helpful to further limit their work opportunities by preventing them from driving.	"No pass, no drive" policies are a workaround of a flawed system. If we want to stop students from dropping out, we should just make it illegal to drop out.

Essay Task

Write a unified, coherent essay in which you evaluate multiple perspectives on "No Pass, No Drive" policies. In your essay, be sure to:

- analyze and evaluate the perspectives given
- state and develop your own perspective on the issue
- explain the relationship between your perspective and those given

Your perspective may be in full agreement with any of the others, in partial agreement, or wholly different. Whatever the case, support your ideas with logical reasoning and detailed, persuasive examples.

Planning Your Essay

Your work on these prewriting pages will not be scored.

Use the space below and on the back cover to generate ideas and plan your essay. You may wish to consider the following as you think critically about the task:

Strengths and weaknesses of the three given perspectives

- What insights do they offer, and what do they fail to consider?
- Why might they be persuasive to others, or why might they fail to persuade?

Your own knowledge, experience, and values

- What is your perspective on this issue, and what are its strengths and weaknesses?
- How will you support your perspective in your essay?

If you need more space to plan, please continue on the back of this page.

News or Entertainment?

Sometimes it can be difficult to tell the difference between news and entertainment. Many programs deliver news-related content, but with a significant emphasis on heated debates, flamboyant personalities, or comedy. They may even distort the truth in the pursuit of an entertaining episode. Considering the importance of an honest news media to the political process, how should we think about programs that blend news and entertainment?

Read and carefully consider these perspectives. Each suggests a particular way of thinking about the blending of news and entertainment.

Perspective 1	**Perspective 2**	**Perspective 3**
The purpose of news programs is to educate the public and deliver important information. To add an entertainment component to such shows risks misleading audiences.	The public are able to tell the difference between fact and fiction, and, what's more, they like to be entertained. These programs are harmless.	There's nothing wrong with a news program being entertaining; it just needs to be intellectually honest as well, citing its sources and checking its facts carefully.

Essay Task

Write a unified, coherent essay in which you evaluate multiple perspectives on the blending of news and entertainment. In your essay, be sure to:

- analyze and evaluate the perspectives given
- state and develop your own perspective on the issue
- explain the relationship between your perspective and those given

Your perspective may be in full agreement with any of the others, in partial agreement, or wholly different. Whatever the case, support your ideas with logical reasoning and detailed, persuasive examples.

Planning Your Essay

Your work on these prewriting pages will not be scored.

Use the space below and on the back cover to generate ideas and plan your essay. You may wish to consider the following as you think critically about the task:

Strengths and weaknesses of the three given perspectives

- What insights do they offer, and what do they fail to consider?
- Why might they be persuasive to others, or why might they fail to persuade?

Your own knowledge, experience, and values

- What is your perspective on this issue, and what are its strengths and weaknesses?
- How will you support your perspective in your essay?

If you need more space to plan, please continue on the back of this page.

Junk Food in Schools

Schools strive to offer healthy choices for students in their cafeterias, but many also offer "junk food" options like potato chips, candy, or sugary beverages in vending machines on school grounds. Offering such foods may enable students to make unhealthy eating choices, and it may limit parents' ability to control what their children eat. However, additional prohibitions may begin to feel too restrictive to students who already have many aspects of their behavior regulated by school rules. How do we balance a school's responsibility to create a healthy environment for students with the desire to offer more choices to students?

Read and carefully consider these perspectives. Each suggests a particular way of thinking about junk food in schools.

Perspective 1	Perspective 2	Perspective 3
Schools have a duty of care, and junk food is always harmful. Selling students junk food violates the school's duty of care, so schools shouldn't be allowed to do it.	Occasional snacking is harmless and enjoyable. Schools that sell snack food to students are providing a service, not harming students.	Junk food is a bad choice, but students can't learn to make good choices if they aren't allowed to make bad ones. Schools should teach students, not coddle them.

Essay Task

Write a unified, coherent essay in which you evaluate multiple perspectives on junk food in schools. In your essay, be sure to:

- analyze and evaluate the perspectives given
- state and develop your own perspective on the issue
- explain the relationship between your perspective and those given

Your perspective may be in full agreement with any of the others, in partial agreement, or wholly different. Whatever the case, support your ideas with logical reasoning and detailed, persuasive examples.

Planning Your Essay

Your work on these prewriting pages will not be scored.

Use the space below and on the back cover to generate ideas and plan your essay. You may wish to consider the following as you think critically about the task:

Strengths and weaknesses of the three given perspectives

- What insights do they offer, and what do they fail to consider?
- Why might they be persuasive to others, or why might they fail to persuade?

Your own knowledge, experience, and values

- What is your perspective on this issue, and what are its strengths and weaknesses?
- How will you support your perspective in your essay?

If you need more space to plan, please continue on the back of this page.

Cloning Extinct Species

Scientists have been able to clone animals for over twenty years. The cellular material required to make a clone does not need to come from a living animal, leading some scientists to suggest the cloning of extinct species. A Spanish team successfully cloned a Pyrenean Ibex, an extinct species of wild goat, but it lived for only seven minutes. Others have speculated about cloning the wooly mammoth, a species that has been extinct for four thousand years, from frozen tissue discovered in Siberia. The difficulties of such projects are immense, and the healthy survival of the cloned animals is in no way guaranteed. Should scientists pursue the cloning of extinct species?

Read and carefully consider these perspectives. Each suggests a particular way of thinking about the cloning of extinct species.

Perspective 1	Perspective 2	Perspective 3
Countless species are dying out due to hunting and habitat destruction caused by humans. Cloning offers humanity a way to restore some of the biodiversity that we have eliminated.	Cloned animals may be unable to adapt to modern ecosystems, or may even cause harm to them. Cloning extinct species comes at too great an ethical cost to be worthwhile.	Cloning could give a new life to extinct species, but we must set limits on the practice. We should only clone recently-extinct species that we can be sure will thrive in today's environment.

Essay Task

Write a unified, coherent essay in which you evaluate multiple perspectives on the cloning of extinct species. In your essay, be sure to:

- analyze and evaluate the perspectives given
- state and develop your own perspective on the issue
- explain the relationship between your perspective and those given

Your perspective may be in full agreement with any of the others, in partial agreement, or wholly different. Whatever the case, support your ideas with logical reasoning and detailed, persuasive examples.

Planning Your Essay

Your work on these prewriting pages will not be scored.

Use the space below and on the back cover to generate ideas and plan your essay. You may wish to consider the following as you think critically about the task:

Strengths and weaknesses of the three given perspectives

- What insights do they offer, and what do they fail to consider?
- Why might they be persuasive to others, or why might they fail to persuade?

Your own knowledge, experience, and values

- What is your perspective on this issue, and what are its strengths and weaknesses?
- How will you support your perspective in your essay?

If you need more space to plan, please continue on the back of this page.

Should Schools Confiscate Cell Phones?

Many schools now prohibit cell phone use during the school day. Students who violate cell phone policies may have their phones confiscated, in some cases for as long as a week or more. Such policies are intended to protect the learning environment by reducing distractions, and they are similar to older policies banning other forms of electronics. However, some students and families have argued that schools don't have the right to confiscate a student's private property. Do schools have a right to confiscate cell phones to help create a better learning environment?

Read and carefully consider these perspectives. Each suggests a particular way of thinking about whether schools should be allowed to confiscate cell phones.

Perspective 1	Perspective 2	Perspective 3
Schools don't have a right to confiscate private property from students. If schools want to prohibit cell phone use during class, they should find a different form of punishment.	Schools aren't entering homes to seize property, they're confiscating devices that students bring to school. A student who uses a prohibited device in class knowingly forfeits his or her right to that device.	Schools may have a limited right to confiscate private property, but only during school hours. Any confiscated devices should be returned no later than the end of the school day.

Essay Task

Write a unified, coherent essay in which you evaluate multiple perspectives on whether schools should be allowed to confiscate cell phones. In your essay, be sure to:

- analyze and evaluate the perspectives given
- state and develop your own perspective on the issue
- explain the relationship between your perspective and those given

Your perspective may be in full agreement with any of the others, in partial agreement, or wholly different. Whatever the case, support your ideas with logical reasoning and detailed, persuasive examples.

Planning Your Essay

Your work on these prewriting pages will not be scored.

Use the space below and on the back cover to generate ideas and plan your essay. You may wish to consider the following as you think critically about the task:

Strengths and weaknesses of the three given perspectives

- What insights do they offer, and what do they fail to consider?
- Why might they be persuasive to others, or why might they fail to persuade?

Your own knowledge, experience, and values

- What is your perspective on this issue, and what are its strengths and weaknesses?
- How will you support your perspective in your essay?

If you need more space to plan, please continue on the back of this page.

P1

O
Rights 2 students

F
Severity = nothing + no other option

O

No student rights
More focused
learning environment

P2

F
Students rights
will sneak
them.

Some
student
No confiscation
overnight

P3
o
F
Different
punishments?

MP

Support:
I'm a student
Technology is vital.

S
Student rights/
choice/
Gives decision &
responsibility
Forces empathy &
consideration

W
Some may abuse / distract
Excuse to get off topic.

Encryption Software

Private information, from conversations with friends to credit card information, is stored on personal electronic devices and transmitted over secure networks. Some of that information could endanger us if it were easily accessible. Encryption protects the information that we store on our personal devices and transmit over networks. However, it may also protect criminals and terrorists. For that reason, law enforcement and others have suggested that we should limit the encryption available to private individuals or provide a 'key' to the government to unlock private encryption. However, some are concerned that such measures would undermine the security of our private communications. Should private individuals have access to encryption that even the government can't unlock?

Read and carefully consider these perspectives. Each suggests a particular way of thinking about encryption.

Perspective 1	Perspective 2	Perspective 3
Law enforcement needs the tools to do its job. The threat of a hacker obtaining government decryption keys is smaller than the threat posed by criminals with uncrackable encryption.	Law enforcement is tasked with ensuring our security, not figuring out how to disable it. Encryption software keeps us safe, and we shouldn't undermine its effectiveness for any reason.	Private citizens should be protected from unwarranted government invasion as well as terrorism. Companies that provide encryption should grant access to investigators on a case-by-case basis.

Essay Task

Write a unified, coherent essay in which you evaluate multiple perspectives on encryption. In your essay, be sure to:

- analyze and evaluate the perspectives given
- state and develop your own perspective on the issue
- explain the relationship between your perspective and those given

Your perspective may be in full agreement with any of the others, in partial agreement, or wholly different. Whatever the case, support your ideas with logical reasoning and detailed, persuasive examples.

Planning Your Essay

Your work on these prewriting pages will not be scored.

Use the space below and on the back cover to generate ideas and plan your essay. You may wish to consider the following as you think critically about the task:

Strengths and weaknesses of the three given perspectives

- What insights do they offer, and what do they fail to consider?
- Why might they be persuasive to others, or why might they fail to persuade?

Your own knowledge, experience, and values

- What is your perspective on this issue, and what are its strengths and weaknesses?
- How will you support your perspective in your essay?

If you need more space to plan, please continue on the back of this page.

Raising the Driving Age

Today, most teens are able to get learner's permits as soon as they are 15 and driver's licenses shortly after they turn 16. In some states, the driving age is as low as 14. Some safety advocates, however, have suggested raising the driving age to 18 nationally. They note that drivers between the ages of 15 and 19 are almost three times as likely to be involved in fatal car accidents as older drivers. One possible explanation for this danger is that younger drivers are learning drivers, and they are in more danger simply because they haven't had as much practice. Another possible explanation is that teens actually engage in more risky behavior, such as texting while driving. Comparing data from states with different driving ages does suggest that higher driving ages reduce rates of traffic deaths. Is this a prudent safety measure, or an undue burden on teens?

Read and carefully consider these perspectives. Each suggests a particular way of thinking about raising the driving age.

Perspective 1	Perspective 2	Perspective 3
When we have a low driving age, more teens die in car accidents. The convenience of a driver's license isn't worth dying for: the driving age should be raised.	Driving is an essential right in modern society. Teens may need to drive themselves to school or work. We shouldn't take away their rights because of exaggerated fears.	Raising the driving age will just delay learning for new drivers. It's sad that people get hurt while learning to drive, but raising the driving age won't solve that problem.

Essay Task

Write a unified, coherent essay in which you evaluate multiple perspectives on raising the driving age. In your essay, be sure to:

- analyze and evaluate the perspectives given
- state and develop your own perspective on the issue
- explain the relationship between your perspective and those given

Your perspective may be in full agreement with any of the others, in partial agreement, or wholly different. Whatever the case, support your ideas with logical reasoning and detailed, persuasive examples.

Planning Your Essay

Your work on these prewriting pages will not be scored.

Use the space below and on the back cover to generate ideas and plan your essay. You may wish to consider the following as you think critically about the task:

Strengths and weaknesses of the three given perspectives

- What insights do they offer, and what do they fail to consider?
- Why might they be persuasive to others, or why might they fail to persuade?

Your own knowledge, experience, and values

- What is your perspective on this issue, and what are its strengths and weaknesses?
- How will you support your perspective in your essay?

If you need more space to plan, please continue on the back of this page.

Free Public Transit for College Students

High school students in many areas are able to rely on school buses for transportation. In some urban areas, students receive free access to public transportation instead. Some colleges and universities also have their own buses, but many do not. Some student advocates have suggested that college students, like high school students, should have free access to public transportation while they are completing their education. However, college students are often a major source of fare revenue for public transit systems, since many do not own cars. Providing free access would cause public transit systems to lose revenue, necessitating additional public funding. Should college students have free access to public transit?

Read and carefully consider these perspectives. Each suggests a particular way of thinking about free public transit for college students.

Perspective 1	Perspective 2	Perspective 3
Public transit is already subsidized: the rest of us shouldn't have to pay more to make it free for adult students. They can work part-time to pay for transportation.	Today, college is as essential as high school and very expensive. Society should make caring for students a priority, and ensure that they can travel to school for free.	College students shouldn't be privileged over working people. Public transit should either be free to all who use it, or remain a fare-based service.

Essay Task

Write a unified, coherent essay in which you evaluate multiple perspectives on free public transit for college students. In your essay, be sure to:

- analyze and evaluate the perspectives given
- state and develop your own perspective on the issue
- explain the relationship between your perspective and those given

Your perspective may be in full agreement with any of the others, in partial agreement, or wholly different. Whatever the case, support your ideas with logical reasoning and detailed, persuasive examples.

Planning Your Essay

Your work on these prewriting pages will not be scored.

Use the space below and on the back cover to generate ideas and plan your essay. You may wish to consider the following as you think critically about the task:

Strengths and weaknesses of the three given perspectives

- What insights do they offer, and what do they fail to consider?
- Why might they be persuasive to others, or why might they fail to persuade?

Your own knowledge, experience, and values

- What is your perspective on this issue, and what are its strengths and weaknesses?
- How will you support your perspective in your essay?

If you need more space to plan, please continue on the back of this page.

Practice Tests

Chapter 7

Practice Test 1

The ACT

This practice test contains tests in English, Math, Reading, and Science. These tests measure skills and abilities related to high school course work and college preparedness. **You can use a calculator on the math test only.**

The questions in each test are numbered, and the suggested answers for each question are lettered. On the answer sheet, the rows are numbered to match the questions, and the circles in each row are lettered to correspond to the suggested answers.

For each question, choose the best answer and fill in the corresponding circle on your answer document. Use a soft lead pencil and make your marks heavy and black. **Do not use a ballpoint pen.**

Fill in only one answer to each question. If you change your mind about an answer, completely erase your first mark before filling in your new answer. For each question, make certain that you mark in the row of ovals with the same number as the question.

Only responses marked on your answer sheet will be scored. Your score on each test will be based only on the number of questions you answer correctly during the time allowed for that test. You will NOT be penalized for guessing. **Even if you are unsure about an answer, you should make a guess.**

You may work on each test ONLY when your proctor tells you to do so. If you complete a test before the end of your allotted time, use the extra minutes to check your work on that section only. Do NOT use the time to work on another section. Doing this will disqualify your scores.

Put down your pencil immediately when time is called at the end of each test. You are not allowed to continue answering questions after the allotted time has run out. This includes marking answers on your answer sheet that you previously noted in your test booklet.

You are not allowed to fold or tear the pages of your test booklet.

Do Not Open This Booklet Until You Are Told to Do So.

NAME: _____

DATE: _____

TEST 1

1 Ⓐ Ⓑ Ⓒ Ⓓ	14 Ⓕ Ⓖ Ⓗ Ⓙ	27 Ⓐ Ⓑ Ⓒ Ⓓ	40 Ⓕ Ⓖ Ⓗ Ⓙ	53 Ⓐ Ⓑ Ⓒ Ⓓ	66 Ⓕ Ⓖ Ⓗ Ⓙ
2 Ⓕ Ⓖ Ⓗ Ⓙ	15 Ⓐ Ⓑ Ⓒ Ⓓ	28 Ⓕ Ⓖ Ⓗ Ⓙ	41 Ⓐ Ⓑ Ⓒ Ⓓ	54 Ⓕ Ⓖ Ⓗ Ⓙ	67 Ⓐ Ⓑ Ⓒ Ⓓ
3 Ⓐ Ⓑ Ⓒ Ⓓ	16 Ⓕ Ⓖ Ⓗ Ⓙ	29 Ⓐ Ⓑ Ⓒ Ⓓ	42 Ⓕ Ⓖ Ⓗ Ⓙ	55 Ⓐ Ⓑ Ⓒ Ⓓ	68 Ⓕ Ⓖ Ⓗ Ⓙ
4 Ⓕ Ⓖ Ⓗ Ⓙ	17 Ⓐ Ⓑ Ⓒ Ⓓ	30 Ⓕ Ⓖ Ⓗ Ⓙ	43 Ⓐ Ⓑ Ⓒ Ⓓ	56 Ⓕ Ⓖ Ⓗ Ⓙ	69 Ⓐ Ⓑ Ⓒ Ⓓ
5 Ⓐ Ⓑ Ⓒ Ⓓ	18 Ⓕ Ⓖ Ⓗ Ⓙ	31 Ⓐ Ⓑ Ⓒ Ⓓ	44 Ⓕ Ⓖ Ⓗ Ⓙ	57 Ⓐ Ⓑ Ⓒ Ⓓ	70 Ⓕ Ⓖ Ⓗ Ⓙ
6 Ⓕ Ⓖ Ⓗ Ⓙ	19 Ⓐ Ⓑ Ⓒ Ⓓ	32 Ⓕ Ⓖ Ⓗ Ⓙ	45 Ⓐ Ⓑ Ⓒ Ⓓ	58 Ⓕ Ⓖ Ⓗ Ⓙ	71 Ⓐ Ⓑ Ⓒ Ⓓ
7 Ⓐ Ⓑ Ⓒ Ⓓ	20 Ⓕ Ⓖ Ⓗ Ⓙ	33 Ⓐ Ⓑ Ⓒ Ⓓ	46 Ⓕ Ⓖ Ⓗ Ⓙ	59 Ⓐ Ⓑ Ⓒ Ⓓ	72 Ⓕ Ⓖ Ⓗ Ⓙ
8 Ⓕ Ⓖ Ⓗ Ⓙ	21 Ⓐ Ⓑ Ⓒ Ⓓ	34 Ⓕ Ⓖ Ⓗ Ⓙ	47 Ⓐ Ⓑ Ⓒ Ⓓ	60 Ⓕ Ⓖ Ⓗ Ⓙ	73 Ⓐ Ⓑ Ⓒ Ⓓ
9 Ⓐ Ⓑ Ⓒ Ⓓ	22 Ⓕ Ⓖ Ⓗ Ⓙ	35 Ⓐ Ⓑ Ⓒ Ⓓ	48 Ⓕ Ⓖ Ⓗ Ⓙ	61 Ⓐ Ⓑ Ⓒ Ⓓ	74 Ⓕ Ⓖ Ⓗ Ⓙ
10 Ⓐ Ⓑ Ⓒ Ⓓ	23 Ⓐ Ⓑ Ⓒ Ⓓ	36 Ⓕ Ⓖ Ⓗ Ⓙ	49 Ⓐ Ⓑ Ⓒ Ⓓ	62 Ⓕ Ⓖ Ⓗ Ⓙ	75 Ⓐ Ⓑ Ⓒ Ⓓ
11 Ⓐ Ⓑ Ⓒ Ⓓ	24 Ⓕ Ⓖ Ⓗ Ⓙ	37 Ⓐ Ⓑ Ⓒ Ⓓ	50 Ⓕ Ⓖ Ⓗ Ⓙ	63 Ⓐ Ⓑ Ⓒ Ⓓ	
12 Ⓕ Ⓖ Ⓗ Ⓙ	25 Ⓐ Ⓑ Ⓒ Ⓓ	38 Ⓕ Ⓖ Ⓗ Ⓙ	51 Ⓐ Ⓑ Ⓒ Ⓓ	64 Ⓕ Ⓖ Ⓗ Ⓙ	
13 Ⓐ Ⓑ Ⓒ Ⓓ	26 Ⓕ Ⓖ Ⓗ Ⓙ	39 Ⓐ Ⓑ Ⓒ Ⓓ	52 Ⓕ Ⓖ Ⓗ Ⓙ	65 Ⓐ Ⓑ Ⓒ Ⓓ	

TEST 2

1 Ⓐ Ⓑ Ⓒ Ⓓ Ⓔ	11 Ⓐ Ⓑ Ⓒ Ⓓ Ⓔ	21 Ⓐ Ⓑ Ⓒ Ⓓ Ⓔ	31 Ⓐ Ⓑ Ⓒ Ⓓ Ⓔ	41 Ⓐ Ⓑ Ⓒ Ⓓ Ⓔ	51 Ⓐ Ⓑ Ⓒ Ⓓ Ⓔ
2 Ⓕ Ⓖ Ⓗ Ⓙ Ⓚ	12 Ⓕ Ⓖ Ⓗ Ⓙ Ⓚ	22 Ⓕ Ⓖ Ⓗ Ⓙ Ⓚ	32 Ⓕ Ⓖ Ⓗ Ⓙ Ⓚ	42 Ⓕ Ⓖ Ⓗ Ⓙ Ⓚ	52 Ⓕ Ⓖ Ⓗ Ⓙ Ⓚ
3 Ⓐ Ⓑ Ⓒ Ⓓ Ⓔ	13 Ⓐ Ⓑ Ⓒ Ⓓ Ⓔ	23 Ⓐ Ⓑ Ⓒ Ⓓ Ⓔ	33 Ⓐ Ⓑ Ⓒ Ⓓ Ⓔ	43 Ⓐ Ⓑ Ⓒ Ⓓ Ⓔ	53 Ⓐ Ⓑ Ⓒ Ⓓ Ⓔ
4 Ⓕ Ⓖ Ⓗ Ⓙ Ⓚ	14 Ⓕ Ⓖ Ⓗ Ⓙ Ⓚ	24 Ⓕ Ⓖ Ⓗ Ⓙ Ⓚ	34 Ⓕ Ⓖ Ⓗ Ⓙ Ⓚ	44 Ⓕ Ⓖ Ⓗ Ⓙ Ⓚ	54 Ⓕ Ⓖ Ⓗ Ⓙ Ⓚ
5 Ⓐ Ⓑ Ⓒ Ⓓ Ⓔ	15 Ⓐ Ⓑ Ⓒ Ⓓ Ⓔ	25 Ⓐ Ⓑ Ⓒ Ⓓ Ⓔ	35 Ⓐ Ⓑ Ⓒ Ⓓ Ⓔ	45 Ⓐ Ⓑ Ⓒ Ⓓ Ⓔ	55 Ⓐ Ⓑ Ⓒ Ⓓ Ⓔ
6 Ⓕ Ⓖ Ⓗ Ⓙ Ⓚ	16 Ⓕ Ⓖ Ⓗ Ⓙ Ⓚ	26 Ⓕ Ⓖ Ⓗ Ⓙ Ⓚ	36 Ⓕ Ⓖ Ⓗ Ⓙ Ⓚ	46 Ⓕ Ⓖ Ⓗ Ⓙ Ⓚ	56 Ⓕ Ⓖ Ⓗ Ⓙ Ⓚ
7 Ⓐ Ⓑ Ⓒ Ⓓ Ⓔ	17 Ⓐ Ⓑ Ⓒ Ⓓ Ⓔ	27 Ⓐ Ⓑ Ⓒ Ⓓ Ⓔ	37 Ⓐ Ⓑ Ⓒ Ⓓ Ⓔ	47 Ⓐ Ⓑ Ⓒ Ⓓ Ⓔ	57 Ⓐ Ⓑ Ⓒ Ⓓ Ⓔ
8 Ⓕ Ⓖ Ⓗ Ⓙ Ⓚ	18 Ⓕ Ⓖ Ⓗ Ⓙ Ⓚ	28 Ⓕ Ⓖ Ⓗ Ⓙ Ⓚ	38 Ⓕ Ⓖ Ⓗ Ⓙ Ⓚ	48 Ⓕ Ⓖ Ⓗ Ⓙ Ⓚ	58 Ⓕ Ⓖ Ⓗ Ⓙ Ⓚ
9 Ⓐ Ⓑ Ⓒ Ⓓ Ⓔ	19 Ⓐ Ⓑ Ⓒ Ⓓ Ⓔ	29 Ⓐ Ⓑ Ⓒ Ⓓ Ⓔ	39 Ⓐ Ⓑ Ⓒ Ⓓ Ⓔ	49 Ⓐ Ⓑ Ⓒ Ⓓ Ⓔ	59 Ⓐ Ⓑ Ⓒ Ⓓ Ⓔ
10 Ⓕ Ⓖ Ⓗ Ⓙ Ⓚ	20 Ⓕ Ⓖ Ⓗ Ⓙ Ⓚ	30 Ⓕ Ⓖ Ⓗ Ⓙ Ⓚ	40 Ⓕ Ⓖ Ⓗ Ⓙ Ⓚ	50 Ⓕ Ⓖ Ⓗ Ⓙ Ⓚ	60 Ⓕ Ⓖ Ⓗ Ⓙ Ⓚ

TEST 3

1 Ⓐ Ⓑ Ⓒ Ⓓ	8 Ⓕ Ⓖ Ⓗ Ⓙ	15 Ⓐ Ⓑ Ⓒ Ⓓ	22 Ⓕ Ⓖ Ⓗ Ⓙ	29 Ⓐ Ⓑ Ⓒ Ⓓ	36 Ⓕ Ⓖ Ⓗ Ⓙ
2 Ⓕ Ⓖ Ⓗ Ⓙ	9 Ⓐ Ⓑ Ⓒ Ⓓ	16 Ⓕ Ⓖ Ⓗ Ⓙ	23 Ⓐ Ⓑ Ⓒ Ⓓ	30 Ⓕ Ⓖ Ⓗ Ⓙ	37 Ⓐ Ⓑ Ⓒ Ⓓ
3 Ⓐ Ⓑ Ⓒ Ⓓ	10 Ⓕ Ⓖ Ⓗ Ⓙ	17 Ⓐ Ⓑ Ⓒ Ⓓ	24 Ⓕ Ⓖ Ⓗ Ⓙ	31 Ⓐ Ⓑ Ⓒ Ⓓ	38 Ⓕ Ⓖ Ⓗ Ⓙ
4 Ⓕ Ⓖ Ⓗ Ⓙ	11 Ⓐ Ⓑ Ⓒ Ⓓ	18 Ⓕ Ⓖ Ⓗ Ⓙ	25 Ⓐ Ⓑ Ⓒ Ⓓ	32 Ⓕ Ⓖ Ⓗ Ⓙ	39 Ⓐ Ⓑ Ⓒ Ⓓ
5 Ⓐ Ⓑ Ⓒ Ⓓ	12 Ⓕ Ⓖ Ⓗ Ⓙ	19 Ⓐ Ⓑ Ⓒ Ⓓ	26 Ⓕ Ⓖ Ⓗ Ⓙ	33 Ⓐ Ⓑ Ⓒ Ⓓ	40 Ⓕ Ⓖ Ⓗ Ⓙ
6 Ⓕ Ⓖ Ⓗ Ⓙ	13 Ⓐ Ⓑ Ⓒ Ⓓ	20 Ⓕ Ⓖ Ⓗ Ⓙ	27 Ⓐ Ⓑ Ⓒ Ⓓ	34 Ⓕ Ⓖ Ⓗ Ⓙ	
7 Ⓐ Ⓑ Ⓒ Ⓓ	14 Ⓕ Ⓖ Ⓗ Ⓙ	21 Ⓐ Ⓑ Ⓒ Ⓓ	28 Ⓕ Ⓖ Ⓗ Ⓙ	35 Ⓐ Ⓑ Ⓒ Ⓓ	

TEST 4

1 Ⓐ Ⓑ Ⓒ Ⓓ	8 Ⓕ Ⓖ Ⓗ Ⓙ	15 Ⓐ Ⓑ Ⓒ Ⓓ	22 Ⓕ Ⓖ Ⓗ Ⓙ	29 Ⓐ Ⓑ Ⓒ Ⓓ	36 Ⓕ Ⓖ Ⓗ Ⓙ
2 Ⓕ Ⓖ Ⓗ Ⓙ	9 Ⓐ Ⓑ Ⓒ Ⓓ	16 Ⓕ Ⓖ Ⓗ Ⓙ	23 Ⓐ Ⓑ Ⓒ Ⓓ	30 Ⓕ Ⓖ Ⓗ Ⓙ	37 Ⓐ Ⓑ Ⓒ Ⓓ
3 Ⓐ Ⓑ Ⓒ Ⓓ	10 Ⓕ Ⓖ Ⓗ Ⓙ	17 Ⓐ Ⓑ Ⓒ Ⓓ	24 Ⓕ Ⓖ Ⓗ Ⓙ	31 Ⓐ Ⓑ Ⓒ Ⓓ	38 Ⓕ Ⓖ Ⓗ Ⓙ
4 Ⓕ Ⓖ Ⓗ Ⓙ	11 Ⓐ Ⓑ Ⓒ Ⓓ	18 Ⓕ Ⓖ Ⓗ Ⓙ	25 Ⓐ Ⓑ Ⓒ Ⓓ	32 Ⓕ Ⓖ Ⓗ Ⓙ	39 Ⓐ Ⓑ Ⓒ Ⓓ
5 Ⓐ Ⓑ Ⓒ Ⓓ	12 Ⓕ Ⓖ Ⓗ Ⓙ	19 Ⓐ Ⓑ Ⓒ Ⓓ	26 Ⓕ Ⓖ Ⓗ Ⓙ	33 Ⓐ Ⓑ Ⓒ Ⓓ	40 Ⓕ Ⓖ Ⓗ Ⓙ
6 Ⓕ Ⓖ Ⓗ Ⓙ	13 Ⓐ Ⓑ Ⓒ Ⓓ	20 Ⓕ Ⓖ Ⓗ Ⓙ	27 Ⓐ Ⓑ Ⓒ Ⓓ	34 Ⓕ Ⓖ Ⓗ Ⓙ	
7 Ⓐ Ⓑ Ⓒ Ⓓ	14 Ⓕ Ⓖ Ⓗ Ⓙ	21 Ⓐ Ⓑ Ⓒ Ⓓ	28 Ⓕ Ⓖ Ⓗ Ⓙ	35 Ⓐ Ⓑ Ⓒ Ⓓ	

Use a soft lead No. 2 pencil only. Do NOT use a mechanical pencil, ink, ballpoint, or felt-tip pens.

Begin WRITING TEST here.

_____

_____

_____

_____

_____

_____

_____

_____

_____

_____

_____

_____

_____

_____

_____

_____

_____

_____

_____

_____

_____

_____

_____

_____

_____

_____

If you need more space, please continue on the next page.

1

WRITING TEST

_____
_____
_____
_____
_____
_____
_____
_____
_____
_____
_____
_____
_____
_____
_____
_____
_____
_____
_____
_____
_____
_____
_____
_____
_____
_____
_____
_____

If you need more space, please continue on the back of this page.

2

WRITING TEST

_____

_____

_____

_____

_____

_____

_____

_____

_____

_____

_____

_____

_____

_____

_____

_____

_____

_____

_____

_____

_____

_____

_____

_____

_____

_____

If you need more space, please continue on the next page.

3

WRITING TEST

_____

_____

_____

_____

_____

_____

_____

_____

_____

_____

_____

_____

_____

_____

_____

_____

_____

_____

_____

_____

_____

_____

_____

_____

_____

_____

_____

STOP!

4

English Test
45 Minutes—75 Questions

DIRECTIONS: In the five passages that follow, certain words and phrases are underlined and numbered. In the right-hand column, you will find alternatives for the underlined part. In most cases, you are to choose the one that best expresses the idea, makes the statement appropriate for standard written English, or is worded most consistently with the style and tone of the passage as a whole. If you think the original version is best, choose "NO CHANGE." In some cases, you will find in the right-hand column a question about the underlined part. You are to choose the best answer to the question.

You will also find questions about a section of the passage, or about the passage as a whole. These questions do not refer to an underlined portion of the passage, but rather are identified by a number or numbers in a box.

For each question, choose the alternative you consider best and fill in the corresponding circle on your answer document. Read each passage through once before you begin to answer the questions that accompany it. For many of the questions, you must read several sentences beyond the question to determine the answer. Be sure that you have read far enough ahead each time you choose an alternative.

Passage I

Idia: The First Queen Mother of Benin

[1]

When the king of Benin, oba Ozolua, died in the late fifteenth century, the kingdom was thrown into a state of chaos as his two sons battled for the monarchy. One son, Esigie, controlled the kingdom's political and cultural center, Benin City while his brother, Ahruaran ruled in the equally important city of Udo.

1. **A.** NO CHANGE
   B. century, as the kingdom
   C. century, when the kingdom
   D. century. The kingdom

2. **F.** NO CHANGE
   G. Benin City, while his brother, Ahruaran
   H. Benin City while his brother, Ahruaran,
   J. Benin City, while his brother, Ahruaran,

[2]

In addition to dividing the country, the war led to the conquest of Benin's northern territories by the neighboring Igala peoples. Faced with the destruction of the country, Esigie made an unprecedented move, he turned to his mother, Idia, to help him gain control by using her mystical powers and providing political counsel.

3. **A.** NO CHANGE
   B. unprecedented move he turned
   C. unprecedented move; he turned
   D. unprecedented move and he turned

GO ON TO THE NEXT PAGE.

[3]

Esigie faced his brother and the Igala, as well as the
<u>　　　　　　　　　　　　　　　　　　</u>
　　　　　　　4

daunting task of reuniting the kingdom and restoring Benin
<u>　　　　　　　　　　　　　　　　　　　　　　</u>
　　　　　　　4

as a regional power.</u> Much of his success was attributed to
<u>　　　　　　　　</u>
　　　4

the counsel and mystical support of his mother, leading to a

significant change in the status of Idia, <u>who was the first</u>
　　　　　　　　　　　　　　　　　　　　　　5

<u>king's mother to become the first Queen Mother of Benin.</u>
　　　　　　　　　　5

[4]

Prior to Idia's elevation to Queen Mother, mothers of

the oba's first-born sons lived according to very strict rules.

They were not allowed to have additional children,

instead devoting <u>herself</u> to the wellbeing of the future rulers
　　　　　　　　　6

and, by extension, the wellbeing of the kingdom. Once their

sons <u>took rulership upon</u> the throne, it was customary to
　　　　7

behead the mothers to prevent them from using their

<u>mystical powers to magically harm the country.</u> Esegie,
　　　　　　　　　8

however, asked that his people reward his mother by not

<u>only allowing her to live but also honoring</u> her with the title
　　　　　　　　　9

4. Which choice most effectively guides the reader from the preceding paragraph into this new paragraph?

　F.　NO CHANGE

　G.　With Idia's guidance and help, Esigie was able to defeat his brother and the Igala, reuniting Benin and securing its role as a regional power.

　H.　Esigie's reliance on his mother's council stood out in a culture in which women typically played more passive roles.

　J.　Idia was reluctant, but eventually she decided to help her son.

5. A.　NO CHANGE

　B.　the first Queen Mother of Benin, Queen Mother Idia.

　C.　who became the first Queen Mother of Benin.

　D.　who became the first Queen Mother of Benin as a result of the counsel and support she provided.

6. F.　NO CHANGE

　G.　hers

　H.　themselves

　J.　oneself

7. A.　NO CHANGE

　B.　undertook

　C.　assumed

　D.　sat down at

8. F.　NO CHANGE

　G.　to cause harm to the country by supernatural means.

　H.　to harm the country.

　J.　OMIT the underlined portion.

9. A.　NO CHANGE

　B.　allowed her to live but also by honored

　C.　allowing her to live but also honored

　D.　allowed her to live but also by honoring

GO ON TO THE NEXT PAGE.

f iyoba, or Queen Mother. Bestowing upon her certain
_____
10
political powers. The people agreed, but only on the
_____
10

condition that Esegie and Idia would never again has direct
                                                   ___
                                                   11
contact.

[5]

Soon after, Idia was installed in her own palace

outside the capital city. It's hard to believe, but she never
                        _____
                                    12
saw her son again! However, from that time forward, iyobas
_____
     12

remained powerful members of society and their sons', the
                                      _____
                                            13
obas, wore carved ivory pendant masks representing the
____
 13
iyoba during ceremonies designed to rid the kingdom of

malevolent spiritual forces.

10. F. NO CHANGE
    G. Queen Mother and bestowing upon her certain
        political powers.
    H. Queen Mother, and bestowing upon her certain
        political powers.
    J. Queen Mother bestowing upon her certain political
        powers.

11. A. NO CHANGE
    B. have
    C. had have
    D. has had

12. Which choice best maintains the tone of the passage?
    F. NO CHANGE
    G. After all she did for him, Idia never saw her son
        again!
    H. While Idia gained power and prestige, she never
        saw her son again.
    J. Although it may seem harsh that Idia never saw her
        son again, at least she wasn't beheaded.

13. A. NO CHANGE
    B. their sons, the obas',
    C. their sons, the obas,
    D. their sons', the obas',

Questions 14 and 15 refer to the preceding passage as a whole.

---

14. Upon reviewing this essay and realizing that some
    information had been left out, the writer composes the
    following sentence, incorporating that information:

    Benin, in what is now Nigeria, was a regional
    power, and the civil war had devastating effects.

    The most logical and effective place to add this sentence
    would be after the last sentence in Paragraph:

    F. 1.
    G. 2.
    H. 4.
    J. 5.

15. Suppose the writer had decided to write an essay
    discussing the role of women in Africa during the 15th
    century. Would this essay successfully fulfill the
    writer's goal?

    A. Yes, because the essay explains the role of women
        during times of conflict in the kingdom of Benin.
    B. Yes, because the essay provides detailed
        information about the lives of certain women that
        allows the reader to determine the roles of most
        women in that time and place.
    C. No, because the essay explains only what happened
        to the women whose sons became kings in one
        specific country.
    D. No, because the essay focuses on modern roles for
        women instead of their traditional roles.

GO ON TO THE NEXT PAGE.

Passage II

Can You Sing the World's Oldest Song?

[1]

Music seems eternal, it is: an art form that transcends
<u>   </u>
                16
time and distance despite shifts in styles and fashion. After

all, people today still flock to hear the works of Mozart,

Beethoven, Ellington, and a growing list of aging rock stars.

<u>Tunes</u> by notable composers like Gershwin and folk
17

musicians whose names have been lost to history are

<u>woven around</u> the fabric of cultures worldwide.
18

[2]

[1] Where did it all begin? [2] Unfortunately, no

traces of those songs remain. [3] No one knows for sure,

though archaeological digs have turned up primitive bone

and ivory flutes that date back some 43,000 years. [4]

Certainly the musicians who played these instruments, and

others lost to the ages, played songs. [19]

[3]

<u>In conclusion,</u> the oldest known sample of musical
20

notations dates from just 4,000 years ago, and that is just a

fragment on a Sumerian clay tablet. Most historians agree that

the oldest known written melody in existence is "Hurrian

16. **F.** NO CHANGE
    G. eternal; it is: an
    H. eternal; it is an
    J. eternal—it is—an

17. Which of the following is the LEAST acceptable
    alternative to the underlined portion?
    A. Ditties
    B. Music
    C. Stuff
    D. Songs

18. **F.** NO CHANGE
    G. weaving in and out of
    H. woven into
    J. weaving through

19. For the sake of the logic and coherence of Paragraph 2
    Sentence 2 should be placed:
    A. where it is now.
    B. before Sentence 1.
    C. after Sentence 3.
    D. after Sentence 4.

20. **F.** NO CHANGE
    G. In summary
    H. In fact
    J. Nevertheless

GO ON TO THE NEXT PAGE.

ymn No. 6," which is intended to be played on a nine-
_____
21

ringed lyre.
____
21

[2] The clay tablets were found in Syria in the 1950s and

include instructions for how to play the song on a type of

lyre.

[4]

However, because Hurrian Hymn No. 6 is just a

fragment, some experts to claim that it cannot be considered
_____
23

the oldest known musical composition. That distinction,

we insisted, belongs to the so-called Seikilos Epitaph.
_____
24

[5]

The Seikilos Epitaph is engraved on a marble

column, or stele, marking the grave of a Turkish woman.

The stele includes complete lyrics in Greek and musical

notations, which was why those who favor it claim it is a
_____
25

21. Given that all of the choices are true, which one is most relevant to the focus of this paragraph?

    A. NO CHANGE

    B. which modern musicians have attempted to reconstruct and play.

    C. which can be transcribed in several ways depending on interpretations of its symbols.

    D. which was composed in cuneiform around the 14th century B.C.

22. At this point, the writer has decided to insert additional information physically describing the clay tablet on which the Hurrian Hymn was inscribed. Which sentence best accomplishes that goal?

    F. Hurrian Hymn No. 6 was written in cuneiform writing in the Hurrian language, which is not completely understood today.

    G. The hymn was inscribed on a tablet that, while cracked and partially illegible, was the most complete of a group of 36 such tablets.

    H. Clay tablets were used before the invention of paper to record business transactions, literature, and—apparently—music.

    J. Cuneiform symbols were pressed into the clay tablet.

23. **A.** NO CHANGE

    B. experts claiming

    C. experts claim

    D. experts having claimed

24. **F.** NO CHANGE

    G. we insist,

    H. I insist,

    J. they insist,

25. **A.** NO CHANGE

    B. has been

    C. is

    D. would be

GO ON TO THE NEXT PAGE.

complete composition. The lyrics and notes facilitate the
 $\overline{}$
 26
ability of modern scholars to translate the words, and
$\overline{}$
26

modern musicians play the song in full, unlike the Hurrian
 $\overline{}$
 27

Hymn. Perhaps because the lyrics are so poignant. The
 $\overline{}$
 28
music is so plaintive, a number of recordings 29 have
$\overline{}$
28

been made of the Seikilos Epitaph. It is after all hard to
 $\overline{}$
 30
resist a song that proclaims, "While you live, shine / Have

no grief at all / Life exists only for a short while / And time

demands its toll."

26. **F.** NO CHANGE
    G. open the door to
    H. create a possibility for
    J. enable

27. **A.** NO CHANGE
    B. to play
    C. playing
    D. played

28. **F.** NO CHANGE
    G. poignant: the music
    H. poignant and the music
    J. poignant. Because the music

29. At this point, the writer is considering adding th
    following parenthetical phrase:

    —you can listen to some recordings online—

    Would this phrase be a relevant addition to th
    paragraph?

    A. Yes, because hearing the actual song woul
    provide more information to the reader than simpl
    reading the passage does.

    B. Yes, because in order to fully understand a song i
    is necessary to hear it.

    C. No, because the passage focuses mainly on th
    Hurrian Hymn No. 6, and additional informatio
    about the Seiklos Epitaph is distracting.

    D. No, because information about where the reade
    can hear the epitaph is an unnecessary addition t
    the point that recordings have been made.

30. **F.** NO CHANGE
    G. It is after all, hard
    H. It is, after all hard
    J. It is, after all, hard

Passage III

Mr. Jones: An American Writer

[1]

In 1952, James Jones won the National Book Award

for his first published novel. Based on his experience during
_____
31

World War II, *From Here to Eternity* is set in Hawaii

just before the Japanese attacked Pearl Harbor, an event it
                                                          ‾‾
                                                          32

witnessed. It was the first book in what would eventually

become known as Jones's war trilogy. [34]
‾‾‾‾‾
33

[2]

[1] Born in Robinson, Illinois, in 1921, James Jones

enlisted in the U.S. Army in 1939 and served in the 25th

Infantry Division, 27th Infantry Regiment. [2] Having taken

some classes at the University of Hawaii while awaiting his

combat assignment; Jones resumed his studies at New York
‾‾‾‾‾‾‾‾‾‾‾‾‾‾‾‾‾
35

University after leaving the military, but eventually returned

to Robinson where he worked on his writing. [3] His first

published story appeared in *Atlantic Monthly* in 1948. [4] He

saw combat on Guadalcanal, where he was injured, and he

was discharged in 1944. [36]

31. **A.** NO CHANGE
    B. novel, based on
    C. novel based on
    D. OMIT the underlined portion.

32. **F.** NO CHANGE
    G. him
    H. they
    J. Jones

33. **A.** NO CHANGE
    B. became
    C. becomes
    D. will become

34. The writer is considering deleting the preceding sentence. If the writer were to make this deletion, the essay would primarily lose information that:
    F. places a novel in the context of other works.
    G. provides details about an author's military background.
    H. provides supporting evidence for a key argument.
    J. repeats a key idea for emphasis.

35. **A.** NO CHANGE
    B. assignment: Jones
    C. assignment, Jones
    D. assignment—Jones

36. For the sake of the logic and coherence of Paragraph 2, Sentence 4 should be placed:
    F. where it is now.
    G. before Sentence 1.
    H. before Sentence 2.
    J. before Sentence 3.

GO ON TO THE NEXT PAGE.

[3]

The book portrays the enlisted men and officers of
$\overline{}$
                              37

the Army, named one of the 100 Best Novels of the 20th
$\overline{}$
                              37

century by the Modern Library Board, not as heroes, but as
$\overline{}$
                              37

flawed human beings struggling to find their way in a world
$\overline{}$
                              37

that is about to be torn asunder by war. *From Here to*
$\overline{}$
                              37

Eternity was such a victory on the reading public that it was
                          $\overline{}$
                              38

made into a movie starring Burt Lancaster, Deborah Kerr,

Montgomery Clift, and Frank Sinatra in 1953.

[4]

After the success of *From Here to Eternity*, Jones

wrote and published *Some Came Running*, which was not
                    $\overline{}$
                              39

as critically acclaimed as *From Here to Eternity* but also
$\overline{}$
        40

became a bestseller. Following his marriage to

Gloria Mosolino, Jones relocated to France, where he
                          $\overline{}$
                              41

37. A. NO CHANGE
  B. The book portrays the enlisted men and officers of the Army not as heroes, but as flawed human beings struggling to find their way in a world that is about to be torn asunder by war, named one of the 100 Best Novels of the 20th century by the Modern Library Board.
  C. The book portrays the enlisted men and officers of the Army not as heroes, but as flawed human beings, named one of the 100 Best Novels of the 20th century by the Modern Library Board, struggling to find their way in a world that is about to be torn asunder by war.
  D. Named one of the 100 Best Novels of the 20th century by the Modern Library Board, the book portrays the enlisted men and officers of the Army not as heroes, but as flawed human beings struggling to find their way in a world that is about to be torn asunder by war.

38. F. NO CHANGE
  G. an impact on
  H. a success with
  J. a triumph over

39. A. NO CHANGE
  B. *Some Came Running* was not
  C. *Some Came Running*, it was not
  D. *Some Came Running*, was not

40. F. NO CHANGE
  G. critical acclaim
  H. critically acclaim
  J. critical acclaimed

41. Which choice is the LEAST acceptable alternative to the underlined portion?
  A. proceeded to
  B. left for
  C. immigrated to
  D. resettled in

GO ON TO THE NEXT PAGE.

write *The Thin Red Line* in 1962, the second book in his war
<u>42</u>
trilogy.

[5]

Jones was close to completing the third book of his

war trilogy, *Whistle*, when he passed away in 1977. Jones
<u>43</u>
left instructions for another writer, Willie Morris, to
<u>43</u>
complete the final novel in his war trilogy, which was
<u>43</u>
posthumously published in 1978.
<u>43</u>

42. **F.** NO CHANGE
    G. wrote
    H. writes
    J. had written

43. Given that all of the choices are true, which one would most effectively conclude this essay?

    A. NO CHANGE
    B. Jones's novels were informed by his own experience—characters in *From Here to Eternity* were based on his platoon—but they also contained fictionalized elements.
    C. In addition to his book awards, Jones was awarded the Purple Heart for his injuries in World War II.
    D. Jones's early work had been supported by a "writer's colony," a place established to provide for the needs of writers while they practice their craft.

Questions 44 and 45 refer to the preceding passage as a whole.

---

44. For the sake of logic and coherence, Paragraph 1 should be placed:

    F. where it is now.
    G. after Paragraph 2.
    H. after Paragraph 3.
    J. after Paragraph 4.

45. Suppose the writer's primary purpose had been to explain the importance of Jones's contributions in helping to shape the genre of war literature. Would this essay accomplish that purpose?

    A. Yes, because it focuses on how James Jones based his war trilogy on his own experiences of war.
    B. Yes, because it describes how James Jones's war trilogy influenced future authors.
    C. No, because the essay mainly focuses on James's life and only briefly mentions Jones's war trilogy.
    D. No, because the essay does not place Jones's writing in a broader context of war literature.

GO ON TO THE NEXT PAGE.

Passage IV

Peddling Yarns

[1]

I once worked at a small company that sold wool and

yarn online. When I started the job, because I didn't realize

how many different fibers were used in yarns and fabrics.

But here I was selling the stuff I had to learn fast!

[2]

One of the first fibers I got to know wasn't wool at

all: it is acrylic.

Acrylic, kind of plastic. It's turned into a spinnable fiber

through a process called "extrusion." Extrusion is used to

make a variety of synthetic fibers, including Kevlar fibers,

which are woven into Kevlar cloth. These are spun into

yarns. Acrylic yarn is inexpensive, strong, and elastic.

46. **F.** NO CHANGE
    G. although
    H. whereas
    J. OMIT the underlined portion.

47. **A.** NO CHANGE
    B. was selling: the stuff I had
    C. was; selling the stuff I had
    D. was, selling the stuff; I had

48. **F.** NO CHANGE
    G. was
    H. had been
    J. will be

49. **A.** NO CHANGE
    B. Acrylic: a kind of plastic.
    C. Acrylic is a kind of plastic.
    D. Kind of plastic.

50. Given that all of the choices are true, which one is most relevant to the focus of the paragraph?
    F. NO CHANGE
    G. The plastic is melted, then forced through tiny holes to form thin strands of spinnable fibers.
    H. In addition to plastics, extrusion is also used to process natural cellulose from trees and bamboo.
    J. Extrusion is used in the food industry to create a variety of products including pasta, sausages, and cereals, but in the textile industry it is used to create spinnable fibers.

51. **A.** NO CHANGE
    B. possesses the attributes of being inexpensive, strong, and elastic.
    C. has the following characteristics: inexpensiveness, strength, and elasticity.
    D. is characterized by inexpensiveness, strength, and elasticity.

GO ON TO THE NEXT PAGE.

Practice Test

Unfortunately, it's also very *déclassé*—we sold high-end
—————
52
fibers, and I only learned about acrylic because our

customers needed to be assured that we weren't using it.

[3]

After learning what we didn't like, I learned about

a fiber we loved: merino wool. There are many different

kinds of sheep and they produce wools with slightly

different characteristics. [53] Merino sheep produce merino

wool, which is soft, somewhat elastic, and very squishy.

The first time I heard this, I was a little confused: how can
                                                   —————
                                                     54
wool be "squishy?" To understand how "squishy" describes
—————
  54
the texture of wool, just grab a ball and give it a squeeze: a

ball of squishy wool doesn't offer much resistance, and

bounces back after you squeeze it. Squishiness makes wool

ideal for garments that have to take a lot of wear-and-tear,

but also need to be comfortable—like socks. We sold to a lot

of sock knitters, merino our most popular product.
        —————
          55

52. Which of the following alternatives to the underlined
    portion would be LEAST acceptable?
    F. However,
    G. Indeed,
    H. Regrettably,
    J. Alas,

53. At this point, the writer is considering adding the
    following sentence:

    White or lightly colored wool is often dyed in an
    array of dazzling colors.

    Should the writer make this addition?

    A. Yes, because it provides interesting additional
       information about merino wool.
    B. Yes, because it helps to explain how different
       breeds of sheep can produce wool with different
       qualities by providing a specific example.
    C. No, because it does not specify the color of wool
       provided by merino sheep.
    D. No, because it does not develop the idea that
       different breeds of sheep produce different kinds of
       wool.

54. F. NO CHANGE
    G. how can wool be "squishy!"
    H. how can wool be "squishy."
    J. how can wool be "squishy:"

55. A. NO CHANGE
    B. knitters, merino was
    C. knitters, so merino was
    D. knitters; merino,

GO ON TO THE NEXT PAGE.

[4]

[1] We also sold some very expensive luxury fibers, like cashmere and silk blends, but my personal favorite was alpaca wool. [2] Alpaca wool is incredibly soft. [3] Alpaca wool is also warmest than sheeps' wool, so garments like scarves and gloves can be made from a finer yarn and still provide just as much warmth as thicker, scratchier sheeps' wool garments. [4] It's never prickly, like some sheeps' wool can be. 58

[5]

I don't sell wool anymore, but I still like it: a hand-knit alpaca wool scarf is one of my most prized possessions.

56. F. NO CHANGE
G. expensively
H. expense
J. expensiveness

57. A. NO CHANGE
B. warmer
C. warm
D. most warm

58. For the sake of the logic and coherence of Paragraph 4, Sentence 4 should be:

F. placed where it is now.
G. placed before Sentence 1.
H. placed after Sentence 2.
J. OMITTED, because the paragraph focuses on alpaca wool, not sheeps' wool.

59. A. NO CHANGE
B. things that I like
C. highly valued holdings
D. articles of clothing

Question 60 refers to the preceding passage as a whole.

60. Suppose the writer's primary purpose had been to describe some of what he learned from a work experience. Would this essay accomplish that goal?

F. Yes, because it describes how the writer learned to manufacture several varieties of fiber from a kind of plastic.
G. Yes, because it explains what the writer learned about a variety of fibers by selling them.
H. No, because it focuses on providing general information about fibers without explaining how the writer learned the information.
J. No, because it provides information about fiber and yarn rather than the business knowledge that a person gains through work.

GO ON TO THE NEXT PAGE.

Passage V

Who is El Niño?

[1]

[1] Weather forecasters often use the term "El
Niño." [2] However, most people have no idea what the term
really means. [3] The name, Spanish for "the boy child,"
arose, because South American fishermen noticed that
coastal waters sometimes warmed up around Christmas. [4]
This linked the event with the child Christ, or "El Niño." [62]

[2]

El Niño is actually one of three states of a single
climate phenomenon known as the El Niño Southern
Oscillation, or ENSO. ENSO includes La Niña, which is a
cooling of the ocean surface, and the neutral state, during
which the temperature of the tropical Pacific is close to
average. The simplest explanation of what happens during
the phase is that the ocean surface warms up, and that
warming affects wind patterns and ocean currents.

[3]

[1] El Niño can cause droughts in western Pacific
countries from Southeast Asia to Australia, while at the
same time bringing potentially severely rain to areas that are
normally dry, like Peru and Ecuador. [2] East African

61. A. NO CHANGE
   B. child," arose
   C. child" arose
   D. child" arose,

62. For the sake of the logic and coherence of Paragraph 1,
   Sentence 4 should be placed:
   F. where it is now.
   G. before Sentence 1.
   H. after Sentence 1.
   J. after Sentence 2.

63. A. NO CHANGE
   B. it
   C. El Niño
   D. this

64. F. NO CHANGE
   G. potentially severe
   H. potential severe
   J. potential severely

GO ON TO THE NEXT PAGE.

countries <u>experience unusually wet conditions,</u> while South
                          65
African countries are drier. [3] During El Niños, winters in

the northern U.S., Canada, and Europe are warmer and drier

than average, while the southern portions of North America

and Europe are cooler and wetter. [4] Though hurricanes are

suppressed in the Atlantic, there's a rise in tropical cyclones

throughout the Pacific. [66]

[4]

<u>Naturally,</u> these changes in global weather patterns
   67

have <u>global effects. El Niño</u> is linked to increases in
            68
mosquito populations and mosquito-borne diseases like

malaria and dengue fever. Economic impacts are also

significant: changes in rain patterns <u>had affected</u> everything
                                          69

from crops to hydroelectric dams, <u>and the prices of</u>
                                         70
<u>everything—from food prices to electricity prices.</u> Some
                           70

65. A. NO CHANGE
   B. have some pretty damp days,
   C. see it raining cats and dogs,
   D. are totally soaked,

66. The writer is considering deleting a sentence from th[e]
   paragraph to improve its focus on the effects that E[l]
   Niño has on different nations of the world. To be[st]
   accomplish this goal, the writer should delete:

   F. Sentence 1.
   G. Sentence 2.
   H. Sentence 3.
   J. Sentence 4.

67. Which of the following choices is the LEAS[T]
   acceptable alternative to the underlined portion?

   A. Obviously,
   B. Of course,
   C. Conversely,
   D. OMIT the underlined portion and capitalize th[e]
   first letter of the next word.

68. F. NO CHANGE
   G. global effects, El Niño
   H. global effects El Niño
   J. global effects, El Niño,

69. A. NO CHANGE
   B. affected
   C. will affect
   D. affect

70. F. NO CHANGE
   G. and the prices of food, and nearly everything else[,]
   including the price of electricity.
   H. and everything from food prices to electricit[y]
   prices, as a result of the effects on things such a[s]
   crops and dams.
   J. and the prices of everything from food t[o]
   electricity.

GO ON TO THE NEXT PAGE.

dies have even claimed that the risk of social problems,
71

en civil wars increases, with El Niño's arrival.
71

[5]

Not all of El Niño's effects are negative: in areas
72

here El Niño reduces rain, rates of mosquito-borne disease

tually was falling, and in many regions some crop yields
73

tually increase. Whatever the effects on a particular

gion. It's good for us to know about them in advance and
74

an for El Niño's arrival. 75

71. A. NO CHANGE
B. problems—even civil wars—increases
C. problems; even civil wars increases
D. problems: even civil wars, increases

72. F. NO CHANGE
G. El Niños effects
H. El Niños effect's
J. El Niño's effect's

73. A. NO CHANGE
B. falls,
C. has fallen,
D. fall,

74. F. NO CHANGE
G. region it's good
H. region it's good,
J. region, it's good

> Question 75 refers to the preceding passage as a whole.

75. Suppose the writer's primary purpose had been to argue that future generations should work to mitigate the negative effects of climate phenomena like El Niño. Would this essay accomplish that goal?

A. Yes, because the passage concludes by indicating that we should make plans based on weather patterns.

B. Yes, because the passage warns about many of the severe consequences of El Niño.

C. No, because the writer does not suggest that there is any way for future generations to prevent El Niño.

D. No, because the author focuses primarily on describing El Niño, rather than making any argument.

END OF TEST 1.

STOP! DO NOT TURN THE PAGE UNTIL YOU ARE TOLD TO DO SO.

Mathematics Test
60 Minutes—60 Questions

DIRECTIONS: For each problem, solve for the correct answer, select your choice and fill in the corresponding bubble on your answer document.

Some problems may take a longer time to solve, but do not take too much time on any single problem. Solve the easier questions first, then return to the harder questions in the remaining time for this test.

A calculator is allowed on this test. While you may be able to solve some problems without a calculator, you

are allowed to use a calculator for all of the problems c this test.

Note: Unless otherwise directed, all of the followin statements are considered correct.

1. All drawn figures are NOT necessarily drawn to sca
2. All geometric figures are in a plane.
3. The word *line*, when used, is the same as a straight lin
4. The word *average*, when used, is the same a arithmetic mean.

---

1. For all nonzero values of x, the expression $-3x^3 \cdot 6x^{-2}$ is equivalent to:

   A. $3x$

   B. $3x^{-6}$

   C. $-18x^{-6}$

   D. $-18x$

   E. $18x$

2. A mole is a unit of measurement in chemistry. If 1 mole contains 6.02×10^{23} particles, how many particles are in $\frac{1}{2}$ of a mole?

   F. $3.01 \times 10^{11.5}$

   G. 3.01×10^{23}

   H. 6.02×10^{23}

   J. $6.02 \times 10^{11.5}$

   K. 3.01×5^{23}

3. 20% of x is 15. What is x% of 120?

   A. 3

   B. 24

   C. 30

   D. 45

   E. 90

4. Maria drives to her aunt's house at an average speed 50 miles per hour. If her trip takes 5 hours and minutes, how many miles does she drive?

   F. 227.5

   G. 257.5

   H. 262.5

   J. 266.5

   K. 275.5

5. A customer uses a coupon to get 16% off the cost of jacket. Due to an in-store promotion, she receives a additional 10% off of the sale price at the register. If th jacket originally cost $237, how much does she pay, the nearest cent?

   A. $173.94

   B. $175.38

   C. $179.17

   D. $199.08

   E. $213.30

6. What is the lowest common denominator $\frac{1}{17}, \frac{1}{12}, \frac{1}{4}$, and $\frac{1}{6}$?

   F. 204

   G. 408

   H. 816

   J. 3,264

   K. 780,336

GO ON TO THE NEXT PAGE.

7. If $x = -2$, what is the value of $(x^3 + 6)(x^2 - 3)$?

   A.   −14

   B.   −3

   C.   −2

   D.   −1

   E.   14

8. 3 points are shown below on a standard (x,y) coordinate plane.

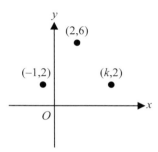

If 3 lines are drawn to connect each of the points, an isosceles triangle is formed. $k = ?$

   F.   5

   G.   3

   H.   2

   J.   1

   K.   0

9. Which values of x satisfy the equation $x^2 - 16x = 0$?

   A. $x = 4$ and $x = -4$

   B. $x = 0$ and $x = 16$

   C. $x = 0$ and $x = -16$

   D. $x = 0$

   E.   There are no real solutions to the equation.

10. Which of the following expressions is equivalent to $3(5x - 2y) + 8\left(\dfrac{1}{2}y - 2x\right)$?

   F. $-x - 2y$

   G. $-2x - 2y$

   H. $-8x + 4y$

   J. $12x - 16y$

   K. $19x - 22y$

11. An artist is constructing a triangular frame out of metal for the City of Calgary. His blueprint is a triangular frame with a ratio of side lengths that is exactly 8:10:15. If the longest side of the real structure is 45 meters, what is the total length of the metal needed to build the triangular frame, to the nearest meter?

   A.   186

   B.   120

   C.   99

   D.   63

   E.   33

12. The distance d, in meters, traveled by a moving object is given by the equation $d = vt + \dfrac{1}{2}at^2$, where v is the velocity in meters per second, a is the acceleration in meters per second per second, and t is the elapsed time in seconds. If an object with velocity 15 meters per second travels 61 meters in 3 seconds, what is its acceleration, a, in meters per second per second?

   F.   0

   G. $\dfrac{9}{32}$

   H. $\dfrac{32}{3}$

   J. $\dfrac{32}{9}$

   K. $\dfrac{212}{9}$

13. A dry cleaning business charges a fee of \$9 for its services, plus \$5 per shirt and \$6 per jacket. Kristin drops off s shirts and j jackets for dry cleaning. Which of the following expressions represents the cost, in dollars, that Kristin must pay for her dry cleaning?

   A. $5j + 6s + 9$

   B. $5s + 6j + 9$

   C. $5s + 6j$

   D. $20(s + j)$

   E. $11(s + j) + 9$

GO ON TO THE NEXT PAGE.

14. What is the sum of the 2 roots in the function shown in the graph below?

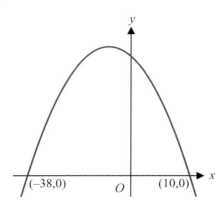

F. −28

G. −3

H. 0

J. 3

K. 28

15. What is the y-intercept of a line that passes through the points $(-2,0)$ and $(1,6)$?

A. −4

B. −2

C. 0

D. 2

E. 4

16. Let $b = x^a$. What happens to the value of b if x is equal to 2 and a is increased by 1?

F. It increases by 2.

G. It doubles.

H. It increases by a.

J. It increases by a^2.

K. It is unchanged.

17. Alex owns 5 shirts, 5 pants, 3 sweaters, and 4 pairs of sandals. A complete outfit consists of a shirt, a pair of pants, a sweater, and a pair of sandals. If he loses a pair of sandals and a shirt, how many complete outfit options does he lose?

A. 120

B. 180

C. 300

D. 360

E. 540

18. Which of the following inequalities is the solution for the inequality $23 \geq -(17 + 5x)$?

F. $x \geq -8$

G. $x \leq -8$

H. $x \geq 8$

J. $x \geq -40$

K. $x \leq -40$

19. In the figure shown below, each pair of intersecting line segments meets at a right angle, and all the lengths are given in meters. What is the perimeter, in meters, of the figure?

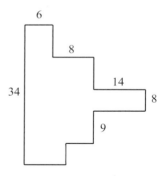

A. 62

B. 79

C. 118

D. 124

E. 952

20. The ratio of x to 3 is x:3. If this ratio of x:3 is equal to 7:10, what is the value of x?

F. 1.0

G. 2.1

H. 2.8

J. 4.3

K. 23.3

GO ON TO THE NEXT PAGE.

Practice Test

1. A mover lowers a piano from a window using a rope, keeping the piano at a right angle to the ground. At the window, the rope bends at a 40° angle, as shown in the figure below. At what angle, with respect to the ground, must the mover hold the rope?

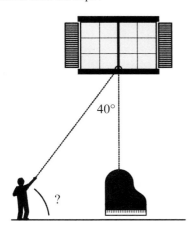

A. 35°
B. 40°
C. 45°
D. 50°
E. 90°

22. What is the correct order of the following fractions, from smallest to largest?

$$\frac{2}{3}, \frac{5}{2}, \frac{11}{12}, \frac{4}{7}$$

F. $\frac{2}{3}, \frac{4}{7}, \frac{5}{2}, \frac{11}{12}$

G. $\frac{2}{3}, \frac{5}{2}, \frac{4}{7}, \frac{11}{12}$

H. $\frac{2}{3}, \frac{4}{7}, \frac{11}{12}, \frac{5}{2}$

J. $\frac{2}{3}, \frac{11}{12}, \frac{4}{7}, \frac{5}{2}$

K. $\frac{4}{7}, \frac{2}{3}, \frac{11}{12}, \frac{5}{2}$

23. If $x^2 - 1 = y$ and $x + y = 1$, which of the following is a possible value for x?

A. −1
B. 0
C. 1
D. 2
E. 3

24. The function $f(x)$ is shown in the standard (x, y) coordinate plane.

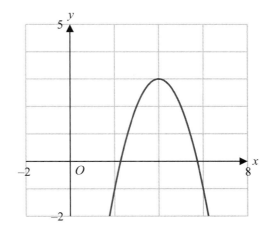

If the point $(4, y)$ lies on the curve of the function $-f(x)$, what is the value of y?

F. 3
G. 2
H. 0
J. −2
K. −3

25. If $3^x = 81^7$, $x = ?$

A. 4
B. 11
C. 10
D. 28
E. 30

26. If the arc length of a sector of a circle with radius 1 is $\frac{\pi}{2}$, what is the measure of the sector's angle, in degrees?

F. 270°
G. 180°
H. 115°
J. 90°
K. 45°

GO ON TO THE NEXT PAGE.

27. A library charges a fine if a book is not returned after 21 days. The fine is $0.25 the first day, and doubles every following day such that the total fine would be $1.00 after the third day. What is the maximum number of days that a book may be borrowed from the library before accumulating a total fine of $4.00?

- **A.** 22
- **B.** 23
- **C.** 24
- **D.** 25
- **E.** 26

28. $|9 - 21| - |8 + 3 - 16| = ?$

- **F.** −17
- **G.** −7
- **H.** 7
- **J.** 8
- **K.** 17

29. What is the value of $\dfrac{\sin \beta}{\cos \beta}$ in the figure below?

- **A.** $\dfrac{1}{2}$
- **B.** $\dfrac{3}{4}$
- **C.** 1
- **D.** $\dfrac{4}{3}$
- **E.** $\dfrac{212}{9}$

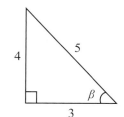

30. A number is doubled, then tripled, and then divided by 4. If n is the original number, which of the following is equal to the new number?

- **F.** $\dfrac{n}{4}$
- **G.** $\dfrac{n}{2}$
- **H.** $\dfrac{3n}{2}$
- **J.** $4n$
- **K.** $6n$

31. What is the value of $\log_2 128 - \log_2 64$?

- **A.** 4
- **B.** 3
- **C.** 2
- **D.** 1
- **E.** 0

32. John is buying candy and soda for a party. Candy cost $4 per bag, and soda costs $3 per bottle. If John has combined total of 40 bags and bottles, and he spend $130, how many bottles does he buy?

- **F.** 5
- **G.** 10
- **H.** 20
- **J.** 30
- **K.** 40

33. The graph below represents which of the following equations?

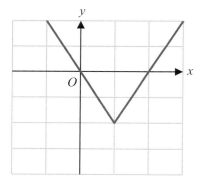

- **A.** $y = (x - 1)^2 - 1$
- **B.** $y = |x - 1| - 1$
- **C.** $y = |x - 1| + 1$
- **D.** $y = 2x - 2$ and $y = -\dfrac{1}{2}x - 1$
- **E.** $y = -2x - 2$ and $y = \dfrac{1}{2}x - 1$

GO ON TO THE NEXT PAGE.

34. $\begin{bmatrix} -1 & 2 \\ 2 & 4 \end{bmatrix} + \begin{bmatrix} 4 \\ 2 \end{bmatrix} = ?$

    F. $\begin{bmatrix} 4 \\ 16 \end{bmatrix}$

    G. $\begin{bmatrix} 16 \\ 4 \end{bmatrix}$

    H. $\begin{bmatrix} -4 & 8 \\ 8 & 8 \end{bmatrix}$

    J. $\begin{bmatrix} 8 & 8 \\ -4 & 8 \end{bmatrix}$

    K. The resulting matrix is undefined.

35. Five consecutive integers add up to 105. What is the smallest of these integers?

    A. 18
    B. 19
    C. 20
    D. 21
    E. 22

Use the following information to answer questions 36-37.

Every day, Fred and Angela make daily deposits, in dollars, into their savings accounts, as shown in the table below.

Day	Fred	Angela
June 1	25	1
June 2	30	2
June 3	35	4
June 4	40	8
June 5	45	16

36. If Fred's deposits continue to increase at the same daily rate, how much money will he have after 10 days?

    F. $70
    G. $250
    H. $350
    J. $475
    K. $950

37. Both Fred and Angela's deposits continue increasing at the same rate. What is the first day on which Angela will deposit more money than Fred?

    A. June 6
    B. June 7
    C. June 8
    D. June 9
    E. October 6

38. A tent uses cables that are 13 feet long to support its structure. If the tent is erected perpendicular to the ground and the cables are secured 5 feet from the base of the tent, as shown below, how tall is the tent in feet?

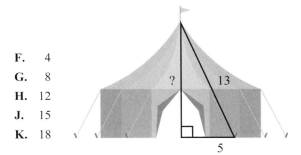

    F. 4
    G. 8
    H. 12
    J. 15
    K. 18

39. Jennifer asks Corwin what his favorite number is. Corwin responds, "If you add 2 to my favorite number, then find the square root of the result, the end result is 5." What is Corwin's favorite number?

    A. −27
    B. 5
    C. 23
    D. 25
    E. 27

40. The function $(x - 15)^2 + (y - 4)^2 = 81$ is graphed on a standard (x,y) coordinate plane. How many times does the function intersect the x-axis?

    F. 0
    G. 1
    H. 2
    J. 3
    K. 4

GO ON TO THE NEXT PAGE.

41. Vector $\overrightarrow{BC}$ is shown in the standard (x,y) coordinate plane below. Which of the following is the component form of $\overrightarrow{BC}$?

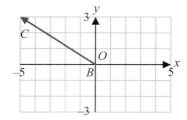

- **A.** $\langle -5,-3 \rangle$
- **B.** $\langle -5, 3 \rangle$
- **C.** $\langle 3,-3 \rangle$
- **D.** $\langle 5,-3 \rangle$
- **E.** $\langle 5, 5 \rangle$

42. If $16^x = 4$, $x = 16^y$, what is the value of xy?

- **F.** $-\dfrac{1}{8}$
- **G.** $-\dfrac{1}{4}$
- **H.** $-\dfrac{1}{2}$
- **J.** $\dfrac{1}{2}$
- **K.** 1

43. The volume of a sphere can be expressed by the equation $V = \dfrac{4}{3}\pi r^3$, where r is the radius. What would happen to the volume of a sphere if its radius were tripled?

- **A.** It would increase by a factor of 6.
- **B.** It would increase by a factor of 9.
- **C.** It would increase by a factor of 27.
- **D.** It would decrease by a factor of 6.
- **E.** If would decrease by a factor of 27.

44. If $f(x) = 2x^2 + 1$ and $g(x) = \dfrac{1}{x}$, what is $f(g(2))$?

- **F.** 9
- **G.** $\dfrac{3}{2}$
- **H.** $\dfrac{2}{3}$
- **J.** $\dfrac{1}{2}$
- **K.** 0

45. Two of the vertices of a square graphed on the standard (x,y) plane are at the points $(-2,3)$ and $(2,-1)$. Which of the following coordinates is NOT a possible vertex of the square?

- **A.** $(6, 3)$
- **B.** $(3, 6)$
- **C.** $(2, 3)$
- **D.** $(-2,-1)$
- **E.** $(-6,-1)$

46. In the quadrilateral shown below, what is the value of x

- **F.** 100
- **G.** 105
- **H.** 110
- **J.** 115
- **K.** 120

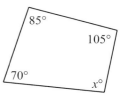

47. A line $\overline{AD}$ is shown below.

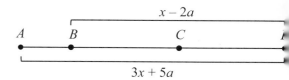

What is the length of $\overline{AB}$?

- **A.** $2x + 7a$
- **B.** $-x + 3a$
- **C.** $-2x + 7a$
- **D.** $-2x - 3a$
- **E.** $-4x - 3a$

GO ON TO THE NEXT PAGE.

48. What is the length of the hypotenuse of the isosceles right triangle shown below?

F. $\dfrac{10}{\sqrt{2}}$

G. $5\sqrt{2}$

H. 10

J. $10\sqrt{2}$

K. 20

$\dfrac{10}{\sqrt{2}}$

50. Caleb decides to string a clothesline along the diagonal from one end of the garden to the other. The clothesline starts 1 foot off the ground at one end, and ends 6 feet off the ground at the other end of the diagonal. What is the total length of the clothesline, in feet?

F. 10

G. $10\sqrt{2}$

H. 15

J. 20

K. 26

51. Caleb no longer wants daffodils or lilies and hires Miu, a carpenter, to build rectangular wooden decks over the daffodils and lilies in his garden. She plans to cover the areas with planks of wood that are 0.2 feet high by 0.5 feet wide by 2.5 feet long to make the deck. What is the minimum number of planks that she will need?

A. 10

B. 20

C. 25

D. 30

E. 50

Use the following information to answer questions 49-51.

Caleb is planting a 10-foot-by-10-foot garden with different flowers, as shown in the figure below. He decides to plant daffodils (D), lilies (L), and pansies (P).

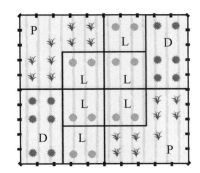

49. What is the area, to the nearest square foot, in which Caleb can plant pansies?

A. 17

B. 25

C. 38

D. 45

E. 75

52. What is the measure of each interior angle in the regular hexagon shown below?

F. 60°

G. 80°

H. 100°

J. 110°

K. 120°

GO ON TO THE NEXT PAGE.

53. If $\dfrac{a}{b} = \dfrac{x - \frac{1}{2}}{x + \frac{1}{3}}$ and $x \neq -\dfrac{1}{3}$, which of the following expressions is equal to ab?

   I. $\ x^2 - \dfrac{1}{6}x - \dfrac{1}{6}$

   II. $\ x^2 - \dfrac{1}{6}$

   III. $\ x^2 + \dfrac{1}{2}x - \dfrac{1}{6}$

   A. I only
   B. II only
   C. III only
   D. I and II
   E. II and III

54. The diagram of a circular target is shown below. The center circle has a radius of 5 cm, and each larger circle has a radius 1 cm larger than the previous circle. Which area is the smallest?

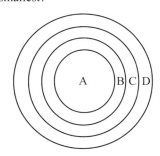

   F. A
   G. B
   H. C
   J. D
   K. The three outer areas are equal in size.

55. Points A, B, C, and D lie on a line. A man starts at point A and walks to point B. He then continues 300 m to point C. After, he walks 400 m back past point B to point D. If his total trip was 900 m, how far apart are points A and D?

   A. 100 m
   B. 200 m
   C. 300 m
   D. 500 m
   E. 1000 m

56. If $\tan \theta = \sqrt{3}$ and $\cos \theta = \dfrac{1}{2}$, what is $\sin \theta$?

   F. $\dfrac{\sqrt{3}}{2}$

   G. $\dfrac{2}{\sqrt{3}}$

   H. $2\sqrt{3}$

   J. $\sqrt{\dfrac{3}{2}}$

   K. $\sqrt{3}$

57. Alan has a square backyard with an area of 64 squares meters. He wants to build the largest possible circula pool in this backyard. What is the area, in square meter of the largest possible pool that Alan can build?

   A. 4π
   B. 8π
   C. 16π
   D. 32π
   E. 64π

58. A local band releases their latest album on cassette tape They decorate each tape with a sticker that covers th entire surface except for the circular shaded region shown in the figure below. If the measurements are i inches, what is the area of the sticker to the nearest tent of an inch?

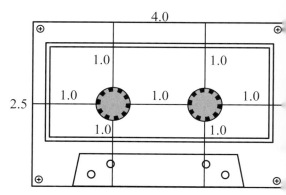

   F. 8.4
   G. 9.2
   H. 9.6
   J. 9.8
   K. 10.0

GO ON TO THE NEXT PAGE.

Practice Test

59. Which of the following number lines represents the solution of the inequality $1 < \dfrac{1}{x}$?

A.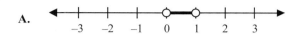

B.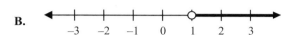

C.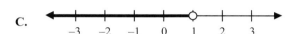

D.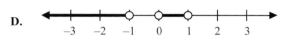

E.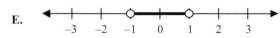

60. Both of the curves graphed below are variants of the same base function, $y = a \cdot \sin[k(x - d)] + c$. What changes were made to $f(x)$ to yield $g(x)$?

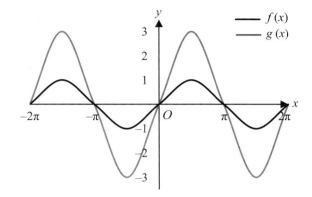

F. a increases

G. a decreases

H. c increases

J. k increases

K. d decreases

END OF TEST 2.

STOP! DO NOT TURN THE PAGE UNTIL YOU ARE TOLD TO DO SO.

DO NOT RETURN TO THE PREVIOUS TEST.

Reading Test
35 Minutes—40 Questions

DIRECTIONS: There are multiple passages in this test. Each one is accompanied by several questions. After reading a passage, choose the best answer to every question and fill in the matching circle on your scoring sheet. You can refer back to the passages as often as necessary.

Passage I

Prose Fiction: This passage is adapted from the story "David's Haircut" by Ken Elkes. The story depicts a boy going to get his haircut with his father accompanying him (©2016 Ken Elkes).

When David steps out of the front door he is blinded for a moment by the white, fizzing sunlight and reaches instinctively for his dad's hand.

It's the first really warm day of the year, an
5 unexpected heat that bridges the cusp between spring and summer. Father and son are on their way to the barbershop, something they have always done together.

Always, the routine is the same. "It's about time we got that mop of yours cut," David's dad will say.
10 "Perhaps I should do it. Where are those shears, Janet?"

Sometimes his dad chases him round the living room, pretending to cut off his ears. When he was young David used to get too excited and start crying, scared that maybe he really would lose his ears, but he has long
15 since grown out of that.

Mr. Samuels' barbershop is in a long room above the chip shop, reached by a steep flight of stairs. There is a groove worn in each step by the men who climb and descend in a regular stream. David follows his father,
20 annoyed that he cannot make each step creak like his old man can.

David loves the barbershop—it's like nowhere else he goes. Black and white photographs of men with various out-of-fashion hairstyles hang above a picture
25 rail at the end of the room, where two barber's chairs are bolted to the floor. They are heavy, old-fashioned chairs with foot pumps that hiss and chatter as Mr. Samuels adjusts the height of the seat. At the back of the room sit the customers.

30 When it is David's turn for a cut, Mr. Samuels places a wooden board covered with a piece of oxblood red leather across the arms of the chair, so that the barber doesn't have to stoop to cut the boy's hair. David scrambles up onto the bench.

35 "The rate you're shooting up, you won't need this soon, you'll be sat in the chair," the barber says.

"Wow," says David, squirming round to look at his dad, forgetting that he can see him through the mirror. "Dad, Mr. Samuels said I could be sitting in the chair
40 soon, not just on the board!"

"So I hear," his father replies, not looking up from the paper. "I expect Mr. Samuels will start charging me more for your hair then."

"At least double the price," says Mr. Samuels,
45 winking at David.

Finally David's dad looks up from his newspaper and glances into the mirror, seeing his son looking back at him. He smiles.

"Wasn't so long ago when I had to lift you onto that
50 board because you couldn't climb up there yourself," he says.

"They don't stay young for long do they, kids," Mr. Samuels declares. All the men in the shop nod in agreement. David nods too.

55 In the mirror he sees a little head sticking out of a long nylon cape that Mr. Samuels has swirled around him and folded into his collar with a wedge of cotton wool. Occasionally he steals glances at the barber as he works. He smells a mixture of stale sweat and aftershave
60 as the barber moves around him, combing and snipping, combing and snipping.

David feels like he is in another world, noiseless except for the scuffing of the barber's shoes on the linoleum and the snap of his scissors. In the reflection
65 from the window he can see the barber's careful movements.

GO ON TO THE NEXT PAGE.

Sleepily, his eyes drop to the front of the cape where his hair falls with the same softness as snow, and he imagines sitting in the chair just like the men and older
70 boys, the special bench left leaning against the wall in the corner.

When Mr. Samuels has finished, David hops down from the seat, rubbing the itchy hair from his face. Looking down he sees his own thick, blonde hair
75 scattered among the browns, greys, and blacks of the men who have sat in the chair before him. For a moment he wants to reach down and gather up the broken blonde locks, to separate them from the others, but he does not have time.

80 The sun is still strong when they reach the pavement outside the shop, but it is less fiery now, already beginning to drop from its zenith.

"I tell you what, lad, let's get some fish and chips to take home, save your mum from cooking tea," says
85 David's dad and turns up the street.

The youngster is excited and grabs his dad's hand. The thick-skinned fingers close gently around his and David is surprised to find, warming in his father's palm, a lock of his own hair.

1. Within the passage, the father's statements, "Perhaps I should do it. Where are those shears, Janet?" (line 10) suggest that:

   A. David's father usually cuts David's hair.
   B. David's mother usually cuts David's hair.
   C. David's father usually jokes that he will cut David's hair.
   D. David's mother usually takes David to the barber's to get his hair cut.

2. As it is used in line 13, the word *excited* most nearly means:

   F. enthusiastic.
   G. thrilled.
   H. angry.
   J. frightened.

3. It can reasonably be inferred that David is "annoyed that he cannot make each step creak" because David:

   A. wants to be like his father.
   B. is a naturally irritable person.
   C. has always dreamt of being tall and athletic.
   D. finds the sound of steps creaking satisfying.

4. David's attitude toward his father can best be characterized as:

   F. cautious and intrepid.
   G. polite and distant.
   H. admiring and fond.
   J. reverent and fearful.

5. The passage suggests that David nods in line 54 because he:

   A. agrees with Mr. Samuels' insight.
   B. seeks to copy the older men in the shop.
   C. is lost in thought.
   D. wants Mr. Samuels to resume cutting his hair.

6. Details in the passage suggest that, for David, Mr. Samuels' barbershop is:

   F. a new place that intimidates him.
   G. a memorable place that has grown a bit dull.
   H. a novel place that fills him with curiosity.
   J. a familiar place that has maintained its wonder.

7. The passage describes Mr. Samuels with the repeated phrase "combing and snipping, combing and snipping" (lines 60-61) to suggest that Mr. Samuels:

   A. combed and snipped David's hair exactly twice.
   B. worked on David's hair with expressive gestures.
   C. cut David's hair with repetitive and practiced movements.
   D. was becoming drowsy as he was cutting David's hair.

8. The comparison between David's hair and snow is included to imply that, like snow, David's hair:

   F. is light in color.
   G. feels cold to the touch.
   H. is plentiful.
   J. falls lightly.

9. The author details how David's father's "thick-skinned fingers close gently around his" (line 87) primarily to:

   A. suggest David's father's age and maturity in comparison to David's.
   B. characterize David's father as tough and resilient.
   C. identify a physical trait that David and David's father share.
   D. indicate David's father's physical weakness.

GO ON TO THE NEXT PAGE.

10. The author's purpose at the end of the passage in depicting David's father holding a lock of David's hair could be to show all of the following about David's father EXCEPT that he:

F. becomes attached to items easily.

G. is sentimental about David's young age.

H. anticipates that David will not always be young.

J. appreciates their father-son haircut outings as much as David does.

Passage II

Social Science: This passage is adapted from the article "An Early Expression of Democracy, the U.S. Patent System is Out of Step with Today's Citizens" by Shobita Parthasarathy (©2015 Shobita Parthasarathy).

The U.S. patent system, first established in the late 18th and early 19th centuries, was made to be fair and equal—particularly compared to the European patent systems of the time. The U.S. encouraged great
5 participation in the system by keeping patent application fees low and creating public displays of patented technologies to inspire others to create, too.

The U.S. system, in other words, made patents, innovation, and entrepreneurship a possibility for every
10 citizen. The idea was to increase innovation, which would help the economy and eventually society as a whole. In many ways, these efforts were successful. Patent application rates grew through the 19th and 20th centuries, and in 2014, the U.S. gave out more than
15 300,000 patents, for things ranging from photocopiers to solar panels. Indeed, many industries have said they owe their success to this early patent system.

This approach has also gone global, buoyed by international legal agreements intended to make it easier
20 for inventions to travel, for inventors to collect rewards across borders, and for markets to span nations. This system has held for hundreds of years and is built on the idea that encouraging innovation through patents will ultimately be good for everyone. It sees every citizen as
25 a potential inventor, and believes that if laws help inventors, they automatically help the public.

But the relationship between the patent system and the people has changed in recent decades. Public health activists have launched lawsuits saying that, rather than
30 making technology easier to get to, patents create monopolies that make good health unaffordable for a lot of people. In 2013, a group of patients, health care workers, and scientists challenged patents on genes linked to breast and ovarian cancer at the U.S. Supreme

35 Court. They argued the patents had led to expensive and low-quality genetic tests available only through one company. Meanwhile, small farmers have organized protests against seed patents, suggesting they speed up big-company control of agriculture in ways that are bad
40 for their businesses, for innovation, for buyers, and for the environment.

Other groups have prompted legal hearings and media campaigns arguing that patents justify working with and earning money from morally controversial
45 areas of research. These campaigns began as early as the 1980s, when environmental activists, animals rights groups, and religious leaders challenged the patenting of genetically engineered animals. They worried that by turning these animals into products, the patent system
50 would change our relationship with the natural environment.

Patent system officials and lawyers tend to view these criticisms as seriously missing the point. They argue that these citizen critics do not understand how the patent
55 system works: the system is focused simply on recognizing the novelty, creativity, and usefulness of inventions. This attitude is also built into the rules and processes of the system, which make it nearly impossible for average citizens to participate, except by applying for
60 patents.

Is it possible to change the system to take into account the newly engaged public? Consider, for example, the pan-European patent system, which is in many ways quite similar to the U.S. patent system. In
65 recent years, it has been open to public participation in its official proceedings, and considered moral and social-economic concerns in its decisions. It has been particularly sensitive to citizens' concerns about patents on software and biotechnology.

70 In 2007, the European Patent Office invited a group of its critics to participate in developing a report that identified the challenges and opportunities it would face over the next 30 years. In response, governments across Europe have followed and taken steps to limit patent
75 monopolies that might hurt public health and agriculture.

It is worth recognizing that while the U.S. system was first created to be a democratic improvement on the European systems of the time, today's pan-European patent system is far ahead of the U.S. patent system in
80 terms of its public engagement and its attention to the issues that citizens care about. If the U.S. patent system wants to keep the public's trust, it has to realize that the 21st-century citizen is very different from the 18th-

GO ON TO THE NEXT PAGE.

century citizen. Today's citizen cares about the moral
85 and social-economic consequences of patents and the
technologies they cover, and is not satisfied to assume
that the system's benefits eventually make their way to
the majority of the population. She also wants to have an
active role in making decisions.

90   Taking this citizen seriously will require significant
patent system reforms, including increasing opportunities
for the public to participate in patent decision-making,
allowing more legal and bureaucratic challenges on behalf
of the public interest, and including more emphasis on
95 moral and social-economic implications into our patent
laws.

11. What is the main purpose of the passage?

  A. To demonstrate the excellence of the U.S. patent
system

  B. To compare and contrast the U.S. patent system
with several European patent systems

  C. To emphasize that the U.S. patent system should
respond to public concerns

  D. To show how patent systems commonly fail to
satisfy public demands

12. According to the passage, the late 18th and early 19th
century U.S. patent system accomplished all of the
following EXCEPT:

  F. making patents affordable by keeping application
fees low.

  G. encouraging economic growth.

  H. championing a select few highly capable inventors.

  J. inspiring later international patent agreements.

13. The term *buoyed* in line 18 most nearly means:

  A. floated.

  B. supported.

  C. uplifted.

  D. emboldened.

14. Both health care professionals and small farmers protest
the current U.S. patent system because it contributes to:

  F. patented material being shared too widely with
other businesses.

  G. heavy control of patents by a limited number of
patent-holders.

  H. violations of guaranteed natural rights.

  J. irreparable damage to the environment.

15. The main function of the fourth and fifth paragraphs
(lines 27-51) is to:

  A. prove that U.S. citizens in the late 18th and 19th
century had concerns about the patent system.

  B. emphasize how the current U.S. patent system
honors the principles of the earlier U.S. patent
system.

  C. assert that the U.S. patent system and medicine are
fundamentally incompatible.

  D. show reasons for and examples of public resistance
to the current U.S. patent system.

16. It is reasonable to infer that patent system officials and
lawyers would respond to criticisms about the moral
implications of the U.S. patent system by saying that:

  F. improvements to the patent system will take time to
implement.

  G. such criticisms misunderstand the structure and
goals of the patent system.

  H. critics should take up their concerns by producing
written complaints.

  J. moral concerns are completely irrelevant to law.

17. As it is used in line 68, the word *sensitive* means:

  A. responsive.

  B. tender.

  C. touchy.

  D. sentient.

18. The author's tone can be characterized as one of:

  F. skeptical disdain.

  G. thoughtful interest.

  H. frenzied concern.

  J. detached observation.

19. The author suggests that compared to the U.S. patent
system, the pan-European patent system is:

  A. an improvement that better takes into account the
public's moral and social concerns.

  B. a near-identical system that also struggles with
addressing public opinions.

  C. an inefficient attempt to build on the basics of the
U.S. patent system.

  D. an institution that further alienates the public.

GO ON TO THE NEXT PAGE.

20. By stating that a possible reform to the U.S. patent system could start "allowing more legal and bureaucratic challenges on behalf of the public interest" (lines 93-94), the author suggests that the U.S. patent system should:

    F. take into account the opinions of non-American politicians.

    G. be more difficult to decipher for the average person.

    H. allow public concerns about patent law to have more influence.

    J. feature more prominently in the government's public speeches.

Passage III

Humanities: This passage is adapted from the article "Picasso the...sculptor? Disputed purchase brings attention to lesser-known aspect of his art" by Enrique Mallen (©2016 Enrique Mallen).

A bust of Picasso's mistress, Marie-Thérèse Walter, is currently being exhibited at New York's Museum of Modern Art. Beyond the astronomical (disputed) sale price—upwards of $106 million—it's also significant
5 news because it's relatively rare for attention to be lavished upon one of Picasso's sculptures.

Pablo Picasso's sculptures remain a mystery to many. The prolific Picasso is probably best known as a painter, although his drawings, ceramics, engravings,
10 and lithographs are also often highlighted in museums, exhibitions, and auctions. What hasn't been very well publicized is the substantial contribution to modern art that Picasso made as a sculptor. In fact, *Picasso Sculpture*, an ongoing exhibition at New York's
15 Museum of Modern Art, is the first time in nearly 20 years that a museum is directing attention squarely on the artist's sculptures.

While nearly all his early experience, training, and prodigious energy went into painting, some have even
20 argued that Picasso was more naturally a sculptor. Admittedly, Picasso's sculptures make up a small fraction of the estimated 50,000 works the artist produced in his lifetime. There's still debate over how many Picasso produced. The famous Picasso biographer
25 Roland Penrose included 284 entries in his extensive exhibition of Picasso sculptures, and Picasso scholar Werner Spies identified 664 items in his catalogue raisonné. Meanwhile, the Online Picasso Project contains 796 sculptures.

30   One reason Picasso's sculptures remain a myster to many is that the artist was averse to selling them According to Trinity College professor Michae Fitzgerald, "trained as a painter, [Picasso] rarel hesitated to sell his paintings." On the other hand, "H
35 developed a deep fondness for his sculptures, an treasured them as if they were members of his family. In fact, Picasso didn't agree to a full-scale exhibition c his sculptures until 1966, when he participated in th large Paris retrospective *Hommage à Picasso*, whic
40 would go on to London and New York in 1967. Onl then did the public fully realize that Picasso had bee creating—and experimenting—in this medium.

"This is the moment Picasso agrees for the first tim to let his sculptures depart from his studio en masse,
45 Anne Umland, curator of painting and sculpture at Ne York's Museum of Modern Art, explained at the time "It's the first time the public has the chance to see th scope and range of his sculptures." Because Picass wasn't willing to exhibit his sculptures until later in hi
50 life, they often went undocumented in the (purportedly comprehensive publications of his work.

While Picasso had been formally trained as a painte (and earned most of his income from selling paintings) sculpture was a medium where the artist coul
55 experiment freely and break established rules withou fear of damaging his reputation or hurting his bottom line. His Cubist sculptures of 1912–1913 wer particularly innovative. As *The Guardian*'s Jason Farag put it, they were a "thunderclap," with the artist upending
60 what, at the time, was the traditional method of sculpture chiseling away at a block of material to achieve a new form. Instead, by fusing pieces of cardboard, Picass "built" his *Guitare* (1912). Constructing objects from sheets of common materials like cardboard, metal, o
65 wood, the artist was able to connect his art to th everyday world, blurring the boundaries between art an life.

For art historian Yve-Alain Bois, the role played by this sculpture lies precisely in its full exploration of th
70 nonrepresentational value of sculpture. In other words he was able to use arbitrary objects and materials t create pictorial signifiers. As the artist once declared, h wanted to "trick the mind"—not simply fool the eye.

In the 1950s, Picasso would return to plana
75 sculptures. These would also start with paper o cardboard models that the artist would cut out and fold He would then have them transferred to sheet metal which he would either paint or leave unpainted, with th

surface of the metal exposed. The play of folds, hollow
80 spaces, and polychromatic tones serves to suggest relief.
Folding and cutting allowed Picasso to superimpose
different points of view and still retain the frontal view;
meanwhile, depth is suggested by the contrast between
filled and empty spaces.

85   Judging by the critics' glowing reception of the
current New York exhibition featuring Picasso, we may
start to see Picasso's sculptures getting the attention they
truly deserve. Perhaps Picasso's sculptures will go the
route of his revolutionary paintings from the late 1960s
90 and early 1970s, including works like *Le vieil homme
assis*, which were widely panned when they were first
exhibited at Avignon's Palais des Papes in 1973.
Nonetheless, these would go on to have a profound
influence on later generations of artists. Today, they're
95 some of the most sought-after Picassos in the world.

21. The main purpose of the passage can best be described
as:

A. arguing that Picasso's sculptures are superior to his
paintings.

B. detailing the sales processes for Picasso's various
sculptures.

C. highlighting a lesser-known area of Picasso's body
of work.

D. discussing some of Picasso's most well-known
sculptures.

22. The author's attitude toward Picasso's sculptures can
best be characterized as:

F. enthusiastic.

G. baffled.

H. dismissive.

J. amused.

23. The author believes Picasso's sculptures did not first
achieve success primarily because:

A. they were inferior in form to his paintings.

B. Picasso was initially hesitant to sell them.

C. art critics were more interested in his paintings.

D. not enough exhibits were open to displaying
sculptures.

24. According to the sixth paragraph (lines 52-67),
compared to his work with paintings, Picasso's work
with sculptures:

F. was not yet ready for public consumption and
criticism.

G. allowed for greater experimentation with less risk.

H. was a much more lucrative if less enjoyable
endeavor.

J. took more time and energy but offered fewer
payoffs.

25. As it is used in line 44, the phrase *depart from his studio
en masse* most nearly refers to:

A. Picasso's destruction of the majority of his
sculptures.

B. the widespread private sale of Picasso's sculptures
after an exhibition.

C. Picasso's participation in a public exhibition.

D. the decision Picasso made to focus primarily on
paintings.

26. The passage claims that Picasso's sculptures differed
from more traditional forms in that his sculptures:

F. focused on everyday rather than religious subjects.

G. involved conversion of a block of material into a
new form.

H. incorporated paintings into their display.

J. consisted of a fusion of different materials.

27. As it is used in line 85, the word *glowing* most nearly
means:

A. lighted.

B. positive.

C. incandescent.

D. radiant.

28. According to the passage, like some of his paintings,
Picasso's sculptures may:

F. attain recognition even if not immediately hailed
for their achievements.

G. cycle between fame and obscurity for a significant
amount of time.

H. face disproportionate criticism that eventually
destroys their potential sales.

J. achieve immediate fame upon initial presentation
in art galleries.

GO ON TO THE NEXT PAGE.

29. The author calls the sale price of one of Picasso's sculptures "astronomical" in line 3 because it:

    A. is extraordinarily high for a piece of artwork.

    B. sold for a price greater than any other Museum of Modern Art piece.

    C. is disproportionate to the quality of the piece.

    D. reflects an unsustainable price that later fell through.

30. The passage identifies Picasso's sculptures as being both:

    F. shocking and overpraised.

    G. revolutionary and underappreciated.

    H. conventional and obscure.

    J. inexpensive and popular.

Passage IV

Natural Science: Passage A is adapted from the article "Primed for Battle: Helping Plants Fight Off Pathogens by Enhancing Their Immune Systems" by Jeannette Rapicavoli (©2015 by Jeannette Rapicavoli). Passage B is adapted from "Hacking Plant 'Blood Vessels' Could Avert Food Crisis" by John Runions (©2013 by John Runions).

Passage A by Jeannette Rapicavoli

A novel area of research in the war against plant pathogens focuses on enhancing the plant's natural immune system. If a plant can fight off an infection on its own, we can reduce the amount of pesticides needed.
5 Just as children are vaccinated to protect against future diseases, plants can be "immunized" against pathogens by plant pathologists, who aim to strengthen the plants' immune defenses against invaders. This method of priming plants' immune systems could be a safe and
10 effective way to save some of the global harvest currently lost to diseases.

Plants are naturally exposed to a variety of pathogenic microbes, such as bacteria, fungi, and viruses. Plants have a multi-tiered immune system that
15 helps them fight off these microorganisms. It works in a manner very similar to the human immune system. Plants detect pathogens by recognizing microbial "patterns." These are unique characteristics of the type of microbe that the plant has evolved to recognize as "non-self."

20 One of our major research goals is to harness these patterns to prime the plant immune system, creating enhanced protection against pathogenic microbes, in lieu of traditional chemical control methods. The principle of "defense priming" is very similar to how we develop

25 vaccines to treat human diseases. A vaccine works by acting as a pathogen impostor. It tricks the immune system into thinking it's being attacked, which stimulates defense responses, such as the production of antibodies. This creates a defense memory, allowing the
30 immune system to remember a particular pathogen if the body encounters it in the future. It can then respond swiftly and robustly, thanks to its primed memory from the vaccine.

We can apply this same principle to a plant-
35 pathogen relationship. For example, once we've identified a pathogen's pattern of interest, we work to isolate and purify it. This step is like manufacturing the vaccine. We can then inoculate the plant with the purified pattern—for instance, by injecting it into the
40 stem or leaves with a syringe. The goal is to stimulate the plant's natural immune response, resulting in a faster or stronger defense response the next time the plant encounters that pathogen.

Primed plants display enhanced tolerance to
45 infection, which is often characterized by fewer symptoms and reduced pathogen populations within the plant. Although primed plants haven't yet been implemented on a large-scale basis in commercial agriculture, scientists are actively conducting research on the use of defense priming
50 in both greenhouse and field settings for protection against bacteria, viruses, and fungi.

Furthermore, the primed state is durable and can be maintained long after the initial stimulus. Current research has also shown that plants can pass on this defense
55 memory to their descendants, providing multigenerational protection without any genetic modification. Further research is needed to improve our understanding of the molecular mechanisms behind this phenomenon, but defense priming looks likely to be a valuable and
60 promising tool in the future of sustainable agriculture.

Passage B by John Runions

In a recent paper, some of the world's leading plant biologists show that, by hacking how plants transport key nutrients into plant cells, we could solve the impending food crisis.

65 Each plant is made of billions of cells, all of which are surrounded by membranes. The pores in these membranes are lined with membrane transporters, which ferry nutrients that plants capture from soil with the help of roots. What scientists have learned is that if such
70 membrane transporters are tweaked, they can enhance plant productivity. When these tweaks are applied to crops, they can produce plants that are high in calories

GO ON TO THE NEXT PAGE.

rich in certain nutrients, or able to better fight pests. All these methods increase food production while using
75 fewer resources.

For example, over two billion people suffer from iron or zinc deficiency in their diets. Simple genetic modification increases the amount of membrane transporters that ferry these minerals. Such plants, when
80 ready for harvest, can have as much as four times the concentration of iron, compared to that of common crop variety.

Another key issue is that disease-causing microorganisms, pathogens, manipulate a plant's
85 functioning and consume the sucrose it produces for energy. Most crops have membrane transporters called SWEETs that move sucrose made by leaves from photosynthesis to other regions where it may be stored. Plant pathogens have evolved to manipulate SWEET
90 genes so that sugars are moved to cells where the pathogens can feed on the goods.

Now scientists have found a way of disrupting this pathogen-induced manipulation by a method called RNA-silencing. This reduces or eliminates the
95 pathogens' ability to feed on the plants' hard work, and in turn helps increase plant productivity.

Researchers have been quietly chugging away in labs working on making such radical improvements to crops. Breeding of plants, a form of untailored genetic
100 modification that bestowed most of the benefits to agriculture a generation ago, is not able to keep up with the pace of change required for an ever-increasing demand for food. That is why it is important that we understand the science behind the process of tinkering
105 with specific genes before making any rash judgments.

32. The language of the first paragraph of Passage A, including "war," "fight off," and "invaders," is most likely intended to convey a sense of:

F. the violence of different plant species towards one another in nature.

G. the possible military uses for the scientists' research.

H. the high stakes involved for plants defending against pathogens.

J. the sophisticated inner machinery of plant pathogens.

33. As it is used in line 1, the word *novel* most closely means:

A. new.

B. literary.

C. narrative.

D. unique.

34. Which of the following best summarizes one of the goals of the researchers mentioned in Passage A?

F. Help plants use their natural immune system to protect against pathogens

G. Improve the chemical control methods of plant protection to ensure good harvests

H. Determine why some plant pathogens are more susceptible to viruses than others

J. Study how plants pass on defense memory to their offspring

Questions 31-34 ask about Passage A.

31. The primary purpose of Passage A is to:

A. argue for using more sustainable agricultural techniques in the future.

B. discuss the benefits of defense priming in protecting plants.

C. show the mechanisms by which most pathogens attract plants.

D. demonstrate the resilience of plants in the face of pesticides.

Questions 35-38 ask about Passage B.

35. According to Passage B, one reason that scientists may manipulate plant genes is to:

A. ensure that plants obtain the proper nutrients from the soil.

B. increase the value of crops so farmers can make a greater profit.

C. produce plants that have increased nutritional value.

D. help protect plants against natural predators like birds.

GO ON TO THE NEXT PAGE.

36. The author of Passage B uses the example of iron and zinc deficiency to:

   F. show that genetic modifications cannot solve all hunger problems.

   G. highlight an issue with which many plants suffer.

   H. underline the author's previous research into ways that plant modifications affect vitamin uptake.

   J. demonstrate one potential area where genetic manipulation of plants may be helpful.

37. The final paragraph of Passage B serves primarily to:

   A. summarize the author's point that plants have a variety of defenses against pathogens.

   B. argue that global hunger is the most pressing issue of the modern era.

   C. suggest why scientists must study and comprehend the genetic modification of plants.

   D. explain the mechanisms behind recent developments in genome editing.

38. The word *ferry*, as it is used in line 68, most nearly means:

   F. ship.

   G. pack.

   H. transport.

   J. travel.

Questions 39 and 40 ask about both passages.

39. Both Passage A and Passage B view potential modifications of plants:

   A. warily.

   B. favorably.

   C. skeptically.

   D. joyously.

40. Passage A and Passage B both discuss:

   F. the impact of genetic modifications on the food supply.

   G. recent policies surrounding genetic modifications.

   H. economic considerations connected to genetically modified crops.

   J. manipulation of plants to protect against pathogens.

END OF TEST 3

STOP! DO NOT TURN THE PAGE UNTIL YOU ARE TOLD TO DO SO

DO NOT RETURN TO THE PREVIOUS TEST

Science Test

35 Minutes—40 Questions

DIRECTIONS: There are several passages in this test, and each is accompanied by several questions. After reading a passage, choose the best answer to each question and fill in the corresponding oval on your answer document. You may refer to the passages as often as necessary.

You are NOT permitted to use a calculator on this test.

Passage I

Sound is a *mechanical wave*, a vibration that moves through a medium at a certain velocity. Students measured the velocity of sound in various media and at different temperatures to determine a relationship between medium, temperature, and the velocity of sound.

Experiment 1

A cylindrical tank with a length of 20 cm and a radius of 4 cm was filled with 1 L of a given liquid at 20°C. A sound velocity probe was inserted into one end of the tank. A sound pulse generator was inserted in the other end. The tank was plugged after it was filled. Ten sound pulses were sent through each given liquid and the average velocity was calculated (see Table 1). The tank was washed with distilled water before this process was repeated with each liquid.

Table 1	
Medium	Velocity (m/s)
Acetic acid	1150
Water	1482
Salt water	1522
Kerosene	1320
Mercury	1438
Octane	1171
Oil	1461

Experiment 2

Experiment 1 was repeated with a cylinder of a given solid at 20°C, with a length of 20 cm and a radius of 4 cm. A sound velocity probe was connected to one end of the cylinder and a sound pulse generator to the other. Ten sound pulses were sent through each given solid and the average velocity was calculated (see Table 2).

Table 2	
Medium	Velocity (m/s)
Brick	4208
Cork	400
Quartz	5980
Glass	3962
Copper	4589
Rubber	100
Hardwood	3954

Experiment 3

Experiment 1 was repeated with 1 L of air in the same cylindrical tank. A thermometer was also inserted into one end of the tank before it was plugged. The air in the tank was heated by immersion in a water bath or cooled in an ice bath. Ten sound pulses were sent through the tank of air at each given temperature and the average velocities were calculated (see Figure 1).

GO ON TO THE NEXT PAGE.

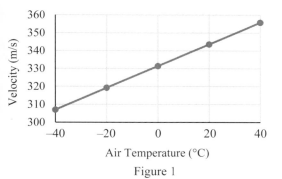

Velocity (m/s) vs Air Temperature (°C)

Figure 1

Experimental design adapted from Martin Greenspan and Carroll E. Tschiegg, "Speed of Sound in Water by a Direct Method." ©1957 by JRNIStand 59.4.

1. Based on Experiment 3, as air temperature increases, sound velocity:

   A. increases only.

   B. decreases only.

   C. increases, then decreases.

   D. decreases, then increases.

2. A *sound dampener* is a material that reduces sound velocity. Which of the following media would be the most effective sound dampener?

   F. Quartz

   G. Air

   H. Rubber

   J. Oil

3. The students conclude from their results that sound travels faster in solids than in liquids. According to Experiments 1 and 2, which two media are the exceptions to the students' conclusion?

   A. Oil and salt water

   B. Salt water and cork

   C. Cork and rubber

   D. Quartz and rubber

4. Assuming that water is frozen at 0°C and is gaseous at 100°C, at which of the following temperatures would the velocity of sound in water be the greatest?

   F. 120°C

   G. 80°C

   H. 40°C

   J. −20°C

5. *Elasticity* (E) is the ability of a material to recover its shape after deformation due to vibration, pressure, or other forces. *Density* (ρ) is the mass per unit volume of a material. The *velocity* of sound (v) in a given medium can be given by the following equation:

$$v = \sqrt{\frac{E}{\rho}}$$

If the density of copper is 8950 kg/m³ and the density of acetic acid is 1049 kg/m³, then the velocity of sound in copper is higher than the velocity of sound in acetic acid because copper:

   A. has a much lower density than acetic acid.

   B. has a much lower elasticity than acetic acid.

   C. has a much greater density than acetic acid.

   D. has a much greater elasticity than acetic acid.

6. Suppose Students A and B stand 50 m from Student C. Students B and C each hold a copper cup, and the two cups are attached by a copper wire measuring 50 m. If Student A shouts at Student C and Student B shouts into the copper cup, who will Student C hear first?

   F. Student C will hear Student A first.

   G. Student C will hear Student B first.

   H. Student C will hear Student A and Student B at the same time.

   J. Student C will hear Student A but will not hear Student B.

7. Suppose that another group of students attempts to replicate the results of Experiment 1. This group of students forgets to plug the cylindrical tank. Were the average velocities higher in the original or in the replicated Experiment 1?

   A. In the original, because the sound traveled through liquid and no gas, and the velocity of sound is higher in liquid than in gas.

   B. In the original, because the sound traveled through liquid and some gas, and the velocity of sound is lower in liquid than in gas.

   C. In the replication, because the sound traveled through liquid and no gas, and the velocity of sound is higher in liquid than in gas.

   D. In the replication, because the sound traveled through liquid and some gas, and the velocity of sound is lower in liquid than in gas.

GO ON TO THE NEXT PAGE.

Passage II

Researchers studied heavy metals in the water, soil, and root systems of mangrove forests to determine if the metals posed ecological risks.

Study 1

The mangrove forests bordered a *mud flat*, which is an area of seafloor left uncovered at low tide. Researchers used the unvegetated mud flat as a control. The mangrove forest was divided into two habitats, each dominated by one species of mangrove: white or black (see Diagram 1). For each habitat, researchers established three sample locations where they collected 15 overlying water samples in acid-washed plastic jars, 15 soil sediment samples in acid-washed plastic pipes, 12 seedling samples, and 15 root samples by plastic scraper. The samples were filtered and tested to determine the pH and conductivity of the overlying water, the soil sediment, and the root systems (see Table 1).

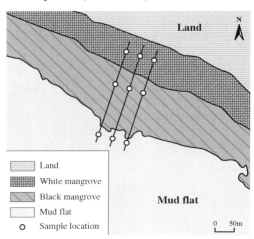

Diagram 1

Mangrove habitat	White	Black	Mud flat
Table 1			
Mangrove habitat	White	Black	Mud flat
Overlying water			
pH	8.21	7.98	8.25
Conductivity (S/m)	1.66	1.44	1.64
Soil sediment			
pH	6.55	6.86	7.06
Conductivity (S/m)	0.51	0.33	0.36
Root system			
pH	6.95	7.18	n/a
Conductivity (S/m)	0.70	0.46	n/a

Note: S/m = Siemens/meter = $kg^{-1}m^{-3}s^3A^2$

Study 2

The same samples tested in Study 1 were tested using mass spectroscopy to determine the concentrations of five heavy metals: chromium (Cr), nickel (Ni), copper (Cu), arsenic (As), and cadmium (Cd). The concentrations (in µg/g) for each heavy metal in each habitat are shown in Table 2.

Table 2			
Mangrove habitat	White	Black	Mud flat
Overlying water			
Cr	20	10	10
Ni	11	10	9
Cu	10	11	9
As	10	14	4
Cd	0.01	0.02	0.05
Soil sediment			
Cr	90	43	74
Ni	52	24	38
Cu	102	52	74
As	98	76	52
Cd	0.96	0.88	0.67
Root system			
Cr	60	50	n/a
Ni	23	18	n/a
Cu	25	51	n/a
As	36	29	n/a
Cd	0.32	0.18	n/a

Study 3

The researchers collected the following data to determine whether the concentrations of heavy metals (in µg/g) in the mangrove forests would have adverse effects on the organisms in each habitat (see Table 3). The *probable effect level* is the concentration above which adverse effects on organisms are frequently observed.

Table 3					
	Cr	Ni	Cu	As	Cd
Background Level	38.80	19.83	9.98	5.90	0.03
Probable Effect Level	111	48.60	149	33	4.98

Data adapted from Ruili Li et al, "Distribution, Fraction, and Ecological Assessment of Heavy Metals in Sediment-Plant System in Mangrove Forest, South China Sea." ©2016 by PLoS One. 10.1371/journal.pone.0147308

GO ON TO THE NEXT PAGE.

8. Which of the following mangrove habitats had the most alkaline pH, and in which part of the habitat was that pH found?

   F. Black; root system
   G. White; overlying water
   H. White; soil sediment
   J. Mud flat; overlying water

9. Why was there no data for the mud flat's root system?

   A. There was no vegetation in the mud flat.
   B. There were many different types of plants in the mud flat.
   C. There were no samples of any kind taken in the mud flat.
   D. There was animal activity in the mud flat.

10. According to Study 2, as the distance between mangrove forests and the mud flat increased, the concentration of arsenic in the soil sediment:

   F. increased only.
   G. decreased only.
   H. increased, then decreased.
   J. decreased, then increased.

11. Researchers performed Study 2 on a new sample of soil sediment. If the heavy metal profile, in μg/g, for the samples are given in the table below, from which mangrove habitat did the researchers most likely take their sample?

Cr	50
Ni	25
Cu	51
As	76
Cd	0.88

   A. Land
   B. Mud flat
   C. Black mangrove
   D. White mangrove

12. Why did the researchers wash their sample collection equipment with acid?

   F. To lower the pH of the samples
   G. To attract heavy metals to the equipment
   H. To destroy bacteria in the soil and water
   J. To ensure no contaminants were introduced to the sample

13. It was discovered that the researchers who performed the mass spectroscopy used contaminated sample containers that released trace levels of copper into the samples. Which of the following measures would correct this error?

   A. Calculate the copper concentration due to the contaminated sample containers and add it to the copper concentrations of the samples.
   B. Calculate the copper concentration due to the contaminated sample containers and subtract it from the copper concentrations of the samples.
   C. Repeat the experiment, using the contaminated samples but different sampling equipment.
   D. Repeat the experiment, using the contaminated sampling equipment but different samples.

14. The roots of the white mangrove are ground into a powder and used as an oral medicine. Based on Studies 2 and 3, is it safe to use the roots of the white mangroves found in this region as a medicine?

   F. Yes; the concentration of arsenic found in the root systems of the white mangroves did not exceed its probable effect level.
   G. Yes; all of the concentrations of heavy metals found in the root systems of the white mangroves did not exceed their probable effect levels.
   H. No; the concentration of arsenic found in the root systems of the white mangroves exceeded its probable effect level.
   J. No; all of the concentrations of heavy metals found in the root systems of the white mangroves exceeded their probable effect levels.

GO ON TO THE NEXT PAGE.

Passage III

A *satellite* is any object that orbits another object in space. Over 2,000 human-made satellites are now orbiting Earth.

All satellites orbit in an *ellipse*—an elongated circle with two focal points—and they orbit faster when they are closer to the object they are orbiting (see Figure 1). The object orbited by the satellite is usually at one of the two focal points of the satellite's elliptical orbit.

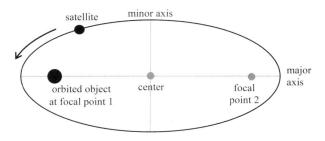

Figure 1

The *orbital period* is the time it takes the satellite to complete one orbit. The *semi-major axis* is half the length of the *major axis*, which is the distance across the long side of the elliptical orbit. For any two satellites, Kepler's Third Law states that the relationship between the orbital period (P) in years and the length of the semi-major axis (A) in Astronomical Units (AU) is constant according to the following equation:

$$\left(\frac{P_1}{P_2}\right)^2 = \left(\frac{A_1}{A_2}\right)^3$$

Students categorized six known satellites in terms of mass, average orbital height, and orbital period (see Table 1).

Table 1			
Satellite	Mass (kg)	Height (AU)	Period (yr)
ISS	4.20×10^5	2.74×10^{-6}	1.71×10^{-4}
GPS	1.47×10^3	1.35×10^{-4}	1.37×10^{-3}
Hubble	1.11×10^4	3.74×10^{-6}	1.81×10^{-4}
Spektr-R	3.60×10^3	2.01×10^{-3}	2.43×10^{-2}
Glonass-M	1.48×10^3	1.28×10^{-4}	1.28×10^{-3}

Note: 1 AU = 1.50×10^8 km.

15. According to Table 1, which of the following satellites has the greatest mass?

    A. ISS
    B. GPS
    C. Hubble
    D. Spektr-R

16. Satellites are classified in three categories based on their average orbital height: Low Earth Orbit, less than 1.34×10^{-5} AU; Medium Earth Orbit, between 1.34×10^{-5} and 5.35×10^{-4} AU; and High Earth Orbit, greater than 5.35×10^{-4} AU. Which of the following satellites would be classified as High Earth Orbit?

    F. GPS
    G. Spektr-R
    H. Glonass-M
    J. Hubble

17. According to Table 1, what is the relationship between satellite mass and orbital period?

    A. As satellite mass increases, orbital period increases.
    B. As satellite mass increases, orbital period decreases.
    C. As satellite mass increases, orbital period increases then decreases.
    D. There is no relationship between satellite mass and orbital period.

18. Suppose the students want to use Table 1 to test Kepler's Third Law. Based on the given equation and Table 1, is their approach correct?

    F. Yes; the given equation only requires the mass, which is given in Table 1.
    G. Yes; the given equation requires the period and the mass, both of which are given in Table 1.
    H. No; the given equation requires the period and the semi-major axis, and only the period is given in Table 1.
    J. No; the given equation requires the period and the height, and only the height is given in Table 1.

GO ON TO THE NEXT PAGE.

19. Suppose the orbit of the moon is analogous to Figure 1, with the moon at the position of the satellite and Earth at focal point 1. The *apogee* is the point of the moon's orbit when it is farthest from Earth. According to Figure 1, the moon's apogee is located:

A. at the left of the ellipse along the major axis.

B. at the right of the ellipse along the major axis.

C. at the top of the ellipse along the minor axis.

D. at the bottom of the ellipse along the minor axis.

20. If the moon has an average orbital period of 7.40×10^{-2} years, approximately how many times greater is the orbital period of the moon than the orbital period of the satellite with the longest orbital period in Table 1?

F. 3

G. 30

H. 300

J. 3,000

GO ON TO THE NEXT PAGE.

Passage IV

Heat tolerance is a highly desirable trait in crop plants. Researchers attempted to improve the heat tolerance of cotton and tobacco plants by introducing the heat shock protein 101 (*AtHSP101*) from the plant species *Arabidopsis thaliana*.

Study 1

Pollen are small grains that carry reproductive material from one plant to another. High temperatures inhibit the ability of tobacco pollen to produce a pollen tube, which transfers reproductive material. Researchers created 3 strains of tobacco containing *AtHSP101* in different locations in the genome (G1, G2, and G3). For comparison, they also used 2 strains of tobacco that did not contain *AtHSP101* (N1 and N2). The pollen tubes were grown from pollen grains in glass dishes filled with water. The researchers measured the lengths of the pollen tubes generated by the 5 different tobacco strains at a normal growing temperature (30°C) and at a higher temperature (60°C). The average tube lengths are shown in Figure 1.

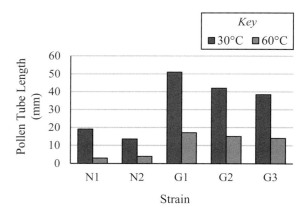

Figure 1

Study 2

Cotton plants produce *bolls*, rounded capsules that, upon opening, release cotton seeds. The researchers studied boll and seed production under high temperatures by conducting a field experiment using 1 unaltered strain of cotton plants (S1) and 1 strain of cotton plants that had the *AtHSP101* gene (S2). The researchers grew 20 plants from each strain and measured the number of bolls per plant, the number of open bolls per plant, the number of seeds per open boll, and the number of closed bolls per plant. The data were collected from Day 1 to Day 46. Daily high and low temperatures over this period are shown in Figure 2. Average boll and seed production data from each strain are shown in Table 1.

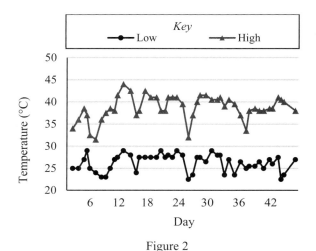

Figure 2

Table 1				
Plant Strain	Bolls/ plant	Open bolls/plant	Seeds/open boll	Closed bolls/plant
S1	22.4	11.75	18.09	10.65
S2	30.35	12.95	18.54	17.4

GO ON TO THE NEXT PAGE.

21. According to Figure 2, from Day 1 to Day 46, the daily high temperature:

    A. remained the same.

    B. decreased only.

    C. increased only.

    D. fluctuated, but with no clear trend.

22. According to Figure 1, which of the following correctly orders the 5 pollen strains from shortest average pollen tube at 30°C to longest average pollen tube at 30°C?

    F. G1, G2, G3, N1, N2

    G. N2, N1, G3, G2, G1

    H. N1, N2, G3, G2, G1

    J. N1, G1, N2, G2, G3

23. In Study 2, the researchers measured the number of seeds produced by each open boll because:

    A. seeds produce energy for the plant by absorbing sunlight.

    B. seeds absorb water for the plant.

    C. seeds allow the plant to reproduce.

    D. seeds protect the plant from predation.

24. Suppose that, while observing the pollen grains in Study 1, one of the researchers notices that the water levels in the 60°C growth dishes are significantly lower than those in the 30°C growth dishes. In order to ensure that both groups of pollen grains have equal water availability, the best solution would be to:

    F. increase the temperature of the 60°C growth dishes.

    G. remove all water from both sets of dishes.

    H. cover the dishes so that the water cannot evaporate.

    J. move the pollen grains from the 60°C growth dishes into the 30°C growth dishes and vice versa.

25. If the researchers from Study 1 had grown pollen grains at a third temperature of 80°C, the average pollen tube length of the G1 strain would most likely have been:

    A. less than 20 mm.

    B. between 20 mm and 40 mm.

    C. between 40 mm and 50 mm.

    D. greater than 50 mm.

26. One researcher hypothesizes that S2 cotton plants grown in an environment with an average daily high temperature between 35°C and 40°C will, on average, produce fewer than 38 bolls. Do the data from Study 2 support this hypothesis?

    F. Yes, because the average daily high temperature from Study 2 fell between 35°C and 40°C.

    G. Yes, because the S2 plants produced more than 38 bolls on average.

    H. No, because the average daily high temperature from Study 2 fell between 35°C and 40°C.

    J. No, because the S2 plants produced more than 38 bolls on average.

27. The *reproductive efficiency* of a cotton plant is defined as the total number of seeds released by a cotton plant divided by the number of bolls produced. The researchers conclude that S2 plants have a lower average reproductive efficiency than S1 plants. Which of the following could explain this observation?

    A. On average, S2 plants produced more bolls that did not open.

    B. S2 plants produced fewer seeds per open boll than S1 plants.

    C. The pollen grains produced by S2 plants produced longer pollen tubes than pollen grains produced by S1 plants.

    D. On average, S2 plants produced fewer bolls.

GO ON TO THE NEXT PAGE.

Passage V

Denaturation is a process by which the two strands of a DNA molecule separate, destroying the structure of the DNA and rendering it functionless. Scientists studied the stability of DNA molecules in the organic solvent dimethylformamide (DMF), which is used in laboratories to dissolve DNA.

First, the scientists measured the amount of UV light absorbed by DNA dissolved in various concentrations of DMF. As DNA becomes less stable and begins to denature, it absorbs more UV light. The scientists tested the UV absorbance of both a linear DNA segment and a circular DNA segment at 25°C. The results are shown in Figure 1.

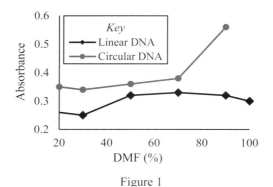

Figure 1

Next, the scientists used UV absorbance to investigate the behavior of circular DNA in DMF solvent at various temperatures. Typically, as temperature increases, DNA stability decreases, and eventually denatures. The scientists measured the UV absorbance of circular DNA in 3 different concentrations of DMF solvent at temperatures between 20°C and 65°C. The results are shown in Figure 2.

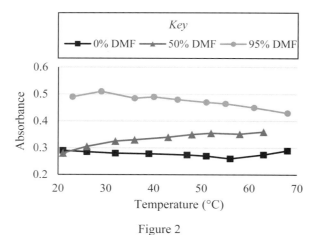

Figure 2

28. According to Figure 1, in which solution did linear DNA have the lowest UV absorbance?

   F. 10% DMF
   G. 20% DMF
   H. 30% DMF
   J. 40% DMF

29. According to Figure 1, as the concentration of DMF increased from 30% to 90%, the UV absorbance of circular DNA:

   A. decreased only.
   B. increased only.
   C. increased, then decreased.
   D. decreased, then increased.

30. Based on Figure 2, if the scientists had measured the UV absorbance of circular DNA in 95% DMF at 75°C, the absorbance would most likely have been:

   F. lower than 0.2.
   G. between 0.2 and 0.35.
   H. between 0.35 and 0.5.
   J. greater than 0.5.

31. A scientist hypothesizes that when concentrations of DMF increase, the UV absorbance of both types of DNA increases as well. Do the data in Figure 1 support this hypothesis?

   A. Yes, because the UV absorbance of circular DNA increases with increasing DMF concentration.
   B. Yes, because the UV absorbance of linear DNA does not have a clear relationship with DMF concentration.
   C. No, because the UV absorbance of circular DNA increases with increasing DMF concentration.
   D. No, because the UV absorbance of linear DNA does not have a clear relationship with DMF concentration.

GO ON TO THE NEXT PAGE.

32. The backbone of the DNA molecule is negatively charged. If a DNA molecule were placed between a negatively charged surface and a positively charged surface, the molecule would:

   F. remain stationary between the two surfaces.

   G. move toward the negatively charged surface.

   H. move toward the positively charged surface.

   J. move erratically, with no particular direction.

33. DNA is considered to be completely denatured if its UV absorbance is greater than 0.4. According to Figure 1 and Figure 2, in which of the following situations would a DNA segment NOT be completely denatured?

   A. Circular DNA in 85% DMF at 25°C

   B. Circular DNA in 95% DMF at 70°C

   C. Circular DNA in 95% DMF at 20°C

   D. Circular DNA in 25% DMF at 25°C

GO ON TO THE NEXT PAGE.

Passage VI

Atoms are a unit of matter, and combinations of atoms form molecules such as water (H_2O) and carbon dioxide (CO_2). Because atoms are very small, it can be difficult to study their structure. Three theories of atomic structure are outlined below.

Theory 1

Atoms are the smallest units of matter. Matter is composed of elements, each of which comprises atoms of a single, unique type. Atoms are indivisible, which means that there are no smaller subunits that compose an atom. Atoms cannot be destroyed or created, but they can be combined in different whole-number ratios to form molecules. Because atoms are indivisible, mass is always conserved during a chemical reaction. All atoms have an overall, uniformly distributed neutral electric charge.

Theory 2

Atoms are divisible. They consist of small, negatively charged particles called *electrons*, which are spread throughout a cloud of positive charge. The electrons are held within the cloud because of the attraction between positive and negative charges. The electrons are free to float within the cloud, but they cannot escape it. As electrons float farther from the center of the atom, the attractive force acting on them increases linearly. Overall, atoms have a neutral charge due to equal positive and negative charges from the cloud and the electrons, respectively.

Theory 3

Atoms are divisible. At the center of the atom lies the *nucleus*, a small, dense cluster of positively charged particles called *protons* and neutral particles called *neutrons*. The attractive forces between the negatively charged electrons and positively charged protons keep the atom together. Electrons are constrained to particular orbits around the nucleus, though they can jump between orbits. As electrons jump to orbits farther from the nucleus, the attractive force acting on them decreases in steps. Protons and electrons have equal and opposite charges, so an atom with an overall neutral charge has equal numbers of protons and electrons. Atoms can gain or lose electrons, thereby becoming negatively or positively charged.

34. According to Theory 3, which of the following conditions are *possible*?

    I. The number of protons in an atom equals the number of electrons.

    II. The number of protons in an atom is greater than the number of electrons.

    III. The number of protons in an atom is less than the number of electrons.

    F. I only
    G. II only
    H. II and III
    J. I, II, and III

35. A researcher discovers a particle that is smaller than the smallest known atom. Which of the 3 theories is contradicted by this evidence?

    A. Theory 1
    B. Theory 2
    C. Theory 3
    D. None of the theories are contradicted by the evidence.

36. In an experiment, positively charged particles were fired at a thin sheet of atoms. Most of the particles passed through the sheet, but some bounced off in different directions. A proponent of Theory 3 would most likely explain this phenomenon by arguing that:

    F. the positively charged particles usually pass through the nucleus. The occasional deflections occur when the particles are repelled by an electron.

    G. the positively charged particles usually pass through the space around the nucleus. The occasional deflections occur when the particles are repelled by the nucleus.

    H. the positively charged particles usually pass through the cloud of positive charge. The occasional deflections occur when the particles are repelled by free-floating electrons.

    J. the positively charged particles usually pass between atoms. The occasional deflections occur when the particles hit an indivisible atom.

GO ON TO THE NEXT PAGE.

37. According to Theory 2 and Theory 3, which of the following pairs of graphs could represent the relationship between an electron's distance from the center of the atom and the attractive force acting upon that electron?

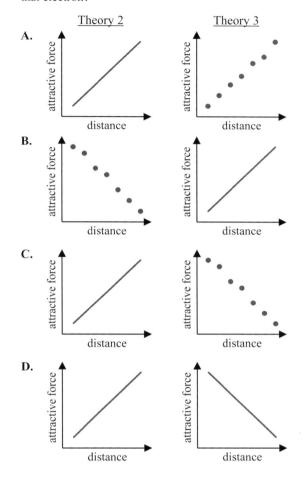

38. With which of the following statements would a proponent of Theory 2 be LEAST likely to agree?

F. An atom's stability depends on the attractive force between positive and negative charges.

G. An atom's negative charge exists in small pockets dispersed throughout a larger space.

H. An atom's positive charge exists in a dispersed cloud.

J. An atom can gain or lose electrons, thus altering its overall charge.

39. A researcher discovers that the distribution of charge throughout an atom is not uniform. How does this evidence affect the strength of the 3 theories?

	Theory 1	Theory 2	Theory 3
A.	strengthen	strengthen	strengthen
B.	strengthen	weaken	weaken
C.	weaken	strengthen	strengthen
D.	weaken	weaken	weaken

40. Which of the following best describes the forces between positively charged particles and negatively charged particles?

F. Positive particles and negative particles are attracted to each other due to electrostatic forces.

G. Positive particles and negative particles are attracted to each other due to frictional forces.

H. Positive particles and negative particles are repelled from each other due to gravitational forces.

J. Positive particles and negative particles are repelled from each other due to electrostatic forces.

END OF TEST 4.

STOP! DO NOT TURN THE PAGE UNTIL YOU ARE TOLD TO DO SO.

DO NOT RETURN TO THE PREVIOUS TEST.

Writing Test
40 Minutes—1 Prompt

Directions: This is a test of your writing ability. You'll have 40 minutes to read the prompt, plan your response, and write your essay. Before you begin, read all of the material in this test section carefully and make sure you understand what is being asked of you.

You should write your essay on the lined pages included in your answer sheet. Only your writing on those pages will be scored. Your work on these pages will not be scored.

Your essay will be graded based on the evidence it provides and your ability to:

- analyze and evaluate different perspectives on complicated issues
- express and develop your own perspective on the issue
- explain and support your arguments with logical reasoning and detailed examples
- clearly and logically organize your ideas in an essay
- effectively communicate your point of view in English

Stop writing and put down your pencil as soon as time is called.

DO NOT BEGIN THE WRITING TEST UNTIL YOU ARE TOLD TO DO SO.

How Much Homework?

A recent study from Spain suggested that the optimal amount of homework for teenagers was about one hour per day. Statistics collected in the United States show that most American high schoolers also do about an hour of homework every day, if not more. Proponents of more homework hope that students will be better prepared for the workloads of postsecondary programs. Critics of assigning more homework cite the many ways teenagers might use more free time: work, volunteering, extracurricular activities, hobbies, or even just relaxing with their friends. Should high schools be assigning more homework, or less?

Read and carefully consider these perspectives. Each suggests a particular way of thinking about the amount of homework assigned by high schools.

Perspective 1	Perspective 2	Perspective 3
We must prepare young people for the amounts of homework they'll encounter in college or university. High schools should assign more homework.	The amount of homework assigned is just right. Students who do about an hour of homework a day will be prepared for higher education. However, they'll also have ample free time to use as they see fit.	Adolescence is a time of personal growth and self-discovery, but high schoolers will miss out on this if they have too much homework. Schools should assign less homework, making up for any gaps by prioritizing more rigorous in-class work.

Essay Task

Write a unified, coherent essay in which you evaluate multiple perspectives on the amount of homework assigned by high schools. In your essay, be sure to:

- analyze and evaluate the perspectives given
- state and develop your own perspective on the issue
- explain the relationship between your perspective and those given

Your perspective may be in full agreement with any of the others, in partial agreement, or wholly different. Whatever the case, support your ideas with logical reasoning and detailed, persuasive examples.

Planning Your Essay

Your work on these prewriting pages will not be scored.

Use the space below and on the back cover to generate ideas and plan your essay. You may wish to consider the following as you think critically about the task:

Strengths and weaknesses of the three given perspectives

- What insights do they offer, and what do they fail to consider?
- Why might they be persuasive to others, or why might they fail to persuade?

Your own knowledge, experience, and values

- What is your perspective on this issue, and what are its strengths and weaknesses?
- How will you support your perspective in your essay?

Note

- Your practice Writing Test includes scratch paper and four lined sheets for your essay.
- Your official ACT exam will include a test booklet with space for planning and four lined sheets to write your essay.
- Review Answers and Scoring for instructions on how to grade your exam.

Practice Test 2

The ACT

This practice test contains tests in English, Math, Reading, and Science. These tests measure skills and abilities related to high school course work and college preparedness. **You can use a calculator on the math test only.**

The questions in each test are numbered, and the suggested answers for each question are lettered. On the answer sheet, the rows are numbered to match the questions, and the circles in each row are lettered to correspond to the suggested answers.

For each question, choose the best answer and fill in the corresponding circle on your answer document. Use a soft lead pencil and make your marks heavy and black. **Do not use a ballpoint pen.**

Fill in only one answer to each question. If you change your mind about an answer, completely erase your first mark before filling in your new answer. For each question, make certain that you mark in the row of ovals with the same number as the question.

Only responses marked on your answer sheet will be scored. Your score on each test will be based only on the number of questions you answer correctly during the time allowed for that test. You will NOT be penalized for guessing. **Even if you are unsure about an answer, you should make a guess.**

You may work on each test ONLY when your proctor tells you to do so. If you complete a test before the end of your allotted time, use the extra minutes to check your work on that section only. Do NOT use the time to work on another section. Doing this will disqualify your scores.

Put down your pencil immediately when time is called at the end of each test. You are not allowed to continue answering questions after the allotted time has run out. This includes marking answers on your answer sheet that you previously noted in your test booklet.

You are not allowed to fold or tear the pages of your test booklet.

Do Not Open This Booklet Until You Are Told to Do So.

NAME: _____

DATE: _____

TEST 1

1 Ⓐ Ⓑ Ⓒ Ⓓ	14 Ⓕ Ⓖ Ⓗ Ⓙ	27 Ⓐ Ⓑ Ⓒ Ⓓ	40 Ⓕ Ⓖ Ⓗ Ⓙ	53 Ⓐ Ⓑ Ⓒ Ⓓ	66 Ⓕ Ⓖ Ⓗ Ⓙ
2 Ⓕ Ⓖ Ⓗ Ⓙ	15 Ⓐ Ⓑ Ⓒ Ⓓ	28 Ⓕ Ⓖ Ⓗ Ⓙ	41 Ⓐ Ⓑ Ⓒ Ⓓ	54 Ⓕ Ⓖ Ⓗ Ⓙ	67 Ⓐ Ⓑ Ⓒ Ⓓ
3 Ⓐ Ⓑ Ⓒ Ⓓ	16 Ⓕ Ⓖ Ⓗ Ⓙ	29 Ⓐ Ⓑ Ⓒ Ⓓ	42 Ⓕ Ⓖ Ⓗ Ⓙ	55 Ⓐ Ⓑ Ⓒ Ⓓ	68 Ⓕ Ⓖ Ⓗ Ⓙ
4 Ⓕ Ⓖ Ⓗ Ⓙ	17 Ⓐ Ⓑ Ⓒ Ⓓ	30 Ⓕ Ⓖ Ⓗ Ⓙ	43 Ⓐ Ⓑ Ⓒ Ⓓ	56 Ⓕ Ⓖ Ⓗ Ⓙ	69 Ⓐ Ⓑ Ⓒ Ⓓ
5 Ⓐ Ⓑ Ⓒ Ⓓ	18 Ⓕ Ⓖ Ⓗ Ⓙ	31 Ⓐ Ⓑ Ⓒ Ⓓ	44 Ⓕ Ⓖ Ⓗ Ⓙ	57 Ⓐ Ⓑ Ⓒ Ⓓ	70 Ⓕ Ⓖ Ⓗ Ⓙ
6 Ⓕ Ⓖ Ⓗ Ⓙ	19 Ⓐ Ⓑ Ⓒ Ⓓ	32 Ⓕ Ⓖ Ⓗ Ⓙ	45 Ⓐ Ⓑ Ⓒ Ⓓ	58 Ⓕ Ⓖ Ⓗ Ⓙ	71 Ⓐ Ⓑ Ⓒ Ⓓ
7 Ⓐ Ⓑ Ⓒ Ⓓ	20 Ⓕ Ⓖ Ⓗ Ⓙ	33 Ⓐ Ⓑ Ⓒ Ⓓ	46 Ⓕ Ⓖ Ⓗ Ⓙ	59 Ⓐ Ⓑ Ⓒ Ⓓ	72 Ⓕ Ⓖ Ⓗ Ⓙ
8 Ⓕ Ⓖ Ⓗ Ⓙ	21 Ⓐ Ⓑ Ⓒ Ⓓ	34 Ⓕ Ⓖ Ⓗ Ⓙ	47 Ⓐ Ⓑ Ⓒ Ⓓ	60 Ⓕ Ⓖ Ⓗ Ⓙ	73 Ⓐ Ⓑ Ⓒ Ⓓ
9 Ⓐ Ⓑ Ⓒ Ⓓ	22 Ⓕ Ⓖ Ⓗ Ⓙ	35 Ⓐ Ⓑ Ⓒ Ⓓ	48 Ⓕ Ⓖ Ⓗ Ⓙ	61 Ⓐ Ⓑ Ⓒ Ⓓ	74 Ⓕ Ⓖ Ⓗ Ⓙ
10 Ⓕ Ⓖ Ⓗ Ⓙ	23 Ⓐ Ⓑ Ⓒ Ⓓ	36 Ⓕ Ⓖ Ⓗ Ⓙ	49 Ⓐ Ⓑ Ⓒ Ⓓ	62 Ⓕ Ⓖ Ⓗ Ⓙ	75 Ⓐ Ⓑ Ⓒ Ⓓ
11 Ⓐ Ⓑ Ⓒ Ⓓ	24 Ⓕ Ⓖ Ⓗ Ⓙ	37 Ⓐ Ⓑ Ⓒ Ⓓ	50 Ⓕ Ⓖ Ⓗ Ⓙ	63 Ⓐ Ⓑ Ⓒ Ⓓ	
12 Ⓕ Ⓖ Ⓗ Ⓙ	25 Ⓐ Ⓑ Ⓒ Ⓓ	38 Ⓕ Ⓖ Ⓗ Ⓙ	51 Ⓐ Ⓑ Ⓒ Ⓓ	64 Ⓕ Ⓖ Ⓗ Ⓙ	
13 Ⓐ Ⓑ Ⓒ Ⓓ	26 Ⓕ Ⓖ Ⓗ Ⓙ	39 Ⓐ Ⓑ Ⓒ Ⓓ	52 Ⓕ Ⓖ Ⓗ Ⓙ	65 Ⓐ Ⓑ Ⓒ Ⓓ	

TEST 2

1 Ⓐ Ⓑ Ⓒ Ⓓ Ⓔ	11 Ⓐ Ⓑ Ⓒ Ⓓ Ⓔ	21 Ⓐ Ⓑ Ⓒ Ⓓ Ⓔ	31 Ⓐ Ⓑ Ⓒ Ⓓ Ⓔ	41 Ⓐ Ⓑ Ⓒ Ⓓ Ⓔ	51 Ⓐ Ⓑ Ⓒ Ⓓ Ⓔ
2 Ⓕ Ⓖ Ⓗ Ⓙ Ⓚ	12 Ⓕ Ⓖ Ⓗ Ⓙ Ⓚ	22 Ⓕ Ⓖ Ⓗ Ⓙ Ⓚ	32 Ⓕ Ⓖ Ⓗ Ⓙ Ⓚ	42 Ⓕ Ⓖ Ⓗ Ⓙ Ⓚ	52 Ⓕ Ⓖ Ⓗ Ⓙ Ⓚ
3 Ⓐ Ⓑ Ⓒ Ⓓ Ⓔ	13 Ⓐ Ⓑ Ⓒ Ⓓ Ⓔ	23 Ⓐ Ⓑ Ⓒ Ⓓ Ⓔ	33 Ⓐ Ⓑ Ⓒ Ⓓ Ⓔ	43 Ⓐ Ⓑ Ⓒ Ⓓ Ⓔ	53 Ⓐ Ⓑ Ⓒ Ⓓ Ⓔ
4 Ⓕ Ⓖ Ⓗ Ⓙ Ⓚ	14 Ⓕ Ⓖ Ⓗ Ⓙ Ⓚ	24 Ⓕ Ⓖ Ⓗ Ⓙ Ⓚ	34 Ⓕ Ⓖ Ⓗ Ⓙ Ⓚ	44 Ⓕ Ⓖ Ⓗ Ⓙ Ⓚ	54 Ⓕ Ⓖ Ⓗ Ⓙ Ⓚ
5 Ⓐ Ⓑ Ⓒ Ⓓ Ⓔ	15 Ⓐ Ⓑ Ⓒ Ⓓ Ⓔ	25 Ⓐ Ⓑ Ⓒ Ⓓ Ⓔ	35 Ⓐ Ⓑ Ⓒ Ⓓ Ⓔ	45 Ⓐ Ⓑ Ⓒ Ⓓ Ⓔ	55 Ⓐ Ⓑ Ⓒ Ⓓ Ⓔ
6 Ⓕ Ⓖ Ⓗ Ⓙ Ⓚ	16 Ⓕ Ⓖ Ⓗ Ⓙ Ⓚ	26 Ⓕ Ⓖ Ⓗ Ⓙ Ⓚ	36 Ⓕ Ⓖ Ⓗ Ⓙ Ⓚ	46 Ⓕ Ⓖ Ⓗ Ⓙ Ⓚ	56 Ⓕ Ⓖ Ⓗ Ⓙ Ⓚ
7 Ⓐ Ⓑ Ⓒ Ⓓ Ⓔ	17 Ⓐ Ⓑ Ⓒ Ⓓ Ⓔ	27 Ⓐ Ⓑ Ⓒ Ⓓ Ⓔ	37 Ⓐ Ⓑ Ⓒ Ⓓ Ⓔ	47 Ⓐ Ⓑ Ⓒ Ⓓ Ⓔ	57 Ⓐ Ⓑ Ⓒ Ⓓ Ⓔ
8 Ⓕ Ⓖ Ⓗ Ⓙ Ⓚ	18 Ⓕ Ⓖ Ⓗ Ⓙ Ⓚ	28 Ⓕ Ⓖ Ⓗ Ⓙ Ⓚ	38 Ⓕ Ⓖ Ⓗ Ⓙ Ⓚ	48 Ⓕ Ⓖ Ⓗ Ⓙ Ⓚ	58 Ⓕ Ⓖ Ⓗ Ⓙ Ⓚ
9 Ⓐ Ⓑ Ⓒ Ⓓ Ⓔ	19 Ⓐ Ⓑ Ⓒ Ⓓ Ⓔ	29 Ⓐ Ⓑ Ⓒ Ⓓ Ⓔ	39 Ⓐ Ⓑ Ⓒ Ⓓ Ⓔ	49 Ⓐ Ⓑ Ⓒ Ⓓ Ⓔ	59 Ⓐ Ⓑ Ⓒ Ⓓ Ⓔ
10 Ⓕ Ⓖ Ⓗ Ⓙ Ⓚ	20 Ⓕ Ⓖ Ⓗ Ⓙ Ⓚ	30 Ⓕ Ⓖ Ⓗ Ⓙ Ⓚ	40 Ⓕ Ⓖ Ⓗ Ⓙ Ⓚ	50 Ⓕ Ⓖ Ⓗ Ⓙ Ⓚ	60 Ⓕ Ⓖ Ⓗ Ⓙ Ⓚ

TEST 3

1 Ⓐ Ⓑ Ⓒ Ⓓ	8 Ⓕ Ⓖ Ⓗ Ⓙ	15 Ⓐ Ⓑ Ⓒ Ⓓ	22 Ⓕ Ⓖ Ⓗ Ⓙ	29 Ⓐ Ⓑ Ⓒ Ⓓ	36 Ⓕ Ⓖ Ⓗ Ⓙ
2 Ⓕ Ⓖ Ⓗ Ⓙ	9 Ⓐ Ⓑ Ⓒ Ⓓ	16 Ⓕ Ⓖ Ⓗ Ⓙ	23 Ⓐ Ⓑ Ⓒ Ⓓ	30 Ⓕ Ⓖ Ⓗ Ⓙ	37 Ⓐ Ⓑ Ⓒ Ⓓ
3 Ⓐ Ⓑ Ⓒ Ⓓ	10 Ⓕ Ⓖ Ⓗ Ⓙ	17 Ⓐ Ⓑ Ⓒ Ⓓ	24 Ⓕ Ⓖ Ⓗ Ⓙ	31 Ⓐ Ⓑ Ⓒ Ⓓ	38 Ⓕ Ⓖ Ⓗ Ⓙ
4 Ⓕ Ⓖ Ⓗ Ⓙ	11 Ⓐ Ⓑ Ⓒ Ⓓ	18 Ⓕ Ⓖ Ⓗ Ⓙ	25 Ⓐ Ⓑ Ⓒ Ⓓ	32 Ⓕ Ⓖ Ⓗ Ⓙ	39 Ⓐ Ⓑ Ⓒ Ⓓ
5 Ⓐ Ⓑ Ⓒ Ⓓ	12 Ⓕ Ⓖ Ⓗ Ⓙ	19 Ⓐ Ⓑ Ⓒ Ⓓ	26 Ⓕ Ⓖ Ⓗ Ⓙ	33 Ⓐ Ⓑ Ⓒ Ⓓ	40 Ⓕ Ⓖ Ⓗ Ⓙ
6 Ⓕ Ⓖ Ⓗ Ⓙ	13 Ⓐ Ⓑ Ⓒ Ⓓ	20 Ⓕ Ⓖ Ⓗ Ⓙ	27 Ⓐ Ⓑ Ⓒ Ⓓ	34 Ⓕ Ⓖ Ⓗ Ⓙ	
7 Ⓐ Ⓑ Ⓒ Ⓓ	14 Ⓕ Ⓖ Ⓗ Ⓙ	21 Ⓐ Ⓑ Ⓒ Ⓓ	28 Ⓕ Ⓖ Ⓗ Ⓙ	35 Ⓐ Ⓑ Ⓒ Ⓓ	

TEST 4

1 Ⓐ Ⓑ Ⓒ Ⓓ	8 Ⓕ Ⓖ Ⓗ Ⓙ	15 Ⓐ Ⓑ Ⓒ Ⓓ	22 Ⓕ Ⓖ Ⓗ Ⓙ	29 Ⓐ Ⓑ Ⓒ Ⓓ	36 Ⓕ Ⓖ Ⓗ Ⓙ
2 Ⓕ Ⓖ Ⓗ Ⓙ	9 Ⓐ Ⓑ Ⓒ Ⓓ	16 Ⓕ Ⓖ Ⓗ Ⓙ	23 Ⓐ Ⓑ Ⓒ Ⓓ	30 Ⓕ Ⓖ Ⓗ Ⓙ	37 Ⓐ Ⓑ Ⓒ Ⓓ
3 Ⓐ Ⓑ Ⓒ Ⓓ	10 Ⓕ Ⓖ Ⓗ Ⓙ	17 Ⓐ Ⓑ Ⓒ Ⓓ	24 Ⓕ Ⓖ Ⓗ Ⓙ	31 Ⓐ Ⓑ Ⓒ Ⓓ	38 Ⓕ Ⓖ Ⓗ Ⓙ
4 Ⓕ Ⓖ Ⓗ Ⓙ	11 Ⓐ Ⓑ Ⓒ Ⓓ	18 Ⓕ Ⓖ Ⓗ Ⓙ	25 Ⓐ Ⓑ Ⓒ Ⓓ	32 Ⓕ Ⓖ Ⓗ Ⓙ	39 Ⓐ Ⓑ Ⓒ Ⓓ
5 Ⓐ Ⓑ Ⓒ Ⓓ	12 Ⓕ Ⓖ Ⓗ Ⓙ	19 Ⓐ Ⓑ Ⓒ Ⓓ	26 Ⓕ Ⓖ Ⓗ Ⓙ	33 Ⓐ Ⓑ Ⓒ Ⓓ	40 Ⓕ Ⓖ Ⓗ Ⓙ
6 Ⓕ Ⓖ Ⓗ Ⓙ	13 Ⓐ Ⓑ Ⓒ Ⓓ	20 Ⓕ Ⓖ Ⓗ Ⓙ	27 Ⓐ Ⓑ Ⓒ Ⓓ	34 Ⓕ Ⓖ Ⓗ Ⓙ	
7 Ⓐ Ⓑ Ⓒ Ⓓ	14 Ⓕ Ⓖ Ⓗ Ⓙ	21 Ⓐ Ⓑ Ⓒ Ⓓ	28 Ⓕ Ⓖ Ⓗ Ⓙ	35 Ⓐ Ⓑ Ⓒ Ⓓ	

Use a soft lead No. 2 pencil only. Do NOT use a mechanical pencil, ink, ballpoint, or felt-tip pens.

Begin WRITING TEST here.

If you need more space, please continue on the next page.

1

WRITING TEST

_____

_____

_____

_____

_____

_____

_____

_____

_____

_____

_____

_____

_____

_____

_____

_____

_____

_____

_____

_____

_____

_____

_____

_____

_____

_____

If you need more space, please continue on the back of this page.

2

WRITING TEST

_____

_____

_____

_____

_____

_____

_____

_____

_____

_____

_____

_____

_____

_____

_____

_____

_____

_____

_____

_____

_____

_____

_____

_____

_____

_____

_____

_____

If you need more space, please continue on the next page.

3

WRITING TEST

_____
_____
_____
_____
_____
_____
_____
_____
_____
_____
_____
_____
_____
_____
_____
_____
_____
_____
_____
_____
_____
_____
_____
_____
_____
_____
_____
_____
_____

STOP!

4

English Test
45 Minutes—75 Questions

DIRECTIONS: In the five passages that follow, certain words and phrases are underlined and numbered. In the right-hand column, you will find alternatives for the underlined part. In most cases, you are to choose the one that best expresses the idea, makes the statement appropriate for standard written English, or is worded most consistently with the style and tone of the passage as a whole. If you think the original version is best, choose "NO CHANGE." In some cases, you will find in the right-hand column a question about the underlined part. You are to choose the best answer to the question.

You will also find questions about a section of the passage, or about the passage as a whole. These questions do not refer to an underlined portion of the passage, but rather are identified by a number or numbers in a box.

For each question, choose the alternative you consider best and fill in the corresponding circle on your answer document. Read each passage through once before you begin to answer the questions that accompany it. For many of the questions, you must read several sentences beyond the question to determine the answer. Be sure that you have read far enough ahead each time you choose an alternative.

Passage I

Study of an Unusual Vermeer

[1]

Although, the Dutch painter Johannes Vermeer was
$\underline{\hspace{3cm}}$
1
considered only modestly successful during his lifetime,

he is now considered one of the most important artists of

the Dutch Golden Age. Part of the reason Vermeer <u>was</u>
 2
<u>underestimated during his lifetime may have been that he did</u>
 2
<u>not paint as much</u> at that time as his contemporaries, a group
 2
that included Frans Hals and Rembrandt. However, such

works as *The Milkmaid* and *The Girl with a Pearl Earring*

have been studied intensely and continue to <u>earned</u> Vermeer
 3
acclaim to this day.

[2]

[1] One painting that has long fascinated art critics

and art historians is his *Study of a Young Woman.* [2] This

piece is an example of a Dutch form called the "tronie,"

1. **A.** NO CHANGE
   B. Although, the Dutch painter Johannes Vermeer,
   C. Although the Dutch painter Johannes Vermeer
   D. Although the Dutch painter, Johannes Vermeer

2. **F.** NO CHANGE
   G. was underestimated may have been that he did not paint as much
   H. was underestimated during his lifetime is he did not paint as much during his lifetime
   J. was underestimated may have been partly that he did not paint as much

3. **A.** NO CHANGE
   B. earning
   C. earns
   D. earn

GO ON TO THE NEXT PAGE.

painted sometime between 1665 and 1667, a painting of
the head and face of a figure thought to be unusual or
striking. [3] This painting is of particular interest, in part,
because the dark background of the painting is very

different than Vermeers usual vividly lit and richly detailed

backgrounds. [6]

[3]

It is also notable that, while the subject of the
painting is certainly striking, I would not call her
conventionally beautiful. This young woman's gaze is

steady and a slight smile tugs at their lips, hinting at a sort of
confidence. Yet she seems to have no eyebrows or

eyelashes. Eyes set extremely wide. That may be the

point, in *Study of a Young Woman,* Vermeer seems to be
more interested in exploring and representing aspects of his
subject's character and expression rather than representing
conventional forms of beauty.

4. The best placement for the underlined phrase would be:
   F. where it is now.
   G. after the word *piece* (revising the punctuation accordingly).
   H. after the word *figure.*
   J. after the word *form.*

5. A. NO CHANGE
   B. Vermeers'
   C. Vermeers's
   D. Vermeer's

6. If the writer were to delete Sentence 2, the essay would primarily lose details that:
   F. describe the form of a painting, giving the reader an idea of what Vermeer painted.
   G. suggest that Dutch painters were mostly concerned with unusual or striking faces of figures.
   H. raise the question of why Vermeer decided to use such an unusual model for his painting.
   J. continue to develop the idea that Vermeer's paintings are widely acclaimed.

7. A. NO CHANGE
   B. we would not regard her as conventionally beautiful.
   C. conventionally beautiful is not what she was.
   D. she is not conventionally beautiful.

8. F. NO CHANGE
   G. one's
   H. her
   J. its

9. A. NO CHANGE
   B. Her eyes are extremely wide-set.
   C. Her eyes being extremely wide-set.
   D. The eyes, set extremely wide.

10. F. NO CHANGE
    G. point: in
    H. point, in,
    J. point in

GO ON TO THE NEXT PAGE.

[4]

The painting itself, instead, is beautiful. There is a gradual transition from light to shadow on the

young woman's face; which is echoed by the subtle shifts of tone in the folds of cloth draped over her shoulder.

Vermeer's exploration of the effect of light on this extraordinary face creates the sense that he has somehow illuminated a dream of moving beyond mere beauty toward a more authentic engagement with the world.

11. **A.** NO CHANGE
    B. however,
    C. therefore,
    D. in the meantime,

12. **F.** NO CHANGE
    G. young woman's face which is
    H. young woman's face which is;
    J. young woman's face, which is

13. Given that all the choices are true, which one most effectively introduces this sentence by describing what technique Vermeer used?

    A. NO CHANGE
    B. Vermeer's use of color
    C. The fact that there are no distracting details like a window or furniture
    D. The use of bold, broad brushstrokes in the painting

Questions 14 and 15 ask about the preceding passage as a whole.

---

14. Upon reviewing notes for this essay, the writer comes across the following true statement:

    Some scholars claim the model for *Study of a Young Woman* was Vermeer's daughter.

    The writer is considering adding the sentence. The most logical choice for the writer is to:

    F. add it at the end of paragraph 1.
    G. add it at the end of paragraph 2.
    H. add it at the end of paragraph 3.
    J. OMIT the sentence, because it is not a relevant addition to any paragraph.

15. Suppose the writer's goal had been to write an essay focusing on the reasons Vermeer is held in such high esteem by art critics and historians. Would this essay fulfill that goal?

    A. Yes, because the essay explains in detail why Vermeer's paintings are considered masterpieces.
    B. Yes, because the essay focuses on Vermeer's use of light.
    C. No, because the essay does not provide enough detail about Vermeer's life.
    D. No, because the essay does not explain the reasons art critics and historians believe Vermeer should be considered an important artist.

GO ON TO THE NEXT PAGE.

Passage II

What Is Music? The Brain Knows.

[1] Though research has found that even the most ancient cultures <u>made music. The reasons</u> behind this
<u>16</u>
universal drive remain unexplained. [2] However, until recently they have been unable to verify this theory. [3] <u>Scientists have long assumed that there must be a neural</u>
<u>17</u>
<u>basis for our love of music, and they have searched for</u>
<u>17</u>
<u>evidence using conventional brain-scanning technology.</u>
<u>17</u>
[4] Now, though, researchers at the Massachusetts Institute

of Technology (MIT) have devised a <u>weird trick for brain</u>
<u>18</u>

imaging that seems to support this long-held hypothesis. 19

These <u>MIT researchers,</u> performed mathematical
<u>20</u>
analyses of scans of the auditory cortex and found that specific groups of neurons in this region, which is located in the temporal lobes, <u>fires</u> in response to music.
<u>21</u>

16. **F.** NO CHANGE
    G. made music, and the reasons
    H. made music; however, the reasons
    J. made music, the reasons

17. **A.** NO CHANGE
    B. Scientists have long assumed, using conventional brain-scanning technology, that there must be a neural basis for our love of music, and they have searched for evidence.
    C. Using conventional brain-scanning technology, scientists have long assumed that there must be a neural basis for our love of music, and they have searched for evidence.
    D. Scientists have long assumed that there must be a neural basis for our love of music using conventional brain-scanning technology, and they have searched for evidence.

18. **F.** NO CHANGE
    G. new approach to
    H. cool new method of
    J. mode of action concerning

19. For the sake of the logic and coherence of this paragraph, Sentence 2 should be placed:
    A. where it is now.
    B. before Sentence 1.
    C. after Sentence 3.
    D. after Sentence 4.

20. **F.** NO CHANGE
    G. These, MIT researchers,
    H. These, MIT researchers
    J. These MIT researchers

21. **A.** NO CHANGE
    B. fire
    C. has fired
    D. is firing

GO ON TO THE NEXT PAGE.

owever, they found a part of the brain that is dedicated
22

distinguishing music from noise in general. They also
                                              23
und that this area is able to recognize music as distinctly
                                         23
parate from speech. During testing, neurons in the area
      23
red in response to everything from Bach to bluegrass and

p-hop but stayed unmoved by other sounds. Different parts

f the auditory cortex responded to such sounds as running

ater and falling trees. 24

After gathering a library of easy recognizable sounds,
                              25
he researchers scanned the brains of a group of volunteers

ho listened to the sound clips. Researchers matched the

ctivation patterns in the brain to the sounds that were

layed. And determined that four basic response patterns
                                           26
vere linked to such properties as pitch, rhythm, and
                              26
requency.
26

Though researchers still can't say which exact
              27
coustic features in music stimulate the music-sensitive

22. **F.** NO CHANGE
    G. Insofar as,
    H. In other words,
    J. Therefore,

23. **A.** NO CHANGE
    B. general. This area, they found, also recognizes music as different.
    C. general, or from such specific other noises as speech.
    D. general, and from speech.

24. The writer is considering deleting the preceding sentence from this paragraph. If the writer made this deletion, the paragraph would primarily lose:
    F. information explaining how parts of the brain recognize music, speech, and other sounds.
    G. examples of non-musical sounds processed by different parts of the brain than those that process music.
    H. scientific proof of the statement that brain scanning technology is effective.
    J. evidence that the sound of running water is not music.

25. **A.** NO CHANGE
    B. easy recognizably
    C. easily recognizably
    D. easily recognizable

26. **F.** NO CHANGE
    G. They determined that four basic response patterns were linked to such properties as pitch, rhythm, and frequency.
    H. And four basic response patterns were linked to such properties as pitch, rhythm, and frequency.
    J. Four basic response patterns were linked.

27. **A.** NO CHANGE
    B. researchers' still can't
    C. researchers still cant
    D. researchers' still cant

GO ON TO THE NEXT PAGE.

areas of the brain, but it's clear that the brain recognizes
<u></u>
₂₈

music when it hears it. Of course, a number of questions
<u></u>
₂₉

remain, including such questions as why humans have music
<u></u>
₂₉

to begin with and why some music moves us to dance. This

discovery, however, opens up the possibility of finally

finding the answers.

28. F. NO CHANGE
    G. and it is
    H. but it is
    J. it's

29. A. NO CHANGE
    B. Of course, a number of questions remain, including
    C. Of course, questions remain, such as those of
    D. A number of questions remain, of course,

> Question 30 asks about the preceding passage as a whole.

30. Suppose the writer's primary purpose had been to describe how a specific study sheds light on a bigger question. Would this essay accomplish that goal?

    F. Yes, because it shows how a study of the brain has revealed music-sensitive areas that may help to answer bigger questions about why we enjoy music.

    G. Yes, because it shows how a study of the brain reveals the areas of the brain that make us respond to music with joy and dance.

    H. No, because it describes a study that ultimately fails to answer any big questions.

    J. No, because it begins by posing questions about why we like music, but focuses instead on how we perceive it.

Passage III

A Very Important Person

[1] A V.I.P. was coming to visit, I had no idea what
<u></u>
₃₁

that meant but everyone else in my family seemed very

excited. [2] The house was subjected to an extra-deep
<u></u>
₃₂

cleaning, a menu was planned, and the phone kept ringing

with people wanting to be invited over on the red-letter day.

[3] My mother apologized to every caller, explaining that

although our guest was a V.I.P. he was also my father's

cousin, and his visit would be strictly a family affair.

31. A. NO CHANGE
    B. visit I had no
    C. visit. I had no
    D. visit, I had no,

32. Which of the following alternatives to the underlined portion would be the LEAST acceptable?

    F. put through
    G. imperiled by
    H. exposed to
    J. made to endure

GO ON TO THE NEXT PAGE.

] Of course, that didn't stop my mother from making me

ractice curtsying. Or reminding my brother about the
___
33

nportance of making eye contact when shaking hands.

] I have to admit I was a little disappointed when the

.I.P. turned out to be an ordinary man. [6] He was wearing

nakis and a blue sports coat just like my dad. [7] The only

ing that set him apart from most men I knew was his

ustache. 34

"It's just a guy," I whispered to my brother, who

ave me a hard nudge in the ribs with his elbow. He smiled
                                                     ___
                                                      35

hen I curtsied and asked if I greeted all our guests this way.

blurted out that, I was only curtsying because he was the
            _____
                   36

.I.P. I heard my mother gasp as a result of this comment.
      _____
                         37

ut the man laughed and asked me, "What is your favorite

hing to do?" I told him that my favorite thing was getting

iggyback rides, he laughed again, got down on one knee,
         _____
              38

33. **A.** NO CHANGE
    B. curtsying or
    C. curtsying;
    D. curtsying; or

34. The writer has decided to divide this opening paragraph into two. The best place to add the new paragraph break would be at the beginning of Sentence:

    F. 4, because at this point the focus shifts to the narrator's mother's expectations.
    G. 4, because at this point the emphasis shifts from the narrator's mother to the narrator.
    H. 5, because at this point the essay shifts from describing the guest as important to describing him as unimportant.
    J. 5, because at this point the essay shifts from events before the VIP's arrival to the event of his arrival.

35. **A.** NO CHANGE
    B. The V.I.P.
    C. My brother
    D. She

36. **F.** NO CHANGE
    G. that I was only,
    H. that I was only
    J. that, I was only,

37. **A.** NO CHANGE
    B. As a result of this comment, my mother gasped.
    C. The fact that I made this comment is what made my mother gasp.
    D. This comment made my mother gasp.

38. **F.** NO CHANGE
    G. rides, and he laughed
    H. rides he laughed
    J. rides, and he laughed;

GO ON TO THE NEXT PAGE.

and told me to climb up. In fact, before my mother could
₃₉

lodge a protest; he galloped across the lawn with me on
₄₀
his back.

Eventually we were called to lunch. My mother

was inside had set the dining room table with the good
₄₁

china and silverware. Having been carefully coached in

table etiquette, I noticed the V.I.P. break the rules several

times—but of upsetting her, instead, this actually seemed
₄₂
to make my mother feel more relaxed!
₄₂

It turned out that the V.I.P was a regular person like us,
₄₃

and the day was truly my families' affair. I will never forget
₄₄
the day the U.S. Ambassador to France gave me a piggyback

ride.

39. **A.** NO CHANGE
    B. However
    C. Then
    D. Finally

40. **F.** NO CHANGE
    G. protest—he
    H. protest, he
    J. protest: he

41. **A.** NO CHANGE
    B. sets
    C. set
    D. setting

42. **F.** NO CHANGE
    G. more relaxed, instead of upsetting her, this actually seemed to make my mother feel!
    H. this seemed to, instead of upsetting her, more relaxed make my mother feel!
    J. instead of upsetting her, this actually seemed to make my mother feel more relaxed!

43. **A.** NO CHANGE
    B. Despite his status, this man was clearly of an egalitarian disposition,
    C. See, he was just a regular guy,
    D. We realized that he wasn't special,

44. **F.** NO CHANGE
    G. family's
    H. family
    J. families

Question 45 asks about the preceding passage as a whole.

45. Suppose the writer's goal had been to write an essay focusing on the behavior of ambassadors when they are off-duty. Would this essay fulfill that goal?

    A. Yes, because the essay focuses on a day when a U.S. ambassador was visiting with family.

    B. Yes, because the essay indicates that ambassadors are just normal people.

    C. No, because the essay primarily focuses on just one person on a specific day.

    D. No, because the essay focuses more on the narrator's opinions than the ambassador's behavior.

GO ON TO THE NEXT PAGE.

Practice Tests

Passage IV

Will You Be My Valentine?

[1]

February 14th is widely celebrated as Valentine's

Day, an occasion for sharing cards, flowers, gifts;
                                                    46
chocolates, and romantic candlelit dinners. Today over 1
                                      46
billion Valentine's Day cards are sent each year.

The origins of this holiday, however, are shrouded in
                                    47

mystery. Who was St. Valentine and why is their day so
                                                48

romantic?

[2]

[1] Simply knowing that the date celebrates St.

Valentine does little to clarify things. [2] There are, after

all, three different martyred saints bearing the name. 49

[3] The most widely held legend is that the one we

celebrate was a priest named Valentine living in Rome
                              50

during the third century. [4] At that time, the Roman

Emperor Claudius II outlawed marriage for young men

---

46. F. NO CHANGE

G. sharing cards, flowers; gifts, chocolates—and romantic candlelit dinners.

H. sharing cards, flowers, gifts chocolates, and romantic—candlelit dinners.

J. sharing cards, flowers, gifts, chocolates, and romantic candlelit dinners.

47. Which of the following alternatives to the underlined portion would be LEAST acceptable?

A. though

B. in addition

C. meanwhile

D. nevertheless

48. F. NO CHANGE

G. there

H. his

J. its

49. If the writer were to delete the preceding sentence, the essay would primarily lose:

A. an introduction of several historical figures who will each be discussed further.

B. a fact that helps to explain why the origin of Valentine's Day is shrouded in mystery.

C. an interpretation of historical events that refutes the common wisdom about Valentine's Day.

D. a possible answer to the questions surrounding the origin of Valentine's Day.

50. F. NO CHANGE

G. whose name was Valentine

H. by the name of Valentine

J. OMIT the underlined portion

GO ON TO THE NEXT PAGE.

because he believed, single soldiers were better soldiers.
—————
51

[5] Valentine defied what he saw as an unjust decree

by continuing to perform marriages for young lovers.

[6] When this was discovered. Claudius had Valentine
                        —————————
                            52

put to death. [53]

[3]

Why celebrate St. Valentine on February 14th! The
                                        —————
                                          54
simplest answer is that this is supposedly the anniversary

of the date when they was either executed or buried.
                    —————
                      55
However, some scholars claim that it was because the

Christian church sought to replace the pagan fertility festival
                        ————————————————————————————
                                        56
of Lupercalia with its own celebration. Lupercalia was
————————————————————
        56
celebrated until the end

of the fifth century when Pope Gelasius, who was the pope
                    ———————————————————————————
                                57
at that time, outlawed the festival and declared February
—————
  57
14th St. Valentine's Day.

51. **A.** NO CHANGE
    B. because he, believed
    C. because he believed
    D. because, he believed

52. **F.** NO CHANGE
    G. discovered, Claudius
    H. discovered; Claudius
    J. discovered, and Claudius

53. For the sake of the logic and coherence of this paragraph, Sentence 4 should be placed:
    A. where it is now.
    B. after Sentence 1.
    C. after Sentence 2.
    D. after Sentence 6.

54. **F.** NO CHANGE
    G. 14th. The
    H. 14th, the
    J. 14th? The

55. **A.** NO CHANGE
    B. he was
    C. it was
    D. they were

56. Given that all of the choices are true, which one provides the most logical cause for the action described in the statement immediately following this underlined portion?
    F. NO CHANGE
    G. to give converts a chance to celebrate a romantic holiday.
    H. to require former pagans to learn about St. Valentine.
    J. to create another joyous Winter holiday to keep morale up until Spring.

57. **A.** NO CHANGE
    B. when Pope Gelasius
    C. when the pope at that time, Gelasius,
    D. when the pope at that time, named Gelasius,

GO ON TO THE NEXT PAGE.

Practice Tests

[4]

During the Middle Ages, tales of romance flourished.
58

e date was also believed to be the beginning of birds'

ting season, which also might had lead to the day being
59

sociated with romance.

[5]

By the 19th century the combination of mass

oduced cards and inexpensive postage made exchanging

alentine's Day greetings very popular. Today, it is second

ly to Christmas in the number of cards exchanged for the

oliday.

58. Given that all the choices are true, which one provides the best opening to this paragraph?

   F. NO CHANGE

   G. St. Valentine became popular during the Middle Ages.

   H. Perhaps because of his dedication to young lovers, St. Valentine's day became associated with romance during the Middle Ages, a time when tales of romance flourished.

   J. Perhaps because the Middle Ages were a time of upheaval and young romance, St. Valentine became very popular during that time.

59. **A.** NO CHANGE

   B. might have led

   C. might have lead

   D. might led

> Question 60 asks about the preceding passage as a whole.

60. Upon reviewing notes for this essay, the writer comes across the following true statement:

> The first mass-produced valentines in America were elaborate creations featuring real lace and colorful graphics made by Esther A. Howland, the "Mother of the Valentine."

If the writer were to use this sentence, the most logical place to add it would be after the first sentence in Paragraph:

   F. 1.

   G. 2.

   H. 3.

   J. 5.

GO ON TO THE NEXT PAGE.

PASSAGE V

How is Paper Made?

[1]

We are surrounded by paper. Books, newspapers,

magazines, the boxes our cereal comes in, and that paper
                                                    61

plates we use to avoid washing dishes all add up to millions

of tons of paper. Even as we move toward "paperless

environment," in the U.S. alone, offices use a so-called
                                                   62

12.1 trillion sheets of paper each year. 63 According to

one study by the American Forest & Paper Association,

they discard 4 million tons of paper every year.
   64

[2]

Where do they all come from? Although paper has
          65

been made using such materials as rice, water plants,

cotton, and even recycled clothing, most of the paper made

today comes from pulpwood logs, recycled paper products,

or by mixing logs and recycled paper into a combination
                                              66

of the two. No matter what material is used, the process is
   66

---

61. A. NO CHANGE
  B. those
  C. them
  D. a

62. The best placement for the underlined phrase would be
  F. where it is now.
  G. after the word *toward*.
  H. after the word *offices*.
  J. before the word *paper*.

63. Given that all the choices are true, which one provides the most relevant information at this point in the essay?
  A. Paper manufacturing also uses a large amount of water.
  B. Further, up to 95% of business information is still recorded on paper.
  C. The global average is much lower, however.
  D. Paper can be recycled up to seven times before it has to be combined with fresh wood pulp.

64. F. NO CHANGE
  G. it discards
  H. Americans discard
  J. the American Forest & Paper Association discards

65. A. NO CHANGE
  B. does he
  C. does it
  D. does they

66. F. NO CHANGE
  G. a combination of the two.
  H. by mixing the two into a combination.
  J. by mixing logs and recycled paper.

GO ON TO THE NEXT PAGE.

Practice Test

asically similar to the process devised by the ancient
67

hinese more than 2,000 years ago. Fibers are mixed in a

quid, then pressed into a flat surface and allowed to dry.

his was once done by hand; however, advances in

manufacturing technology had transformed papermaking
68

om a fledgling industry into a large-scale industrial
69

rocess.

[3]

The story begins in the forest. After harvesting trees,
70

emoving the bark, and milling the wood into lumber, there

s a lot left over. These leftovers are converted into small

vood chips, and the small wood chips are then either ground
71

lown or mixed with chemicals to create a pudding-like pulp.

Obviously, there's a lot of liquid in the pulp that must be

emoved.

[4]

So the next step is to spray it onto moving wire
72

creens that can be up to 20 feet wide. These screens move

67. **A.** NO CHANGE
   B. basic similarly
   C. basically similarly
   D. basic similar

68. **F.** NO CHANGE
   G. will have transformed
   H. transform
   J. have transformed

69. At this point, the writer wants to add a statement that would effectively contrast the old process of papermaking with the process that it is today. Given that all of the choices are true, which one would best accomplish that purpose?
   A. NO CHANGE
   B. a small-scale craft
   C. a natural process
   D. an art-form

70. Given that all of the choices are true, which one would most effectively introduce this paragraph?
   F. NO CHANGE
   G. When paper is made from wood, the first step is to harvest trees.
   H. As I've already mentioned, paper can be made from recycled paper or from wood.
   J. Here, we are concerned only with paper that is made from wood.

71. **A.** NO CHANGE
   B. those little wood chips are then either further ground
   C. the chips are then either
   D. the chips, already small, are then either ground

72. **F.** NO CHANGE
   G. the wet paper pulp
   H. the liquid portion
   J. that

GO ON TO THE NEXT PAGE.

at speeds as fast as 60 miles <u>per hour which forces the water</u>
                                        73

to drop away and makes the cellulose fibers mat together to

form paper. While the paper is still damp, it is fed through

heated rollers that press and dry it.

[5]

The completed paper is wound into reels. These paper

reels can be so large it takes a crane to move them. The

paper on the reels is cut into whatever size is needed

to create the final paper product. 74

73. A. NO CHANGE
   B. per hour which forces,
   C. per hour, which forces,
   D. per hour, which forces

74. Which of the following sentences, if added here, would provide the best conclusion to the paragraph and make it most consistent with the main focus of the essay?

   F. Whether that product is a book or a paper plate made of recycled paper or from a newly-cut tree, the process of creating the material from which it is made is essentially the same.

   G. The fact that paper reels are so large means that huge storage facilities must be maintained to handle it all.

   H. There are a trillion reasons to choose paper goods made from recycled paper instead of chopping down trees.

   J. Imagine what the ancient Egyptians would think about that!

> Question 75 asks about the preceding passage as a whole.

75. The writer is considering combining Paragraphs 3 and 4 into a single paragraph. Should the writer make this change?

   A. Yes, because Paragraphs 3 and 4 are concerned with the same subject.

   B. Yes, because Paragraph 4 is only three sentences.

   C. No, because Paragraph 3 describes how water is removed from paper pulp, while Paragraph 4 describes how paper is stored.

   D. No, because combining the paragraphs will result in a single paragraph with more than 5 sentences.

END OF TEST 1

STOP! DO NOT TURN THE PAGE UNTIL YOU ARE TOLD TO DO SO

Mathematics Test
60 Minutes—60 Questions

DIRECTIONS: For each problem, solve for the correct answer, select your choice and fill in the corresponding bubble on your answer document.

Some problems may take a longer time to solve, but do not take too much time on any single problem. Solve the easier questions first, then return to the harder questions in the remaining time for this test.

A calculator is allowed on this test. While you may be able to solve some problems without a calculator, you are allowed to use a calculator for all of the problems on this test.

Note: Unless otherwise directed, all of the following statements are considered correct.

1. All drawn figures are NOT necessarily drawn to scale
2. All geometric figures are in a plane.
3. The word *line*, when used, is the same as a straight line
4. The word *average*, when used, is the same as arithmetic mean.

---

1. In scientific notation, $0.00000729 = ?$

    A. 7.29×10^{-8}
    B. 7.29×10^{-6}
    C. 7.29×10^{-5}
    D. 7.29×10^{-4}
    E. 0.729×10^{-3}

2. The average of 2 numbers is 184. The smaller of the 2 numbers is 170. What is the value of the larger number?

    F. 192
    G. 195
    H. 198
    J. 199
    K. 201

3. What is the greatest common factor of 72, 88, and 120?

    A. 2
    B. 3
    C. 4
    D. 6
    E. 8

4. If $6z + 2 = 5 - 11z$, then $z = ?$

    F. $\dfrac{3}{17}$
    G. $\dfrac{17}{3}$
    H. 3
    J. $\dfrac{7}{17}$
    K. $-\dfrac{7}{5}$

5. The rectangular field shown below has an area of 320,000 square feet. If the field is 400 feet wide, as shown below, what is the perimeter of the field?

    A. 800 feet
    B. 1,200 feet
    C. 1,600 feet
    D. 1,800 feet
    E. 2,400 feet

    400 feet

6. Which of the following ratios is equivalent to $\dfrac{2}{5} : \dfrac{1}{8}$?

    F. 1:20
    G. 2:5
    H. 8:5
    J. 16:5
    K. 5:16

GO ON TO THE NEXT PAGE.

If $f(x) = (a^4b^3)^{2x+1}$, what is the value of $f(2)$?

A. a^9b^8

B. $a^{10}b^9$

C. $a^{15}b^{20}$

D. $a^{20}b^{15}$

E. $a^{24}b^{18}$

A recipe for 5 cupcakes calls for $1\frac{1}{4}$ cups of flour. A bag of flour contains $7\frac{1}{2}$ cups. How many cupcakes can be made with 1 bag of flour?

F. 5

G. 6

H. 7

J. 25

K. 30

9. If n is a positive integer, which of the following *must* be odd?

A. n

B. $n + 1$

C. $2n$

D. $2n + 1$

E. $3n$

10. A student creates a circle graph to help plan her homework time over the course of 24 hours, as shown below. If she sleeps for 8 hours, which of the of the following is the closest angle measure for the time she spends on homework?

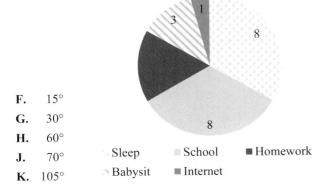

Sleep   School   Homework
Babysit   Internet

F. 15°

G. 30°

H. 60°

J. 70°

K. 105°

11. For all x, $(x - 5)(x + 2) = ?$

A. $x^2 + 3x - 10$

B. $x^2 - 3x - 10$

C. $x^2 - 3x + 10$

D. $x^2 - 10$

E. $x^2 - 3x$

12. If a is half of b, and c is 3 times a, how many times greater than b is c?

F. $\frac{1}{2}$

G. $\frac{2}{3}$

H. $\frac{3}{2}$

J. 2

K. 3

13. If $|x - 5| = 3$ and $4x + 1 = y$, which of the following is a possible value for y?

A. 42

B. 9

C. 0

D. −9

E. −33

14. A blueprint depicts the floor of a treehouse. The blueprint is a rectangle measuring 6 inches by 10 inches, and the floor's longer side measures 15 feet. To the nearest foot, what is the length of the shorter side of the floor?

F. 4

G. 6

H. 9

J. 10

K. 15

GO ON TO THE NEXT PAGE.

15. In the figure below, A, C, and E are collinear, B, C, and D are collinear, and $\overline{AB}$ is parallel to $\overline{DE}$. What is the sum of the measures of the angles marked x and y?

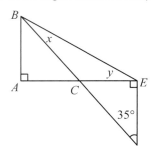

A. 35°
B. 45°
C. 55°
D. 125°
E. 135°

16. If x is a real number such that $\sqrt{x} = 2$, then $x^2 + x^3 = ?$

F. 4
G. 16
H. 32
J. 64
K. 80

17. In the scale model of the solar system shown below, the distance from the Sun to Jupiter is 65 cm, the distance from the Sun to Mars is 20 cm, and the distance from Mercury to Jupiter is 60 cm. What is the distance from Mercury to Mars?

Sun   Mercury   Mars   Jupiter

A. 45 cm
B. 40 cm
C. 25 cm
D. 15 cm
E. 5 cm

18. The smaller of two numbers is 6 less than 2 times the larger number. When the smaller number is subtracted from the larger number, the result is 1. If y is the larger number, which equation below determines the correct value of y?

F. $y - 2y - 6 = 1$
G. $(2y - 6) - y = 1$
H. $y - (2y - 6) = 1$
J. $2y - (2y - 6) = 1$
K. $y - (2y - 6) = 0$

19. The expression $(x^6 - x^5)^{\frac{1}{2}}$ is equivalent to:

A. 1
B. $x\sqrt{x - 1}$
C. $\sqrt{x^5 + x - 1}$
D. $x^2\sqrt{x^2 - x}$
E. $x^2\sqrt{2x - 1}$

20. A right triangle has a base of 4 units and hypotenuse of 6 units. What is its height?

F. $2\sqrt{5}$
G. $5\sqrt{2}$
H. $\sqrt{10}$
J. $2\sqrt{10}$
K. 20

Use the following information to answer questions 21-22.

Nathan budgets $100 for iced tea and spends $10 on iced tea every day.

21. Which of the following expressions represents the amount of money remaining in Nathan's iced tea budget after w weeks?

A. $100 + 5w$
B. $100 + 70w$
C. $100 - 50w$
D. $100 - 70w$
E. $70w$

22. Nathan decides to increase how much he spends on iced tea by $10 per day, starting on day 2 and ending when he spends 100% of his budget. During which day will Nathan run out of money?

F. Day 3
G. Day 4
H. Day 5
J. Day 6
K. Day 7

GO ON TO THE NEXT PAGE.

23. Which of the following equations represents the line below?

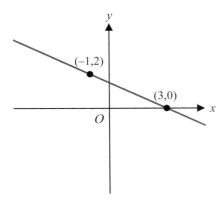

A. $y = -2x + \dfrac{3}{2}$

B. $y = -\dfrac{1}{2}x + \dfrac{3}{2}$

C. $y = \dfrac{1}{2}x + \dfrac{3}{2}$

D. $y = \dfrac{1}{2}x - \dfrac{3}{2}$

E. $y = 2x + \dfrac{3}{2}$

24. A chimpanzee receives a maximum of 63 bananas each week. Some weeks, the chimpanzee does not eat the maximum number of bananas. If b is its average daily banana consumption for a 1 week period, which of the following inequalities best describes b?

F. $b \le 9$

G. $b \ge 9$

H. $b \le 63$

J. $b \ge 63$

K. $b \ge 441$

25. Which of the following expressions is equivalent to $-\left(\dfrac{(z^2 - 4)}{16z^3 - 64z}\right)$?

A. $-\dfrac{1}{4}z$

B. $-\dfrac{1}{4}x^2z^2$

C. $-\dfrac{1}{32z}$

D. $\dfrac{1}{4z}$

E. $-\dfrac{1}{16z}$

26. A door-stopper is a triangle with a height increase of 2 inches for every 5-inch increase in the length of the horizontal base. The top corner of the door-stopper fits exactly in the 3-inch space between the bottom of a door and the floor. What is the length, in inches, of the base of the door-stopper?

F. 1.2

G. 2.5

H. 5.0

J. 7.5

K. 15.0

27. $(8x^2y^3)^2 \cdot (-2x)^3 = ?$

A. $-512x^7y^6 - 2y^3$

B. $-512x^{12}y^5 - 2y^3$

C. $-512x^{12}y^6 + 2y^3$

D. $-512x^{12}y^5 + 2y^3$

E. $-512x^7y^6$

28. Which of the following is the solution to the system of equations below?

$$y = x + 1$$
$$y = -3x - 3$$

F. $(-1, 0)$

G. $(1, 2)$

H. $\left(\dfrac{1}{2}, \dfrac{5}{4}\right)$

J. $\left(-\dfrac{1}{2}, \dfrac{3}{4}\right)$

K. There are no solutions to the system of equations.

29. In order to win an election, the top candidate must receive at least 30 votes more than the runner-up candidate. If the top candidate receives a votes, and the runner-up candidate receives b votes, which of the following expresses this rule?

A. $a - b \ge 30$

B. $a - b \le 30$

C. $a - b = 30$

D. $a - b > 30$

E. $a - b < 30$

GO ON TO THE NEXT PAGE.

30. $32^{\frac{2}{5}}$ is equivalent to which of the following?

   F. $2^{\frac{7}{5}}$

   G. 2^2

   H. $2^{\frac{5}{2}}$

   J. 2^5

   K. 2^7

31. What is the area of the parallelogram, in units squared?

   A. 20

   B. 25

   C. 32

   D. 40

   E. 120

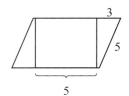

32. If the pattern below continues to increase, what will be the total number of circles in the first 9 rows?

   F. 21

   G. 63

   H. 117

   J. 130

   K. 189

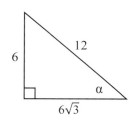

33. In the triangle below, what is the value of sin α?

   A. 3

   B. 2

   C. $\dfrac{5}{6}$

   D. $\dfrac{\sqrt{3}}{2}$

   E. $\dfrac{1}{2}$

34. In a drama class of 60 students, $\dfrac{1}{4}$ participate in musical theater. Of the students in musical theater, $\dfrac{1}{3}$ do not play an instrument. How many students in the class participate in musical theater and play an instrument?

   F. 15

   G. 10

   H. 8

   J. 5

   K. 3

35. A fundraiser sells cookies for \$2 each. Its goal is to average \$100 per day over 1 full week. On the first 6 days the fundraiser made \$52, \$84, \$106, \$66, \$94, and \$98. How many cookies must be sold on the last day in order to reach this goal?

   A. 28

   B. 38

   C. 50

   D. 54

   E. 100

36. The table below shows values of x and $f(x)$ for the function $f(x) = mx + 4$. What is the value of m?

x	$f(x)$
0	4
1	7
2	10
3	13
4	16
5	19

   F. 1

   G. 2

   H. 3

   J. 4

   K. 5

37. Parallelogram $ABCD$ is divided into 4 triangles. $\triangle AEL$ and $\triangle BCF$ are congruent isosceles triangles. $\triangle ABF$ and $\triangle ECD$ are congruent right triangles. If angle $\angle EDC$ measures 50°, what is the measure of $\angle FBC$?

   A. 20°

   B. 30°

   C. 45°

   D. 50°

   E. 60°

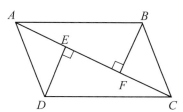

GO ON TO THE NEXT PAGE.

38. Two perpendicular lines on a standard (x,y) coordinate plane intersect at the point $(2,1)$. If one of the lines crosses the y-axis at the origin, at what point does the other line intersect the y-axis?

  F. $(0,0)$

  G. $(0,2)$

  H. $(0,5)$

  J. $(5,0)$

  K. $(2,0)$

39. A local sports store sells baseballs, hockey sticks, and footballs. For every hockey stick sold, it sells 3 baseballs. For every baseball sold, it sells 5 footballs. If the store sold 720 footballs, how many hockey sticks did it sell?

  A. 43

  B. 48

  C. 90

  D. 144

  E. 240

40. A square is inscribed in another square, as shown in the figure below. What percentage of the larger square's area is the smaller square's area?

  F. 33%

  G. 43%

  H. 50%

  J. 52%

  K. 64%

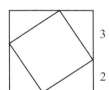

41. If $c = 2x^2 - 10x - 28$ and $d = 4x + 8$, which expression is equivalent to $\dfrac{c}{d}$?

  A. $x - 7$

  B. $\dfrac{x - 7}{2}$

  C. $x - \dfrac{7}{2}$

  D. $\dfrac{x + 7}{2(x + 2)}$

  E. $\dfrac{(x + 7)(x - 2)}{2(x + 2)}$

42. Which of the following systems of inequalities represents the shaded region on the graph below?

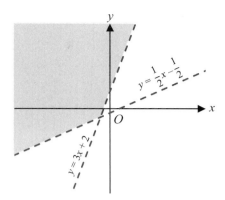

  F. $y > \dfrac{1}{2}x - \dfrac{1}{2}$ and $y > 3x + 2$

  G. $y > \dfrac{1}{2}x - \dfrac{1}{2}$ or $y < 3x + 2$

  H. $y < \dfrac{1}{2}x - \dfrac{1}{2}$ and $y < 3x + 2$

  J. $y > \dfrac{1}{2}x - \dfrac{1}{2}$ and $y < 3x + 2$

  K. $y > \dfrac{1}{2}x - \dfrac{1}{2}$ or $y > 3x + 2$

43. Given that $i^2 = -1$, what is the value of $(i + 2)(i - 2)$?

  A. 5

  B. $4 + i$

  C. -5

  D. $-4 + i$

  E. $-4 - i$

44. The unit vector notations for vectors **u** and **v** are given by $\mathbf{u} = 7\mathbf{i} + 4\mathbf{j}$ and $\mathbf{v} = 3\mathbf{i} - 2\mathbf{j}$. What is the value of $2\mathbf{u} - 3\mathbf{v}$?

  F. $4\mathbf{i} + 6\mathbf{j}$

  G. $5\mathbf{i} + 14\mathbf{j}$

  H. $8\mathbf{i} + 12\mathbf{j}$

  J. $10\mathbf{i} + 2\mathbf{j}$

  K. $20\mathbf{i} + 6\mathbf{j}$

GO ON TO THE NEXT PAGE.

45. If $\sin \theta = \dfrac{1}{2}$ and $\cos \theta = \dfrac{\sqrt{3}}{2}$, $\theta = ?$

   A. 15°

   B. 30°

   C. 45°

   D. 60°

   E. 90°

46. A square window with a perimeter of 16 inches and a piece of colored glass is shown in the standard (x,y) coordinate plane below.

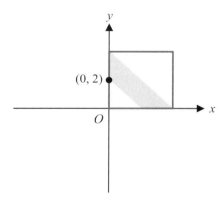

If the edge of the colored glass that connects with the point $(0,2)$ has a slope of -1, what is the perimeter, in inches, of the colored glass?

   F. 12

   G. 8

   H. $6 + 2\sqrt{3}$

   J. $4 + 6\sqrt{2}$

   K. $4 + 2\sqrt{2}$

47. $x^{\log_x a} = ?$

   A. a

   B. $a \cdot \log_a x$

   C. 0

   D. 1

   E. $\log_x 2a$

Use the following information to answer questions 48-50.

A gold company melts gold and forms it into bars. They have 100,000 cubic centimeters of gold, and they plan to make gold bars in the shape of trapezoidal prisms, each with a volume of 1,040 cubic centimeters and an expected pure weight of approximately 12.55 kilograms, as shown in the figure below. All measurements are in centimeters.

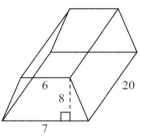

48. The company covers the bottom and top of each gold bar in wax paper to prevent scratching. To the nearest square centimeter, how much wax paper would it need to cover 1 gold bar?

   F. 130

   G. 140

   H. 260

   J. 420

   K. 1,040

49. After the company makes the maximum number of gold bars from its gold, what volume, in cubic centimeters, of gold will be left over?

   A. 96

   B. 100

   C. 160

   D. 320

   E. 884

50. The purity of gold is its actual weight divided by its expected weight. If the company makes a gold bar with the dimensions above that weighs 12.52 kg, what is its purity, to the nearest tenth of a percent?

   F. 52.0%

   G. 94.5%

   H. 98.9%

   J. 99.6%

   K. 99.8%

GO ON TO THE NEXT PAGE.

1. Which of the following is NOT infinite?

   A. Line

   B. Line segment

   C. Ray

   D. Plane

   E. All of the above are infinite.

2. Centripetal force can be modeled by the equation $F = \dfrac{mv^2}{r}$, where m is mass, v is velocity, and r is the distance to the center of the circle. If the centripetal force is doubled and the mass and distance from the object to the center remain the same, how does the velocity change?

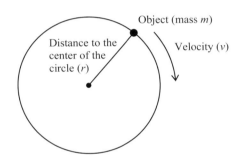

Object (mass m)

Distance to the center of the circle (r)

Velocity (v)

   F. v is multiplied by a factor of $\sqrt{2}$.

   G. v is multiplied by a factor of 2.

   H. v is multiplied by a factor of 4.

   J. v is divided by a factor of 2.

   K. v is divided by a factor of 4.

53. Let u, v, and w be positive integers such that $u = \dfrac{3v}{5}$ and $v = \dfrac{4}{w}$. Which of the following expresses w in terms of u?

   A. $\dfrac{12}{5u}$

   B. $\dfrac{5}{12u}$

   C. $\dfrac{4}{u}$

   D. $\dfrac{5u}{12}$

   E. $\dfrac{12u}{5}$

54. Two congruent triangles are drawn on a standard (x,y) coordinate plane, as shown below.

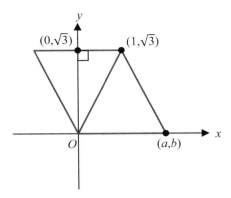

What is the value of $\dfrac{b}{a} + a$?

   F. $\dfrac{3}{2}$

   G. 0

   H. 1

   J. $\dfrac{3}{2}$

   K. 2

55. A radar on a boat records the positions of 2 islands, A and B, and the angle between them, as shown in the diagram below. If the units on the diagram are in miles, what is the distance d between islands A and B to the closest mile?

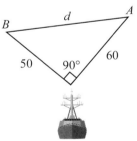

(Note: For a triangle with sides of length a, b, and c, and opposite angles $\angle A$, $\angle B$, and $\angle C$, respectively, the law of cosines states $c^2 = a^2 + b^2 - 2ab \cos \angle C$.)

   A. 10

   B. 78

   C. 100

   D. 110

   E. 6,100

GO ON TO THE NEXT PAGE.

56. If the statement "If a wagon is red, then it is painted" were true, which of the following statements must be true?

   F. "If a wagon is red, then it is not painted."

   G. "If a wagon is not red, then it is not painted."

   H. "If a wagon is painted, then it is red."

   J. "If a wagon is not painted, then it is red."

   K. "If a wagon is not painted, then it is not red."

57. A pool with a base of 30 feet by 15 feet is filled to a uniform depth of 5 feet, as shown below. The walls of the pool are 5.5 feet high. Three people enter the pool and it overflows. Which of the following, to the nearest cubic foot, is the minimum volume displaced by the 3 people?

   A. 2,475

   B. 2,250

   C. 1,650

   D. 450

   E. 225

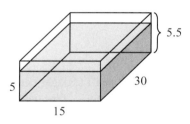

58. Which of the following graphs functions $f(x)$, $g(x)$, and $h(x)$ for $-2 < 2x \leq 2$?

$$f(x) = -x^2 - 1$$

$$g(x) = \frac{x}{2} + \frac{1}{2}$$

$$h(x) = 1 - x$$

   F.

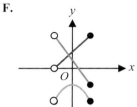

   J.

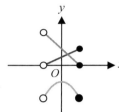

   G.

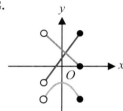

   K.

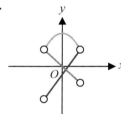

   H.

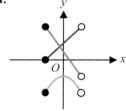

GO ON TO THE NEXT PAGE.

Practice Test

59. A restaurant cuts a circular table so it has a flat edge that can rest against a wall, as shown in the figure below. The radius of the table is 40 centimeters, and the distance from the center to the flat edge is 32 centimeters. To the nearest centimeter, how long is the flat edge of the table?

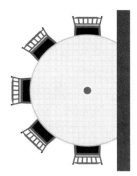

A. 24
B. 48
C. 64
D. 80
E. 96

60. An oceanographer records the height of the tides at a beach at regular intervals throughout the week. She plots the data on a graph and finds that it can be modeled by the function $y = a \cos(kx) + c$, where y is height and x is time. If the time between high tides decreased, which constant in the function would change?

F. a
G. k
H. c
J. x
K. y

END OF TEST 2.

STOP! DO NOT TURN THE PAGE UNTIL YOU ARE TOLD TO DO SO.

DO NOT RETURN TO THE PREVIOUS TEST.

Reading Test

35 Minutes—40 Questions

DIRECTIONS: There are multiple passages in this test. Each one is accompanied by several questions. After reading a passage, choose the best answer to every question and fill in the matching circle on your scoring sheet. You can refer back to the passages as often as necessary.

Passage I

Prose Fiction: This passage is adapted from the story "Metropolis" by Crystal Gail Shangkuan Koo. The story focuses on a young woman's recollection of her time in Beijing. (©2016 Crystal Gail Shangkuan Koo).

This is how you talk about a city you love. You talk about it as if it's the only place in the world where this story can happen.

The postcard I look at most often now was a picture
5 of a language university in Beijing that specialized in teaching Mandarin to foreigners. Once in the Philippines, when I was eleven, I had to recite the week's lesson from memory in Mandarin class.

Eight years later I was sent to Beijing with my
10 parents' blessings. I met my language partners every Friday in the school library, two girls who wanted to practice their English with me, but they frequently slipped back to Mandarin. *How can you be Chinese? How can you be Filipino? How can you speak English?*
15 *You speak Filipino too, right? How do you say, 'How do you do?'* Xin Feng spoke English with recklessness and confidence; Miao Ban was made of inquisitiveness, looking at Xin Feng for frequent translation.

Xin Feng and Miao Ban brought me out for dinner.
20 Across the restaurant was a frozen lake, fenceless, unwatched. I had never stood on iced water before. Figures whispered and laughed softly around me, but the lake was quiet and the world was calm.

I went walking in a *hutong* during lunch hour in
25 spring. Pots of rice and cabbage boiled outside sheds made of iron sheets. The aroma of garlic and meat coming from the makeshift vents smelled of a home.

Once, after one of my lunch hour walks, I stood before the Imperial Palace in the Forbidden City, hat in
30 my hands, waiting for a realization to engulf me. It had only been in Beijing that I learned to say 'ancestors' without feeling too self-aware. But tourists jostled around me, shoving each other to see the Imperial Throne, and the realization never came.

35 I went to parks often to escape the crowds. One of them had a small pavilion. When I reached it, a few lights were turned on softly and old fifties music was playing and middle-aged people were dancing. Some wore cocktail dresses; others office clothes. Swing, tango,
40 waltz. They would take each other's arms and twirl over the floor, lost in the sepia-colored music. Spring was turning to summer. I sat on a nearby bench, feeling the air turn humid, and a dragonfly landed on my shoulder.

Once, an old man and his wife stopped me on the
45 way back to the university. His accent was missing the Beijing growl. He said they had come to the city because his wife needed a surgical operation. The wife was moaning to herself and her husband was close to tears. They were hungry and needed money for a subway ticket
50 to the hospital.

I went to a small restaurant nearby and bought them two meals and bottled tea. Both of them were crying. I gave them money for the trip, and as the old man took the coins he whispered to his wife in a dialect before
55 thanking me and turning away.

The months passed quickly. Beijing was a detour to keep off the hunger till we reached home. That is why we write stories of it, so we won't forget. If I had found a home in Beijing, where I am a nameless unit in a sea
60 of faces, where I am finally part of the majority—until I speak and the accent reveals everything—I would have forgotten all my wonder.

Toward the end of my trip, I went to see my friend. She had been watching the sandstorm when I arrived.

65 She looked at me and asked: "So what's waiting for you after Beijing?"

"Looking for work in the Philippines, I suppose. Or maybe I'll go to Hong Kong and teach English there. Something. How are you doing?"

70 She shrugged. "I think he's going to call it quits before I leave. It's difficult. I mean, if it all just falls apart in the future, it won't be completely unexpected."

GO ON TO THE NEXT PAGE.

My friend left Beijing three days before I did. I heard from friends that she and her boyfriend did break up. I wonder how he could stay there seeing everything that would remind him of her.

This is how you talk about something you love. You tell *why*. And in the end it's really all about remembering. How the sun rose above the granite and concrete. How the pigeon flew above you, its tail feathers trilling. Sometimes I remember it so well I can feel the sand being crunched between my teeth.

The author's tone can be described as:

A. resentful.

B. distraught.

C. worshipful.

D. reflective.

The main purpose of the passage is to:

F. describe a nostalgia for one's hometown.

G. show the process of learning a language.

H. relate the meaningfulness of a place.

J. demonstrate a good deed.

It can be reasonably inferred from the passage that the narrator:

A. grew up in Beijing, lived for a while in the Philippines, and then visited Beijing.

B. grew up in the Philippines and visited Beijing.

C. grew up in and still lives in Beijing.

D. grew up in Hong Kong and visited Beijing.

4. Details in the passage suggest that the context for the narrator's meeting with Xin Feng and Miao Bian is that the three of them:

F. are family friends.

G. have been acquaintances since high school.

H. met by chance in a restaurant.

J. study at the same university.

5. The passage mentions all of the following in relation to Beijing EXCEPT:

A. local foods.

B. public leisure activities.

C. art festivals.

D. historical sites.

6. When the narrator says she is waiting for a "realization" (line 30), she means she was:

F. waiting for her language lessons to take hold.

G. hoping to be overtaken in a crowd.

H. wishing to feel a profound connection to her heritage.

J. looking for inspiration for her writing in the Forbidden City.

7. The scene where the narrator encounters the old man and his wife could have all of the following purposes EXCEPT:

A. to contrast with the more serene picture of Beijing in the previous paragraph.

B. to illustrate a tragic aspect of Beijing's busy atmosphere.

C. to give a fuller impression of the narrator's emotions during her stay.

D. to emphasize the narrator's fear of falling ill.

8. In saying that "Beijing was a detour" (line 56), the author suggests that:

F. she only stayed in Beijing for a couple of weeks.

G. Beijing was a popular destination spot for tourists.

H. she felt Beijing could only be a temporary home.

J. Beijing had many winding routes.

9. The narrator notes that not making a home in Beijing allows her to:

A. return early to the Philippines.

B. write a renowned story about Beijing.

C. begin a life of luxurious travel.

D. keep Beijing something of a mystery.

10. The story of the friend's breakup serves to:

F. mirror the narrator's complex feelings about leaving Beijing.

G. illustrate the romantic nature of relationships in Beijing.

H. provide a scenario of which the author is jealous.

J. prove that the author is a good friend.

GO ON TO THE NEXT PAGE.

Passage II

Social Science: Passage A is adapted from the article "Why Do Oil Prices Keep Going Down?" by Marcelle Arak and Scheila Tschinkel (©2016 Marcelle Arak and Scheila Tschinkel). Passage B is adapted from the article "We Need to Rethink the Financial Future of Oil" by Andreas Goldthau and Benjamin Sovacool (©2016 Andreas Goldthau and Benjamin Sovacool).

Passage A by Marcelle Arak and Scheila Tschinkel

A glut of crude oil in the global economy has led to the sharp declines in oil prices. Additional supplies of oil have ended up in storage tanks, because consumption of oil has barely budged. In tandem with price, oil revenues
5 of producing countries have dropped. If prices have fallen so much, why doesn't demand increase? It's because oil use in the short run is determined by factors that cannot be changed quickly.

Economists look at the responsiveness of demand
10 to price changes in terms of "the elasticity of demand." Demand for oil consumption in the short run is inelastic, in that it is not significantly affected by changes in price. To illustrate, a consumer driving a gas-guzzling SUV in excellent condition will not trade it in right away just
15 because prices rise. Or if you are a manufacturer and your equipment is still in good condition, you cannot quickly adjust this equipment to use less energy or buy different machines.

With demand for oil inelastic, the price decline does
20 not generate enough of an increase in sales volume to raise revenue for any seller. Nonetheless, producers and individual nations keep trying to increase revenue by producing and selling even more oil.

If demand is inelastic in the short run, would
25 withholding supply (in hopes prices will rise) lead to more revenue? If a cooperating group of sellers account for a large enough share of total sales, cutting back on supply will generate a large-enough price increase that these sellers can improve their revenue, even if sales
30 volume declines. In the 1970s, the Organization of Petroleum Exporting Countries controlled more than half of the global supply of crude oil. When it cut production, prices rose and all its members benefited. All it would take today is two or three major suppliers
35 working together to restrict supply sufficiently to raise prices by enough to increase their total revenue. This would also improve revenues of countries and producers who did not cut back.

That said, today's oil-producing countries don't

40 appear interested or even able to work together to rais prices—let alone to do so unilaterally—due in part varying foreign policy interests and economic structure Producers may also be thinking long-term and waitin out the lower prices in hopes of either pushing U.S
45 marginal suppliers into bankruptcy or reversing the tren toward fuel efficiency.

In the long run, the price elasticity of demand higher, because consumers are more responsive to pric changes. If prices go up, consumers and businesse
50 eventually find ways to cut back. If prices are low demand will eventually rise to a level commensurat with the reduced cost. Meanwhile, though, as long a supply continues to rise and demand remains inelastic o unresponsive, the price of oil is likely to continue it
55 slide.

Passage B by Andreas Goldthau and Benjami Sovacool

The price of oil keeps moving in one direction— down. Oil assets are on the losing side and the futur does not bode well for global oil. This, however, is fo reasons related to climate change, not because o
60 tumbling prices. Two actors are key: the U.S government and financial investors.

In the U.S., "independents" have become squeezed "Independents" are small- to mid-sized companies tha form the backbone of the recent shale-to-gas revolution
65 So far, they have shown a remarkable ability to cope wit an oil price spiraling downward, thanks to thei innovative nature and their ability to cut costs and streamline production processes. Now, they have hi their limits, and find themselves in the red.

70 The U.S. government's decarbonization strategy meanwhile, has a strong incentive to keep thes independents alive and well. By and large the strategy relies on replacing coal with gas, in addition to implementing tougher power plant regulation. This
75 strategy has worked so far thanks to lots of additional gas coming online as a byproduct of oil production, keeping the market oversupplied and gas cheap.

The finance industry, in turn, shows signs of a serious rethink over whether oil remains as attractive for
80 investment as it has been in the past. Already in 2013, Citibank, a global financial firm, declared that global oil demand was "approaching a tipping point" and that "the end is nigh" for growth. It cited the trends of substituting natural gas for oil, coupled with improvements in the fue
85 economy of vehicles, as the reasons.

GO ON TO THE NEXT PAGE.

Moreover, 196 world parties to the 2015 Paris Climate Conference acknowledged that humanity must, for climate reasons, manage its remaining "carbon budget." This means that it needs to limit, and eventually
90 end, the use of fossil fuels, including oil. As a consequence, many barrels of oil will need to stay in the ground as "stranded assets." Reacting to this, the global insurance companies Allianz and Axa already announced an end to investing in coal. Oil is likely to
95 follow. With the global divestment movement gaining further traction, there will be additional impetus from civil society to abandon oil. This is why some observers have already called on established international oil companies "to sell their existing oil reserves as quickly
00 as possible."

Ultimately, the future politics of oil present a fundamental and inescapable paradox. Ironically, it is the very same climate change imperatives that are helping to stabilize America's oil industry in the short
05 term that will sound its death knell in the long term.

14. According to the passage, all of the following are reasons countries that supply oil are unwilling to deliberately increase oil prices EXCEPT:

F. confidence that oil prices will increase naturally over time.
G. satisfaction with current strong oil revenues.
H. political relations among countries.
J. different economic structures within nations.

Questions 15-17 ask about Passage B.

15. It is reasonable to infer from the passage that the U.S. government:

A. prefers shale to gas as an energy source.
B. has policies in place to reduce uses of carbon.
C. is uninvolved with private oil companies' activities.
D. is creative in streamlining production of oil.

Questions 11-14 ask about Passage A.

11. According to the passage, demand for oil in the short term is "inelastic" in response to price (line 11) because:

A. oil is a non-renewable natural resource.
B. all car models use relatively the same amount of oil.
C. consumers are slow to adjust consumption in the short term.
D. consumers actively resist economic pressures.

12. The authors would most likely characterize suppliers' efforts to increase revenue by selling still more oil as:

F. necessary.
G. inventive.
H. ineffective.
J. disastrous.

13. The passage states that decreasing oil supply sufficiently will cause:

A. a decrease in demand for oil.
B. an increase in demand for oil.
C. a decrease in price of oil.
D. an increase in revenues from oil.

16. The passage mentions Citibank's declarations (lines 80-83) primarily in order to:

F. prove that automobiles use fuel more efficiently than before.
G. highlight the environmental leadership of major investors.
H. emphasize a collaboration between financial investors and the U.S. government.
J. cite an example of how investors are turning away from oil.

17. It is reasonable to infer from the passage that a paradox of lowered financial investment in oil is that:

A. investors are writing off oil, while consumers remain optimistic about it.
B. the long-term decrease in oil's value is protecting the oil industry in the short term.
C. coal is in high demand, but oil is not.
D. oil prices are going down, while oil supplier revenues are going up.

GO ON TO THE NEXT PAGE.

Questions 18-20 ask about both passages.

18. Both Passage A and Passage B are concerned with:

  F. patterns of decreasing prices of oil.

  G. trends of increasing revenues of oil suppliers.

  H. implications of climate change on oil sales.

  J. the effects oil price has on demand.

19. Which of the following is a reason for the oversupply of oil mentioned by Passage A but not by Passage B?

  A. Alternative natural sources of oil

  B. Lower financial investment in oil

  C. Oil reserves that have to be sold off

  D. Oil suppliers' efforts to increase revenues

20. The authors of Passage A suggest that in the long run, for oil, "If prices are low, demand will eventually rise to a level commensurate with the reduced cost" (lines 50-52). The authors of Passage B would most likely respond by saying that:

  F. long-term demand for oil is also inelastic.

  G. oil reserves will be used until they run out.

  H. the U.S. will mandate a ban on oil in the future.

  J. total oil usage will decline in the long run.

GO ON TO THE NEXT PAGE.

Passage III

Humanities: This passage is adapted from the article "Explainer: the History of Jazz" by Alexander Hunter (©2015 Alexander Hunter).

After more than 100 years of history, it's clear the word "jazz" means many different things to many different people. Depending on who's doing the talking, it can either mean a highly specific musical style, or almost
5 nothing. The early timeline of jazz is spotty, vague, and disputed, as one might expect of a musical movement that grew from a group that was both marginalized and exploited. Jazz evolved from the fringes of American society into one of the most influential, and enduring,
10 musical movements of the 20th century.

New Orleans in the late 1800s was a remarkably cosmopolitan city, with a more racially egalitarian society than the rest of the American south. In that city, distinct musical trends began to develop, fusing
15 elements of West African musical traditions with European harmonic structures.

Jelly Roll Morton claimed to have invented what we call "jazz" in 1902, and did much to popularize the New Orleans sound through newly available recording
20 technologies. By the time he recorded his "Black Bottom Stomp" in 1926, this new music had travelled as far as Chicago. In 1917 the cultural hub known as Storyville was closed, which coincided with The Great Migration, in which more than a million African Americans travelled
25 from rural communities in the South to major cities between 1910 and 1930. That migration, combined with recording technology and Prohibition, brought jazz to an unprecedented number of black and non-black audiences.

During this time, Louis Armstrong was at the
30 forefront of jazz. He altered the performance practice of jazz from the traditional texture in which multiple musicians play melody lines simultaneously, to what we now recognize as the individualist, soloist-plus-ensemble format. Later, the period between 1935 and
35 1946, generally referred to as the "Swing Era," saw small, soloist-plus-ensemble bands of Armstrong and others largely give way to big bands, consisting of about 18 musicians.

In the early 1940s, a schism occurred in jazz that
40 forever changed the face of pop music. Many black musicians resented the success of white bands and, led by Charlie Parker and Dizzy Gillespie, returned to the virtuosic combo setting. "Bebop" was faster and more complicated than anything that had come before it. This
45 was the first time jazz audiences sat down and listened, moving out of the dance halls and into smoky bars. Jazz

was becoming art music. Just as bebop musicians were getting the hang of their new ideas, the Musicians Union in the U.S. enforced a ban on new commercial recordings
50 as part of a dispute over royalties. For more than a year, starting in August 1942, almost no instrumental musicians were permitted to make new recordings (vocalists were exempt from the ban).

Before the ban, vocalists were special soloists with
55 big bands, and usually sang a verse or two in the middle of the song. But Tommy Dorsey's trombone, not Sinatra's voice, was the important feature. During the ban, audiences became accustomed to vocal pop music, and haven't looked back. From this split in the early 40s
60 between jazz as art music, and popular music with a vocal focus, the history of jazz follows the art branch.

Jazz musicians tend not to stay in one genre too long. Out of the rejection of the fast-paced, complex bebop emerged the late 40s new West Coast scene.
65 "Cool Jazz" had a more relaxed tempo, with less focus on soloing and a return to ensemble playing. This caused yet another reaction, resulting in what is known as "hard bop," which fuses bebop practices with R&B, Gospel, and Blues influences, and is generally
70 recognized as the default style practiced and taught around the world today.

In 1958, when bebop had taken chord progressions and virtuosity to its extreme, Miles Davis began experimenting with the other logical extreme. Jazz
75 musicians had been playing the same standard repertoire since the days of early bebop, and had become very adept at what is called "running the changes."

If bebop had the maximum number of chord changes, what might happen when there were no, or very few, chord
80 changes? Miles Davis's *Milestones* (1958) has only two chords. Davis sought to encourage melodic improvising by removing the "crutches" of complex changes. This "Modal Jazz" represented a huge shift in the techniques utilized by soloists, encouraging space in solos.

85 This focus in attention to space and melody, combined with new techniques and ideas coming out of the classical avant-garde, gave rise to a new avant-garde, and eventually "free," jazz. Starting with *The Shape of Jazz to Come* in 1959, Ornette Coleman did away with
90 chords altogether, encouraging musicians to play without being constrained by ideas of Western harmonic and melodic conventions.

As electronic instruments and funk gained in popularity, jazz musicians quickly jumped on new trends
95 and innovations, starting in 1968 with Miles Davis's

GO ON TO THE NEXT PAGE.

Filles de Kilamanjaro. As jazz moved through the 70s and 80s various elements of pop music seeped in, with just as many jazz elements seeping out.

When speaking of jazz in academia today we are
100 using the vocabulary set out by the pioneers of bebop. As with all music, jazz had to be codified, and classicized, in order to be studied, integrated into education, and understood.

21. Which of the following statements best characterizes the author's attitude toward jazz?

    A. It is an impressive form of music that has remained largely uniform through its short history.

    B. It is an outdated and largely forgotten form of music that should be revived.

    C. It is a fascinating and multifaceted form of music with many different eras in its evolution.

    D. It is a baffling form of music that achieved prominence largely because of bans on vocal music in the mid-century.

22. The passage devotes the LEAST attention to which of the following topics?

    F. The history of jazz music

    G. Popular jazz musicians

    H. Divisions within jazz

    J. Sales of jazz records

23. Which of the following developments does the passage indicate occurred first chronologically?

    A. Miles Davis experiments with "Modal Jazz."

    B. The cultural center of Storyville closes.

    C. Elements of pop music make their way into jazz.

    D. The "Swing Era" sees a shift towards larger bands.

24. What does the author name as the type of jazz that brings R&B, Gospel, and Blues infusions to bebop styles?

    F. Bebop

    G. Hard bop

    H. Modal jazz

    J. Free jazz

25. According to the passage, early precursors to jazz were influenced by:

    A. The Great Migration and the cultural hub of Storyville.

    B. New Orleans art and West African culture.

    C. African musical traditions and European harmonic structures.

    D. early R&B music and European classical music.

26. As it is used in line 28, the word *unprecedented* most nearly means:

    F. irreplaceable.

    G. unique.

    H. exclusive.

    J. record.

27. It is most reasonable to infer that in line 53 the phrase "exempt from the ban" refers to the fact that jazz vocalists:

    A. could still make new recordings.

    B. were still allowed to perform in bars.

    C. could make use of imported music.

    D. were not prevented from selling their work.

28. According to the passage, one of the effects of the ban imposed by the Musicians Union in the USA was that:

    F. jazz boomed as a genre as a result of restrictions on other forms of music.

    G. bebop trends started to veer more towards hard bop music.

    H. vocal music gained preeminence as audiences grew familiar with it.

    J. musicians moved from a focus on recordings to a focus on live performances.

29. The author notes that "free" jazz encouraged musicians to:

    A. offer public performances and concerts for free.

    B. shed the restrictions of traditional music conventions.

    C. collaborate with musicians in other genres.

    D. record songs that did not rely on contributions from vocalists.

30. The author refers to *Filles de Kilamanjaro* as an example of a work that:

    F. utilized new trends like electronic instruments and funk.

    G. infused classical jazz with many elements of pop music.

    H. found popularity only decades after its initial release.

    J. pushed the boundaries of conventional jazz with mixed results.

GO ON TO THE NEXT PAGE.

Passage IV

Natural Sciences: This passage is adapted from the article "What can beagles teach us about Alzheimer's disease?" by Elizabeth Head (©2015 Elizabeth Head).

Every 67 seconds, someone in the United States is diagnosed with Alzheimer's disease, and new estimates suggest that it may be the third leading cause of death for older people. Alzheimer's disease is associated with memory loss in older people that becomes severe enough over time to interfere with normal daily functions. Other signs of Alzheimer's include changes in the ability to communicate, losses in language, decreased ability to focus and to pay attention, impairments in judgment, and other behavioral changes.

People with Alzheimer's disease experience changes in their brains, which we can see in autopsies. Over the course of the disease, clumps of protein (called senile plaques) and tangles in neurons (called neurofibrillary tangles) accumulate. These plaques and tangles interfere with how the brain works and disrupt connections that are important for intact learning and memory ability.

The majority of studies to develop treatments for Alzheimer's disease use mice that are genetically modified to produce human proteins with mutations. But these mutations are usually present in less than 5% of people with Alzheimer's disease. This limitation can make it difficult to translate benefits of a treatment tested in mouse studies to people. However, there are several animals, including dogs, that naturally develop human-like brain changes that look much like Alzheimer's disease.

Old dogs may teach us a great deal about aging. As dogs get older, some develop learning and memory problems, much like we do. And like people, not all old dogs become impaired. Indeed, some old dogs remain bright and able to learn just as well as younger dogs, although they may be a little slower in reaching high levels of performance.

When aged dogs show cognitive changes not caused by other systemic illnesses, they are related to brain changes that are strikingly similar to people's. For example, old dogs develop senile plaques in their brains that are made of a protein that is identical to one that humans produce. This protein, called beta-amyloid, is toxic to cells in the brain. Unlike mice and rats, old dogs naturally develop significant brain pathology like we see in people. In this way, aging dogs may resemble aging humans in a more natural or realistic way than mice with genetic mutations.

Dogs may be very well suited to help us understand how different lifestyle factors help our brains as we get older. Our lab initially began studying beagles in the early 1990s, as there was interest in developing a drug to treat "dog dementia" based on pet owners' observations of changes in behavior in their older dogs. At that time, little was known about learning and memory changes in aging dogs (beagles over eight years of age) and our earliest research was designed to find ways to systematically measure these changes.

The first step in doing this was to teach dogs to look at different objects (for example a Lego block or a toy truck) and learn that one of the two always hid a food reward. When we switched the food reward to the object that was previously not rewarded, older dogs kept choosing the wrong object. Young dogs very quickly switched over to the new object.

When we counted the number of errors dogs make to learn the problem, old dogs made many more errors overall. Interestingly, not all old dogs were impaired. Another subset of old dogs showed significant losses in their ability to remember information and some showed changes in their ability to be "flexible" in changing behaviors.

This is very similar to people. Not everyone ages in the same way—some people remain sharp as tacks well into their older years. After measuring learning and memory changes in dogs, we next studied the brain changes that were most strongly linked to these cognitive losses. We found that senile plaques in the brains of old dogs were more frequent in the animals that had learning and memory problems. In our more recent studies, we have been seeking ways to improve brain health in old dogs with the hope that these approaches can translate to healthy aging in people.

For instance, in several studies of aging in beagles, we have found that a diet rich in antioxidants that includes vitamins E and C, and importantly, fruits and vegetables, can lead to wonderful benefits in learning and memory ability that can be maintained for years. Dogs that had trouble remembering where they had seen a food reward (this is an example of spatial memory) showed significant improvements in their memory over time when following this diet. Also, old dogs showed rapid improvements in their ability to modify their behaviors (an example of enhanced executive function)

GO ON TO THE NEXT PAGE.

when the rules had changed in the task they were learning. In addition, providing dogs with physical
95 exercise, social enrichment, and "brain games," like the food reward game, can also significantly improve cognition as they get older.

If we take these factors into account, we may be able to engage in strategies and lifestyle changes that
100 will be good for both species. If we participate in exercise, social interaction, and learning new tricks with our aged companion animals, the benefits will be twofold: for them and for us.

31. In the context of the passage as a whole, it is most reasonable to infer that the phrase "lifestyle factors" (line 48) includes:

  A. diet and exercise.
  B. memory and cognition.
  C. sleep and stress.
  D. strength and endurance.

32. The passage implies that Alzheimer's disease can cause:

  F. changes in the brain and behavior that may affect quality of life.
  G. a massive stroke due to the accumulation of neurofibrillary tangles.
  H. disruptions in long-term memory and ability to recall childhood memories.
  J. alterations in speech patterns and the favoring of short, simple words.

33. The passage suggests that dogs may be more useful than mice for studying Alzheimer's disease because:

  A. their age-related brain changes are more similar to humans'.
  B. they are mammals and so suffer from the same diseases.
  C. most dogs remain bright and intelligent through their old age.
  D. dogs have longer life spans than mice and can be studied for longer.

34. Which of the following findings, if true, would best support the idea that brain games "can significantly improve cognition" in aging dogs (lines 96-97)?

  F. Dogs that consumed more vitamin E and C outperformed others on cognitive tests.
  G. Dogs that exercised outdoors with their human owners developed better spatial memory.
  H. Dogs that engaged in memory-related tasks saw cognitive impairment at a later age than dogs that did not.
  J. Dogs that performed well on brain-related games typically continued to do so throughout their lives.

35. As described in the passage, people who suffer from Alzheimer's may experience all of the following EXCEPT:

  A. impairments in judgment.
  B. changes in behavior.
  C. loss of focus.
  D. improvements in language.

36. The passage makes clear that the senile plaques humans develop are made up of:

  F. beta-amyloid.
  G. vitamins E and C.
  H. neurons.
  J. neurofibrillary fibers.

37. According to the passage, in a study by the author, dogs were tested on their ability to:

  A. distinguish between numerous objects.
  B. sniff out a hidden treat.
  C. locate a food reward.
  D. follow verbal commands.

38. The central idea of the hypothesis proposed by the author is that:

  F. Alzheimer's can be cured with a proper regimen of diet and exercise.
  G. dogs and humans are more alike in cognition than previously recognized.
  H. specific lifestyle changes may delay some Alzheimer's symptoms.
  J. the buildup of plaque in dogs' brains can be treated with careful therapy.

GO ON TO THE NEXT PAGE.

9. As it is used in line 80, the word *translate* most nearly means:

   A. change.

   B. apply.

   C. transform.

   D. decode.

40. In their experiments with dogs on locating food rewards, the researchers measured their results by counting the number of:

   F. food rewards found by young versus old dogs.

   G. mistakes made before dogs found the reward.

   H. errors made before dogs gave up on the task.

   J. young dogs that performed better than old dogs.

END OF TEST 3.

STOP! DO NOT TURN THE PAGE UNTIL YOU ARE TOLD TO DO SO.

DO NOT RETURN TO THE PREVIOUS TEST.

Science Test

35 Minutes—40 Questions

DIRECTIONS: There are several passages in this test, and each is accompanied by several questions. After reading a passage, choose the best answer to each question and fill in the corresponding oval on your answer document. You may refer to the passages as often as necessary.

You are NOT permitted to use a calculator on this test.

Passage I

In honey bee colonies, there are 3 *castes*, or types of bees. The queen produces eggs at a rate of 2,000 per day. The workers care for the eggs, gather food, and defend the colony. The drones fertilize the eggs. Scientists investigated how bees maintain environmental conditions in the hive.

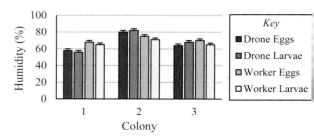

Figure 2

Experiment 1

Three honey bee colonies (Colonies 1–3) were placed in separate hives. A queen was placed in a cage in the center of each hive, and 800 worker eggs and 800 drone eggs were harvested from her over a period of 24 hrs. Worker larvae and drone larvae were taken from a different hive. Each of the 3 experimental hives contained 4 frames: one with worker eggs, one with worker larvae, one with drone eggs, and one with drone larvae. Three sensors were stripped of their plastic cases and inserted between each pair of frames. Temperature and humidity were recorded at intervals of 30 minutes over a period of 5 days (see Figure 1 and Figure 2).

Experiment 2

Honeycomb—wax cells full of honey—is often found in hives. Three hives were used to study how the presence of bees and honeycomb affects hive humidity. Each hive had frames, sensors, and queens inserted as in Experiment 1. Hive 1 contained no honeycomb and no bees. Hive 2 contained honeycomb but no bees. Hive 3 contained both honeycomb and bees. Humidity was recorded in each hive at intervals of 30 minutes over a period of 24 hrs (see Figure 3).

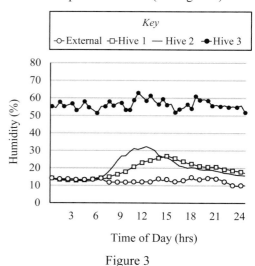

Figure 3

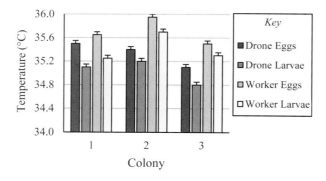

Figure 1

Data adapted from Zhiyong Li et al, "Drone and Worker Brood Microclimates Are Regulated Differently in Honey Bees, *Apis mellifera*." ©2016 by PLoS One. 10.1371/journal.pone.0148740

GO ON TO THE NEXT PAGE.

1. Based on the results of Experiment 1, frames containing which of the following had the highest average temperature?

   A. Drone eggs

   B. Drone larvae

   C. Worker eggs

   D. Worker larvae

2. In Experiment 1, did the scientists use all the eggs that each of the 3 queens could have produced that day?

   F. Yes; each queen could have produced 1,600 eggs per day.

   G. Yes; each queen could have produced 2,000 eggs per day.

   H. No; each queen could have produced 1,600 eggs per day.

   J. No; each queen could have produced 2,000 eggs per day.

3. Based on the results of Experiment 2, which of the following is the most important factor influencing humidity in the hive?

   A. Frames

   B. Sensors

   C. Combs

   D. Bees

4. The scientists place their sensor between two frames in another hive. It records an average temperature of 35.7°C and an average humidity of 65% at 30-minute intervals over a period of 5 days. If there were eggs and larvae in these frames, in which caste do they belong?

   F. Drones only

   G. Workers only

   H. Both drones and workers

   J. Neither drones nor workers

5. Which of the following claims about temperature and humidity is consistent with both Experiments 1 and 2?

   A. Temperature is dependent on caste, and humidity is dependent on the presence of bees.

   B. Temperature is dependent on the queen, and humidity is dependent on the presence of honeycomb.

   C. Humidity is dependent on caste, and temperature is dependent on the presence of bees.

   D. Humidity and temperature are both dependent on caste.

6. Which of the following is the best explanation for why the sensors were stripped of their plastic cases before they were inserted between the frames?

   F. The plastic cases were foreign to the honey bee hives.

   G. The plastic cases were too large to fit between the frames.

   H. The plastic cases increased the sensors' precision.

   J. The plastic cases increased the sensors' range.

7. When the temperature of the hive falls below 35.6°C, bees contract their thoracic muscles to heat it. When the temperature of the hive rises above 35.6°C, bees fan their wings to cool it. In Colony 2, which of these two methods would be more prevalent in the worker and drone frames?

	Drone	Worker
A.	thoracic contraction	thoracic contraction
B.	thoracic contraction	wing fanning
C.	wing fanning	thoracic contraction
D.	wing fanning	wing fanning

GO ON TO THE NEXT PAGE.

Passage II

Concrete is the most widely used building material in the world. It is relatively inexpensive but vulnerable to explosive blasts. New buildings can be reinforced against blast damage as they are built, but old buildings must be *retrofitted*—reinforced after construction with additional material.

Figure 1 shows the stress-strain curves of various materials. *Stress* is force per unit area, measured in kilopascals (kPa), and *strain* is percent deformation, which describes how much the shape of the material changes under stress. Materials fail at a certain combination of stress and strain, indicated by an *x* on the figure.

Figure 2 shows the displacement-time graph for concrete retrofitted with different 8 mm layers of spray-on polyurethane (PU) during and after the explosion of 2 kg of trinitrotoluene (TNT) from 1.6 m away over a duration of 1.05 ms. *Displacement* is the distance the material moves in response to a force.

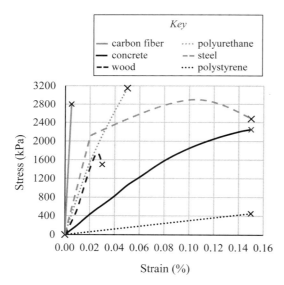

Figure 1

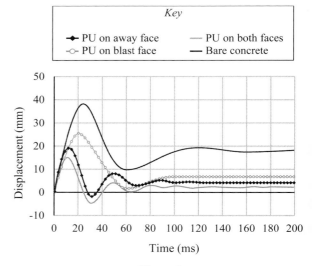

Figure 2

Figures adapted from S. N. Raman et al, "Elastomeric Polymers for Retrofitting of Reinforced Concrete Structures against the Explosive Effects of Blast." ©2012 by Advances in Material Science and Engineering. 10.1155/2012/754142

8. Based on Figure 2, the average displacement for bare concrete for the 200 ms during and after the explosion of 2 kg of TNT was closest to which of the following?

   F. 0 mm
   G. 12 mm
   H. 18 mm
   J. 39 mm

9. According to Figure 1, if polystyrene did not fail and its stress-strain curve had maintained its constant slope, its strain under 600 kPa of stress would most likely have been:

   A. less than 0.16%.
   B. between 0.16% and 0.20%.
   C. between 0.20% and 0.24%.
   D. greater than 0.24%.

GO ON TO THE NEXT PAGE.

10. Based on Figure 2, which of the following methods of retrofitting concrete was the most effective at reducing displacement?

    F. PU on away face

    G. PU on blast face

    H. PU on both faces

    J. Bare concrete

11. According to Figures 1 and 2, how do displacement and strain differ?

    A. Displacement is a distance, and strain is a percent change.

    B. Displacement is a percent change, and strain is a distance.

    C. Displacement is measured in kPa, and strain is a percent change.

    D. Displacement is a distance, and strain is force.

12. At the *yield point* of a given material, the relationship between stress and strain for a given material ceases to be linear. Prior to the yield point, a deformed material will return to its original shape. After the yield point, a material will maintain its deformed shape. If a steel plate experiences a stress of 2400 kPa, will it return to its original shape after deforming?

    F. Yes; this stress occurs before the yield point of steel.

    G. Yes; this stress occurs after the yield point of steel.

    H. No; this stress occurs before the yield point of steel.

    J. No; this stress occurs after the yield point of steel.

13. The *ultimate strength* of a material is the maximum amount of stress that it can bear without failing. Which of the following materials has an ultimate strength that is greater than the stress at its fail point?

    I. Carbon fiber

    II. Steel

    III. Wood

    A. I only

    B. II only

    C. II and III

    D. I, II, and III

GO ON TO THE NEXT PAGE.

Passage III

Harmful oral microbes cause infections and ferment sugars into acids, which erode the minerals of the teeth. They also form *plaque*, a film that covers the teeth and can lead to tooth decay and gum disease. Students studied how various toothpastes affect the growth of these microbes.

Experiment 1

The students prepared 12 plates with a standard nutrient broth before transferring microbes and toothpaste to the plates. They prepared 3 plates for each of 3 strains of oral microbes: *Streptococcus mutans*, *Candida albicans*, and *Escherichia coli*. They also prepared 3 plates without microbes. Each plate received the same 5 treatments: 0.2 mL droplets of 4 different types of toothpaste (Toothpastes 1–4) and a 0.2 mL droplet of distilled water. The plates were then incubated at 37°C for 48 hrs to allow the microbes to grow. The diameter of the *inhibition zone*—the area around the treatment where no microbes grew—was measured for each of the 12 plates as shown in Diagram 1. The averages of the diameters of the inhibition zones for each group of 3 plates are shown in Table 1.

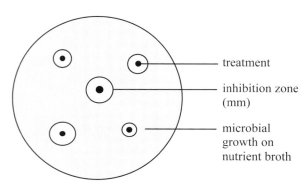

treatment

inhibition zone (mm)

microbial growth on nutrient broth

Diagram 1

Table 1

	S. mutans	C. albicans	E. coli	No Microbes
	Inhibition Zone Diameter (mm)			
Toothpaste 1	2.80	3.62	2.62	0.00
Toothpaste 2	1.25	3.21	2.00	0.00
Toothpaste 3	0.09	0.12	0.23	0.00
Toothpaste 4	2.21	1.30	1.36	0.00
Distilled Water	0.08	0.07	0.08	0.00

Experiment 2

The students repeated Experiment 1 using different dilutions of Toothpaste 1. Each plate received the same 5 treatments: 0.2 mL droplets of 4 different dilutions of Toothpaste 1 and a 0.2 mL droplet of distilled water. The dilutions were 1:2, 1:4, 1:8, and 1:16. The results are shown in Table 2.

Table 2

	S. mutans	C. albicans	E. coli	No Microbes
	Inhibition Zone Diameter (mm)			
1:2	2.49	3.14	2.31	0.00
1:4	1.41	1.78	1.32	0.00
1:8	0.86	1.20	0.75	0.00
1:16	0.40	0.55	0.38	0.00
Distilled Water	0.07	0.07	0.08	0.00

Experimental design adapted from Manupati Prasanth, "Antimicrobial Efficacy of Different Toothpastes and Mouthrinses: An In Vitro Study." © 2011 by Dental Research Journal PMC3177399

14. According to Experiment 1, which toothpaste was most effective at inhibiting microbial growth?

   F. Toothpaste 1
   G. Toothpaste 2
   H. Toothpaste 3
   J. Toothpaste 4

15. According to Experiment 2, when the concentration of toothpaste decreased, the growth of the microbes in the treatment area:

   A. increased only.
   B. decreased only.
   C. increased, then decreased.
   D. decreased, then increased.

16. If the *corrected diameter* of the inhibition zone is the average diameter of the distilled water inhibition zone subtracted from the average diameter of the treatment inhibition zone, what was the corrected diameter of the inhibition zone for Toothpaste 4 on *C. albicans*?

   F. 1.30 mm
   G. 1.28 mm
   H. 1.23 mm
   J. 0.05 mm

GO ON TO THE NEXT PAGE.

17. Distilled water is water that:

    A. has no chemical or biological contaminants.

    B. has been added to the toothpastes.

    C. is found in glaciers.

    D. has no microbial inhibition zone.

18. Suppose that, in Experiments 1 and 2, only treatments using toothpaste were conducted. What effect would the absence of a distilled water treatment have on the results of both experiments?

    F. The students would be unable to determine the differences between toothpaste treatments.

    G. The students would be unable to determine the type of microbes affected by the toothpaste.

    H. The students would be unable to determine the type of toothpaste used.

    J. The students would be unable to determine the cause of the inhibition zone.

19. In another experiment, a student treated *E. coli* with a 1:4 dilution of Toothpaste 4. Based on the data in Tables 1 and 2, which of the following was most likely the average inhibition zone diameter in this experiment?

    A. 0.65 mm

    B. 1.01 mm

    C. 1.32 mm

    D. 1.36 mm

20. Based on the results of Experiment 1, a student concludes that Toothpaste 2 was the second-most effective toothpaste against *all* 3 types of oral microbes. Do the data from Table 1 support this conclusion?

    F. No; Toothpaste 4 produced a larger inhibition zone against *S. mutans*.

    G. No; Toothpaste 3 produced a larger inhibition zone against *S. mutans*.

    H. Yes; Toothpaste 2 produced the second-smallest inhibition zones against all 3 types of oral microbes.

    J. Yes; Toothpaste 2 produced the second-largest inhibition zones against all 3 types of oral microbes.

GO ON TO THE NEXT PAGE.

Passage IV

Chemical reactions often move in only one direction, but can also move forward and backward. Le Chatelier's Principle states that if a reactant is added to a chemical reacton, more products will be produced, and if a product is added to a chemical reaction, more reactants will be produced.

Researchers performed two experiments to investigate Le Chatelier's Principle. They studied a reaction involving observable color changes. The equation of this reaction is as follows:

$$[CoCl_4]^{2-} + 6H_2O \rightleftharpoons [Co(H_2O)_6]^{2+} + 4Cl^-$$

Reactants	Products
(Clear)	(Pink)

Study 1

Researchers added 4 g of $CoCl_4^{2-}$ to 40 mL of water at 25°C. The resulting solution was a dark pink color. The researchers divided the solution into 5 vials (Vials 1–5) and added various amounts of hydrochloric acid (HCl), which contains Cl^-, to each vial (excluding Vial 1, which received no HCl). The researchers measured the light absorbance of each solution at 425 nm. The researchers also noted the color of each vial. The results are shown in Table 1.

Table 1			
Vial #	# HCl drops added	Color	Absorbance at 425nm
1	0	Dark pink	0.652
2	1	Medium pink	0.508
3	2	Light pink	0.348
4	3	Very light pink	0.211
5	4	Clear	0.046

Study 2

The researchers added 4 g of $CoCl_4^{2-}$ to 40 mL water at 25°C. They measured the absorbance of the solution and then heated the reaction vial over a flame, measuring the absorbance of the solution at 10°C intervals. They then cooled the vial in an ice bath and measured the absorbance at temperatures below 25°C. The results are shown in Table 2.

Table 2	
Temperature (°C)	Absorbance at 425 nm
25	0.648
35	0.604
45	0.555
55	0.505
65	0.447
15	0.696
5	0.749

21. According to Table 1, as more drops of hydrochloric acid were added to the reaction, the color of the solution

   A. became darker only.
   B. became lighter only.
   C. became darker, then lighter.
   D. did not change.

22. During Study 2, one of the researchers measured the absorbance of the solution at 50°C. The absorbance of the solution was most likely:

   F. 0.501.
   G. 0.525.
   H. 0.549.
   J. 0.576.

23. If the researchers from Study 2 had continued to heat the reaction vial to 85°C, the color of the solution would have been closest to:

   A. light pink.
   B. medium pink.
   C. dark pink.
   D. very light pink.

GO ON TO THE NEXT PAGE.

24. Suppose the researchers repeated Study 1, but instead of adding drops of HCl, they added drops of water (H_2O). Which of the following graphs shows the relationship between the number of water drops added and the absorbance of the solution?

F.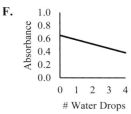

H.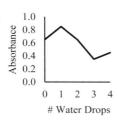

G.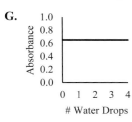

J.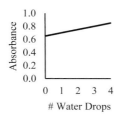

25. In Study 1, the addition of HCl to the reaction vials:

A. increased the concentration of one of the products, producing more products.

B. increased the concentration of one of the products, producing more reactants.

C. decreased the concentration of one of the reactants, producing more products.

D. decreased the concentration of one of the reactants, producing more reactants.

26. Based on the results of Study 2, one of the researchers concludes that, in this chemical reaction, heat is a product. Do the data in Table 2 support this conclusion?

F. No; as heat was added, more products were produced.

G. No; as heat was added, more reactants were produced.

H. Yes; as heat was added, more products were produced.

J. Yes; as heat was added, more reactants were produced.

27. After Study 1 was completed, it was discovered that the HCl used was contaminated with an unknown amount of pink dye, which absorbs light at 425 nm. What effect, if any, did this contamination have on the results of Study 1?

A. The pink dye increased the absorbance measurements of Vials 1, 2, 3, 4, and 5.

B. The pink dye decreased the absorbance measurements of Vials 1, 2, 3, 4, and 5.

C. The pink dye increased the absorbance measurements of Vials 2, 3, 4, and 5, but had no effect on Vial 1.

D. The pink dye had no effect on the absorbance measurements of Vials 2, 3, 4, and 5, but increased the absorbance of Vial 1.

GO ON TO THE NEXT PAGE.

Passage V

Scientists analyzed the climate change vulnerability of 82 species of fish and marine invertebrates found in the Northeast United States Continental Shelf region. Figure 1 shows a map of the region, which consists of 4 distinct sub-regions: Cape Hatteras, Mid-Atlantic Bight, Georges Bank, and the Gulf of Maine.

The scientists outlined 7 climate exposure factors to describe the extent to which a species experiences the effects of climate change. They then rated each marine species on a scale of 1–4 for each of these 7 factors. Table 1 shows the average score among all species for each factor.

The climate exposure factors were used to create an overall climate vulnerability score. The species were then divided into 6 general categories. Figure 2 shows the distributions of climate vulnerability scores for each category.

Table 1	
Climate Exposure Factor	Average Score
Surface temperature	3.95
Surface salinity	1.79
Air temperature	2.09
Precipitation	1.18
Ocean acidification	3.99
Currents	1.20
Sea level rise	1.27

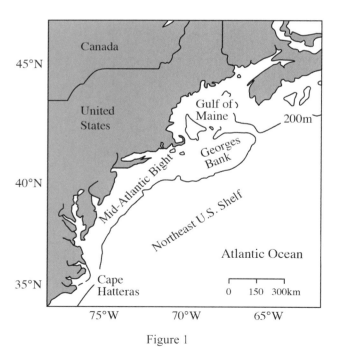

Figure 1

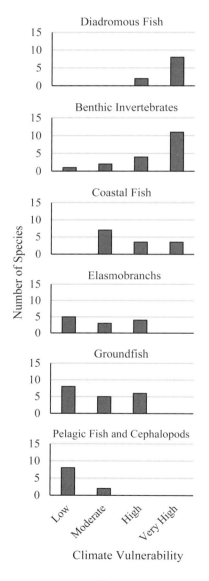

Figure 2

GO ON TO THE NEXT PAGE.

28. The witch flounder scores below average on its exposure to surface salinity. Which of the following could be the surface salinity exposure score of this species?

    F. 1.00
    G. 2.00
    H. 3.00
    J. 4.00

29. According to Figure 2, among the benthic invertebrates, which climate vulnerability score describes the largest number of species?

    A. Low
    B. Moderate
    C. High
    D. Very High

30. There were no species from Cape Hatteras that scored Very High on climate vulnerability. Which of the following categories of marine animal is LEAST likely to have been sampled from Cape Hatteras?

    F. Groundfish
    G. Pelagic fish and cephalopods
    H. Diadromous fish
    J. Elasmobranchs

31. Ocean acidification causes seawater to become more acidic. Which of the following statements best describes this phenomenon?

    A. The density of the seawater increases.
    B. The viscosity of the seawater decreases.
    C. The pH of the seawater increases.
    D. The pH of the seawater decreases.

32. A researcher hypothesizes that, because groundfish are found in the widest range of habitats, they will have the highest variability in climate vulnerability scores. Do the data from Figure 2 support this hypothesis?

    F. No; the diadromous fish show a wider range of climate vulnerability scores.
    G. No; the benthic invertebrates show a wider range of climate vulnerability scores.
    H. Yes; the groundfish show the widest range of climate vulnerability scores.
    J. Yes; the groundfish and elasmobranchs both show the widest range of climate vulnerability scores.

33. According to Figures 1 and 2, and assuming that climate change is more extreme in more northerly regions, which of the following populations is most vulnerable to climate change effects?

    A. Benthic invertebrates in Georges Bank
    B. Benthic invertebrates in the Gulf of Maine
    C. Elasmobranchs in the Gulf of Maine
    D. Groundfish in Cape Hatteras

GO ON TO THE NEXT PAGE.

Passage VI

A *supernova* is a star explosion, during which a star launches all its particles into space except its neutrons, which form a *neutron star*. Scientists debate whether neutron stars form *black holes*—objects with gravity so strong that no matter or radiation can escape them, making them difficult to detect.

(Note: The force of gravity depends on mass, and increases proportionally with it.)

Scientist A

Massive stars have too much gravity to launch all their particles into space. When a massive star explodes and forms a neutron star, some of the supernova debris accumulates on the neutron star and increases its mass. The neutron star's gravity, which pulls the debris inward, then exceeds its *neutron degeneracy* pressure, which pushes outward. The neutron star collapses into a black hole.

Black holes can be detected via distorted light, which occurs when light from stars close to a black hole is bent, forming halos, arcs of light, and duplicate star images. They can also be detected via *Hawking radiation*, which is the appearance of pairs of particles and antiparticles. These pairs negate each other and cease to exist—except when a particle appears outside a black hole and its antiparticle appears inside a black hole. The antiparticle cannot escape and negate the particle, so the particle exists and can be detected from Earth.

Scientist B

Massive stars explode with such force that all their particles are launched a great distance into space. Scientist A is incorrect in stating that the neutron star will accumulate supernova debris, because too few particles remain to accumulate on the neutron star. Therefore, it will not gain significant mass, and its gravity will not overcome its neutron degeneracy pressure. No black hole will form.

Distorted light does not indicate a black hole because galaxies and star clusters are massive enough to distort light from nearby stars. Any observed halos, arcs, or duplicate images are due to the force of gravity of galaxies or star clusters. There is no method to determine whether a particle came into existence through Hawking radiation at the edge of a black hole or elsewhere. Furthermore, single particles cannot be detected from Earth.

34. Which of the following observations would indicate the presence of a black hole, in Scientist A's view?

   F. The same star appears twice in a given region of space.

   G. A large neutron star is observed with gas and dust around it.

   H. A supernova is detected near the edge of a star cluster.

   J. A massive star orbits a neutron star.

35. Based on Scientist A's view, which of the following figures best depicts the change in mass of a massive star as it undergoes supernova and black hole formation?

   (Note: In each figure, S represents the star before the supernova occurs, N represents the time of neutron star formation, and B represents the time of black hole formation.)

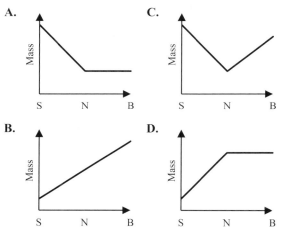

36. With which of the following statements would Scientist B be LEAST likely to agree?

   F. Neutron stars are often formed by supernova.

   G. Distorted light can be observed from Earth in the form of halos and arcs of light.

   H. Hawking radiation occurs in the universe.

   J. A neutron star's gravity always overcomes neutron degeneracy pressure.

GO ON TO THE NEXT PAGE.

37. Which scientist(s), if any, assert(s) that a neutron star will form after a massive star undergoes a supernova?

   A. Scientist A only

   B. Scientist B only

   C. Both Scientist A and B

   D. Neither Scientist A nor B

38. If a black hole were to form near a star, it would accumulate matter from that star. The accumulated matter would then emit single particles. Which scientist, if any, would be likely to claim that these particles would be observable from Earth?

   F. Scientist A only

   G. Scientist B only

   H. Both Scientist A and B

   J. Neither Scientist A nor B

39. Suppose a study of a nearby lone star, isolated from star clusters and galaxies, produced a double image and a nearby halo of light. How would this study most likely affect the scientists' viewpoints?

	Scientist A	Scientist B
A.	strengthen	strengthen
B.	strengthen	weaken
C.	weaken	strengthen
D.	weaken	weaken

40. Suppose a black hole had the same mass as the Sun. Which of the following statements accurately describes the relationship between the black hole's force of gravity and the Sun's force of gravity?

   F. The black hole's force of gravity would be smaller than the Sun's force of gravity.

   G. The black hole's force of gravity would be larger than the Sun's force of gravity.

   H. The black hole's force of gravity would be equal to the Sun's force of gravity.

   J. The black hole would not have a force of gravity.

END OF TEST 4.

STOP! DO NOT TURN THE PAGE UNTIL YOU ARE TOLD TO DO SO.

DO NOT RETURN TO THE PREVIOUS TEST.

Writing Test
40 Minutes—1 Prompt

Directions: This is a test of your writing ability. You'll have 40 minutes to read the prompt, plan your response, and write your essay. Before you begin, read all of the material in this test section carefully and make sure you understand what is being asked of you.

You should write your essay on the lined pages included in your answer sheet. Only your writing on those pages will be scored. Your work on these pages will not be scored.

Your essay will be graded based on the evidence it provides and your ability to:

- analyze and evaluate different perspectives on complicated issues
- express and develop your own perspective on the issue
- explain and support your arguments with logical reasoning and detailed examples
- clearly and logically organize your ideas in an essay
- effectively communicate your point of view in English

Stop writing and put down your pencil as soon as time is called.

DO NOT BEGIN THE WRITING TEST UNTIL YOU ARE TOLD TO DO SO.

Group Work or Individual Projects?

t's quite common for students in college and university classes to have group assignments. In a science class, several students might be responsible for a single lab experiment and report; in the humanities and social sciences, students might work together on a class presentation. Supporters of group assignments say that cooperation encourages students to share ideas and perspectives, and to get to know one another better. They also emphasize the importance of learning how to work well with others. Those who favor individual projects cite the potential for unfairness in groups, such as one or two students being given all of a group's work. Others question why particularly introverted students should be compelled to participate in group projects if they don't want to. Should college and university classes encourage group work, or should they encourage individual projects?

Read and carefully consider these perspectives. Each suggests a particular way of thinking about the merits of group work and individual projects.

Perspective 1	Perspective 2	Perspective 3
Working together is an important skill in many workplaces and academic fields. It is therefore important to encourage this behavior in undergraduates by assigning group projects.	It's more fair on students, who often have clashing schedules and differing personal investments in a class, to be given individual assignments only. This way, everyone will be judged solely on their own efforts.	Everyone is different. Some people love working in groups, and others are happiest working on their own. College and university educators should be mindful of this, and ensure that everyone's preferences are reasonably accommodated.

Essay Task

Write a unified, coherent essay in which you evaluate multiple perspectives on the merits of group work and individual projects. In your essay, be sure to:

- analyze and evaluate the perspectives given
- state and develop your own perspective on the issue
- explain the relationship between your perspective and those given

Your perspective may be in full agreement with any of the others, in partial agreement, or wholly different. Whatever the case, support your ideas with logical reasoning and detailed, persuasive examples.

Planning Your Essay

Your work on these prewriting pages will not be scored.

Use the space below and on the back cover to generate ideas and plan your essay. You may wish to consider the following as you think critically about the task:

Strengths and weaknesses of the three given perspectives
- What insights do they offer, and what do they fail to consider?
- Why might they be persuasive to others, or why might they fail to persuade?

Your own knowledge, experience, and values
- What is your perspective on this issue, and what are its strengths and weaknesses?
- How will you support your perspective in your essay?

Note

- Your practice Writing Test includes scratch paper and four lined sheets for your essay.
- Your official ACT exam will include a test booklet with space for planning and four lined sheets to write your essay.
- Review Answers and Scoring for instructions on how to grade your exam.

Practice Test 3

The ACT

This practice test contains tests in English, Math, Reading, and Science. These tests measure skills and abilities related to high school course work and college preparedness. **You can use a calculator on the math test only.**

The questions in each test are numbered, and the suggested answers for each question are lettered. On the answer sheet, the rows are numbered to match the questions, and the circles in each row are lettered to correspond to the suggested answers.

For each question, choose the best answer and fill in the corresponding circle on your answer document. Use a soft lead pencil and make your marks heavy and black. **Do not use a ballpoint pen.**

Fill in only one answer to each question. If you change your mind about an answer, completely erase your first mark before filling in your new answer. For each question, make certain that you mark in the row of ovals with the same number as the question.

Only responses marked on your answer sheet will be scored. Your score on each test will be based only on the number of questions you answer correctly during the time allowed for that test. You will NOT be penalized for guessing. **Even if you are unsure about an answer, you should make a guess.**

You may work on each test ONLY when your proctor tells you to do so. If you complete a test before the end of your allotted time, use the extra minutes to check your work on that section only. Do NOT use the time to work on another section. Doing this will disqualify your scores.

Put down your pencil immediately when time is called at the end of each test. You are not allowed to continue answering questions after the allotted time has run out. This includes marking answers on your answer sheet that you previously noted in your test booklet.

You are not allowed to fold or tear the pages of your test booklet.

Do Not Open This Booklet Until You Are Told to Do So.

NAME: _____

DATE: _____

TEST 1

1 Ⓐ Ⓑ Ⓒ Ⓓ	14 Ⓕ Ⓖ Ⓗ Ⓙ	27 Ⓐ Ⓑ Ⓒ Ⓓ	40 Ⓕ Ⓖ Ⓗ Ⓙ	53 Ⓐ Ⓑ Ⓒ Ⓓ	66 Ⓕ Ⓖ Ⓗ Ⓙ
2 Ⓕ Ⓖ Ⓗ Ⓙ	15 Ⓐ Ⓑ Ⓒ Ⓓ	28 Ⓕ Ⓖ Ⓗ Ⓙ	41 Ⓐ Ⓑ Ⓒ Ⓓ	54 Ⓕ Ⓖ Ⓗ Ⓙ	67 Ⓐ Ⓑ Ⓒ Ⓓ
3 Ⓐ Ⓑ Ⓒ Ⓓ	16 Ⓕ Ⓖ Ⓗ Ⓙ	29 Ⓐ Ⓑ Ⓒ Ⓓ	42 Ⓕ Ⓖ Ⓗ Ⓙ	55 Ⓐ Ⓑ Ⓒ Ⓓ	68 Ⓕ Ⓖ Ⓗ Ⓙ
4 Ⓕ Ⓖ Ⓗ Ⓙ	17 Ⓐ Ⓑ Ⓒ Ⓓ	30 Ⓕ Ⓖ Ⓗ Ⓙ	43 Ⓐ Ⓑ Ⓒ Ⓓ	56 Ⓕ Ⓖ Ⓗ Ⓙ	69 Ⓐ Ⓑ Ⓒ Ⓓ
5 Ⓐ Ⓑ Ⓒ Ⓓ	18 Ⓕ Ⓖ Ⓗ Ⓙ	31 Ⓐ Ⓑ Ⓒ Ⓓ	44 Ⓕ Ⓖ Ⓗ Ⓙ	57 Ⓐ Ⓑ Ⓒ Ⓓ	70 Ⓕ Ⓖ Ⓗ Ⓙ
6 Ⓕ Ⓖ Ⓗ Ⓙ	19 Ⓐ Ⓑ Ⓒ Ⓓ	32 Ⓕ Ⓖ Ⓗ Ⓙ	45 Ⓐ Ⓑ Ⓒ Ⓓ	58 Ⓕ Ⓖ Ⓗ Ⓙ	71 Ⓐ Ⓑ Ⓒ Ⓓ
7 Ⓐ Ⓑ Ⓒ Ⓓ	20 Ⓕ Ⓖ Ⓗ Ⓙ	33 Ⓐ Ⓑ Ⓒ Ⓓ	46 Ⓕ Ⓖ Ⓗ Ⓙ	59 Ⓐ Ⓑ Ⓒ Ⓓ	72 Ⓕ Ⓖ Ⓗ Ⓙ
8 Ⓕ Ⓖ Ⓗ Ⓙ	21 Ⓐ Ⓑ Ⓒ Ⓓ	34 Ⓕ Ⓖ Ⓗ Ⓙ	47 Ⓐ Ⓑ Ⓒ Ⓓ	60 Ⓕ Ⓖ Ⓗ Ⓙ	73 Ⓐ Ⓑ Ⓒ Ⓓ
9 Ⓐ Ⓑ Ⓒ Ⓓ	22 Ⓕ Ⓖ Ⓗ Ⓙ	35 Ⓐ Ⓑ Ⓒ Ⓓ	48 Ⓕ Ⓖ Ⓗ Ⓙ	61 Ⓐ Ⓑ Ⓒ Ⓓ	74 Ⓕ Ⓖ Ⓗ Ⓙ
10 Ⓕ Ⓖ Ⓗ Ⓙ	23 Ⓐ Ⓑ Ⓒ Ⓓ	36 Ⓕ Ⓖ Ⓗ Ⓙ	49 Ⓐ Ⓑ Ⓒ Ⓓ	62 Ⓕ Ⓖ Ⓗ Ⓙ	75 Ⓐ Ⓑ Ⓒ Ⓓ
11 Ⓐ Ⓑ Ⓒ Ⓓ	24 Ⓕ Ⓖ Ⓗ Ⓙ	37 Ⓐ Ⓑ Ⓒ Ⓓ	50 Ⓕ Ⓖ Ⓗ Ⓙ	63 Ⓐ Ⓑ Ⓒ Ⓓ	
12 Ⓕ Ⓖ Ⓗ Ⓙ	25 Ⓐ Ⓑ Ⓒ Ⓓ	38 Ⓕ Ⓖ Ⓗ Ⓙ	51 Ⓐ Ⓑ Ⓒ Ⓓ	64 Ⓕ Ⓖ Ⓗ Ⓙ	
13 Ⓐ Ⓑ Ⓒ Ⓓ	26 Ⓕ Ⓖ Ⓗ Ⓙ	39 Ⓐ Ⓑ Ⓒ Ⓓ	52 Ⓕ Ⓖ Ⓗ Ⓙ	65 Ⓐ Ⓑ Ⓒ Ⓓ	

TEST 2

1 Ⓐ Ⓑ Ⓒ Ⓓ Ⓔ	11 Ⓐ Ⓑ Ⓒ Ⓓ Ⓔ	21 Ⓐ Ⓑ Ⓒ Ⓓ Ⓔ	31 Ⓐ Ⓑ Ⓒ Ⓓ Ⓔ	41 Ⓐ Ⓑ Ⓒ Ⓓ Ⓔ	51 Ⓐ Ⓑ Ⓒ Ⓓ Ⓔ
2 Ⓕ Ⓖ Ⓗ Ⓙ Ⓚ	12 Ⓕ Ⓖ Ⓗ Ⓙ Ⓚ	22 Ⓕ Ⓖ Ⓗ Ⓙ Ⓚ	32 Ⓕ Ⓖ Ⓗ Ⓙ Ⓚ	42 Ⓕ Ⓖ Ⓗ Ⓙ Ⓚ	52 Ⓕ Ⓖ Ⓗ Ⓙ Ⓚ
3 Ⓐ Ⓑ Ⓒ Ⓓ Ⓔ	13 Ⓐ Ⓑ Ⓒ Ⓓ Ⓔ	23 Ⓐ Ⓑ Ⓒ Ⓓ Ⓔ	33 Ⓐ Ⓑ Ⓒ Ⓓ Ⓔ	43 Ⓐ Ⓑ Ⓒ Ⓓ Ⓔ	53 Ⓐ Ⓑ Ⓒ Ⓓ Ⓔ
4 Ⓕ Ⓖ Ⓗ Ⓙ Ⓚ	14 Ⓕ Ⓖ Ⓗ Ⓙ Ⓚ	24 Ⓕ Ⓖ Ⓗ Ⓙ Ⓚ	34 Ⓕ Ⓖ Ⓗ Ⓙ Ⓚ	44 Ⓕ Ⓖ Ⓗ Ⓙ Ⓚ	54 Ⓕ Ⓖ Ⓗ Ⓙ Ⓚ
5 Ⓐ Ⓑ Ⓒ Ⓓ Ⓔ	15 Ⓐ Ⓑ Ⓒ Ⓓ Ⓔ	25 Ⓐ Ⓑ Ⓒ Ⓓ Ⓔ	35 Ⓐ Ⓑ Ⓒ Ⓓ Ⓔ	45 Ⓐ Ⓑ Ⓒ Ⓓ Ⓔ	55 Ⓐ Ⓑ Ⓒ Ⓓ Ⓔ
6 Ⓕ Ⓖ Ⓗ Ⓙ Ⓚ	16 Ⓕ Ⓖ Ⓗ Ⓙ Ⓚ	26 Ⓕ Ⓖ Ⓗ Ⓙ Ⓚ	36 Ⓕ Ⓖ Ⓗ Ⓙ Ⓚ	46 Ⓕ Ⓖ Ⓗ Ⓙ Ⓚ	56 Ⓕ Ⓖ Ⓗ Ⓙ Ⓚ
7 Ⓐ Ⓑ Ⓒ Ⓓ Ⓔ	17 Ⓐ Ⓑ Ⓒ Ⓓ Ⓔ	27 Ⓐ Ⓑ Ⓒ Ⓓ Ⓔ	37 Ⓐ Ⓑ Ⓒ Ⓓ Ⓔ	47 Ⓐ Ⓑ Ⓒ Ⓓ Ⓔ	57 Ⓐ Ⓑ Ⓒ Ⓓ Ⓔ
8 Ⓕ Ⓖ Ⓗ Ⓙ Ⓚ	18 Ⓕ Ⓖ Ⓗ Ⓙ Ⓚ	28 Ⓕ Ⓖ Ⓗ Ⓙ Ⓚ	38 Ⓕ Ⓖ Ⓗ Ⓙ Ⓚ	48 Ⓕ Ⓖ Ⓗ Ⓙ Ⓚ	58 Ⓕ Ⓖ Ⓗ Ⓙ Ⓚ
9 Ⓐ Ⓑ Ⓒ Ⓓ Ⓔ	19 Ⓐ Ⓑ Ⓒ Ⓓ Ⓔ	29 Ⓐ Ⓑ Ⓒ Ⓓ Ⓔ	39 Ⓐ Ⓑ Ⓒ Ⓓ Ⓔ	49 Ⓐ Ⓑ Ⓒ Ⓓ Ⓔ	59 Ⓐ Ⓑ Ⓒ Ⓓ Ⓔ
10 Ⓕ Ⓖ Ⓗ Ⓙ Ⓚ	20 Ⓕ Ⓖ Ⓗ Ⓙ Ⓚ	30 Ⓕ Ⓖ Ⓗ Ⓙ Ⓚ	40 Ⓕ Ⓖ Ⓗ Ⓙ Ⓚ	50 Ⓕ Ⓖ Ⓗ Ⓙ Ⓚ	60 Ⓕ Ⓖ Ⓗ Ⓙ Ⓚ

TEST 3

1 Ⓐ Ⓑ Ⓒ Ⓓ	8 Ⓕ Ⓖ Ⓗ Ⓙ	15 Ⓐ Ⓑ Ⓒ Ⓓ	22 Ⓕ Ⓖ Ⓗ Ⓙ	29 Ⓐ Ⓑ Ⓒ Ⓓ	36 Ⓕ Ⓖ Ⓗ Ⓙ
2 Ⓕ Ⓖ Ⓗ Ⓙ	9 Ⓐ Ⓑ Ⓒ Ⓓ	16 Ⓕ Ⓖ Ⓗ Ⓙ	23 Ⓐ Ⓑ Ⓒ Ⓓ	30 Ⓕ Ⓖ Ⓗ Ⓙ	37 Ⓐ Ⓑ Ⓒ Ⓓ
3 Ⓐ Ⓑ Ⓒ Ⓓ	10 Ⓕ Ⓖ Ⓗ Ⓙ	17 Ⓐ Ⓑ Ⓒ Ⓓ	24 Ⓕ Ⓖ Ⓗ Ⓙ	31 Ⓐ Ⓑ Ⓒ Ⓓ	38 Ⓕ Ⓖ Ⓗ Ⓙ
4 Ⓕ Ⓖ Ⓗ Ⓙ	11 Ⓐ Ⓑ Ⓒ Ⓓ	18 Ⓕ Ⓖ Ⓗ Ⓙ	25 Ⓐ Ⓑ Ⓒ Ⓓ	32 Ⓕ Ⓖ Ⓗ Ⓙ	39 Ⓐ Ⓑ Ⓒ Ⓓ
5 Ⓐ Ⓑ Ⓒ Ⓓ	12 Ⓕ Ⓖ Ⓗ Ⓙ	19 Ⓐ Ⓑ Ⓒ Ⓓ	26 Ⓕ Ⓖ Ⓗ Ⓙ	33 Ⓐ Ⓑ Ⓒ Ⓓ	40 Ⓕ Ⓖ Ⓗ Ⓙ
6 Ⓕ Ⓖ Ⓗ Ⓙ	13 Ⓐ Ⓑ Ⓒ Ⓓ	20 Ⓕ Ⓖ Ⓗ Ⓙ	27 Ⓐ Ⓑ Ⓒ Ⓓ	34 Ⓕ Ⓖ Ⓗ Ⓙ	
7 Ⓐ Ⓑ Ⓒ Ⓓ	14 Ⓕ Ⓖ Ⓗ Ⓙ	21 Ⓐ Ⓑ Ⓒ Ⓓ	28 Ⓕ Ⓖ Ⓗ Ⓙ	35 Ⓐ Ⓑ Ⓒ Ⓓ	

TEST 4

1 Ⓐ Ⓑ Ⓒ Ⓓ	8 Ⓕ Ⓖ Ⓗ Ⓙ	15 Ⓐ Ⓑ Ⓒ Ⓓ	22 Ⓕ Ⓖ Ⓗ Ⓙ	29 Ⓐ Ⓑ Ⓒ Ⓓ	36 Ⓕ Ⓖ Ⓗ Ⓙ
2 Ⓕ Ⓖ Ⓗ Ⓙ	9 Ⓐ Ⓑ Ⓒ Ⓓ	16 Ⓕ Ⓖ Ⓗ Ⓙ	23 Ⓐ Ⓑ Ⓒ Ⓓ	30 Ⓕ Ⓖ Ⓗ Ⓙ	37 Ⓐ Ⓑ Ⓒ Ⓓ
3 Ⓐ Ⓑ Ⓒ Ⓓ	10 Ⓕ Ⓖ Ⓗ Ⓙ	17 Ⓐ Ⓑ Ⓒ Ⓓ	24 Ⓕ Ⓖ Ⓗ Ⓙ	31 Ⓐ Ⓑ Ⓒ Ⓓ	38 Ⓕ Ⓖ Ⓗ Ⓙ
4 Ⓕ Ⓖ Ⓗ Ⓙ	11 Ⓐ Ⓑ Ⓒ Ⓓ	18 Ⓕ Ⓖ Ⓗ Ⓙ	25 Ⓐ Ⓑ Ⓒ Ⓓ	32 Ⓕ Ⓖ Ⓗ Ⓙ	39 Ⓐ Ⓑ Ⓒ Ⓓ
5 Ⓐ Ⓑ Ⓒ Ⓓ	12 Ⓕ Ⓖ Ⓗ Ⓙ	19 Ⓐ Ⓑ Ⓒ Ⓓ	26 Ⓕ Ⓖ Ⓗ Ⓙ	33 Ⓐ Ⓑ Ⓒ Ⓓ	40 Ⓕ Ⓖ Ⓗ Ⓙ
6 Ⓕ Ⓖ Ⓗ Ⓙ	13 Ⓐ Ⓑ Ⓒ Ⓓ	20 Ⓕ Ⓖ Ⓗ Ⓙ	27 Ⓐ Ⓑ Ⓒ Ⓓ	34 Ⓕ Ⓖ Ⓗ Ⓙ	
7 Ⓐ Ⓑ Ⓒ Ⓓ	14 Ⓕ Ⓖ Ⓗ Ⓙ	21 Ⓐ Ⓑ Ⓒ Ⓓ	28 Ⓕ Ⓖ Ⓗ Ⓙ	35 Ⓐ Ⓑ Ⓒ Ⓓ	

Use a soft lead No. 2 pencil only. Do NOT use a mechanical pencil, ink, ballpoint, or felt-tip pens.

Begin WRITING TEST here.

If you need more space, please continue on the next page.

1

WRITING TEST

_____
_____
_____
_____
_____
_____
_____
_____
_____
_____
_____
_____
_____
_____
_____
_____
_____
_____
_____
_____
_____
_____
_____
_____
_____
_____

If you need more space, please continue on the back of this page.

2

WRITING TEST

_____
_____
_____
_____
_____
_____
_____
_____
_____
_____
_____
_____
_____
_____
_____
_____
_____
_____
_____
_____
_____
_____
_____
_____
_____
_____

If you need more space, please continue on the next page.

WRITING TEST

_____
_____
_____
_____
_____
_____
_____
_____
_____
_____
_____
_____
_____
_____
_____
_____
_____
_____
_____
_____
_____
_____
_____
_____
_____
_____
_____
_____
_____
_____
_____

STOP!

4

English Test

45 Minutes—75 Questions

DIRECTIONS: In the five passages that follow, certain words and phrases are underlined and numbered. In the right-hand column, you will find alternatives for the underlined part. In most cases, you are to choose the one that best expresses the idea, makes the statement appropriate for standard written English, or is worded most consistently with the style and tone of the passage as a whole. If you think the original version is best, choose "NO CHANGE." In some cases, you will find in the right-hand column a question about the underlined part. You are to choose the best answer to the question.

You will also find questions about a section of the passage, or about the passage as a whole. These questions do not refer to an underlined portion of the passage, but rather are identified by a number or numbers in a box.

For each question, choose the alternative you consider best and fill in the corresponding circle on your answer document. Read each passage through once before you begin to answer the questions that accompany it. For many of the questions, you must read several sentences beyond the question to determine the answer. Be sure that you have read far enough ahead each time you choose an alternative.

Passage I

Milton's Style: A Critical Controversy

[1]

The English poet John Milton is best known for his biblical epic poem *Paradise Lost*—a work that has provoked centuries of debate about the suitability of its style. Although Milton differed, from his immediate peers by refusing to use rhyme, his most heated critics appeared

1. **A.** NO CHANGE
   B. Although Milton differed from
   C. Although, Milton differed from
   D. Although, Milton, differed from

later, and starting in the eighteenth century. Readers of

2. **F.** NO CHANGE
   G. and, starting
   H. and, started
   J. starting

Paradise Lost have most commonly objected to the poems' complicated sentence structure and unusual word choices.

3. **A.** NO CHANGE
   B. poems
   C. poem's
   D. poem

[2]

The critic Samuel Johnson, in a series of essays written in 1751, argued that Milton's poetic language was often too harsh and jarring. He claimed that Milton chose

GO ON TO THE NEXT PAGE.

and arranged words in ways that <u>fail</u> to create a
₄

<u>pleasant effect and a musical effect.</u> However, Johnson did
₅

very modestly admit that he still might "fall below the

illustrious writer" of *Paradise Lost*, suggesting his continued

high regard for Milton in other ways. Although Johnson was

an important tastemaker in his time, in spite of an

appearance marred by scars from a childhood illness, the

pendulum swung back strongly in Milton's favor in

subsequent decades. ⑥

[3]

In the nineteenth century, Milton's poetry received

acclaim from important figures like Mary Shelley, Percy

Bysse Shelley, Thomas Coleridge, and William <u>Blake and in</u>
₇

<u>fact</u> many poets of the Romantic period in English literature
₇

chose to write in a similar way—a high form of praise!

[4]

<u>However,</u> many readers in the twentieth century once
₈

again found fault with Milton's style. T.S. Eliot, one of the

most famous poets <u>within</u> his generation, was among the
₉

4. **F.** NO CHANGE
    G. fails
    H. failed
    J. had failed

5. **A.** NO CHANGE
    B. pleasant, musical effect.
    C. pleasant effect, and a musical one.
    D. pleasant effect which would be musical.

6. The writer is considering deleting the following clause from the preceding sentence:

> in spite of an appearance marred by scars from a childhood illness,

Should the writer make this deletion?

    F. No, because the clause establishes Johnson's unusual authority as a tastemaker.
    G. No, because it prevents confusion with other eighteenth-century writers named Samuel Johnson.
    H. Yes, because it suggests that Johnson's unusual appearance was a hindrance rather than an asset.
    J. Yes, because it introduces material that is not immediately relevant.

7. **A.** NO CHANGE
    B. Blake and, in fact
    C. Blake. In fact,
    D. Blake, in fact

8. **F.** NO CHANGE
    G. Also,
    H. Meanwhile,
    J. Furthermore,

9. **A.** NO CHANGE
    B. at
    C. amongst
    D. of

GO ON TO THE NEXT PAGE.

most greatest critical. In a 1946 essay, he called Milton both
10
"great artist" and a "bad influence." According to Eliot,

Milton led other poets astray by encouraging them to focus

rather than their meanings, on the sounds of words. He cited
11
a number of examples in *Paradise Lost* where, he claimed,

the poem did not make any sense. Yet Milton continued to

have his defenders; Christopher Ricks, in his 1965 book

Milton's Grand Style, implicated Eliot of simply
12
misunderstanding the passages that he claims are nonsense.

C.S. Lewis and William Empson, two additional critics,
13
were less concerned with the style of Milton's poem than
13
they were with its religious themes.
13

[5]

Scholars of literature today have broadened their

horizons and are less likely to focus on style solely when
14

they make claims about Milton. [15]

---

10. F. NO CHANGE
   G. most
   H. most great
   J. greater

11. A. NO CHANGE
   B. rather on their meanings, than the sounds of words.
   C. on the sounds of words, rather than their meanings.
   D. on, rather their meanings, the sounds of words.

12. F. NO CHANGE
   G. implied
   H. prosecuted
   J. accused

13. Given that all of the following choices are true, which one would best maintain the focus of the preceding paragraph?

   A. NO CHANGE
   B. Ricks then went on to receive considerable praise and awards throughout his career, later becoming the president of the Association of Literary Scholars and Critics.
   C. Ricks' book remains well-regarded, and his opinions have helped to shape current thinking on Milton's work.
   D. Milton also wrote a great deal of nonfiction, including treatises on government, religion, and education.

14. F. NO CHANGE
   G. solely less likely to focus on style
   H. less solely likely to focus on style
   J. less likely to focus solely on style

15. Given that all of the following choices are true, which option provides the best concluding sentence for the passage was a whole?

   A. However, this critical history is still widely taught, and scholars continue to discuss and critique Milton's *Paradise Lost*.
   B. With its rich critical history, I can strongly recommend *Paradise Lost* to anyone who enjoys poetry.
   C. Samuel Johnson's essays, as public domain documents, can be read by all.
   D. *Paradise Lost* is still widely anthologized and translated.

GO ON TO THE NEXT PAGE.

Passage II

The Science of Chocolate Chip Cookie Perfection

Few things are more delicious than a perfect chocolate chip cookie. Some prefer a chewy cookie, while some want their cookies crisp; and others find a cake-like texture is the best.

Though there is room for debate about the definition of "perfection," what cannot be argued is this: achieving one's personal chocolate chip cookie ideal all comes down to science. More specifically, it all comes down to chemistry.

[1] Most recipes, for chocolate chip cookies, start with the same basic ingredients. [2] These ingredients include butter, sugar, vanilla, eggs, flour, salt, and some kind of chemical leavening agent such as baking soda, baking powder, or a combination of the two. [3] However, making cookies is about much more than combining a list of ingredients. [4] It's the ways these ingredients are handled during preparation and the techniques used to combine them that determine what type of chocolate chip cookie will be achieved. [5] Changing the way one ingredient is used can have a significant effect.

As a result, consider how butter is used. The first step in most recipes called for combined the butter with sugar. They are beaten together, and the moisture in the butter dissolves some of the sugar, which will leaven the

16. **F.** NO CHANGE
    G. Some prefer a chewy cookie, while some want their cookies crisp, and
    H. Some prefer a chewy cookie; while some want their cookies crisp, and
    J. Some prefer a chewy cookie; while some want their cookies crisp; and

17. **A.** NO CHANGE
    B. achieved
    C. achieves
    D. to achieve

18. **F.** NO CHANGE
    G. recipes for chocolate chip cookies start
    H. recipes, for chocolate chip cookies start
    J. recipes for chocolate chip cookies, start

19. Which of the following true statements, if added here, would provide the most effective link between Sentences 2 and 4?
    A. NO CHANGE
    B. The quality of individual ingredients can vary, and each ingredient must be of the highest quality.
    C. Baking is a fine art, and the greatest bakers can dedicate their lives to learning it.
    D. That would be like saying that painting is just a matter of putting colors on canvas!

20. **F.** NO CHANGE
    G. Therefore
    H. For example
    J. In contrast

21. **A.** NO CHANGE
    B. called for combining
    C. calls for combines
    D. calls for combining

GO ON TO THE NEXT PAGE.

Practice Test

ookies as they bake or, in other words, make them rise.
22

you combines melted butter and sugar, however, the result
23

a denser cookie. Browning butter, which evaporates the

ater content of the butter so that it won't dissolve sugar,

akes even more of a difference. 24

Then there's the effect of butter on gluten, the web of
25

iterconnected proteins that sets up when something is
25

aked. Gluten makes cookies crispier, and butter affects its

ormation. Butter inhibits gluten to produce a more tender
26

ookie, which cannot form in fat. As a result, more butter
26

iakes for a chewier cookie.

Conversely, less water also equals less gluten
27

22. **F.** NO CHANGE
  G. or make them rise.
  H. in other words, make them rise.
  J. DELETE the underlined portion.

23. **A.** NO CHANGE
  B. one
  C. they
  D. we

24. At this point, the writer is considering adding the following true statement:

  The browned milk solids can also be removed to create clarified butter, which is often used as a dipping sauce for crab and other delicacies.

  Should the writer make this addition here?

  F. Yes, because it provides important information about another form of butter.
  G. Yes, because it helps the reader better understand how to use different types of butter.
  H. No, because it distracts the reader from the main focus of the paragraph.
  J. No, because it is inconsistent with the style and tone of the essay.

25. **A.** NO CHANGE
  B. on gluten. The web of interconnected proteins
  C. on gluten; the web of interconnected proteins
  D. on gluten the web of interconnected proteins

26. **F.** NO CHANGE
  G. The butter, which cannot form in fat, inhibits gluten to produce a more tender cookie.
  H. The butter inhibits gluten, which cannot form in fat, to produce a more tender cookie.
  J. Unable to form in fat, butter inhibits gluten to produce a more tender cookie.

27. **A.** NO CHANGE
  B. Therefore,
  C. However,
  D. Furthermore,

GO ON TO THE NEXT PAGE.

development so a cookie made with browned butter will be
____
28

softer and chewier than one made with creamed butter or

even melted butter.

    If different ways of dealing with the butter make such

an enormous difference, then it's clear that the role of each
____
29

ingredient must be considered when thinking about

chocolate chip cookies.

28. **F.** NO CHANGE
    G. development, so
    H. development so,
    J. development, so,

29. **A.** NO CHANGE
    B. a jumbo
    C. an epic
    D. a very, very big

Question 30 asks about the preceding passage as a whole.

---

30. Suppose the writer had chosen to write a brief essay comparing the health benefits of chocolate chip cookies made with sweet butter with those made with salted butter. Would this essay successfully fulfill the writer's goal?

    F. Yes, because the essay does explain how different forms of butter affect the final cookies.
    G. Yes, because the essay includes salt in the list of ingredients used in most recipes.
    H. No, because the essay presents theories that do not reflect the effect of salt in butter on health.
    J. No, because the essay focuses only on the chemical effects of various forms of the ingredient in a recipe.

Passage III

Crab Fishing on the Pier

[1]

    I grew up next to the Pacific Ocean, where, it was
____
31

common to see people fishing for crabs on the pier. Even in

wet weather there would often be one or two dedicated

families standing at the railing in their raincoats, waiting to
____
32

31. **A.** NO CHANGE
    B. Pacific Ocean, where it
    C. Pacific Ocean where, it
    D. Pacific Ocean where it

32. The best placement for the underlined phrase would be:
    F. where it is now.
    G. after the word *Even*.
    H. after the word *weather*.
    J. after the word *traps*.

GO ON TO THE NEXT PAGE.

ıl up their traps. I can remembering my own
_____
33

nily going crab fishing as a family just once, though.
_____
34

[2]

I was only about five years old at the time, and the

ạ, cumbersome crab trap looked to me like some sort of
_____
35

ird metal basket. I also thought it was funny that my dad

ed, leftover chicken from lunch, as the bait. He tossed the
_____
36

ıp over the edge of the pier, and then the boring part
_____
37

ırted, we waited.
_____
37

ıerefore, my dad let me hold the yellow nylon line that led
_____
38

ıwn to the trap on the seabed, and I felt proud to have such

ı important job.

[3]

After a few unsuccessful hauls with nothing in the

ıp, we finally pulled up a load of crabs. This was quite an
_____
39

ıciting moment for me. 40 I'm not sure if I'd been to the

ıquarium yet, but I had definitely gone to the pet store to

ıok at the fish, and I loved everything to do with the

33. A. NO CHANGE
B. remembers
C. remembered
D. remember

34. F. NO CHANGE
G. family going crab fishing just once, though.
H. going crab fishing as a family just one time, though.
J. family going crab fishing just once, though, as I recall.

35. A. NO CHANGE
B. onerous
C. clumsy
D. manageable

36. F. NO CHANGE
G. used leftover chicken from lunch as the bait.
H. used leftover chicken, from lunch as the bait.
J. used leftover, chicken from lunch, as the bait.

37. A. NO CHANGE
B. and then: the boring part started, we
C. and then the boring part started: we
D. and then the boring part started we

38. F. NO CHANGE
G. Occasionally,
H. Otherwise,
J. Consequently,

39. A. NO CHANGE
B. he
C. I
D. they

40. Given that all the following statements are true, which one provides the most relevant information at this point in the essay?
F. It had been a long wait.
G. I stifled a yawn as my father pulled the yellow nylon line.
H. There were real crabs in the trap!
J. I'd never experienced a successful haul up close before this.

GO ON TO THE NEXT PAGE.

undersea world. [41] The crabs waved their claws at us

41. The writer is considering deleting the preceding sentence from the paragraph. If the writer made this deletion, the paragraph would primarily lose:

   A. information that distracts from the main point of the paragraph.

   B. a detail that relates the narrator's previous experiences with crabs.

   C. a detail that helps explain why the narrator was excited to see the crabs in the pot.

   D. the repetition of a detail that is clearly stated elsewhere in the paragraph.

through the metal basket, so I wondered if they'd enjoyed

                            42

our chicken.

42. **F.** NO CHANGE

   G. while

   H. for

   J. yet

[4]

Oddly enough, I don't remember us keeping or eating

the crabs, boiled, fried, or steamed that we caught that day.

                 43

They may simply have been too small, but I have an even

more likely theory. My dad is a very tender-hearted man, and

I think that once he saw the crabs he chose to let them go

back into the sea unharmed. That would also explain why we

never went crab fishing again.

43. **A.** NO CHANGE

   B. the crabs—boiled, fried, or steamed,

   C. the crabs—boiled, fried, or steamed—

   D. the crabs boiled, fried, or steamed—

Questions 44 and 45 ask about the preceding passage as a whole.

---

44. Upon reviewing the essay and realizing that some key information has been left out, the writer composes the following sentence incorporating that information:

    At other times, I amused myself by trying to read the signs that explained which crabs were too small to keep.

The sentence would most logically be placed after the last sentence in Paragraph:

   F. 1

   G. 2

   H. 3

   J. 4

45. Suppose the writer's goal had been to write an essay focusing on the various ways in which people forage for wild foods. Would this essay fulfill this goal?

   A. Yes, because the essay explains that people who live near the Pacific Ocean regularly go crab fishing.

   B. Yes, because the essay focuses on the methods used to haul crabs from the ocean.

   C. No, because the essay focuses on the narrator's childhood fascination with all things aquatic.

   D. No, because the essay primarily focuses on a single event from the narrator's past.

GO ON TO THE NEXT PAGE.

Practice Test

Passage IV

Olmec Heads: A Marvel of Mesoamerican Sculpture

[1]

Three thousand years ago, the Olmec civilization lived in the tropical forests of southeastern Mexico. We do not know what the Olmec called themselves; "Olmec" was a term used by their neighbors, and refers to the numerically abundant supply of natural rubber in
46

their homeland. While much else about the civilization
47

remain a mystery, archaeologists have uncovered a number
48

of magnificent works of Olmec art. Perhaps, the most
49

impressive of these artworks is seventeen colossal head
50
sculptures.

[2]

The heads. Which date to before 900 BCE, are carved
51
out of huge blocks of basalt. These heads probably depict

important rulers even though the blocks weigh between six
52
and fifty tons, the Olmec carried them over ninety miles in

swampy and uneven terrain to their final destination at

46. **F.** NO CHANGE
    G. abundant, numerically,
    H. abundant in number
    J. abundant

47. **A.** NO CHANGE
    B. their
    C. they're
    D. they are

48. **F.** NO CHANGE
    G. remains
    H. remained
    J. OMIT the underlined portion

49. **A.** NO CHANGE
    B. Perhaps:
    C. Perhaps
    D. Perhaps;

50. **F.** NO CHANGE
    G. was
    H. are
    J. is being

51. **A.** NO CHANGE
    B. The heads which
    C. The heads; which
    D. The heads, which

52. **F.** NO CHANGE
    G. rulers, even though
    H. rulers. Even though
    J. rulers. Even though,

GO ON TO THE NEXT PAGE.

multiple sites in the area. The Olmec did not have wheels or
<u>draft animals, and it is unclear how they accomplished such</u>
53

a feat. 54

[3]

The heads are very realistic, with a wide range of
detailed facial features and expressions. Each also depicts

headgear that, in life, <u>will likely have been made of fabric.</u>
55
Based on pigments found on one of the heads, archaeologists
speculate that the pieces were originally painted.

[4]

[1] <u>Therefore, the cultural purpose</u> of the Olmec
56
heads is another topic of speculation. [2] Many were found
buried and show signs of alteration, and the anthropologist
David C. Grove offers a possible explanation in a chapter of
the 1981 book *The Olmec and Their Neighbours*. [3] Grove
notices that the marks on the sculptures are similar across
<u>multiple sites, and implying</u> a deliberate practice. [4]
57
However, some other scholars think they were simply
damaged during a conflict. [5] He suggests that the marking
and burial were part of a ceremony to record the passage of

53. At this point in the essay, the writer wants to provide specific information about the location of the colossal head sites. Given that all of the choices are true, which one best conveys that information?

    A. NO CHANGE

    B. present-day Veracruz and Tabasco.

    C. Southeastern Mexico.

    D. Mexico.

54. At this point, the writer is considering deleting the final sentence of the second paragraph. Should the writer make this deletion?

    F. Yes, because deleting the sentence preserves a captivating sense of mystery about the Olmec heads.

    G. Yes, because the sentence provides information that is already addressed more clearly in another paragraph.

    H. No, because the sentence anticipates questions the reader might have about how the Olmec transported the blocks.

    J. No, because the sentence shows how draft animals were important to the Olmec artistic process.

55. **A.** NO CHANGE

    B. would

    C. will have

    D. was

56. **F.** NO CHANGE

    G. However, the cultural purpose

    H. Alternately, the cultural purpose

    J. The cultural purpose

57. **A.** NO CHANGE

    B. sites and implying

    C. sites, and, implying

    D. sites, implying

GO ON TO THE NEXT PAGE.

ne or acknowledge a change in ruling dynasties. [58]

58. For the sake of logic and coherence, sentence 4 should be placed:

    F. where it is now.

    G. after sentence 1.

    H. after sentence 2.

    J. after sentence 5.

[5]

While the original purpose of the Olmec heads
                            59

mains open to scholarly debate, it is clear that the great
    59

59. Which of the following would be the LEAST logical alternative for the underlined portion?

    A. Thought it remains unclear what needs Olmec heads fulfilled for ancient people,

    B. While it is unclear what role Olmec heads might play in present-day society,

    C. Although the ancient role of the Olmec heads remains a mystery,

    D. Even though we can't be totally certain about why the Olmec built their heads millennia ago,

ne colossi have a new role in our time: they make
                                60

velers and museum-goers worldwide say, "Wow!"
             60

60. F. NO CHANGE

    G. captivate the imaginations of travelers and museum-goers worldwide.

    H. are really, really impressive to tourists and travelers.

    J. are a super interesting tourist attraction, and are very appealing to people from around the world.

PASSAGE V

The Platypus: A Creature Full of Surprises

[1]

The platypus is an Australian mammal that lays eggs,

akes venom, and has a bill like a duck. This has long given

a reputation as a very unusual animal. In a story told by

digenous Australians, birds, water animals, and land

nimals all invite the platypus to join them, but because it is
                                     61

independent-minded it rejects them all. Early scientists

lso recognized the singularity of the platypus, and some

61. Which of the following alternatives to the underlined portion would be LEAST acceptable?

    A. but since

    B. but as

    C. and although

    D. yet because

GO ON TO THE NEXT PAGE.

even refuse to believe that such a creature could exist: when
‾‾
62

the English zoologist George Shaw first saw a preserved

specimen in 1799, he thought that somebody was trying to

play the prank on him. No one doubts the platypus's
‾‾‾‾‾
63

existence now, but its awesome abilities continue to surprise
‾‾‾‾‾‾‾
64

us.

[2]

Venomous mammals, are also very unusual. The only
‾‾‾‾‾‾‾‾‾
65

other mammals to share this quality are certain shrews and
‾‾‾
66

bats—venom is otherwise mostly found in: reptiles and fish.
‾‾‾‾‾
67

The male platypus carries a powerful venom amidst the
‾‾‾‾‾‾
68

hollow spurs on its hind legs.

[3]

Egg-laying mammals, known as "monotremes," are

very rare. This category includes, along with the platypus,

the echidna—a hedgehog-like animal also found in

---

62. F. NO CHANGE
   G. refused
   H. refuses
   J. refusing

63. A. NO CHANGE
   B. his prank
   C. the pranks
   D. a prank

64. F. NO CHANGE
   G. remarkable
   H. wicked
   J. wonderful

65. A. NO CHANGE
   B. mammals are
   C. mammals, are,
   D. mammals are,

66. F. NO CHANGE
   G. is
   H. as
   J. was

67. A. NO CHANGE
   B. in;
   C. in
   D. in,

68. F. NO CHANGE
   G. among
   H. within
   J. about

GO ON TO THE NEXT PAGE.

stralia. Australia's biodiversity is among the greatest on

th. Platypus eggs are soft, much like a reptile's. Once
69

ty hatch, likewise, baby platypuses drink their mother's
70

lk like other mammals.

[4]

The snout of the platypus gives it the uncommon

nse of "electrolocation." It is covered with highly sensitive

ectroreceptors. These sensors allow the platypus to sense

e electrical fields set off by the muscle movements of prey,

ch as shrimp and larvae. Only a few other mammals
71

hidnae and dolphins share this sense. When the platypus
71

ints underwater, it keeps its eyes, ears, and nose closed; its

ectroreceptors are its only means of finding food.

[5]

The platypus is not the only mammal to lay eggs,

crete venom, or use electrolocation, but it is the only one

do all three. It can proudly take it's place as one of the
72

ost uniquest animals in the world.
73

69. At this point, the writer is considering deleting the underlined sentence. Should the writer make this deletion?

    A. Yes, because the sentence does not relate to the subject of the paragraph at large.

    B. Yes, because it introduces a boastful tone that is inappropriate when writing about animals.

    C. No, because it relates logically to the previous sentence in the paragraph.

    D. No, because it helps to explain why the platypus evolved in Australia.

70. F. NO CHANGE
    G. however,
    H. too,
    J. similarly,

71. A. NO CHANGE
    B. mammals echidnae, and dolphins
    C. mammals—echidnae and dolphins—
    D. mammals: echidnae and dolphins

72. F. NO CHANGE
    G. its'
    H. it is
    J. its

73. A. NO CHANGE
    B. uniquer
    C. uniquest
    D. most unique

GO ON TO THE NEXT PAGE.

Questions 74 and 75 ask about the preceding passage as a whole.

74. Suppose the writer intends to produce a passage describing cultural responses to the platypus. Does the preceding passage fulfill that goal?

    F. Yes, because it explains how indigenous Australians and 18th-century English scientists reacted to the platypus's famous duck-bill.

    G. Yes, because it begins by discussing the historical role of the platypus in Australian pranks.

    H. No, because the passage is much more closely focused on the platypus's physical features.

    J. No, because the passage devotes most of its attention to the place of dolphins, birds, and echidnae in culture.

75. For the sake of logic and coherence, Paragraph 2 should be placed:

    A. where it is now.

    B. after paragraph 3.

    C. after paragraph 4.

    D. after paragraph 5.

END OF TEST 1

STOP! DO NOT TURN THE PAGE UNTIL YOU ARE TOLD TO DO SO

Mathematics Test

60 Minutes—60 Questions

DIRECTIONS: For each problem, solve for the correct answer, select your choice and fill in the corresponding bubble on your answer document.

Some problems may take a longer time to solve, but do not take too much time on any single problem. Solve the easier questions first, then return to the harder questions in the remaining time for this test.

A calculator is allowed on this test. While you may be able to solve some problems without a calculator, you are allowed to use a calculator for all of the problems on this test.

Note: Unless otherwise directed, all of the following statements are considered correct.

1. All drawn figures are NOT necessarily drawn to scale.
2. All geometric figures are in a plane.
3. The word *line*, when used, is the same as a straight line.
4. The word *average*, when used, is the same as arithmetic mean.

---

1. How many real solutions exist for the equation $0 = x^2 + x$?

  A. 0

  B. 1

  C. 2

  D. 3

  E. Infinitely many

2. $C + D - 2(C + D) = ?$

  F. $3C + 3D$

  G. $-C + 3D$

  H. $-C - D$

  J. $-C$

  K. $-D$

3. For all nonzero values of x, $\dfrac{4x^4 + 8x^3 + 16x^2}{4x^2} = ?$

  A. $x^2 + 2x$

  B. $x^2 + 2x + 4$

  C. $x^2 + 2x^{\frac{3}{2}} + 4$

  D. $4x^4 + 8x^3 + 12x^2$

  E. $4x + 12$

4. Gabriella purchases tickets to a baseball game on sale for $6.00 each. She spends $42.00 on her tickets, which is $56.00 less than if she had bought them at regular price. What was the regular ticket price?

  F. $ 8.00

  G. $10.00

  H. $12.00

  J. $14.00

  K. $16.00

5. What is the greatest common factor of 51, 68, and 119?

  A. 3

  B. 4

  C. 7

  D. 13

  E. 17

6. Henry wants to paint the 4 walls of his bedroom and has enough paint for 175 square feet. If the walls of the bedroom are each 9 feet high and 13 feet long, and Henry uses all of his paint, what is the area of his walls, in square feet, that will remain unpainted?

  F. 0

  G. 175

  H. 293

  J. 468

  K. 936

GO ON TO THE NEXT PAGE.

7. If $\frac{2}{x} + \frac{3}{x} = 40$, what is the value of x?

A. $\frac{1}{2}$

B. $\frac{1}{4}$

C. $\frac{1}{6}$

D. $\frac{1}{8}$

E. $\frac{1}{40}$

8. In the diagram below, $\overline{AB}$ and $\overline{CD}$ are parallel. What is the value of q?

F. 47
G. 60
H. 73
J. 81
K. 120

9. Alex works as an unpaid intern at an office for a month for college credit. She does the work that the company would otherwise pay an employee $12 per hour to do. If there are twenty 8-hour work days in this month, how much money does the company save by having Alex work instead of a paid employee?

A. $ 336
B. $ 836
C. $1,920
D. $2,420
E. $2,920

10. In the standard (x,y) coordinate plane, point Q has coordinates $(1,4)$ and point R has coordinates $(5,a)$, where a is an unknown number. If the distance between Q and R is 4, which of the following is the value of a?

F. 1
G. 2
H. 3
J. 4
K. 5

11. How many prime numbers are there between 80 and 100?

A. 3
B. 4
C. 5
D. 6
E. 7

12. In the diagram below, lines $\overline{LM}$ and $\overline{NP}$ are parallel to each other. What is the value of c, in degrees?

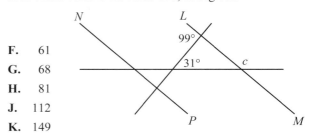

F. 61
G. 68
H. 81
J. 112
K. 149

13. Which of the following is equal to $20x + 8y - 80$?

A. $3x + y - 10$
B. $5x + 2y - 20$
C. $4(5x + 2y - 20)$
D. $4(5x + 2y - 40)$
E. $4(5x + 8y - 20)$

14. In the standard (x,y) coordinate plane, a line segment has its endpoints at $(-10,-4)$ and $(6,8)$. What are the coordinates of the midpoint of the line segment?

F. $(-2,2)$
G. $(-2,6)$
H. $(2,2)$
J. $(2,6)$
K. $(8,6)$

GO ON TO THE NEXT PAGE.

15. The following chart shows the current enrollment in Grade 11 science classes offered by Centennial High School.

Grade 11	
Biology	55
Chemistry	41
Physics	28
Total	124

If there are only 84 Grade 11 students enrolled in science classes, what is the maximum number of Grade 11 students who are enrolled in more than one science class?

- **A.** 28
- **B.** 40
- **C.** 55
- **D.** 61
- **E.** 84

16. A large triangle is composed of 16 equal smaller triangles, as shown below. What is the ratio of the shaded area to the area of the whole triangle?

- **F.** 1:2
- **G.** 1:3
- **H.** 1:4
- **J.** 1:5
- **K.** 1:6

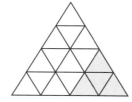

17. Herb is building a fence around his field. On the first day, he builds 15 fence-posts. He plans to build 5 more fence-posts on each successive day than he built the day before. If Herb will finish his fence on the first day he builds 60 fence-posts, how many fence-posts will he have built in total?

- **A.** 60
- **B.** 75
- **C.** 375
- **D.** 600
- **E.** 750

18. In the standard (x,y) coordinate plane, shape A contains points that are all the same distance from its center. Which of the following figures is shape A?

- **F.** Square
- **G.** Line segment
- **H.** Triangle
- **J.** Circle
- **K.** Plane

19. The expression $(3a^2 - 4b)(3a^2 + 4b)$ is equivalent to:

- **A.** $9a^2 - 16b^2$
- **B.** $9a^4 - 16b^2$
- **C.** $9a^2 - 16b^4$
- **D.** $6a^2 - 8b^2$
- **E.** $9a^2 + 16b^2$

20. A salesman sells suits for $200 each. As a weekly promotion, he offers a shirt at a discount price of $20 to anyone who purchases a suit. If he sells a discount shirt with 10% of the suits he sells and makes a total of $8,080, how many suits does he sell?

- **F.** 4
- **G.** 20
- **H.** 40
- **J.** 202
- **K.** 220

21. A kite is constructed by sewing together two triangular pieces of fabric. The two triangles share a base with length of 20 inches. What is the length of h, to the nearest inch?

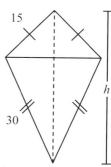

- **A.** 22
- **B.** 28
- **C.** 30
- **D.** 39
- **E.** 41

GO ON TO THE NEXT PAGE.

Practice Test

22. What 3 numbers could be placed in the blanks below so that the difference between consecutive numbers is the same?

$$\_\_ , 12, \_\_ , 22, \_\_$$

F. 2, 22, 32

G. 6, 16, 26

H. 7, 17, 27

J. 9, 19, 29

K. 10, 14, 24

23. Howard is baking a cake. He has half a bag of flour and 1 liter of milk. There are 14 cups in 1 bag of flour and 4 cups in 1 liter of milk. If Howard needs $1\frac{2}{3}$ cups of flour and $\frac{3}{4}$ cups of milk per cake, what is the maximum number of whole cakes he can bake?

A. 3

B. 4

C. 5

D. 6

E. 8

24. Martin and Robert share a pizza. If Martin eats $\frac{1}{3}$ of the pizza and Robert eats $\frac{2}{7}$ of the pizza, what is the ratio of Martin's share to Robert's share?

F. 7:6

G. 6:7

H. 3:7

J. 3:2

K. 3:1

25. A square is inscribed in a second square, as shown in the figure below. What must the value of x be, in degrees?

A. 45

B. 90

C. 110

D. 125

E. 135

26. The table below shows the weekly crate production of a factory for month A and month B.

	Production (crates/week)	
	Month A	Month B
Week 1	2,000	2,000
Week 2	3,000	1,000
Week 3	2,000	3,000
Week 4	3,000	0

What is the percent decrease in average weekly crate production from month A to month B?

F. 25%

G. 39%

H. 40%

J. 50%

K. 66%

27. If x is a negative integer, which of the following expressions, if any, are equal for all possible values of x?

I. $-x$

II. $-|x|$

III. $|-x|$

A. I and II

B. I and III

C. II and III

D. I, II, and III

E. None of the expressions are equal for all values of x.

28. What is the value of $\left(\dfrac{g^2}{g+1}\right)+\left(\dfrac{g+1}{g^2}\right)$ when $g = 4$?

F. 1

G. $\dfrac{271}{80}$

H. $\dfrac{281}{80}$

J. $\dfrac{153}{40}$

K. $\dfrac{281}{40}$

GO ON TO THE NEXT PAGE.

29. Last month, 200 people donated food items to the Downtown Food Bank as shown in the figure below.

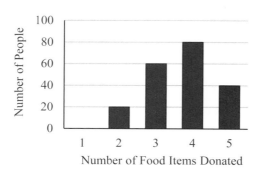

Number of People (y-axis, 0 to 100)

Number of Food Items Donated (x-axis, 1 to 5)

Which of the following statements is justifiable from the given information?

A. The mode is greater than the median.

B. The mean is greater than the median.

C. The median is greater than the mode.

D. The mode is equal to the median.

E. The mean is equal to the median.

30. If a and b are integers such that $a < 0$ and $b < 0$, then which of the following inequalities *must* be true?

F. $\dfrac{a}{b} > 1$

G. $ab > 2$

H. $a^2 > b^2$

J. $a^2 b^3 > 0$

K. $a^2 b^2 > 0$

31. Two horses—Cleo and Jordan—race against 8 other horses. Each horse has an equal chance to win the race. If Cleo finishes first, what is the probability, to the nearest percent, that Jordan finishes second?

A. 1%

B. 10%

C. 11%

D. 20%

E. 47%

32. Joanne bounces a basketball as shown in the figure below. It bounces off the ground at time $t = 0$, and its height during its first bounce, h, at time t, in seconds, is given by $h = -t^2 + 4t$. After what time, in seconds, does the basketball hit the ground again?

F. 2

G. 4

H. 6

J. 8

K. 16

33. If $f(x) = x^2 + 2x$ and $g(x) = \sqrt{2x}$, what is the value of $f(g(8))$?

A. $32 + 16\sqrt{2}$

B. 32

C. 24

D. 16

E. $4\sqrt{2}$

34. The number line shown below represents which of the following systems of inequalities?

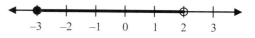

F. $x < -3$ and $x \le 2$

G. $x > -3$ and $x \le 2$

H. $x \ge -3$ and $x < 2$

J. $x \ge -3$ or $x < 2$

K. $x > -3$ or $x \le 2$

GO ON TO THE NEXT PAGE.

Practice Test

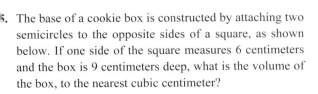
5. The base of a cookie box is constructed by attaching two semicircles to the opposite sides of a square, as shown below. If one side of the square measures 6 centimeters and the box is 9 centimeters deep, what is the volume of the box, to the nearest cubic centimeter?

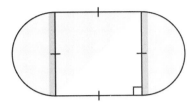

   A.   149

   B.   494

   C.   578

   D. 1,072

   E. 1,342

6. Which of the following expressions is equivalent to

$$\frac{\sqrt{x^2 + 6x + 9}}{x^2 - 9} \ ?$$

   F. $(x + 3)(x - 3)$

   G. $\dfrac{x + 3}{x - 3}$

   H. $\dfrac{\sqrt{x + 3}}{x - 3}$

   J. $\dfrac{\sqrt{x^2 + 6x + 9}}{x - 3}$

   K. $\dfrac{1}{x - 3}$

7. Two parallel lines l and m are graphed in the standard (x,y) coordinate plane below. If these lines extend infinitely in both directions, which of the following statements is FALSE?

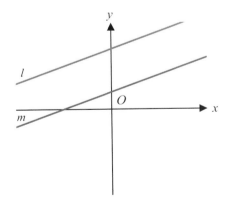

   A.   Line l and line m never intersect.

   B.   The y-intercept of line m is positive.

   C.   Line l does not intersect the x-axis.

   D.   Line l and line m may both contain positive and negative y-coordinates.

   E.   Line l and line m have the same slope.

Use the following information to answer questions 38–40.

The exponential growth of bacterial populations is modeled by the following function, where A, f, and r are constants, and P and t are variables:

$$P(t) = A\,(f)^{rt}$$

P is the population size at time t, in hours. A is the initial size of the population when $t = 0$, f is the factor by which the population is multiplied in every growth interval, and r is the number of growth intervals per hour.

38. One strain of bacteria grows according to the equation $P(t) = 20(10)^t$. What would be the size of this bacterial population after 3 hours of growth?

   F.   200

   G.   500

   H.   6,000

   J.   10,000

   K. 20,000

39. If a strain of bacteria doubles during every half-hour and began with an initial population of 50 bacteria, which of the following equations would accurately express the growth of the strain per hour?

   A. $P = 50(2)^{2t}$

   B. $P = 50(2)^{0.5t}$

   C. $P = 50(2)^{2}$

   D. $P = 2(50)^{2t}$

   E. $50 = A(2)^{2t}$

40. Another type of bacteria grows by a factor of 5 during each growth interval. If a population of 1000 of these bacteria grew from an initial population of 40 over a period of 5 hours, how many growth intervals did the bacteria undergo per hour?

   F. $\dfrac{1}{5}$

   G. $\dfrac{2}{5}$

   H.   1

   J.   2

   K.   5

GO ON TO THE NEXT PAGE.

41. A square with one side measuring 3 units is inscribed in a circle, as shown below. What is the area of the circle, in square units?

A. $\dfrac{19\pi}{4}$

B. $\dfrac{\sqrt{18}}{2}\pi$

C. $\sqrt{18}\pi$

D. $\dfrac{9\pi}{2}$

E. 18π

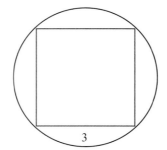

3

42. Four identical overlapping rectangles are drawn, as shown in the figure below. Each rectangle is 10 inches long and 3 inches wide. What is the sum, in inches, of the inner and outer perimeters formed by these rectangles?

F. 28
G. 40
H. 44
J. 56
K. 64

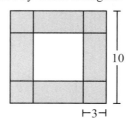

10

├─3─┤

43. For 2 consecutive integers, the result of adding twice the smaller integer and half the larger integer is 33. What are the 2 integers?

A. 10, 11
B. 11, 12
C. 12, 13
D. 13, 14
E. 14, 15

44. Which of the following is the equation of a line perpendicular to the line $y = 5x - 3$ and passing through the point $(-4,4)$ in the standard (x,y) coordinate plane?

F. $y = \dfrac{1}{5}x + \dfrac{16}{5}$

G. $y = \dfrac{1}{5}x - \dfrac{24}{5}$

H. $y = -\dfrac{1}{5}x + \dfrac{24}{5}$

J. $y = -\dfrac{1}{5}x + \dfrac{16}{5}$

K. $y = -5x$

45. Matrix A, $\begin{bmatrix} 7 & -2 \\ -1 & 8 \end{bmatrix}$, can be multiplied by a constant, to yield matrix B, $\begin{bmatrix} -21 & 6 \\ 3 & -24 \end{bmatrix}$. What is the value of k?

A. 3
B. −3
C. 2
D. −2
E. 5

46. Triangle BFG with vertices B, F, and G is shown in the standard (x,y) coordinate plane below.

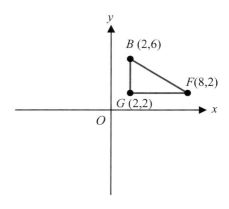

Triangle BFG is reflected across the y-axis and translated 4 units to the right. Which of the following graphs shows the result of these transformations?

F.
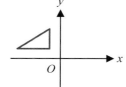

J.
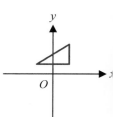

G.
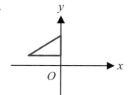

K.
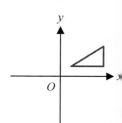

H.
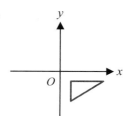

GO ON TO THE NEXT PAGE.

47. An exam room seats a maximum of 9 students. Which of the following expressions gives the number of permutations for 120 students who are taking a test in this exam room?

   A. 120(9)

   B. 9!

   C. $\dfrac{120!}{9!}$

   D. $\dfrac{120!}{(120\text{-}9)!}$

   E. $\dfrac{120!}{(9!)(120\text{-}9)!}$

48. Which of the following is the graph of the equation $y = \dfrac{x^2 - 7x - 8}{x + 1}$ in the standard (x,y) coordinate plane?

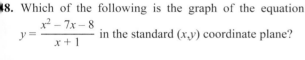

F.
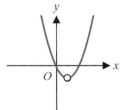

J.
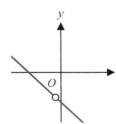

G.
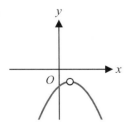

K.
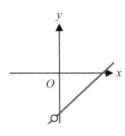

H.
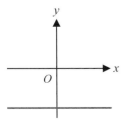

49. If $\log_2 x = a$ and $\log_2 y = b$, then $\log_2 xy = ?$

   A. ab

   B. $\dfrac{a}{b}$

   C. $a - b$

   D. $a + b$

   E. $2ab$

50. Bricks with uniform dimensions of 18 inches by 7 inches are laid to form a wall such that the edge of the brick on top of the row below it lies at the midpoint of the brick directly beneath it, as shown in the figure below. A brick is cut in half if it is too long for the edge of the wall, and its other half is used on the other side of the wall. How many bricks need to be used to make a wall that is 42 inches tall by 126 inches long?

   F. 40

   G. 41

   H. 42

   J. 43

   K. 44

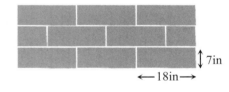

51. When graphed in the standard (x,y) coordinate plane, the lines $x = \dfrac{2y - 7}{5}$ and $y = 6 - x$ intersect at what point?

   A. $\left(\dfrac{2}{5}, -1 \right)$

   B. $\left(\dfrac{37}{7}, \dfrac{5}{7} \right)$

   C. $\left(\dfrac{5}{7}, \dfrac{37}{7} \right)$

   D. $(\ 0, \ 6)$

   E. $\left(-\dfrac{37}{7}, \dfrac{5}{7} \right)$

GO ON TO THE NEXT PAGE.

52. A triangular prism is placed in a box, which measures 14 inches by 14 inches by 6 inches, as shown in the diagram below.

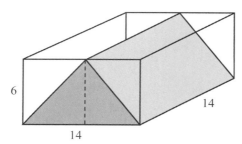

6

14

14

After the prism is placed in the box, how much empty space remains in the box, in inches cubed?

F. 84
G. 588
H. 980
J. 1,092
K. 1,176

53. A rectangle is graphed such that each of its vertices are located in a different quadrant of the standard (x,y) coordinate plane below. The rectangle is then rotated 180 degrees and reflected across the x-axis.

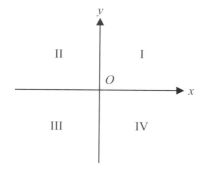

Quadrants of the Standard
(x,y) Coordinate plane

If vertex A of the rectangle was originally located in quadrant I, in which quadrant is it located after the rectangle's rotation and reflection?

A. I
B. II
C. III
D. IV
E. The quadrant cannot be determined.

54. Xiao the lumberjack leans a ladder against a vertical tre as shown in the figure below. If the ladder reaches height of 12 feet up the tree trunk and makes an angle 25° with the ground, which of the following expressio represents the length of the ladder?

F. 12sin(25)

G. 12sin(65)

H. $\dfrac{12}{\sin(25)}$

J. $\dfrac{12}{\cos(25)}$

K. 12tan(25)

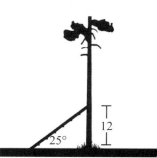

55. In the circle shown below in the standard (x,y) coordinat plane, the center lies at $(4,-2)$ and the point $(7,-1)$ lies c the circle. Which of the following points must also lie o the circle?

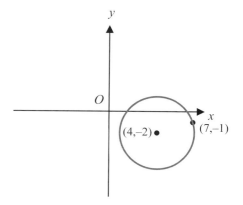

A. $(4,-3)$
B. $(1,-4)$
C. $(1,-3)$
D. $(1,-2)$
E. $(-1,-3)$

GO ON TO THE NEXT PAGE.

Practice Test

. Triangle ABC is shown below. The length of a is 16 and $\cos(B) = \dfrac{4}{5}$. What is the length of c?

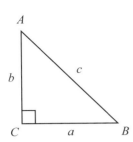

F. 4
G. 5
H. 16
J. 18
K. 20

Use the following information to answer questions 57–58.

s such that $0 < \theta < \dfrac{\pi}{2}$.

7. Which of the following statements must be true?

  I. $\sin\theta < 0$
  II. $\cos\theta < 0$
  III. $\tan\theta > 0$

A. I only
B. II only
C. III only
D. I and II
E. I, II, and III

8. The expression $\dfrac{2(\sin^2(\theta) + \cos^2(\theta))}{4}$ is equivalent to:

F. 0

G. $\dfrac{1}{2}$

H. 1

J. $\sin x$

K. $\tan x$

59. A rectangle has 2 diagonals, a pentagon has 5 diagonals, and a hexagon, with 6 sides, has 9 diagonals. If a nonagon has 9 sides, how many diagonals does it have?

A. 9
B. 12
C. 17
D. 27
E. 35

60. The volume for a pyramid with a square base is calculated with the equation $v = \dfrac{l^2 h}{3}$, where v is volume, l is the length of one side of the base, and h is the pyramid's height from the center of the base to its top. Measurements of the square-based pyramid below are given in meters. What is the volume, in cubic meters, of the pyramid?

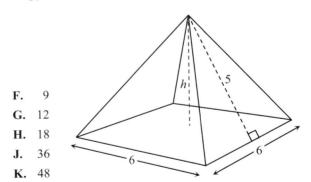

F. 9
G. 12
H. 18
J. 36
K. 48

END OF TEST 2.

STOP! DO NOT TURN THE PAGE UNTIL YOU ARE TOLD TO DO SO.

DO NOT RETURN TO THE PREVIOUS TEST.

Reading Test

35 Minutes—40 Questions

DIRECTIONS: There are multiple passages in this test. Each one is accompanied by several questions. After reading a passage, choose the best answer to every question and fill in the matching circle on your scoring sheet. You can refer back to the passages as often as necessary.

Passage I

Prose Fiction: This passage is adapted from the short story "Arrangement" by Rob Morris (©2003 by Rob Morris).

After they moved the fold-out sofa into the den and the old bed into the guest room, the men from the furniture store carried two new beds into the bedroom and arranged them side by side, leaving a corridor the
5 width of the night table between them. She tipped the men and sent them away, and now it seemed to her that their heavy steps had stirred up a layer of dust.

She was sure the house needed cleaning, and she set to work with a rag and a can of furniture polish.

10 She felt industrious, the way she felt on the first mild day in April. In fact it was January. Snow had drifted into their driveway. Window panes made tiny cracking noises. She bent over the dining room table, wiping firmly in small circles. Even from a low angle,
15 even with the sallow afternoon light illuminating the table's surface, she had to admit that the table—and every other surface in the room—was remarkably clean.

And yet this fact made her work seem all the more necessary. The silver picture frame on the side table
20 cried out to be held and buffed and set down at a jaunty angle. Her hands begged to wipe the candlesticks. The weight of the sugar bowl, the crust around its rim, the curve of the rocking chair's legs—the house gathered itself up and called to her, and she responded, moving
25 with a sure step from room to room.

In the den she discovered that her husband's files were poorly kept, and she applied herself to the task of straightening them. But as she opened first one folder and then another, their contents seemed alien and brittle.
30 There were ancient carbons the color of bad teeth, knickknacks and gifts from students and secretaries. A frog made from green felt dropped from a folder and into her lap. The frog had bubble eyes with black discs for pupils, and they made a weak rattle. The weight of his

35 life at the school pressed down on her shoulders. She had pulled out a file drawer, and now she saw it stretch before her like tracks laid across a prairie—all that distance covered with files, all those files filled with material that she could not improve. She tried to shut the door as she
40 stood, and in her hurry she caught the tip of a finger in the drawer's path.

She considered the benefit of yelling. It might release the hot thumping pulse in her finger, which she now held to her side.

45 She yelled. It was an orderly yell, and it offered no relief. Her finger still pulsed. She convinced herself that any swelling or injury would be less important than finishing the project she had started, so she picked up her rag and began again.

50 Now evening hung outside—the drifts were the color of light from television—and she went upstairs to start in on their bedroom. She imagined a traveler passing the house on foot and noticing the square of yellow light—their bedroom window—set against the dusk. He
55 would gaze at her industry as if it were a fire.

She stood and squared herself to look at the beds. She gave them the face she would give an errant child. The mattresses had the sheen and smell of satin. The beds needed sheets, so she went to the hall linen closet to find
60 them.

The closet needed straightening too, and she set it to rights while looking for single sheets. She refolded towels and stacked them neatly on one shelf. Washcloths were folded into squares and set on top of pillowcases,
65 which looked as smooth and fine as party gloves. Sheets were held out and examined, then folded and set in separate stacks—one for top sheets, one for bottom sheets. All of the sheets were made for king-size beds.

"Well," she said, shutting the closet door and
70 holding two sets of sheets against her chest, "I guess we'll just have to look a little baggy."

GO ON TO THE NEXT PAGE.

As she readied herself to spread out the first bottom sheet, a door clicked shut downstairs.

She set the sheets down on one bed, still folded.

5   Her husband wore soft-soled shoes, so she could hardly hear him come up the stairs. But she knew his pace well enough to count it off; she knew the exact moment when his head would poke around the corner of the stairwell. And there it was. And there, too, was the
10 sigh he let out as he pulled himself to the top step, exaggerating the effort.

"Oh, the banker's wife, the banker's wife," he said. "You could have been the banker's wife." He said this facing the bathroom door, so she saw him in profile, like
15 a president on a coin. Now he turned to her and said, "Instead, you got me. How does it feel? How does it feel to be the principal's wife?"

He looked into the room. "Ah hah," he said. He pressed past her and slid into the room.

20 "Now this is something new."

\. The passage focuses mainly on:

A. the protagonist's last-minute efforts to prepare the spare room for the arrival of an unexpected guest.

B. the conflicted feelings the protagonist experiences when her husband changes careers.

C. the protagonist's tenseness and consequent desire to clean and rearrange her house.

D. the protagonist's anguish about the cold and foreboding winter weather.

\. As used in line 45, the word "orderly" most nearly means:

F. commanding.

G. clinical.

H. neat.

J. restrained.

\. The passage implies that there are only king-sized sheets in the closet because:

A. the protagonist and her husband cannot afford other sizes of sheets.

B. before the time of the story, there were only ever king-sized beds in the house.

C. the family who lives in the house is forgetful and a little disorganized.

D. the furniture store made a mistake and sent the wrong size of sheets.

4. Compared with the way she felt while cleaning the rest of the house, when the protagonist tries to clean up her husband's files, she feels:

F. more welcome.

G. less comfortable.

H. more confident.

J. less rushed.

5. In the context of the passage, lines 34-35 most likely indicate that the protagonist:

A. resents how often she had to help her husband finish his schoolwork when he was younger.

B. is fatigued after spending so much time arranging her husband's files.

C. feels dejected that she is unable to engage with her husband's work life.

D. has sympathy for the student who gave her husband the frog as a gift.

6. Based on the passage, the protagonist would most likely describe her husband as:

F. unsentimental and distant.

G. genial and compassionate.

H. stately and dignified.

J. world-weary and hopeless.

7. The third paragraph (lines 10-17) primarily serves to:

A. depict the desolate weather, which suggests the coldness of the characters.

B. clarify that the protagonist's wish to clean is because of her inner emotional state, not the house's untidiness.

C. describe the protagonist's superior technique, which reveals an important aspect of her personality.

D. establish a timetable of events that foreshadows a later tragedy.

8. Which of the following questions is NOT answered by information in the passage?

F. How long have the husband and protagonist been married?

G. What is the protagonist's husband's occupation?

H. Does the husband expect to see the new single beds?

J. Does the protagonist stop cleaning after she hurts her finger?

9. As used in the passage in line 55, the word "industry" most nearly means:

A. machinery.

B. business.

C. skilled trade.

D. work.

GO ON TO THE NEXT PAGE.

10. The protagonist would most likely agree with which of the following statements?

F. Cleaning is a tedious necessity, best avoided for as long as possible.

G. Through life's changes, it can be reassuring to have control over something like cleanliness.

H. There's no point trying to clean your house when it is already tidy.

J. Receiving new furniture can cause a mess, so it is a good idea to clean up after a delivery.

Passage II

Social Science: This passage is adapted from the article "In Our Wi-Fi World, the Internet Still Depends on Undersea Cables" by Nicole Starosielski (©2015 by Nicole Starosielski).

Not many people realize that undersea cables transport nearly 100% of transoceanic data traffic. These lines are laid on the very bottom of the ocean floor. They're about as thick as a garden hose and carry the

5 world's internet, phone calls, and even TV transmissions between continents at the speed of light. A single cable can carry tens of terabits of information per second. While researching my book *The Undersea Network*, I realized that the cables we all rely on to send everything

10 from email to banking information across the seas remain largely unregulated and undefended. Although they are laid by only a few companies and often funneled along narrow paths, the ocean's vastness has often provided them protection.

15 The fact that we route internet traffic through the ocean—amidst deep sea creatures and hydrothermal vents—runs counter to most people's imaginings of the internet. Didn't we develop satellites and Wi-Fi to transmit signals through the air? Haven't we moved to

20 the cloud? Undersea cable systems sound like a thing of the past. The reality is that the cloud is actually under the ocean. Even though they might seem behind the times, fiber-optic cables are actually state-of-the-art global communications technologies. Since they use light to

25 encode information and remain unfettered by weather, cables carry data more quickly and cheaply than satellites can. They crisscross the continents too—a message from New York to California also travels by fiber-optic cable. These systems are not going to be

30 replaced by aerial communications anytime soon.

The biggest problem with cable systems is not technological—it's human. Because they run underground, underwater, and between telephone poles,

cable systems populate the same spaces we do. As a resul

35 we accidentally break them all the time. Local constructio projects dig up terrestrial lines. Boaters drop anchors o cables. And submarines can disturb systems under the sea Are global communications networks at risk of disruption What would happen if these cables were cut? The answe

40 to this is not black and white. Any individual cable always at risk, but likely far more so from boaters an fishermen than any saboteur. Over history, the singl largest cause of disruption has been people unintentional dropping anchors and nets.

45 The International Cable Protection Committee ha been working for years to prevent such breaks. As result, cables today are covered in steel armor and burie beneath the seafloor at their shore-ends, where the huma threat is most concentrated. This provides some level c

50 protection. In the deep sea, the ocean's inaccessibilit largely safeguards cables—they need only to be covere with a thin polyethelene sheath. It's not that it's muc more difficult to sever cables in the deep ocean, it's jus that the primary forms of interference are less likely t

55 happen. The sea is so big and the cables are so narrow the probability isn't that high that you'd run across one

Sabotage has actually been rare in the history c undersea cables. There have been occurrences, but thes are disproportionately publicized. The World War

60 German raid of the Fanning Island cable station in th Pacific Ocean gets a lot of attention. And there wa speculation about sabotage in the cable disruption outside Alexandria, Egypt, in 2008, which cut off 70% c the country's internet, affecting millions. Yet we hea

65 little about the regular faults that occur, on average, abou 200 times each year. The fact is it's incredibly difficul to monitor these lines. Cable companies have been tryin to do so for more than a century, since the first telegrap lines were laid in the 1800s. But the ocean is too vast an

70 the lines simply too long. It would be impossible to sto every vessel that came anywhere near critica communications cables. We'd need to create extremel long "no-go" zones across the ocean, which itself woul profoundly disrupt the economy.

75 Fewer than 300 cable systems transport almost a transoceanic traffic around the world. And these ofte run through narrow pressure points where sma disruptions can have massive impacts. Since each cabl can carry an extraordinary amount of information, it'

80 not uncommon for an entire country to rely on only handful of systems. In many places, it would take only few cable cuts to take out large swathes of the internet. the right cables were disrupted at the right time, it cou!

GO ON TO THE NEXT PAGE.

disrupt global internet traffic for weeks or even months. The thing that protects global information traffic is the fact that there's some redundancy built into the system. Since there is more cable capacity than there is traffic, when there is a break, information is automatically rerouted along other cables. Because there are many systems linking to the United States, and a lot of internet infrastructure is located here, a single cable outage is unlikely to cause any noticeable effect for Americans.

Any single cable line has been and will continue to be susceptible to disruption. And the only way around this is to build a more diverse system. But as things are, even though individual companies each look out for their own network, there is no economic incentive or supervisory body to ensure the global system as a whole is resilient. If there's a vulnerability to worry about, this is it.

1. The passage suggests that a single cable outage would cause:

A. significant disruptions for Americans, but limited disruptions elsewhere.

B. significant disruptions for both Americans and people elsewhere.

C. moderate disruptions for both Americans and people elsewhere.

D. negligible disruptions for Americans, but potentially significant disruptions elsewhere.

2. As used in the third paragraph, the word "populate" (line 34) most closely means:

F. popularize.

G. produce.

H. occupy.

J. exit.

3. The author's tone can be described as:

A. sarcastic.

B. informative.

C. surprised.

D. excited.

4. The main point of the second paragraph (lines 15–30) is that:

F. oceanic cables are mostly a thing of the past.

G. satellites are the fastest and cheapest way to send signals.

H. deep-sea creatures cause excessive traffic in the ocean.

J. undersea cables are still the best way to carry data.

15. The passage states that, compared to the risk of accidental damage, the risk of deliberate sabotage of undersea cables is:

A. slightly higher.

B. about the same.

C. slightly lower.

D. significantly lower.

16. According to the passage, undersea cables are buried and surrounded by steel armor as a result of:

F. the International Cable Protection Committee's struggles to protect cables from deliberate cutting.

G. efforts by the International Cable Protection Committee to protect cables from nets and anchors.

H. a cable company's special initiative to stop seawater from eroding cables.

J. British attempts to deter German raids on Fanning Island during World War I.

17. As used in the fifth paragraph, the word "critical" (line 71) most nearly means:

A. perilous.

B. important.

C. disparaging.

D. broken.

18. The purpose of the final paragraph is to show that:

F. the largest potential weakness of the world's undersea cable networks is a lack of global cooperation.

G. the world's undersea cable system is more resilient, as a whole, than its individual parts.

H. cable lines remain vulnerable to snipping, crushing, and corrosion.

J. a more diverse system must incorporate satellites and cloud computing to improve transmission speeds.

19. The passage states that outages affecting 70% of a nation's internet access occurred in:

A. Egypt in 2008.

B. Germany during World War I.

C. France in 2011.

D. The United States in 1999.

GO ON TO THE NEXT PAGE.

20. Based on the fifth paragraph (lines 57–74), which of the following statements would the author most likely agree with regarding the protection of undersea cables from damage?

F. Governments must cooperate to stop ships from sailing too close to communications cables.

G. The media has not done enough to warn citizens to be vigilant about the sabotage of cables.

H. It would be a waste of time and money to focus efforts on preventing damage from ships.

J. Emulating telegraph companies of the 1800s would allow for more efficient monitoring of cables.

Passage III

Humanities: Passage A is adapted from the article "When it Comes to Comics, Let's Put Literary Criticism Back on the Shelf" by David Sweeney (©2014 by David Sweeney). Passage B is adapted from "Teaching Graphic Novels as Literature: *The Complete Maus* Enters the Curriculum" by Catherine Beavis (©2013 by Catherine Beavis).

Passage A by David Sweeney

The absorption of comic books into a culturally highbrow setting should not go unquestioned. Some believe that a "high-quality" text can only be enjoyed by a similarly sophisticated audience, and something
5 similar often happens when comics are discussed as "graphic novels."

I have always disliked the term "graphic novel." I have found that it is often used in an attempt to elevate certain comics, and their readers, to a more legitimate
10 social position. Deploying the notion of the novel in this way demonstrates an ignorance of its cultural history. After all, the novel as we know it today only achieved preeminence relatively recently, beginning in the 18th century. Hitherto it was considered inferior to poetry and
15 drama, and was seen to be a form of entertainment for the lower classes, rather than "serious" literature. The novel rose to its current status in parallel with the rise of the bourgeoisie, for whom it became their original literary form.

20 Alan Moore, one of the best-known and most highly regarded writers in the comics field, has remarked that growing up in Britain in the 1950s and 1960s, comics were "just something you have, like rickets." In this comment, the association of a lowly textual form with a
25 lowly social class—rickets being a condition associated in Britain with the working class—is explicit. Moore is credited with bringing depth and maturity to comics with his "revisionist" superhero series *Watchmen*, illustrated

by Dave Gibbons, which attempted to present a reali[s]
30 view of the superhero genre.

Several other British writers, most notably Ne[i]l Gaiman, offered radical reinterpretations of existin[g] comic book characters, which challenged and ultimatel[y] redefined the superhero genre. Gaiman in particular wa[s]
35 marketed as a novelist who just so happened to b[e] working in the comic book field; Gaiman's image as [a] "serious" writer was further emphasized by th[e] forewords and endorsements from prose novelists whic[h] accompanied the collected editions of his wor[k]
40 including Norman Mailer's description of his *Sandma[n]* series as "a comic strip for intellectuals."

But the success of comics has also increased th[e] number of "readers" who seek to identify som[e] intellectual merit in comic books. This is particularly tru[e]
45 in academia, where comparative literature program[s] place comics alongside works of literary and popula[r] prose fiction. On the surface this appears to be [a] progressive step, but I wonder whether this inclusion, an[d] seeming elevation, of comic books is not in fact [a]
50 reduction.

In being absorbed into highbrow literary discours[e] the comic book form is often treated, at best, as a versio[n] of the prose novel. I am not saying that comic book[s] aren't worthy of academic inquiry, but they should b[e]
55 taken on their own terms and not those of establishe[d] literary criticism. They require no elevation.

Passage B by Catherine Beavis

As a literary and artistic form, graphic novel[s] combine the visual with text to create rich and comple[x] narratives. But they also require a different kind o[f]
60 "reading" than the school texts students might be used t[o] The recent move to include graphic novels in th[e] curriculum invites a new examination of kinds of literac[y] and their demands on teachers, students, and examiners[.]

The Victorian Curriculum and Assessmen[t]
65 Authority (VCAA) provides a list of approved texts fo[r] study as part of English and English as an Additiona[l] Language. The text list includes a selection of texts in [a] range of categories—novels, short stories, poetry [o]r songs, plays, nonfiction texts and, from 201[4]
70 "multimodal," formerly the "film" category.

The move to expand the category "film" t[o] "multimodal," and to provide teachers and students wit[h] the opportunity to study a graphic novel, is significan[t] For some time now, teachers and education bodies hav[e]

GO ON TO THE NEXT PAGE.

75 been conscious of the changing nature of literacy, and
the need for students to be confident and competent users
of both traditional and more contemporary forms.

The decision suggests two significant shifts in
thinking. First, the graphic narrative now stands
80 alongside plays, poetry, and novels as a sophisticated
and complex text form worthy of study and close
analysis, meeting the common criteria for all texts on the
list. Second, graphic novels are recognized as unique
forms in their own right, with their own types of logic
85 and organization which differ significantly from both
print-based genres and from film. This means that
teachers and students will have the opportunity to
explore and analyze the text, but also to recognize the
importance of the visual elements of the story.

90 Pages in graphic novels and graphic narratives are
made up of words, images, and panels. To read them
effectively, and to understand their complex and subtle
meanings, requires attention to the ways in which both
images and words work independently and together.
95 Each has its own logic and way of organizing meaning.

In writing, one thing usually follows another.
Theorist Gunther Kress describes the "logic" of writing
as about time and sequence. With images, on the other
hand, lots of information is presented at once. The
00 "logic" of the image is of "space and simultaneity".

Graphic narratives are quintessentially multimodal,
and require new ways of reading that call on both visual
and verbal modes. As the field has matured, a canon of
sophisticated, multilayered graphic novels and
05 narratives has developed. They are worthy of study in
senior secondary English classes alongside other forms
of literature in more familiar print and multimedia
genres.

Questions 21-25 ask about Passage A.

1. One of the main arguments the author is trying to make
in Passage A is that:

A. all forms of writing, from novels to comic books,
are worthy of academic study.

B. comic books do not need to be elevated to "serious
literature" in order to have merit.

C. critics should spend more time analyzing a comic
book's form rather than its narrative.

D. comic books should be taught alongside novels and
other prose fiction in schools.

22. The author of Passage A indicates that he feels that the
term "graphic novel" is:

F. unnecessary and misleading.

G. confusing and esoteric.

H. suitable and practical.

J. clear and explanatory.

23. In Passage A, the repetition of words like *lowly* and
lower (lines 16–25) is most likely intended by the author
to convey:

A. the historical association of popular forms of
literature with the lower classes.

B. the relative inexpensiveness of comics as compared
to other forms of literature.

C. the general critical classification of comics based on
length and subject matter.

D. the place of literature in comparison to other forms
of art, such as painting and music.

24. As it is used in line 36, the word *image* most nearly
means:

F. appearance.

G. copy.

H. portrait.

J. reputation.

25. The author states that the elevation of comic books may
actually be a "reduction" (line 50) because:

A. academic analysis tends to lump comic books in
with other prose fiction.

B. critics have historically viewed comic books as a
lowbrow form of fiction.

C. academics rarely treat comic books with the same
rigor as novels and short stories.

D. most critics tend to forget about comic books in
their literary analyses.

Questions 26-28 ask about Passage B.

26. Passage B best supports which of the following
conclusions about graphic novels?

F. Graphic novels have replaced videos as the most
popular multimodal form of storytelling.

G. Graphic novels have their own form of presentation
that relies heavily on visual elements.

H. Graphic novels are a simpler form of storytelling
than novels and film.

J. Graphic novels are now included in major curricula
because of their strong moral themes.

GO ON TO THE NEXT PAGE.

27. Within Passage B, the author brings up the theorist Gunther Kress in lines 96–100 in order to:

   A. offer evidence of the usefulness of academic conversation about graphic novels.

   B. argue that graphic novels represent a less serious form of literature.

   C. contrast the logic of writing with the logic of images.

   D. suggest that the logic of comic books is less clear than the logic of novels.

28. The second paragraph of Passage B states that one of the changes instituted by the VCAA was that:

   F. schools were mandated to include at least three different forms of literature in each class.

   G. comic books were banned from inclusion in high school courses.

   H. graphic novels replaced prose fiction in most school curricula.

   J. the "film" category was transformed into the "multimodal" category.

Questions 29 and 30 ask about both passages.

29. The authors of both passages would likely agree with which of the following statements?

   A. Comic books have yet to become a serious form of literature.

   B. Critics should give more attention to comics.

   C. Comic books have literary qualities unique to the form.

   D. More authors than ever are now experimenting with graphic novels.

30. Unlike Passage A, Passage B views the inclusion of comic books in academic curricula as:

   F. praiseworthy.

   G. foolish.

   H. ambitious.

   J. detrimental.

GO ON TO THE NEXT PAGE.

Passage IV

Natural Science: This passage is adapted from the article "The ultimate in stealth, puff adders employ camouflage at every level" by Ashadee Kay Miller and Graham Alexander (©2016 Ashadee Kay Miller and Graham Alexander).

The puff adder (*Bitis arietans*) is one of the most widespread and venomous snakes in Africa. It is responsible for more deaths on the continent than any other snake. It is an extreme ambush forager, often lying
5 motionless for days at a time, waiting for prey to pass within striking range.

Unlike other snakes, puff adders spend most of their lives above ground, seldom seeking refuge beneath rocks or down burrows. During these long bouts in
10 ambush, an easily detectable puff adder would be a sitting duck to any predator, its ability to flee limited by its squat body. Instead, puff adders must rely on their ability to hide in plain sight using their astonishingly good camouflage.

15 The puff adder's risk of being eaten is remarkably high. It has as many as 42 documented species of predators, and in some years, annualized mortality rates can approach 50% of the adult population. In a system like this, the selective pressures acting on a species are
20 great, and may result in an evolutionary arms race between predator and prey. The puff adder's impressive visual camouflage is testament to this; its cryptic coloration and patterning are highly effective.

The puff adder has an additional survival
25 mechanism that, until now, has been little known: it doesn't carry a scent. This makes it undetectable to even the most keenly nosed predators. Not all of the puff adder's predators rely on vision to locate their prey. As many as 15, including dogs, meerkats, and mongooses,
30 rely on their keen sense of smell to find their food. This hunting style simply bypasses the effectiveness of the puff adder's visual camouflage.

Yet, from our observations in the field, it is clear that in response to an approach by predators, resting and
35 ambushing puff adders choose to remain motionless. In fact, they are so committed to this that we have observed dogs and mongooses walking directly over puff adders with no response from the snakes.

These observations led us to a very intriguing
40 question. Are puff adders evading their scent-orientated predators by hiding or reducing their scent? To answer this question, our research team implemented a novel approach. We enlisted a team of scent-matching dogs and meerkats. These puff adder predators were trained to
45 test whether they could locate puff adders using smell alone.

The use of detection dogs as research tools is growing in popularity within the field of ecology. They are now routinely used to locate rare, elusive, or invasive
50 species. Dogs are trained onto a specific target scent, which they must reliably and repeatedly indicate to gain reward.

But in this case the research team needed their dogs and meerkats to do much more. You can't train a dog or
55 meerkat onto a species' target scent if the species is scentless. So, the dogs and meerkats were required to match pairs of new scents to each other among a line-up of scent options. This is much more challenging, and it took the dogs and meerkats months to learn this skill. But
60 once they had, the researchers were able to test how smelly some snake species were to these sniffer extraordinaires.

It turned out that of the six snake species tested, one stood out as being undetectable. In 100 scent-matching
65 trials, puff adders stumped both the dog and meerkat teams every time. These teams failed to correctly match the puff adder scent pairs to each other at rates greater than chance.

The results from the other snake species were very
70 different. Both dogs and meerkats were able to match pairs of these smelly snake scents around 90% of the time. This makes the puff adder the first terrestrial vertebrate species for which chemical crypsis—the art of being scentless—has been demonstrated.

75 Although these findings are a world first, we believe that this phenomenon is likely to be common in the animal world. Ambushing animals that experience high mortality rates as a result of predation, and animals that remain in an exposed locality, such as incubating,
80 ground-nesting birds and newly born fawns, are likely to derive great benefit from being scentless or being able to mask their odor in some way.

Chemical crypsis has probably not been shown before simply due to research focus being biased toward
85 our own primary sense—vision. We hope that the findings act as a springboard for research on chemical crypsis in other systems. For now, we are focused on figuring out how puff adders are doing it.

GO ON TO THE NEXT PAGE.

31. The authors' purpose in writing this passage is most likely to:

   A. describe the discovery of a new species of snake.

   B. argue for increased research on chemical crypsis.

   C. detail the unusual camouflage abilities of puff adders.

   D. summarize recent research conducted on dogs and meerkats.

32. It can reasonably be inferred from the passage that puff adders' natural defenses:

   F. have weakened over time in response to decreased predation.

   G. are based mainly on their poisonous bodies.

   H. include fierce attacks on predators that discover them.

   J. still do not protect them from substantial population losses.

33. What does the passage offer as evidence that puff adders and their predators are engaged in an "evolutionary arms race" (line 20)?

   A. Annualized mortality rates of puff adders can reach 50%.

   B. Chemical crypsis may actually be more common than once believed.

   C. Over 42 different species have been known to prey upon puff adders.

   D. Puff adders have developed camouflaged coloring and patterning.

34. According to the passage, the use of detection dogs to locate species is:

   F. unprecedented.

   G. unpopular.

   H. revered.

   J. customary.

35. As it is used in line 11, the phrase *sitting duck* most nearly refers to the fact that puff adders would be:

   A. helpless in evading detection from skilled predators.

   B. easy prey without their camouflage defenses.

   C. less effective hunters if they carried a scent.

   D. mostly harmless if not for their chemical defenses.

36. The main purpose of the study described in the passage was to determine:

   F. the biological mechanisms behind the puff adders' chemical crypsis defense.

   G. whether puff adders were using chemical crypsis to avoid predators.

   H. how predators like dogs and meerkats hunted puff adders.

   J. whether puff adders could be trained to use chemical rather than camouflage defenses.

37. The passage suggests that unlike other snakes, the puff adder is unusual in that it:

   A. makes use of camouflage to avoid predators.

   B. can defend itself against dogs and meerkats.

   C. uses stealth to capture its prey.

   D. can avoid detection through chemical crypsis.

38. Within the passage, the statement in lines 77–82 serves mainly to:

   F. list some of the key results from the study discussed in the passage.

   G. provide support for the theory that chemical crypsis is common among animals.

   H. show that scentless animals are actually much rarer than once thought.

   J. offer evidence that puff adders prey upon a wide variety of creatures.

39. It can most reasonably be inferred that the word *stumped* in line 65 refers to puff adders' ability to:

   A. baffle their natural predators.

   B. confuse the researchers.

   C. engineer defenses against dogs and meerkats.

   D. flee from dangerous threats.

40. The authors indicate that research into chemical crypsis has sometimes been overlooked due to:

   F. a lack of available research funds.

   G. a bias towards researching visual camouflage.

   H. a focus on more common defenses.

   J. ignorance of the science behind it.

END OF TEST 3

STOP! DO NOT TURN THE PAGE UNTIL YOU ARE TOLD TO DO SO.

DO NOT RETURN TO THE PREVIOUS TEST.

Science Test

35 Minutes—40 Questions

DIRECTIONS: There are several passages in this test, and each is accompanied by several questions. After reading a passage, choose the best answer to each question and fill in the corresponding oval on your answer document. You may refer to the passages as often as necessary.

You are NOT permitted to use a calculator on this test.

Passage I

Paper chromatography is a laboratory technique used to study mixtures. This technique uses a solvent to carry compounds through the fibers of a piece of paper. Different compounds will travel different distances through the paper according to their affinity for the solvent. Compounds with a higher affinity will travel farther, relative to the distance traveled by the solvent.

Students performed two experiments to determine the chemical composition of an unknown mixture, Mixture Z.

Study 1

The students collected 8 pure compounds (Compounds 1–8) from around the laboratory. They placed one drop of each compound near the bottom edge of a rectangular sheet of filter paper, as shown in Diagram 1. The bottom edge of the filter paper was placed in a beaker of acetone. As the acetone moved up the filter paper, it carried the samples of Compounds 1–8 with it. When the acetone neared the top of the filter paper, the students removed the filter paper from the acetone bath. The final positions reached by the acetone and by Compounds 1–8 are shown in Figure 1.

For each compound, the students measured the distance traveled and calculated a *retention factor* (R_f) value, which describes how far the compound traveled relative to the acetone solvent. The R_f values were calculated using the following formula:

$$R_f = \frac{\text{distance traveled by compound}}{\text{distance traveled by solvent}}$$

All results are shown in Table 1.

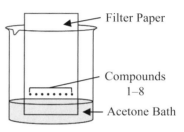

Diagram 1

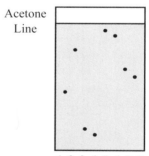

Acetone Line

1 2 3 4 5 6 7 8

Figure 1

Table 1		
Compound	Distance traveled (cm)	R_f
Acetone	9.8	n/a
Compound 1	3.4	0.347
Compound 2	7.6	0.776
Compound 3	1.1	0.114
Compound 4	0.8	0.082
Compound 5	9.3	0.949
Compound 6	8.8	0.898
Compound 7	5.1	0.520
Compound 8	4.7	0.480

GO ON TO THE NEXT PAGE.

Study 2

The students repeated Study 1 using Mixture Z. Unlike the pure compounds from Study 1, Mixture Z separated into three spots (Z_1, Z_2, and Z_3) as it traveled through the filter paper. The final positions reached by the acetone and by the various components of Mixture Z are shown in Figure 2. The students measured the distances traveled and calculated the R_f values for Z_1, Z_2, and Z_3. The results are shown in Table 2.

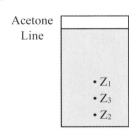

Figure 2

Table 2		
Compound	Distance traveled (cm)	R_f
Acetone	9.7	n/a
Z_1	5.1	0.525
Z_2	0.7	0.076
Z_3	3.3	0.351

1. When attempting to replicate Studies 1 and 2, one of the students decides to use water, instead of acetone, as her solvent. Will she be able to compare her results to the results of Studies 1 and 2?

   A. No; the affinity of the compounds for water and acetone are the same.

   B. No; the affinity of the compounds for water and acetone may not be the same.

   C. Yes; the affinity of the compounds for water and acetone are the same.

   D. Yes; the affinity of the compounds for water and acetone may not be the same.

2. Based on the results of Study 1, which of the following compounds had the highest affinity for acetone?

   F. Compound 3

   G. Compound 4

   H. Compound 5

   J. Compound 6

3. One of the students finds another pure substance, Compound 9, in the lab. Compound 9 is known to have a higher affinity for acetone than Compound 2 and a lower affinity than Compound 6. The R_f value of Compound 9 is most likely:

   A. less than 0.520.

   B. between 0.520 and 0.776.

   C. between 0.776 and 0.898.

   D. greater than 0.898.

4. In both Studies 1 and 2, if the acetone had traveled farther up the filter paper, the distances traveled by Compounds 1–8 and Mixture Z would most likely have:

   F. decreased only.

   G. stayed the same.

   H. increased only.

   J. changed with no apparent trend.

5. A student makes a mixture of Compound 1, Compound 2, and Compound 3. In order to most effectively separate the components of this mixture, he should use:

   A. a solvent for which the three compounds have very different affinities.

   B. a solvent for which the compounds have very similar, but not identical, affinities.

   C. a solvent for which the compounds have identical affinities.

   D. a solvent for which the compounds have unknown affinities.

6. According to Table 2, Mixture Z is most likely composed of which of following sets of compounds?

   F. Compound 1, Compound 4, Compound 7

   G. Compound 1, Compound 4, Compound 8

   H. Compound 1, Compound 2, Compound 7

   J. Compound 6, Compound 7, Compound 8

7. The students most likely calculated R_f in addition to measuring the distances traveled by the compounds in order to:

   A. ensure that the distances traveled by the acetone were identical in both Study 1 and Study 2.

   B. compare the results of Study 1 and Study 2, even though the distances traveled by the acetone were not identical.

   C. calculate the density of acetone.

   D. determine the order in which Z_1, Z_2, and Z_3 were mixed to produce Compound Z.

GO ON TO THE NEXT PAGE.

Passage II

Biological aging involves a decrease in *metabolism*, the processes of chemical breakdown and synthesis necessary for life. It also involves a decrease in reproductive capability and in the ability to maintain *homeostasis*, a state in which cell and organ systems function at optimal capacity. Aging eventually leads to cell and organismal death. Four scientists discuss the causes of aging.

Scientist 1

Genes are composed of nucleic acids and instruct cells to produce proteins. When genes are active, their proteins are produced; when they are inhibited, their proteins are not produced. Regulatory genes, which are responsible for the activation and inhibition of other genes, are programmed to increasingly suppress metabolism, reproduction, and homeostasis genes over time. This process results in a gradual decrease in protein production, and eventual cell and organismal death.

Scientist 2

Free radicals are reactive oxygen-based chemicals that cause damage to important cellular components and to nucleic acids, and this damage accumulates over time. Eventually, this damage renders cellular components functionless and mutates nucleic acids, which means cells are no longer able to produce proteins involved in metabolism, reproduction, and homeostasis. Free radicals are produced as a byproduct of metabolic processes and can also be absorbed from the environment.

Scientist 3

Telomeres are nucleic acid structures that do not instruct cells to produce proteins. Instead, they are found at the end of protein-producing nucleic acids and protect them from damage. Every time a cell divides, its telomeres get shorter. When a telomere is too short, it can no longer protect protein-producing nucleic acids from damage. Over time, these nucleic acids are damaged and mutated, which means they are no longer able to produce proteins involved in metabolism, reproduction, and homeostasis.

Scientist 4

Hormones are chemical signals that circulate through an organism and initiate protein production in specific cells and tissues. Hormones are produced by endocrine glands, which gradually stop producing most hormones over time. Without hormones to initiate metabolic, reproductive, and homeostatic protein production, these processes cease. Other hormones signal these processes to slow and gradually stop.

8. Which scientist asserts that aging is caused by the shortening of nucleic acids?

   F. Scientist 1
   G. Scientist 2
   (H) Scientist 3
   J. Scientist 4

9. Which scientist(s) claim(s) that decreased protein production is a part of the cause of aging?

   A. Scientist 1 only
   B. Scientist 3 only
   C. Scientists 1 and 2
   (D) Scientists 1, 2, 3, and 4

10. *Antioxidants* are chemicals that inhibit the activity of reactive oxygen. Which scientist would agree with the claim that antioxidants slow the aging process?

    F. Scientist 1
    (G) Scientist 2
    H. Scientist 3
    J. Scientist 4

11. Which of the following experimental discoveries is consistent with Scientist 1's viewpoint?

    (A) The inhibition of the *Indy* regulatory gene allows fruit flies to live twice as long.
    B. The absence of the *IGF-1* hormone allows roundworms to live twice as long.
    C. Shortening telomeres with x-ray radiation causes yeast to live half as long.
    D. Damage to endocrine glands causes lab mice to live half as long.

12. There are two classes of aging hypotheses. The *Program Hypothesis* states that aging is biologically determined. The *Error Hypothesis* states that aging is caused by damage accumulated over time. Which scientist(s) would agree with the *Error Hypothesis*?

    F. Scientist 2 only
    G. Scientist 3 only
    (H) Scientists 2 and 3
    J. Scientists 2, 3, and 4

GO ON TO THE NEXT PAGE.

13. Another scientist claims that aging is caused by the loss of immune system function over time. The immune system protects organisms from disease and damage. How would Scientist 4 respond to this claim?

A. Immune system function is regulated by genes. When these genes inhibit the immune system, it ceases to function.

B. Immune system function is impaired by telomere shortening. When telomeres are too short, the immune system ceases to function.

C. Immune system function is triggered by hormones. When hormones are no longer produced, the immune system ceases to function.

D. Hormones are damaged by the loss of immune function. When the immune system ceases to function, hormones are no longer produced.

14. Metabolism produces molecules that store energy in an easily usable form. Which of the following molecules is produced during metabolism?

F. DNA

G. RNA

H. ATP

J. Chlorophyll

GO ON TO THE NEXT PAGE.

Passage III

Global warming has increased vegetation cover across northern *tundra*—regions with frozen subsoil, shrubs, and no trees. From the year 1880 to the present, the Alaskan moose (*Alces alces gigas*) has extended its range from *boreal* regions, which are heavily forested, across the *treeline* and into the northern tundra.

Moose bones were recovered from eroding *permafrost*, which is a subsurface layer of earth that remains frozen year-round. The bones were dated using carbon isotopes and were found to be from between 1880 and 1950. After 1940, a moose tracking program was established in Alaska. Figure 1 shows the locations of moose bones and sightings and the extent of moose habitats.

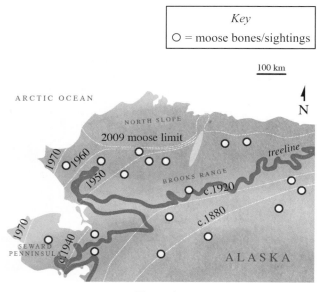

Figure 1

Moose require shrubs protruding above the snow in late winter for their habitat and food. The trend line in Figure 2 shows the mean shrub height, and Figure 3 shows the mean July temperature in Alaska since 1860. Figure 4 shows the average foliage mass of *A. gigas's* preferred shrubs, *Salix alaxensis* and *Salix richardsonii*.

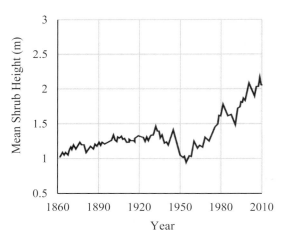

Figure 2

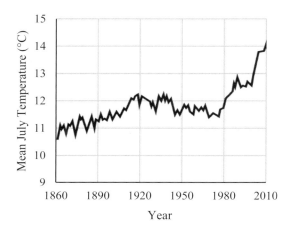

Figure 3

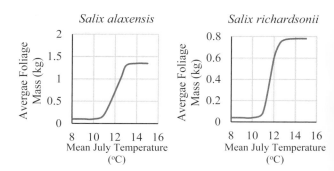

Figure 4

All figures adapted from Ken D. Tape et al., "Range Expansion of Moose in Arctic Alaska Linked to Warming and Increased Shrub Habitat." ©2016 by PloS One. 10.1371/journal.pone.0152636.

GO ON TO THE NEXT PAGE.

Practice Test

15. According to Figure 3, the greatest increase in mean July temperature observed in Alaska was between the years:

   A. 1890 and 1920.

   B. 1920 and 1950.

   C. 1950 and 1980.

   D. 1980 and 2010.

16. According to Figure 2, the greatest mean shrub height observed between the years 1860 and 1980 was:

   F. less than 1.5 m.

   G. between 1.5 m and 2.0 m.

   H. between 2.0 m and 2.5 m.

   J. greater than 2.5 m.

17. Which of the following figures best depicts the location of the treeline?

   A.

   B.
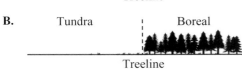

   C.

   D.

18. If the trend observed in Figure 3 continues, then the habitat of *A. gigas* will:

   F. extend into the North Slope.

   G. extend into the Seward Peninsula.

   H. contract into the Brooks Range.

   J. contract south of the treeline.

19. Suppose that the mean July temperature in 2016 was approximately the same as the mean July temperature in 2010. What will be the average foliage mass of *S. richardsonii* in 2016?

   A. 1.50 kg

   B. 1.25 kg

   C. 0.78 kg

   D. 0.65 kg

20. According to Figure 4, which of the shrubs preferred by *A. gigas* exhibited a greater increase in average foliage mass when the mean July temperature increased?

   F. *S. alaxensis* exhibited the greater increase in average foliage mass.

   G. *S. richardsonii* exhibited the greater increase in average foliage mass.

   H. Both *S. alaxensis* and *S. richardsonii* exhibited the same increase in average foliage mass.

   J. Neither *S. alaxensis* nor *S. richardsonii* exhibited an increase in average foliage mass.

GO ON TO THE NEXT PAGE.

Passage IV

Students studied *surface tension*, which is caused by the attraction of the particles in the surface of a solution to the bulk of the solution. The higher the surface tension, the more force will be required to break the surface of the solution.

Activity 1

Four beakers (Beakers 1–4) at 25°C were filled with 200 mL of distilled water, 200 mL of salt water, 200 mL of glycerol, and 200 mL of acetone, respectively. The students used a single-beam balance with an 8 cm-long needle suspended horizontally from its beam end. The length of the string holding the needle was adjusted so that the needle rested on the surface of the substance. Masses, in mg, were added to the tray of the balance until the needle was pulled from the surface of the substance, as shown in Diagram 1. The results are recorded in Table 1.

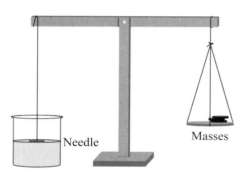

Diagram 1

Table 1	
Beaker	Mass required to remove needle (mg)
1	1175
2	1210
3	1145
4	1015

Activity 2

Each beaker was placed on a hot plate with a thermometer. Activity 1 was repeated and the mass required to remove the needle was measured at 4 temperatures, as shown in Figure 1.

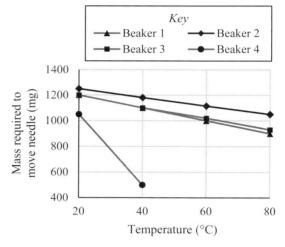

Figure 1

Activity 3

The surface tensions, s, of the substances at 25°C were calculated using the formula $s = \dfrac{2d}{F}$, where d is the length of the needle and F is the force required to remove the needle from the surface of the substance. The results are recorded in Table 2.

Table 2	
Beaker	Surface tension (dyn/cm)
1	71.97
2	74.09
3	70.18
4	62.32

Note: dyn = 1 g·cm/s²

GO ON TO THE NEXT PAGE.

21. According to Activity 1, which of the following substances had the greatest surface tension?

    A. Distilled water

    B. Salt water

    C. Glycerol

    D. Acetone

22. The students predicted that increasing the temperature of a substance would decrease its surface tension. Are the results of Activity 2 consistent with this prediction?

    F. No; for each substance tested, the mass required to remove the needle was greater at a higher temperature.

    G. No; for each substance tested, the mass required to remove the needle was lower at a higher temperature.

    H. Yes; for each substance tested, the mass required to remove the needle was greater at a higher temperature.

    J. Yes; for each substance tested, the mass required to remove the needle was lower at a higher temperature.

23. In Activity 3, force (F) equals $m \times g$, where m is the mass required to pull the needle from the surface of the solution, and g is the acceleration due to gravity. Which of the following equations allows the students to correctly calculate surface tension?

    A. $s = 2dmg$

    B. $s = \dfrac{2d}{mg}$

    C. $s = \dfrac{mg}{2d}$

    D. $s = \dfrac{dm}{2g}$

24. Activity 1 differed from Activity 2 in which of the following ways?

    F. Only different substances were tested in Activity 1, whereas different temperatures were also tested in Activity 2.

    G. Only different temperatures were tested in Activity 1, whereas different substances were also tested in Activity 2.

    H. Surface tension was calculated in Activity 1 and not in Activity 2.

    J. Surface tension was calculated in Activity 2 and not in Activity 1.

25. Suppose that during Activity 1, the students forgot to rinse and dry the needle between Beaker 3 and Beaker 4. Compared to the *measured* mass required to pull the needle from the surface of the substance in Beaker 4, the *actual* mass would be:

    A. significantly greater.

    B. slightly greater.

    C. slightly less.

    D. exactly the same.

26. Of the following facts about acetone, which best explains the lack of data points at 60°C and 80°C for Beaker 4 in Figure 1?

    F. Acetone boils at 56°C.

    G. Acetone has a 10-day half-life.

    H. Acetone is an organic solvent.

    J. Acetone's chemical formula is C_3H_6O.

27. Suppose the students tested acetic acid using the same procedure as in Activity 1. They then calculated the surface tension using the formula in Activity 3, and found it to be 64.52 dyn/cm. What is the order of the substances, from the substance with the lowest surface tension to the substance with the highest?

    A. Salt water, distilled water, glycerol, acetone, acetic acid

    B. Salt water, distilled water, glycerol, acetic acid, acetone

    C. Acetone, acetic acid, glycerol, distilled water, salt water

    D. Acetic acid, acetone, glycerol, distilled water, salt water

GO ON TO THE NEXT PAGE.

Passage V

Researchers studied how the Saharan silver ant, *Cataglyphis bombycina*, tolerates high temperatures using small hairs that cover its body. The hairs reflect light and emit heat, which allows *C. bombycina* to survive in a temperature range uninhabitable by many other species of ants.

Study 1

Researchers collected 200 Saharan silver ants from sand dunes in Morocco and anesthetized the ants through exposure to carbon dioxide (CO_2), a non-toxic gas. Next, they removed the hairs on 100 of the ants' abdomens using a scalpel, and divided the ants into two groups: one of 100 shaved ants, and one of 100 unshaved ants. Each group of ants was placed in a gray *well plate* (a plate containing a matrix of round depressions), one ant per well. Each ant was then illuminated by 9 wavelengths of light for 90 seconds using a fitted bulb. The *reflectance*—percent of light reflected—of each ant at each wavelength was measured using a spectrophotometer, and the results for the two groups were averaged. Researchers recorded these results in Table 1.

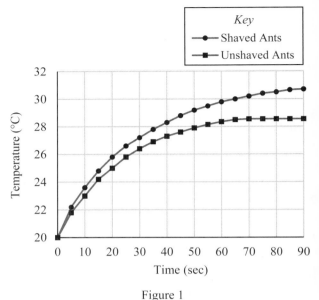

Figure 1

Table and figures adapted from Quentin Willot et al., "Total Interna Reflection Accounts for the Bright Color of the Saharan Silver Ant. ©2016 by PLOS One. 10.1371/journal.pone.0152325.

Table 1		
Wavelength (nm)	Reflectance of Shaved Ants	Reflectance of Unshaved Ants
400	2.2%	5.9%
450	2.6%	5.5%
500	2.9%	5.5%
550	3.3%	5.5%
600	3.4%	5.3%
650	3.6%	5.1%
700	3.8%	5.0%
750	3.9%	5.0%
800	4.0%	4.9%

Study 2

Using the same gray well plates, researchers exposed the abdomens of both the 100 shaved Saharan silver ants and the 100 unshaved ants from Study 1 to light from a solar simulator for 90 seconds, and measured the ants' internal temperature using a digital thermometer. The internal temperatures of each group were averaged and recorded in Figure 2.

28. Based on Table 1, which of the following groups has the highest reflectance?

   F. Shaved ants exposed to light of 500 nm
   G. Shaved ants exposed to light of 750 nm
   H. Unshaved ants exposed to light of 500 nm
   J. Unshaved ants exposed to light of 750 nm

29. What was the dependent variable in Study 1?

   A. Heat emission
   B. Amount of hair
   C. Wavelength
   D. Reflectance

30. Suppose that an additional trial in Study 1 had been performed using a wavelength of 350 nm. The reflectance of shaved ants would most likely be:

   F. less than 1.7%.
   G. between 1.7 and 2.2%.
   H. between 2.2 and 2.7%.
   J. greater than 2.7%.

GO ON TO THE NEXT PAGE.

Practice Test

31. The researchers had predicted that shaving ants' hair would make them more likely to be affected by a temperature increase. Are the results of Study 2 consistent with this prediction?

A. No; the internal temperature of shaved ants rose more rapidly than the internal temperature of unshaved ants.

B. No; the internal temperature of unshaved ants rose more rapidly than the internal temperature of shaved ants.

C. Yes; the internal temperature of shaved ants rose more rapidly than the internal temperature of unshaved ants.

D. Yes; the internal temperature of unshaved ants rose more rapidly than the internal temperature of shaved ants.

32. One way Study 1 differed from Study 2 was that in Study 1:

F. ants with only one type of hair were measured under different conditions, while in Study 2, ants with different types of hair were measured.

G. ants with different types of hair were measured, while in Study 2, ants with only one type of hair were measured under different conditions.

H. ants' internal temperature was measured, while in Study 2, ants' reflectance was measured.

J. ants' reflectance was measured, while in Study 2, ants' internal temperature was measured.

33. A researcher discovers that Saharan silver ants perish when their internal temperature reaches 30°C. Based on the results of Study 2, which of the following groups would not survive?

A. Shaved ants after 70 seconds of exposure

B. Shaved ants after 50 seconds of exposure

C. Unshaved ants after 70 seconds of exposure

D. Unshaved ants after 50 seconds of exposure

34. One group of ants reached an internal temperature of 30°C after 65 seconds of exposure to light from a solar simulator. At 450 nm, what would the reflectance of these ants most likely be?

F. 2.6%

G. 4.0%

H. 5.5%

J. It is impossible to determine from the given information.

GO ON TO THE NEXT PAGE.

Passage VI

The *Coriolis effect* is the deflection of a moving object from its original path due to the inertial force caused by the counterclockwise rotation of the Earth. Figure 1 shows that an object is deflected to the east of its original path in the Northern Hemisphere and to the west of its original path in the Southern Hemisphere. Figure 2 shows the change in the rate of Earth's rotation from the Equator (0°N) to the North Pole (90°N). Figure 3 shows the strength of the inertial force that causes the Coriolis effect when the mass and velocity of the affected object varies.

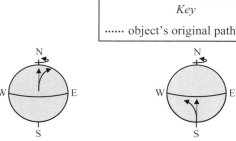

Deflection to the east in the Northern Hemisphere

Deflection to the west in the Southern Hemisphere

Figure 1

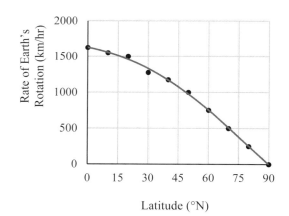

Figure 2

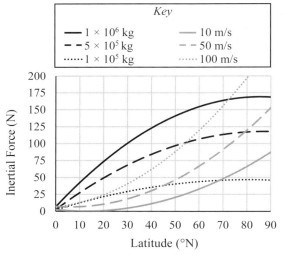

Figure 3

Note: An object with a mass of 5×10^5 kg was measured at different velocities, and objects of different masses were measured at 50 m/s.

35. If an object travels south in a straight line from Point A in the Northern Hemisphere then, due to the Coriolis effect, which point will the object most likely reach?

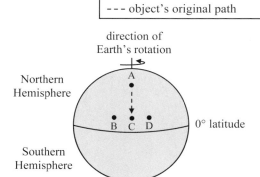

A. Point A
B. Point B
C. Point C
D. Point D

GO ON TO THE NEXT PAGE.

Practice Test

36. According to Figure 2, as latitude increases from the Equator to the North Pole, the rate of Earth's rotation:

    F. increases only.

    G. decreases only.

    H. remains constant, then decreases.

    J. remains constant, then increases.

37. According to Figure 3, the inertial force acting on an object with a mass of 7.5×10^5 kg traveling at 50 m/s at 90°N latitude would be:

    A. less than 50 N.

    B. between 50 and 100 N.

    C. between 100 and 150 N.

    D. greater than 150 N.

38. According to Figures 2 and 3, for an object of uniform mass and velocity, as the rate of the Earth's rotation increases, the Coriolis effect:

    F. increases only.

    G. decreases only.

    H. increases, then decreases.

    J. varies, but with no clear trend.

39. Which of the following properties of a moving object changes due to the Coriolis effect?

    A. Velocity

    B. Weight

    C. Mass

    D. Density

40. Which of the following objects would be most significantly affected by the Coriolis effect?

    F. An object with a mass of 1×10^6 kg, traveling at 50 m/s at 0°N latitude.

    G. An object with a mass of 1×10^6 kg, traveling at 100 m/s at 0°N latitude.

    H. An object with a mass of 1×10^6 kg, traveling at 50 m/s at 60°N latitude.

    J. An object with a mass of 1×10^6 kg, traveling at 100 m/s at 60°N latitude.

END OF TEST 4.

STOP! DO NOT TURN THE PAGE UNTIL YOU ARE TOLD TO DO SO.

DO NOT RETURN TO THE PREVIOUS TEST.

Writing Test
40 Minutes—1 Prompt

Directions: This is a test of your writing ability. You'll have 40 minutes to read the prompt, plan your response, and write your essay. Before you begin, read all of the material in this test section carefully and make sure you understand what is being asked of you.

You should write your essay on the lined pages included in your answer sheet. Only your writing on those pages will be scored. Your work on these pages will not be scored.

Your essay will be graded based on the evidence it provides and your ability to:

- analyze and evaluate different perspectives on complicated issues
- express and develop your own perspective on the issue
- explain and support your arguments with logical reasoning and detailed examples
- clearly and logically organize your ideas in an essay
- effectively communicate your point of view in English

Stop writing and put down your pencil as soon as time is called.

DO NOT BEGIN THE WRITING TEST UNTIL YOU ARE TOLD TO DO SO.

Repatriation of Museum Artifacts

Visitors to museums don't often stop to think about how artifacts from distant places make their way into collections. Yet archaeologists sometimes acquire pieces through dishonest or illegal means. Consider the Elgin Marbles: originally part of the Parthenon in Greece, they were removed by a Scottish aristocrat without permission. They remain in the British Museum despite two centuries of controversy. Those who support the "repatriation," or return, of stolen artifacts to their points of origin argue that to keep them would be unjust. They also emphasize the educational value of encountering artifacts in their original settings. Critics of the return of artifacts like the Elgin Marbles worry that it would set a precedent for the return of all museum holdings. Additionally, they cite the convenience of concentrating many of the world's artifacts in one place. Should museums return artifacts to their places of origin if they were acquired unethically, or should they keep them?

Read and carefully consider these perspectives. Each suggests a particular way of thinking about the repatriation of museum artifacts.

Perspective 1	Perspective 2	Perspective 3
If we looked closely at the collections of most museums, we would probably find that a great many of their pieces were gained unethically. It would be impractical to return them all, and an inconvenience for museum-goers.	Returning a dishonestly acquired artifact to its home country or indigenous community rights a historical wrong, and allows the piece to be appreciated in its original context.	In cases where a museum considers it too impractical to return a stolen artifact, they should be compelled to make, at their own expense, a high-quality replica for the country of origin as compensation.

Essay Task

Write a unified, coherent essay in which you evaluate multiple perspectives on the return of unethically acquired artifacts in museums. In your essay, be sure to:

- analyze and evaluate the perspectives given
- state and develop your own perspective on the issue
- explain the relationship between your perspective and those given

Your perspective may be in full agreement with any of the others, in partial agreement, or wholly different. Whatever the case, support your ideas with logical reasoning and detailed, persuasive examples.

Planning Your Essay

Your work on these prewriting pages will not be scored.

Use the space below and on the back cover to generate ideas and plan your essay. You may wish to consider the following as you think critically about the task:

Strengths and weaknesses of the three given perspectives
- What insights do they offer, and what do they fail to consider?
- Why might they be persuasive to others, or why might they fail to persuade?

Your own knowledge, experience, and values
- What is your perspective on this issue, and what are its strengths and weaknesses?
- How will you support your perspective in your essay?

Note

- Your practice Writing Test includes scratch paper and four lined sheets for your essay.
- Your official ACT exam will include a test booklet with space for planning and four lined sheets to write your essay.
- Review Answers and Scoring for instructions on how to grade your exam.

Answers
Chapter 8

English

Grammar Practice Questions (Pages 71–73)

1. D	4. G	7. D	10. J	13. B
2. H	5. D	8. H	11. B	14. H
3. B	6. J	9. A	12. J	15. A

Sentence Structure Practice Questions (Pages 91–93)

1. D	4. G	7. D	10. J	13. D
2. G	5. C	8. G	11. B	14. H
3. B	6. H	9. C	12. J	15. C

Punctuation Practice Questions (Pages 105–107)

1. B	4. J	7. A	10. H	13. C
2. F	5. D	8. H	11. C	14. F
3. B	6. F	9. B	12. G	15. D

Writing Strategy Practice Questions (Pages 121–126)

1. A	4. G	7. A	10. G	13. A
2. J	5. B	8. J	11. C	14. G
3. C	6. H	9. D	12. F	15. C

Organization Practice Questions (Pages 138–142)

1. C	4. J	7. D	10. H	13. B
2. G	5. C	8. H	11. B	14. G
3. A	6. J	9. A	12. G	15. C

Style Practice Questions (Pages 151–153)

1. D	4. J	7. B	10. G	13. D
2. H	5. D	8. J	11. A	14. F
3. C	6. J	9. C	12. G	15. B

 For answer explanations, please visit **ivyglobal.com/study**.

Pre-Algebra Practice Questions (Pages 196–199)

1. C	5. E	9. C	13. D	17. D
2. H	6. F	10. K	14. K	18. G
3. B	7. A	11. E	15. D	19. A
4. J	8. G	12. J	16. G	20. J

Elementary Algebra Practice Questions (Pages 216–218)

1. B	5. D	9. A	13. A	17. B
2. G	6. H	10. K	14. H	18. K
3. C	7. E	11. C	15. D	19. A
4. H	8. G	12. J	16. J	20. K

Intermediate Algebra Practice Questions (Pages 243–245)

1. D	5. E	9. C	13. B	17. B
2. F	6. H	10. J	14. J	18. G
3. B	7. A	11. D	15. D	19. A
4. G	8. J	12. J	16. J	20. F

Coordinate Geometry Practice Questions (Pages 282–286)

1. D	5. D	9. B	13. D	17. D
2. F	6. H	10. G	14. G	18. G
3. A	7. D	11. A	15. C	19. D
4. J	8. J	12. G	16. K	20. J

Plane Geometry Practice Questions (Pages 313–316)

1.	E	5.	B	9.	B	13.	B	17.	C
2.	J	6.	K	10.	G	14.	J	18.	J
3.	C	7.	C	11.	A	15.	C	19.	D
4.	H	8.	G	12.	K	16.	F	20.	J

Trigonometry Practice Questions (Pages 331–334)

1.	B	5.	D	9.	D	13.	D	17.	D
2.	J	6.	G	10.	G	14.	J	18.	K
3.	D	7.	D	11.	C	15.	D	19.	E
4.	K	8.	H	12.	J	16.	G	20.	F

For answer explanations, please visit **ivyglobal.com/study**.

Reading

Approaching the Reading Test

Marking up a Passage (Pages 344–345)

Social Science: This passage is adapted from the article, "Paid Sick Days and Physicians at Work: Ancient Egyptians Had State-Supported Health Care" by Anne Austin (©2015 by Anne Austin).

We might think of state-supported health care as an innovation of the 20th century, but it's a much older tradition than that. In fact, texts from a village dating back
5　to Egypt's New Kingdom period, about 3,100–3,600 years ago, suggest that in ancient Egypt there was a state-supported health care network designed to ensure that workers making the king's tomb were
10　productive.

The village of Deir el-Medina was built for the workmen who made the royal tombs during the New Kingdom (1550–1070 BCE). During this period, kings were buried in the
15　Valley of the Kings in a series of rock-cut tombs, not the enormous pyramids of the past. The village was purposely built close enough to the royal tomb to ensure that workers could hike there on a weekly basis.
20　These workmen were not what we normally picture when we think about the men who built and decorated ancient Egyptian royal tombs—they were highly skilled craftsmen. The workmen at Deir el-Medina were given a
25　variety of amenities afforded only to those with the craftsmanship and knowledge

necessary to work on something as important as the royal tomb. The village was allotted extra support: the Egyptian state
30　paid them monthly wages in the form of grain and provided them with housing and servants to assist with tasks like washing laundry, grinding grain, and porting water. Their families lived with them in the village,
35　and their wives and children could also benefit from these provisions from the state.

Among these texts are numerous <u>daily records detailing when and why individual workmen were absent</u> from work. Nearly
40　one-third of these absences occur when a workman was too sick to work. Yet, monthly ration distributions from Deir el-Medina are consistent enough to indicate that these <u>workmen were paid even if they were out</u>
45　<u>sick for several days</u>. These texts also identify a workman on the crew designated as the *swnw*, physician. The <u>physician</u> was given an assistant and both were allotted <u>days off to prepare medicine and take care of</u>
50　<u>colleagues</u>. The Egyptian state even gave the physician extra rations as payment for his services to the community of Deir el-Medina.

This physician would have most likely <u>treated the workmen with remedies and</u>
55　<u>incantations</u> found in his <u>medical papyrus</u>. About a dozen extensive medical papyri have been identified from ancient Egypt,

including one set from Deir el-Medina. These texts were a kind of reference book for the ancient Egyptian medical practitioner, listing individual treatments for a variety of ailments. The longest of these, Papyrus Ebers, contains over 800 treatments covering anything from eye problems to digestive disorders. Just like today, <u>some</u> of these ancient Egyptian medical treatments <u>required expensive and rare ingredients</u> that limited who could actually afford to be treated, but the <u>most frequent ingredients</u> found in these texts tended to be <u>common household items</u> like honey and grease. One text from Deir el-Medina indicates that the state rationed out common ingredients to a few men in the workforce so that they could be shared among the workers.

<u>Despite</u> paid sick leave, medical rations, and a state-supported physician, it is clear that in <u>some cases</u> the workmen were actually <u>working through their illnesses</u>. For <u>example</u>, in one text, the workman <u>Merysekhmet</u> attempted to go to work after being sick. The text tells us that he descended to the King's Tomb on two consecutive days, but was unable to work. He then hiked back to the village of Deir el-Medina where he stayed for the next ten days until he was able to work again. Though short, these hikes were steep: the trip from Deir el-Medina to the royal tomb involved an ascent greater than climbing to the top of the Great Pyramid. Merysekhmet's movements across the Theban valleys were likely at the expense of his own health. This suggests that <u>sick days and medical care</u> were <u>not</u>

<u>magnanimous gestures</u> of the Egyptian state, but were rather <u>calculated</u> health care provisions designed to ensure that men like Merysekhmet were <u>healthy enough to work</u>.

In cases where these provisions from the state were not enough, the <u>residents</u> of Deir el-Medina <u>turned to each other</u>. Personal letters from the site indicate that family members were expected to take care of each other by providing clothing and food, especially when a relative was sick. These documents show us that <u>caretaking was a reciprocal relationship between direct family members</u>, regardless of gender or age. Children were expected to take care of both parents just as parents were expected to take care of all of their children. When family members <u>neglected these responsibilities</u>, there were <u>financial and social consequences</u>. In her will, the villager Naunakhte indicates that even though she was a dedicated mother to all of her children, four of them abandoned her in her old age. She admonishes them and disinherits them from her will, punishing them financially, but also shaming them in a public document made in front of the most senior members of the Deir el-Medina community.

This shows us that health care at Deir el-Medina was <u>a system with overlying networks of care</u> provided through the state and the community. While workmen <u>counted on the state</u> for paid sick leave, a physician, and even medical ingredients, they were equally dependent on their <u>loved ones</u> for the care necessary to thrive in ancient Egypt.

Summarizing (Pages 346–348)

Paragraph 3:   paid sick days + physician

Paragraph 4:   papyrus gives common treatments

Paragraph 5:   illness impacts work

Paragraph 6:   family support essential

Paragraph 7:   state + community support

Active Reading (Pages 357–358)

1. B   2. F   3. C   4. H   5. C

electing Your Answers (Pages 359–360)

1. D 2. F 3. A

ull Length Practice (Pages 361–366)

1. D	5. B	9. C	13. C	17. B
2. H	6. G	10. F	14. H	18. J
3. B	7. D	11. B	15. A	19. B
4. F	8. F	12. J	16. H	20. F

assage Types Practice Questions

rose Fiction (Page 382)

1. C 2. J 3. A

ocial Science (Pages 383–384)

1. B 2. F 3. B

umanities (Pages 384–385)

1. B 2. G 3. C

atural Science (Pages 385–386)

1. D 2. F 3. B

aired Passages (Pages 386–388)

1. D 2. H 3. A

Details and Implicit Meaning Practice Questions

etails (Pages 398–399)

1. A 2. G 3. D

mplicit Meaning (Pages 399–400)

1. D 2. F 3. A 4. H

Generalization and Main Ideas Practice Questions (Pages 409–410)

1. D 2. G 3. A 4. H

Author's Voice and Method Practice Questions (Pages 423–424)

1. B 2. G 3. A 4. H

Meanings of Words and Phrases Practice Questions (Pages 436–437)

1. C   2. G   3. D   4. G

Relationships Practice Questions (Pages 449–450)

1. A   2. G   3. C

 For answer explanations, please visit **ivyglobal.com/study**.

Science

assage Types

ata Representation Practice Questions (Pages 471–476)

1. C	5. B	9. D	13. C	17. C
2. G	6. G	10. J	14. J	18. J
3. A	7. A	11. B	15. D	
4. H	8. F	12. J	16. G	

esearch Summaries Practice Questions (485–490)

1. C	6. J	11. C	16. J	21. A
2. H	7. A	12. F	17. D	
3. A	8. G	13. B	18. H	
4. G	9. C	14. H	19. C	
5. A	10. F	15. B	20. H	

onflicting Viewpoints Practice Questions (Pages 498–503)

1. A	6. J	11. D	16. H	21. C
2. H	7. C	12. G	17. D	
3. B	8. F	13. B	18. F	
4. F	9. C	14. F	19. C	
5. C	10. J	15. B	20. J	

Question Types

nderstanding Practice Questions (Pages 510–511)

1. B	2. H	3. D	4. G	5. B

nalysis Practice Questions (Pages 516–517)

1. B	2. F	3. C	4. F	5. D

Synthesis Practice Questions (Pages 522–523)

1. B   2. G   3. D   4. H   5. A

Experimental Design Practice Questions (Pages 528–529)

1. D   2. H   3. D   4. J   5. A

 For answer explanations, please visit **ivyglobal.com/study**.

Practice Tests

English Test

1. A	12. H	23. C	34. F	45. D	56. F	67. C
2. J	13. C	24. J	35. C	46. J	57. B	68. F
3. C	14. F	25. C	36. H	47. D	58. H	69. D
4. G	15. C	26. J	37. D	48. G	59. A	70. J
5. C	16. H	27. B	38. H	49. C	60. G	71. B
6. H	17. C	28. H	39. A	50. G	61. B	72. F
7. C	18. H	29. D	40. F	51. A	62. F	73. D
8. H	19. D	30. J	41. A	52. G	63. C	74. J
9. A	20. H	31. A	42. G	53. D	64. G	75. D
10. H	21. D	32. J	43. A	54. F	65. A	
11. B	22. G	33. A	44. G	55. C	66. J	

Math Test

1. D	10. F	19. D	28. H	37. B	46. F	55. A
2. G	11. C	20. G	29. D	38. H	47. A	56. F
3. E	12. J	21. D	30. H	39. C	48. H	57. C
4. H	13. B	22. K	31. D	40. H	49. C	58. H
5. C	14. F	23. C	32. J	41. B	50. H	59. A
6. F	15. E	24. K	33. B	42. F	51. E	60. F
7. C	16. G	25. D	34. K	43. C	52. K	
8. F	17. A	26. J	35. B	44. G	53. A	
9. B	18. F	27. D	36. J	45. B	54. G	

Reading Test

1. C	7. C	13. B	19. A	25. C	31. B	37. C
2. J	8. J	14. G	20. H	26. J	32. H	38. H
3. A	9. A	15. D	21. C	27. B	33. A	39. B
4. H	10. F	16. G	22. F	28. F	34. F	40. J
5. B	11. C	17. A	23. B	29. A	35. C	
6. J	12. H	18. G	24. G	30. G	36. J	

Science Test

1. A	7. A	13. B	19. B	25. A	31. D	37. C
2. H	8. J	14. H	20. F	26. F	32. H	38. J
3. C	9. A	15. A	21. D	27. A	33. D	39. C
4. J	10. F	16. G	22. G	28. H	34. J	40. F
5. D	11. C	17. D	23. C	29. B	35. A	
6. G	12. J	18. H	24. H	30. H	36. G	

Practice Test 2 (Pages 669–726)

English Test

1. C	12. J	23. D	34. J	45. C	56. F	67. A
2. G	13. A	24. G	35. B	46. J	57. B	68. J
3. D	14. J	25. D	36. H	47. B	58. H	69. B
4. G	15. D	26. G	37. D	48. H	59. B	70. G
5. D	16. J	27. A	38. G	49. B	60. J	71. C
6. F	17. A	28. J	39. C	50. J	61. B	72. G
7. D	18. G	29. B	40. H	51. C	62. G	73. D
8. H	19. C	30. F	41. D	52. G	63. B	74. F
9. B	20. J	31. C	42. J	53. A	64. F	75. A
10. G	21. B	32. G	43. A	54. J	65. C	
11. B	22. H	33. B	44. G	55. B	66. G	

Math Test

1. B	10. H	19. D	28. F	37. C	46. J	55. B
2. H	11. B	20. F	29. A	38. H	47. A	56. K
3. E	12. H	21. D	30. G	39. B	48. H	57. E
4. F	13. B	22. G	31. C	40. J	49. C	58. J
5. E	14. H	23. B	32. H	41. B	50. K	59. B
6. J	15. C	24. F	33. E	42. F	51. B	60. G
7. D	16. K	25. E	34. G	43. C	52. F	
8. K	17. D	26. J	35. E	44. G	53. A	
9. D	18. H	27. E	36. H	45. B	54. K	

1. D	7. D	13. D	19. D	25. C	31. A	37. C
2. H	8. H	14. G	20. J	26. J	32. F	38. H
3. B	9. D	15. B	21. C	27. A	33. A	39. B
4. J	10. F	16. J	22. J	28. H	34. H	40. G
5. C	11. C	17. B	23. B	29. B	35. D	
6. H	12. H	18. F	24. G	30. F	36. F	

cience Test

1. C	7. B	13. C	19. A	25. B	31. D	37. C
2. J	8. H	14. F	20. F	26. J	32. G	38. F
3. D	9. B	15. A	21. B	27. C	33. B	39. B
4. G	10. H	16. H	22. G	28. F	34. F	40. H
5. A	11. A	17. A	23. A	29. D	35. C	
6. G	12. J	18. J	24. J	30. H	36. J	

ractice Test 3 (Pages 727–784)

nglish Test

1. B	12. J	23. B	34. G	45. D	56. J	67. C
2. J	13. C	24. H	35. A	46. J	57. D	68. H
3. C	14. J	25. A	36. G	47. B	58. J	69. A
4. H	15. A	26. H	37. C	48. G	59. B	70. G
5. B	16. G	27. D	38. G	49. C	60. G	71. C
6. J	17. A	28. G	39. A	50. H	61. C	72. J
7. C	18. G	29. A	40. J	51. D	62. G	73. D
8. F	19. A	30. J	41. C	52. H	63. D	74. H
9. D	20. H	31. B	42. G	53. B	64. G	75. B
10. G	21. D	32. F	43. D	54. H	65. B	
11. C	22. J	33. D	44. G	55. B	66. F	

Math Test

1. C	10. J	19. B	28. H	37. C	46. J	55. C
2. H	11. A	20. H	29. D	38. K	47. D	56. K
3. B	12. J	21. D	30. K	39. A	48. K	57. C
4. J	13. C	22. H	31. C	40. G	49. D	58. G
5. E	14. F	23. B	32. G	41. D	50. H	59. D
6. H	15. B	24. F	33. C	42. J	51. C	60. K
7. D	16. H	25. E	34. H	43. D	52. G	
8. G	17. C	26. H	35. C	44. J	53. B	
9. C	18. J	27. B	36. K	45. B	54. H	

Reading Test

1. C	7. B	13. B	19. A	25. A	31. C	37. D
2. J	8. F	14. J	20. H	26. G	32. J	38. G
3. B	9. D	15. D	21. B	27. C	33. D	39. A
4. G	10. G	16. G	22. F	28. J	34. J	40. G
5. C	11. D	17. B	23. A	29. C	35. B	
6. F	12. H	18. F	24. J	30. F	36. G	

Science Test

1. B	7. B	13. C	19. C	25. C	31. C	37. C
2. H	8. H	14. H	20. F	26. F	32. J	38. G
3. C	9. D	15. D	21. B	27. C	33. A	39. A
4. H	10. G	16. G	22. J	28. H	34. F	40. J
5. A	11. A	17. B	23. B	29. D	35. D	
6. F	12. H	18. F	24. F	30. G	36. G	

For answer explanations, please visit **ivyglobal.com/study**.

Fill out your answers on **cloud.ivylobal.com**
to get a detailed score report for each test.

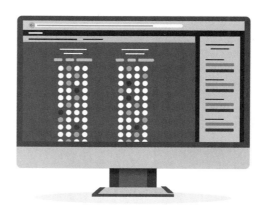

Section 6
How to Score Your Practice Tests

Scoring of your practice test can either be done manually using the following charts or automatically by using our online resources. In the previous chapter, you can find all of the answers to the practice problems and practice tests found in this book. Remember, if you are having any troubles with these questions, you can always look at our online answer explanations for help.

For additional resources, please visit **ivyglobal.com/study**.

In order to calculate your ACT composite score, you first need to find your scaled scores in each of the four test areas: English, mathematics, reading, and science. Start by counting the number of correct answers that you got in each area; this is called your raw score. In order to find each of these areas' scaled score, you need to find your raw score on the chart below and then read your scaled score from the same row.

Because each of the four areas of the ACT are calculated differently, they each need to be scored independently. The same raw score for reading and mathematics, for example, will not give you the same scaled score in these areas.

Scaled Score					
Scaled Score	English	Math	Reading	Science	Writing
36	75	60	40	40	47-48
35	72-74	58-59	39	39	46
34	71	57	38	38	44-45
33	70	55-56	37	37	42-43
32	68-69	54	35-36	—	41
31	67	52-53	34	36	40
30	66	50-51	33	35	38-39

Scaled Score	English	Math	Reading	Science	Writing
29	65	48-49	32	34	37
28	63-64	45-47	31	33	35-36
27	62	43-44	30	32	34
26	60-61	40-42	29	30-31	33
25	58-59	38-39	28	28-29	32
24	56-57	36-37	27	26-27	31
23	53-55	34-35	25-26	24-25	29-30
22	51-52	32-33	24	22-23	28
21	48-50	30-31	22-23	21	26-27
20	45-47	29	21	19-20	25
19	43-44	27-28	19-20	17-18	24
18	41-42	24-26	18	16	23
17	39-40	21-23	17	14-15	21-22
16	36-38	17-20	15-16	13	20
15	32-35	13-16	14	12	—
14	29-31	11-12	12-13	11	18-19
13	27-28	8-10	11	10	17
12	25-26	7	9-10	9	16
11	23-24	5-6	8	8	—
10	20-22	4	6-7	7	14-15
9	18-19	—	—	5-6	13
8	15-17	3	5	—	12
7	12-14	—	4	4	—
6	10-11	2	3	3	10-11
5	8-9	—	—	2	9
4	6-7	1	2	—	—
3	4-5	—	—	1	—
2	2-3	—	1	—	—
1	0-1	0	0	0	8

Once you have found all your scaled scores from the table, simply average your four scaled scores to get your ACT composite score out of 36.

If you took the optional writing portion of the practice test, you will also want to calculate your score for this area; the scoring chart for writing is located in the next section, right after the scoring charts for the other areas. If you are calculating writing, make sure that you get another person to also score the four areas of this section; each section will therefore be scored from 2–12. To determine your Writing score, from 2–12, take the average of these four sections. In order to calculate your ELA subscore, you will also need to determine your scaled score (out of 36) for this area, using the scaling charts that follow.

Practice Test 1

Part 1

Raw Score

English	_____	out of 75
Math	_____	out of 60
Reading	_____	out of 40
Science	_____	out of 40

Writing Score

Ideas and Analysis	_____
+ Development & Support	_____
+ Organization	_____
+ Language Use & Conventions	_____
Total Score	_____

$\div 4 =$ [_____] out of 12

ELA Score

English Scaled Score	_____
+ Reading Scaled Score	_____
+ Writing Scaled Score	_____
Total Score	_____

$\div 3 =$ [_____] out of 36

Scaled Score

English	_____	out of 36
Math	_____	out of 36
Reading	_____	out of 36
Science	_____	out of 36

Composite ACT Score

English Scaled Score	_____
+ Math Scaled Score	_____
+ Reading Scaled Score	_____
+ Science Scaled Score	_____
Total Score	_____

$\div 4 =$ [_____] out of 1

STEM

Math Scaled Score	_____
+ Science Scaled Score	_____
Total Score	_____

$\div 2 =$ [_____] out of 3

Practice Test 2
Part 2

Raw Score		
English	_____	out of 75
Math	_____	out of 60
Reading	_____	out of 40
Science	_____	out of 40

Scaled Score		
English	_____	out of 36
Math	_____	out of 36
Reading	_____	out of 36
Science	_____	out of 36

Writing Score	
Ideas and Analysis	_____
+ Development & Support	_____
+ Organization	_____
+ Language Use & Conventions	_____
Total Score	_____
÷ 4 = [_____]	out of 12

Composite ACT Score	
English Scaled Score	_____
+ Math Scaled Score	_____
+ Reading Scaled Score	_____
+ Science Scaled Score	_____
Total Score	_____
÷ 4 = [_____]	out of 12

ELA Score	
English Scaled Score	_____
+ Reading Scaled Score	_____
+ Writing Scaled Score	_____
Total Score	_____
÷ 3 = [_____]	out of 36

STEM	
Math Scaled Score	_____
+ Science Scaled Score	_____
Total Score	_____
÷ 2 = [_____]	out of 36

Practice Test 3

Part 3

Raw Score		
English	_____	out of 75
Math	_____	out of 60
Reading	_____	out of 40
Science	_____	out of 40

Scaled Score		
English	_____	out of 36
Math	_____	out of 36
Reading	_____	out of 36
Science	_____	out of 36

Writing Score

Ideas and Analysis	_____
+ Development & Support	_____
+ Organization	_____
+ Language Use & Conventions	_____
Total Score	_____

÷ 4 = [_____] out of 12

Composite ACT Score

English Scaled Score	_____
+ Math Scaled Score	_____
+ Reading Scaled Score	_____
+ Science Scaled Score	_____
Total Score	_____

÷ 4 = [_____] out of 12

ELA Score

English Scaled Score	_____
+ Reading Scaled Score	_____
+ Writing Scaled Score	_____
Total Score	_____

÷ 3 = [_____] out of 36

STEM

Math Scaled Score	_____
+ Science Scaled Score	_____
Total Score	_____

÷ 2 = [_____] out of 36

Comparing Your Scores
Part 4

Scaled Scores	Test 1	Previous Test	Percent Change in Score	
English			(Previous Test ÷ Test 1 − 1) × 100 =	_____ %
Math			(Previous Test ÷ Test 1 − 1) × 100 =	_____ %
Reading			(Previous Test ÷ Test 1 − 1) × 100 =	_____ %
Science			(Previous Test ÷ Test 1 − 1) × 100 =	_____ %
ACT Composite			(Previous Test ÷ Test 1 − 1) × 100 =	_____ %
Writing			(Previous Test ÷ Test 1 − 1) × 100 =	_____ %
ELA			(Previous Test ÷ Test 1 − 1) × 100 =	_____ %
STEM			(Previous Test ÷ Test 1 − 1) × 100 =	_____ %

Scaled Scores	Test 2	Previous Test	Percent Change in Score	
English			(Previous Test ÷ Test 1 − 1) × 100 =	_____ %
Math			(Previous Test ÷ Test 1 − 1) × 100 =	_____ %
Reading			(Previous Test ÷ Test 1 − 1) × 100 =	_____ %
Science			(Previous Test ÷ Test 1 − 1) × 100 =	_____ %
ACT Composite			(Previous Test ÷ Test 1 − 1) × 100 =	_____ %
Writing			(Previous Test ÷ Test 1 − 1) × 100 =	_____ %
ELA			(Previous Test ÷ Test 1 − 1) × 100 =	_____ %
STEM			(Previous Test ÷ Test 1 − 1) × 100 =	_____ %

Scaled Scores	Test 3	Previous Test	Percent Change in Score	
English			(Previous Test ÷ Test 1 − 1) × 100 =	_____ %
Math			(Previous Test ÷ Test 1 − 1) × 100 =	_____ %
Reading			(Previous Test ÷ Test 1 − 1) × 100 =	_____ %
Science			(Previous Test ÷ Test 1 − 1) × 100 =	_____ %
ACT Composite			(Previous Test ÷ Test 1 − 1) × 100 =	_____ %
Writing			(Previous Test ÷ Test 1 − 1) × 100 =	_____ %
ELA			(Previous Test ÷ Test 1 − 1) × 100 =	_____ %
STEM			(Previous Test ÷ Test 1 − 1) × 100 =	_____ %